AMERICAN POLITICAL PARTIES: A READER

AMERICAN POLITICAL PARTIES:

A READER

Eric M. Uslaner, Editor

University of Maryland

 F. E. PEACOCK PUBLISHERS, INC.
ITASCA, ILLINOIS

For Debbie, Avery, and Bo

CONTENTS

Contents

ABOUT THE CONTRIBUTORS

Eric M. Uslaner, the editor, is Professor of Government and Politics, University of Maryland—College Park.

David W. Brady is Professor in the Department of Political Science and the Graduate School of Business, Stanford University.

Bernadette A. Budde is Vice-President for Political Education of the Business-Industry Political Action Committee.

David T. Canon is Assistant Professor of Political Science, University of Wisconsin–Madison.

Allan J. Cigler is Professor of Political Science, University of Kansas.

William Crotty is Professor of Political Science, Northwestern University.

Leon D. Epstein is Professor Emeritus of Political Science, University of Wisconsin and a former president of the American Political Science Association.

Jo Freeman is a legislative analyst for the New York General Assembly.

William Galston is Deputy Assistant to the President for Domestic Policy and Professor of Public Affairs, University of Maryland–College Park.

John G. Geer is Assistant Professor of Political Science, Arizona State University.

James L. Gibson is Distinguished University Professor of Political Science, University of Houston.

Benjamin Ginsberg is Professor of Political Science, Johns Hopkins University.

Paul S. Herrnson is Associate Professor of Government and Politics, University of Maryland–College Park.

Patricia A. Hurley is Associate Professor of Political Science, Texas A & M University.

Elaine Ciulla Kamarck is Senior Fellow, Progressive Policy Institute.

Xandra Kayden is a political consultant.

Everett Carll Ladd is Professor of Political Science, University of Connecticut.

Eddie Mahe, Jr., is President of the Eddie Mahe Company.

About the Contributors

Sidney M. Milkis is Assistant Professor of Politics, Brandeis University.

Warren E. Miller is Professor of Political Science, Arizona State University and a former president of the American Political Science Association.

Norman Ornstein is Resident Scholar, American Enterprise Institute for Public Policy Research.

John R. Petrocik is Professor of Political Science, University of California–Los Angeles.

Howard L. Reiter is Professor of Political Science, University of Connecticut.

Robert H. Salisbury is Professor and Chair of the Department of Political Science, Washington University.

Susan E. Scarrow is Assistant Professor of Political Science, University of Houston.

Martin Shefter is Professor of Government, Cornell University.

Martin P. Wattenberg is Professor of Politics and Society, University of California–Irvine.

Jim Weber is Vice-President of the Eddie Mahe Company.

SOURCES OF THE READINGS

Leon D. Epstein, "What Happened to the British Party Model?" *American Political Science Review* 54 (1980): 406–27. Reprinted with permission of the American Political Science Association.

Robert H. Salisbury, "Parties and Pluralism." Prepared especially for this volume.

Benjamin Ginsberg and Martin Shefter, "Political Parties, Electoral Conflict, and Institutional Combat" in Larry Berman, ed., *Looking Back on the Reagan Presidency* (Baltimore: Johns Hopkins U. Press, 1991), pp. 241–67. Updated by the authors. Reprinted with permission of Johns Hopkins U. Press and the authors.

David W. Brady, "Critical Elections, Congressional Parties and Clusters of Policy Changes." *British Journal of Political Science* 8 (1978): 79–99. Reprinted with permission of Cambridge U. Press.

Martin P. Wattenberg, "The Decline of Political Partisanship in the United States: Negativity or Neutrality." *American Political Science Review* 75 (1981): 941–50. Reprinted with permission of the American Political Science Association.

John R. Petrocik, "Realignment: New Party Coalitions and the Nationalization of the South." *Journal of Politics* 49 (1987): 347–75. Reprinted with permission of the U. of Texas Press.

Warren E. Miller, "Party Identification, Realignment, and Party Voting." *American Political Science Review* 85 (1991): 557–68. Reprinted with permission of the American Political Science Association.

Xandra Kayden and Eddie Mahe, Jr., "Back from the Depths: Party Resurgence," Chapter 3 in Kayden and Mahe, *The Party Goes On* (New York: Basic Books, 1985). Reprinted with permission of HarperCollins Publishers.

Paul S. Herrnson, "Do Parties Make a Difference? The Role of Party Organizations in Congressional Elections." *Journal of Politics* 48 (1986): 589–615. Reprinted with permission of the U. of Texas Press.

James L. Gibson and Susan E. Scarrow, "State and Local Party Organizations in American Politics." Prepared especially for this volume.

William Crotty, "Party Reforms and Party Adaptability." Prepared especially for this volume.

Everett Carll Ladd, "Party Reform and the Public Interest." *Political Science Quarterly* 101 (1987): 355–69. Reprinted with permission of the Academy of Political Science.

Howard L. Reiter, "The Limitations of Reform: Changes in the Nominating Process." *British Journal of Political Science* 15 (1987): 399–417. Updated by the author. Reprinted with permission of Cambridge U. Press.

Warren E. Miller, "A New Context for Presidential Politics: The Reagan Legacy." *Political Behavior* 9 (1987): 91–113. Reprinted with permission of Plenum Publishers.

John G. Geer, "Assessing the Representativeness of Electorates in Presidential Primaries." *American Journal of Political Science* 32 (1988): 929–45. Reprinted with permission of the U. of Texas Press.

Jo Freeman, "The Political Culture of the Democratic and Republican Parties." *Political Science Quarterly* 100 (1986): 327–56. Reprinted with permission of the author.

Allan J. Cigler, "Political Parties and Interest Groups: Competitors, Collaborators, and Uneasy Allies." Prepared especially for this volume.

Sidney M. Milkis, "The Presidency and Political Parties" in Michael Nelson, ed., *The Presidency & The Political System*, 3d ed. (Washington, D.C.: Congressional Quarterly Press, 1992). Reprinted with permission of Congressional Quarterly Press.

David T. Canon, "The Institutionalization of Leadership in the U.S. Congress." *Legislative Studies Quarterly* 14 (1989): 415–43. Reprinted with permission of the Comparative Legislative Research Center, U. of Iowa.

Patricia A. Hurley, "Partisan Representation and the Failure of Realignment in the 1980s." *American Journal of Political Science* 33 (1989): 240–61. Reprinted with permission of the U. of Texas Press.

Norman Ornstein, "A Modest Proposal for Campaign Finance Reform." Prepared especially for this volume.

Bernadette A. Budde, "Campaign Finance Revision: A Framework for the Discussion." Prepared especially for this volume.

William Galston and Elaine Ciulla Kamarck, "The Politics of Evasion: Democrats and the Presidency." Prepared for the Progressive Policy Institute. Reprinted with permission of the authors.

Eddie Mahe, Jr., and Jim Weber, "The Road to Nowhere? Political Parties in the Next Millennium." Prepared especially for this volume.

PREFACE

This anthology follows a standard set of topics covered in courses on party politics: party theory, party identification and realignment, party organizations, party reform, parties and representation, and parties in the government. The two concluding sections depart from the traditional. The two essays on campaign finance reform are advocacy pieces, one by a Democrat and the other by a Republican. Neither author is a party official, and both depart from their party's conventional wisdom. The concluding section offers views on what the Democratic and Republican parties should do in the coming decade, authored by political consultants in each party. Each section begins with my summary of the essays to follow.

Typically, a collection of essays contains either all new essays or all reprints from scholarly journals. I have purused a middle course, coming up with a melange that should be more interesting and accessible than usual. I have selected many articles from the leading professional journals in political science, focusing on those that abjure heavy statistics in favor of more comprehensible exposition. I have also asked prominent scholars in the field to write or revise original chapters for this volume. Finally, two contributions have been previously published in other edited volumes and one is a chapter from a previously published book.

I have greatly benefited from the comments of colleagues and reviewers in putting this collection together. Allan J. Cigler and Paul S. Herrnson offered particularly valuable advice on multiple occasions. The comments of John F. Bibby, Malcolm Jewell, Patricia Hurley, and James Hutler were also very useful. Leo Wiegman and Ted Peacock of Peacock Publishers were a real pleasure to work with. The General Research Board of the University of Maryland, College Park, provided much appreciated support over a series of years that gave me time to collect the thoughts that are represented here. Debbie, Avery, and Bo provided the even more essential love that sustains such an endeavor.

Eric M. Uslaner
College Park, Maryland

PART ONE

PARTY THEORY

American political parties have traditionally been far weaker than their counterparts in other democratic societies. The United States has no tradition of viable socialist parties. Nor have we had the far right parties or electoral blocs based on religious or ethnic ties that have been common in Europe. Moderate parties socialize conflict, but they also restrict the scope of policy debate in the United States. Our parties pale by comparison with others in terms of policy innovation.

Have we missed something? Would we be better off with sharper conflicts that lead to more bursts of innovative policy? Leon Epstein in "What Happened to the British Party Model?" suggests not. Epstein considers the British parliamentary system with its history of strong parties and the capacity to make large-scale shifts in policy-making. He concludes that the British system is no longer the model of "responsible party government" that it once was, and that the prescriptions of strong parties and structural reform are far less appealing to Americans now.

Why are American parties weak? The conventional wisdom, according to Robert H. Salisbury in "Parties and Pluralism," is that American interest groups are very powerful, and where there are strong interest groups there cannot be robust parties. The proliferation of interest groups in the United States reflects the diversity of the society and widely dispersed resources for affecting politics—or pluralism. Salisbury contests the thesis that pluralism is incompatible with strong parties. He traces the relationships between parties and interest groups throughout American history. He finds, perhaps surprisingly, that interest groups have traditionally aligned themselves with parties and have not stood outside the party system as independent entrepreneurs.

Innovative policy-making becomes far more difficult when control of the executive and legislative branches is split between the Republicans and the Democrats, as it has been for most of the post–World War II era. Benjamin Ginsberg and Martin Shefter, in "Political Parties, Electoral Conflict, and Institutional Combat," argue that divided control of the federal government is now a virtually permanent fixture of the political landscape. The two parties have now retreated from electoral combat. Political conflict has come to rest in the bureaucracy, the courts, and the media as each party attempts to seize the political momentum from the other. The decline of social consensus since the war in Vietnam has legitimized these struggles outside the electoral arena.

Reading 1

WHAT HAPPENED TO THE BRITISH PARTY MODEL?

Leon D. Epstein

My discussion of our profession's changing views of the British party model is not a way to develop generalizations of the kind that distinguished earlier presidential addresses on the nature and responsibility of political science. I find it difficult to offer general advice now that political scientists identify with increasingly specialized subjects and employ more disparate methods. Hence, I present an intellectual case history from which, at the end, I seek to draw only a few broad inferences about how transient circumstances and ideological concerns influence our political perceptions, and how the diminished appeal of a particular model may illustrate a wider skepticism about political systems.

The British party model is familiar from the works of several generations of scholars. Its essence is a sufficiently, but not an absolutely, cohesive parliamentary majority in support of executive office-holding leaders and so of policies accepted by those leaders as well as by the bulk of their partisan followers. Often associated with the model is a mass membership organized in constituency units and represented in national committees and conferences. Their policy-making role is disputed, in fact and in principle, but the model is that of "responsible-party government" whether the crucial parliamentary majority regards itself as mandated by its organized followers, its largely unorganized voters, or its own judgments. In one way or another, that party majority has been the centerpiece of modern British parliamentary government and of the "Westminster model" of strong cabinet leadership adapted and developed by certain Commonwealth nations. While not forgetting the vital linkage of a cohesive governing party with British-style parliamentary institutions, I concentrate here on the party model because of its salience in American political science. Given an almost chronic dissatisfaction with the relative weakness of American parties, our descriptions of British parties have often suggested a special admiration. Moreover, the admiration has occasionally been strong enough to imply that American adaptations were possible even without the transplantation of the parliamentary system in which Britain's strong parties had thrived. The disjunction is observable despite the historical tendency of many American intellectuals, if not the larger American public, to admire British government more generally rather than just for its party model. That tendency among political scientists is excellently and comprehensively reviewed by Dennis Kavanagh.[1]

In addition to exploring the reasons for the British party model's attractiveness in the past, I shall try to explain its apparently diminished appeal during the 1970s although we have been more troubled than ever about the increasingly porous qualities of American parties. My concern here is mainly with changes in the model's appeal to liberal reformers prominent in American political science and in the search for strong party government. A different intellectual possibility would arise insofar as American conservatives were now to look to Prime Minister Thatcher's new parliamentary party majority for the doctrinal policy accomplishments to which her leadership is committed. But whether they or anyone else will be attracted to the model may also depend on the substantial changes in its operation during the 1970s. I describe these changes after discussing the use and disuse of the conventional model.

WHEN AND HOW THE MODEL WAS USED

Thanks to Ranney's analysis,[2] many of us realize that the British party model attracted the attention of American political scientists by the turn of the century. Both Wilson and Lowell appreciated that a parliamentary party majority supported an executive leadership's policies to an extent that an American congressional party majority did not.[3] One of the first scholarly students of American parties, Henry Jones Ford (1898), cited the British model, apart from the direct influence of Woodrow Wilson. These founders of American political science, however, were not single-minded advocates of the transfer of British institutions to the United States, and Lowell explicitly recognized that British responsible-party government was incompatible with an American constitutional order designed to protect minority rights against a legislative majority.[4] Ours is not the first generation to understand the difficulty of transplanting institutions, and British institutions in particular.[5]

However sophisticated the early American exposition of the British party model, it usually reflected admiration—explicitly in Wilson's presentation and implicitly in Lowell's despite its non-imitative character. But old British hands, sorry now to realize the diminished importance of our subject, should not exaggerate the place that British politics once occupied in the profession. To be sure, academic courses on Britain were fairly common before the study of comparative politics included many other nations, and Lowell's early text[6] was followed by others, notably Ogg's standard treatment.[7] Judging, however, from old volumes of the *American Political Science Review,* one finds little evidence that any large number of scholars ever focused heavily on British affairs. Although in the past American political scientists would have been likely to know much more about Britain than about any other foreign nation, their dominant empirical interest then as later was in the American field.

Despite ordinarily limited attention from most American political scientists, the British political system provided our most convenient comparative benchmark. During the first half of this century, Britain's cultural prestige, imperial power, stable governmental institutions, and linguistic accessibility combined to make its political experience more familiar than that of other foreign nations. In addition, the programmatic and policy-oriented discussion of British politics appealed particularly to academics who esteemed such discussion and found it lacking in the United States. Insofar as British parties were based on ideas, even on ideologies, they had room for intellectual activity that seemed less welcome in Republican or Democratic politics. Admiration on this score dates back to Wilson's reading of Bagehot[8] and it may be found among conservative as well as liberal writers. Certainly it was implicit and occasionally explicit in the American academic approach to the Labour party; a fairly early case in point is Dean McHenry's *Labour Party in Transition.*[9]

Not all earlier American academic writing about British parties or the rest of the British system was favorable. Being a familiar benchmark for comparison meant that the British model could also be cited invidiously. So it was in well-known works by Pendleton Herring[10] and by Don K. Price.[11] Each thought that Britain's disciplined party leadership had produced bad policy results during the 1930s, at the very time that American presidential leadership appeared to have been relatively successful. Probably the period about which Herring and Price wrote was exceptional in the first half of this century, but their penetrating rejection of the model tells us something about its presence in American political science. As Herring and Price realized, the British model had American champions even in the wake of its failures in the 1930s.

American championship of the British model, it should be stressed, was more widespread not just when the model looked better than it did in the 1930s but also when there was greater dissatisfaction with our own political system and particularly with the role of parties in that system. Fading during the early years of the presidencies of Wilson and Franklin Roosevelt, as partisan congressional majorities enacted innovative policies, dissatisfaction rose in the years between World War II and the early 1960s. No consistently effective party majority functioned to enact the kind of domestic program that liberal intellectuals wanted, and political frustration tended to focus around the inadequacy of party when (in 1949–53, for example) Democrats nominally held both houses of Congress and the presidency. We remember this period in political science for the flourishing of responsible-party advocacy.

If any time were opportune to cite the British model, as it had been cited 50 years before, it was in the first 15 or 20 years after World War II. The American desire for a democratic alternative was strong, and, particularly from 1945 to 1951, the British model was widely thought to have worked effectively to achieve moderate socialist policies. Even in the decade or so after 1951, when Labour left office, British responsible-party government retained its aura of success partly because the Conservative majorities accepted most of Labour's legislation and partly because of Labour's expected, though delayed, return to power. Furthermore, the British political system generally was again held in great esteem. It had survived World War II, as had no other major Western European regime, and its interwar failures looked less important than its maintenance through such bad times and its rapid peaceful adaptation to social-democratic purposes after the 1945 general election. Newly self-governing nations, especially those in the Commonwealth, sought to adapt British political institutions, not without encouragement from Britons confident of the virtues of their own system.

A few of us can remember that glad confident postwar British morning in which democratic hopes rested heavily on parliamentary government and its responsible-party mainspring. The interest of American political scientists in Britain was as always much less than pervasive, but there was an increased awareness of British political institutions. Books by British scholars like Ivor Jennings provided full accounts of how these institutions worked,[12] often stressing the importance of parties. Others like Herman Finer[13] presented British parties and other political institutions in a favorable comparative context. Interest was even reflected in a small increase in the number of articles on British subjects that the *American Political Science Review* published in the early 1950s. The British party model became a standard reference point in the comparative politics courses that developed in American universities after World War II, and new textbooks treated it as working successfully in contrast to the experience with multiparty arrangements in most continental European nations. In the teaching of American government, the capacity of a British party to enact a program was contrasted to the description of brokered politics in the American system.

At the same time, most political scientists understood the difficulties that would impede American adoption of the British party model, or even of significant portions of it. However much the American responsible-party school now admired the model, it could not readily suggest explicit emulation without also recommending apparently utopian constitutional changes that it sought ordinarily and realistically to avoid. I have in mind the famous advocates of responsible American parties, E. E. Schattschneider and the APSA's own Committee on Political Parties. Although a member of the committee, Schattschneider most clearly and fully stated his case in *Party Government*,[14] a widely used book in the immediate postwar years, and *The Struggle for Party Government*,[15] an influential series of short essays. After searching in these two works for references to British experience, I am struck with their approving character, even in 1942 before the advent of the postwar Labour government, but also with their small number, brevity, and limited applicability to the author's main argument. Schattschneider approvingly contrasted British cabinet government, under the effective control of the leaders of a majority parliamentary party, with the American situation in which the Constitution makes such a government impossible.[16] Because he proposed no constitutional change, the contrast served only to help explain the nature of the American problem of securing responsible parties. Elsewhere, Schattschneider only implied possible American emulation of British practices by emphasizing the virtues of a less locally oriented parliamentary candidate-selection process,[17] the more limited role of pressure groups in the House of Commons,[18] and the British acceptance of *party* politics as respectable activity.[19]

The APSA's controversial committee report, "Toward a More Responsible Two-Party System," said even less about the British model.[20] The cabinet system was mentioned only to be quickly put aside,[21] and there was a brief though admiring description of the substantial permanent central staffing of British parties.[22] Limited though these references surely were, we have the written evidence of one who served on the committee, E. M. Kirkpatrick, that "the British model was significant for a number of its members."[23] Furthermore, Kirkpatrick devoted two pages of his devastatingly critical analysis of the report to the proposition that the committee had seriously misunderstood the actual operation of British parties and had, consequently, advocated changes in accord with a partly fictitious model.[24] I might temper that criticism, but I can hardly challenge Kirkpatrick's recollection of the significance that the British model had for committee members. It should be emphasized, however, that even Kirkpatrick's account did not assert that the committee thought that the United States could or should adopt the full British party model. At most, the committee wanted American parties to follow certain British practices despite the constraints of the American constitutional setting.

In stressing that the much-abused APSA committee report was innocent of wholesale imitation of the British model, I am trying to sustain my view that American political scientists who used the model did not often let their admiration, when it existed, lead them to think that we could or should fully copy it in the United States. Not only were most Americanists among us wary of wholesale imitation of the British model but so also were most comparativists. Samuel Beer, the leading postwar American scholar of British parties, is illustrative. Admiring generally though not wholly the British party model that he explicated so well, and often seeming to want more effective and coherent American policy making, Beer nevertheless remained dubious about the importation of British-inspired reforms.[25] Writing when British governmental prestige was still high, he did no more than favorably contrast "the concentration of power in the British system" with the American system's "dispersion of power" that creates tendencies toward "incoherence and immobilism."[26]

UNDERSTANDING THE MODEL

Particularly during the postwar years, several specialized American and British scholars sought to rectify suspected misconceptions and misinformation about how parties worked in Britain. Rectification of this kind became a thriving, though small, academic industry, and I confess to a part in it. Little of the criticism, however, sought to refute the view that party government existed in Britain in a form or to an extent unknown in the United States. The essence of the model, as we had known it since Wilson and Lowell, remained securely in place. Most critics argued that American party reformers in the postwar years had tended, on the basis of limited acquaintance, to exaggerate the admittedly high degree of parliamentary party cohesion, and, more significantly, to attribute it to greater ideological commitment, stronger central party control, fuller mass-membership participation in policy making, and more clearcut electoral mandates than actually existed in Britain. Although in retrospect I am inclined to stress the limitations of the criticism, much of it was certainly substantial and useful. One of the earliest and best corrective pieces was by David Butler; he contended that "British parties are in fact much less differentiated and much less democratic than is often supposed, and that it is a good thing that this should be so."[27] He thought that their differences, ideologically and programmatically, were not nearly so great in the postwar years as they had seemed to be in the 1930s. Butler also believed that parliamentary leaders, not rank-and-file party members, were predominant as policy makers even in the Labour party. Here Butler's theme resembled that of McKenzie's major party organizational study.[28] Their stress on the leadership's policy-making power, it should be noted, would not have troubled all American responsible-party advocates; Schattschneider, for example, did not rest his case on intra-party democracy.

In any event, there is a respectable argument to be made for important occasional influence flowing from organized British party members.[29] It cannot be so confidently dismissed as wrong even by those of us who have accepted most of McKenzie's analysis and preferences. From time to time, a party conference representing a dues-paying membership, or an executive committee acting in its behalf, affected the policies of an election manifesto. So it seemed in one important particular of Labour's 1945 election program,[30] notable also for the fact that so much of the program was subsequently enacted. No doubt, the salience of this experience in the immediate postwar years led too readily to generalizations not just about intra-party democracy but also about clear-cut electoral mandates and government policy accomplishments that could not be supported by experience in other periods. Such mistaken generalizations, however, strike me as exaggerations, often temporary, of certain characteristics of the model, rather than as basic misunderstandings.

American party reformers might have had reasons of their own for highlighting whatever role the mass membership played in party affairs. Without the benefit of a parliamentary system that could itself produce the legislative cohesion necessary for an effective programmatic governing party, it was natural to look to whatever else seemed to encourage party loyalty among British MPs. The ideological and programmatic commitments of their organized followers were plausible encouragements especially insofar as these commitments were enforced in one way or another—that is, if MPs were threatened with loss of place for significantly deviating from the wishes of their party's dues-paying members. On this score, one did not have to believe that the organized external membership made or even heavily influenced policies imposed on the parliamentary party. No more had to be assumed than that the organized membership shared the commitments (often more zealously) of its parliamentary leaders and was willing to select as candidates those who would act in accord with those commitments. With rare exceptions, British party members fulfilled those conditions, and, without the hurdle of a direct primary, their bestowal of the party label on candidates remained definitive. If at first in the postwar years the candidate-selection process was incorrectly perceived as highly centralized, the picture of committed party persons in control of the process was not critically changed by learning that constituency-party activists were effectively the selectors.[31] These activists, while choosing candidates in constituency organizations, remained national rather than local in their policy orientations. American responsible-party advocates could still envy the programmatic enforcement that the system thus allowed, and they might even hope in the United States to mobilize similar programmatic followers capable of selecting loyal candidates and of helping them to win direct primaries.

The postwar American party reformers ordinarily realized that those who cared about national party policies would have to control or exert great influence in the congressional nominating process if they were to have a responsible-party system. Moreover, in the 1950s new ideological or programmatic American party organizations, called amateur, non-patronage, and voluntary, developed in several states mainly for this purpose. The fact that they could not regularly fulfill the purpose, in the British manner, tells us what even many responsible-party advocates have always known: the American political structure imposes formidable obstacles to the development of programmatically cohesive parties on a national scale. The experience does not tell us that there was an ill-informed effort to imitate British practices. Not only were the new American programmatic activists probably unaware of any British model, but also their intellectual supporters among political scientists, while more likely to have the model in mind, may not have misunderstood it in thinking that Americans should try to emulate its organizational and candidate-selection features. At most, it seems to me, they might have overestimated the degree to which extra-parliamentary organizations, in contrast to the pressures of the parliamentary system itself, were responsible for British party cohesion.

Turning from party reformers, what can be said about the way in which comparative politics specialists understood the British party model during the first two postwar decades? We can fairly assume that they, whether American or British, would have been a principal source of knowledge for the rest of the profession. Their emphases vary, of course, and it is risky to generalize. Textbook chapters, I believe, properly stressed the parliamentary discipline that characterized the two major parties in the 1950s and early 1960s although the qualifications might not always have been as fully spelled out as we should now prefer. Among specialized works, Beer's influential *British Politics in the Collectivist Age* (1965) devoted more attention to the ideological character of both major parties than did several other close observers, but Beer's description of

British party government was representative in depicting its relative strength and cohesion, and carefully tempered by an appreciation of the importance of interest groups in the system. To be sure, this appreciation was mainly reserved for the way in which interest groups were accommodated within or through the major parties and the ministries, in contrast to the more direct legislative influence of interest groups in the United States.

Here, in relation to interest groups, we should note a more basic problem concerning the American understanding of the British party. Customarily it was perceived as majoritarian in the sense of being much more capable than an American party of enacting a program or set of policies in behalf of a majority of citizens. Beer's description was not at odds with this perception; it filled it out, sensibly, by showing how a British party aggregated diverse interests compatibly with the maintenance of its legislative cohesion. Did that aggregating function make it possible for American pluralists to admire the British party model? I raise the query because without an affirmative answer to it we might conclude that American pluralists should have rejected the British party model. No doubt, many did reject it even during its heyday. Admiration would always have been easier for an unabashed majoritarian like Schattschneider.

DECLINING ATTRACTIVENESS

The decline in the model's attractiveness is, I believe, readily apparent. Along with Britain's political institutions generally, its parties have suffered new blows from American and British critics during the last 10 or 15 years. Effective and coherent policy making is no longer perceived as the predominant result of the British system. Party government is blamed for many of Britain's new failures. Kavanagh captured the spirit as well as the substance of the recent American criticism in his broader review article.[32] He cited several important works rejecting the once-supposed superiority of the British model. Among them is Kenneth Waltz's major assault (1967) on Britain's political leadership in foreign policy since 1945. While critical of the whole British political system, Waltz regarded the prime minister's concern for party unity as a principal cause of neglect of a broader public interest.[33] Moreover, he contrasted this feature of the British party model unfavorably with the American arrangement that allows for a less party-oriented foreign policy leadership.[34] If few other political scientists went so far as Waltz, there were widespread doubts about the British system after the mid-1960s. As

Kavanagh notes, they appear in Beer's epilogue chapter,[35] written for the paperback edition of his 1965 book, and the doubts refer particularly to the efficacy of British party government.

Certain American criticism probably originated in this country, perhaps as reaction against a perceived anglophile tradition, but American political scientists were hardly unaware that British writers had begun to express a new dissatisfaction with their own political institutions and with parties in particular. Bernard Crick's proposals for parliamentary reform,[36] strengthening MPs and the Commons as a whole in relation to the party-based executive leadership, were well known in this country, and so, a little later, were the critical opinions of John Mackintosh on the way in which party cohesiveness actually functioned.[37] Indeed, it would have been hard for any American student of British politics in the 1970s to escape what had become a prevailing current of adverse commentary on party government by British political scientists and related intellectual publicists. The commentary could be said to have culminated in *The Economist's* well-publicized five-page editorial leader marking Guy Fawkes Day[38]; the leader recommended the figurative blowing up of the system of government that allows "two alternating party political tyrannies."[39] *The Economist* would free Britain from these tyrannies—that is, from the likelihood of responsible party government—by a form of proportional representation that would preclude a majority party without a majority of popular votes, by a constitutional bill of rights limiting the scope of governmental action, and by a parliament whose members, committees, and resources would more nearly resemble those of the U.S. Congress than those of the much less powerful House of Commons. To be sure, these recommendations were not out of line with *The Economist's* nineteenth-century liberal tradition, but the ground had now been well prepared by numerous academic critics of the system.

We should not, therefore, expect many favorable references to British party performance in the most recent proposals for the reform of American political parties. Certain proposals did not even use the old "responsible party" theme that might have drawn, implicitly or explicitly, on the British model. Saloma and Sontag, for example, avoided the language of the responsible-party school. They sought to distinguish themselves from its principal advocates[40] although they did recommend several features of responsible parties—for example, more policy-coherent congressional parties, and more issue-oriented citizen participation in electoral party organizations. On the other hand, the actual post-1968 Democratic party reforms moved, in vital respects, away from responsible-party goals. Whatever its model, the McGovern-Fraser Commission, seeking more open and wider participation in party affairs, helped to demolish what there was of regularized control of nomination processes. The shift was in the progresive anti-organizational direction. If the Democratic reformers wanted to build a new, stronger, and more ideological organization after destroying old and inappropriate structures, their intentions were seldom explicit enough to cite a responsible-party model, British or any other.[41]

Yet many American students of parties continued to prefer responsible parties in the 1970s although some avoided, as did Saloma and Sontag, an identification with the responsible-party school. Others, like W. D. Burnham,[42] were less optimistic about the possibilities than were political scientists of an earlier generation. Now and then the responsible-party school itself received a favorable reexamination. Pomper[43] argued that the APSA committee of 1950 had often been correct in its projections of the consequences of continuing to function without responsible parties, and that certain conditions required for such parties were more fully met in the 1970s than in the 1950s. While thus being relatively optimistic, Pomper did not cite the British model. Of course, that is not evidence that he rejected it—any more than a similar absence of the British model from J. M. Burns' earlier popular book advocating responsible American parties[44] indicates such rejection. The model, along with Britain generally, may just command less attention when the old favorable image dims. So it is possible to account for the absence of British experience in Broder's well-known book[45] and in his very recent writing.[46] In urging that we develop much stronger parties, Broder[47] drew heavily from the APSA's report of 1950, as well as from other political scientists, but he did not specify anything about the British model that might have been in the minds of certain earlier writers. Insofar as Broder had a working model, it was of a responsible-party government that he believed once existed in more substantial degree in the United States.[48]

Lest we conclude that all American reformers abandoned discussion of the British party model, we should note Charles Hardin's case for a new American constitution[49] redesigned on principles so close to those of British parliamentary government that it would produce the kind of strong party that had existed in modern Britain. Not only did Hardin insist with good reason, if with unrealistic hope, that parliamentary-type institutions must be adopted in order to produce British-type parties; but also, in so arguing, he responded to a large portion of the recently adverse criticism of the performance of British party government.[50] Significantly, Hardin liked the British party model not merely because party government promises coherent policy making but especially because such policy making is collective rather than individual in the manner of the American presidency. Writing when the presidency had been darkened by Nixon and by failures in Vietnam, Hardin wanted a chief execu-tive who would, like a British prime minister, be a party leader subject to control by his or her legislative followers. Executive authority could thus be strong and yet effectively limited.[51]

Other Americans, less interested than Hardin in strengthening par-ties, similarly discovered in British experience a means for restraining American executive authority in the 1970s. It is hard to say that they found the British party model attractive as had the older responsible-party school or even Hardin. For example, Groth[52] concentrated on the restraints imposed on British prime ministers because they shared decision-making power with the cabinet and had to answer for it in the Commons. Groth's admiration is primarily for the traditional parliamen-tary institutions that limited the executive and not for the strong party support that others had supposed those institutions to have helped pro-duce. Later post-Watergate critics occasionally looked enviously to Bri-tian's conventional vote of no-confidence as a way to limit chief executives. These ideas, critically reviewed by Livingston,[53] are tangen-tial to my analysis but interesting because they indicate that in the early and mid-1970s Americans could be attracted to British practices that are distinguishable from those usually associated with the party model itself.

The period for that kind of attraction may already have ended when the Watergate scandal receded and Americans began again to search for a strong president who would lead Congress rather than being limited by it. Probably, too, not very many political scientists even in the early and mid-1970s looked to the restraining features of British institutions. In-stead, the relatively strong and cohesive parliamentary parties remained familiar benchmarks for elucidating, by comparison, the increasingly great independence-from-party of American congressional representa-tives. Thus Mayhew explained the American situation by a highly so-phisticated reference to the British.[54] Although at least implicitly critical of a good deal of American congressional behavior, Mayhew stressed the way in which such behavior is a consequence of a system basically differ-ent from Britain's. So neutrally objective an account of the British party model, without the old admiration and certainly without recommenda-tions for emulation, strikes me as typical, despite the exceptions cited, of those American political scientists who used the British comparison at all in the 1970s and even the late 1960s. I admit, however, that I do not find numerous contemporary discussions of British experience in the kind of American context that Mayhew provides.

My impression is that American academic interest in many aspects of British politics declined in the last two decades, or, more precisely, that it declined relative to other interests. There is no disconfirmation of that impression in the rough counting that I described in my earlier foot-note; rather, the proportion of *APSR* articles on all British subjects dropped to two percent in the 1960s and 1970s from six percent in the 1950s and four to eight percent in preceding decades. Counting only *APSR* articles may underestimate the recent British interest on the part of American political scientists because they could now be contributing works on Britain to several new specialized journals. Hence the general significance of the reported small decline is uncertain. For the professional journal serving the largest political science readership, strictly scholarly developments, like the growth of research on many other nations and on new topics unconnected with any particular nations, could help explain any lessened relative interest in British subjects. But there is also the plain fact that Britain as a nation has become much less powerful and important in the world during the last few decades. We have less cause to look at Britain's foreign policy making, either for its successes or failures, when it no longer plays a major role in international affairs. Moreover, Britain's economy has grown less rapidly than the economies of most continental nations and has now fallen below several of them in an absolute sense. Whether or not national failures are blamed on party government or any other political institution, Britain is a struggling medium-sized industrial country much less likely than in its great-power days to provide models for us.

A probable ideological cause for turning away from the British party model also appears in the late 1960s and 1970s. These were years of disappointment for democratic socialism. Unlike the period immediately following 1945, the American Left—socialist, crypto-socialist, or just welfare-statist—could now see little in Britain by way of major change or promise of major change. Thus the British party model lacked much of the allure of preceding decades. I do not suggest that conservative Americans have never been attracted to the party model, as they were to other British political institutions, but I believe that the particular model had appealed especially to left-of-center reformers who sought a means effectively to mobilize a majority to support domestic economic and social legislation. I tried to make the point in discussing the use of the model in the late 1940s and 1950s, and I believe that it can also be made about Woodrow Wilson's admiration for British party government as he himself became a reformer. Like Wilson, relatively few Americans who, after 1945, looked hopefully to British Labour were socialists, even in the loose British sense. But in the postwar years they saw Labour using its parliamentary party majority to enact large-scale economic and social changes within a stable democratic society. Without that use, the British party model lost a substantial portion of its old American constituency.

The loss—that is, the diminished ideological appeal—is explicable from several standpoints. British socialism and the Labour party were themselves often associated with Britain's decline and failures—being largely blamed for *The Future That Doesn't Work*.[55] So perhaps fewer observers now favored British socialism and the political means for its accomplishment. Thus the American Left might itself have diminished or have become a still less explicitly socialist Left. But even among those seeking socialist solutions—including many seeking these solutions for the first time—the British parliamentary means for achieving socialism had come to look even more pragmatic and so less "socialist" than earlier; furthermore, Labour party leadership had become more prominently middle-class. Harold Wilson's 13 years (1963–1976) as Labour leader, eight of them as prime minister, were uninspiring for socialists.

Likelier than earlier, socialists could find credible, or at least plausible, the far-Left's persistent rejection of the established parliamentary means for the political advancement of working-class objectives. Leninists were not alone among socialists rejecting British Labour's credentials and methods. More popular among intellectuals in Britain and the United States during the late 1960s and 1970s were those who used Marxist arguments against parliamentary socialism without adopting the explicitly Leninist alternative of revolutionary action to create a dictatorship of the proletariat. Well known among these critics of the Labour party is Ralph Miliband. His books,[56] widely circulated in both Britain and the United States, argued that the failures of Labour governments to be more socialist lay in the party's too-exclusive reliance on conventional parliamentary means. Miliband did not want to abandon those means, or the political liberties associated with them, but he did want the mobilization of working-class participants in a network of organizations supplementing state power.[57] Still more sharply, another British leftist critic, David Coates, following Miliband's earlier writing, contended that Labour's faith in the reforming potential of a parliamentary majority is misplaced and that now, as in the past, Labour's failures illustrate "the impossibility of the Parliamentary road to socialism."[58]

No doubt, few American political scientists would have turned away from the British party model because of Marxist-influenced criticism of Labour's use of that model. Nevertheless, I cite these critics to indicate the breadth of disillusionment with the conventional hopes for the model. The point can also be illustrated by turning to a more moderate critic of Labour's inability to achieve working-class objectives. Andrew Martin, an American political scientist asking only whether democratic control—defined as organized labor's control—of capitalist economies is possible,[59] argued that Swedish Social Democrats may have succeeded in a way that British Labour had not. His case, ingeniously made, rests on the possibly crucial usefulness of continuous long-term power for the party representing organized labor. Thus the Swedish Social Democrats, dominating governments for over four decades, could accomplish objectives impossible for British Labour because of its enforced alternation in office. In other words, the very election system that provided the Labour party with a parliamentary majority also deprived it of a sufficiently long-run opportunity to carry out its program successfully. Britain's kind of two-party competition, resting on single-member plurality elections and ordinarily perceived as advantageous for enactment of a socialist program, is in Martin's view less useful than Sweden's multipartyism, associated with proportional representation, which allowed Social Democrats to control governmental policies as the largest single party, although not often with a majority of parliamentary seats. Hence, in a special way Martin saw defects in the British party model.

Regardless of the election system and the number of effectively competing parties, it may have become harder for a labor or social democratic party in any highly developed society to mobilize an electoral majority for strictly working-class objectives. The industrial working class no longer appears large enough in any homogeneous sense to provide such a majority. As Inglehart declared, "The Left *must* go beyond a working-class base if it hopes to win elections."[60] As white-collar workers are beginning to outnumber blue-collar workers, he believed that a party of the Left would have little chance if it depended on class-based voting. Its hopes, he argued, lie in attracting votes from "a relatively large Post-Materialist section of the middle class."[61] Such hopes may well be realizable in Britain or elsewhere, but it is not clear that their realization in an electoral sense would mean realization in the old working-class socialist sense. A majority now would be more diverse in its composition and interests, and perhaps more transient. The party model thus becomes more pluralist in character than it was for those socialists who conceived of a majority party as representative of the working-class majority of the population.

It is true that most advocates of stronger American parties never adopted the class-based majoritarianism found in the European socialist tradition. They tended to be majoritarian only in the sense of believing that a party could mobilize a set of interests constituting an effective majority supporting a given program. Insofar as British Labour might have seemed a class-based party in the European tradition, it could not so readily serve as a model in the United States. But, as I have suggested, the Labour party had impressed American reformers, correctly, I believe, as a less thoroughly majoritarian, even a quasi-pluralist, means for achieving socialist or certain non-socialist purposes.

The point that remains is that American reformers as well as socialists recently became impressed with perceived failures rather than successes of the British Labour party. Hence, an important mid-century reason for the American Left to admire the British party model disappeared, at least temporarily. It is too soon to know whether any comparable admiration will develop on the American right if the British Conservative party's parliamentary majority of 1979 should successfully enact its anti-socialist policies.

CHANGES IN THE MODEL

For those interested in broadly programmatic policies, left or right, the British party model's attractiveness always rested on its actual operations; British responsible-party government was a working model rather than an abstraction. So it was also for many of its new critics in the late 1960s and the 1970s; for example, the *Economist's* attack of 1977, previously cited, assumed that party government remained powerful. On the other hand, political scientists, in Britain and the United States, began in the 1970s to observe changes in the characteristics of British parties. In their eyes, the system could no longer be counted on to produce a cohesive party majority as it had during the previous three or four decades of Conservative-Labour competition. Some observers also challenged the earlier description for overlooking or down-playing past deviations from cohesive party government. The emphasis, however, was on changes evident in the 1970s even if they were treated as implicit in earlier experiences.[62]

Important changes were found in electoral behavior, parliamentary parties, and extra-parliamentary organizations. All indicated a weakening of the capacity of the two major parties, Conservative and Labour, to dominate British politics and government. Least crucial, in my opinion, was the decline in the direct individual dues-paying membership of the extra-parliamentary party organizations. Having by the 1960s already dropped from peaks achieved in the early 1950s, both the Conservative and Labour parties continued the generally downward trends in such memberships. The Conservative total, however, apparently remained over one million, after having been over two million, and Labour's, while roughly half of what it had been and down to about 300,000, was augmented by over six million indirectly affiliated trade-union memberships.[63] It is not clear that diminished numbers of direct dues-paying members lessened the always-disputed policy-making role of the external organizations. Insofar as the extra-parliamentary party organization might reinforce the parliamentary party loyalty achieved and achievable as a result of other causes, a smaller membership could be just as effective. Where, however, a diminished organization would be less effective is in campaigning. Systematic volunteer canvassing, long so conspicuous an activity of British constituency parties,[64] requires a substantial regularized membership. Its decline itself may thus make it harder for the major parties to mobilize voters although the membership decline itself may also have been caused by a weakening of the parties for other reasons or by the deliberate substitution of mass-media campaigning for individual canvassing. I do not, therefore, treat party membership declines as generally insignificant when I contend that they have not themselves basically altered the British party model.

Much more fundamental was the inability of either major party to win and hold a secure majority of parliamentary seats during about half of the 1970s. From February to October 1974, when Labour governed after winning less than half the seats in the February general election, and also during the next four and one-half years, when Labour had either the barest of majorities or, in the last three years, had none at all except with the help of minor parties, there could simply be no strong party government in the conventional sense. The duration of minority-party government in the 1970s was especially striking. During the preceding decades of two-party dominance, not to mention the 1920s, governments had rested on slim and insecure majorities. They were, however, short-lived and more readily viewed as transitional than the Labour governments of 1974–1979. Admittedly, those governments too may later be regarded as transitional if several years of party majorities now follow the May 1979 election.

Nevertheless, the experience of the 1970s suggests continued departures from the postwar two-party order. It is true that Britain's use of the simple-plurality, single-member election system still helps mightily to produce a majority parliamentary party on a minority of national popular votes for its candidates. But as is shown by long Canadian experience, even more than by Britain's in the 1970s, the election system's magnification, or distortion, of a major party's popular vote has not always been sufficient to provide a secure majority, if any majority at all. In Britain, it was insufficient in the 1974 elections when neither major party received 40 percent of the total popular vote, and it was just sufficient for a safe parliamentary majority in 1979 when the Conservatives received almost 44 percent of the vote. The popular democratic credentials of that parliamentary majority, it should be noted, are suspect in greater degree than they were for earlier party majorities that rested on about 48 percent of the voters (or on an actual voting majority, last achieved in 1935). But in the 1970s it was hard for a major party to come close to winning half of the popular vote. Third-party Liberals, various regional parties, and minor parties together polled between a tenth and a quarter of the votes in the four general elections of the decade, including almost a fifth in the 1979 election that produced the substantial Conservative majority in the House of Commons. The persistence of Liberal electoral strength, still at almost 14 percent in 1979 after its postwar highs of 18 and 19 percent in 1974, is notable. So too, as evidence of the limitations of the major parties, is the increased volatility of support for Labour and the Conservatives.[65] The erosion of electoral commitment to the major parties became most apparent in the 1970s although it may well have begun a decade or more earlier. Voters identified less strongly and less constantly with Conservatives and Labour without always substituting any more durable third-party commitments. Perhaps British two-partyism suffered in the 1970s because the class basis for the earlier mobilization of Conservative and Labour voters had diminished.[66] Whatever the reason, achieving the kind of electoral support requisite for majority-party government was now much more uncertain than it had been in the postwar years.

Still more disruptive of the party model in the 1970s was a decreasing cohesiveness in each parliamentary party even when it had a majority. The way in which the European Economic Community (EEC) issue cut across party lines was only the most highly visible of these signs. The critical parliamentary decisions on EEC in both 1971 and 1975 rested on cross-party majorities, and in 1975 the governing Labour party split sharply and widely when it held a national referendum on Britain's continued membership.[67] Even if the EEC issue had been alone in producing intra-party parliamentary divisions, it could not readily be treated as of little general relevance. Deciding whether the nation should belong to the EEC was the most significant British policy making of the decade and perhaps of the last 40 years. Probably, however, less conspicuous divisions than those on the EEC issue are more persuasive with respect to decreased parliamentary-party cohesion.

The increasing frequency of intra-party dissent in parliamentary voting has been carefully tabulated and analyzed by Philip Norton of the University of Hull. His recording of all cross-voting from 1945 to 1974 shows a sharp rise in both the number and proportion of divisions involving dissenting votes from the earlier parliaments (especially those of the 1950s) to the parliament of 1970–74. Norton finds the Conservative government of 1970–74 to have been actually defeated on five occasions as a result of dissenting votes, including abstentions, and to have suffered on one occasion from the adverse votes of two-thirds of its party's

MPs on a whipped division.[68] These examples are especially telling because the Conservative government of 1970–74 did have a parliamentary majority at just the level of modesty once thought most likely to ensure solidarity and so its policy-making effectiveness. The rising intra-party dissension of the early 1970s makes it unlikely that the better-known dissension during the Labour governments of 1974–79 could be characteristic only of circumstances in which there was either the barest party majority or none. Instead, Norton's later analyses[69] display the post-1974 intra-party voting dissension as a continuation of tendencies previously established. Between 1974 and 1979, several Labour MPs helped, crucially on occasion, to defeat their government's parliamentary policies on expenditures, taxes, Scottish devolution, and wage restraint. They rallied back to the flag only on votes of confidence, thus helping to keep their party leaders in office.

Of course, from 1976 to 1979, their party's lack of a parliamentary majority meant that Labour MPs needed the support or least the abstention of certain minor-party MPs in order to win confidence votes. Accordingly, when almost all the minor-party MPs voted with the Conservative opposition on the April 1979 confidence motion, Labour's solidarity, though complete, was not enough to keep the government in office. Losing a vote of confidence, as Callaghan's government thus did in 1979, was not at odds with any previously expected operation of the system. Although there had been no other such loss for over 50 years, it was well understood that a minority governing party might always be defeated by a combination of opposing parties. During the three preceding years, however, the system had worked differently from the way in which many of us had told our students that it had worked in the postwar decades. Prime Minister Callaghan remained in office, 1976–79, despite unreversed parliamentary defeats of several of his government's important policies. Moreover, they were defeats that he might well have suffered, as had Heath in 1970–74, even if his party had held a majority rather than almost a majority of seats.

It is clear that in the 1970s both Conservative and Labour MPs voted more independently, and more consequently so, than their predecessors of the 1950s. The change need not have been overwhelming in order to be important. We can still appreciate that MPs, while never as regularly docile as the most extreme picture of party discipline might have implied, remained in the 1970s much more regularly loyal to their parties than American congressional representatives ever have been. We can also appreciate that the decline in parliamentary party cohesion might, like that of the electoral capacity of the major parties, be reversible. But, at least for the 1970s we must say that the British party model itself substantially changed. A cohesive party as well as a majority party became less certain.

CONCLUDING INFERENCES

The *first* of the broad inferences to be drawn from my review of the place of the British party model in political science comes most directly from the last section. It concerns the time-bound nature of our studies, about which I also wrote when reviewing works on American presidential nominations.[70] In that fascinating area, generalizations based on the politics of 1940–1968 were evidently shaken by experiences in 1972 and 1976. Here and elsewhere, political scientists must now be aware of changes in patterns discerned only a decade or so earlier. The awareness is notably acute in recent scholarship in the highly developed study of voting behavior.[71] Yet we like to write in the present tense, so describing behavior and the operation of political institutions in terms that allow readers to think that there is and will be a continuity in what we have found to exist over the past decade or two. It is one of the ways in which we distinguish ourselves from most historians. When we desert the present tense, we often still imply that recently observed developments will remain in effect. I may have come close to doing that in describing the weakened grip of British parties during the 1970s, and I am certain that many of us treated the dominant and cohesive Conservative and Labour parties of the first postwar years as though they would remain so into an indefinite future. Now their great power in the years soon after World War II looks to have been something of a period piece, expressing a simpler, more complete two-party division between classes and ideologies that had prevailed during earlier decades, or that would prevail in the 1970s. At least from the standpoint of 1979, the capacity of the British system to mobilize almost all political interests into two major parties, each cohesive in its purposes, seems a transient phenomenon rather than a durable culmination of long-run developments. Although Americans still have good reason to view each major British party as relatively cohesive and capable of responsible government, now as in the rest of the last century, we must qualify the sharper picture that we had a little earlier.

My *second* inference relates to the perspective of time in a different sense. Even if we have accurately described the British party model in reasonably qualified form, as I believe that political scientists have usually done, its attractiveness rose and fell especially with the policy successes and failures that the American Left identified with it. As I have observed, it was on the left, a moderate Left to be sure, that the model usually had its American champions. While embraced by British tories as well as by British socialists (but not always by British liberals), the majoritarian feature of responsible-party government might have had less appeal for American conservatives. So far at least, it is mainly the ideological perspective of the Left that helps to explain the rise and decline of the British party model's attractiveness in the United States.

Third, the diminished attractiveness of the British party model parallels experience with other once-popular working political models. I am thinking especially but not only of socialist models like those provided by the USSR and other nations governed by Communist parties. It seems to me that Western Marxists now seldom regard any of these nations as suitable models for the United States or other advanced industrial societies. The socialist goals that they retain do not appear to be based on working models elsewhere, as they often were, for instance, in the 1930s. We do not live in a time when the desire for a better political world characteristically finds its fulfillment in a happy experience elsewhere. What hopes we still have must evidently depend on using our own political institutions rather than trying to reshape them according to an operating model in another country. Political scientists may have played a part in bringing about this change, specifically in the case of the British party model by explaining how it actually works, but I should think that their part has been modest relative to other changing perspectives that have made the British experience less compelling.

These new perspectives, it should be added, need not mark the end of our discipline's long-standing treatment of British party government as a principal comparative benchmark for the exposition of the American political system. The model could thus remain useful analytically even without its old appeal as a superior political instrument.

NOTES

1. Dennis Kavanagh, "An American Science of British Politics," *Political Studies* 22 (1974): 2251-70.

2. Austin Ranney, *The Doctrine of Responsible Party Government* (Urbana, Ill.: U. of Illinois Press, 1962).

3. Woodrow Wilson, *Congressional Government* (Boston: Houghton Mifflin, 1885); Lawrence A. Lowell, "The Influence of Party Upon Legislation in England and America," *Annual Report of the American Historical Association* (Washington, D.C.: U.S. Government Printing Office, 1902); Lowell, *The Government of England* (New York: Macmillan, 1908).

4. Lawrence A. Lowell, *Essays on Government* (Boston: Houghton Mifflin, 1889), pp. 78-96.

5. Lawrence A. Lowell, "The Physiology of Politics," *American Political Science Review* 4 (1910): 3.

6. Lowell, *The Government of England.*

7. Frederic A. Ogg, *English Government and Politics* (New York: Macmillan, 1929).

8. Walter Bagehot, *The English Constitution and Other Political Essays* (New York: Appleton, 1877).

9. Dean E. McHenry, *His Majesty's Opposition* (Berkeley, Calif.: U. of California Press, 1940).

10. Pendleton Herring, *Presidential Leadership* (New York: Rinehart, 1940), pp. 129–30, 142.

11. Don K. Price, "The Parliamentary and Presidential Systems," *Public Administration Review* 3 (1943): 317–34.

12. Ivor W. Jennings, *Cabinet Government* (Cambridge: Cambridge U. Press, 1936); Jennings, *Parliament* (Cambridge: Cambridge U. Press, 1939).

13. Herman Finer, *The Theory and Practice of Modern Government* (New York: Henry Holt, 1949).

14. E. E. Schattschneider, *Party Government* (New York: Holt, Rinehart and Winston, 1942).

15. Schattschneider, *The Struggle for Party Government* (College Park, Md.: U. of Maryland Press, 1948).

16. Schattschneider, *Party Government*, pp. 123–27.

17. Ibid., pp. 99–100.

18. Ibid., p. 107.

19. Schattschneider, *The Struggle for Party Government.*

20. ASPA Committee on Political Parties, "Toward a More Responsible Two-Party System," *American Political Science Review* 44 (1950): Supplement.

21. Ibid., p. 35.

22. Ibid., p. 49.

23. Evron M. Kirkpatrick, "Toward a More Responsible Two-Party System: Political Science, Policy Science, or Pseudo-Science?" *American Political Review* 65 (1971): 965–90.

24. Ibid., pp. 974–76.

25. Samuel H. Beer, "New Structures of Democracy" in William N. Chambers and Robert H. Salisbury, eds., *Democracy Today* (New York: Collier, 1962), pp. 55, 76.

26. Ibid., p. 78.

27. David Butler, "American Myths about British Parties," *Virginia Quarterly Review* 31 (1955): 47.

28. Robert McKenzie, *British Political Parties* (London: William Heinemann, 1955).

29. Lewis Minkin, *The Labour Party Conference* (London: Allen Lane, 1978).

30. Samuel H. Beer, *British Politics in the Collectivist Age* (New York: Random House, 1965), pp. 174–78.

31. Austin Ranney, *Pathways to Parliament* (Madison, Wis.: U. of Wisconsin Press, 1965).

32. Dennis Kavanagh, "An American Science of British Politics," *Political Studies* 22 (1974): 263–65.

33. Kenneth Waltz, *Foreign Policy and Democratic Politics: The American and British Experience* (Boston: Little, Brown, 1967), p. 62.

34. Ibid., p. 307.

35. Samuel H. Beer, *British Politics in the Collectivist Age* (New York: Vintage Books, Random House, 1969).

36. Bernard Crick, *The Reform of Parliament* (London: Weidenfeld and Nicholson, 1964).

37. John P. Mackintosh, "The Declining Respect for the Law" in Anthony King, ed., *Why Is Britain Becoming Harder to Govern?* (London: British Broadcasting Corporation, 1976).

38. *Economist*, 22 November 1975.

39. Ibid., p. 11.

40. John S. Saloma and Frederick H. Sontag, *Parties: The Real Opportunity for Effective Citizen Politics* (New York: Random House, 1972), p. 10.

41. William J. Crotty, *Political Reform and the American Experiment* (New York: Crowell, 1977).

42. Walter Dean Burnham, *Critical Elections and Mainsprings of American Politics* (New York: Norton, 1970).

43. Gerald Pomper, "Toward a More Responsible Two-Party System? What, Again?" *Journal of Politics* 33 (1971): 916–40.

44. James MacGregor Burns, *The Deadlock of Democracy: Four-Party Politics in America* (Englewood Cliffs, N.J.: Prentice-Hall, 1963).

45. David S. Broder, *The Party's Over* (New York: Harper & Row, 1972).

46. David S. Broder, "Parties in Trouble," *Today*, 11 May 1979, pp. 10–11.

47. Broder, *The Party's Over*, pp. 182, 244–46.

48. Ibid., p. 170.

49. Charles E. Hardin, *Presidential Power and Accountability: Toward a New Constitution* (Chicago: U. of Chicago Press, 1974).

50. Ibid., pp. 131–41.

51. Ibid., pp. 2–5.

52. Alexander Groth, "Britain and America: Some Requisites of Leadership Compared," *Political Science Quarterly* 85 (1970): 217–39.

53. William S. Livingston, "Britain and America: The Institutionalization of Accountability," *Journal of Politics* 38 (1976): 879–94.

54. David Mayhew, *Congress: The Electoral Connection* (New Haven, Conn.: Yale U. Press, 1974), pp. 19–27.

55. Emmett R. Tyrrell, ed., *The Future That Doesn't Work: Social Democracy's Failures in Britain* (Garden City, N.Y.: Doubleday, 1977).

56. Ralph Miliband, *Parliamentary Socialism* (London: Allen and Unwin, 1961); Miliband, *The State in Capitalist Society* (London: Quartet Books, 1973); Miliband, *Marxism and Politics* (Oxford: Oxford U. Press, 1977).

57. Miliband, *Marxism and Politics*, pp. 188–89.

58. David Coates, *The Labour Party and the Struggle for Socialism* (London: Cambridge U. Press, 1975), pp. 144, 229.

59. Andrew Martin, "Is Democratic Control of Capitalist Economics Possible?" in Leon N. Lindberg, Robert Alford, Colin Crouch, and Claus Offe, eds.,

Stress and Contradiction in Modern Capitalism (Lexington, Mass.: D. C. Heath, 1975), pp. 13–56.

60. Ronald Inglehart, *The Silent Revolution* (Princeton, N.J.: Princeton U. Press, 1977), p. 215.

61. Ibid.

62. Jorgen S. Rasmussen, "Was Guy Fawes Right?" in Isaac Kramnick, ed., *Is Britain Dying?: Perspectives on the Current Crisis* (Ithaca, N.Y.: Cornell U. Press, 1979), pp. 97–125.

63. *Economist,* 22 November 1975, p. 22.

64. John E. Turner, *Labour's Doorstep Politics in London* (Minneapolis, Minn.: U. of Minnesota Press, 1978).

65. Ivor Crewe, "Party Identification Theory and Political Change in Britain" in Ian Budge, Ivor Crewe, and Dennis Fairlie, eds., *Part Identification and Beyond* (London: Wiley, 1976), pp. 31–61.

66. David S. Butler and Donald Stokes, *Political Change in Britain* (London: Macmillan, 1974), p. 208.

67. Anthony King, *Britain Says Yes* (Washington, D.C.: American Enterprise Institute, 1977).

68. Phillip Norton, *Dissension in the House of Commons: Intra-Party Dissent in the House Commons' Division Lobbies 1945–1974* (London: Macmillan, 1975), pp. 609–10.

69. Phillip Norton, "The Government Defeat: 10 March 1976," *The Parliamentarian* 57 (1976): 174–75; Norton, "Intra-Party Dissent in the House of Commons: The Parliament of 1974," *The Parliamentarian* 58 (1977): 240–45; Norton, "Govern Defeats in the House of Commons: Three Restraints Overcome," *The Parliamentarian* 59 (1978): 231–38.

70. Leon D. Epstein, "Political Science and Presidential Nominations," *Political Science Quarterly* 93 (1978): 177–95.

71. Norman H. Nie, Sidney Verba, and John R. Petrocik, *The Changing American Voter* (Cambridge, Mass.: Harvard U. Press, 1976); Butler and Stokes, *Political Change in Britain.*

REFERENCES

APSA Committee on Political Parties (1950). "Toward a More Responsible Two-Party System." *American Political Science Review* 44: Supplement.

Bagehot, Walter (1877). *The English Constitution and Other Political Essays.* New York: Appleton.

Beet, Samuel H. (1962). "New Structures of Democracy." In William N. Chambers and Robert H. Salisbury (eds.), *Democracy Today.* New York: Collier, pp. 45–79.

_____ (1965). *British Politics in the Collectivist Age.* New York: Random House.

_____ (1969). *British Politics in the Collectivist Age.* New York: Vintage Books, Random House.

Broder, David S. (1972). *The Party's Over*. New York: Harper & Row.

———— (1979). "Parties in Trouble." *Today*, May 11, 1979, pp. 10–11.

Burnham, Walter Dean (1970). *Critical Elections and the Mainsprings of American Politics*. New York: Norton.

Burns, James MacGregor (1963). *The Deadlock of Democracy: Four-Party Politics in America*. Englewood Cliffs, N.J.: Prentice-Hall.

Butler, David (1955). "American Myths about British Parties." *Virginia Quarterly Review* 31: 46–56.

————, and Donald Stokes (1974). *Political Change in Britain*. London: Macmillan.

Coates, David (1975). *The Labour Party and the Struggle for Socialism*. London: Cambridge University Press.

Crewe, Ivor (1976). "Party Identification Theory and Political Change in Britain." In Ian Budge, Ivor Crewe, and Dennis Fairlie (eds.), *Party Identification and Beyond*. London: Wiley, pp. 31–61.

Crick, Bernard (1964). *The Reform of Parliament*. London: Weldenfeld and Nicolson.

Crotty, William J. (1977). *Political Reform and the American Experiment*. New York: Crowell.

Economist (1975). Nov. 22, 1975, p. 22.

———— (1977). "Blowing Up a Tyranny." Nov. 5, 1977, pp. 11–16.

Epstein, Leon D. (1978). "Political Science and Presidential Nominations." *Political Science Quarterly* 93: 177–95.

Finer, Herman (1949). *The Theory and Practice of Modern Government*. New York: Henry Holt.

Ford, Henry Jones (1898). *The Rise and Growth of American Politics*. New York: Macmillan.

Groth, Alexander (1970). "Britain and America: Some Requisites of Leadership Compared." *Political Science Quarterly* 85: 217–39.

Hardin, Charles E. (1974). *Presidential Power and Accountability: Toward a New Constitution*. Chicago: University of Chicago Press.

Herring, Pendleton (1940). *Presidential Leadership*. New York: Rinehart.

Inglehart, Ronald (1977). *The Silent Revolution*. Princeton: Princeton University Press.

Jennings, W. Ivor (1936). *Cabinet Government*. Cambridge: Cambridge University Press.

———— (1939). *Parliament*. Cambridge: Cambridge University Press.

Kavanagh, Dennis (1974). "An American Science of British Politics." *Political Studies* 22: 251–70.

King, Anthony (1977). *Britain Says Yes*. Washington: American Enterprise Institute.

Kirkpatrick, Evron M. (1971). "Toward a More Responsible Two-Party System: Political Science, Policy Science, or Pseudo-Science?" *American Political Science Review* 65: 965–90.

Livingston, William S. (1976). "Britain and America: The Institutionalization of Accountability." *Journal of Politics* 38: 879–94.

Lowell, A. Lawrence (1889). *Essays on Government.* Boston: Houghton Mifflin.

———— (1902). "The Influence of Party Upon Legislation in England and America." *Annual Report of the American Historical Association.* Washington: Government Printing Office.

———— (1908). *The Government of England.* New York: Macmillan.

———— (1910). "The Physiology of Politics." *American Political Science Review* 4: 1–15.

Mackintosh, John P. (1976). "The Declining Respect for the Law." In Anthony King (ed.), *Why is Britain Becoming Harder to Govern?* London: British Broadcasting Corporation, pp. 74–95.

Martin, Andrew (1975). "Is Democratic Control of Capitalist Economies Possible?" In Leon N. Lindberg, Robert Alford, Colin Crouch, and Claus Offe (eds.), *Stress and Contradiction in Modern Capitalism.* Lexington, Mass.: D. C. Heath, pp. 13–56.

Mayhew, David (1974). *Congress: The Electoral Connection.* New Haven: Yale University Press.

McHenry, Dean E. (1940). *His Majesty's Opposition.* Berkeley: University of California Press.

McKenzie, Robert (1955). *British Political Parties.* London: William Heinemann.

Miliband, Ralph (1961). *Parliamentary Socialism.* London: Allen and Unwin.

———— (1973). *The State in Capitalist Society.* London: Quartet Books.

———— (1977). *Marxism and Politics.* Oxford: Oxford University Press.

Minkin, Lewis (1978). *The Labour Party Conference.* London: Allen Lane.

Nie, Norman H., Sidney Verba, and John R. Petrocik (1976). *The Changing American Voter.* Cambridge, Mass.: Harvard University Press.

Norton, Philip (1975). *Dissension in the House of Commons: Intra-Party Dissent in the House of Commons' Division Lobbies 1956–1974.* London: Macmillan.

———— (1976). "The Government Defeat: 10 March 1976." *The Parliamentarian* 57: 174–75.

———— (1977). "Intra-Party Dissent in the House of Commons: The Parliament of 1974." *The Parliamentarian* 58: 240–45.

———— (1978). "Government Defeats in the House of Commons: Three Restraints Overcome." *The Parliamentarian* 59: 231–38.

Ogg, Frederic A. (1929). *English Government and Politics.* New York: Macmillan.

Pomper, Gerald (1971). "Toward a More Responsible Two-Party System? What, Again?" *Journal of Politics* 33: 916–40.

Price, Don K. (1943). "The Parliamentary and Presidential Systems." *Public Administration Review* 3: 317–34.

Ranney, Austin (1962). *The Doctrine of Responsible Party Government.* Urbana: University of Illinois Press.

———— (1965). *Pathways to Parliament.* Madison: University of Wisconsin Press.

Rasmussen, Jorgen S. (1979). "Was Guy Fawkes Right?" In Isaac Kramnick (ed.), *Is Britain Dying?: Perspectives on the Current Crisis.* Ithaca, N.Y.: Cornell University Press, pp. 97–125.

Saloma, John S., and Frederick H. Sontag (1972). *Parties: The Real Opportunity for Effective Citizen Politics.* New York: Random House.
Schattschneider, E. E. (1942). *Party Government.* New York: Holt, Rinehart and Winston.
_____ (1948). *The Struggle for Party Government.* College Park: University of Maryland Press.
Turner, John E. (1978). *Labour's Doorstep Politics in London.* Minneapolis: University of Minnesota Press.
Tyrrell, R. Emmett, ed. (1977). *The Future That Doesn't Work: Social Democracy's Failures in Britain.* Garden City, N.Y.: Doubleday.
Waltz, Kenneth (1967). *Foreign Policy and Democratic Politics: The American and British Experience.* Boston: Little, Brown.
Wilson, Woodrow (1885). *Congressional Government.* Boston: Houghton Mifflin.

PARTIES AND PLURALISM

Robert H. Salisbury

The relationship between political parties and interest groups in American politics has often been discussed, but for the most part in quite general terms. For many commentators it has been almost axiomatic that parties are, or at least can be, desirable institutions in a democracy, aggregating citizen preferences and shaping them into more or less coherent programs of action that voters may then approve or vote against, and thereby exercise meaningful control over their government. Interest groups, on the other hand, are often portrayed as centrifugal, fragmenting forces pursuing narrow policy goals outside the electoral process, escaping the judgment of the voters while generating an assemblage of policies full of inconsistencies and, however beneficial to particular groups, harmful to the overall progress of the nation. Moreover, it has long been held that political parties and interest groups vary inversely in their relative strength and autonomous ability to fulfill their respective purposes; that is, a strong party system dominates interest groups so that they must work through and be constrained by the parties. Whereas, if the parties are weak and unable to keep control of the processes of electing candidates to office or to discipline their members in office, then interest groups will flourish unchecked.

If this is more or less the conventional wisdom in modern political science, it need only be added that indeed almost everyone agrees that American political parties, never all-powerful, are today in very poor health, whereas in the last thirty years we have seen a veritable explosion in the number and variety of interest groups actively pursuing policy interests.

This would seem to provide ample grounds for pessimism, and for many it has done so. Before we embrace such a gloomy conclusion, however, it might be worth looking more closely and carefully at just what the key concepts—parties and interest groups—mean and how, in both past and present, they have actually been connected. We shall confront in this process a considerably more complicated set of relationships than so far suggested and perhaps derive a more uncertain and less clearly dour set of expectations.

Not all the politically relevant or effective interests in American politics are represented by organized groups. Hence, although I will certainly take interest organizations into account, the more inclusive and accurate term to employ for my purposes is pluralism. And because pluralism has been a hotly disputed concept in political science, it is necessary to say at the outset what I mean by it. I do *not* regard pluralism, as many seem to, as synonymous with organized interest groups. Nor do I suppose, as is sometimes said of pluralists, that because the American political order is pluralist, all interests can effectively make a sufficient noise that "some official will have to listen or else suffer."[1]

Pluralism entails four necessary elements. First, and most obvious, there must be a diversity of interests in the system, a heterogeneity of values from which political action springs. If there is substantial consensus—as in a middle-class suburb, perhaps[2]—or a polity divided into two or three socioeconomic classes or ethnic groups whose conflicts dominate every political question and shape every policy answer, the system should not be regarded as pluralist. Second, as Dahl stressed in his study of New Haven,[3] for pluralism to be meaningful there must be multiple resources of relevance to public decisions—money, votes, legal authority, expertise, and so on—and control of these resources must be dispersed, not concentrated in one or two groups. In New Haven, some interests had votes but little money, while others were wealthy but were not always able to convert their resources into political clout. What resources there are, which ones really count, and what groups control them are, of course, empirical questions, not to be settled by assertion. For a system to be regarded as pluralist—whether it is a nation, a state, or a local community—there must not only be a diversity of interests but also widely dispersed resources of potential influence.

A third necessity in a pluralist order involves the institutional structures through which the collective decisions of public policy are made. If diverse interests are to articulate their preferences with regard to collective or policy choices and retain their separate identities for future rounds of play, there must be an institutional arena, or perhaps several, in which those interests are present, either as such or through representation. Moreover, that presence must be a matter of continuing right, lest a majority vote to exclude or suppress some minority. Even if some interests lose every time out, in a pluralist order they must retain the possibility of securing representation and do so perhaps in defiance of centralized leadership. For a political leader or a party to be able to control the effective selection of legislators is to reduce and possibly destroy authentic pluralism. The selection of decision makers must be rooted in the same ground that generates the pluralist diversity of values.

Within the institutional arena(s) employed to make public policy decisions, a pluralist order proceeds through bargaining to create coalitions large enough to meet the criteria of action specified by the institution's rules. There are a good many institutional variations that would satisfy the requirement, but a single-chamber parliament with two strong, centralized, and disciplined parties does not. No room is left for bargaining within the framework of the parliament, and diversity of interests will have to be preserved, if at all, through articulation and bargaining elsewhere, in party conferences perhaps or even in the cabinet. The classic pluralist institution is the characteristic American legislature in which autonomous constituencies select their representatives who, in turn, tend to be insulated against command from party leaders and may therefore choose to represent whatever combination of interests suits their own purposes. Added to this, of course, is the further institutional fragmentation brought about by the separation of powers and federalism. The result is enormously to increase the amount of pluralist bargaining required to enact and implement almost any policy choice.

Finally, for a system properly to be called pluralist, there can be no permanent winners. There may well be perennial losers. In the U.S., racial minorities endured decades of abject political failure. Many causes today may appear quite hopeless to all but the most devoted true believer. Yet, the system may still be regarded as thoroughly pluralist as long as the roster of winners changes from time to time. This question, too, is an empirical one, and different investigators have read the historical record differently. My point here is definitional; in a pluralist order the same groups cannot always prevail. If they do—if big business, or the Catholic Church, or the local political machine dominates every policy outcome—the system is not pluralist.

Now before we move on, let us consider briefly several criteria by which the interaction of a pluralist universe of interests and the institutional structures of political parties might be and has been assessed. I want to stress that the vast majority of the voluminous literature bearing on this general topic carries normative baggage in either text or subtext, and I suspect that in many cases it is largely its normative bias that keeps the argument alive. E. E. Schattschneider, in his *Party Government*,[4] provides a splendid example of this tendency with an urgent attack on pluralist politics and a plea for party reform in order to make rational voter judgment possible and thereby strengthen effective popular control over the substance of public policy. Although the reader may suspect that

Schattschneider had the horrors of his earlier study of the Smoot-Hawley tariff (1935) in mind or, perhaps more broadly, the unrealized policy goals of the New Deal, he does not say so or suggest that his opposition to interest group politics is derived from his concern that the wrong groups won. Herring (1940a), by contrast, insists that to assess rationally the performance of political institutions, one must determine which interests are served. Who wins and who loses is crucial to possible evaluation. His primary normative criterion, however, is system order and stability. Contrasting the American party experience with the interwar instabilities of France and Weimar Germany and the fascist repressions of Mussolini and Hitler, Herring elevates the middling moderation of inclusive pluralism to a high station among the political virtues.

E. E. Schattschneider treats the parties primarily as structures of power and concludes that they are much too weak and fragmented to serve adequately the need to aggregate an effective majority he believes to be waiting, like prosperity, just around the corner, ready when called to overcome the special interests and to articulate and enact the policy needs of the people. For Herring the parties are primarily institutional arenas in which diverse interests contend for representation, and that is also the main analytic perspective he brings to the study of other institutions, including administrative agencies[5] and the presidency.[6] He sees these interest struggles as tending toward rough equilibrium in which most of the participating interests seem to reach an adequate *modus vivendi*. Truman (1951) followed in this tradition, arguing that an equilibrating tendency is characteristic of interest group dynamics and one of the key mechanisms for securing system stability. Ironically, it is precisely this stability, this balance among contending "special" interests, that constitutes the core of the indictment in Schattschneider's later work and in that of such other critics of pluralism as McConnell and Lowi.

In *The Semisovereign People*,[7] Schattschneider condemns what he regards as the inherent "upper class" bias of substantive policy in a pluralist regime, in contrast to what he believes would be more egalitarian results in a system directed by more centralized structures of authority. Grant McConnell[8] argues that American pluralist politics produces policy results that favor the status quo and the already prosperous, but he holds different institutional mechanisms responsible. He has little to say about the party system except perhaps by indirection, and focuses instead on the hegemonic power of major sectoral interest groups and their domination of particular segments of the institutional machinery of government, which they use to turn public authority into private domain. Theodore Lowi, too, sees the stability of the pluralist order as a grievous fault, arguing that the inability to transcend distributive politics makes it impossible to address many serious problems of the society, but also, somewhat paradoxically, encourages a generalized long-term drift in the polity's development, which ultimately must cause derangement if not disintegration of the system.[9] Lowi proposes that policy makers be bound by firm administrative standards and so accepts one pluralist requirement, limited government. For both Schattschneider and McConnell, on the other hand, the power of a mobilized majority is (*contra* Madison) the preferred mechanism for controlling the excesses of pluralist interest group demands. All three agree, however, that autonomous group demands for differentiated public policy action in their respective interests are dangerous, if not ruinous, to democracy and perhaps to the very survival of the republic.

The ranks of those who criticize pluralism on the basis of its alleged substantive policy bias are chiefly informed by the view that American pluralism operates primarily to the advantage of business interests or, in some versions, more generally to the advantage of society's elites. There is, in this view, no redistribution of values by virtue of the workings of the political process, and there should be. The political arena is supposed to be utilized for the pursuit of justice and redress to which turn those who find other arenas of life inadequate or unsatisfactory. This perspective is reasonable as long as the primary units of action in the political arena are individuals and the principal instrument of action is the vote. It is logical, given these assumptions and concerns, to place at the center of one's argument the electoral process and political parties, as Schattschneider did. But it is perhaps more appropriate to ask first whether the assumptions are valid, which is essentially what McConnell and Lowi did. To ask with Herring whether distributive justice is really the first question to raise in reaching normative judgments about the political order, is to challenge that position.

A pluralist must certainly be sensitive to issues of equity of interest representation, but system stability has been more salient to most pluralists. And by system the pluralist means to include the continued viability of all the articulate groups. In pluralist politics none of the losers is required to leave or remain silent. The game goes on and they all keep on playing. Effective pluralism is often extremely frustrating to political winners because they soon discover that their victory was incomplete. Institutional bastions are still controlled by others, and bargaining is still required to accomplish policy purposes. It is this continuity, this maintenance of politically relevant group life, that constitutes the first principle of pluralist evaluation, from Madison to the present.

WHAT PLURALISM DOES TO PARTIES

Let us now turn to consider the effects of pluralism on the party system—and vice versa. We have advanced a conception of pluralism sufficiently wide in its compass to leave out very few factors of any importance whatever, so a comprehensive answer to any question would incorporate practically every conceivable dimension of the American experience. To make our task more manageable, therefore, we will focus on the component of pluralism most often identified as its core, the heterogeneity of interests.

GROUP INTERESTS AND PARTISAN ATTACHMENTS

A hallmark of American political parties is the extent to which voters have developed enduring attachments to them on the basis of their respective identification with various social groups, especially those of ethnocultural origin. The broad structure of these commitments developed in the nineteenth century, especially during the second (1828–56) and third party systems (1856–96), and despite considerable attenuation of some of those attachments, a substantial residuum survives and has been added to by newer arrivals among ethnocultural interests.[10] Ethnocultural groups have by no means been the only kind whose devoted adherents have concluded that group loyalty should be the basis also of party loyalty. Regional interests such as the long commitment to the Democratic party by Southerners and ex-Southerners have given distinctive accents to the parties. So also since the late 1920s have the interests concentrated in the larger core cities. Some economic groups, notably organized labor, have often found themselves inextricably entangled with one party or the other, and this recognition leads us to an important point.

In principle, well-organized interest groups might be expected to prefer bipartisanship, keeping their commitments contingent and their options open so as to bargain with both parties (or perhaps more than two), and extracting the best deal possible in each election cycle. Samuel Gompers's historic advice—reward friends and punish enemies—embodied this strategic premise and so implicitly does the contemporary contribution pattern of business PACs.[11] Much of the academic commentary on interest groups and parties, especially the normatively critical part, postulates fundamental opposition between them, asserting that where one is strong, the other will be weak or subordinate. Yet, the historic experience suggests that quite substantial parts of the pluralist world of interest groups operate through partisan commitment, developing and reinforcing group attachment by means of party identification. There is a paradox here requiring some explanation.

Which groups serve as builders of partisan attachment and which ones bargain pragmatically looking for the best advantage? The answer would seem to depend on the extent to which commitment to the group itself is a product of ascriptive social identity and hence, in most cases, of significant and more or less self-conscious early socialization. One learns early what it means to be a Virginian, a Cuban-American, or an Irish Catholic, and when each of those identities carries an implicit partisan preference, as it surely has for much of American history, that preference is also learned. Not only is it engraved in the cognitive part of the persona, it is enriched by the affect in which such dimensions of identity are embedded. For some, the status of worker, farmer, or business executive is also invested with a good deal of affect, though it may not be learned until adulthood. When that is true, it too may be accompanied by a comparably strong commitment to one party or the other. Certainly there have been many business executives who felt a near religious devotion to the Republican party, and labor's romance with the Democrats, though not without conflict, has been deep and longlasting. But where the group is primarily concerned with substantive policy advantage rather than reinforcing through political commitment its status and identity, partisanship tends to be muted and relatively contingent.

While groups that are based on the pragmatic pursuit of economic self-interest may try to avoid long-term partisan commitment and seek advantageous concessions from both sides, at the same time the very composition of each party's following is substantially shaped by group attachments, especially those associated with primary groups. Group pressures external to the parties may force them together, not so much because voters are centrists but because party leaders and candidates compete by means of policy promises to essentially the same audience of the uncommitted to attract support or minimize opposition. Group attachments to party that are inside, however, help to keep the parties apart. If black voters are overwhelmingly committed to the Democrats, that fact assures a consequential difference between the Democratic and Republican parties. And if party activists generally are ideologically distinct and intense in their convictions, as they have been in recent years, this too will deepen the partisan gulf.[12] Thus group pluralism provides much of the foundation for both the substantive tilt of each party and the strategic imperative each party faces not to permit too wide a policy gap to develop between it and its opponent.

Party response to interest hetereogeneity is not exclusively expressed in the form of policy promises, of course. Particularly with regard to ethnocultural group identifiers, parties have long sought to construct "balanced" tickets that would be composed of representatives of the various groups prominent within the core of the party's support. The ethnic medleys traditional in the local slates of candidates in Chicago are illustrative of the principle. While each party may occasionally reach out to the rival coalition by nominating a representative of a group generally supportive of the other side, the dominant criterion in slatemaking, especially at local levels, has been the representation of the principal groups and factions within the ranks of the party faithful. There have been substantive policy issues now and then that exercise ethnocultural groups, and parties try through platform declarations and other expressive modes to cater to these concerns. This has been most apparent on certain issues of foreign policy and on some items of what today we call the social agenda. U.S. support for Baltic independence, Israeli military strength, and Irish unification illuminates the former; bilingual education in the schools and prohibition the latter. Few would contend, however, that these constitute a very substantial share of the total array of policy concerns, now or formerly. Rather, most policy issues fall into that space that neither party occupies unchallenged, and insofar as the policy options are expressed in terms of opposing or supporting a particular group or coalition, both parties must compete with policy offers.

This is the more pragmatic side of pluralist group-party relationships, and there is a profoundly important consequence that follows from the point. When a party tries to secure support from a pragmatic interest group, it is likely to couch its offer in the narrowest terms it can use and still remain credible. To assuage the construction industry, party candidates do not need to promise an end to the full budget deficit; defense contractors want defense contracts, not a new balance of international power; school teachers want higher salaries, not enhanced technological performance by U.S. industry. In each case, the latter goal—the macro-policy objective—may be very attractive, but it is not what motivates the group's lobbying effort nor is it likely to be the form in which party politicians express their response. What this means, and it has long been familiar to anyone conversant with American politics, is that because of the existence of heterogeneous interests outside the framework of partisan commitment, policy makers, needing their support, will seek it by making policy offers expressed in disaggregated, often group-specific terms. The rhetoric of a strong defense is converted into the realities of military contracts and bases; farm policy is formulated in terms of commodity supports and marketing orders; and education is improved by raising teacher salaries and mandating physical education. Much policy is enacted in the highly fungible form of money and allocated amongst the diverse groups. Very often, the result is to reinforce the autonomy of the groups who are enabled by earmarked policy benefits to stay alive and resist incorporation by larger aggregates. Beekeepers are a good current example, but so are the defenders of threatened military bases and the many other policy beneficiaries determined to retain the perquisites of past political success.

Is it fair or accurate to lay the prevalence of distributive policies in American politics on the doorstep of party interaction with uncommitted interest groups? I think the answer is no, not completely. One needs to incorporate an additional element of the pluralist order, the fragmented institutional structure of public authority. In particular, the autonomy of every member of Congress vis-à-vis each other, the president, and any national party apparatus that may exist assures not only that the parties in office will be weak and decentralized, but also that policies will tend to be put into forms that can be disaggregated to the state and congressional district level so that members of Congress can claim credit for them.[13] Again, money itself is the most readily fungible form for policy to take, but jobs can also be directly matched to votes so employment-generating expenditures are always attractive.

Many programs can also be defended, of course, in terms of service to the national interest, and they are routinely subjected to macro-level critiques. Does this tank development program increase defense efficiency? Does that crop subsidy stabilize farm income? Does another lock-and-dam project appreciably worsen the budget deficit? Macro-policy considerations are entailed in micro-policy decisions and vice versa. Autonomous members of Congress and heterogeneous interest groups combine to generate policy outcomes that are largely defined and enacted in terms that emphasize their distributive character and make difficult any substantial shifts in the direction—the particular pattern of winners and losers—U.S. public policy has taken.

TWO HISTORIC EPISODES

The interaction of pluralist interests and the party system can be illuminated by examining two critical periods in American party development. One is the Jacksonian era, when the first really "modern" party system took shape, and the other is the late nineteenth and early twentieth century when the foundations of the modern "interest system" were constructed. I rely in each case on the data gathering and primary interpretations of others, adding my own gloss to serve the needs of this essay.

THE EMERGENCE OF PLURALIST PARTIES

Whether or not it is accurate to call the pre-Jacksonian years the era of good feelings, it is plain that politics then was not dominated by partisanship, either in name or in effective form.[14] While the particular labels continued to fluctuate, by the 1840s reasonably stable organizational structures had been established by which candidates were nominated for public office, election campaigns were organized and managed, voters were aroused and mobilized, and, to a considerable extent, the policy-making process itself was conducted.[15] There was still a good deal of anti-party sentiment around, but the popularity of party politics was unmistakable. Even though every dimension of American life change seems to have been more rapid then than now, it is startling to contemplate the emergence of a nearly complete nationwide system of party politics in the space of less than two decades. How did it happen?

The record is reasonably clear that the primary motivating force behind party creation was the drive to elect Andrew Jackson as president. Having been outmaneuvered in 1824, the Jackson forces were determined to succeed at the next opportunity and to do so by mobilizing the electorate, now considerably expanded as a result of both franchise extensions and population growth, with a combination of personalized Jackson appeals and broader partisan sloganizing that picked up the Jeffersonian traditions.

But the party structure, developed for a quadrennial presidential contest, quickly took on a more permanent and pervasive existence. One important reason for this was that there was a swift enlargement not only of the voting electorate but also of the array of elective offices. During the period from the mid-1820s to the mid-1840s a vast number of new communities were founded, new counties were created, and several new states entered the union.[16] Moreover, the roster of public officials grew to perform the expanding tasks of governments and more and more of these officials were chosen by the voters, often on an annual basis. This huge increase in the number and variety of officials to be selected by popular vote provided a rich opportunity and perhaps even the functional necessity for some kind of coordinating mechanism, some common rhetoric and shared symbolic language with which to simplify and consolidate the electoral investments required of the citizenry having to vote on who was to fill so many thousands of positions.

For the Democrats, Jackson provided much of the needed symbolism, and the indefatigable Van Buren put together much of the coordinating structure. The Whigs lacked a full measure of either but found it politically necessary to follow along. When they had military heroes to serve as candidates they could win the presidency and their group interest foundations, in part carried over from the old Federalist base, gave them regional pockets of strength. Van Buren was especially skillful at one of the essentials of managing a party that had been constructed to organize the electoral process in a context of a weak, almost minimal state. He understood the point that the stakes at issue in these contests were, first and foremost, jobs. Patronage appointments and individuals slated for election had to be allocated shrewdly in order to maximize support for the party, and at this process Van Buren was a master. Henry Clay, for his part, fashioned a strategy for assembling a policy agenda that was nicely calculated to serve the kind of party system that had been created. His American System involved distributing internal improvements broadly throughout the land, and the Whigs also employed both the tariff and the revenue surplus it generated in a distributive fashion, explicitly disaggregated to serve the interests of distinct economic and political groups. In those days government did relatively little at the national or even the state level, but the relatively modest stakes of patronage and internal improvements were sufficient to attract the eager efforts of many Americans who discovered that by investing their energy and enthusiasm in electioneering might obtain employment that was more remunerative, less risky, and, on the whole, pleasanter work than could be had in field or factory. And although some of the most lucrative appointments were under federal control, the bulk of the opportunities were at state and, increasingly, local levels, and were affected only indirectly by the tides of national elections. Thus, by mid-century, a party system had developed based upon mobilizing a mass electorate, through the use of strongly affective, highly personified appeals combined with strategically distributed patronage and differentiated policy benefits, and organized and managed largely by people for whom the principal stakes were jobs for themselves and their supporting cadres. This system flourished in the sense that it successfully mobilized the electorate, not only inducing high levels of turnout, but also achieving a remarkable degree of civic attention among the voters. To be sure, alternative mass entertainments had not yet developed, but if one puts aside such blemishes as the exclusion of women and blacks and the inebriation of some of the local worthies, the depictions of enthusiastic political involvement recorded by George Caleb Bingham's paintings in the early 1850s bespeak a highly attractive politically activated community.

And yet the stakes were so small. By present-day standards most of the issues in campaigns and in Congress were marginal to the lives of most people. However exercised people got about elections, the outcomes had remarkably little impact upon their interests. Of course, there were exceptions, most notably involving the struggle to preserve the union by means of party strategies to bridge the widening gulf between North and South. The pluralist parties developed to accommodate diverse interests and permit a united search for public office and its spoils were relatively effective in managing also to postpone the sectional breach, outlasting by nearly two decades the Methodist, Presbyterian, and Baptist church structures. But eventually, of course, they failed. The political agenda became too heated and too inflated to be manageable through pluralist methods of distributive accommodation. Secession and war were the result.

THE FLOWERING OF THE ORGANIZATIONAL SOCIETY

Political scientists[17] have focused so much attention on the party realignment centered in 1896 that, by comparison at least, they have neglected what were from a pluralist perspective, more fundamental changes in the party system and the interest structures of American society. The development of large-scale heavy industry and the accompanying explosive growth of cities during the late nineteenth century are well known, of course. In the Schattschneider-Burnham view, it was essentially the social tensions generated by the twin forces of industrialization and urbanization that triggered the realignment of 1896, producing one-party hegemonies that enabled the industrial elite to stave off any serious threat of using the political order, as socialists tried to do in Europe, to redress the balance of economic power. But in addition to this story there were several other more or less simultaneous developments that had the effect of changing profoundly the meaning of electoral politics, indeed of politics altogether.[18]

One of these was the emergence of ideologically intense political conflict. Agrarian populism, labor union militancy, and corporate conservatism all took on greatly intensified expressive forms replete with mass protests, strikes, and riots. The electoral arena did not feel the full brunt of this conflict, before or after 1896. Some of it found expression in the courts as throughout the 1890s the Supreme Court issued one extreme pro-business decision after another.[19] Many state and local governments were deeply involved; particularly when the police were called upon to defend "society" against the forces of protest.[20] But to a substantial extent, the protests were not political at all. Most of them were expressed in terms of organizing to improve conditions in the work place, creating ameliorative institutions like the YMCA and the settlement houses in the cities, and to developing cooperative market power and more skillful management on the farms. What needs to be understood, if we are to make sense politically of 1896 and thereafter, is that much of what mattered to Americans was not a part of the electoral agenda and was addressed elsewhere. It was the transformation of the private sector toward the end of the century that made the real difference and provided the foundation of twentieth-century politics.

This transformation had several aspects, all interrelated, but here I want to focus attention on two: (1) the growth of autonomous institutions and associations that came to provide the contexts in and through which more and more individual Americans pursued the things they valued; and (2) the expansion of the service state, which provided a much enriched array of opportunities for obtaining distributive benefits. The symbiosis of private institutions and the service state required for its effective survival that the party system not threaten to disrupt established relationships every time there was an election. This could be accomplished in either of two very different ways. One was by establishing one-party hegemony over any jurisdiction that dispensed significant service benefits. The other was by "reform" that removed partisan electoral effects from the implementation of governmental services. Both these paths were taken.

The most dramatic institutional blossoms of the latter nineteenth and early twentieth centuries were business corporations.[21] Beginning with the railroads, which achieved "big business" status following the post-bellum consolidations of earlier lines, and stimulated by the innovative practices of financial and market manipulation developed in the 1870s and 1880s, corporate business manifested impressive structures of economic power by the end of the century. Indeed, the power of the trusts had already stimulated such widespread concern that political rhetoric routinely made symbolic gestures of opposition as in the Sherman Antitrust Act of 1890. Corporate growth was not simply a matter of increased size and scope, however. Fueled by incredibly rapid changes in technology, there was a truly vast increase in the kinds of goods and services produced and marketed nationally. Business by 1900 was a far more diverse and complex phenomenon than it had been a decade or two earlier.

While the trusts and other business enterprises were being built, so also were other institutions.[22] Colleges and universities began to have more than local followings and to constitute centers of scientific and technical research as well as sources of social engineering advice.

Church hierarchies grew, creating such subsidiary institutions as schools and settlement houses as well as ever-larger edifices of worship. Cultural institutions such as opera companies, symphony orchestras, theater and vaudeville circuits, and professional baseball were established.[23] In nearly every case, the earliest traces of institutional development lay back in the years immediately after the Civil War, but it is remarkable, nevertheless, how dense the institutional forest became in a brief span at the very end of the nineteenth century.

There was a further organizational development of this period that also had profound effects on American politics and on the way the party system functioned. This was the growth of voluntary associations. In the 1830s Tocqueville had said that the voluntary association was the characteristic method by which Americans tried to address situations calling for collective action. There were numerous examples then and thereafter to support his claim, but there was not yet, in his day, so much need for collective action as to generate the volume of associational activity that developed half a century later. The first business-trade association[24] and the first "modern" national farm organizations[25] were formed right after the Civil War, when reduced transportation and communication costs made feasible the intensified interactions of associational life. Trade associations were mechanisms to facilitate exchanges of information and the cultivation of self-consciousness and trade-related norms of conduct as much as, and apart from, any market-rigging effects. In the 1880s a spate of professional associations for historians, economists, and other types of academics came into being, and the national organizations of lawyers and doctors were revitalized and redirected. Many of these associations were to have important constraining impacts on their members, and the whole congeries of trade and professional associations has continued to grow in number and variety throughout the twentieth century. But by 1900 the essential form of what would come to be labeled pejoratively as the "special interests" had been well established.

Business corporations and other kinds of institutions shared with trade and professional associations the tendency to articulate organizational interests, identifying how what government did or did not do would affect matters of value and concern to the corporate entity or the members of the association. These corporate or collective organizations possessed the resources to study such matters and then to act politically to advance what they had concluded were their interests. With this capability they were far more effective than individuals, even wealthy businessmen or prestigious professionals, were likely to be and far less troubled by any potential "overlapping memberships" which might dilute the purposeful intensity of individuals' political action.

As interest groups took modern shape, their concerns, to one degree or another, came to include the ways in which actions of government affected or might affect them. Some of those interests were quite ad hoc, needing only a brief foray into politics to accomplish the desired result. Others, however, were more enduring and called for long-term, stable relationships between the group and the relevant public authority. Robert Wiebe[26] has called the whole period from 1877 to 1920 "the search for order," and his meaning is very close to, though more inclusive than, the interpretation advanced here. In any case, group interests called for lobbying, and though there had been the occasional antecedent, the emergence of lobbying in recognizably modern form is a development of the late nineteenth and early twentieth century.[27]

The growth of organized interests, both institutions and associations, meant that for their respective inhabitants there were mechanisms for the pursuit of political interests which were far more efficient, though often narrower in policy focus, than the electoral franchise. Moreover, the political stakes at issue had expanded enormously in importance, partly as a result of the successes of interest group efforts, and partly reflecting the unavoidable externalities of rapid industrial and urban expansion. Government at every level increased its spending and the scope of its regulations. As public functions increased beyond the historic range of minimal service and promotion, partisan elections became a less useful device to guide decision.

To put the matter more precisely, the social costs of switching the administration of public services from one party's faithful cohort to that of the other escalated as the scale of those services increased. Merit system personnel management and other anti-party devices could reduce those costs, but so could one-party control. It may seem paradoxical, but it is nonetheless true that in one city after another the expansion of governmental services—paving streets, building schools, enlarging police and fire protection, and so on—was closely and functionally associated with the decline of party competition. The growth of party machines in their full glory followed close on the heels of service expansion. On the one hand, more government services meant more jobs and other Plunkitt-type[28] "opportunities" for the machine to feed upon. On the other hand, the recipients of these services, especially those in the local business community, did not find advantage in switching back and forth between political rivals. Government had become too important to leave it to competing politicians. So the structure of party competition and the incentives to political participation were transformed.

At the national level the expansion of governmental functions was somewhat slower and more halting, but, as Skowronek[29] has shown, from the 1890s on federal promotional and service activities increased in scope and significance, and, for the most part, they did so in ways that were unaffected by actual or potential shifts in partisan sentiment. The party system was irrelevant to the development of a professional military following the embarrassments of the Spanish-American War, for example. The enlargement of the federal bureaucracy in this era was tied to interest group concerns with which the parties could only deal, if at all, by trying to outbid each other. Not until the New Deal, and only partially even then, could party competition attain a reasonable degree of congruence with a broader bimodal structure of socioeconomic interests and values in the society such that the electoral choice between parties provided meaningful instruction as to the main lines of what government was to do.

I do not mean to imply that the elections of the 1890s and thereafter had no importance other than distinguishing the superficial identities of who was in and who was out. At the very least, electoral politics made it possible, by shielding governments from partisan change, for the service state and its bureaucratic infrastructure to grow and mature. More than that, the Republican triumphs that followed the severe 1893 depression provided the foundation for changes in the structure and operation of Congress[30] that, traveling a rather dialectical path, led ultimately to a legislative system that for some decades has been remarkably insulated from the vicissitudes of partisan fortunes. The pre-1896 party system was largely based on ethnocultural conflicts. It could not provide effective representation to the "new generation" of pluralist forces. The interest groups and associations of this new system were pragmatic and narrowly focused on how government might affect them.

The precipitous decline in the relevance of political party competition was accompanied by a sharp drop in voter participation. Much of this drop was concentrated among those segments of the electorate that were least well represented in and through the newly emerging interest groups. These groups were and are predominantly composed of the better off and the socially advantaged. But an ethnoculturally based party system was never very effective at representing the economic interests of the less fortunate in society either, however much enthusiasm the latter displayed in the torchlight parades and high turnouts of nineteenth-century elections. A pluralist society generates a pluralist party system, not one that offers programmatically coherent dichotomous alternatives to which an electorate, more or less bimodally distributed along the main programmatic dimension, can rationally respond.

One other point should be added to this argument. Just because most of the organized groups do not include or speak in behalf of the interests of the dispossessed and the downtrodden, and a pluralistic party system cannot effectively aggregate group interests so as to incorporate the unorganized and underrepresented, individual political entrepreneurs are not precluded from doing so. One feature of pluralist politics—free market politics, if you will—is that there are few entry barriers to entrepreneurship. It takes some capital to start a new group, to be sure, or to advocate a hitherto neglected cause, but individual members of Congress, to take several hundred examples, are provided by their offices with a fair amount of capitalization of the rhetorical and other components of political enterprise. If a viable political enterprise can be constructed by raising new issues or appealing to new groups, a pluralist system makes it far easier to do so, and hence ultimately to permit social dynamics to be registered in public policy decisions, than disciplined parties or juridical standards.

THE CONTEMPORARY SCENE: THE CONSTRAINED PARTISANSHIP OF INTEREST GROUPS

Ethnocultural attachments and perspectives, in the United States and elsewhere in the world, are remarkably vital and long-lasting, and any theoretical stance that does not accord them a significant place is likely to get things wrong. Both the party system in the United States and diverse aspects of public policy continue to bear the imprint of these orientations. We are also the heirs to the organizational revolution that so profoundly reshaped the structure of economic life and led to a modern world in which much of the population is embedded in large bureaucratic enterprises of one kind or another. These institutions and their associations articulate organizational interests that make up a sizable chunk of the agendas of public concern. To these are added the issues that spring from the diverse consumption values of the individuals who live their productive economic lives inside these economic institutions. The latter (including many academics) constitute a major "market" for the formation of citizens groups and other exponents of various versions of the public interest which have flourished in abundance since the 1950s.[31] This "new class" has been a significant constituency supporting the democratizing reforms of political parties.[32] In the last two or three decades, therefore, there has been not only continued vitality and expansion of organizational manifestations of the ethnocultural and corporate and associational phases of pluralist development. There has also been a significant shift in the structural balance of organized interest groups with many more citizens groups, public interest champions, externality/ alternative advocates, and ideological enthusiasts than before.

Earlier we stressed that the emergence of organized interest groups was associated with the joint effects of one-party hegemonies and anti-party reforms of various kinds. The changing shape of the interest group universe in recent decades has been accompanied also by a changing party system with renewed competition along a rather sharply drawn ideological dimension having to do with economic concerns. It is ironic that these developments have occurred amidst laments over the decay of party institutions, the weakening of party loyalty in the mass electorate, and the failure of predicted realignments to take place.

Yet, there has in fact been a realignment of sorts, primarily among political elites, who have divided into two quite clearly defined and internally cohesive groups with clear lines of descent from the New Deal. On one side are those who take a consistently conservative position on such questions of economic policy as the place of labor unions, corporate profits, and business power. On the other are those who take a liberal view. The conservatives are Republicans and the liberals are Democrats. Among political activists there is not much ambivalence on these issues as there is on many items of the so-called social agenda. Southern conservative Democrats have largely disappeared or converted, and that is true also of liberal Republicans from the northeast. Accordingly, party unity votes in Congress are at thirty-year peaks,[33] and, whatever the mass electorate may think, for the past three decades the system has generated quite clear and consistent election alternatives on the dimension of economic policy. Moreover, inasmuch as activists have a disproportionate voice in choosing party nominees, and activists tend to be the most ideologically committed among the party identifiers, the structure of partisan, especially presidential, contests is likely to continue indefinitely to take liberal v. conservative form.[34]

What has pluralism to do with this? Arguably, the continuing ethno-cultural basis of much party attachment has retarded the shift to a more complete ideological dichotomy between Republicans and Democrats. What about the pragmatism toward partisanship which is so often associated with the rise of interest group politics? Here we encounter another paradox. There is no doubt that today there are far more organized groups present in Washington. Nor is there reason to think that the strategic wisdom of interest group bipartisanship, supporting friends on both sides of the aisle and avoiding being shut off from access if the election goes sour, has paled. Yet, a substantial majority of interest group lobbyists active in Washington are rather strong partisans. In our study of lobbyists in four policy domains, my colleagues and I found that they tend generally to be activists.[35] Many of them have been involved in partisan campaigns, they often have held political or partisan office themselves, and they have both contributed money to campaigns and raised it from others. If their political background and present commitment are Republican, they tend quite strongly to be conservatives on economic questions. Interest-group representatives who are or have been active Democrats are generally quite strongly liberal. Moreover, liberal Democrats tend to know and work with other liberal Democrats, and the opposite is true of conservative Republicans. Working colleagues tend to share the same partisan and ideological perspective, and their network connections with notable lobbyists follow similar paths.[36]

Thus lobbyists tend to display a high degree of partisan commitment, reflecting both their personal values and those of the organization that hires or retains them. What does this tell us regarding their behavior? The answer is not entirely clear or consistent. On the one hand many of them claim that partisan affiliation has no bearing on their lobbying work. Specifically, they tend to deny that the shift from Carter to Reagan appreciably affected their access to relevant government officials, presumably the *sine qua non* of effective lobbying. On the other hand, the patterns of coactivation of groups within a policy domain—which groups become active for or against whom—reveal a partisan division of varying clarity but present in all four of the policy domains we examined.[37]

This does not mean that all the groups participating in the political struggles of a policy domain are clustered into two close-knit coalitions, one liberal Democratic and the other conservative Republican. Only in the labor domain was that pattern unmistakably present. The others were much more segmented, with several clusters of groups in each domain, each differentiated from the others not only by the positions taken but by their agendas of concern. Nevertheless, whenever they were active on the same issue consumer groups, labor unions, some commodity and farmer organizations, environmentalists, health care professionals, and the like were consistently closer to one another and more distant from business and trade association interests. Common partisanship and relatively abstract ideology were not powerful enough to pull each set into complete harmony of action, but party and belief certainly constrained lobbyist behavior.

One must hasten to supplement this assertion with the acknowledgment that powerful constituency-based interests continue to persuade members of Congress to disregard both party and ideology so that not always but often there are defectors from the partisan majority. Constituency-responsive defectors and other mavericks have been comparatively rare in recent years, however. For their part, some interest groups play both sides of the partisan aisle, notably business PACs, which contribute substantially to incumbents regardless of their party.

Despite this bipartisan, transideological quest for access, however, the actual policy positions espoused by the business groups have followed a more consistent conservative pattern. Partisanship constrains much group behavior and thus keeps pluralist diversity from breaking down into chaotic shapelessness. In turn, the substance of what partisanship has come to mean at the federal level is importantly defined by the positions taken by each partisan constellation of groups and politicians.

SOME SUMMARY MUSINGS

In a schematic and oversimplified way I have argued that there are three quite distinct layers of pluralist heterogeneity and linked each to a distinct phase of party system development. Each of these interacting pairs is very much with us as we approach the century's conclusion, and that certainly makes it difficult and perhaps inappropriate to talk about either pluralism or the party system as a singular phenomenon. In this summary I want to recapitulate the schematic components and then offer a brief homily that looks toward the future.

The oldest stratum of politically meaningful pluralism is that combination of ethnocultural identity and local/regional location, which has served as the breeding ground of so much of what Americans value. The version of party politics most closely associated with this form of pluralism has been one in which the parties cultivate affective attachments that reinforce group identity and provide disaggregated policy benefits as further incentives to loyal participation. A long ballot of elective officials and decentralized "congressional-type" policy-making institutions are well matched to this combination of party and pluralism and help mightily to perpetuate it long after its origins in the Jacksonian era have been forgotten. Thus we still observe the distributive particularism of so much public policy and the strength of partisan affect among ethnocultural groups such as African-Americans whose political bargaining position might be enhanced if their votes were not already largely committed.

The second dimension of American pluralism we identified was organizational. Large-scale organizations came to dominate major segments of life, especially economic life. The late nineteenth century and thereafter witnessed the growth of both public and private institutions and of associations linking them together to provide the mechanisms for collective action. It is in this period that the secondary association component of interest group pluralism with its distinctive feature of lobbying for public policy objectives comes into full view. To accommodate this new and insistent layer of pluralist (substantively diverse) development, the party system was adapted to allow long-term stability in mutually advantageous relationships between government and group. The substance of policy was still largely distributed in disaggregated form, but the benefits were considerably more substantial and sought on a more permanent basis. One-party domination made long-term bargains easier and more dependable. Removing functions from the jurisdiction of partisan officials and giving them over to nonpartisan experts, independent agencies, and the like had the same effect, and accordingly the scope of the party system was narrowed.

The third wave of pluralist growth has been marked by the emergence of citizens groups, externality/alternative interests, and assorted other organizations including ideological think tanks. At the foundation of this "wave" of enlargement of the pluralist universe are relative affluence and individual job security, often provided by the protective cocoon of employment within a large bureaucracy. This situation permits the pursuit of a wide variety of consumption goods, among which may be expressive values with public policy implications. Consumer protection, the many forms of environmentalism, subsidizing the arts, abortion pro and con, and dozens of other causes can be and are pursued through the mechanism of organized groups with little or no direct connection to the economic self-interests of the enthusiasts.

There is much irony in the notion that there is substantial ideological coherence and consistency in the values espoused by these "nonself-interested" groups but not as much in the economic interest sectors. The latter, in the context of American politics, have chosen generally to be pragmatic rather than ideological, avoiding partisan commitments for fear of the high cost of losing. If the substance of a partisan defeat is "only" one's cherished beliefs, however, and not one's purse, the risk may more often be worth it. In any case, the party system that has lately emerged contains a substantial amount of ideologically framed conflict, at least among activists, while at the same time failing to engage even the attention, much less the commitment, of considerable portions of the electorate. Interest group pursuit of policy objectives is constrained by elite polarization, of course, but not so completely as to preclude pragmatic adjustments in behalf of economic self-interest.

What this all means, it seems to me, is this: American pluralism and the American party system are both richly compounded phenomena. They defy attempts at analysis which employ singular verb forms. *The* bias of pluralism and *the* realignment of party strength are not very meaningful phrases unless one not only specifies a particular aspect of pluralism or part of the party system but also makes sure that the assessment is kept in the larger context of the compound structure. Political scientists and lots of other folks too often have been inclined to suppress observed complexity in order to fit results into theoretical schemas or conventional language sets that are simply inadequate. New and improved versions of social theory are announced with the frequency and fanfare that characterize the introduction of new breakfast cereals, and one suspects that the discernible improvement of our intellectual diet has been of approximately equivalent value. It might be well, therefore, to devote more of our labor to the fuller and more systematic mapping of the observables of pluralism and partisanship and the exploration of their empirical connections and try not to rush to judgment. Later, in the improved light yielded by well-crafted research, we can return to the tasks of normative evaluation.

NOTES

1. Robert Dahl, *A Preface to Democratic Theory* (Chicago: U. of Chicago Press, 1956), p. 145.

2. Wood, 1959.

3. Robert Dahl, *Who Governs* (New Haven, Conn.: Yale U. Press, 1961).

4. E. E. Schattschneider, *Party Government* (New York: Farrer and Rinehart, 1942).

5. E. Pendleton Herring, *Public Administration and the Public Interest* (New York: McGraw-Hill, 1936).

6. E. Pendleton Herring, *Presidential Leadership* (New York: Farrer and Rinehart, 1940b).

7. E. E. Schattschneider, *The Semisovereign People* (New York: Holt, Rinehart and Winston, 1960).

8. Grant McConnell, *Private Power and American Democracy* (New York: Knopf, 1966).

9. Theodore Lowi, *The End of Liberalism* (New York: Norton, 1969).

10. Lawrence H. Fuchs, *The American Kaleidoscope: Race, Ethnicity, and the Civic Culture* (Hanover, N.H.: U. Press of New England, 1990).

11. Norman Ornstein, Thomas E. Mann, and Michael J. Malbin, *Vital Statistics on Congress, 1989–1990* (Washington, D.C.: Congressional Quarterly Press, 1990).

12. Byron Shafer, *Bifurcated Politics: Evolution and Reform in the National Party Convention* (Cambridge, Mass.: Howard U. Press, 1988).

13. David Mayhew, *Congress: The Electoral Connection* (New Haven, Conn.: Yale U. Press, 1974).

14. Richard L. McCormick, *The Party Period and Public Policy* (New York: Oxford U. Press, 1986).

15. Joel H. Sibley, *The American Political Nation, 1838–1893* (Stanford, Calif.: Stanford U. Press, 1991).

16. Daniel J. Boorstin, *The Americans: The National Experience* (New York: Vintage Books, 1965).

17. Schattschneider, *Semisovereign People;* Burnham; James Sunquist, *Dynamics of the Party System* (Washington, D.C.: The Brookings Institution, 1973).

18. McCormick, *The Party Period and Public Policy.*

19. Arnold M. Paul, *Conservative Crisis and the Rule of Law,* 1960.

20. Paul Avrich, *The Haymarket Tragedy* (Princeton, N.J.: Princeton U. Press, 1984).

21. Thomas Cochran, *200 Years of American Business* (New York: Delta, 1977); Alfred Chandler, *The Visible Hand: The Managerial Revolution in American Business* (Cambridge, Mass.: Belnap Press, 1977); Louis Galambos and Joseph Pratt, *The Rise of the Corporate Commonwealth* (New York: Basic Books, 1988).

22. Alan Trachtenberg, *The Incorporation of America, Culture and Society in the Gilded Age* (New York: Hill and Wang, 1982); Peter Dobkin Hall, *The Organization of American Culture, 1700–1900: Private Institutions, Elites, and the Origin of American Nationality* (New York: New York U. Press, 1984).

23. Gunther Barth, *City People: The Rise of Modern City Culture in Nineteenth Century America* (New York: Oxford U. Press, 1980).

24. Louis Galambos, *Competition and Cooperation: The Emergence of a National Trade Association* (Baltimore: Johns Hopkins U. Press, 1966).

25. Theodore Saloutos, *Farmer Movements in the South, 1865–1933* (Berkeley, Calif.: U. of California Press, 1960).

26. Robert Wiebe, *The Search for Order, 1877–1920* (New York: Hill and Wang, 1967).

27. Margaret Susan Thompson, *The ''Spider Web'' Congress and Lobbying in the Age of Grant* (Ithaca, N.Y.: Cornell U. Press, 1985); Scott Ainsworth, *The Evolution of Interest Representation and the Emergence of Lobbyists,* Ph.D. dissertation, St. Louis, Washington U., 1989.

28. Riordan, 1948.

29. Steven Skowronek, *Building a New American State* (Cambridge, England: Cambridge U. Press, 1982).

30. David Brady, *Critical Elections and Congressional Policy Making* (Stanford, Calif.: Stanford U. Press, 1988).

31. Jack Walker, "The Origins and Maintenance of Interest Groups in America," *American Political Science Review* 77 (June 1983): 390–406; Andrew McFarland, *Common Cause* (Chatham, N.J.: Chatham House, 1984).

32. Byron Shafer, *Quiet Revolution: The Struggle for the Democratic Party and the Shaping of Post-Reform Politics* (New York: Russell Sage, 1983); Shafer, *Bifurcated Politics.*

33. David Rhode, *Parties and Leaders in the Post-Reform House* (Chicago: U. of Chicago Press, 1991).

34. Shafer, *Bifurcated Politics;* Shafer, *The End of Realignment? Atrophy of a Concept and Death of a Phenomenon?* (Madison, Wis.: U. of Wisconsin Press, 1991).

35. Robert L. Nelson, John P. Heinz, Edward O. Laumann, and Robert H. Salisbury, "Private Representation in Washington: Surveying the Structure of Influence," *American Bar Foundation Research Journal* (Winter 1987): 141–200.

36. John P. Heinz, Edward O. Laumann, Robert H. Salisbury, and Robert L. Nelson, "Inner Circles or Hollow Cores? Elite Networks in National Policy Systems," *Journal of Politics* 52 (May 1990): 356–90.

37. Robert H. Salisbury, John P. Heinz, Edward O. Laumann, and Robert L. Nelson, "Who Works With Whom? Interest Group Alliances and Opposition," *American Political Science Review* 81 (December 1987): 1217-34.

REFERENCES

Ainsworth, Scott, 1989. *The Evolution of Interest Representation and the Emergence of Lobbyists*, Ph.D. dissertation. St. Louis: Washington University.

Avrich, Paul, 1984. *The Haymarket Tragedy*. Princeton, N.J.: Princeton U. Press.

Barth, Gunther, 1980. *City People: The Rise of Modern City Culture in Nineteenth Century America*. New York: Oxford U. Press.

Boorstin, Daniel J., 1965. *The Americans: The National Experience*. New York: Vintage Books.

Brady, David, 1988. *Critical Elections and Congressional Policy Making*. Stanford, Calif.: Stanford U. Press.

Burnham, Walter Dean, 1970. *Critical Elections and the Mainsprings of American Politics*. New York: Norton.

Chandler, Alfred, 1977. *The Visible Hand: The Managerial Revolution in American Business*. Cambridge, Mass.: Belknap Press.

Cochran, Thomas, 1977. *200 Years of American Business*. New York: Delta.

Dahl, Robert A., 1956. *A Preface to Democratic Theory*. Chicago: U. of Chicago Press.

_____ , 1961. *Who Governs?* New Haven, Conn.: Yale U. Press.

Fuchs, Lawrence H., 1990. *The American Kaleidoscope: Race, Ethnicity, and the Civic Culture*. Hanover, N.H.: U. Press of New England.

Galambos, Louis, 1966. *Competition and Cooperation: The Emergence of a National Trade Association*. Baltimore: Johns Hopkins U. Press.

_____ , and Joseph Pratt, 1988. *The Rise of the Corporate Commonwealth*. New York: Basic Books.

Hall, Peter Dobkin, 1984. *The Organization of American Culture, 1700–1900: Private Institutions, Elites, and the Origins of American Nationality*. New York: New York U. Press.

Heinz, John P., Edward O. Laumann, Robert H. Salisbury, and Robert L. Nelson, 1990. "Inner Circles or Hollow Cores? Elite Networks in National Policy Systems." *Journal of Politics* 52 (May 1990): 356–90.

Herring, E. Pendleton, 1936. *Public Administration and the Public Interest*. New York: McGraw-Hill.

_____ , 1940a. *The Politics of Democracy*. New York: Rinehart.

_____ , 1940b. *Presidential Leadership*. New York: Farrer and Rinehart.

Lowi, Theodore, 1969. *The End of Liberalism*. New York: Norton.

Mayhew, David, 1974. *Congress: The Electoral Connection*. New Haven, Conn.: Yale U. Press.

McConnell, Grant, 1966. *Private Power and American Democracy*. New York: Knopf.

McCormick, Richard L., 1986. *The Party Period and Public Policy*. New York: Oxford U. Press.

McCormick, Richard P., 1982. *The Presidential Game.* New York: Oxford U. Press.

————, 1966. *The Second America Party System, Party Formation in the Jacksonian Era.* New York: Norton.

McFarland, Andrew, 1984. *Common Cause.* Chatham, N.J.: Chatham House.

Nelson, Robert L., John P. Heinz, Edward O. Laumann, and Robert H. Salisbury, 1987. "Private Representation in Washington: Surveying the Structure of Influence." *American Bar Foundation Research Journal* (Winter 1987): 141–200.

Ornstein, Norman, Thomas E. Mann, and Michael J. Malbin, 1990. *Vital Statistics on Congress, 1989–1990.* Washington, D.C.: Congressional Quarterly Press.

Paul, Arnold M., 1960. *Conservative Crisis and the Rule of Law.*

Rhode, David, 1991. *Parties and Leaders in the Post-Reform House.* Chicago: U. of Chicago Press.

Riordan, William, 1948. *Plunkitt of Tammany Hall.* New York: Knopf.

Salisbury, Robert H., John P. Heinz, Edward O. Laumann, and Robert L. Nelson. "Who Works With Whom? Interest Group Alliances and Opposition." *American Political Science Review* 81 (December 1987): 1217–34.

Saloutos, Theodore, 1960. *Farmer Movements in the South, 1865–1933.* Berkeley, Calif.: U. of California Press.

Schattschneider, E. E., 1942. *Party Government.* New York: Farrer and Rinehart.

————, 1935. *Politics, Pressures and the Tariff.* New York: Prentice-Hall.

————, 1960. *The Semisovereign People.* New York: Holt, Rinehart and Winston.

Shafer, Byron, 1988. *Bifurcated Politics: Evolution and Reform in the National Party Convention.* Cambridge, Mass.: Howard U. Press.

————, 1991. *The End of Realignment? Atrophy of a Concept and Death of a Phenomenon?* Madison, Wis.: U. of Wisconsin Press.

————, 1983. *Quiet Revolution: The Struggle for the Democratic Party and the Shaping of Post-Reform Politics.* New York: Russell Sage.

Sibley, Joel H., 1991. *The American Political Nation, 1838–1893.* Stanford, Calif.: Stanford U. Press.

Skowronek, Steven, 1982. *Building a New American State.* Cambridge, England: Cambridge U. Press.

Sundquist, James, 1973. *Dynamics of the Party System.* Washington, D.C.: The Brookings Institution.

Thompson, Margaret Susan, 1985. *The "Spider Web:" Congress and Lobbying in the Age of Grant.* Ithaca, N.Y.: Cornell U. Press.

Trachtenberg, Alan, 1982. *The Incorporation of America, Culture and Society in the Gilded Age.* New York: Hill and Wang.

Truman, David B., 1982. *The Governmental Process.* New York: Knopf.

Walker, Jack, 1983. "The Origins and Maintenance of Interest Groups in America." *American Political Science Review* 77 (June 1983): 390–406.

Wiebe, Robert, 1967. *The Search for Order, 1877–1920.* New York: Hill and Wang.

Reading 3

Political Parties, Electoral Conflict, and Institutional Combat

Benjamin Ginsberg and Martin Shefter

Ronald Reagan and George Bush won landslide Electoral College victories in the presidential contests of 1980, 1984, and 1988. Republicans, nevertheless, failed to win control of the House of Representatives, and though they captured the Senate in 1980 they lost their majority in the middle of Reagan's second term. Democratic control of Congress was confirmed in the elections of 1990.

This pattern of divided outcomes has confirmed a major change that has been taking place over the past two decades in the very role and significance of elections in American politics. Rather than continuing to rely primarily upon voter mobilization, contending forces have come increasingly to use such mechanisms as congressional investigations, alliances with foreign governments, and judicial proceedings to gain political power.

The growing use of one nonelectoral weapon of political combat—the criminal sanction—is suggested by the tenfold increase between the early 1970s and the mid-1980s in the number of indictments brought by federal prosecutors against national, state, and local officials (see Figure 3.1). Although many of those indicted were lower level civil servants, large numbers were prominent figures—among them more than a dozen members of Congress, several federal judges, and a substantial number of high-ranking executive officials including Michael Deaver and Lyn Nofziger, and Labor Secretary Raymond Donovan. These data, of course, do not even take into account the many other top-ranking officials such as Attorney General Edward Meese and House Speaker Jim Wright who were targets of investigations that did not result in indictments.

There is no reason to believe that the level of political corruption in the United States has actually increased tenfold over the past decade and a half, but it could be said that this sharp rise in the number of criminal indictments of government officials reflects a heightened level of public concern with governmental misconduct. However, both the issue of gov-

Figure 3.1 Federal indictments and convictions of public officials, 1970–86.
Reporting procedures were modified in 1983 so that pre- and post-1983 data
are not strictly comparable. *Indictments* are of federal, state, and local officials
by U.S. prosecutors; *convictions* are of federal, state, and local officials in the
U.S. courts. (*Source:* Reports of the U.S. Department of Justice Public
Integrity Section, 1971–88.)

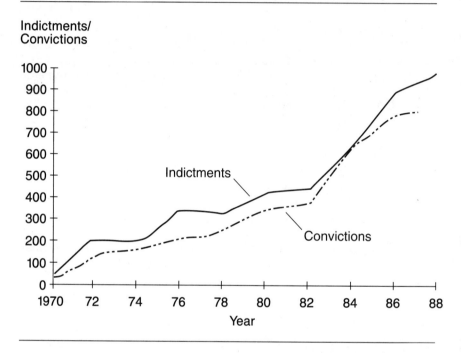

Indictments/
Convictions

ernment ethics and the growing use of criminal sanctions against public
officials have been closely linked to struggles for political power in the
United States. In the aftermath of Watergate, institutions were established and processes created to investigate allegations of unethical conduct on the part of public figures. Increasingly, political forces have
sought to make use of these mechanisms to discredit their opponents.
When scores of investigators, accountants, and lawyers are deployed to
scrutinize the conduct of an Ed Meese or a Jim Wright, it is all but certain
that something questionable will be found. It is the creation of these
processes more than changes in the public's moral standards which explains why public officials increasingly are being charged with ethical
and criminal violations.

Three arenas of nonelectoral conflict have become especially important in the United States over the past two decades. First, contending political forces have sought to make use of the powers of Congress and the presidency as political weapons and to that end have attempted to strengthen the branch of government to which they have access while weakening the branch controlled by the opposition. Second, competing groups have undertaken to gain control over other institutions such as the judiciary and the national security apparatus and to use these as instruments of governance and political combat. Third, competing groups have used techniques including exposés, lawsuits, covert operations, and the imposition of regulatory controls to disrupt and undermine organizations and social forces upon which their opponents depend for support while strengthening the organizations and forces with which they are allied.

INSTITUTIONAL COMBAT: CONGRESS AND THE PRESIDENCY

Institutional conflict is built into the American governmental structure by the separation of powers. This form of political struggle has intensified over the past two decades, however, as the Republicans have gained a solid hold on the White House, and the Democrats have strengthened their grip on Congress. The GOP has reacted to its inability to win control of Congress by seeking to enhance the powers of the executive branch and to circumvent legislative restrictions on presidential conduct. The Democrats, in turn, have responded to the Republican presidential advantage by seeking to strengthen the Congress while reducing the powers and prerogatives of the presidency through legislative investigations, media exposés, and judicial proceedings as well as through the imposition of statutory limits on executive power. Ironically, the very techniques that allowed the Republicans to dominate presidential elections left them vulnerable to these tactics. The GOP depended for its electoral success on money and the new capital-intensive techniques of polling, television, advertising, and direct mail fund-raising, which enabled them to win elections without engaging in the long and arduous task of constructing grass roots electoral organizations. Had they possessed strong organizational ties to their supporters, the Republicans would not have been as vulnerable to investigations and allegations aired through the media. At any rate, the two parties now have become locked in a struggle whose outcome will be decided more by the institutional weapons and power at their disposal than by their capacity to mobilize additional voters.

INSTITUTIONAL POWER AND POLITICS

The power of any governmental institution is a function of both the strength of its alliances with social forces or with other institutions that can support its assertions of authority, and its internal capacities for coercion, extraction, distribution, and administration. These two sources of institutional power may be mutually reinforcing because an institution can use the support of its constituency to increase its coercive or extractive authority and then employ this enhanced authority to add new groups to its constituency.

For example, the presidency gained power in the 1930s and 1940s through both of these processes. The first has been emphasized by Samuel P. Huntington.[1] As he notes, presidents during the New Deal and postwar eras pursued domestic and foreign policies that won the support of a nexus of powerful national political forces: national labor unions, corporations, banks, law firms, news media, foundations, and universities. These political forces were thus prepared to support presidential policy initiatives—initiatives that characteristically added to the power of the executive branch—and to back the president in his conflicts with Congress and other governmental institutions. The votes, campaign assistance, money, publicity, and expertise they brought to bear on behalf of the president and his initiatives often enabled him to prevail over (or reach acceptable accommodations with) his opponents in other governmental institutions.

Equally important to the building of presidential power, however, was the second of the mechanisms mentioned above: the enormous growth of federal revenues, expenditures, and employment during the Depression and World War II gave the president access to resources he could use to induce members of Congress, state and local officials, party politicians, and private interests to follow his lead. At the same time, the growth of the federal government's coercive capacity—a capacity recorded in the Code of Federal Regulations and the corpus of federal statutory, administrative, and case law and enforced by an army of administrators, investigators, attorneys, special agents, and military personnel—enabled presidents to compel would-be resistors to come to terms. To enhance their control over this new federal leviathan and limit the ability of their opponents to draw resources and political advantages from it, Franklin Roosevelt and his successors created the "institutionalized presidency" and undertook to reorganize the executive establishment (Milkis 1985). Precisely because they recognized that questions of institutional and political power were at stake, forces that enjoyed better access to the Congress, administrative agencies, or courts than to the

White House often resisted these efforts at executive reorganization. This conflict over the expansion of presidential power during the 1930s and 1940s is a useful backdrop for examining the institutional struggles of the past twenty years.

FROM WATERGATE TO CONTRAGATE

As just indicated, during the New Deal and postwar periods efforts to strengthen the presidency had received the support of a broad coalition of national political forces. In the late 1960s, however, this constituency split over the issue of Vietnam. The Nixon administration retained the backing of those elements that believed the United States should use its military resources to fight communism in Southeast Asia. At the same time, President Nixon attacked what he regarded as costly and socially disruptive excesses in federal domestic programs. Opponents of the Vietnam War and defenders of domestic social programs looked to Congress to support their point of view.

Many congressional Democrats, and some Republicans as well, allied with these dissident forces and sought to prevail over the White House on issues of both foreign and domestic policy. A combination of developments in the 1960s and 1970s enabled these members of Congress to fight, and ultimately defeat, the president. In the first place, during this period, Congress essentially acquired a distributive capacity of its own. As Morris Fiorina has noted,[2] Congress enacted an enormous number of new domestic programs in these years; its members regularly intervened in the bureaucracy to channel the benefits generated by these programs to their constituents and then claimed credit for this largess. Fiorina attributed to this process the increased electoral advantage that incumbents came to enjoy at this time—an advantage that largely insulated congressional from presidential elections. This made it politically possible for congressmen to take on the president.

In addition, by establishing close linkages with other institutions, Congress effectively acquired administrative, mobilizing, and coercive capacities during the 1960s and 1970s. In a return to nineteenth-century practice, Congress enacted very detailed regulatory statutes and authorized private citizens to sue in the federal courts to secure their implementation[3]; that is, by allying with the judiciary, Congress was able to assure the interests enjoying access to it that the policies they favored would be implemented regardless of the political sympathies of the administration in power.

In a similar fashion, by establishing linkages with the national news media—especially through nationally televised hearings—members of

Congress were able to mobilize nationwide constituencies in support of various policy initiatives and to stampede Congress into enacting and the president into signing legislation designed to remedy the evils the hearings in question publicized.[4] The 1962 thalidomide hearings, chaired by Senator Estes Kefauver, were a pattern-setting example of this technique. Televised hearings could also be used to mobilize national constituencies against the White House. The 1967 Senate Foreign Relations Committee hearings on Vietnam, chaired by William Fulbright, for example, played a crucial role in legitimizing opposition to presidential policies in Southeast Asia.

Finally, alliances with the media and the judiciary provided Congress with a coercive capacity. In the 1950s, Senators Kefauver, McCarthy, and McClellan had demonstrated how televised hearings could be used to harass—and, in conjunction with perjury trials, imprison—gangsters, left-wingers, and union leaders. In the 1960s and early 1970s, other senators used these precedents to pillory and politically weaken employers of migrant labor, corporate polluters, and Nixon administration officials. After the Watergate episode entered its final stages and a special prosecutor was appointed, the congressional-media-judicial nexus achieved its full coercive capacity and was able to imprison errant administration officials.

These developments enabled Congress to strengthen its base of political support by increasing the range of governmental services it was in a position to provide to members of its constituency. Liberal political forces benefitted especially from this and, in a reversal of their prior stance, became quite vocal in defending the prerogatives of Congress and attacking the "imperial presidency."[5] Thus, they were prepared to rally in support of Congress as tensions between the legislative and executive branches increased during the Nixon years.

President Nixon, especially after his reelection in 1972, responded to these developments by attempting to undermine the new capacities of Congress and the institutions with which it was allied. The President impounded billions of dollars appropriated by Congress and sought to sever its ties with the bureaucracy by reorganizing executive agencies without seeking legislative approval. The White House established the plumbers squad to plug leaks of information to Congress and the press, and, its opponents claimed, it sought to undermine the legitimacy of the Supreme Court by appointing justices who were completely unqualified. The administration's opponents also claimed that it sought to limit Congress's influence over foreign policy by keeping vital information from it, most notably in the so-called "secret bombing" of Cambodia.

The President's opponents declared these actions to be abuses of power, and this animated their attack upon Richard Nixon in the Watergate controversy. Congress scored a total victory in that institutional conflict. It won because the bulk of the constituency that had supported assertions of presidential power during the New Deal and postwar period ultimately abandoned Richard Nixon and because the combination of media exposure, congressional investigation, and judicial process enabled the President's opponents to divide, delegitimate, and disrupt his administration. During the course of this constitutional conflict and in its immediate aftermath, Congress undertook to institutionalize its victory by imposing statutory limits on executive power in the War Powers Act, the Budget and Impoundment Act, the Freedom of Information Act, the Arms Export Control Act, and the Ethics in Government Act and by subjecting domestic and foreign intelligence agencies to much stricter congressional scrutiny. These restraints were quite effective and contributed to the difficulties that Gerald Ford and Jimmy Carter faced in asserting their leadership in the mid- and late-1970s.

After his election in 1980, Ronald Reagan undertook to strengthen the presidency by putting together a new constituency for presidential power and rebuilding the capacity of the executive to act independently of Congress. This endeavor enjoyed reasonable success during his first half-dozen years in office until Congress and the institutions with which it is allied counterattacked in the Iran-contra affair.

The budget and tax cuts enacted at the President's behest were at the heart of the Reaganite effort to solidify Republican control of the White House.[6] The Reagan spending cuts diminished the flow of resources to—and promised to weaken politically—groups and organizations that had a stake in federal domestic expenditures and were closely tied to the Democrats. Chief among these were the poor and near-poor, public employees and their unions, blacks (who disproportionately are poor or employed in the public sector), and those members of the middle class who were working for universities and other institutions in the nonprofit sector of the economy (institutions that depend upon federal grants and tax subsidies). At the same time, the Reagan tax cuts generated enormous budget and trade deficits. The economic dislocations caused by these deficits weakened two other institutions linked to the Democrats: labor unions in import-sensitive industries, and municipal governments in the nation's industrial belt.

On the other hand, those members of the middle class who were working in the private sector—and even more clearly, upper-income individuals—benefitted from the Reagan tax cuts. The President's tax and budget policies thus divided the middle class and joined the largest segment of it with upper class. In addition, the administration's assault on unions broke the entente between labor and management which had emerged in many sectors of the economy during the late 1930s and 1940s and, as much as anything, explains the overwhelming support the Republicans now receive among businessmen. As a result, the GOP not only won two-thirds of the votes of the middle and upper classes in the 1984 presidential election, but also through Political Action Committees (PACs) and direct contributions, it solidified its enormous advantage in campaign finance.[7] By weakening established centers of power and reorganizing interests in these (among other) ways, the Reaganites sought to solidify Republican control of the White House and create a new constituency for presidential power.

In addition, the Reaganites sought to restrict the distributive and extractive capacities of Congress. The tax cuts enacted in 1981 were designed to serve the first of these purposes.[8] The enormous budget deficits created by those tax cuts limited Congress's ability to enact new spending programs by subjecting such proposals to the charge of exacerbating the deficit problem, and the 1986 tax reform reduced the extractive capacities of Congress by eliminating many of the exemptions, deductions, and preferences that in prior decades had made it politically possible to increase tax rates.

At the same time, the Reaganites undertook to increase the coercive and administrative capacities of the executive branch, especially in the realm of national security policy. Reagan sought to reassert the prerogative of the president unilaterally to deploy military force abroad by invading Grenada and bombing Libya. In both of these episodes, the duration of American involvement was brief, casualties were minimal, victory was assured, and hence public support for the President was extremely high. Senators and representatives who disapproved of the President's conduct thus found it politically impossible to criticize him, and he was able to act without securing the prior approval of Congress. In addition, the administration undertook to rebuild the CIA's capacity to engage in covert operations by greatly increasing its budget and personnel and by attempting to circumvent congressional scrutiny of intelligence operations.

During Ronald Reagan's first six years in office, these efforts enjoyed considerable success. Congress did not enact a single major new social program; the administration oversaw the largest peacetime military buildup in the nation's history; and the President demonstrated that it was possible, despite the trauma of Vietnam, for a politician to increase his popularity at home by using American forces abroad. Observers generally agreed that Reagan had gone a long way toward restoring the prestige and power of the presidency.[9]

Nonetheless, the President did suffer a number of reversals. After 1982, the Congress refused to cut domestic spending any further and required the administration to slow the pace of its rearmament program. In addition, Congress restricted the President's efforts to aid the contras in Nicaragua by enacting a series of amendments—the Boland amendments —to foreign military assistance bills. Congressional Democrats further limited that effort by compelling the CIA to stop mining Nicaragua's harbors, insisting that the agency withdraw a training manual that advocated the assassination of Sandinista cadres, and publicizing charges that the contras violated human rights.

THE IRAN-CONTRA AFFAIR

It was in this context that the Reagan administration undertook to build an alternative intelligence apparatus, attached to the National Security Council. This apparatus enabled the White House to conduct covert operations (such as aid to the contras) which the Congress had refused to approve and activities (such as the Iranian weapons sales) which Congress almost certainly would not countenance.

Critics in Congress called the network put together by Oliver North and others a "state within the state." This characterization is not inappropriate because that apparatus had some of the administrative, extractive, and coercive capacities of a governmental intelligence agency. North's network was able to conduct covert operations because it was staffed by retired military officers and CIA operatives with experience in this realm and had ties to foreign intelligence officials and arms merchants. Lacking access to tax revenues, it was financed by gifts from foreign governments, contributions from wealthy American conservatives, and the profits from weapons sales to Iran. Furthermore, depending upon how one chooses to characterize its relationship with the anti-Sandinista forces to which it provided political and military guidance as well as financial and logistical support, it might be said to have had coercive capacities as well.

The eruption of the Iran-contra scandal did more than destroy this intelligence network. It disrupted the entire Reagan administration and to a significant degree shifted the balance of the national political power toward institutions that compete with the presidency. The President's difficulties cannot, however, simply be attributed to the fact that his administration committed a major blunder in selling arms to Iran in exchange for the release of American hostages and in diverting some of the proceeds from those sales to the contras. Scandals such as the Iran-contra affair must be understood as political events. Politically damaging revelations are a consequence of efforts by investigators to uncover facts that will embarrass an administration politically as much as they are a source of that administration's difficulties. After all, prior to November 1986, there were reports in the press that Israel was shipping arms to Iran and that Oliver North was helping the contras secure weapons, but neither the media nor Congress undertook to discover the source of these arms. As with Watergate, one must look to changes within political constituencies and to institutional factors to account for the emergence and success of challenges to the Reagan presidency.

As for changes within political constituencies, two developments weakened the coalition Ronald Reagan had constructed and served to energize the institutions through which his opponents operated. The first of these was the Democratic recapture of the U.S. Senate in the mid-term elections of 1986. (The great benefits of incumbency in House elections had enabled the Democrats to retain control of that chamber, of course, despite the GOP landslides in the 1980 and 1984 presidential elections.) The Democrats' success in 1986 emboldened the President's opponents in Congress. In addition, it emboldened the press, which up to that point had treated the Reagan administration quite gingerly for fear of alienating its middle-class audience.

The second development weakening the President was the emergence of a cleavage between the White House and the nation's foreign policy establishment. The institutions comprising that establishment—the State Department, Council on Foreign Relations, organs of elite opinion—had been upset by the White House's actions during and after the Reykjavik summit, which had caused strains in the Atlantic alliance, and they were appalled by revelations of the extent to which the White House had made policy and conducted sensitive operations in the Mideast and Central America through Oliver North's alternative foreign policy network. The communications media most closely associated with the foreign policy establishment denounced the "cowboys" in the White House for constructing this alternative network, supported the State Department's virtual declaration of independence after the Iran scandal erupted, and joined in the attack on the Reagan administration.

As for institutional factors, the President was weakened by the very way in which the Iranian weapons deal was conducted. The White House made use of a network of retired military officers and arms merchants to deal with Iran because its policy was opposed by the State and

Defense Departments and would certainly have evoked the same hostile reaction in Congress. This expedient was self-defeating, however, because after the weapons deal was revealed and the President came under attack, that network was not powerful enough to sustain him. Reagan could neither rely upon it to maintain his Iranian initiative (which he continued to insist was a good idea), nor was that network linked to powerful social forces to which he could turn for political support.

The administration's opponents, by contrast, were able to make use of the formidable iron triangle of institutions—Congress, the national news media, and the federal judiciary—which had triumphed over the White House in the Watergate affair. The extent to which this nexus has become institutionalized is indicated by the fact that after the diversion of funds to the contras was revealed, it was almost universally assumed that Congress should conduct televised hearings and the judiciary should appoint an independent counsel to investigate the officials involved in the episode. Yet this procedure is really quite remarkable: officials who in other democracies would merely be compelled to resign from office are in the United States threatened with imprisonment. The threat of imprisonment plays a crucial role in legislative-executive conflicts because it leads administration officials to testify against one another, that is, it gives Congress the coercive capacity to do battle with the imperial presidency.

By making use of these weapons of institutional combat—coercion, investigation, and publicity—in the Iran-contra affair, congressional Democrats were able to weaken the Reagan administration during its final two years. For example, the President was compelled to appoint a national security advisor, director of central intelligence, White House chief of staff, and ultimately to select a nominee for the Supreme Court acceptable to the opposition in Congress. In the realm of policy, the President was unable to advance his conservative agenda any further. Indeed, he only found it possible to take major initiatives—most notably arms control—when these coincided with the agenda of his liberal opponents. Thus, through institutional combat, the Democrats were able to contain the effects of Reagan's 1984 landslide electoral victory.

By the same token, the effects of the Democrats' success in the arena of congressional elections have been limited by the deficits that Republican fiscal policies produced. In 1990, of course, congressional Democrats engaged in a fierce battle with President Bush over the federal budget, seeking to make more money available for domestic spending programs. This struggle, however, ended in a stalemate. Thus, the consequences of each party's electoral victories have been contained by the weapons of institutional combat its opponents have developed and deployed.

INSTITUTIONAL COMBAT: COURTS AND THE NATIONAL SECURITY APPARATUS

In addition to exploiting the powers of the presidency and Congress, competing forces in recent years have sought to develop other weapons of institutional combat. In particular, liberal political forces have undertaken to gain control over or ally themselves with the courts and conservatives with the national security apparatus—institutions whose personnel and decisions are not directly subject to electoral review or challenge.

Of course, the use of such institutions as instruments of governance and political struggle is not without precedent in the United States. During the decades prior to the 1930s, for example, business interests relied upon the federal courts to check the hostile forces that controlled state legislatures, particularly in the Midwest and West. It was precisely to circumvent the influence that business exercised through the courts that Progressive reformers sponsored the creation of what then was a novel institution—the independent regulatory commission. Despite these precedents, what is distinctive about the present period is the extent to which competing forces have come to rely upon nonelective institutions and the scope of the powers that these institutions have come to exercise.

The alliance between liberal political forces and the federal judiciary dates back to the late 1930s and 1940s.[10] Faced with the threat of Franklin Roosevelt's court-packing plan, the Supreme Court found it prudent to abandon its ties to the conservative camp and align itself with liberals on issues of economic policy, civil rights, and freedom of speech. During the 1950s, 1960s, and 1970s, the federal judiciary took a leading role on behalf of school desegregation, reform of the criminal justice system, women's rights, affirmative action, and environmental and consumer regulation. The courts have been a valuable ally for liberal forces because they provide a channel for exerting influence that is not (at least in the short run) contingent upon victories in the electoral arena. From the perspective of the judiciary, this alliance has been valuable because liberals —including important members of Congress—have been willing to defend the courts in struggles with opponents who seek to limit their jurisdiction or enforcement powers. In recent years, efforts to limit the power of the federal judiciary have been resisted by coalitions of civil rights organizations, women's groups, educators, liberal Jewish and Protestant organizations, bar associations, law professors, and congressional liberals.

The support that the federal judiciary has received from these quarters enabled it to expand its powers greatly over the past twenty-five years.[11] Beginning in the 1960s, the Supreme Court substantially changed the rules governing justiciability—the conditions under which courts will hear a case—to permit the federal judiciary to play a larger and more active role in the governmental and political processes. For example, the Court liberalized the doctrine of "standing" to permit taxpayers' suits where First Amendment issues were involved. Similarly, the Supreme Court effectively rescinded the "abstention" doctrine which had called for federal judges to decline to hear cases that rested on questions of state law not yet resolved by the state courts. Moreover, the Supreme Court relaxed the rules governing determinations of "mootness" and, for all intents and purposes did away with the "political question" doctrine that for many years had functioned as limits on judicial activism. This liberalization of rules governing justiciability gave a wider range of litigants access to the courts, rendered a wider range of issues subject to judicial settlement, and made the courts more valuable as an institutional ally.

Equally important in expanding access to the judiciary was the Supreme Court amending the federal rules of civil procedure to facilitate class-action suits. Claims that might have been rejected as *de minimis* if asserted individually could now be aggregated against a common defendant. Class-action suits became critical weapons in the arsenals of the civil rights consumer and of the environmental, feminist, and antinuclear movements.

Accompanying this increased use of class actions was an expansion of judicial remedies including injunctions and the broad use of equitable powers for innovative forms of relief. Class actions challenging conditions in mental institutions, prisons, and other public facilities, for example, produced a host of detailed judicial decrees setting forth the minimum standards of care required of public agencies. Increasingly, judges made use of special masters under the control of the court to take charge of the day-to-day operations of institutional defendants such as the Boston school system and Alabama state prison system. Thus, by the 1970s, the federal judiciary provided litigants with remedies of the sort that were previously only available from either the executive or legislative branches. The chief beneficiaries of these new judicial powers were liberal political forces that, in turn, could be counted upon to rally to the support of the federal judiciary when it came under fire.

The support of the federal judiciary became critically important to liberal forces during their struggles with the Nixon and Reagan administrations. During the Nixon presidency, the Supreme Court refused to halt the desegregation of southern school districts. Most important, of course, was the Court's decision in the Watergate tapes case which compelled Nixon to resign from office or face certain impeachment. During the Reagan era, the Supreme Court opposed the administration on abortion rights, church-state relations, voting rights, and affirmative action, thus helping to block the implementation of important segments of the conservative agenda. The Supreme Court also served the interests of liberal forces by offering the media substantial protection from the laws of libel and increasing the liability of officials of the executive branch to civil suits.

The Nixon, Reagan, and Bush administrations sought to disrupt this alliance between the federal judiciary and liberal political forces. During his six years in office, President Nixon appointed a number of conservatives to the district and circuit courts as well as four justices including Chief Justice Warren Burger to the Supreme Court. Because of the importance liberals attached to the federal judiciary, especially to the Supreme Court, they resisted these efforts to create a more conservative bench. Liberal forces scored their most significant victories when Democrats in Congress blocked Nixon's efforts to appoint Clement Haynsworth and G. Harrold Carswell, both of whom were likely to oppose liberal interests, to the Supreme Court. The judges Nixon was able to appoint were, for the most part, moderate Republicans whose views on key issues were not sufficiently intense to impel them to seek to move the federal judiciary from its alliance with the liberal camp.

President Reagan, for his part, attempted to curb the ability of liberal forces to exercise influence through the federal judiciary by appointing notable conservative legal scholars such as Ralph K. Winter of Yale and Richard Posner of the University of Chicago to federal appeals courts. Through such appointments, Reagan sought not simply to ensure that conservative judges would replace liberals on the federal bench, but sought also to stage an intellectual revolution by enhancing the impact of conservative ideas on American jurisprudence. In the case of the Supreme Court, Reagan was able to appoint Sandra Day O'Connor, a Republican moderate; Antonin Scalia, a conservative appeals court judge and former University of Chicago law professor; and to elevate Nixon appointee William Rehnquist to the position of chief justice. However, after a bitter campaign, Senate Democrats defeated Reagan's next nominee, arch-conservative Judge Robert Bork; and conservative Judge Douglas Ginsburg, whom Reagan nominated in Bork's place, was compelled to withdraw his name from consideration. Reagan was forced to name a somewhat more moderate jurist, Judge Anthony Kennedy, to fill the Court's vacant position.

After his election in 1988, George Bush continued Reagan's efforts to name conservatives to the Supreme Court. In 1989 Bush secured the appointment of David Souter, a conservative federal judge. In 1991, after a bitter struggle, Bush was able to appoint Judge Clarence Thomas, a black conservative, to replace retiring liberal Justice Thurgood Marshall. Liberal forces saw the Thomas nomination battle as their last opportunity to prevent conservative domination of the Court and made an all-out effort to block Thomas. However, after nationally televised hearings in which Thomas was accused of having sexually harassed a female subordinate while director of the federal Equal Employment Opportunity Commission, Thomas was confirmed by the Senate.

Just as liberal forces were able to exercise influence through the federal courts, conservatives sought to use the military and national security apparatus as political weapons. From the 1940s into the 1960s, America's "military-industrial complex"—the national security apparatus and the economic sectors associated with it—had ties to both the Democratic and Republican parties. At the end of World War II, the dominant forces within the two major parties were able to achieve an accord on questions of foreign and military policy. This bipartisan consensus included the need to contain the Soviet Union and to maintain a powerful military establishment for this purpose. Presidents and members of Congress, Democrats and Republicans alike, supported high levels of military spending, the construction of new weapons systems, and the use of American military force abroad. Indeed, if there was any difference between the parties during this period it was the Democrats who were more consistent advocates of high levels of defense spending. Prior to the Vietnam War, the two largest military buildups of the postwar decades were sponsored by the Democratic administration of Harry Truman and John F. Kennedy, whereas it was the Republican administration of Dwight Eisenhower which was most diligent in seeking to economize on defense.

Conflict over the Vietnam War shattered this bipartisan consensus. Factions that eventually came to play a dominant role in the Democratic party turned against the use of American military force abroad and sought to slash defense spending. Conservative Republicans saw the new Democratic stance on defense issues as a threat to America's security and at the same time as an opportunity to expand the GOP's social and political base.

By promoting an enormous military buildup, the Reagan administration moved to attach to the Republican party political institutions, social forces, and economic interests with a stake in defense programs. The goal of this endeavor was not simply to secure campaign contributions and votes; the administration's larger purpose was to create a governing apparatus that could supplant the institutions of the domestic state linked to the Democrats. During the New Deal and postwar periods, Democrats had constructed a number of domestic welfare, regulatory, and fiscal institutions through which they could manage the nation's economy, shape its social structure, and provide a steady flow of public services and benefits to their party's constituent groups. The institutions of the domestic state fashioned by the Democrats thus served both as mechanisms of governance and as the political institutions through which the party perpetuated its power.

Although the Reaganites might have wished to do so, the experience of the Nixon administration revealed that any effort to seize control of these institutions and use them for their own purposes would have encountered overwhelming resistance. The president, to be sure, can appoint top agency administrators, but the commitment of domestic agencies to liberal programs is fiercely defended by congressional committees and by the constituency groups the agencies serve. Thus, when the Nixon administration sought to reorganize and reorient a number of domestic bureaucracies, it generated a firestorm of opposition. Indeed, this effort was one of the major reasons that President Nixon's opponents undertook to drive him from office. Similarly, when President Reagan attempted to bring about major changes in the policies of the Environmental Protection Agency (EPA), the congressional and constituency forces that supported existing EPA programs launched a counterattack that not only blocked Reagan's efforts but also resulted in investigations of two of the President's top EPA appointees, Rita Lavelle and Anne Gorsuch Burford—investigations that in Lavelle's case led to criminal indictment, prosecution, and imprisonment.

Recognizing that at least in the short term, it would be unable to seize control of the agencies of the domestic state, the Reagan administration endeavored, instead, to weaken and supplant them. The first of these aims was served by the administration's budget and tax policies that reduced the revenues and resources available to domestic agencies and thereby limited their administrative and political capabilities.

In addition, however, the Reagan administration sought to enhance the size and power of America's military and national security apparatus and to use it as an instrument for governing and perpetuating the power of the GOP in a manner parallel to the Democratic use of the agencies of the domestic state. Democratic administrations used domestic spending programs to solidify the party's ties to its numerous constituency groups. At the same time, as specified by the Keynesian theory, these federal spending programs stimulated economic growth and employment, thereby identifying the Democrats as the party of prosperity.

Thus, even many interests that were not direct recipients of federal spending were given reason to support the Democrats. Although professing to reject the economic theory associated with Democratic spending programs, the Reagan administration adopted what might be described as "military Keynesianism." The administration's military programs directly benefited segments of the business community, regions of the country, and elements of the electorate whose fortunes were tied to the military sector. At the same time, the Republicans expected that the economic growth, high levels of employment, and healthy corporate profits promoted by these programs would provide Americans more generally with reason to support the GOP.

The Democrats, of course, sought to block Republican efforts to use the national security apparatus as a political weapon. Congressional Democrats resisted the President's military buildup and ultimately succeeded in reducing the growth rate of military spending to a level considerably below that desired by the President. Opposition to the Republican efforts to enhance the role of the national security apparatus was one reason that liberal Democrats opposed President Bush's use of American military forces in the Persian Gulf in the wake of Iraq's invasion of Kuwait in 1991. Many Democrats feared the domestic consequences of Republican military success more than they feared the foreign policy implications of an American defeat.

SOCIAL COMBAT

In addition to institutional combat, political forces in recent years have engaged in another mode of struggle outside the electoral arena. They have used such weapons as criminal prosecutions, domestic intelligence operations, and media exposés to attack organizations and social forces linked to their opponents while employing subsidies, regulation, and deregulation to strengthen organizations and social groups with which they are allied.

After entering the White House, President Reagan and his supporters systematically began to attack the organizational bases of their opponents. Reagan appointees in executive agencies sought to "defund the left"—for example, halting the flow of federal funds to legal services agencies that file class-action suits on behalf of the poor. In addition, the Internal Revenue Service threatened to withdraw the tax exemptions of nonprofit organizations that engaged in political activism. These advocacy groups sought to defend themselves and their constituents by conducting a major voter registration drive among the poor in 1984, and

President Reagan's appointees on the board of the Legal Services Corporation responded by initiating an investigation to determine whether this constituted a violation of the rights of poor people to make their own decisions concerning whether or not to register and vote.

In a similar vein, the Reagan administration launched a systematic campaign of criminal investigations and prosecutions of Democratic mayors, legislators, and judges. Thus, Republican United States attorneys initiated investigations of corruption and wrongdoing in such Democratically controlled cities as Chicago, New York, Washington, D.C., and Atlanta. Several of these probes were aimed at prominent black elected officials including Marion Barry, Julian Bond, Andrew Young, and Harold Ford. Investigations by the Justice Department's Public Integrity Section targeted federal judges such as Frank Battisti of Ohio and Alcee Hastings of Florida.

The Reagan administration also sought to weaken organized labor—probably the most important organizational mainstay of the Democratic party. It encouraged employers to resist union demands, itself setting an example by destroying the Professional Air Traffic Controllers Organization (PATCO). In addition, the President appointed individuals hostile to organized labor to the National Labor Relations Board (NLRB), an agency formerly dominated by union sympathizers. Moreover, the fiscal and monetary policies that Reagan pursued in his first term drove up real interest rates and the value of the dollar, eroding the international competitiveness of the most heavily unionized sectors of the American economy, increasing unemployment in these sectors, and reducing labor's bargaining power.

Finally, the administration supported policies of deregulation which provided business firms with a strong incentive to seek to rid themselves of their unions. During the New Deal period, the federal government had established a regime of regulation over numerous sectors of the American economy—airlines, telecommunications, petroleum, coal, banking, securities, railroads, and trucking. Characteristically, regulation was used to restrict price competition among firms within regulated industries and to create barriers to the entry of new firms. To the extent that firms within such industries could pass added costs on to the customers without having to worry about being undersold by competitors, they lost an incentive to control their labor costs. Consequently, union-management relations in most regulated industries were less adversarial than cooperative in character: rather than fight one another over wages and work rules, unions and employers entered the political arena as allies to defend and extend the regulatory regime and to secure direct or indirect public subsidies for their industry.

During the late 1970s, an unlikely coalition of conservatives and consumer advocates, asserting that these accommodations served special interests at the expense of the public interest, secured a substantial measure of deregulation in these industries. Through deregulation, conservatives sought to get business to break its accommodations with organized labor, and consumer advocates sought to weaken the labor unions and business interests that were among their chief rivals for influence within the Democratic party. Conservatives have had more reason to be satisfied with the consequences of deregulation. Especially in airlines, telecommunications, and trucking, deregulation led to the emergence of nonunion firms that sought to undersell the established giants in their industry, and this in turn compelled those giants to demand "givebacks" from their unions so as to lower their labor costs. It is little wonder then that the Reagan administration sought to maintain the momentum of deregulation and thereby to undermine the economic and political power of organized labor.

The national news media also became targets of conservative political forces during the Reagan era. Conservatives regarded the media as among the chief institutions through which their opponents exercised political influence. The key conservative weapons in this campaign were libel suits filed against the national news media, the best known example of which was the Westmoreland suit against CBS in the early 1980s. These suits were encouraged and often financed by conservative organizations such as the Capitol Legal Foundation, the American Legal Foundation, and Accuracy in Media Inc. When journalists and liberals charged that the threat of such suits could discourage attacks on public officials, these conservative organizations were quite forthright in saying that this was precisely their intention. For example, in a December 11, 1984 letter to the *New York Times* on the Westmoreland case, Reed Irvine, head of Accuracy in Media, asserted that Westmoreland's legal bills were "footed by contributions by individuals and foundations who believe that CBS deserves to be chilled for the way it treated the general.... What is wrong with chilling any propensity of journalists to defame with reckless disregard of the truth?"

Finally, through its domestic spending restrictions, the Reagan administration attacked urban service bureaucracies and municipal governments—agencies controlled overwhelmingly by the Democrats. The domestic programs whose budgets suffered the deepest cuts were those that had provided local governments with funds and the capacity to dispense a large number of jobs such as the Comprehensive Employment and Training program. In addition, the administration's 1986 tax reform package reduced the deductibility of local sales taxes and restricted the ability of local governments to issue tax-free bonds. These changes in the tax code further diminished the resources available to the administration's foes.

In recent years, liberals as well as conservatives have sought to strengthen organizations and groups with which they are allied while seeking to undermine those upon which their opponents depend. Liberals, of course, rely upon the support of labor unions and civil rights and women's groups. In addition, among the most important instruments of social combat they have fashioned in recent decades are public interest groups—organizations devoted to political reform such as Common Cause and Ralph Nader's Public Interest Research Groups, environmental groups such as the Sierra Club and Friends of the Earth, and consumer and health groups such as the Center for Auto Safety and Action for Smoking and Health. Public interest groups and other liberal organizations have sustained themselves not only through membership contributions and foundation grants but also through grants from the federal government. The recipients of federal funding have included such liberal groups as the Reverend Jesse Jackson's Operation PUSH, the Women's Equity Action League and the Conservation Foundation.

One weapon that these organizations have used very effectively has been the exposé alleging wrongdoing on the part of their foes. The best-known of these was Ralph Nader's book *Unsafe at Any Speed*, which asserted that the American auto industry was indifferent to the safety defects of its vehicles. The nuclear power industry has been another major target of such exposés. Indeed, this industry has been brought to its knees by highly publicized changes of safety hazards in nuclear plants.

Litigation is an equally important weapon in the arsenal of liberal organizations. Most obviously through federal court suits, civil rights groups launched a successful assault on southern school systems, state and local governments, and political arrangements that they could not possibly have altered in the electoral arena. In a similar vein, environmental groups have used the courts to block the construction of highways, dams, and other public projects that not only threatened to damage the environment but would also have provided money and other resources to their political rivals. Similarly through the courts, women's groups have succeeded in overturning state laws that restricted abortion as well as statutes discriminating against women in the labor market.

In a number of ways, Democrats in Congress helped liberal interest groups make use of the federal courts for these purposes. For example, regulatory statutes enacted during the 1970s gave public interest groups legal standing—the right to bring suits—challenging the decisions of executive agencies in environmental cases. Congress also authorized public interest groups to serve as "private attorneys general" and to finance their activities by collecting legal fees and expenses from their opponents —generally business firms or government agencies—in such suits. Similarly, by securing the enactment of the Civil Rights Act of 1991, Democrats hope to give women and disabled persons, as well as members of minority groups, a greater opportunity to use the courts against employers in the private sector.

POLITICS IN THE POST-ELECTORAL ERA

Political analysts both in the press and in academe devote an enormous amount of attention to analyzing America's national elections. America, however, has now entered an era in which institutional combat has increased in importance relative to electoral competition. This is not to say that electoral outcomes can make no difference. If the Republicans were able to break the Democratic stranglehold on Congress or the Democrats were able more than occasionally to overcome the GOP's advantage in the presidential arena, the stalemate that has characterized American electoral politics for the past quarter-century would be broken, and the patterns of institutional combat we describe would become less prominent.

Even under present conditions, elections can have an impact. In 1980, the Republican capture of the White House and Senate and the party's unusually strong gains in House races enabled Ronald Reagan to secure the enactment of major changes in tax and budget policy. President Reagan's dominance of American government lasted for little more than a year, however, before the momentum of the Reagan Revolution was broken by institutional struggles.

The one election in the past two decades which gave a single party control over the presidency and both houses of Congress—the election of 1976—had little effect on prevailing patterns of American government. Although a member of their party occupied the White House, congressional Democrats had acquired such a stake in legislative power and had so little confidence in their ability to maintain control of the presidency that they refused to follow Carter's leadership and continued their attack on presidential power. More than a short-term break in the electoral deadlock that has endured now for nearly a generation would be required to shift the focus of American politics from institutional combat back to the electoral arena.

NOTES

1. Samuel P. Huntington, "Congressional Response to the Twentieth Century" in David Truman, ed., *Congress and America's Future* (Englewood Cliffs, N.J.: Prentice-Hall, 1973).

2. Morris Fiorina, *Congress: Keystone of the Washington Establishment* (New Haven, Conn.: Yale U. Press, 1977).

3. Jeremy Rabkin, *Public Law, Constitutional Disorder* (New York: Basic Books, 1988).

4. James Q. Wilson, "The Politics of Regulation" in Thomas Ferguson and Joel Rogers, eds., *The Political Economy* (Armonk, N.Y.: M. E. Sharpe, 1984).

5. Arthur Schlesinger, *The Imperial Presidency* (Boston: Houghton Mifflin, 1973).

6. Martin Shefter and Benjamin Ginsberg, "Institutionalizing the Reagan Regime" in Benjamin Ginsberg and Alan Stone, eds., *Do Elections Matter?* (Armonk, N.Y.: M. E. Sharpe, 1986).

7. Thomas Edsall, *The New Politics of Inequality* (New York: W. W. Norton, 1984); Gary Jacobson, "The Republican Advantage in Campaign Finance" in John Chubb and Paul Peterson, eds., *The New Direction in American Politics* (Washington, D.C.: The Brookings Institution, 1985).

8. David Stockman, *The Triumph of Politics* (New York: Harper & Row, 1986).

9. John Chubb and Paul Peterson, eds., *The New Direction in American Politics* (Washington, D.C.: The Brookings Institution, 1985).

10. Martin Shapiro, "The Supreme Court's Return to Economic Regulation," *Studies in American Political Development* 1 (1986): 91–142.

11. Mark Silverstein and Benjamin Ginsberg, "The Supreme Court and the New Politics of Judicial Power," *Political Science Quarterly* 102 (1987): 371–88.

REFERENCES

Burnham, Walter Dean. 1982. *The Current Crisis in American Politics*. New York: Oxford U. Press.

Chubb, John, and Paul Peterson. 1985. *The New Direction in American Politics*. Washington, D.C.: The Brookings Institution.

Edsall, Thomas. 1984. *The New Politics of Inequality*. New York: W. W. Norton.

Ferejohn, John, and Morris Fiorina. 1985. "Incumbency and Realignment in Congressional Elections." In *The New Direction in American Politics*, edited by John Chubb and Paul Peterson. Washington, D.C.: The Brookings Institution.

Fiorina, Morris. 1977. *Congress: Keystone of the Washington Establishment*. New Haven, Conn.: Yale U. Press.

Huntington, Samuel P. 1973. "Congressional Response to the Twentieth Century." In *Congress and America's Future*, edited by David Truman. Englewood Cliffs, N.J.: Prentice-Hall.

Jacobson, Gary. 1985. "The Republican Advantage in Campaign Finance." In *The New Direction in American Politics,* edited by John Chubb and Paul Peterson. Washington, D.C.: The Brookings Institution.

Milkis, Sidney. 1987. "The New Deal, Administrative Reform, and the Transcendence of Partisan Politics." *Administration and Society* 18 (January 1987): 433–72.

Rabkin, Jeremy. 1988. *Public Law, Constitutional Disorder.* New York: Basic Books.

Reich, Robert. 1985. "High Tech, a Subsidiary of Pentagon Inc." *New York Times,* 29 May, p. A23.

Schlesinger, Arthur. 1973. *The Imperial Presidency.* Boston: Houghton Mifflin.

Shapiro, Martin. 1986. "The Supreme Court's Return to Economic Regulation." *Studies in American Political Development* 1: 91–142.

Shefter, Martin, and Benjamin Ginsberg. 1986. "Institutionalizing the Reagan Regime." In *Do Elections Matter?* edited by Benjamin Ginsberg and Alan Stone. Armonk, N.Y.: M. E. Sharpe.

Silverstein, Mark, and Benjamin Ginsberg. 1987. "The Supreme Court and the New Politics of Judicial Power." *Political Science Quarterly* 102: 371–88.

Stockman, David. 1986. *The Triumph of Politics.* New York: Harper & Row.

Wilson, James Q. 1984. "The Politics of Regulation." In *The Political Economy,* edited by Thomas Ferguson and Joel Rogers. Armonk, N.Y.: M. E. Sharpe.

PART TWO

PARTY IDENTIFICATION AND REALIGNMENT

What are parties? To a considerable extent, they are the men and women who identify themselves as Democrats and Republicans. Unlike the "British party model," the American parties issue no membership cards. Nor do they charge people for the privilege of using the monickers. Yet, most Americans identify with one of the two major parties, and those who call themselves Democrats are generally more liberal on a wide range of issues than people who identify themselves as Republicans.

Despite those linkages, the moderation of American parties rarely means that a Democratic-controlled government will depart sharply from the policies of its Republican-controlled predecessor. Periodically, large-scale shifts in party identification among voters occurs. These realignments occur in response to shifting values among voters and a "triggering event" (usually an economic collapse) that destroys an old political order. Following a realignment, the American party system performs very much as the British party model is supposed to behave. David Brady, in "Critical Elections, Congressional Parties and Clusters of Policy Changes," finds that the 1896 and 1932 realignments brought large numbers of new members into the Congress. The old power structures give way to more vigorous leadership and party cohesion on roll calls dramatically increases. The emerging majority party controls the agenda and enacts wide-ranging policy innovations, largely because of the support of the new members elected.

Realignments, and hence major policy initiatives, occur when an old political order wanes and a fresh new one takes its place. Yet, as Ginsberg and Shefter suggest in the previous section, our current order has already frayed. Is a new regime in sight? Martin P. Wattenberg, in "The Decline of Political Partisanship in the United States: Negativity or Neutrality?," suggests that Americans have become less passionate about parties. In the 1950s and 1960s Americans tended to like one party and dislike the other. By the 1970s, they were more likely to have neutral feelings about both parties. Instead, their attention shifted to candidates. The fundamental bases of partisanship had atrophied. What many have called an "era of dealignment" was upon us. The dominance of Democrats in Congress and Republicans in the presidency indicates that the electorate has moved beyond partisanship in voting, perhaps for the long run.

Yet, not all observers were so pessimistic. John R. Petrocik, in "Realignment: New Party Coalitions and the Nationalization of the South," argues that the Democratic dominance that emerged from the New Deal realignment has not given way to a Republican majority. Yet, party coalitions have shifted, especially in the South. Southern whites have shifted from Democratic to Republican ties and these changes cannot be explained by either migration or generational accounts.

Warren E. Miller, in "Party Identification, Realignment, and Party Voting: Back to the Basics," challenges this argument. He asserts that the best measure of party identification is one that emphasizes how people label themselves, not how strongly one feels about partisanship. Miller finds little volatility in party identification and no decrease in party line voting between 1952 and 1988. The growth of Republican strength comes from less-than-loyal Democrats changing their affiliations.

CRITICAL ELECTIONS, CONGRESSIONAL PARTIES AND CLUSTERS OF POLICY CHANGES

David W. Brady

Profound changes in American public policy have occurred only rarely and have been associated with "critical" or "realigning" elections in which "more or less profound readjustments occur in the relations of power within the community."[1] Since the appearance of V. O. Key's seminal articles on critical elections, an increasing number of political scientists have attributed great importance to such elections.[2] Schattschneider views the structure of politics brought into being by critical elections as systems of action. Thus, during realignments, not only voting behavior but institutional roles and policy outputs undergo substantial change.[3] Burnham, perhaps the most important analyst of realignment patterns, alleges the existence of an intimate relationship between realigning elections and "transformations in large clusters of policy."

In other words, realignments are themselves constituent acts: they arise from emergent tensions in society which, not adequately controlled by the organization or outputs of party politics as usual, escalate to a flash point; they are issue-oriented phenomena, centrally associated with these tensions and more or less leading to resolution adjustments; they result in significant transformations in the general shape of policy; and they have relatively profound after effects on the roles played by institutional elites.[4]

The importance of the relationship between certain elections and clusters of policy changes is considerable because, if such a relationship in fact exists, then at such times there also exist relatively clear relationships between mass electoral behavior and public-policy changes. This is, of course, contrary to "normal" politics, when there is little if any relationship between elections and public policy. If such a connection between elections and policy changes can be established for realigning periods, then we can better account both for change in the American political system and for the linkages that are responsible for change.

A peculiar feature of the discussion of the relationships between critical elections, institutional changes and clusters of policy changes is that, while there are studies available of the effects of critical elections on the "party in the electorate"[5] and on the "party as organization,"[6] there are no studies available of the effect of such elections on the vehicle through which policy changes are legitimized: the congressional parties. Whatever connections exist between critical elections and changes in public policy occur in large part within the institutional context of building legitimating congressional majorities. That is, in order for "clusters of policy changes" to become policies a majority of the Congress must vote for them. The relationship between critical elections, changes in congressional parties and clusters of policy changes remains unexplored. This paper examines some of these relationships on the understanding that the theoretical contribution to be made is middle-range, namely a specification only of the major variables and relationships.

The fact that profound changes in public policy have occurred only rarely presents a problem to researchers seeking connections between mass electoral behavior, Congress and policy changes. The limited number of cases available makes it difficult for the researcher to generalize. In this paper the strategy is to compare two realignments, those of 1896 and 1932, in an attempt to determine whether any similarities exist between them and then, in the discussion section, to outline possible connections between types of election and policy changes. The realignment eras of the 1890s and 1930s were chosen because there is universal agreement that both were benchmarks in American political history. The policy changes associated with the election of 1896 were the crystallization of policies favoring industrialization. Expansionism, protective tariffs and the gold standard were the critical issues and each favored industrial interests.[7] After 1896 the industrial future of America was assured. The policy changes associated with the New Deal involved increased governmental action in the hitherto private sphere. Welfare policies, government involvement in the economy and increased regulation of the private sector are prime examples of the major changes associated with the 1930s realignment.[8] These two realignments thus ought to be good examples of eras in which there should exist connections between elections and policies.

It is the thesis of this paper that critical elections have the effect of creating conditions which facilitate the building of partisan majorities in the legislature capable of enacting clusters of policy change. In order to demonstrate this thesis, the effects of the critical elections of 1896 and 1932 on the congressional parties in the United States' House of Representatives will be examined. The analysis will show that the effect of critical elections on the congressional parties is to diminish the two major drawbacks to party government in the House, i.e., party-constituency cross-pressuring and the nature of the committee system.[9] Specifically, critical elections change the constituency bases of the congressional parties along a continuum which reflects the changes that are occurring in the "party in the electorate," thereby helping to diminish party-constituency cross-pressures. Such elections also effectively rearrange the committees of the House so that the party leadership is able to perform its function of organizing coherent majorities for legislative programs. Given these conditions, levels of party voting in the House rise. Party voting on the programs central to the policy changes is especially high.

Both the 1896 and the 1932 realignments can be said to have begun in the congressional elections prior to the presidential realigning election. The research design therefore includes Houses before the presidential election years of 1896 and 1932 as well as a "normal" House prior to the realigning elections themselves. The study of the 1890s realignment includes the 53rd House (1892) and the 54th and 55th (1894 and 1896 respectively), while the study of the 1932 realignment includes the 70th House (1926) as well as the 71st, 72nd and 73rd (1928 through 1932 respectively). Data analysis occurs at two levels, institutional and individual. At the institutional level, it will be shown that in both realignments the congressional parties are changed along a socio-economic continuum; that there is a drastic turnover in committee membership and leadership, thus disrupting committee continuity; and that these two developments are associated with a rise in the level of both majority-party cohesion and party voting in the realignment Houses. At the individual level, data analysis separates the roll call votes into issue dimensions and then shows that over the realignment period party competition and party identification are highly related to support for the new clusters of policy changes. This combination of institutional and individual data analysis will clearly demonstrate the relevance of party during realignment eras.

Finally, the data analysis includes a section on switched-seat congressmen, i.e., those Representatives elected from districts that switched in the direction of the realignment. It will be demonstrated that they are a critical linkage between election results and party voting, which helps to account for the clusters of policy changes. In Clausen's words "the main impetus for changes in the overall policy posture of the Congress comes in the new membership."[10] In sum it will be shown that at both the institutional and the individual level the effect of critical elections is to increase party cohesion and party voting, thus facilitating legislative responsibility and legitimizing the clusters of changes.

The data will be presented as follows: (1) a brief discussion of the cross-cutting issues in the realignment and a sketch of the realignment in the party in the electorate; (2) presentation of the aggregate-level data showing the changes in constituency composition of the parties, the breakdown of committee continuity, and the concomitant rise in majority-party cohesion and party voting; and (3) analysis at the individual level showing the increasing importance of party identification and competition in predicting individual voting behavior.

Proving the thesis outlined above depends upon establishing that party-constituency cross-pressuring and the nature of the committee system are in fact major drawbacks to party voting. Thus it is necessary first to discuss cross-pressuring and the committee system.

In the American system, congressmen's relationships to their constituencies are paramount, and to the extent that party positions conflict with real or perceived constituency interests cross-pressuring occurs. Cross-pressured Representatives will often vote constituency interests, not party position. Constituency interests are so important that both parties' caucuses have formalized the Representative's right to vote in accordance with them. Huitt sums it up nicely: "If the member pleases it (the constituency), no party leader can fatally hurt him; if he does not, no national party organ can save him."[11] In the modern House a large number of Representatives are cross-pressured; for example, southern Democrats from rural districts have constituency pressures on them not to vote with the Democratic leadership on certain welfare issues. During realignments the freshmen members of the new congressional majority are elected from constituencies where the issues of the realignment are causing shifts in party identification; for example, in 1932 the Democratic majority in Congress represented blue-collar and ethnic urbanites who were switching to the Democrats. The number of cross-pressuring districts is thus likely to be substantially reduced.

The committee system is a drawback to party government because committee chairmen, immunized until the 94th Congress by seniority, "are chieftains to be bargained with, not lieutenants to be commanded."[12] And their power to decide is based on the fact that committees have a continuous life of their own. Change in committee membership is "never complete and seldom dramatic."[13] Under these conditions committee norms and decision styles which affect or control public policy can be transmitted to the new members. Committees are normally stable in both membership and norms. Thus public policy decisions are incremental. It will be shown that during realignments committee stability and continuity are affected by a drastic turnover in membership. It follows that, if both cross-pressuring and committee stability are reduced, the level of party voting should increase dramatically —i.e., that the necessary conditions for party government should be fulfilled.

THE 1896 AND 1932 REALIGNMENTS

The agrarian revolt that culminated in the critical election of 1896 was the product of the crises of industrialization. Western and southern farmers allied with western silver interests and sought to enlist the "toiling masses" of the industrial East and Midwest, thereby recapturing America from the foreign monied interests responsible for industrialization. The crisis of industrialization squarely placed an agrarian-fundamentalist view of life against an industrial-progressive view of life, and the issue positions taken on this division were polar.[14]

The specific issues that cut across party preferences in the 1890s were the gold-silver question, the protective tariff, and expansionism. These specific issues were subsumed under the more general "crisis of vulnerability" in which urban industrial interests were pitted against rural anti-industrialist forces. The election of McKinley and the Republicans assured America's industrial future. Never again would the agricultural interests capture a major party and come so close to winning control of the government. The crisis of vulnerability was resolvable only by one side or the other winning out. Thus the 1896 realignment resolved the question of whether the northern and eastern industrial interests or the southern and western agricultural and mining interests would be victorious. The effect of the realignment was that it "eventually separated the Southern and Western agrarians and transformed the most industrially advanced region of the country into a bulwark of industrial Republicanism."[15]

Sundquist's analysis of the voters who switched their allegiance to the Republicans during the realignment showed that those who switched were mainly northern, urban and blue-collar, residing in the industrial East and Midwest.[16] In contrast, Bryan did not increase the Democrats' support compared with 1892 in the rural Midwest and East; thus the Democratic party after 1896 was essentially southern and border-state agrarian in its constituency base.

The political revolution that Franklin Roosevelt led was, unlike the 1896 realignment, the product of a single event—the Great Depression.

The underlying issue-dimension which separated and distinguished the parties was the question of whether the government would *actively* deal with the problems facing the country. Hoover and the majority of the Republican party came down against greatly increased governmental activity: "Economic depression cannot be cured by legislative action or executive pronouncement. Economic wounds must be healed by . . . the producers and the consumers themselves."[17] The Democrats, while not entirely sure in which direction to move, had formulated activist programs. John Garner, the conservative Speaker of the House, had advocated a $900 million federal public-works program, a billion dollar RFC loan fund and a $100 million mercy-money fund. The Democratic platform in 1932 differed markedly from the Republican on issues regarding the aggregation of wealth, control over the distribution of wealth and the exercise of governmental power. Benjamin Ginsberg's content analysis of party platforms from 1844-1968 showed the above issues to be both salient to parties and divisive across them during the 1932 election.[18] In sum, the parties differed markedly over the role the government was to play in curing the Depression. The Democrats favored active government involvement; the Republicans favored voluntarism and non-intervention.

The voters switching to the Democrats in the 1932 election came primarily from those groups most affected by the Depression: farmers and city dwellers. The farm depression of the 1920s had continued long after industry had recovered. The Republican leadership had done little to deal with the problem and seemed relatively unconcerned; President Coolidge commented: "Well, farmers never have made money [and] I don't believe we can do much about it."[19] This policy resulted in a number of farm protests, such as McNary-Haugenism, and may be viewed as a harbinger of the political revolution precipitated by the Depression. In fact, Sundquist suggests that these farm protests were an integral part of the realignment of the 1930s.[20] We would expect the congressional Democratic party over the 1926-32 period to reflect this change in voter sentiment.

The second and larger group of voters switching to the Democratic party is most readily identifiable by place of residence. The cities, populated by workers, ethnics and blacks, moved into the Democratic column during this period. In cities formerly Democratic such as New York, the Republicans ceased to be competitive, while in cities such as Boston which had voted for Al Smith in 1928 the Democrats became the dominant party from 1932 onward. Working-class ethnics and northern blacks were hard hit by the Depression and voted for the Democrats. We would also expect to see this change reflected in the congressional Democratic party.

CONSTITUENCY CHANGES DURING REALIGNMENTS

If realignments in the parties in the electorate are reflected in the composition of the congressional parties, then the constituency bases of the congressional parties should show dramatic shifts. Accordingly one would expect that from the 53rd House to the 55th the congressional Republican party would suddenly come to over-represent industrial and eastern constituencies. The shift in the congressional Democratic party during the New Deal should be toward northern industrial urban districts.

In order to test these hypotheses, the following data were collected for the 1896 and 1932 periods. The numbers of farmers and blue-collar workers were collected from the appropriate county sections of the 1890 census and then mapped onto congressional districts. The number of blue-collar workers, the value added by manufacture and the population density were collected from the appropriate county sections of the 1930 census and likewise mapped onto congressional districts. Since in both periods congressional districts varied in size, percentages were used. These percentage data were then arrayed and divided by mean and median and into quartiles. Table 4.1 presents the results of this analysis. The results in both cases show a dramatic shift in the constituency bases of the new majority congressional party.

In 1896 the percentage of Republican congressmen from labor districts increased from 44 to 79 percent, while the ratio of increase in absolute numbers of Republicans from such districts was 1.91. In agricultural districts the Republican percentage decreased by 3 percent over the period; the ratio of absolute change was .95. Moreover, the switch in the constituency base of the Republican party was also highly sectional, with over three-fourths of Republicans elected from the East and the North Central region by 1896. Analysis of the same figures for the congressional Democrats showed a shift toward highly agricultural districts located in the southern and border states. In short, the 1896 realignment yielded two relatively homogeneous congressional parties, with distinct centers of gravity on both a sectional and an agricultural-industrial continuum.

During the 1932 realignment Democratic gains were proportionately greater in urban blue-collar industrial districts than in more rural, less industrial districts. During the New Deal realignment the Democrats increased their share of urban seats from 30 to 66 percent; in industrial and

Table 4.1 Shifts in Congressional Majority Party Composition During the 1896 and 1932 Realignments in Percentages and Absolute Ratio of Increase

District composition	1896 Realignment		Percent increase	Absolute ratio
	53rd Congress	55th Congress		
Percent Republican congressmen from:				
Labor				
Low	35	31	−4	.93
High	44	79	+35	1.91
Agricultural				
Low	40	71	+31	1.78
High	36	33	−3	.95
Region				
Dem. from southern and border states	47	64	+17	
Rep. from East and North Central region	62	76	+14	

District composition	1932 Realignment		Percent increase	Absolute ratio
	70th Congress	73rd Congress		
Percent Democratic congressmen from:				
Labor				
Low	57	82	25	1.37
High	32	64	32	1.97
Industry				
Low	54	81	27	1.40
High	34	67	33	1.89
Urban				
Low	53	77	24	1.38
High	30	67	37	1.96

labor districts the increase was from 34 and 32 percent respectively to 65 and 64 percent. The ratio of increase, which measures absolute change, shows that in each category the more urban, more industrial, more blue-collar the district, the greater the increase in Democratic strength. The effect of the Roosevelt realignment on the congressional Democratic party was to add a large number of congressmen representing urban blue-collar districts to the solid rural non-industrial southern base that the

Democrats had had since 1896. A secondary effect was to increase the Democrats' share of northern farm districts. This, of course, meant a corresponding reduction in the number of Republican Congressmen from urban and northern farm districts. Thus, the "New Deal" coalition so often studied in the party in the electorate was reflected directly in the composition of the congressional Democratic party.

In both realignments the shifts in voter sentiment were reflected in the composition of the majority congressional party. These shifts created relatively homogeneous congressional parties, organized in effect around substantive partisan divisions of policy. Such stable over-time "partisan alignments form the constituent bases for governments committed to the translation of the choices made by the electorate during critical periods into public policy."[21] Under such conditions there is a reduction in party/constituency cross-pressuring because party and constituency are relatively homogeneous. Thus, if our analysis is correct, party voting should rise over the realignment period. However, before we test the party-voting hypothesis it is necessary to determine the effect of realignments on the second obstacle to party government—the committee system.

REALIGNMENT AND THE STABILITY OF THE COMMITTEE SYSTEM

In this section it is argued that the effects of this second obstacle are substantially reduced—specifically, that the turnover rates on House committees during the realignments were drastic enough to disturb committee continuity, and that the new members were more partisan than the members they replaced. The result of the realignments was thus the replacement of old committee members with new members more predisposed to partisan voting.

In the modern House of Representatives the committee system has reigned in no small part because of committee continuity. Committee continuity assures gradual changes in leadership and that committee norms can be transmitted easily to new members. The result is incrementalism in policy decisions rather than clusters of policy changes. Professor Fenno observed the importance of personnel turnover for committee decision-making in his study of the congressional appropriations process: "The two occasions on which the greatest amount of open dissatisfaction, threatened rebellion, and actual rebellion occurred coincided with the two greatest personnel turnovers...the tendency to rebellion increases as personnel turnover increases, the very stability of committee membership appears, once again, as a vital condition of (the style of decision making)."[22] Huitt and others have also commented on the importance of committee continuity for policy stability.[23]

Demonstrating that committee continuity is drastically affected by realignments and that the change in membership results in more partisanship requires it to be shown:

(1) that turnover on House Committees during the realignments is high;

(2) that a substantial portion of the committee leaders in the 55th (1896) and 73rd (1932) Houses was not prominent immediately prior to the realignment;

(3) and that the new members of the Ways and Means and Appropriations Committees, in particular, were more party-oriented than the members they replaced.

In order to demonstrate the drastic nature of committee turnovers in both realignments, membership lists from thirteen committees were collected for the 53rd through 55th Houses and the 70th through 73rd Houses. A turnover rate for each of these committees was computed both over the whole committee and for the party components of each committee.[24] The turnover rates were computed by taking the number of holdover members on the committee and dividing it by the number of committee members. For example, in the 55th House the Appropriations Committee had seventeen members only six of whom had served on the committee in the 53rd House. The total turnover was thus 64.7 percent; conversely the percentage of carryovers was 35.3 percent. Party turnover rates on these committees were arrived at in the same fashion and are included to demonstrate that the high turnover figures were not solely the result of changes in the relative positions of the majority and minority parties. Table 4.2 shows the results of this analysis for the thirteen committees.

The results are striking. The lowest of any of the rates of turnover was 50 percent. Excluding the Republicans on Rules, Appropriations and Merchant Marine, the lowest turnover rates were 62.5 percent. Thus, during both realignments all thirteen committees found themselves with majorities consisting of new members. Committee continuity was greatly disrupted. Comparing committee turnover during the realignments to turnover in the period immediately preceding them reveals that turnover was much greater during the realignment periods. The average turnover for the thirteen committees from the 52nd House to the 53rd was slightly over 30 percent, while the average turnover from the 53rd to the 55th was over 80 percent. The same pattern holds for the 1930s realignment. Average committee turnover during the pre-alignment Houses was slightly over 20 percent, while during the realignment it was

Table 4.2 Committee and Partisan Committee Turnover for Thirteen
Selected House Committees in the 1896 (53rd to 55th Houses) and
1932 (70th to 73rd Houses) Realignments in Percentages

Committee	1896 Realignment			1932 Realignment		
	Total turnover	Dem. turnover	Rep. turnover	Total turnover	Dem. turnover	Rep. turnover
Agriculture	100.0	100.0	100.0	85.2	89.5	75.0
Appropriations	64.7	66.6	50.0	74.3	67.0	85.7
Banking and Currency	76.5	88.9	62.5	79.2	81.2	75.0
Education	100.0	100.0	100.0	85.7	80.0	100.0
Foreign Affairs	86.7	87.5	85.7	80.0	88.2	62.5
Commerce	82.4	100.0	71.4	64.0	85.7	62.5
Judiciary	82.4	100.0	62.5	88.0	88.2	87.5
Labor	76.9	85.7	66.7	85.0	85.7	83.3
Merchant Marine	91.7	100.0	83.3	73.9	82.4	50.0
Mines and Mining	84.6	85.7	100.0	95.5	100.0	83.3
Public Lands	86.7	100.0	71.4	95.7	100.0	83.3
Rules*	80.0	100.0	50.0	67.0	62.5	75.0
Ways and Means	76.5	88.9	62.5	80.0	93.3	60.0

*During the 1890s' realignment the Rules Committee had only five members.

over 80 percent. Comparisons with turnover figures for the modern
House of Representatives reveal the same pattern.[25] It seems clear that,
no matter how turnover rates are computed, the 1896 and 1932 realignments effected drastic changes in committee composition.

COMMITTEE LEADERS

Important components of the committee system, facilitating committee
continuity and stability, are the seniority and specialization norms. Committee leadership positions come available relatively rarely; leaders are
brought along slowly. A committee's leaders serve on the same committee for long periods of time, acquiring expertise and becoming keepers of
committee norms and policy.

   If in a very short time there are drastic turnovers in membership, one
would expect the norms of seniority and specialization to be affected—
specifically, that during realignment periods committee turnover would be
so drastic that many of the committee leaders in the realignment Houses
would not have acquired much seniority. Any committee chairman in the

55th and 73rd Houses who was either not on that committee in the 53rd or 70th Houses or who was below the median rank of seniority in those Houses was considered to have advanced rapidly to committee leadership. Obviously a chairman in the realignment Houses who had not been on the committee two or three terms before could not have acquired either much seniority or much expertise in the intervening period.

During the period of the 1890s realignment, forty-nine House Committees with more than five members were continuously in existence. Of these forty-nine committees, in the 55th House, twenty-eight, or 57 percent, had chairmen who were not on the committee in the 53rd House. Another eleven had chairmen who were below the median seniority in the 53rd. Thus thirty-nine of forty-nine committees, or 80 percent of House committees in the 1896 House, had committee chairmen who had not acquired much seniority and were not likely to be subject-matter experts. Of course at this time the Speaker had the power to appoint committees and chairmen. Thus the effect of turnover, which gave the party leadership flexibility in appointments, was further enhanced by the Speaker's power to jump members to committee chairmanships. However, most of these thirty-nine committee chairmen were not the result of the Speaker's appointive powers.[26]

During the period of the 1930s realignment, there were forty-four House committees with more than five members, and analysis of these forty-four committees shows that, within the short period of three elections, eighteen of them acquired chairmen who were either not on the committee at all at the end of the 70th House or were below the median minority rank. Robert Doughton of North Carolina, for example, was the tenth-ranking Democrat, the last, on the Ways and Means Committee in January 1929; he was chairman of Ways and Means in January 1933. Representative Ragon of Arkansas was not a member of Ways and Means in the 70th House; he was the ranking majority member in the 73rd House. Representative Sabath of Illinois was not on the Rules Committee in the 70th House; by the 73rd House he was the fourth-ranking member. The influx of new members plus the high turnover on committees facilitated the kind of rapid committee advancement noted in the above examples. Rather than continue the argument by enumeration, Table 4.3 shows, for both realignments, the committees whose chairmen had risen to power rapidly. The table shows that both important and unimportant committees in both realignment Houses had chairmen who had not acquired long committee seniority and were not the keepers of committee norms. The most obvious effect of the discontinuities in committee leadership was that the committee system became more flexible or pliable in providing party voting cues. Committee leaders and members had not acquired the norms and expertise necessary to provide the committee voting cues so prominent in the modern House of Representatives. The negative effect of committee continuity on party voting was thus diminished.

The final stage of the argument concerning the committee system and party government entails demonstrating the increased partisanship of the new committee members. In order to demonstrate this, party-support scores for majority-party members of the Ways and Means and Appropriations committees were computed for each of the seven Congresses. The score was computed by scoring a 1 each time the member voted with the majority of his party on all roll calls in which a majority of one party opposed a majority of the other. For example, if out of twenty such votes a member voted with the majority of his party on eleven occasions his support score was 55. Only majority-party members were analyzed because of course "clusters of policy changes" are voted through by a cohesive majority party.[27] In the 53rd House the average partisan predispositions of the Republicans on both committees was 65.5, while in the 54th and 55th realignment Houses the equivalent partisan predispositions were 85.0 and 86.0 percent respectively. Thus the influx of new members increased the committees' partisan predispositions. This finding would be strengthened if the new members were found to have higher support scores than the carryovers. The average partisan predisposition of the carryovers was 75.5 in the 55th House, while the same figure for the new members (54th House plus 55th) was 86.7. The average party support score for Democrats on Ways and Means and Appropriations in the 70th House was slightly below 60 percent. In contrast Democratic committee members' support scores in the 72nd and 73rd Houses were over 80 percent. Thus, as in the 1890s, the influx of new members increased the committee's partisan predispositions. However, in contrast to the 1890s, when the new committee members' party scores were compared to the carryover members', the results showed no significant differences. Nevertheless, the results show clearly that during both realignments the majority-party members of both committees became markedly more partisan.

REALIGNMENTS AND PARTY VOTING

The realignments of the 1890s and 1930s resulted in shifts in the constituency bases of the new congressional majority parties, and a drastic turnover in committee membership and leadership. If the thesis of this paper is correct, this combination of factors reduced constituency/party

Table 4.3 (A) House Committees in the 55th House Whose Chairman Had Either Not Been on Committee, or Had Been Low Ranking, in 53rd House

	Committees	Chairman
*	Accounts	Odel (N.Y.)
*	Agriculture	Wadsworth (N.Y.)
*	Alcohol Liquor Traffic	Brewster (N.Y.)
	Appropriations	Cannon (Ill.)
*	Claims	Brumm (Penn.)
	District of Columbia	Babcock (Wis.)
*	Education	Grow (Penn.)
*	Election of President	Corliss (Mich.)
*	Expenditures in Agriculture	Gillet (N.Y.)
	Expenditures in Interior	Curtiss (Kan.)
*	Expenditures in Justice	Sullaway (N.H.)
*	Expenditures in Navy	Stewart (N.J.)
*	Expenditures in Post Office	Wanger (Penn.)
*	Expenditures in State	Guigg (N.Y.)
*	Expenditures in Treasury	Cousins (Iowa)
*	Expenditures in War Department	Grout (Vt.)
*	Expenditures on Public Buildings	Colson (Ky.)
*	Immigration and Naturalization	Danford (Ohio)
	Indian Affairs	Sherman (N.Y.)
	Commerce	Hepburn (Iowa)
*	Invalid Pensions	Ray (N.Y.)
*	Irrigation	Ellis (Ore.)
*	Judiciary	Henderson (Iowa)
	Labor	Gardner (N.J.)
*	Levees on Mississippi	Bartholdt (Mo.)
*	Manufacturers	Faris (Ind.)
*	Merchant Marine	Payne (N.Y.)
*	Militia	Marsh (Ill.)
*	Mines and Mining	Grosvenar (Ohio)
	Pacific Railroads	Powers (Vt.)
	Patents	Hicks (Penn.)
*	Private Land Claims	Smith (Ill.)
	Public Buildings	Mercer (Neb.)
	Reform in Civil Service	Brosius (Penn.)
*	Revisions of Laws	Warner (Ill.)
*	Rivers and Harbors	Burton (Ohio)
*	Territories	Knox (Mass.)
	War Claims	Mahon (Penn.)
	Ways and Means	Dingley (Me.)

*Chairman had not been on the committee in the 53rd House.

Table 4.3 (B) House Committees in the 73rd House Whose Chairman Had
Not Been on Committee, or Had Been Low Ranking, in 70th
House

	Committees	Chairman
	Accounts	Warren (N.C.)
	District of Columbia	Norton (N.J.)
	Election of President	Carley (N.Y.)
*	Elections – 1	Clark (N.C.)
*	Elections – 2	Gauagan (N.Y.)
*	Enrolled Bills	Parsons (Ill.)
	Expenditures in Executive	Cochran (Mo.)
	Foreign Affairs	McReynolds (Tenn.)
*	Insular Affairs	McDuffie (Ala.)
*	Irrigation and Reclamation	Chavez (N.M.)
*	Library	Keller (Ill.)
	Military Affairs	McSwain (S.C.)
*	Mines and Mining	Smith (W. Va.)
	Patents	Sirovich (N.Y.)
*	Public Lands	DeRoven (La.)
*	Revision of Laws	Harlan (Ohio)
	Territories	Kemp (La.)
	Ways and Means	Doughton (N.C.)

*Chairman had not been on the committee in the 70th House.

cross-pressuring and disrupted committees' policy continuity, thereby enhancing the ability of the majority party to build partisan majorities.[28] Given these conditions, there should have been a sharp rise in party cohesion and party voting. The hypothesis to be tested in this section is that the elimination of Huitt's two obstacles to responsible parties—constituency/congressman relationships and the continuity of the committee system—will have resulted in a sharp rise in party voting during both realignment eras.

To test this hypothesis the percentage of roll calls on which a majority of one party opposed a majority of the other party, and the party-unity scores on party-majority versus party-majority roll calls, were calculated for the 52nd through the 55th and the 70th through the 73rd Houses. Further, for each of the Houses an average Index of Likeness (IPL) was computed by adding the IPL values for each roll call and dividing by the total number of roll calls in the House. The results should show a rise in party unity, a decline in the average Index of Likeness (an

Table 4.4 The Changing Levels of Party Unity and Party Voting Over the Realignments of 1890–96 and 1924–32

Congress	Average index of party likeness	Percent of votes with IPL ≤ .20	Percent of votes with Maj. vs. Maj.	Party unity average on Maj. vs. Maj. votes	
				Dem.	Rep.
1896 Realignment					
52nd (1890)	61.0	10.9	45.4	76.2	79.6
53rd (1892)	59.6	20.0	44.8	85.1	86.1
54th (1894)	46.1	30.3	68.5	86.9	83.2
55th (1896)	30.8	53.6	79.8	89.3	93.3
% increase or decrease 52nd–55th Congress	−30.2	42.7	34.4	13.1	13.7
1932 Realignment					
69th (1924)	63.7	10.5	43.9	74.7	86.0
70th (1926)	61.8	9.5	48.6	80.5	81.8
71st (1928)	50.9	27.2	58.3	85.1	86.0
72nd (1930)	61.0	19.5	57.7	80.9	78.6
73rd (1932)	42.3	33.6	70.6	87.6	88.5
% increase or decrease 69th–73rd Congress	−21.4	23.1	26.7	12.9	2.5

increase in party voting) and a sharp rise in the number of party votes. Table 4.4 shows the results of this analysis, using an Index of Likeness of .20 or less, and majority of one party versus a majority of the other party, as measures of party voting.

The results substantiate the hypothesis. The party-unity scores on majority versus majority votes rose from 79.6 to 93.3 for the Republicans during the 1890s while the comparable figures for the Democrats in the 1930s were 76.2 to 89.6—rises of 13.1 and 12.9 respectively. All three measures of party voting show a sharp increase over the realignment period. During the 1890s the percentage of party votes rose from 45.4 to 79.8, while the proportion of party votes with an IPL of ≤20 rose from 10.9 to 53.6. The results for the Roosevelt realignment shows the same pattern. The proportion of party votes rose from 43.9 to 70.6, while the percentage of IPL ≤20 roll calls rose from 10.5 to 33.6. Party cohesion and party voting increased rapidly during both realignments.

Some scholars have suggested that the crucial election in the 'thirties realignment was the 1936 election in which Roosevelt defeated Alf Landon of Kansas. Their argument holds that in this election the party realignment crystallized and urban ethnics became Democratic identifiers. It may well be the case that among the party in the electorate the realignment was not crystallized until 1936. The linkage between electoral results and the congressional parties, however, does not change significantly between 1933 to 1936. That is, the major thrust of change in the congressional parties occurred with the election of the 73rd House in 1932. In the 75th (1936) House the congressional Democratic party represented the same type of constituencies as in the 73rd and committee turnover and committee leadership turnover was not high. The Democratic committee leaders in the 75th House were by and large —almost 90 percent of them—those who had been the leaders of the 73rd House. Levels of party voting and of Democratic party unity were not as high in the 75th House as in the 73rd. For example, the percentage of majority versus majority votes in the 75th House was 62.9 as compared to 70.6 in the 73rd House, and Democratic party unity scores dropped over seven points to a little less than 80.0. Thus, while it may have been the case that the 1936 election crystallized the effects of the realignment on the party in the electorate, the effects of the 1936 election on the congressional party in the House were not of the same magnitude as the changes that occurred between 1928 and 1932.

PARTY AND ISSUES DURING REALIGNMENTS

One of the major points being made in this paper is that during realignments the policy issues central to the realignment are decided in a highly partisan manner. Since our interest is in the changing role of party in connection with the policy dimensions central to the realignment, Clausen's technique for identifying policy dimensions was utilized, and the resulting scores were then correlated with both party affiliation and party competition.[29] Briefly, the technique for determining policy dimensions is, first, to classify roll calls into issue domains on the basis of their substantive content. Secondly, a type of cluster analysis is applied to the role calls within each domain, the result taking the form of several homogeneous issue dimensions. The most comprehensive such dimension issued to represent each domain in the analysis that follows.

This analysis for the 53rd, 54th and 55th Houses yielded three dimensions. The first concerned monetary policy and the question of whether monetary policy should be inflationary—i.e., based on the silver standard or stable—i.e., based on the gold. This issue dimension occurred in all three Houses. The second dimension was tariff policy, the issue being whether or not tariff policy should be protective. The third policy dimension common to all three Houses was foreign policy. This area was dominated by the question of expansionism or isolationism. Each of these policy dimensions was of course central to the 1890s realignment.

During the 1930s realignment the policy dimensions common to the 71st, 72nd and 73rd Houses were social welfare and governmental activism in the economy. The social-welfare dimension included such legislation as providing hardship loans for the unemployed and the relief of hardship in the District of Columbia. The governmental-activism dimension included the National Recovery Act and legislation dealing with bankruptcy proceedings and a uniform coinage. The result of the analysis for both realignments resulted in the homogeneous issue dimensions mentioned above and also a score for each Representative in each House measuring his support for the policies in question.

If the aggregate-level analysis presented earlier in the paper is correct, then the same broad findings should also obtain at the individual level. Namely, during both realignments party affiliation and party competition should become more highly correlated with support for policy changes.

In order to test this hypothesis, the party-affiliation variable was measured by assigning the majority party in each realignment era a one and the minority party a zero (Republicans a one during the 1890s, Democrats a one during the 1930s). The party-competition variable used was the Hasbrouck-Jones measure of how many times in a five-election period (one census) a congressional seat changes hands.[30] The result was a five-point scale, which is comparable over time because it is not subject to changes in voting percentages patterns as are the Ranney-Kendall and Pfieffer indexes.[31] A district that was Republican four out of five times in the 1890-1900 period is comparable to a district that was Republican four out of five times in the 1920-30 period. The values for the scale are as follows:

1890s	1930s
1 = Democratic 5 times	Republican 5 times
2 = Democratic 4 of 5 times	Republican 4 of 5 times
3 = Democratic or Republican 3 of 5 times	Republican or Democratic 3 of 5 times
4 = Republican 4 of 5 times	Democratic 4 of 5 times
5 = Republican 5 times	Democratic 5 times

Table 4.5 Simple Correlation (r) between Party Identification, Party Competition and Issue Positions Over the Realignments of 1890–96 and 1924–32

| | 1890s Policy dimensions | | | | | |
| | Monetary | | Tariff | | Foreign policy | |
Congress	Party	Comp.	Party	Comp.	Party	Comp.
53rd (1892)	.62	.51	.69	.57	.64	.50
54th (1894)	.83	.69	.79	.72	.81	.63
55th (1896)	.91	.74	.89	.75	.90	.74

| | 1930s Policy dimensions | | | |
| | Social welfare | | Government activism | |
Congress	Party	Comp.	Party	Comp.
71st (1928)	.56	.42	.49	.41
72nd (1930)	.66	.57	.79	.56
73rd (1932)	.88	.67	.90	.70

The level of policy support score was operationalized by determining the number of times an individual member voted in the direction of the policy change. For the 1890s this means that on the monetary dimension the higher the score the more the Representative favored non-inflationary or hard-monetary policy; on the tariff and foreign-policy dimensions, the greater the score, the greater the support for protective tariffs and expansionism. In the 1930s high support scores on the social welfare and government-activism dimensions represents support for welfare programs and support for increased government management of the economy. Table 4.5 presents the correlations between party affiliation, party competition and policy support over the 1890s and 1930s realignments.

The analysis shows clearly the increased strength of the relationship between both party affiliation and party support over the two realignments. Just as party voting over all roll calls increased during both realignments, so does the importance of party increase on the policy dimensions associated with the realignments. Another way to interpret the table is to argue that it shows that over both realignments party improves as a predictor of voting on realignment-related policy dimensions. Our analysis shows that the issues central to the realignment are decided on a highly partisan basis. There is a coming together of party and policy such that many of the elements of a responsible party system are present during realigning eras. Our findings at both the aggregate and individual levels corroborate this thesis.

SWITCHED-SEAT DISTRICTS

If "the main impetus for change in the overall policy posture of the Congress comes in the new membership,"[32] then the new members from districts that changed during the realignments are critical for understanding policy change. It is from these switched-seat districts that new party majorities are formed. The replacement of senior congressmen by freshmen members of the same party does not realign the constituency bases of the parties. Rather, it was districts that switched from Democratic to Republican during the 1892–96 period and from Republican to Democratic during the 1926–32 period that built the "new" congressional parties which supported the respective clusters of policy changes. The congressmen from the switched districts were elected around the issues of the realignment and their high levels of party support provided the majorities necessary to pass the significant policy changes. In this section, after a brief description of their constituencies, the party-support and policy-support scores of switched-district congressmen will be analyzed.

Switched-seat districts in the 55th House are defined as those districts that switched from the Democratic party in the 53rd House to the Republican party in either the 54th House or 55th House and remained Republican through the 56th House. There were forty-nine such districts and they reflected the shift in constituency bases noted in the first section of this paper. Over 85 percent of the switched districts were located in the industrial areas of the East and Midwest. The remaining districts were located in the industrial area in border states such as Maryland and West Virginia. Switched-seat districts in the 73rd House are defined as those districts that switched from the Republican party to the Democrats in either the 72nd or 73rd Houses and remained Democratic through the 75th House. There were 113 such districts and they also reflected the shift in constituency bases noted above. The largest proportion of these districts was urban and industrial while the next largest proportion was largely rural and agricultural and was located

Table 4.6   A Comparison of Party-Support Levels between Switched-Seat and Non-Switched Seat Republicans in the 55th House and Democrats in the 73rd House

Party support scores	1896		1932	
	Switched-seat Republican congressmen	Non-switched Republican congressmen	Switched-seat Democratic congressmen	Non-switched Democratic congressmen
Percent above party mean*	76	47	65	48
Percent below party mean	24	53	35	52
Total	100	100	100	100
Mean support scores†	77.7	69.9	75.0	67.7

*Mean Republican support score in 55th House is 71.8; mean Democratic support score in 73rd House is 69.8.

† *t* test significant for both houses at .05 level.

in the Midwest. It is clear that the change in Democratic strength during the 1930s realignment was reflected in the switched-seat districts.

The specific hypothesis is that switched-seat Representatives will have higher party-support scores than Representatives from districts that have not changed hands. Testing this hypothesis entailed calculating a mean party-support score for the entire majority party and then comparing switched-seat congressmen to the non-switched seat members. The results support the hypothesis (see Table 4.6). Switched-seat congressmen in both realignments were more supportive of the party position than their counterparts. The same analysis was run for each of the policy dimensions discussed above and the results were similar. Congressmen from switched-seat districts in both realignments were highly supportive of the policy changes associated with the respective realignments. The *t* tests were all significant at the .10 level or below. Congressmen from districts switching their party affiliation thus provided critical support for both clusters of policy changes.

DISCUSSION

This paper has demonstrated that the realigning elections of 1896 and 1932 shifted the constituency bases of the new congressional majority party, thereby reducing constituency/party cross pressuring. In addition, the turnover in membership resulting from the two elections disrupted committee continuity. With these two major obstacles to party government removed, the level of party unity and party voting in the House increased dramatically. The realigning elections of 1896 and 1932 created the conditions for party government, and the clusters of policy changes associated with these realignments were enacted by cohesive, unified majority parties. They were likewise opposed by the minority parties.

While the specific question addressed in this paper concerned the nature of the relationship between these two realigning elections and the House of Representatives' legitimation of the clusters of policy changes associated with them, another broader question was implicit in the analysis: namely, are realigning elections a necessary condition of major policy changes?

In order to answer this question, it is imperative that we analyze the vehicle for the legitimation of policy changes—the congressional majority party. In both the 1896 and the 1932 realignments, it was the newly created, cohesive majority party that voted through the shifts in policy. The cohesiveness of the new majority party was the result of the turnover in membership (switched-seat districts) which reduced cross pressuring and disrupted committee continuity. The new members had high party-support scores and provided the votes that enacted the policy changes. Thus, on this reasoning, any election that generates a substantial turnover in membership can create the conditions necessary for major shifts in policy. The 1912 and 1964 elections resulted in major policy changes, and both were characterized by substantial membership turnover. In the 89th House elected in 1964, members representing switched-seat districts were highly supportive of their party's position and provided the votes necessary to enact the major policy changes that occurred.[33] Committee turnover in that Congress was the highest in over fifteen years, and the level of party voting and party unity rose by over five percentage points in its first session. The 1964 election, which may or may not have been a realigning election, brought in a substantial number of new members, who increased the cohesiveness of the majority party and facilitated the passage of policy changes. Further evidence supporting the assertion that the "impetus for policy changes is the new membership" comes from a recent work which shows that during the period 1886 to 1966 the correlation between the percentage of new members and the level of party voting was .46.[34] That is, the effect of new members is to create the conditions for party government, and over time the larger the percentage of new members the higher the levels of party voting. Thus elections characterized by a high turnover of membership seem to be a necessary if not sufficient condition for significant policy changes. It is interesting to note that the 94th House of Representatives, which had seventy-five new Democratic members, was the most partisan in recent years.

Elections that bring to the House a substantial number of new members are not sufficient to ensure policy changes for a number of reasons. The most important is that there must exist a program; either party or both must propose major changes.[35] Another such condition is unified control of Congress and the presidency. The 1920 election of Warren Harding brought to the House a large number of new members, and the percentage of party votes rose from forty-five in the 66th House to 60 percent in the 67th. However, as Charles O. Jones has shown, the lack of a program prohibited that Congress from distinguishing itself by passing significant policy changes. The most recent Congress, the 94th, might well have passed legislation that might have been considered major, but the threat and the fact of a conservative President's veto prohibited major shifts in policy. Clearly presidential programs and the President's involvement, as well as unified control of the policy-making institutions, are factors affecting the likelihood of policy shifts.

Major shifts in public policy are most likely to occur during periods when the parties and the candidates take divergent issue positions and the electorate sends to Washington a new congressional majority party and a president of the same party. Since 1896 this set of conditions has occurred only four times—1896, 1912, 1932-36 and 1964—and in each instance there were major shifts in policy.[36] When these conditions are met, there are relatively strong connections between the electorate, representatives and public policy. During such periods the American system of government exhibits many of the characteristics of responsible party government.

NOTES

1. V. O. Key, Jr., "A Theory of Critical Elections," *Journal of Politics*, XVII (1955), 3–18, p. 4.

2. Key, "A Theory of Critical Elections," and V. O. Key, Jr., "Secular Realignment and the Party System," *Journal of Politics* XXI (1959): 198–210.

3. E. E. Schattschneider, *The Semisovereign People: A Realist's View of Democracy in America* (New York: Holt, Rinehart and Winston, 1960), pp. 78–96.

4. Walter Dean Burnham, *Critical Elections and the Mainsprings of American Politics* (New York: W. W. Norton, 1970), p. 10. This book is the most comprehensive work but see the exchange between Burnham, Phillip Converse and

Jerrold Rusk, "Political Change in America," *American Political Science Review* LXVIII (1974): 1002–58.

5. Burnham, *Critical Elections and the Mainsprings of American Politics*; Key, "A Theory of Critical Elections" and "Secular Realignment and the Party System"; and James L. Sundquist, *Dynamics of the Party System: Alignment and Realignment of Political Parties in the United States* (Washington, D.C.: The Brookings Institution, 1973).

6. Benjamin Ginsberg, "Critical Elections and the Substance of Party Conflict: 1844–1968," *Midwest Journal of Political Science* XVI (1972), 603–26.

7. Walter Dean Burnham, "The Changing Shape of the American Political Universe," *American Political Science Review* LIX (1965), 7–29; and Paul Glad, *McKinley, Bryan and the People* (Philadelphia: Lippincott, 1964).

8. Arthur M. Schlesinger, Jr., *The Coming of the New Deal* (Boston: Houghton-Mifflin, 1958), and *The Politics of Upheaval* (Boston: Houghton-Mifflin, 1960).

9. Ralph Huitt, "Democratic Party Leadership in the Senate," *American Political Science Review* LV (1961): 333–44.

10. Aage Clausen, *How Congressmen Decide: A Policy Focus* (New York: St. Martin's Press, 1973), pp. 231–2.

11. Huitt, "Democratic Party Leadership in the Senate."

12. Ralph Huitt, "The Congressional Committee: A Case Study," *American Political Science Review* XLVIII (1954); 340–65, 341.

13. Huitt, "The Congressional Committee," p. 341.

14. Burnham, *Critical Elections*; Burnham, "The Changing Shape"; Glad, *McKinley, Bryan and the People*; Stanley L. Jones, *The Presidential Election of 1896* (Madison: U. of Wisconsin Press, 1964); V. O. Key, Jr., *Politics, Parties and Pressure Groups* (New York: Thomas Y. Crowell, 1967), pp. 232–6.

15. Burnham, "Changing Shape," p. 18, pp. 7–29.

16. Sundquist, *Dynamics of the Party System*, pp. 232–6.

17. Cited in Sundquist, *Dynamics of the Party System*, p. 185.

18. Ginsberg, "Critical Elections and the Substance of Party Conflict," pp. 603–26.

19. William Allen White, *A Puritan in Babylon: The Story of Calvin Coolidge* (New York: Capricorn, 1965), p. 344; also cited in Sundquist, *Dynamics of the Party System*, p. 172.

20. Sundquist, *Dynamics of the Party System*, pp. 181–2.

21. Benjamin Ginsberg, "Elections and Public Policy," *American Political Science Review* LXX (1976): 41–9, 49.

22. Richard Fenno, *The Power of the Purse* (Boston: Little, Brown, 1966), pp. 226–7.

23. Huitt, "Congressional Committee: A Case Study"; and Malcolm E. Jewell and Samuel C. Patterson, *The Legislative Process in the United States* (New York: Random House, 1966), pp. 442–9.

24. While it is certainly true that as an institution the House in the 1890s differed from the House in the 1930s, committees were already well defined

and important. In fact Woodrow Wilson called congressional government committee government. Thus turnover on committees was an important component of the system. For an analysis of the House as an institution in the 1890s see David W. Brady, *Congressional Voting in a Partisan Era: A Comparison of the McKinley Houses to the Modern House* (Lawrence: U. of Kansas Press, 1973). For the influence of the Speaker on committees see note 26.

25. For data on turnover in recent Houses see Richard Fenno, *Congressmen in Committees* (Boston: Little, Brown, 1973).

26. The committee system in the 1890s was centralized under the Speaker who had power to appoint committees. Thus seniority norms were more likely to be violated during this era. However, the Speaker's power to appoint in violation of seniority cannot account for a large portion of either the committee or committee leadership turnover. The two major papers on seniority in the House, Michael Abram and Joseph Cooper, "The Rise of Seniority in the House of Representatives," *Polity* I (1969), 52–85 and Nelson Polsby et al., "The Growth of the Seniority System in the U.S. House of Representatives," *American Political Science Review* LXIII (1969): 787–807, both show a lower level of seniority violation than could account for the turnover in committee membership. For example, Abram and Cooper say that on major committees only two seniority violations occurred in the 55th House. Polsby et al. show that Speaker Reed followed seniority on thirty-six of fifty-two committee appointments and of the sixteen violations eleven were compensated. Both these figures are far too low to account for the 80 percent turnover.

27. The same analysis was run over the minority party members of the two committees and the partisan predispositions of these members increased.

28. The term "party leadership" is intended to include the President as well as House leaders.

29. Clausen, *How Congressmen Decide*, Chaps. 1 and 2 for the technique to determine issue domains. Product moment correlation was chosen to test the hypotheses because the correlation model assumes strong monotonicity and independence as the null value condition. See Herbert Weisberg, "Models of Statistical Relationships," *American Political Science Review* LXVIII (1974): 1638–51. Moreover in each case reported below regression analysis was run on the same variables to corroborate whether or not real change had taken place. The unstandardized Bs in each case changed in the same direction as did the correlation coefficients.

30. Charles O. Jones, "Inter-Party Competition for Congressional Seats," *Western Political Quarterly* XVII (1964): 461–76; Paul Hasbrouck, *Party Government in the House of Representatives* (New York: Macmillan, 1927), Chap. 9

31. Austin Ranney and Willmoore Kendall, "The American Party Systems," *American Political Science Review* XLVIII (1954): 477–85, and David G. Pfeiffer, "The Measurement of Inter-Party Competition and Systemic Stability," *American Political Science Review* LXI (1967): 457–67. Both measures developed in these articles are based on arrays of data which are time based.

32. Clausen, *How Congressmen Decide*, pp. 231–2.

33. David W. Brady and Naomi Lynn, "Switched-Seat Congressional Districts: Their Effect on Party Voting and Public Policy," *American Journal of Political Science* LXVII (1973): 528–43; and Jeff Fischel, *Party and Opposition: Congressional Challengers in American Politics* (New York: David McKay, 1973), pp. 162–4.

34. David W. Brady, Joseph Cooper and Pat Hurley, "An Analysis of the Decline of Party Voting in the U.S. House of Representatives: 50th to 90th Houses" (unpublished manuscript, 1976).

35. Ginsberg, "Critical Elections and the Substance of Party Conflict."

36. There have been other instances when new majorities and a new president came to Washington, e.g., Eisenhower in 1953. However, in each of these instances Ginsberg's content analysis of issue differences between parties shows little ideological difference between parties.

THE DECLINE OF POLITICAL PARTISANSHIP IN THE UNITED STATES: NEGATIVITY OR NEUTRALITY?

Martin P. Wattenberg

One of the most widely discussed topics in political science over the last decade has been the decline of partisanship in the American electorate. Increasing numbers of voters are declaring themselves political independents and splitting their tickets. Many read in these trends "the end of parties," at least as we know them. That we now live in an "anti-party age" is beyond dispute, according to many authorities. As Jeff Fishel[1] has noted, both proponents of parties as vote-maximizing and consensus-building institutions, such as Jeane Kirkpatrick and Austin Ranney, and those who favor the responsible party government model, such as Gerald Pomper and David Broder, agree that American parties have come to a "shambles."

Yet evidence indicates that in certain respects there has been no decline of parties at all. As organizations, parties have suffered from the disappearance of the big city machines, but overall there are indications of continued organizational vitality. Data from the national election studies conducted by the Survey Research Center/Center for Political Studies (SRC/CPS) at the University of Michigan show that an increasing percentage of citizens have been reporting that they have been exposed to local party organizational contacts.[2] According to Jewell and Olson,[3] state political party organizations have been revitalized, with the result being a more active role for the state parties. And on the national level, Cotter and Bibby[4] have concluded from their extensive study of the history of national party organizations that both parties have undergone processes of institutionalization and nationalization in recent years. As for parties in government, party affiliation remains an excellent predictor of voting behavior in Congress. In addition, recent congressional reforms have served to increase the potential for party leadership and have restored the party caucus.[5] Thus it is evident that the decline of parties in the electorate is a much clearer trend than the decline of parties as organizations or in government. Therefore, to make generalizations about parties being in a shambles may lead us to overlook the importance of aspects of party strength which have not declined.

What is most curious about all of these counter-trends, however, is how they can be occurring at the same time when voters are not only displaying a greater independence from party, but also becoming more and more alienated from them according to Nie, Verba and Petrocik.[6] It is the central point of this article that the increase in alienation towards the parties has been minimal. The major change which has taken place in the public's evaluations of the parties has been towards a neutral attitude rather than a negative one. This is not to say that there has not been a decline of parties *in the electorate*, but instead that the nature of the decline has been different from what many have assumed. Such a distinction is crucial for any understanding of the future of American political parties. If voters are alienated from political parties, then the parties' chances for recovery in the near future are doubtful, but if people are only neutral towards them, then the door remains open for party renewal.

Indeed, a good deal of speculation about the future of the political party system rests on the assumption that voters have rejected parties. For example, Kristi Andersen[7] writes that a major difference between the 1920s and 1970s is that in the 1920s those not affiliated with a party were largely apathetic while in the 1970s "there appears to be a more principled rejection of parties." Such a repudiation, she argues, will make the capture of Independents by one of the parties "exceedingly difficult." It is thus crucial to first assess whether such an alienation process has in fact been responsible for party decline in the electorate.

AN EXAMINATION OF THE ALIENATION HYPOTHESIS

The alienation hypothesis concerning party decline in the electorate contains two basic components. First, it has been asserted that voters increasingly see fewer important differences between the Democrats and the Republicans. Or, as George Wallace said in 1968, "There's not a dime's worth of difference between the two major parties." Second, it has been presumed that as distrust of government—i.e., political cynicism—has increased concurrently with the rise in voter independence, that the two trends are related. One of the clearest arguments for the joint impact of these casual factors has been offered by Nie, Verba and Petrocik.[8] They attribute the increased expression of disenchantment with the government to the troubles of the late 1960s and proceed to describe the following sequence of events:

> The issues of the 1960s...do not clearly coincide with party lines; thus the parties offer no meaningful alternatives that might tie citizens more closely to them. Thus the political parties reap the results of the disaffection. Citizens come to look at the parties in more negative terms; they also begin to abandon the parties in greater numbers.

However, the data which are available from the SRC/CPS election studies do not provide much support for such an interpretation. To begin with, as Table 5.1 (A.) shows, the proportion of respondents who thought that there were "important differences in what the Republican and Democratic parties stand for"[9] has remained quite stable over the years. Between 1952 and 1976 the proportion seeing important differences fluctuates minimally in the range from 46 to 52 percent. The data for 1980 show a significant change from 1976, but it is in the opposite direction from what would be predicted by the alienation hypothesis, with 58 percent now perceiving important differences between the parties.

Nevertheless, the fact that the electorate continues to see important differences in what the parties stand for does not necessarily mean that citizens continue to see the differences as meaning anything in terms of government performance. Since 1960 the election studies have asked respondents what they considered to be the most important problem facing the country. Those who mention a problem are subsequently asked which of the two parties would be the most likely to do what they want on this problem.[10] As can be seen in Table 5.1 (B.), the percentage who feel that one of the parties will do better on the problem which most concerns them has declined since 1964. In that year, 65.7 percent thought that either the Democrats or Republicans would be the most likely to do what they wanted, even though only 50.8 percent said that there were important differences in what the parties stand for. In contrast, in 1980 only 50.3 percent thought one party would be better on the problem they considered most important—which for the first time is significantly lower than the proportion seeing important differences between the parties.

One possible interpretation of this finding is that it represents a growing disenchantment with political parties and the government in general. Black and Rabinowitz,[11] for instance, note that it bears a striking similarity to trends in trust in government. They write that "if neither party can provide desirable alternative solutions to the problems an individual feels are most important for the government to do something about, it is reasonable for the individual to view the parties unfavorably

Table 5.1 The Electorate's Perception of Differences between the Two Major Parties, 1952–1980 (Percent)

A. Percent seeing important differences in what the Democrats and the Republicans stand for

	Important differences	No differences, don't know[a]
1952	49.9	50.1
1960	50.3	49.7
1964	50.8	49.2
1968	52.0	48.0
1972	46.1	53.9
1976	47.2	52.8
1980	58.0	42.0

B. Percent seeing one of the parties as doing the best job on the problem they consider most important

	Party mentioned[b]	About the same	Don't know
1960	62.0	25.0	13.0
1964	65.7	25.3	9.0
1968	51.6	38.7[c]	9.8
1972	49.0	42.4	8.6
1976	46.3	46.0	7.7
1980	50.3	42.7	7.1

Source: National election studies conducted by the University of Michigan's Survey Research Center/Center for Political Studies.

[a]In 1964 and 1968 "don't know" was not on the questionnaire; thus the percentage coded as "no difference" was artificially inflated. To make all results comparable, I have combined responses of "no difference" and "don't know."

[b]Respondents mentioned either the Democratic or Republican party.

[c]Included are those who saw no difference between the major parties but believed that Wallace would do what they wanted.

and lose faith in the government." According to such an interpretation, respondents may still see major differences between the parties, but many are so dissatisfied with the opposing alternatives that they have become alienated.

However, those respondents who believe that there wouldn't be any difference between the parties in handling the problem they feel is most important are no more cynical than those who believe that there would be a difference. On a cynicism scale ranging from +100 to –100, the former group is never more than two points more cynical than the latter. In fact, those respondents who feel that there would be no difference between the parties are actually somewhat less cynical in both 1976 and 1980 compared to their counterparts in these years.

Such a null finding brings into question whether there is any relationship between the respective declines in political partisanship and trust in government, as is often presumed. One simple way to establish whether there is such a relationship is to correlate the cynicism scale with strength of party identification. Only in 1968 is there a relationship worth noting. The Pearson correlation between the two variables varies from a high of .11 in 1968 to a low of –.02 in 1972, averaging about .04. Therefore, it may be plausible to infer that the initial declines in both party identification and trust in government between 1965 and 1968 were slightly intertwined, but there has been no consistent relationship between the two variables.

Yet cross-sectional data can hide systematic changes over time. As Nie et al. emphasize, panel data are necessary to establish or reject a causal link. Fortunately one panel is now available in which there are substantial declines in both party identification and trust in government —the 1965-1973 Jennings-Niemi socialization panel. This data set is particularly interesting because it contains a large sample of new entrants into the electorate who have contributed so much to the growth of political independents.[12]

If it is true that the decline in party identification is due to the growth of cynicism, then it would be expected that those in the panel who became more distrustful between 1965 and 1973 would also be the respondents who showed the greatest decline in partisanship. But, as Table 5.2 demonstrates, this was not the case. For example, data on the younger generation (first interviewed as high school seniors in 1965) shows that there was a substantial decline in strength of party identification in every cell of the table with very little variation depending on whether the cell represents those whose cynicism score increased, stayed the same, or decreased. Even the youth who were *least* cynical in both years showed a sizable decline of 24.4 points on the strength of party identification measure. In comparison, those who shifted from trusting to cynical during the eight-year interval showed only an 18.5-point drop. For their parents, the decline in strength of party identification is much less, but there is a similar lack of any consistent pattern of changes by cynicism scores. Indeed, some of the cells show changes which are the reverse of what would be expected.

Thus there is no evidence in this panel to suggest that the rise in cynicism towards the government has been responsible for the decline of

Table 5.2   Change in Strength of Party Identification by Change in Cynicism
Toward the Government, 1965–1973

	1973 Cynicism		
1965 Cynicism	Trusting	In-between	Cynical
Youth			
Trusting	− 24.4	− 36.3	− 18.3
N	(206)	(307)	(281)
In-between	− 16.3	− 29.4	− 22.1
N	(49)	(108)	(160)
Cynical	*	− 24.8	− 30.2
N	(8)	(28)	(63)
Parents			
Trusting	− 9.9	+ 4.3	− 13.9
N	(153)	(206)	(137)
In-between	+ 2.1	− 12.2	0.0
N	(51)	(132)	(157)
Cynical	*	− 6.1	− 17.7
N	(16)	(84)	(154)

*Insufficient data.

Note: Table entries represent change in strength of party identification from 1965 to 1973. Strength of party identification is calculated by scoring the percentage of Strong Democrats and Strong Republicans as + 2, Weak Democrats and Weak Republicans as + 1, Independent Democrats and Republicans as 0, and Pure Independents and Apoliticals as − 1.

Source: Panel Study of Generations and Politics conducted by M. Kent Jennings and Richard G. Niemi.

partisanship. It must therefore be concluded that the growth of cynicism and political independence are roughly parallel trends but which have little relationship to each other in both a static and dynamic sense.

In summary, what has been found thus far suggests that a reexamination of citizens' attitudes towards the parties is in order. The alienation hypothesis depends largely on two assumptions for which little support has been found here: that voters no longer see important differences in what the parties stand for and that the decline in strength of party identification has been an outgrowth of the decay of public trust in the government.

It is true that there has been a decline in the percentage of the electorate which believes that one party would do a better job in handling whatever they perceive to be the most important problem facing the government. However, the fact that such feelings are not related to political distrust indicates that this trend may not necessarily reflect negative attitudes towards the parties. An equally plausible alternative explanation is that citizens simply see the parties as less relevant than in the past and hence their feelings towards them are more neutral than negative. With the growth of the mass media and candidate-centered campaigns, the importance of parties in the presidential selection process and government in general has been weakened. The ideological differences between the parties may remain, but on the crucial short-run policy issues of the day it is the candidates which now matter most. Because of these changes, there is reason to expect that the electorate should be less positive about the two parties than in the past but that the shift in attitudes will be toward neutrality rather than negativity. Just such a possibility will be examined next.

AN EVALUATIVE PERSPECTIVE ON PARTY DECLINE

One major weakness in the literature on party decline is that the research has been nearly wholly concerned with the affective (party identification) and behavior (voting by party line) aspects of the electorate's relationship to political parties. This is not to demean the importance of the rise of Independents and split-ticket voting. Clearly such trends may forebode significant systemic consequences, most notably the rise in political volatility and instability in the U.S. The problem is that without proper evidence such trends have been grafted onto the description of the evaluative dimension of parties as well. That more people choose to call themselves Independents may not mean that they are "rejecting" parties, or, as James Sundquist puts it,[13] "calling down a plague on both their houses." Being an Independent may mean to most voters just what it says—being independent of parties. Choosing to split one's ticket also does not necessarily imply a long-term rejection of parties. As Miller and Levitan have argued (1976), much of the increase in ticket splitting simply reflects the fact that specific presidential candidates have been nominated whom many party members could not support. Thus it may well be a better indicator of the ability of each party to select its nominee than of voters' evaluation of the parties.

What is sorely lacking is an analysis of just how positive, neutral or negative Americans are towards the parties and what they like or dislike about them. Such an evaluative approach is presented here. In every presidential election year since 1952, the SRC/CPS election studies have asked respondents in the pre-election wave what they liked and disliked about the two political parties. Up to five responses have been coded in each year for each of the four questions. By simply subtracting the number of negative comments from the number of positive ones, we can classify respondents as either positive, neutral or negative toward each of the parties, depending on whether the number of likes exceed, equal or are fewer than the number of dislikes.

After collapsing the data into negative, neutral and positive ratings on each of the two parties, I created a sixfold classification representing respondents' ratings of both parties combined. The six categories are as follows: (1) *negative-negative*: those who have negative attitudes towards both parties; (2) *negative-neutral*: those who report negative ratings of one party, a neutral evaluation of the other; (3) *neutral-neutral*: those who are neutral with respect to both parties; (4) *positive-negative*: those who report a positive evaluation of one party, a negative evaluation of the other; (5) *positive-neutral*: those who are positive towards one party and neutral towards the other; and (6) *positive-positive*: those who rate both parties positively. It should be noted that in all of these categories it is irrelevant which party the respondent feels warm, neutral or cold to. For example, some of the *positive-negative* respondents rate the Democrats positively and the Republicans negatively and some vice versa, but what is important here is that these respondents see the parties in a polarized warm-cool fashion, not which party they are positive towards.

The percentage of respondents falling into each of the six categories of attitudes towards the two major parties on the basis of these open-ended likes/dislikes questions from 1952 to 1980 is shown in Table 5.3. If it is true that citizens are alienated from the parties and have come to perceive them in far more negative terms than in the past, then one would expect to find a large increase in the proportion of *negative-negatives* and *negative-neutrals* in the post-1964 period. Certainly this is the case in 1968, the first measurement point available after party identification began to decline. From 1964 to 1968 there is a 5.6 percent increase in those negative towards both parties and a 2.6 percent rise in the *negative-neutral* category. Given that partisanship continued to erode after 1968, it might be hypothesized that the percentage of the electorate with negative attitudes towards the parties would also continue to rise. However, Table 5.3 clearly shows just the reverse. Since 1968 both the *negative-negatives* and *negative-neutrals* have declined. Thus, the 1968 election stands out as an aberrant year with respect to negative attitudes about the parties rather than the beginning of a trend.

What does change dramatically after 1968 involves the large increase of the *neutral-neutrals* and the decline of polarized partisans, i.e., the *positive-negatives*. In 1968 the proportion of polarized partisans was over

115

twice that of the *neutral-neutrals;* in both 1972 and 1976 the proportion of *neutral-neutrals* is roughly equal, and in 1980 over 9 percent higher. But what is most fascinating about Table 5.3 is that the increase of those having neutral attitudes towards both parties is a trend which is evident throughout the entire 28-year period—in what Converse (1976) has termed the "steady state" period as well as in the period of weakening ties to the parties. From 1952 to 1964, while strength of party identification showed little change, the proportion of *neutral-neutrals* increased with each election, from 13.0 percent in 1952 to 20.2 percent in 1964. Only in 1968 is the linearity of the trend broken due to the largely short-term increase in negative attitudes towards the parties in that year.

It is also evident from Table 5.3 that the decline of polarized partisans began well before strength of party identification started to drop off. This is especially apparent between 1952 and 1956 when the proportion of *positive-negatives* fell by over 10 percent. One would intuitively have to hypothesize that the issues of the New Deal, on which the party system is generally considered to have been aligned upon, were sharply declining in salience from 1952 to 1956. Through 1960 many of these polarized partisans apparently moved to the less polarized categories of *positive-neutral* and *positive-positive*, both of which reach their high points during the years of the Eisenhower presidency. But after 1960 these groups decline in numbers as well as the *positive-negatives*. Overall, from 1952 to 1980 the percentage of *positive-negatives* falls from 50.1 to 27.3 percent. Except for the slight increase during the Eisenhower years, the percentage of respondents positive towards both parties remains fairly stable at about 5 percent.

Given the evidence from Table 5.3, the reader may wonder how Nie, Verba and Petrocik concluded that citizens had come to look upon parties in more negative terms—especially because they also analyzed responses to the party likes/dislikes questions.[14] The answer simply is that Nie et al. combined the categories of *negative-negative, negative-neutral* and *neutral-neutral* into a single group which they label variously throughout the book as "negative evaluations of both parties," "alienated from the parties," or "nonsupporters of the parties." Only the third phrase is an accurate description of what they are measuring. To infer that neutral evaluations of the parties represents alienation is to make an extremely tenuous assumption.

The question which this finding poses is of course what have been the forces causing members of the electorate to be more neutral towards the two parties. Data from the likes/dislikes probes are particularly useful for investigating this question because respondents are free to express exactly what their likes and dislikes concerning the parties actually are. It

Table 5.3 Trends in the Public's Evaluations of the Two Major U.S. Parties, 1952–1980 (Percent)

	Negative-negative	Negative-neutral	Neutral-neutral	Positive-negative	Positive-neutral	Positive-positive	N
1952	3.6	9.7	13.0	50.1	18.1	5.5	1799
1956	2.9	9.0	15.9	40.0	23.3	8.9	1762
1960	1.9	7.5	16.8	41.4	24.2	8.3	1164
1964	4.4	11.2	20.2	38.4	20.6	5.0	1571
1968	10.0	13.8	17.3	37.5	17.4	4.1	1557
1972	7.9	12.6	29.9	30.3	14.7	4.7	1372
1976	7.5	11.8	31.3	31.1	13.7	4.5	2248
1980	5.0	8.6	36.5	27.3	17.7	4.8	1614

Source: National election studies conducted by the University of Michigan's Survey Research Center/Center for Political Studies.

is these substantive comments which we will examine next in order to find a fuller explanation for the trends which have been discovered thus far.

A DIMENSIONAL ANALYSIS OF THE LIKES/DISLIKES DATA COMPARING PARTY AND CANDIDATE RESPONSES

As suggested earlier, one possible explanation for why parties have declined in importance is that for various reasons candidates no longer need the parties in order to win elections. As Lester Seligman has written,[15] "Deprived of presidential support, political parties are losing their meaning to the voters. Increasingly, Presidents are no longer making political parties and parties are no longer making Presidents." Also, previous voting research[16] has shown that the effect of candidate images on the vote has increased over the years, while the effect of party images has declined.

The question which therefore needs to be examined concerns the type of open-ended responses on which candidates have assumed greater saliency, i.e., importance, than parties. Just such a pattern might be expected on specific issues. It will be recalled that when respondents are asked which major party would do best in solving whatever they consider to be the most important problem of the day, an increasing proportion have been responding that there would be no difference. This trend cannot be explained by an increase in the perception that there are no longer important differences between the parties, for there has not been any such increase. Nor can it be attributed to the decline in trust in government. Thus it might be hypothesized that more citizens are now exclusively conceptualizing issues in terms of candidates only and less in terms of party alone. In other words, the stands which candidates take on the issues may no longer be linked to voters' perceptions of the parties. The parties may still stand for certain broad principles and groups, but when it comes to specific policies, candidates now stand above parties rather than with them.

To test this hypothesis, we can compare the frequency of responses to the candidates likes/dislikes questions to the frequency of likes and dislikes expressed about the parties on four substantive dimensions or response categories: domestic issues, foreign issues, benefits provided to groups, and general political philosophy. If such a hypothesis is correct, then one would expect an increase over time in the proportion of the population commenting about issues with respect to the candidates but not with respect to the parties. Such a pattern would indicate that issues are irrelevant to the citizen in evaluating parties but relevant with regard to the candidates.

Table 5.4 provides evidence which shows that such a pattern has become much more prevalent over the years, especially on domestic and foreign policy. For example, domestic issues were overwhelmingly associated with the parties in 1952, with only 2.7 percent making such comments with reference only to candidates compared to 53.5 percent for only parties. But by 1964 the balance had shifted dramatically to the point where more respondents were mentioning domestic issues only in terms of candidates than parties only, and in 1980 the ratio is over two to one in favor of the candidate-only response pattern. References to parties and candidates on foreign policy were roughly balanced in 1952, but the same trend is nevertheless apparent. By 1964 the percentage in the candidate-only category was twice that of the party-only group, and in 1980 41.6 percent of the sample mentioned foreign policy in reference to a candidate but not with respect to either party, while only 3.5 percent displayed the reverse pattern. Finally, while there is a slight decrease in the party-only response pattern for the dimensions of group benefits and general philosophy of government, these attitudes still remain predominantly the domain of the parties, and thus probably account for the lack of any drop in the percentage of the population perceiving major differences between the parties.

Thus it seems that leadership is one crucial variable in determining why the electorate has become more neutral towards the political parties. As candidates have come to assume a much larger share of the spotlight on domestic and foreign policy the parties have seen much of their base of support erode. Apparently the likes and dislikes which citizens perceive for leaders on the issues are not being translated into similar attitudes towards the parties as well.

In an attempt to advance the argument that leadership is one of the key reasons behind the rise in neutrality, we can also examine responses concerning leaders on the *party* likes/dislikes questions. If the explanation for party decline is simply that candidates have become more salient, then one might expect that more people would be referring to leaders when asked about their likes and dislikes of the parties, even though other types of responses on the party likes/dislikes questions have decreased. But if the decline is also due to the fact that the link between parties and candidates has been weakened, then it is probable that fewer people would be mentioning leaders when probed for their opinions about the parties, despite the fact that candidates have become increasingly salient to the electorate.

In working with these responses, one must be careful to compare years in which the leadership situation was as similar as possible. Otherwise the results might simply be due to some exogenous factor such as whether the incumbent was running for reelection or not. The best set of comparisons which can be made are those between 1956 and 1972, when a popular incumbent was seeking reelection, and between 1964 and 1976, when recent mid-term successors to the presidential office sought a term of their own.

These two comparisons support the hypothesis that the party-candidate link has deteriorated. In 1956, 34.4 percent of the respondents mentioned a party figure as a reason for liking or disliking a party while only 19.0 percent did so in 1972. The comparable figures for 1964 and 1976 are 20.4 and 14.5 percent, respectively.[17] The first comparison is particularly interesting, for Eisenhower was a far less partisan figure than Nixon. However, one plausible explanation could be Eisenhower's great personal popularity in 1956. Yet it is not merely positive responses about party leaders which were more prevalent in 1956; dislikes were more frequently mentioned as well. In fact, more people, when asked what they disliked about the Democratic party, mentioned party leaders in 1956 than in 1972 even though Stevenson was a far more popular standard-bearer than McGovern. Regarding the incumbent party, 9.4 percent expressed some dislike of its leaders in 1956 compared to only 3.4 percent in 1972. Although most of the negative comments concerning the Republicans in 1956 were directed at Nixon rather than Eisenhower, it is somewhat unexpected that fewer people would give similar comments about him in 1972—when he was an incumbent president.

Table 5.4 A Comparison of the Frequency of Substantive Responses to the Party and Candidate Likes/Dislikes Questions, 1952–1980 (Percent)

	Mentioned for neither	Mentioned for party only	Mentioned for candidate only	Mentioned for both
Domestic issues				
1952	36.7	53.5	2.7	7.1
1956	49.9	31.8	7.8	10.4
1960	51.7	31.0	7.2	10.1
1964	46.8	15.9	20.5	16.7
1968	54.1	22.0	11.2	12.7
1972	49.6	14.2	21.6	14.7
1976	50.9	19.8	16.6	12.7
1980	46.6	11.0	27.7	14.7
Foreign issues				
1952	55.6	17.4	16.2	10.8
1956	59.9	12.1	16.8	11.2
1960	56.9	13.1	18.8	11.1
1964	64.3	9.0	19.5	7.2
1968	54.7	13.9	20.0	11.4
1972	46.1	6.6	39.1	8.2
1976	74.3	9.1	11.5	5.1
1980	46.0	3.5	41.6	8.8
Benefits provided to groups				
1952	54.0	33.2	4.7	8.1
1956	51.1	32.7	5.3	10.9
1960	56.8	28.3	4.3	10.6
1964	54.4	27.2	7.4	10.9
1968	58.5	25.4	5.5	10.6
1972	54.7	23.8	8.5	12.9
1976	55.0	24.3	9.1	11.6
1980	59.7	28.3	5.2	6.9
General political philosophy				
1952	65.1	20.9	8.8	5.2
1956	76.3	15.7	4.9	3.1
1960	68.1	15.9	9.5	6.5
1964	54.6	14.8	16.5	14.1
1968	54.2	19.3	13.7	12.7
1972	62.8	16.7	12.3	8.2
1976	63.6	17.8	10.9	7.7
1980	69.7	13.2	9.1	7.9

Source: National election studies conducted by the University of Michigan's Survey Research Center/Center for Political Studies.

In summary, at least a partial answer to the question, "Why the growing neutrality towards the parties?" seems to be that fewer people are translating their likes and dislikes about the candidates and the candidates' stands on specific issues into likes and dislikes about the parties. Future research should concentrate on further examining the linkage of candidates and their stands on the issues to voters' perceptions of the parties over time.

CONCLUSION

The results presented in this article offer more hope for the revitalization of American political parties than most previous work on the subject. However, one can also extrapolate reasons to be doubtful about such a prospect based on the interpretation of party decline which has been argued here.

Taking the positive side first, the most important new finding is that there has been little increase in the proportion of the population holding negative attitudes towards the parties. It is quite possible that the initial decline in strength of party identification may have been due to the large jump in negativity apparent in 1968. But since that time negative attitudes towards the parties have subsided. Positive attitudes have also continued to decline, but what has increased has been neutrality rather than negativity.

In addition to the fact that parties do not have to overcome largely negative attitudes towards them, it is also encouraging to note that their recovery probably does not hinge on a restoration of trust in government. Like other institutions, political parties are viewed more cynically than in the past. Specifically, more citizens now believe that parties are more interested in votes than in people's opinions. However, this sort of cynicism is apparently not being translated into negativity towards the parties. People may be more skeptical about the motives of parties, but that does not necessarily mean that they dislike parties in general or that they will not identify with a party in the future. This point is supported by the fact that hardly any relationship was found between strength of party identification and trust in government, except for the .11 correlation in 1968. And in a dynamic sense, panel data show that the two trends are quite independent of one another. Given that the decline of partisanship has been a reflection of growing neutrality instead of negativity on the part of the electorate, such null findings are quite explicable. If negative attitudes about parties were at the root of the rise of independence, then one would expect that other negative attitudes such as cynicism would be related to it, as indeed the case of 1968 appears to show. But, overall, the evidence demonstrates that the decline of parties in the electorate has been more a function of a reduction in salience than an increase in negative attitudes.

However, turning to the reason to be pessimistic about any revitalization of parties in the electorate, there seems to be little prospect for reversing the trend toward neutrality in the immediate future. One of the most important findings in this article is that the decline of parties in the electorate can be traced back much further than the mid-1960s in terms of party evaluations. The decline of polarized views of the parties and the increase in neutrality is visible throughout the election study time series. Thus it can undoubtedly be considered as a long-term secular trend, and such trends are usually difficult to reverse. In addition, these altered public attitudes have themselves become a major reason why it will be difficult to re-institutionalize political parties.

Furthermore, the appearance of a major realigning issue—which is so often considered to be the best hope for reviving the parties—may not have any strengthening effect on partisanship in the electorate. The reason for party decline has not been that people no longer see any important differences between the parties. Indeed, the trend towards neutrality would have been even sharper if the frequency of comments concerning the general philosophies and group benefits offered by the parties had not remained fairly stable. Rather, the problem which the parties must face is that they are considered less relevant in solving the most important domestic and foreign policy issues of the day. In the voters' minds, the parties are losing their association with the candidates and the issues which the candidates claim to stand for. Thus major new issues which arise will probably not help the parties rebuild their base of support unless voters are convinced that the parties can provide a meaningful function which candidates alone cannot.

NOTES

1. Jeff Fishel, ed., *Parties and Elections in an Anti-Party Age* (Bloomington, Ind.: Indiana U. Press, 1978).

2. Michael W. Wolfe, "Personal-Contact Campaigning in Presidential Elections: Who's Been Talking to All Those Voters and What Have They Accomplished?" Presented at the annual meeting of the Midwest Political Science Association, 1979.

3. Malcolm E. Jewell and David M. Olson, *American State Political Parties and Elections* (Homewood, Ill.: Dorsey Press, 1978).

4. Cornelius P. Cotter and John F. Bibby, "Institutional Development of Parties and the Thesis of Party Decline," *Political Science Quarterly* 95 (1980): 1–27.

5. Lawrence C. Dodd and Bruce I. Oppenheimer, eds., *Congress Reconsidered* (New York, Praeger, 1977).

6. Norman H. Nie, Sidney Verba, and John R. Petrocik, *The Changing American Voter* (Cambridge, Mass.: Harvard U. Press, 1976), pp. 57–58.

7. Kristi Andersen, "Generation, Partisan Shift, and Realignment: A Glance Back to the New Deal" in Norman H. Nie, Sidney Verba, and John R. Petrocik, *The Changing American Voter* (Cambridge, Mass.: Harvard U. Press, 1976), p. 95.

8. Nie et al., *The Changing American Voter*, p. 283.

9. The wording of this question has changed slightly over the years. Listed below are the different versions which have been asked:

1952: "Do you think there are any important differences between what the Democratic and Republican parties stand for, or do you think they are about the same?"

1960, 1964, 1972–1980: "Do you think there are any important differences in what the Democrats and Republicans stand for?"

1968: "Do you think there are any important differences between the Democratic and Republican parties?"

10. This question has also undergone slight changes in wording over the years. In 1960, 1964, and 1968 respondents were asked which party they thought would be the most likely to do what they wanted on whichever problem they mentioned. In 1972 this was changed to asking which party would be the most likely to get the government to be helpful on the problem, and in 1976–1980 the wording was again changed to which party would be the most likely to do a better job in dealing with the problem.

11. Merle Black and George Rabinowitz, "American Electoral Change: 1952–1972 (with a note on 1976)" in William Crotty, ed., *The Party Symbol: Readings on Political Parties* (San Francisco: W. H. Freeman, 1980), p. 241.

12. Paul Abramson, "Generational Change and the Decline of Party Identification in America 1952–1974," *American Political Science Review* 70 (1976): 469–78.

13. James L. Sundquist, *Dynamics of the Party System: Alignment and Realignment of Political Parties in the United States* (Washington, D.C.: The Brookings Institution, 1973), p. 343.

14. There are several technical differences which should be noted between the likes/dislikes which I have used and those Nie et al. use. First, Nie et al. use only the three responses in all years, while I employ all five. Second, they fail to filter out the 100 respondents in the 1952 and the 17 in 1960 who were not interviewed in the pre-election wave. As these respondents were not asked the likes/dislikes questions, they should be excluded from the analysis. Finally, Nie et al. include responses from the black supplements in 1964 and 1968. Subsequent analysis at CPS has shown that these supplements actually introduce a greater degree of bias into the sample. Hence, I have not used them.

15. Lester G. Seligman, "The Presidential Office and the President as Party Leader (with a Postscript on the Kennedy-Nixon Era)" in Jeff Fishel, ed., *Parties*

and Elections in an Anti-Party Age (Bloomington, Ind.: Indiana U. Press, 1978), p. 300.

16. Samuel Kirkpatrick, William Lyons, and Michael Fitzgerald, "Candidates, Parties and Issues in the American Electorate: Two Decades of Change" in Samuel Kirkpatrick, ed., *American Electoral Behavior: Change and Stability* (Beverly Hills, Calif.: Sage Publications, 1976; Arthur H. Miller and Warren E. Miller, "Rejoinder: Ideology in the 1972 Election," *American Political Science Review* 70 (1976): 832–49.

17. In 1980 the comparable figure reached a new low of 12.9 percent. Given that both Carter and Reagan were perceived negatively—i.e., more dislikes than likes were expressed about both—this may be considered as fortunate for the parties. However, as an continuation of a long-term weakening of the party-candidate link in the voters' minds, this development implies that even should popular candidates emerge, their popularity is not likely to have much of a positive impact on attitudes towards the parties.

REFERENCES

Abramson, Paul (1976). "Generational Change and the Decline of Party Identification in America: 1952–1974." *American Political Science Review* 70: 469–78.

Andersen, Kristi (1976). "Generation, Partisan Shift, and Realignment: A Glance Back to the New Deal." In Norman Nie et al., *The Changing American Voter*. Cambridge, Mass.: Harvard U. Press.

Black, Merle, and George Rabinowitz (1980). "American Electoral Change: 1952–1972 (with a note on 1976)." In William Crotty (ed.), *The Party Symbol: Readings on Political Parties*. San Francisco: W. H. Freeman.

Converse, Philip E. (1976). *The Dynamics of Party Support: Cohort-Analyzing Party Identification*. Beverly Hills, Calif.: Sage Publications.

Cotter, Cornelius P., and John F. Bibby (1980). "Institutional Development of Parties and the Thesis of Party Decline." *Political Science Quarterly* 95: 1–27.

Dodd, Lawrence C., and Bruce I. Oppenheimer (eds.) (1977). *Congress Reconsidered*. New York: Praeger.

Fishel, Jeff, ed. (1978). *Parties and Elections in an Anti-Party Age*. Bloomington: Indiana U. Press.

Jewell, Malcolm E., and David M. Olson (1978). *American State Political Parties and Elections*. Homewood, Ill.: Dorsey Press.

Kirkpatrick, Samuel, William Lyons, and Michael Fitzgerald (1976). "Candidates, Parties and Issues in the American Electorate: Two Decades of Change." In Samuel Kirkpatrick (ed.), *American Electoral Behavior: Change and Stability*. Beverly Hills, Calif.: Sage Publications.

Miller, Arthur H., and Warren E. Miller (1976). "Rejoinder: Ideology in the 1972 Election." *American Political Science Review* 70: 832–49.

Nie, Norman H., Sidney Verba, and John R. Petrocik (1976). *The Changing American Voter*. Cambridge, Mass.: Harvard U. Press.

Seligman, Lester G. (1978). "The Presidential Office and the President as Party Leader (with a Postscript on the Kennedy-Nixon Era)." In Jeff Fishel (ed.), *Parties and Elections in an Anti-Party Age*. Bloomington: Indiana U. Press.

Sundquist, James L. (1973). *Dynamics of the Party System: Alignment and Realignment of Political Parties in the United States*. Washington, D.C.: The Brookings Institution.

Weisberg, Herbert F. (1980). "A Multidimensional Conceptualization of Party Identification." *Political Behavior* 2: 33–60.

Wolfe, Michael W. (1979). "Personal-Contact Campaigning in Presidential Elections: Who's Been Talking to All Those Voters and What Have They Accomplished?" Presented at the annual meeting of the Midwest Political Science Association.

REALIGNMENT: NEW PARTY COALITIONS AND THE NATIONALIZATION OF THE SOUTH

John R. Petrocik

Kevin Phillips' *Emerging Republican Majority* (1969) was an early entry in a soon-to-burgeon literature on realignment.[1] While Phillips' prophesy was widely discussed, it failed to persuade many scholars because it required Democrats or the offspring of Democrats to become Republicans, and two decades of surveys had found the disavowal of party attachments as uncommon, so the analogy went, as religious conversion. The conventional wisdom foretold a future of modest changes from a present which had barely changed in a quarter of a century. Social mobility might turn some children of working-class Democrats into Republicans, but the weak link between social and political differences would ensure that most socially mobile voters retained the partisanship of their families. Migration to the South would increase its Republican contingent; again, however, most native southerners were expected to retain their Democratic proclivities.

Neither Phillips nor his critics have fared well. The conventional orthodoxy which dismissed Phillips' prediction has been reformulated. While there is no consensus on the magnitude of the changes that have taken place (and even some belief in their exaggeration), there is at least general agreement that the electorate of the 1980s is different from that of the 1950s. Voters seem less partisan, and elections lack the predictability that was made possible by the partisanship of earlier decades. Presidential elections have oscillated between narrow margins and lopsided victories. Defection at least seems higher, and incumbents are immune to all but the most massive short-term surges. In a few words, the party system doesn't show the stable and robust popular foundation invoked by Phillips' critics to reject his prediction of an emerging Republican majority. At the same time, Phillips' prediction is still only a GOP hope.

Figure 6.1   Distribution of party identification.

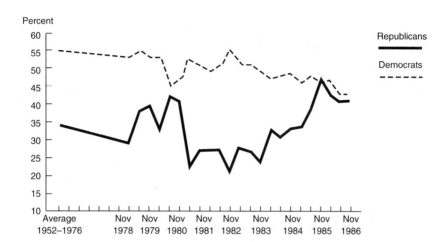

Note: This figure uses data from the National Election Studies and the national surveys of Market Opinion Research. The data are not completely comparable, nor does either series always agree with other national studies (see Table 6.1, for example). The November time points for even years are from the NES data, all others are from MOR.

A DECLINE IN DEMOCRATIC IDENTIFICATION?

However, history has been kinder to Phillips than were his original critics. Although the Republicans have not become the majority party, there has been both a substantial decline in the familiar 20-percentage-point Democratic plurality and a reshaping of the popular foundations of the parties.

Prior to 1980 there was no discernible trend in the balance of Republican and Democratic identifiers. The Democratic lead shrank slightly under the pressures that produced strong Republican presidential victories such as Eisenhower's in 1956, only to grow when the Democrats enjoyed a strong balance of popular support for their candidate (e.g., 1964). Changes were occurring, but they produced no net shift in the partisan balance. The dealignment that reduced the percentage of Democrats and Republicans left the competitive balance between the parties almost unchanged. Since 1980, however, there appears to have been a substantial movement toward the Republicans. Some data (Table 6.1) show a 20-

Table 6.1 Changing Partisanship of the American Electorate

Survey organization	1979/1980			1985/1986			Change in party bias
	Dem.	Rep.	Party bias	Dem.	Rep.	Party bias	
Harris	44	23	+21	41	31	+10	−11
CBS/*New York Times*	42	26	+16	35	30	+ 5	−11
ABC/*Washington Post*	45	22	+23	35	30	+ 5	−18
Time magazine	51	28	+23	48	33	+15	− 8
NBC	35	29	+ 6	35	33	+ 2	− 4
Roper	50	22	+28	48	26	+22	− 6
Gallup	46	22	+24	36	34	+ 2	−22
Center for Political Studies	41	22	+19	36	27	+ 9	−10
Market Opinion Research	43	22	+21	31	29	+ 2	−19
Average	44	24	+20	38	30	+ 8	−12

Source: Market Opinion Research data provided by MOR; Center for Political Studies data were calculated by the author; all other data were adapted from *Public Opinion* (1985). In this table Democrats and Republicans are only those who are categorized as strong or weak identifiers. In all other tables leaning, weak, and strong identifiers are considered partisans. The treatment of leaning identifiers in this table was required by the published data, which defined leaning partisans as independents.

point drop (Gallup), while others (Roper) show very little change (only 6 points), but the median estimate of the Democratic decline is about 12 percentage points, and six of the nine series in Table 6.1 show a change of at least 10 points in the party bias of the electorate. The 20-point Democratic advantage in late 1979 and early 1980 withered to an average of 8 percentage points in late 1985 and early 1986.[2]

The decline was irregular. Surveys conducted during 1981 found a similar Republican tilt, which was quickly reversed by the recession of 1982 (Figure 6.1). Hopeful Republicans insist that the post-1984 levels are permanent, but many interpret the changes as a "performance realignment" that will not persist beyond Reagan or a significant downturn in the economy (Sussman, 1985). Other equivocate, but even some Democrats (pollster Peter Hart, for example) believe that at least some of the pro-Republican movement is rooted in policy preferences that are not likely to be undone by short-lived economic dislocations.[3]

Table 6.2 Party Bias of Age Cohorts, 1952–1984

Respondent became eligible to vote	1950s	1960s	1970s	1980	1982	1984a	1984b
Prior to 1948	– 18	– 22	– 18	– 25	– 27	– 11	– 8
Between 1949–1959	– 25	– 29	– 13	– 10	– 18	– 19	– 21
In 1960	– 27	– 24	– 15	– 11	– 23	– 8	– 6
Between 1961–1976		– 21	– 16	– 18	– 26	– 3	– 1
Between 1977–1980				– 25	– 14	– 4	– 6
After 1980					– 22	– 9	– 1
Average	– 19	– 23	– 20	– 20	– 23	– 8	– 6

Note: Table entries are percentage differences. Negative values indicate a plurality of Democrats; positive values indicate a plurality of Republicans. Leaning partisans are considered identifiers of the party toward which they lean. The studies for 1952, 1956, 1958, and 1960 are grouped as the 1950s; the studies for the years from 1962 through 1970 are considered the 1960s; the studies for 1972 through 1978 are considered the 1970s. The 1984a column uses party identification measures collected in the pre-election survey, while 1984b refers to post-election data.

All data are from the National Election Studies of the Center for Political Studies, unless otherwise indicated.

CONVERSION AND PERSAUSION

Whatever the future of this partisan shift, there is no evidence in Table 6.2 that the current GOP success has depended upon volatile younger voters (but see Helmut Norpoth, 1985, for data which contradict this finding). While those who came of age prior to 1960 changed less than the post-1960 cohort, the erosion of Democratic partisanship occurred among all ages.[4] Conversion has contributed more than the biased mobilization of younger cohorts to the recent surge in Republican identification. This result may not be permanent: As the strong pro-Republican sentiment of the moment recedes, older Democrats could return to their partisan habits while younger voters, whose political tendencies are less well-rooted, remain Republican (the rationale for this is developed in McPhee and Ferguson, 1962; Beck, 1974). At present, however, all age groups have contributed to the declining Democratic plurality.

Yet, while the Democratic decline is not specific to certain age cohorts, it is not unstructured or undifferentiated. It is unequally distributed among ethnic groups and regions, and the older cohorts who appear to have changed their party identification are largely from certain segments of the electorate. This paper presents an analysis of these partisan changes in terms of the social groups which constitute the party coalitions. The first part presents the rationale for examining the social foundations of the American parties, while the second part uses this social-group model of the parties to describe their realignment. The third part of the paper considers recent elections (especially 1984) in terms of the still-underway realignment.[5]

CONCEPTIONS OF REALIGNMENT

James Sundquist's *Dynamics of the Party System* (1983) documents dissent and inattention to even conventional understandings of realignment. While the diversity has contributed to a fuller appreciation of the complexity of party systems and their processes of transformation, it has not been costless. The focus on the complexity of historical realignments has yielded concepts which aid analyses of prior realignments at the expense of sensitivity to contemporary changes. Earlier party transformations have become benchmarks for diagnosing current changes, to the loss of our ability to analyze the latter. These event-based definitions have also limited our sensitivity to the variability of the links among various aspects of party system change. In consequence we have generally come to regard realignments as clusters of causes, symptoms, and consequences, rather than phenomena with diverse causes, several symptoms, and many consequences—some of which may not occur because of the limitations inherent in the prevailing social and political context.

If we are to avoid judging present realignments for their similarity with past realignments, a more limited conception of the phenomena is needed. Several alternatives are possible, but one which is theoretically and empirically satisfying conceives of realignments as transformations of the social group profile of party supporters. The theoretical rationale for this definition arises from the social cleavage theory of parties and party systems; its practical merit is its correspondence with the way in which parties conceive of their electoral base.

SOCIAL DIVISIONS AND POLITICAL PARTIES

Religious, economic, ethnic, linguistic, and regional differences provide the social "fault lines" which have been the most common source of so-

cial conflict. Parties have been the organized expression of these conflicts, and it contradicts none of the conventional ways of thinking about
parties to view them as the traditional (although not the only) instruments of collective action with which groups promote and protect interests that are unmet by the social structure and markets. While the
number, salience and centrality, and political significance of the cleavages vary among societies (in the U.S. and Great Britain social differences and political preference are weakly aligned; in Holland and
Austria the link is strong), the existence of group differences, their politi-
cization through ideological and policy disputes are virtual constants
(LaPalombara and Weiner, 1966; Dahl, 1966; Lipset and Rokkan, 1967;
Rose and Unwin, 1969).[6] While programmatic differences among parties
do not always reflect social group differences and conflicts, one is hard
pressed to find instances where issue conflict is independent of social
cleavages. Issue and ideology may be the language of party conflict, but
group needs and conflicts are its source in modern party systems.

The importance of this conception of parties as, to quote Lipset and
Rokkan (1967), "coalitions in conflict over policies and value commitments within the. . . body politic" is that it leads directly to a conception
of realignments as reformulations of the "coalitions in conflict." The re-
formulation might be a product of massive changes in a group's party affiliation; it may reflect the development of a partisan cleavage within a
new group in the society (immigrants, for example); it might also come
about as a highly aligned group loses its partisan distinctiveness (a major
component of coalition changes in the U.S. through the middle 1970s).
The outcome in any of these cases—and many unmentioned possibilities
—is a realignment of the parties and the electorate.[7]

THE POLITICIAN'S MODEL OF THE ELECTORATE

Practical politicians deal with groups of voters through the issues which
they believe to be of concern to members of the group. When Democratic
or Republican office-seekers "talk about the issues" and otherwise
present a policy agenda to the electorate, they are soliciting support in
several ways. But the central purpose of "dealing with the issues" is to
rally groups which normally support the party's candidates. The candidates present themselves as faithful proponents of the interests of the
groups which constitute the party coalitions. The "generic Democrat"
talks about the social safety net, affirmative action, the need to maintain
momentum against racial injustice, and the essential commitment to
provide jobs and a decent standard of living to all Americans; the Repub-

lican opponent urges reductions in government waste, lower taxes, economic growth, strong opposition to a "predatory" Soviet Union, and a renewal of traditional values and institutions.

Through time and across elections, what the party stands for and the issues its candidates address reflect the preferences of the groups which constitute the core support of the party. Leaders innovate; issues beyond the concerns of their core constituency are placed by them on the party agenda. But over the long run, the programmatic face of the party arises from its constituency, and parties develop reputations for differential issue competence as a result of this constituency-based issue specialization (Budge and Farlie, 1983).

THE REALIGNMENT OF THE COALITIONS

Table 6.3, which presents the partisanship of each group from the 1950s through 1984, shows major changes in the party identification of the groups which have defined the New Deal party coalitions (for the historical origins of these coalition groups as well as their empirical identification, see Petrocik, 1981). The GOP surge documented in Table 6.1 reflects an abrupt lurch in a 20-year-long shift of the partisanship of the New Deal party coalition groups. Table 6.4, which traces the social group profile of the Democratic and Republican parties for the past three decades, shows the results of this creeping transformation of the partisanship of the groups. By the end of the 1970s, the Democratic and Republican coalitions had developed social bases that were unlike those of the 1950s.[8] Changes continued into the eighties. By 1984 northern, white Protestants had declined to about 40% of all Republican identifiers; white southerners, Catholics, and labor households—the mainstays of the New Deal Democracy—represented almost half of all Republicans.

Changes in the Democratic coalition have been even larger. Catholics and white union members—the core of the northern faction of the New Deal Democrats—represented a third of the party in the 1950s, southern whites represented another third, northern white Protestants contributed a fifth of the Democratic base, and Jews and blacks added another 15% or so. By 1984, southern whites constituted barely a fifth of Democratic identifiers while the black contribution doubled.

A summary estimate of these changes is not easily calculated simply because there is no obvious denominator against which the coalitional shift can be compared. A reasonable one (given the emphasis on dealignment) might be changes which leave the party coalitions identical; that is, a realignment which leaves the social base of the Democrats virtually identical to that of the Republicans. Against such a standard, the 15- and 20-

Table 6.3 Changing Party Bias of Major Segments of the Party Coalitions, 1952–1984

	1950s	1960s	1972	1974	1976	1978	1980	1982	1984
White Northern Protestants									
Upper SES	59	39	42	35	39	24	34	31	41
Middle SES	36	18	28	31	21	22	25	5	35
Lower SES	9	-9	-4	6	8	-10	-6	-14	14
White Southerners									
Border states									
Middle-upper SES	-40	-10	-21	-18	11	-24	6	29	-16
Lower SES	-29	-37	-11	0	-16	-25	-24	-54	-27
Deep South									
Middle-upper SES	-71	-30	-26	-51	-22	-11	-21	-31	9
Lower SES	-58	-50	-41	-34	-48	-62	-49	-51	-2
Catholics									
Upper SES	-22	-18	-22	-34	-15	-17	-1	-20	5
All others	-34	-45	-44	-36	-39	-54	-36	-61	-21
Jews	-62	-74	-62	-56	-38	-65	-75	-47	-52
Blacks	-37	-70	-65	-79	-77	-72	-73	-93	-67
Northern union households	-31	-37	-26	-27	-30	-35	-21	-39	-13
Average	-17	-23	-18	-21	-18	-23	-20	-27	-8

Note: Table entries are percentage differences. Negative values indicate a plurality of Democrats; positive values indicate a plurality of Republicans. Leaning partisans are considered identifiers of the party toward which they lean.

Table 6.4 Changing Party Coalitions, 1950s through 1984

	1950s	1960s	1970s	1980	1981	1982	1983	1984	1985
Democrats									
White Northern Protestants	18%	20%	17%	16%	20%	16%	20%	17%	19%
Catholics	14	16	17	14	15	16	14	14	15
Northern union households	22	16	19	23	18	16	11	16	17
White Southerners	31	26	23	17	18	25	24	22	21
Jews	4	4	3	5	4	2	3	3	5
Blacks	9	13	16	18	18	17	18	17	19
Hispanics	1	2	2	3	2	4	6	7	4
All others	2	2	3	4	2	5	5	5	2
Total	100%	100%	100%	100%	100%	100%	100%	100%	102%
Republicans									
White Northern Protestants	51%	50%	43%	37%	38%	40%	38%	38%	31%
Catholics	10	12	12	14	18	12	13	14	20
Northern union households	16	11	14	16	18	12	11	12	15
White Southerners	15	21	23	22	22	28	26	25	26
Jews	1	1	1	1	1	1	2	1	1
Blacks	5	2	2	3	3	1	3	2	3
Hispanics	0	—	1	2	—	1	2	4	2
All others	2	3	3	5	1	5	5	5	2
Total	100%	100%	100%	100%	100%	100%	100%	100%	100%

Source: The 1981, 1983, and 1985 data were supplied by Market Opinion Research. All other years use NES data. Leaning partisans are considered identifiers of the party toward which they lean. Totals may not equal 100% because of rounding.

Table 6.5   Group Contribution to Democratic Plurality, 1950–1984

	1952–1960	1962–1970	1972–1978	1980	1984
Southern whites	+ 12	+ 8	+ 5	+ 5	+ 1
Jews	+ 1	+ 2	+ 1	+ 3	+ 1
Blacks	+ 3	+ 6	+ 7	+ 9	+ 7
All others	+ 1	+ 7	+ 7	+ 3	− 1
Total Democratic plurality	+ 17	+ 23	+ 20	+ 20	+ 8

Note: Table numbers are the net contribution of each group to the Democratic plurality as it appears at the bottom of each column. Leaning partisans are considered identifiers of the party toward which they lean.

percentage-point shift in the Democratic and Republican coalitions, respectively, constitute over 50% of the change that is possible.[9]

SOUTHERN WHITES AND THE SHIFTING PARTY BALANCE

The coalition changes in Table 6.4 have been underway for at least two decades. They are not specific to the 1984 election, and they are not just a reflection of the shifting identification of southern whites.[10] However, the contribution of the South to these changes has been disproportionate; the realignment would have been dramatically smaller without the decline of the southern Democracy. In addition, the programmatic distinctiveness of the region, its historical importance for the Democrats, its pivotal role in recent elections, and the increasing influence of southern whites within the Republican party argue for a fuller documentation of their shift toward the Republican party and a better understanding of their impact on the parties.

THE SOUTHERN IMPACT

By the middle of the 1970s, southern whites were only marginally different from the total electorate. Not only had the Democratic bias of southern whites declined, but the structure of party preference had taken on a national character, with, for example, the class cleavage reversing itself and assuming the northern pattern of greater Republican support among the better-off.[11] Their drift from the Democrats was neither reversed nor slowed by Carter's candidacy. A majority of white southerners voted for Ford, and their party identification continued to move toward the Republicans (see Table 6.3).

Southern realignment is the major component of the changes in the Democratic-Republican balance. As Table 6.5 shows, the white South was critical to Democratic dominance in the 1950s, providing over 70% of the Democratic plurality. If white southerners had been as Democratic as the average white voter of the period, the Democrats would have enjoyed a more modest four-point to six-point lead (about 48 or 49 to 43 percent). The decline of the Southern Democracy was apparent in the 1960s, if not before. Had it not been for the growth of Democratic strength among blacks and white northerners in the sixties (partly attributable to Goldwater's candidacy in 1964), a decline in Democratic identification would have been visible 20 years ago. The persistence of the 20-point Democratic plurality for the next two decades depended upon blacks and the erosion of Republican identification among northern whites, especially middle and upscale WASPs. When northern whites resumed their slightly Republican tilt in 1980, and southern whites became equally divided between the parties in 1984, the Democratic lead dropped to only about 8 points (see Table 6.5), and virtually all of it came from blacks.

Further changes between late 1984 and early 1985, when a GOP plurality was reported by some polls, were not an exclusively southern white phenomenon. The widely reported post-election surge in Republican fortunes depended upon enthusiasm for the GOP among northern whites. However, even these post-1984 changes were insufficient to alter the preeminent place of the South in the transformation of the party coalitions.

THE SOURCES OF THE SOUTHERN REALIGNMENT

Contrary to earlier speculation and even some recent essays on the subject, migration did not cause the decline of the Southern Democracy. Native southern whites are and, even in the 1960s and 1970s, were the major component of the region's realignment. Further, while the relative importance of conversion and mobilization in the formation and realignment of party systems is an unsettled question (see Campbell et al., 1960; Przeworski, 1975; Andersen, 1979; Wanat, 1979; Niemi et al., 1980; Erikson and Tedin, 1981; Petrocik, 1981; Wanat and Burke, 1982; Campbell, 1983; and Petrocik and Brown, 1986), the switching of loyalties among older southerners has figured prominently in the realignment of the region.

THE INSIGNIFICANCE OF MIGRATION

Early studies expected the Democratic bias of the South to change as a result of the migration of much less Democratic northern whites. In fact little of the change has depended upon migration. Virtually all of it rests on the increasing Republicanism of native white southerners.[12]

The data in Table 6.6 present the partisanship of three different groups of southern whites—migrants to the region, native residents of the border southern states, and native residents of the ten states of the Deep South for the 1950s, the 1960s, the 1970s, 1980, and 1984. On average, for the decade of the 1950s, migration had reduced the Democratic identification of white southerners about three percentage points, from the 74% Democratic among natives to 71% among all whites in the region. After that point, the effect of migration on the partisanship of the region becomes even smaller. The second half of Table 6.6 summarizes the data in the first part of the table by decomposing the total change in the partisanship of the region into the contribution of natives and migrants. For every pair of decades, the migrants add one percentage point or less to the total shift. Between the 1950s and the 1960s Democratic identification declined 11 points and Republican affiliation increased 7 points; migrants (who changed 2 points) contributed almost nothing to the net Democratic decline and only 1 of the 7 points of the Republican increase. The pattern of the change from the sixties to the seventies is identical. Between the 1970s and 1984, the relatively weaker Republicanism of the migrants actually produced a roll-back in southern partisanship (although this change may be measurement fluctuation). In the 1950s, Republicans outnumbered Democrats by 12 percentage points among migrants; in 1984 they were only 8 points more numerous.[13] What might have been a 48-point decline in the Democratic bias of the white South became, instead, a 45-point change.[14]

OLD SOUTHERNERS ARE REPUBLICAN, TOO

Throughout the 1970s, the South was distinctive for the growing Republicanism of its younger cohort. The difference was small, but measurable, and striking for its variance from the national pattern. In the North, independence increased as partisans on both sides declined. In the South, at least a third of the Democratic decline resulted in an increase in Republicans (Petrocik, 1981, pp. 86–87). But that growth in Republican identification was not confined to new cohorts; older white southerners were also more Republican. The trend accelerated in the late 1970s. As Table 6.7 shows, by 1984 the younger cohort of native white southerners was more Republican than Democratic, and the overwhelming (71% to 22%) Democratic allegiance of the pre-1960 cohort had declined to a more modest 52 to 39 percent. The older cohort contributed over 70% of the decline in Democratic identification and more than 80% of the increase in Republican partisanship.

Table 6.6A Changing Partisanship of Native Southern Whites

	1952–1960		1962–1970		1972–1978		1980		1984	
	D	R	D	R	D	R	D	R	D	R
All white Southerners	71	22	60	29	53	32	54	33	45	43
Native Southerners	74	19	63	25	56	29	58	30	47	41
Deep South	78	15	64	22	61	22	60	25	40	47
Border South	62	33	60	32	47	42	51	41	58	34
Non-native South	36	53	34	51	26	56	45	43	40	47

Note: Table entries are percentages. Within any time grouping the numbers would sum to 100% with the inclusion of independents. Leaning partisans are considered identifiers of the party toward which they lean.

Table 6.6B Components of Partisan Change among White Southerners

	Democrats			Republicans		
	Net change	Change among		Net change	Change among	
		Natives	Migrants		Natives	Migrants
Change from:						
1950s to 1960s	−11	−11	−2	+7	+6	−2
1960s to 1970s	−7	−7	−8	+3	+4	+5
1970s to 1984	−8	−9	+9	+11	+12	−13

Note: Changes are calculated by subtracting the appropriate percentages. The 11-point estimated total change from the fifties to the sixties among all southerners is calculated by 60% who were self-identified Democrats during 1962–1970 from the 71% Democrat in 1952–1960.

Table 6.7 Effect of Post-1960 Cohort on the Realignment of Native Southern Whites as of 1984

	1950s	1984		
			Voters entering:	
	All voters	Through 1960	After 1960	All voters
Democrats	71%	52%	38%	45%
Independents	6	9	15	12
Republicans	22	39	46	43
	100%	100%	100%	100%
	Total change 1950 to 1984	Contribution of pre-1960 cohort	Contribution of post-1960 cohort	
Democrats	− 26	− 19	− 7	
Independents	+ 6	+ 3	+ 3	
Republicans	+ 21	+ 17	+ 4	

Note: Numbers in the last two columns do not sum to zero because of rounding errors. Leaning partisans are considered identifiers of the party toward which they lean.

"Total change" is calculated by subtracting the proportions in the "All voters" column for 1984 from the "All voters" column for the 1950s. The values are then signed as appropriate. The contribution of the pre-1960s voters is determined by subtracting their proportion of Democrats, Independents, and Republicans in 1984 from the equivalent proportions for the 1950s. The method of defining the cohorts makes this an appropriate calculation. The difference between the percentage point change of the pre-1960s cohort and the total change is the share contributed by the post-1960 cohort. This method of calculating the differences allows the size of groups and their partisanship to enter into the estimate of the change.

NET EFFECTS

Table 6.8 summarizes the data for the white South, and includes the contribution of migrants. Without migration or the post-1960 voters, there would have been a 36-point shift in the party bias of the white South in favor of the Republicans: Democratic identification would have declined 19 points and Republican identification would have increased 17 points. Voters who entered the electorate after 1960 pushed Democratic identification down a further 7 points and added another 4 points to the Republican proportion. Migration, as noted above, reversed some of these changes, adding a point to the Democrats and subtracting 2 percentage points from Republican identification. (See Norpoth and Rusk, 1982, for their estimates of the components of partisan change.)

Table 6.8 Summary of the Effect of the Post-1960 Cohort and Migration on the Realignment of the South, 1950s to 1984

	Percentage point change in:	
	Democrats	Republicans
Deep South		
Pre-60 cohort	− 12	+ 19
Post-60 cohort	− 19	+ 8
Net change	− 31	+ 27
Border South		
Pre-60 cohort	− 3	+ 6
Post-60 cohort	− 5	+ 2
Net change	− 8	+ 8
All white Southerners		
Pre-60 cohort	− 18	+ 18
Post-60 cohort	− 8	+ 4
Immigrants	+ 1	− 2
Net change	− 25	+ 20

Note: Leaning partisans are considered identifiers of the party toward which they lean.

THE PROGRAMMATIC ALIGNMENT OF THE PARTIES

This coalitional shift has affected the programmatic distance between the parties on several issues. A complete analysis of the policy consequences of the realignment documented above demands a full treatment by itself (some analysis is present in Petrocik, 1981), but a brief illustration of what these changes are likely to mean for policy divisions between the parties, especially with regard to race issues, is worthwhile. Consider the data in Figure 6.2.

During the 1950s, Democrats and Republicans differed over questions of economic regulation and social welfare; they were indistinguishable on race issues. By 1984 not only had Democrats and Republicans become more distinctive on welfare questions, but the policy differences between the parties had acquired a racial dimension. While smaller than differences on welfare policy, party differences on race questions were large nonetheless. The realignment is responsible for a significant fraction of this greater programmatic distinctiveness.

Figure 6.2 Effect of realignment on the issue preferences of party identifiers.

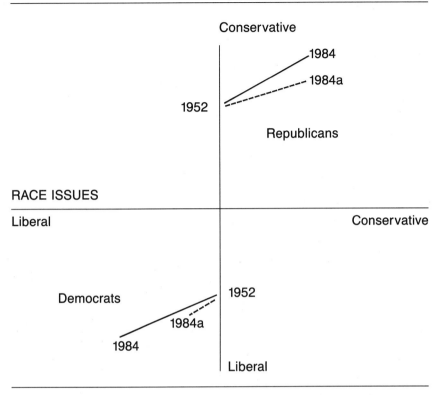

The solid line in Figure 6.2 connects the race-welfare coordinates for the 1950s with similar coordinates for 1984. The length and slope of the line measures the changes. The hatched line in Figure 6.2 presents the race-welfare coordinates that might have been observed if Democrats and Republicans had retained their New Deal coalitions through 1984.[15] The realignment increased the programmatic differences between the parties.

The effect is uneven. The GOP, even without its enlarged white southern constituency, would have become more conservative on both race and welfare issues; white southerners simply increased GOP conservatism on welfare issues. The Democrats, however, have become much more liberal, reflecting—in part—the decline of white southerners among Democratic identifiers and the increased contribution of blacks.[16]

Table 6.9 Republican Vote of Party Coalitions Groups, 1952–1984

				Election year					
	1952–1956	1960	1964	1968a	1968b	1972	1976	1980	1984
White Northern Protestants	77%	79%	51%	75%	76%	77%	64%	66%	76%
Catholics	61	19	27	41	45	67	48	57	65
Northern union households	50	37	18	51	57	60	41	43	48
White Southerners	50	53	42	65	75	78	57	60	69
Jews	25	11	11	7	16	31	29	37	31
Blacks	28	29	1	3	3	13	5	7	9

Note: 1968a presents the Republican vote only; 1968b presents Republican vote and the Wallace vote of the group.

ELECTIONS AND THE NEW COALITIONS

The group voting patterns for 1984 and other recent presidential elections reflect these changes. Reagan's vote in 1984 (and in 1980) was typical of the vote of Republican candidates. His 76% support among WASPs in 1984 was typical of what winning Republican candidates have received from this group. Seven of the last ten Republican candidates drew at least 75% of the votes of WASPs. In 1980 Reagan did not do quite so well with these voters; nor did Ford in 1976, but both carried two-thirds of the group. Only the hapless Goldwater failed to carry WASPs by a strong majority. Catholics and union members were unusually supportive of Reagan, but, as Table 6.9 shows, their Republican vote was not unprecedented. White southern support for Reagan was also quite normal. The "solid South" has been solidly ambiguous for thirty years. Eisenhower split their votes in the 1950s, Nixon won with a small majority in 1960, Wallace held Nixon to 50% in 1968, and native-son Carter kept Ford's majority to 55% in 1976. On the other hand, Nixon won with a large majority in 1972 and Reagan carried the white southerners with wide margins in both of his elections. Goldwater is the only recent Republican presidential candidate to lose the white southern vote. These party identification data simply illustrate that southern partisanship has begun to match southern presidential voting, with consequences for other offices. Only blacks and Jews have remained staunchly Democratic.

The 1984 election was an unexceptional expression of a realignment which has been underway for several years. Reagan's success in 1984 resulted from his substantial appeal to every group which has supported Republican candidates in recent presidential elections. He did not construct an unusual winning coalition; 1984 was not an unanticipated or "critical" election; it was one in a series. The new party alignment pits a Republican core of middle and up-scale northern WASPs and southern whites against a Democratic core of blacks and Jews. Union families and Catholics represent a target group for both parties; neither can depend upon them for a majority although the Democrats are stronger with both, especially union families. Table 6.10 summarizes the partisanship of the groups and their share of the new party coalitions as of 1984.

SOUTHERN REALIGNMENT AND THE ELECTION OF 1986

The parties reassembled their normal coalitions in 1986. Typically Republican voters rallied around Republican candidates; typically Democratic voters supported Democratic candidates.[17] The correspondence between the vote and partisanship was very strong, with only 11% of

Table 6.10 The Group Foundation of the Parties, 1984

	Party identifcation			Group profile of the parties	
	Dem.	Ind.	Rep.	Democrats	Republicans
White Northern Protestants					
Upper SES	28	4	69	2%	6%
Middle SES	28	9	63	7	20
Lower SES	38	10	53	6	10
White Southerners Border states					
Middle-upper SES	54	9	38	5	4
Lower SES	61	6	33	5	3
Deep South Middle-upper SES	41	9	50	6	9
Lower SES	42	18	40	6	7
Immigrants	35	22	43	2	2
Catholics					
Upper SES	42	11	47	6	8
All others	55	12	33	7	5
Jews	73	8	19	3	1
Blacks	79	12	10	17	2
Northern union households	52	10	39	13	12
Hispanics	57	19	24	7	4
All others				8	7
Total				100%	100%

Note: The first three columns can be summed to 100% horizontally. Leaning partisans are considered identifiers of the party toward which they lean.

Democrats voting for Republican Congressional candidates and less than 10% of Republicans voting for Democrats. Party loyalty in the Senate and gubernatorial elections, though not quite as high overall and differing from state to state, was sufficiently great to allow the 1986 campaigns to be characterized as "normal" off-year elections (however frenzied the candidates and parties in their attempt to win the Senate seats at risk).

The "normality" of the outcome is apparent in Table 6.11, which compares the 1986 House, Senate, and Gubernatorial vote of party coalition groups with their presidential votes from 1960 through 1984. The votes of most of the groups match their recent record, and none significantly departs from the historical record.

Republican candidates received three-fifths of the votes of WASPs, with slightly greater support for House candidates and, perhaps, slightly less support for Republican gubernatorial candidates. Recent Republican presidential candidates have done better among them, but the similarity between 1986 and previous elections is undeniable. The Catholic vote was Republican. The 53% support Republican Congressional candidates received from Catholics was exactly the vote to be expected given their partisan balance.

Democrats enjoyed overwhelming support from blacks, Jews, and Hispanics. Union members, reverting to an earlier Democratic affinity, gave less than 40% of their votes to Republicans, a decline that is more than an off-year sag. A comparison of their vote with their partisanship shows an eight-point shortfall. It seems likely that the vote among union members this year registered dissatisfaction with the Republicans.

The striking feature of Table 6.11, given the media emphasis on Democratic success in the South, is the overwhelming Republican vote of white southerners. There is no evidence that southern whites have returned or are returning to their Democratic partisanship of an earlier era. On the contrary, all of the data indicate a continuation of their preference for the Republicans (although, to be sure, not always Republican candidates, especially at the local level). As a group they were at least as Republican as WASPs, the traditional Republican core constituency.

WHY THE SOUTHERN REPUBLICANS LOST

Republicans lost the Senate races in the South not because the realignment of the past two decades was reversed, but because the parallel effort to enfranchise southern blacks has been exceptionally successful. The CBS exit poll of southern Senate races found whites voting 61% to 38% for Denton in Alabama, 59% to 39% for Mattingly in Georgia, 60% to 39% for Moore in Louisiana, and 56% to 42% for Broyhill in North Carolina. In the gubernatorial races they voted 68% to 30% for Hunt in Alabama, 55% to 43% for Martinez in Florida, and 58% to 39% for Clements in Texas. In 1986, blacks—lopsidedly Democratic—turned out at a high enough rate to overcome the Republican advantage among whites.

Table 6.12 summarizes the data and illustrates the structure which yielded the 1986 results and which is likely to handicap future Republican statewide candidates in the South. The first column reports the share of the electorate that was black, the next two report their vote. The last column is particularly significant because it indicates the size of the

Table 6.11 Republican Vote of Party Coalition Groups, 1952–1986

	Election year							1986	
	1960	1964	1968	1972	1976	1980	1984	House	Senate
White Northern Protestants	79%	51%	75%	77%	64%	66%	76%	62%	58%
Catholics	19	27	41	67	48	57	65	53	52
Northern union households	37	18	51	60	41	43	48	36	34
White Southerners	53	42	65	78	57	60	69	61	64
Jews	11	11	7	31	29	37	31	25	34
Blacks	29	1	3	13	5	7	9	9	8
Total Republican vote	49	39	44	61	49	51	59	48	47

Note: 1968 percentages present the Republican vote. The vote for Wallace and Humphrey is the missing percentage. The 1986 data are from an election eve survey conducted by Market Opinion Research as a part of its post-election analysis.

Table 6.12 Southern Black Voting and Its Impact on Statewide Elections in 1986

		Vote		
	Percent of voters	Republican	Democrat	Democratic advantage
Senate races				
Alabama	21	7	88	19
Florida	10	16	80	8
Georgia	24	18	75	18
Louisiana	29	12	85	25
North Carolina	16	6	88	14
Gubernatorial races				
Alabama	21	4	91	19
Florida	10	10	85	9
Texas	9	21	74	7

Source: CBS News Exit Polls.

handicap with which Republicans begin every election in these states because of the Democratic loyalty of blacks. Consider Louisiana, where the
Democratic advantage was greatest in 1986: black voters elected John
Breaux. Given the overwhelmingly Democratic commitment of blacks,
Breaux effectively had almost half of a winning vote before the polls
opened (25% of the total vote was blacks voting for Breaux). To win, Hen-
son Moore had to hold the non-black vote for Breaux to about 34%. The
39% of the white vote that Breaux actually achieved was more than he
needed to win. Louisiana is not unique. Denton started 19 points behind
in Alabama, Mattingly began 18 points behind in Georgia. None was
able to overcome these deficits because the electorate was not so polarized that whites were prepared to vote Republican as heavily as blacks
voted Democrat.

RULES OF THUMB FOR SOUTHERN REPUBLICANS

In the future, in the absence of a racial polarization in the vote and in the
presence of similar black-white turnout rates, Republican statewide candidates will be severely handicapped whenever the black population approaches 20%. In practice, this means that virtually every southern state
and several border states as well (e.g., Maryland) will be marginal Demo-

cratic states despite massive changes in their underlying partisanship. To succeed, Republicans must depend upon atypical support from blacks or huge white majorities. For example, Thad Cochran's win in Mississippi in 1984 was made possible by an 81 to 10% vote among whites. With a 30% black electorate—voting 80% for Winter (and likely to vote equally Democratic in most elections)—Cochran began the election about 24 points behind. To overcome this disadvantage he needed to hold Winter to 37% of the white votes. He did better than that, and won.

In general it seems to be the case the Republicans must draw in the area of 65% of the non-black vote to win in any of the heavily black southern states. Where this target is missed—as it was in 1986 in Alabama, Georgia, Louisiana, North Carolina, and Florida (where Hawkins lost the white vote)—Republicans cannot win despite the continuing (and probably increasing) vitality of the Republican party.

CONCLUSION

This analysis of the social group foundations of the American parties provides both a descriptive and a theoretical improvement over discussions of realignment which focus upon a search for a new majority party. Theoretically, the recognition that a realignment can occur without the emergence of a new majority party incorporates the dominant social cleavage theory of electoral parties with analyses of party system change. All too frequently the latter have been dealt with sui generis, as a phenomenon worth attention simply because it involves a major political institution. While the social value of an institution should be sufficient to legitimize attention to it, social value will not provide a conceptual grasp or, perhaps, even the practical implications of what is recorded.

The wait for a new majority party can too easily blind scholars to the merit of investigating the dynamics and consequences of the changes described above. The wait for a realignment should end because one has occurred and is continuing. Whether it will yield a Republican majority remains to be seen, but that it has significantly affected the parties and conditioned recent presidential elections is beyond question. If, therefore, the post-1984 surge in Republican fortunes recedes (as it seems to have done as of late 1986), leaving the Democrats with only a reduced plurality, the non-critical realignment of the last two decades will not become insignificant. Although the party balance may continue to favor the Democrats, the programmatic underpinnings of the new alignment distinguish it from the New Deal alignment. To the extent that party systems are notable for their axes of agreement and cleavage as well as for their party balance, the United States has undergone the formation of a new party system, and the altered coalitions are the core of the transformation.

NOTES

1. The literature on realignment is too lengthy to cite fully. Moreover, any attempt to do so would surely leave out related, important work. Suffice it to say that if Phillips' book was a major nonacademic statement, the work of Burnham (1970), Ladd (1970), Ladd and Hadley (1975, with a revised edition in 1978, cited below), and Sunquist (1973, with a revised edition in 1983, cited below) were the most comprehensive academic treatises on the topic. Sundquist (1983) is a good source for the literature. All, of course, owe a debt to V. O. Key (1955, 1959).

2. The connection between dealignment and realignment may be quite strong. It is possible that the early period of the transformation of a party system will be characterized by a general loosening of the partisan attachments of the electorate. This dealignment might persist until subsequent events facilitate the reestablishment of a stable equilibrium. The common expectation was that the dealignment of the 1970s would create a party politics marked by nonpartisanship and a peripheral electorate for the indefinite future. The apparently greater partisanship of young voters since 1980 and the southern realignment cast doubt on this prediction of a dealigned, peripheral electorate. It also suggests that there might be merit in examining the extent to which dealignment is a harbinger of realignment.

3. While others have since used the ideas of performance and policy realignment, I first heard this distinction from Frederick Steeper of Market Opinion Research, to whom I am indebted for it.

4. The finding may also have substantive significance. This cohort averages about 56 years of age. It was also common during 1982 and 1983 to find that Reagan's lowest job approval was provided by voters in the 55 to 64 age group. The suspicion was that those voters, nearing retirement, were the most anxious over discussions of the administration's plans for the social security system. The retired segment of the electorate was, on balance, supportive of Reagan. That group knew that whatever the future might hold, the social security system had not reduced their benefits. Further, they did not believe that their benefits would be affected.

5. The 1984 NES survey seriously underrepresented men and white southerners. Since the analysis makes over-time comparisons of the groups in terms of their share of the parties, it was important to compensate for this sampling error by reweighting the sample so that it would conform to population parameters.

6. The weaker alignment of social and party cleavages in the United States is at the root of several distinctive features of the American polity, among which we might include the frequency with which the American parties have realigned and rebuilt their popular foundations. As coalitions of often competing groups, incompatible policies and programs have occasionally divided coalition groups and sent one or more to the opposite party. Just as frequently, and perhaps with

greater net effect, the programmatic orientation of the parties has allowed them to differentially mobilize new entrants into American Politics. The result of this coalition expansion is first a larger party, but also a coalition measurably more diverse and subject to internal differences that may precipitate subsequent realignments.

7. This straightforward definition of realignment is theoretically compatible with the coalitional (Lipset and Rokkan, 1967) definition of parties, it corresponds to practitioners' perspectives on the electoral foundations of parties, and it is easily measured. It also provides purchase on related, problematic phenomena. It allows, for example, an ordering of realignments in terms of their magnitude. Some will be "critical" as Burnham (1970) has used the term, filled with consequences and secondary effects of many kinds; others will be more modest in their by-products. A few will yield a new majority and an alteration of the policy agenda of the society; others may produce only one of these changes. Some realignments will follow major social upheavals, while others will issue from more modest policy failures or intraparty divisions. Some realignments will depend upon a change in the party preference of several large groups, while others will reflect changes of one or a few small segments of the electorate. Some realignments will occur quickly, taking on the qualities of Key's "critical" election; still others will be long-term conflicts producing extended, "secular" realignments. Contemporary party system change in the United States is of the latter type. For more on this see chapter two of Petrocik (1981).

8. Unless otherwise indicated, the 1950s refer to the years between 1952 and 1960, inclusive; the 1960s cover the years from 1962 through 1970, and the 1970s refer to the years from 1972 through 1978.

9. This method of calculating changes is fully described in Petrocik (1981, p. 94).

10. Several different types of analyses have been done of changes in the South. See, for example, Beck (1977), Campbell (1977a, 1977b), and Rabinowitz et al. (1984). Other important and useful analyses of the transformation of southern politics would include Topping, Sazarek, and Linder (1966), Bass and DeVries (1976), and Black (1976). Some of this work, especially Bass and DeVries and Black, focuses on the politics of the South directly. Southern politics is more complex and deserving of fuller attention than it can be given in this paper. The white South for the purpose of this analysis is simply one element, albeit a very important one, of the several which have reshaped the party coalitions.

11. The greater correlation between class and party identification that has been noted in recent years (see Edsall, 1984, as an example) is heavily dependent upon these changes among southern whites. The greater Democratic preference of blacks has also played a part in the stronger correlation between class and party preference.

12. This conclusion is not as contradictory as it seems. Obviously migrants are still more Republican than natives, and they do contribute to the Republicanism of the region. However, migrants since the 1950s are relatively less Republican than migrants who entered the region prior to 1960. As a result, the relative

effect of the increase in migrants as a percent of the population is to make the area less Republican than it would be if the recent migrants had retained the Republicanism of previous migrants.

13. The net effect of migrants is greater than the apparently modest 4-point difference because migrants have increased as a share of the white population of the South. Once less than 10%, they now number approximately 14% of the white population of the region.

14. These over-time differences in the partisanship of migrants are small; it is possible that migrants were not a counter-trend during the 1980s; it is certain that they were an insignificant contributor to the decline in the partisanship of the region. (For more on this, see Petrocik, 1981, pp. 85–86. Thad Brown, 1987, also has relevant data on the political consequences of migration.) Wolfinger and Hagen (1985) argue that migration was a major component of partisan change in the South through the late 1970s. They do not present data that are sufficiently detailed to evaluate that claim. It is certainly contradicted by the NES data presented above, which they claim to have used in their analysis. Moreover, on their face the data seem unlikely to support such a conclusion. A combination of the magnitude of the southern white change and the small fraction migrants are of the total population simply would not allow migrants to be so consequential. Other than this discrepancy most of their analysis parallels findings in Petrocik (1981) and Beck (1977).

15. The second set of coordinates is created by weighting the 1984 data so that each group is represented among all Democratic and Republican identifiers in proportion to their share of the parties in the years from 1952 through 1960.

16. This effect should not be surprising. Racial conflict precipitated southern white flight from the Democratic party. But the transformation has been sustained by other issues, and by the recognition of white southerners that the Democrats do not represent their more conservative positions. Southern whites have not become more conservative in recent years. Relative to the national norm they are actually less conservative than they were 25 years ago. But in 1984 they do not believe, as they did in the 1950s, that the Democratic party better represents their preferences on the issues. The effect of their migration out of the Democratic party has been to intensify the liberal preferences of Democrats on social welfare and, especially, racial questions. This changed perception of the issue stance of the parties and its role in realigning the white South appears in chapters 8 and 9 of Petrocik (1981). A similar analysis of the role of issues in the realignment of the parties appears in Carmines and Stimson (1981). Wolfinger and Hagen (1985) emphasize the substantial similarity of the attitudes of southern whites with that of other groups in the electorate. Their conclusion seems to be based on comparisons between older and younger southern whites, and on the apparent similarity between southern whites and other white voters in the correlation of the issues with the vote. Their findings do not bear on the importance of race and other issue perceptions of the parties among southerners during the 1960s and 1970s. Also, while younger southern whites are, as noted above, more liberal than older southern whites they are still less liberal than comparable non-southern whites.

17. References to 1986 data other than the CBS exit polls refer to an election-eve survey of 1201 respondents conducted by Market Opinion Research of Detroit as a part of their post-election analysis. This was a PPS survey that was stratified by region. Sex quotas were imposed on the sample, but otherwise random procedures were used for respondent selection within households that were called by a random-digit dialing procedure.

REFERENCES

Andersen, Kristi J. 1979. *The Creation of a Democratic Majority: 1928–1936*. Chicago: U. of Chicago Press.

Bass, Jack, and Walter DeVries. 1976. *The Transformation of Southern Politics: Social Change and Political Consequence since 1945*. New York: Basic Books.

Beck, Paul Allen. 1974. A Socialization Theory of Realignment. In Richard G. Niemi and Associates, eds., *The Politics of Future Citizens*. San Francisco: Josey-Bass.

_____. 1977. "Partisan Dealignment in the Post-War South." *American Political Science Review* 71:477–96.

Black, Earl. 1976. *Southern Governors and Civil Rights: Racial Segregation as a Campaign Issue in the Second Reconstruction*. Cambridge, MA: Harvard U. Press.

Brown, Thad A. 1987. Forthcoming. *Migration and Politics*.

Budge, Ian, and Dennis J. Farlie. 1983. *Explaining and Predicting Elections*. London: Allen and Unwin.

Burnham, Walter Dean. 1970. *Critical Elections and the Mainsprings of American Politics*. New York: W. W. Norton.

Campbell, Angus, Philip Converse, Warren Miller, and Donald Stokes. 1960. *The American Voter*. New York: Wiley.

Campbell, Bruce. 1977a. "Change in the Southern Electorate." *American Journals of Political Science* 21:37–64.

_____. 1977b. "Patterns of Change in the Partisan Loyalties of Native Southerners: 1952–1972." *Journal of Politics* 39:730–61.

Campbell, James E. 1983. "Sources of the New Deal Realignment: The Contributions of Conversion and Mobilization to Partisan Change." Paper delivered at the annual meeting of the Southern Political Science Association, Birmingham, AL, November 3–5, 1983.

Carmines, Edward G., and James A. Stimson. 1981. "Issue Evolution, Population Replacement, and Normal Partisan Change." *American Political Science Review* 75:107–18.

Dahl, Robert A. 1966. *Political Oppositions in Western Democracies*. New Haven: Yale U. Press.

Edsall, Thomas B. 1984. *The New Politics of Inequality*. New York: W. W. Norton.

_____. 1985. "Even the Democrats Say the Republicans Have Caught Up." *The Washington Post National Weekly Edition*. August 12:11.

Erikson, Robert S., and Kent L. Tedin. 1981. "The 1928–1936 Partisan Realignment: The Case for the Conversion Hypothesis." *American Political Science Review* 75:951–62.

Kelley, Robert. 1979. *The Cultural Pattern in American Politics: The First Century.* New York: Alfred A. Knopf.

Key, V. O. 1955. "A Theory of Critical Elections." *Journal of Politics* 17:3–18.

———. 1959. "Secular Realignment and the Party System." *Journal of Politics* 21:198–210.

Ladd, Everett C. 1970. *American Political Parties: Social Change and Political Response.* New York: W. W. Norton.

Ladd, Everett C., and Charles Hadley. 1978. *Transformations of the American Party Systems,* 2d ed. New York: W. W. Norton.

LaPalombara, Joseph, and Myron Weiner. 1986. *Political Parties and Political Development.* Princeton: Princeton U. Press.

Lipset, Seymour Martin, and Stein Rokkan. 1967. *Party Systems and Voter Alignments.* New York: Free Press.

McPhee, William N., and Jack Ferguson. 1962. "Political Immunization." In William N. McPhee and William A. Glaser, eds., *Public Opinion and Congressional Elections.* New York: Free Press.

Niemi, Richard S., Richard S. Katz, and David Newman. 1980. "Reconstructing Past Partisanship: The Failure of Party Identification Recall Questions." *American Journal of Political Science* 24:633–51.

Norpoth, Helmut. 1985. "Change in Party Identification: Evidence of a Republican Majority." Paper presented at the 1985 annual meeting of the American Political Science Association, New Orleans, LA, August 29– September 1.

Norpoth, Helmut, and Jerrold Rusk. 1982. "Partisan Dealignment in the American Electorate: Itemizing the Deductions Since 1964." *American Political Science Review* 76:522–37.

Petrocik, John R. 1981. *Party Coalitions: Realignments and the Decline of the New Deal Party System.* Chicago: U. of Chicago Press.

Petrocik, John R., and Thad A. Brown. 1986. "Electoral Mobilization and Party System Change." Unpublished paper.

Phillips, Kevin P. 1969. *The Emerging Republican Majority.* New Rochelle, NY: Arlington House.

Powell, G. Bingham. 1979. "Voting Turnout in Thirty Democracies: Effects of Partisan, Legal, and Socio-economic Environments." Paper delivered at the Conference on Vote Turnout, May 16–19. Half Moon Inn, San Diego, CA.

Przeworski, Adam. 1975. "Institutionalization of Voting Patterns, or Is Mobilization the Source of Decay." *American Political Science Review* 69:49–67.

Rabinowitz, George, Paul-Henri Gurian, and Stuart Elain MacDonald. 1984. "The Structure of Presidential Elections and the Process of Realignment, 1944–1980." *American Journal of Political Science* 28:611–35.

Rose, Richard, and Derek Unwin. 1969. "Social Cohesion, Political Parties, and Strains on Regimes." *Comparative Political Studies* 2:7–67.

Sorauf, Frank J. 1963. *Party and Representation: Legislative Politics in Pennsylvania*. New York: Atherton Press.

Sundquist, James L. 1983. *Dynamics of the Party System*. Rev. ed. Washington, D.C.: The Brookings Institution.

Sussman, Barry. 1985. "Fragile Realignment: As the Economy Goes, So Goes the GOP." *The Washington Post National Weekly Edition*, March 18:37.

Topping, John C., John R. Sazarek, and William H. Linder. 1966. *Southern Republicanism and the New South*. Cambridge, MA.

Wanat, John. 1979. "The Application of a Non-Analytic Most Possible Estimation Technique: The Relative Impact of Mobilization and Conversion of Votes in the New Deal." *Political Methodology* 6:357–74.

Wanat, John, and Karen Burke. 1982. "Estimating the Degree of Mobilization and Conversion in the 1890s: An Inquiry into the Nature of Electoral Change." *American Political Science Review* 76:360–70.

Wolfinger, Raymond, and Michael G. Hagen. 1985. "Republican Prospects Southern Comfort." *Public Opinion* 8:8–13.

PARTY IDENTIFICATION, REALIGNMENT, AND PARTY VOTING: BACK TO THE BASICS

Warren E. Miller

I argue the utility of distinguishing between the overlapping concepts of partisanship and party identification. I do so by presenting some of the consequences of limiting the measurement of party identification to the responses evoked by the classic root questions, "Generally speaking, do you usually think of yourself as a Republican, a Democrat, an independent, or what?" In presenting this set of findings as a research note, I will not attempt to add to the literature on the differences between strong identifiers and weak identifiers, nor will I reexamine the many interpretations of the partisan sympathies of "independent leaners."

Even without undertaking such tasks, my mode of presenting data on the historical record of party identification, narrowly defined, calls into question at least a portion of the current conventional wisdom about the nature of party identification and about the responsiveness of party identification to economic and social events in the lives of individual voters. I shall question the conclusion that a national party realignment preceded the election of 1984. I shall also question the conclusion that dealignment has reduced the relevance of party identification for the vote choice. Finally, in pursuing these conclusions I shall question some revisionist arguments concerning the impact of short-term influences on party identification.

PARTY IDENTIFICATION AND ITS OPERATIONAL MEASURE

My approach to encouraging reconsideration of some of the conventional wisdom about party identification has three major structural components. First, I employ a conceptual definition of Democrats and Republicans that rests entirely on answers to the root question, "Generally speaking, do you usually think of yourself as a Republican, a

Democrat, an independent, or what?" People who answer "independent" or "no preference" or "some other party" are not treated as Republicans or Democrats, even though they may subsequently admit to being closer to one of the two parties. Moreover, I will not distinguish between strong or weak partisans. Thus my basic measure is restricted to separating party identifiers (Democrats and Republicans) from nonidentifiers.

The reasons for this strict interpretation of the meaning of party identification are more firmly grounded in theory than in data. There is little question that variations in the "strength of partisanship" have reflected variations in the short-term fortunes of the respective parties, and have led to changes in the sheer intensity of partisan enthusiasms. It has also been well documented that the same short-term forces have both attracted and repelled many citizens who, while *not* major party identifiers, have on different occasions seen themselves to be closer to one of the two major party alternatives. However, neither of these considerations speaks directly to the question of individuals responding to the same short-term influences by self-consciously moving *across the boundary* separating identifiers from nonidentifiers. The question is not whether "independent leaners" may, from time to time, be more partisan in their voting or their issue preferences than are weak identifiers. And the question is not whether independent leaners are covert partisans; they are demonstrably and overtly partisan. The question is the stability (and the meaningfulness) on one's self-identification as a Democrat, a Republican, or as something else.

In searching for an answer to this question I "return to the basics" as I reconsider the original treatment of the concept and the measurement procedures reported in *The American Voter*.[1] A return to the source places the original measurements in context. It is clear that the effort in *The American Voter* was to build on the concept of group (party) identification, but *also* to create an indicator that would differentiate among degrees of "partisan-ship" or partisan coloration." With hindsight, it now seems that the effort to maximize the versatility of an operational measure blurred the clarity of the basic concept of identification with a political party. On the one hand, going beyond the root question to differentiate additional degrees of partisanship muddled the dimensionality of the resulting measure. It introduced intransitivity into a presumed continuum. Most important here, it also created indicators of *partisanship* that were reflective of short-term influences of preferences for issues or for candidates as well, perhaps, as variations in the relatively enduring sense of partisan political self that is the explicit heart of the concept of identification.[2]

The significance of attending to "details" of measurement when analyzing party identification has recently been forcefully argued by Converse and Pierce. They emphasize that there are "two elements which
have been absolutely central to the whole notion of party identification:
an *extended time horizon* and some engagement of partisan feelings with
self-identity.... These two elements... imply... that numerous forms of
partisan feelings may be experienced by an individual, and reported
upon to investigators, which *do not* constitute the possession of a party
identification as such" (emphasis added).[3] In this exercise we have set
aside the differentiation of independent leaners. We have done so in part
because in the original interview sequence the independent leaners
clearly deny a "temporally extended self-identity" as Democrat or Republican. It is also true that the follow-up question, "Do you think of
yourself as closer to the Republican or Democratic party?" does not attempt to elicit a qualified or limited sense of an "enduring engagement of
partisan feelings with self-identity"; the question is asked only in the
present tense, and it calls only for a cognitive assessment of current circumstance.[4] The answers may indicate partisanship but they do not reflect a sense of party identification. I agree with Converse and Pierce
when they note that there may be no "right" way to measure *partisanship*
but "it is of great importance not to treat diverse measures of partisanship as functional equivalents of one another. Partisanship has multiple
facets, and keeping clear which facet is being measured, is a basic inves-
tigator responsibility."[5]

One result of the common practice of attending to variations in
strength of party identification (strong or not so strong), and variations
in the partisan sympathies of nonidentifiers (the so-called independent
leaners) has been to obscure the relative stability of the basic sense of the
political self, elemental party identification. Short-term enthusiasms for
a Lyndon Johnson, Democratic dismay with a George McGovern, and
Republican distress with Watergate are clearly reflected in abrupt
changes in the now traditional *seven point* measure of partisanship; I
shall document the very limited impact of such phenomena on answers
to the basic identification question, "Generally speaking, do you usually
think of yourself as a Republican or a Democrat?"[6]

In a related development, attention to variations on the strength dimension of partisanship had focused interest on what has come to be
called dealignment. At some point in the reconsideration of party identification, the role of microlevel dealignment as a forerunner to systemic
realignment must be taken up anew. Because of the limited goal of this
research note I shall not present, nor follow the implications of, data connecting dealignment to realignment. It is enough to be concerned with

the historical record of party alignments, e.g., the empirical record of the numerical balance between those who are self-identified Republicans and Democrats. That record will be based on the classic definition of *party identification* rather than on reflections of the broader construct of *partisanship* (Miller, 1991).

THE HISTORICAL RECORD

The second major structural component of my analysis is the decision to exploit the full 36-year time series array of National Election Studies presidential election study data, 1952–88. Examining the full sweep of the period covering 10 elections provides a historical context essential to the analysis of party realignment, as well as to the simple study of aggregate indicators of stability and change through time.

SUBGROUP DIFFERENCES

The third element in my strategy of inquiry is to consider, more or less in tandem, several strands of evidence that are usually presented in isolation, one from the other, in the literature. To this end I shall "disaggregate" the electorate and examine such constituent segment in the presence of all other segments; the parts will sum to the whole, but I will be able to assess the contribution of each part to the whole.

ELECTORAL PARTICIPATION

My first disaggregation separates voters from nonvoters. I shall note that the party identifications of nonvoters among various subgroups in the electorate differ from the party identifications of voters in the same subgroups. I shall also note that combining the two often obscures patterns that characterize voters alone. This must certainly mean that analyses relating aggregate national distributions of party identification in the total electorate to aggregate national election outcomes have missed the mark insofar as the divergent distributions of *nonvoters* have been permitted to intrude on the interpretation of the electoral divisions among *voters*.

RACE

My second disaggregation comes from separating the electorate on the dimension of race. Ideally I would like to examine each of the contributions to the nation's growing ethnic diversity. Because of the limited numbers of Hispanics, Asians, and other minorities in the samples, I trace only the black citizenry over the past four decades. However, separate attention to the partisanship of black citizens is crucial because of the dramatic changes in their contribution to the nation's politics. Even so, the numbers in the national samples are too small to disaggregate blacks into categories other than voters and nonvoters.

REGION

The third focus for disaggregation of nonblacks in my historical reconstruction of stability and change in party identification adds the theme of regional differences. At least since Converse's discussion, party realignment in the South has been an acknowledged topic of importance in contemporary political analysis.[7] Earl and Merle Black added to the work of Converse, Campbell, Beck, Petrocik, Wolfinger, and others and analyzed the continuation of change in the South during the Reagan years.[8] Curiously, however, there was no immediate follow-up to the Blacks' work to ask what the analytic removal of the South did to the remaining national estimates of party identification. I shall ask and answer the question immediately by adding a South/non-South comparison to our comparisons of voters and nonvoters among nonblacks.[9]

GENDER

In my "return to basics," as I examine the record of party identification distributions over the past 10 elections, I shall add one more dimension, *gender*. Gender-related differences usually drew comment in the 1950s to explain how widows were responsible for the slightly pro-Republican cast to the female vote of the 1950s. In more recent years, the persistent pro-Democratic, presumably liberal, cast of women's votes (when compared to male votes) has been labeled "The Gender Gap." As an empirical matter, it is real. In all of the recent elections the female vote has been more Democratic than has the male vote, and this contrasts rather sharply with both the 1950s and 1960s. Our last question, therefore is: "Is there now a 'gender gap' among nonblack voters—South or non-South—that constitutes an element of party realignment?"

Still other dimensions of interest to both practical politics and political theory, such as religion and age, could be added to this list. However, it is not necessary to go beyond the set I have selected in order to make the point that a reassessment of the historical record of the nature and role of party identification is needed. Among the dimensions of disaggregation I have specified, the distinction between voters and nonvoters is the most important.[10]

THE DISTRIBUTION OF PARTY IDENTIFICATION

Somewhat arbitrarily, I first draw attention to evidence related to party realignment and the regional contrast, South and North, depicted among white voters in Table 7.1. Between the elections of 1952 and 1980, outside the South, neither men nor women voters revealed any significant change in the net balance of their partisan sentiments across the 30-year interval. With gender differences exceeding two percentage points during this period only in 1964 and 1976, this is a remarkable demonstration of stability. For Northern whites, the "steady state" period of relatively unchanging party identification apparently lasted not 12 years— 1952 to 1964—but a full 30 years and was finally interrupted only *after* the first Reagan election.[11]

This extraordinary display of persistence in the net party balance among the Northern white voters, who made up between 75% and 80% of all white voters over the past four decades, provides a striking implicit commentary on the literature on the stability of party identification and party alignment. It does not, of course, necessarily negate analyses of short-term fluctuations between the quadrennial readings, although both Green and Palmquist[12] and Abramson and Ostrom[13] have recently spoken to this point. However, the evidence of pervasive, long-term, aggregate stability outside the South is so dramatic that it would seem to call for a reexamination of many conclusions about the origins of change in party identification. It at least calls into question analyses that have, for example, used changes in *national* economic indicators to explain *national* changes in party identification, when electorally relevant change in party identification apparently did not take place outside the South.

It raises more direct questions about the implications of the thesis that party identification changes incrementally as the consequence of prior voting behavior. From 1952 to 1980, according to National Election Studies data, the Northern vote division among white voters averaged *57% Republican*. Despite very large Republican pluralities in virtually every year except 1964, the Republican share of party identifiers did not increase as a simple extrapolation of the work of Markus and Converse[14] might have suggested.

The same evidence of stability in the partisan balance of party identification calls attention to the absence of any cumulative impact of a series of "running tallies" that should have produced a Republican increment between 1952 and 1980 (Fiorina, 1981). The aggregate stabilities may, of course, conceal compensatory changes that have offset a drift away from

Table 7.1 Partisan Balance of Party Identification within Selected Groups of Voters and Nonvoters,[a] 1952–88

Election year	Non-South		South		Nation	
	Men	Women	Men	Women	Blacks	All
Voters[b]						
1952	4	3	57	54	52	15
1956	3	2	57	43	36	12
1960	1	3	58	43	30	15
1964	10	6	39	39	75	32
1968	3	4	28	39	87	22
1972	1	0	21	23	68	13
1976	3	-3	25	14	70	12
1980	3	5	3	21	80	15
1984	-10	-3	5	19	73	5
1988	-9	-7	-3	23	80	4
% Distribution						
1952	41	38	8	9	4	100
1988	30	36	11	13	10	100
Nonvoters						
1952	24	22	49	50	43	39
1956	14	-4	53	46	41	24
1960	10	20	44	59	30	34
1964	31	47	49	35	69	48
1968	8	18	21	27	71	32
1972	12	16	19	29	55	24
1976	-4	12	16	48	52	24
1980	0	24	28	18	60	24
1984	7	8	20	13	52	17
1988	-2	-1	8	26	43	14
% Distribution						
1952	19	27	9	24	20	100
1988	21	29	14	20	17	100

[a]Each entry is the proportion of Democratic identifiers (strong plus weak) minus (−) the proportion of Republicans identified (strong plus weak). A negative sign indicates a Republican plurality.

[b]Voters defined as "validated voters" in 1964, 1976, 1980, 1984, 1988; in all other years the definition is provided by the respondents' self-reports in the postelection interview.

the Democrats and into the Republicans' camp. No reasons for, or evidence of, such compensatory, pro-Democratic changes come immediately to mind. Consequently, it seems fair to conclude that the evidence of aggregate stability among nonblack voters outside the South should prompt further study of the dynamics of microlevel change in party identification.[15]

REALIGNMENT IN THE SOUTH

Equally clear evidence of the mutability of partisan loyalties is provided by Table 7.1 and its description of change among Southern white voters in general, and white Southern males in particular, across the same time span. Apparently the beginning of the end of single-party dominance among Southern white male voters started shortly after the Kennedy election of 1960. By the time of the first Reagan presidency, 20 years later, a virtual 80-20 division favoring the Democratic party had been replaced by near parity for the Republican party. This would seem to be evidence of a classic version of the realignment of partisanship. It was a realignment of massive proportions, involving a Democratic-to-Republican switch of at least 3 out of every 10 Southern nonblack male voters. It was apparently a secular realignment as defined by V. O. Key, Jr.[16] and introduced in the current discussion by Converse.[17]

Further analysis is needed to determine the relative importance of contributions from conversion, mobilization, and cohort replacement among Southern white voters over the 36 years included in Table 7.1, but the net effect is unmistakable. While conditions outside the South did not provoke any net change in the party alignment of nonblack voters between 1952 and 1980, changes within the South produced a virtual revolution. A closer examination of both sets of circumstance should tell us more about party identifications. Earl and Merle Black[18] have suggested major themes to be explored in the analysis of the South. Outside the South suggestions of cohort replacement in the changing composition of the electorate offer a promising first line of inquiry.

THE GENDER GAP

The possible unitary nature of regional factors capable of producing such party realignment among Southern white male voters is initially reflected in the parallel shift among nonblack Southern female voters across the seven elections between 1952 and 1976. A complicating anomaly then appears. Changes in party identification among Southern female voters after 1976 do not match the pattern of any other set of nonblack voters. This is striking because the other three groupings all reveal a shift to small Republican pluralities at the conclusion of the Reagan era in 1988, while white Southern women continuously exhibit a set of clearly pro-Democratic preferences throughout the 1980s. Moreover, their Democratic plurality in 1988 matches the figures from 1972 and results from a clear increase, not a decrease, in relative Democratic strength after the election of 1976. Why this should be so is not obvious.

The importance of explaining the male-female differences among nonblack Southern voters is accentuated by the realization that those differences in the 1980s are primarily responsible for the much discussed "gender gap" for those years.[19] Even without "understanding" these gender differences, it seems possible that the appearance of the gender gap in the Reagan years was not as much a function of a liberal, pro-Democratic growth in the partisan sentiments of women as a function of the sharply conservative pro-Republican move among men.[20] The Republicans have not had a new problem with women; the Democrats have had a continuing problem among men. And once regional data are sorted out, the specification of the gender problem is largely confined to the South.

BLACK VOTERS

Turning away from region and gender differences within white voters to consider the partisan sympathies of the black citizenry, the separation of black voters and black nonvoters from the remainder of the electorate highlights the recent contributions of black voters to partisan national elections. The apparent impact of the Kennedy-Johnson era was more dramatic among black voters than nonvoters. And, given their mobilization beginning in the mid-sixties, black voters across the nation were ultimately only slightly fewer in number than were Southern white male voters. As a consequence, the fact that black voters across the nation almost tripled their margin of support for the Democratic party between 1960 and 1968 by itself more than offset, in sheer numbers, the 50% decline in the Democratic plurality among Southern white males.

The countervailing moves within these two politically significant segments of the electorate underline the hazards of drawing conclusions based on national aggregations. National totals did not suggest any net change in the national balance of party identifications between 1956 and 1980. This is true, in general, because the precipitously real pro-Republican shift in the white (male) South was counterbalanced by the large growth in Democratic pluralities among newly mobilized black citizens.

VOTERS AND NONVOTERS

A suggestion that variations in the nature and meaning of party identification may be associated with variations in political awareness and involvement is provided by the comparison of voters with nonvoters
among blacks. Although changes within each group were similar between 1960 and 1964, sharp differences appear after 1968. Those differences are accentuated by the contrary movements between 1984 and 1988.
It was black *nonvoters*, but not black voters, who contributed to the aggregate evidence suggestive of party realignment during the Reagan years.[21]

More generally, my analytic separation of voters from nonvoters ex-
poses relatively well-ordered evidence of stability among Northern white
voters, stability that contrasts with greater volatility among Northern
nonvoters. Both in the unevenness of patterns of change across time and
in the variability of gender differences, party identification among nonvoters seems less a matter of stable, long-term predispositions and more
a matter of responsiveness to short-term, election-by-election fluctuation
of circumstance than is true for voters. A similar contrast appears both
among black citizens and among Southern whites, although it is less
striking on first inspection because of the pervasive patterns of change
within these groups. While pondering the reason for these differences
between voters and nonvoters, it should also be recognized that the differences may contain the basis for reconciling other scholars' conclusions
about the apparent general responsiveness of party identification to
short-term influences with the new evidence of interelection stability
among Northern white voters.

As a final comment on Table 7.1, it may be noted that the particular
disaggregations that are so revealing of different patterns of stability and
change between 1952 and 1980 do not serve particularly well to cast new
light on the more recent changes in the distributions of party identifications that reflect a limited national realignment during the Reagan era.
The 1980–84 and 1984–88 changes in party balance were primarily a
Northern, white phenomenon and were not apparent at all among black
voters or Southern white women voters. A detailed analysis of the realignment of the Reagan years, developed elsewhere, indicates two quite
distinct stages of change in which Reagan's personal leadership and then
his partisan ideology first moved the younger, less politicized voters and
then the older, more politicized into the Republican party. In neither
stage of the realignment after 1980 were race, region, or gender as relevant as age, ideology, and political involvement.[22] The narrowest point to
be drawn from my introductory analysis is, quite simply, that systematic
inspection of disaggregated time series data may have been a good start-

Table 7.2 Correlations of Party Identification with the Presidential Vote Choice, 1952–88

Election year	Bivariate	Partial[a]
1952	.69	.64
1956	.67	.65
1960	.68	.60
1964	.57	.48
1968	.69	.55
1972	.52	.43
1976	.69	.64
1980	.73	.63
1984	.74	.65
1988	.75	.68
Mean	.67	.60

[a]Partial correlation with controls on race, education, gender, religion, income, and union membership.

ing point for questioning much conventional wisdom about party realignment and the stability of party identification, but it does not provide answers to many of the questions that it raises or that I have posed. The broader points of theoretical interest in the analysis are the many implications for shaping future inquiry into the nature of party identification and into the conditions that facilitate its stability, or provoke change.

PARTY IDENTIFICATION AND THE VOTE

Just as conventional wisdom about the stability of Democratic and Republican party identifications has encouraged some dubious interpretations of changing *distributions* in party identification, questions have also been raised concerning the meaningfulness of party identification as a *determinant* of the vote during the 1970s and 1980s. It seems reasonable to presume that two notable deviations in the correlation of party identification with preferences for presidential candidates, first in 1964 and then again in 1972, have been the remembered evidence for presuming a generally diminished importance for party following the elections of the 1950s.[23] A systematic examination of the simple national bivariate relationships between party identification and vote choice over time, presented in Table 7.2, documents both episodes of declining correlation; it also documents the atypicality of the 1964 and 1972 elections.

The left hand column of Table 7.2 reveals only two elections in which the unstandardized bivariate correlation falls well below the 10-election average of .67. They were the Johnson-Goldwater contest, in which Republicans voted against their conservative senator from the desert, and the Democrats' disastrous experiment with the radical liberal McGovern challenge to an immensely popular Republican incumbent, Richard Nixon. After having risen steadily from the 1972 low, the party identification/vote choice correlation was up to postwar highs by 1984 and 1988. There is no indication from any recent election that party identification is less relevant to the vote decision in the 1980s than it was three decades earlier.

As a further test of the constancy of correlations with the vote, the second column of Table 7.2 presents the *partial* correlations of party identifications and vote choice after the simultaneous imposition of controls on race, gender, religion, education, income, and union membership. The dual message of the partial correlations is clear: (1) year after year very little of the party-vote correlation can be considered the spurious consequence of their sharing these common antecedents; and (2) the passage of time has seen no diminution in the total effect of party identification on vote choice.

The casual role of party identification in the shaping of the attitudes and perceptions that are the immediate or proximate causes of a voter's preference for one candidate over the other had been a continuous topic of inquiry among students of electoral behavior. Evidence that the casual role of party identification as an antecedent to the vote is largely indirect through its influence on policy preferences and appraisals of presidential performance and candidate traits is provided by the Shanks and Miller[24] analyses of the Reagan elections. Such inquires can continue to be motivated, at least in part, by the knowledge that over time the *correlational* evidence is stronger, not weaker, for assigning a major explanatory/causal role for party identification in the context of presidential elections.[25]

PARTY VOTING

The more general conclusion that there has been no across-time decrease in the extent to which the national presidential vote is a party vote is neither challenged nor further illuminated by our disaggregation of voters by gender, region, or race. Year in and year out, women have been no more likely than men to cast a party vote *nor* to defect and cross party lines to vote for a president. After 1960, the black vote was as unwaveringly Democratic as were black voters' partisan loyalties. And within regional comparisons, as with the others, party voting in the 1980s was every bit as common—or uncommon—as it had been in the 1950s. Voting in line with one's party in 1984 and 1988 was as common as it had been in 1952 and 1956.

This conclusion holds for partisans on both sides of the aisle. Republicans in the South have an almost perfect record; they have reported voting for Republican candidates an average of at least 95% of the time from the days of Eisenhower and Nixon to the era of Reagan and Bush. Outside the South the Republican vote has been slightly more variable, but Northern Republicans have reported more than 90% support for their party's presidential candidates. The most noticeable, if still minor, occasions for defections came in 1964 and 1976, but the Republican figures for 1984 and 1988, both South and non-South, and among both men and women, were fully equal to their reported party votes in 1952 and 1956.

The record of Democratic identifiers at the polls is a persistent record of substantially *less* party support than given by Republicans, and it is somewhat more varied than the record of Republicans. Nevertheless, the Democratic patterns of regional party voting do not appear to have changed at all over three decades. Democrats, regardless of either region or sex, were just as faithful—or unfaithful—to party in their 1984 and 1988 votes as in earlier decades. There is no evidence pertaining to either party in either region of any difference in the level of party voting among party identifiers that would distinguish the 1980s from the 1950s.

There are real world consequences of this observation that extend well beyond what it says to political scientists about the more or less enduring nature and role of party identification. The data presented in Table 7.1, and my earlier discussion, indicate that Democrats quite apparently declined in numerical strength in the South between 1960 and 1980, and across the entire nation during the Reagan era, 1980–88. This happened without the emergence of greater loyalty or more faithful voting performance from those who *remained* as Democrats. At the same time, Republicans increased their numbers among party identifiers without suffering any dilution of party loyalty at the polls. Even in the changing South, the party identification/vote choice relationship has been stable for more than three decades for *both* Democratic and Republican identifiers. Thus it would appear that there as elsewhere typically less-than-faithful Democrats have converted to become typically faithful Republicans. Because Republican identifiers are substantially more faithful party voters than are Democratic identifiers, both elements in the exchange argue a greater increase in the election day strength of Republicans than implied by the simple distributional shifts in party identifications. The potentially good news for the Republican party rests on the validity of my deductions based on a return to the basics. Even though a massive regional realignment, followed by a limited national realignment, has cost the Democrats their one-time advantage in the distribution of party identification, the implications of party identification for the presidential vote have not changed materially with the passage of time and the change of political circumstance. And in 1984 and 1988 the Republican ticket benefited doubly from the leveling of the partisan playing field.

NOTES

1. Angus Campbell, Philip E. Converse, Warren E. Miller, and Donald E. Stokes, *The American Voter* (New York: John Wiley & Sons, 1960), pp. 121–28.

2. Richard A. Brody, "Change and Stability in the Components of Partisan Identification." Prepared for the NES Conference on Party Identification, Tallahassee, Florida, 1978; Bruce E. Keith, David B. Magleby, and Raymond E. Wolfinger, "The Partisan Affinities of Independent Leaners," *British Journal of Political Science* 16 (1986): 155–84; Warren E. Miller, "Party Identification" in Sandy Maisel, ed., *Encyclopedia of American Political Parties and Elections* (New York: New York Garland Publishing, Inc., 1991).

3. Philip E. Converse and Roy Pierce, "Measuring Partisanship," *Political Methodology* 11 (1987): 143.

4. The emphasis on an extended time horizon is properly the center of the recent Abramson and Ostrom critique of "Macropartisanship" by MacKuen, Erikson, and Stimson (1989).

5. It should be noted here that the authors of *The American Voter* have, both early and late, contributed to the conventional wisdom against which this note is directed. For example, in *The Dynamics of Party Support* (Converse, 1976) weak identifiers were often combined with independent leaners in the measurement of "strength"; and in the *American National Election Studies Data Sourcebook* (Miller and Traugott, 1989) summary measures of the partisan balance of party identifiers, as in Table 2.32, pp. 103–104. It might also be noted, however, that the definition of party identification groups in tables in *The American Voter* usually followed the orthodoxy being promoted in this note, and the *Data Sourcebook* treats party identification as separate and distinct from party preference, as in Table 2.34, pp. 105–106.

6. In this regard my conclusion is on all fours with the analysis of Abramson and Ostrom who demonstrate that the temporal stability of party identification can be missed—and often has been missed—when Gallup-like questions that emphasize the current moment ("In politics as of today...") are used as indicators of party identification (Abramson and Ostrom, 1991).

7. Philip E. Converse, "On the Possibility of Major Political Realignment in the South" in Allan P. Sindler, ed., *Change in the Contemporary South* (Durham,

N.C.: Duke U. Press, 1963); Raymond Wolfinger and Michael C. Hagan, "Republican Prospects: Southern Comfort," *Public Opinion* (October–November 1985): 8–13.

8. Earl Black and Merle Black, *Politics and Society in the South* (Cambridge, Mass.: Harvard U. Press, 1987).

9. It should be noted that for simplicity of expression I shall, at times, refer to the non-South as the North, even though I mean Westerners, Mid-Westerners as well as "Northerners"; and, taking somewhat greater liberties, I shall refer to nonblacks as whites even though this group includes Hispanics and other ethnic minorities in very small numbers.

10. Laurily K. Epstein, "The Changing Structure of Party Identification," *PS* 13 (1985): 48–52; Wolfinger and Hagan, "Republican Prospects"; Stanley Kelley, "Democracy and the New Deal Party System" in Amy Gutmann, ed., *Democracy and the Welfare State* (Princeton, N.J.: Princeton U. Press, 1988).

11. My earlier comment on measurement comes into play here. If one focuses on "strength of partisanship" and takes variations in the proportions of "strong" identifiers and the proportions with no partisan preference into account, one sees the aggregate evidence that prompted discussions of dealignment. These variations are *not* reflected in root self-identification for nonblack voters outside the South. For an elaboration of this discussion, see Miller, 1990.

12. Donald P. Green and Bradley Palmquist, "Of Artifacts and Partisan Instability," *American Journal of Political Science* 34 (1990): 872–902.

13. Abramson and Ostrom, "Macropartisanship: An Empirical Assessment," *American Political Science Review* 85 (1991): 181–92.

14. Gregory B. Markus and Philip E. Converse, "A Dynamic Simultaneous Equation Model of Electoral Choice," *American Political Science Review* 73 (1979): 1055–70.

15. Further work on the responsiveness of party identification to short-term forces should also take into account the analyses by Donald P. Green and Bradley Palmquist (1990). Their analyses suggest the importance of taking measurement error into account when looking for evidence of partisan instability in nonrecursive models.

16. V. O. Key, Jr., "Secular Realignment and the Party System," *Journal of Politics* 17 (1959): 3–18.

17. Philip E. Converse, *The Dynamics of Party Support: Cohort Analyzing Party Identification* (Beverly Hills, Calif.: Sage, 1976).

18. Black and Black, *Politics and Society in the South*.

19. Sandra Baxter and Marjorie Lansing, *Women and Politics* (Ann Arbor, Mich.: U. Of Michigan Press; Kathleen Frankovic, "Sex and Politics—New Alignments, Old Issues," *PS* 3 (1982): 439–49.

20. Daniel Wirls, "Reinterpreting the Gender Gap," *Public Opinion Quarterly* 50 (1986): 316–30.

21. One consequence of our separation of voters and nonvoters should be a reinvigoration of interest in citizen turnout. It is quite possible, for example, that some portion of the apparent pro-Republican swing among Southern, nonblack,

male voters in the 1980s may have been caused by declining turnout among Southern, nonblack *Democratic* males rather than by pro-Republican conversions within a constant, unchanging population of voters.

22. Warren E. Miller, "The Electorate's View of the Parties" in Sandy Maisel, ed., *The Parties Respond* (Boulder, Colo.: Westview Press, 1990).

23. Arthur H. Miller, Warren E. Miller, Alden E. Raine, and Thad D. Brown, "A Majority Party in Disarray: Policy Polarization in the 1972 Election, "*American Political Science Review* 70 (1976): 753–78.

24. Merrill J. Shanks and Warren E. Miller, "Policy Direction and Performance Evaluation: Complementary Explanations of the Reagan Election," *British Journal of Political Science* 20 (1990): 143–235.

25. Paul A. Beck, "Partisan Development in the Postwar South," *American Political Science Review* (1977): 477–96; Beck, "Realignment Begins? The Republican Surge in Florida," *American Politics Quarterly* 10 (1982): 421–38; Morris P. Fiorina, "An Outline for a Model of Party Choice," *American Political Science Review* 21 (1977): 601–25; Fiorina, *Retrospective Voting in American National Elections* (New Haven, Conn.: Yale U. Press, 1981); Markus and Converse, "A Dynamic Simultaneous Equation"; Benjamin I. Page and Calvin C. Jones, "Reciprocal Effects of Policy Performance, Party Loyalties, and the Vote," *American Political Science Review* 73 (1979): 1071–89; John R. Petrocik, *Party Coalition* (Chicago: U. of Chicago Press, 1981); Martin P. Wattenberg, *The Decline of the American Political Parties 1952–1980* (Cambridge, Mass.: Harvard U. Press, 1984); Paul F. Whiteley, "The Causal Relationships Between Issues, Candidate Evaluations, Party Identification, and Vote Choice—the View from 'Rolling Thunder,' " *Journal of Politics* 50 (1988): 961–84; William G. Jacoby, "The Impact of Party Identification on Issue Attitudes," *American Journal of Political Science* 32 (1988): 643–61.

REFERENCES

Abramson, Paul, and Charles W. Ostrom, Jr. 1991. "Macropartisanship: An Empirical Assessment." *American Political Science Review* 85:181–92.

Baxter, Sandra, and Marjorie Lansing. 1983. *Women and Politics*. Ann Arbor: U. of Michigan Press.

Beck, Paul A. 1977. "Partisan Development in the Postwar South." *American Political Science Review* 71:477–96.

Beck, Paul A. 1982. "Realignment Begins? The Republican Surge in Florida." *American Politics Quarterly* 10:421–38.

Black, Earl, and Merle Black. 1987. *Politics and Society in the South*. Cambridge: Harvard U. Press.

Brody, Richard A. 1978. "Change and Stability in the Components of Partisan Identification." Prepared for the NES Conference on Party Identification, Tallahassee, Florida.

Campbell, Angus, Philip E. Converse, Warren E. Miller, and Donald E. Stokes. 1960. *The American Voter*. New York: John Wiley & Sons.

Campbell, Bruce A. 1977a. "Change in the Southern Electorate." *American Journal of Political Science* 21:37–64.

Campbell, Bruce A. 1977b. "Patterns of Change in the Partisan Loyalties of Native Southerners: 1952–1972." *Journal of Politics* 39:730-61.

Clagget, William. 1981. "Partisan Acquisition Versus Partisan Intensity: Life Cycle, Generation and Period Effects, 1952–1976." *American Journal of Political Science* 25:193–214.

Converse, Philip E. 1963. "On the Possibility of Major Political Realignment in the South." In *Change in the Contemporary South*, Allan P. Sindler, ed. Durham, N.C.: Duke U. Press.

Converse, Philip E. 1976. *The Dynamics of Party Support: Cohort Analyzing Party Identification*. Beverly Hills, Calif.: Sage.

Converse, Philip E. and Roy Pierce. 1987. "Measuring Partisanship." *Political Methodology* 11:143-66.

Epstein, Laurily K. 1985. "The Changing Structure of Party Identification." *PS* 13:48–52.

Fiorina, Morris P. 1977. "An Outline for a Model of Party Choice." *American Journal of Political Science* 21:601–25.

Fiorina, Morris P. 1981. *Retrospective Voting in American National Elections*. New Haven, Conn.: Yale U. Press.

Frankovic, Kathleen. 1982. "Sex and Politics—New Alignments, Old Issues. *PS* 3:439–49.

Green, Donald P. and Bradley Palmquist. 1990. "Of Artifacts and Partisan Instability." *American Journal of Political Science* 34:872–902.

Jacoby, William G. 1988. "The Impact of Party Identification on Issue Attitudes." *American Journal of Political Science* 32:643–61.

Keith, E. Bruce, David B. Magleby, Candice J. Nelson, Elizabeth Orr, Mark K. Westlye, and Raymond E. Wolfinger. 1986. "The Partisan Affinities of Independent Leaners." *British Journal of Political Science* 16:155–84.

Kelley, Stanley. 1988. "Democracy and the New Deal Party System." In *Democracy and the Welfare State*, Amy Gutmann, ed. Princeton: Princeton U. Press.

Key, V. O. Jr. 1959. "Secular Realignment and the Party System." *Journal of Politics* 17:3–18.

MacKuen, Michael B., Robert S. Erikson, and James A. Stimson. 1989. "Macropartisanship." *American Political Science Review* 83:1125–43.

Markus, Gregory B. and Philip E. Converse. 1979. "A Dynamic Simultaneous Equation Model of Electoral Choice." *American Political Science Review* 73:1055–70.

Miller, Arthur H., Warren E. Miller, Alden E. Raine, and Thad D. Brown. 1976. "A Majority Party in Disarray: Policy Polarization in the 1972 Election." *American Political Science Review* 70:753–78.

Miller, Warren E. 1990. "The Electorate's View of the Parties." In *The Parties Respond*, Sandy Maisel, ed. Boulder: Westview Press.

Miller, Warren E. 1991. "Party Identification." In *Encyclopedia of American Political Parties and Elections*, Sandy Maisel, ed. New York: New York Garland Publishing, Inc.

Miller, Warren E., and Santa M. Traugott. 1989. *American National Elections Studies Data Sourcebook*. Cambridge: Harvard U. Press.

Page, Benjamin I., and Calvin C. Jones. 1979. "Reciprocal Effects of Policy Performance, Party Loyalties, and the Vote." *American Political Science Review* 73: 1071–89.

Petrocik, John R. 1981. *Party Coalitions*. Chicago: U. of Chicago Press.

Petrocik, John R. 1987. "Realignment: The South, New Party Coalitions and the Elections of 1984 and 1986." *Where's the Party?* Washington, D.C.: Center for National Policy.

Shanks, J. Merrill, and Warren E. Miller. 1990. "Policy Direction and Performance Evaluation: Complementary Explanations of the Reagan Election. *British Journal of Political Science* 20:143–235.

Shively, E. Phillips. 1979. "The Development of Party Identification Among Adults: Exploration of a Functional Model." *American Political Science Review* 73:1039–54.

Wattenberg, Martin P. 1984. *The Decline of the American Political Parties 1952–1980*. Cambridge: Harvard U. Press.

Whiteley, Paul F. 1988. "The Causal Relationships Between Issues, Candidate Evaluations, Party Identification, and Vote Choice—the View from 'Rolling Thunder.' " *Journal of Politics* 50:961–84.

Wirls, Daniel. 1986. "Reinterpreting the Gender Gap." *Public Opinion Quarterly* 50:316–30.

Wolfinger, Raymond, and Michael C. Hagen. 1985. "Republican Prospects: Southern Comfort." *Public Opinion* Oct./Nov.:8–13.

PART THREE

PARTY ORGANIZATION

Political parties are more than clusters of people who call themselves Democrats or Republicans. They are also men and women who toil behind the scenes to maintain organizations that help candidates run campaigns. Even as party identification has waned among voters (see the previous section), party organizations have grown and are now stronger than they have been.

Xandra Kayden and Eddie Mahe, in "Back from the Depths: Party Resurgence," argue that the 1960s and 1970s were rough years for American parties. Americans lost confidence in a wide range of institutions, including political parties (see also Ginsberg and Shefter, "Political Parties, Electoral Conflict, and Institutional Combat" in the first section). Yet, national party organizations coped with their new environments by fighting back. Both parties, but especially the Republicans, strengthened their national party organizations through extensive fundraising and candidate support. The Democrats have lagged considerably behind the Republicans.

Paul S. Herrnson, in "Do Parties Make a Difference? The Role of Party Organizations in Congressional Elections, " finds that congressional elections in the 1980s are not simply candidate-centered contests. The national party organizations have come to assist congressional candidates through a wide array of services, ranging from fundraising to connections to the Washington community. State and local party organizations provide polling assistance and help to mobilize the electorate. As Kayden and Mahe found, the Republican party has been far more active than the Democrats.

The party resurgence has hardly been restricted to national politics. James L. Gibson and Susan E. Scarrow, in "State and Local Party Organizations in American Politics," demonstrate a remarkable growth in state and local party organizational strength in the 1970s and 1980s. Prior to those years, many states had weak organizations for one party and many localities had no party structures at all. State and local parties were strengthened in the 1970s and 1980s, often working hand in hand. State parties took a more active role in recruiting candidates for both state and federal offices. They also provided many of the same services identified by Herrnson for national parties. Once again, Republicans have far outpaced the Democrats.

All three studies indicate that reports of the death of parties are greatly exaggerated. Even as party ties in the electorate are weaker than they were in the 1950s and 1960s, party organizations have come into their own.

BACK FROM THE DEPTHS: PARTY RESURGENCE

Xandra Kayden and Eddie Mahe, Jr.

The political parties in America reached a crisis in the late 1960s and early 1970s. It was then that political pressure tore at the traditional coalition of the Democratic party. It was then that Watergate cast such a pall on the Republican party. It was then that David Broder wrote *The Party's Over*.[1] He was not alone in describing the desperate straits into which the parties had fallen. Every election seemed to bring more evidence of party decline. Every reform effort on the part of the Democrats seemed to lead the party into a further morass of confusion and hostility.

In this chapter we will describe what happened then and how both parties addressed the crises before them. We will explain what the parties do—how that vague machinery operates in American political life— and what steps have been taken to make the parties more than they have been before. It is our view that the party system emerging in the 1980s is different than what existed before: it performs more functions than we have been accustomed to expect from the parties, and in order to perform those functions, it has dramatically increased its tasks and leadership role.

Most of our description will be about the activities of the Republican party because it is further along in organizational development, but the party resurgence is due to the efforts of both parties. The Democratic reforms, while painful at the time, were consistent with the needs of the organization to adjust itself to a changing environment and play an important role in the developing strength of the system as a whole. The activities within both parties did not go unnoticed by the other and so, while each focused on a separate problem, both benefited by the solutions found to the other's search: the Republicans became more sensitive to participation, and the Democrats began to develop different expectations about the relationship between the party and its candidates.

THE DEMOCRATIC REFORMS

Political parties are rarely staid organizations flowing smoothly from election to election. They are, after all, contesting for power and seek to benefit from the political divisions within the society. The Democrats have been more fractious than the Republicans because they are the majority party (and hence have more to fight over), and because they are composed of a coalition of groups within the population that do no necessarily share the same values and expectations. The changes the Democrats made reflected their coalitional base and the need the party had to respond equitably to groups seeking influence. The changes were directed at the core of the national party's traditional function: the selection of the presidential nominee.

THE HISTORY

The first strains, which appeared in the 1950s, were over questions of civil rights. Black and white liberals expected more because of the New Deal hopes of a better life and because of the horrors of the war, which revealed the consequences of intolerance. On the other hand, part of the coalition was drawn from conservative whites in the South who valued their supremacy and their states' right to determine their own course. The battle lines within the party were drawn on questions of qualification for the national committee and the presidential nominating convention. It reached the boiling point in 1968, when the entire Mississippi delegation and half the Georgia delegation were refused their seats at the Democratic national convention because the state parties had violated a four-year-old rule against racial discrimination.[2]

Also, 1968 was the year in which the peace movement was added to the turmoil of the civil rights movement and the lines were drawn for a major cleavage within the party. The assassinations of Martin Luther King, Jr., and Robert F. Kennedy added to the despair of many who had hoped for resolution within the party, and the division within the convention hall and the nation were reflected in the riots in the streets of Chicago. Losing the election that year forced the Democratic party to take a serious look at itself, and it began the cumbersome process of reform by creating a series of commissions, which met between the conventions and were answerable to the national committee.

THE DEMOCRATIC COMMISSIONS

There were four formal commissions between 1968 and 1982, all designed to develop rules for selecting delegates to the national presidential nominating convention (a fifth commission dealt with the convention itself). It may be one of the ironies of political life that the national party should have succeeded in altering the flow of influence and the structure of the system on the one issue in which it has all of the responsibility and almost none of the control.

During the 1968 primary period, Connecticut supporters of Senator Eugene McCarthy recognized there were no rules to prevent the strong regular party forces from giving them a fair share of representation in the state delegation to the national convention. The McCarthy campaign formed an Ad Hoc Commission on Democratic Selection of Presidential Nominees, chaired by Governor Harold Hughes of Iowa. The commission report concluded that neither the system of selecting delegates by the states, nor the procedures of the convention itself were in keeping with democratic principles and proposed a number of reforms which came in time to form the basis of the party-authorized McGovern-Fraser Commission.

A major theme of the Ad Hoc Commission was the need to include more people in the decision-making process. It was a theme that would be repeated in the next several years, and although it created a great deal of controversy, it led to the inclusion of many more women, blacks, Hispanics, and other minorities within the mainstream of the party.

MCGOVERN-FRASER

After the 1968 election, Senator Fred Harris of Oklahoma, with the support of Hubert Humphrey, was chosen as the new chairman of the Democratic National Committee (DNC). Harris, in turn, chose Senator George McGovern of South Dakota to chair a study of the 1968 presidential nominating process, the report of the Ad Hoc Commission, and make recommendations for the future. When McGovern resigned in order to run for the presidency, Representative Don Fraser of Minnesota was appointed to take his place.

According to Byron Shafer, a political scientist at the Russell Sage Foundation, the commission Harris put together amounted in the end to a replacement of the party regulars with the party reformers, some of whom had come from the reform movement of the 1950s, but most of whom came from the candidacies and issues of the 1968 presidential campaign. The recommendations of the Commission on Party Structure and Delegate Selection led to one of the most far-reaching reforms in American party politics ever instituted from the inside.[3]

At the structural level, the commission called for the codification of national standards to govern state and local parties. This was a sharp departure from the American experience of party "stratarchy," with little influence exercised from one level of party structure to another, and what leverage there was, going from the local to the national, not the other way around. From the very beginning, the focus was on participation in the process, and beyond that, on the inclusion of specific groups which were traditionally underrepresented in the party and in the decision making of society as a whole. Among the specific recommendations were the following:

- Requiring representation of women, young people, and minorities in reasonable relationship to their presence in the state's population.
- Requiring delegate candidates to identify their presidential choices.
- Prohibiting a presidential candidate or a party leader from naming individuals who would make up the slate of delegates, whether pledged to a candidate or not.
- Prohibiting ex-officio delegates.
- Requiring each step in the delegate selection process to begin in the calendar year of the convention.
- Limiting party committee selection of the delegates to 10 percent of the total delegation.[4]

The McGovern-Fraser Commission had a dramatic effect on the presidential selection process in particular and on the make-up of party activists in general, but other factors contributed in a major way to the overall changes in American presidential politics in the years to follow: the increase in the number of state primaries and caucuses (fostered in part by the reforms, and in part by the economic incentives and media attention such events generate); changes in federal campaign finance law, which placed an emphasis on small donations and centralized campaign organizations; and the technology of raising money and running for office. In 1972, however, when the reforms were put into practice, they were extraordinarily controversial and costly to the electoral coalition that constituted the base of the Democratic party. Many of the old guard, particularly organized labor, were hostile to George McGovern and his followers and deserted the party by the tens of thousands.

THE MIKULSKI COMMISSION

After the 1972 campaign, a new commission was created by the Democratic party to refine the reforms of the McGovern-Fraser Commission. It was led by Barbara Mikulski, a Maryland party leader who was later elected to Congress from Baltimore.

The Mikulski Commission relaxed some of the new requirements and was less hostile to party involvement. It allowed the state committees to select 25 percent of their delegation to the national convention, and eliminated the rule that committee members identify their presidential preferences. It also abolished winner-take-all primaries and encouraged proportional representation in caucuses and conventions in an effort to keep relatively strong candidates in the running who might not have done well in early primaries (a reform that seemed less controversial when the party did not have an incumbent president running for reelection).

THE WINOGRAD COMMISSION

Following the 1976 campaign, a third commission, named after its leader, Michigan state party chairman Morely Winograd, was established to continue refining the rules in the face of accrued electoral experience.

Whereas the 25 percent at-large portion of the state's delegation under Mikulski was designed to assure affirmative action goals, the Winograd Commission added another 10 percent to the delegation for party and elected officials. It was the first recognition that the party establishment ought to have a role, and the Winograd Commission might have ended the reform cycle except for the election of Jimmy Carter who, having won under one system, did not want to see it changed. The recommendations of this commission were, therefore, largely ignored by the national party committee run by Carter supporters.[5]

THE HUNT COMMISSION

After Carter's defeat in 1980, yet another commission on delegate selection was created under the chairmanship of North Carolina Governor James B. Hunt. The charge of this commission was to do more than refine the process, it was to try to find a way to heal the wounds inflicted on the party by years of reform battles and the antiparty attitude of the defeated president. Included in the responsibilities were a review of a recent court decision that gave greater weight to the national party in defining state rules; analyses of the mixed caucus/primary system; consideration of the number and scheduling of caucuses and primaries with an eye toward shortening the prenomination season; review of affirmative action at all levels of party activity; and again, a look at the role of the party and elected officials in the nominating process, which this time appeared to be more concerned with finding a better way to choose a leader than guaranteeing a balance of representation in the process.[6]

Losing the White House was a fate to which reforming Democrats had grown accustomed since 1968; losing control of the Senate had a chastening impact. When the Hunt Commission met for the first time, party leaders were also recovering from four years of neglect if not out-

179

right hostility from the Carter presidency. There was a strong desire for rapprochement among the factions which fell prey along the way to the demands of supporters of the leading contenders for the next presidential race—a factor that colored all of the commissions. Winning the presidency, after all, is the best guarantee of getting one's views turned into policy, so designing the process to advance the interests of one candidate over another is an inevitable part of the effort.

A "balanced" commission, such as the Hunt Commission, is found when the Kennedy interests are matched equally against the Mondale interests. The process is considered unbalanced, or at least unfair, when another candidate comes along who might have done better under another arrangement of the rules. Both Jesse Jackson and Gary Hart had cause for complaint after the 1984 primary season, each of whom would have done better under another set of rules.

Among the major changes made by the Hunt Commission were a reorganization of the primary season, making it shorter, in the hope that it would be less likely to bore the American public; and expanding the size of the state delegation once again with the creation of "super delegates" representing the party leaders and elected officials in the continuing effort to tie the selection of the president to the party in the other branches of government.

The complaint was registered after the 1984 election that the super delegates abdicated their deliberative role by declaring their candidate preferences as soon as they were named to the position, instead of waiting until the convention to assess the relative merits of the candidates and back the strongest potential nominee. Both Gary Hart and Jesse Jackson complained that Mondale would not have had the nomination "sewed up" had the super delegates not behaved so. On the other hand, if the super delegates are selected because they represent the party proper—the mainstream of party workers—it would have been very surprising if they had chosen someone other than Walter Mondale who, more than any Democratic candidate running for the nomination in 1984, represented the mainstream of the Democratic party.

Many of the reforms made by the various commissions did not have the impact on the political process their advocates would have wanted. Patrick Caddell, a leading political pollster, in a letter to fellow members of the Hunt Commission written shortly before the end of their work, made the following observations about the reform efforts:

> History instructs us on three points. One: Changes cannot be tallied in a vacuum, i.e., it is impossible to assess changes individually, each must be viewed in relation to all others and to the system as a whole. Two:

Changes are not imposed on a static system, each change also alters the behavior and performance of the entire system, normally in ways severely underestimated at the time. Three: The goals sought by changes are often and regularly undone by consequences unanticipated and unplanned and thus reformers must always be vigilant and sensitive to such possible unintended consequences.[7]

Rick Stearns, a participant in all of the Democratic commissions, drew an interesting conclusion about the impact of the reforms on the relationship between the candidates and the party in another memo to the Hunt Commission:

Curiously, simultaneously with the consolidation of its grip on the nominating process, the national party has surrendered in equal measure the actual power to enforce the purposes of its rules on the presidential candidates. While custom still requires the candidate to come to the convention in the guise of seeking its nomination, the candidate's role at the convention in fact is to enforce the rules that he or she has largely implemented. . . .

While the rules have served these purposes as well as others (most notably, insuring that the composition of the convention conforms to an aggregate ideal), they are also the source of unanticipated frictions. The most important of these is the conflict generated between the state party and the candidate in the exercise of the add-on powers. . . . While these purport to be grants of power to the state parties, in fact considerations of affirmative action on fair reflection require that the selection of add-on delegates be managed by the candidate or his agent. A second source of friction lies in the obvious inconsistency between universal binding provisions, candidate vetting of delegates, and the theory of a deliberative convention. While a deliberative convention is theoretically possible under present party rules (so long as no candidate enters the convention with a first ballot majority), the natural tendency of presidential candidates or their organizations to fill the ranks allotted to delegates with candidate loyalists, suggests instead that any second ballot deliberation would more likely be the result of negotiations among contending candidates than among delegates themselves. This result, of course, is no different from that achieved by the so-called "bossed conventions," simply fewer bosses participate in the brokering. A third source of potential friction may arise from among those who are the intended beneficiaries of the party's affirmative action rules. . . . It remains to be seen whether positions without power will long satisfy the proponents of aggregate reflection.[8]

In the decade and a half that the Democratic party sought to resolve the conflicts which so visibly beset it in 1968, it uncovered other problems. It tried excluding party regulars from the nominating process and it moved back and forth on the role of elected officials. It moved more surely toward the inclusion of those who had been underrepresented, but it tried toward the end to overcome the alienation of those who were threatened by affirmative action.

Whether or not the reforms succeeded in creating a system that will insure the selection of strong candidates, or whether they have succeeded in giving back to the national party the function of controlling the nomination of its presidential candidate, they have succeeded in making substantial changes in the make-up of Democratic party activists. Byron Shafer has called it a "quiet revolution," in which the elites "different in social background, political experience, and policy preference from the coalition which had previously dominated the national Democratic party" came to power.[9] It is a new generation—to be found in both parties—that others have described as "organizers," individuals concerned about the processes of change, who came out of the movements of the sixties, or at least out of that generation.[10]

Some might dispute Shafer's view that it was a "quiet" revolution, given the visibility in the press of the disputes within the party, but it was a revolution and it left the leadership of the Democratic party in a markedly different position in the 1980s than it had been in for some time. When Charles Manatt assumed the chairmanship of the party, after the defeat of Jimmy Carter, he brought in talented people who stayed through the next four years (there had been almost 100 percent turnover in the first two years of the Carter presidency at the DNC) and began the process of building a stronger organization based on many of the techniques used in the Republican party. One small measure of his success was his ability to withstand Mondale's effort to unseat him in the 1984 convention.

THE REPUBLICANS

While the Democrats focused their attention on organizational processes, the Republicans rebuilt their party with money and technology, although they, too, went through a major shift in political generations. Historically, the Republican party has always been better organized that its Democratic opponent. Some have attributed the stronger GOP structure to the inherent business nature of the party, others to the reliance Republican candidates have placed on the party for campaign support in contrast to the Democrats who have relied on labor to provide the organizational backbone of their campaigns thereby lessening the need for a strong party organization. The Republicans are also more homogeneous than Democrats and may, therefore, be more at ease relying on a permanent organization of like-minded people than Democrats who structure both the party and their campaigns on the basis of the separate constituencies which make up the party. The Democratic structure makes for an easy distribution of tasks, but a difficult process of communication which would weaken any organization.

The difference in focus between the two major parties appears to put the Republicans in a stronger position, but the reader should bear in mind that the contests between the parties are far more balanced than the relative party strength suggests. The Republican party outspends the Democratic party, but Democratic candidates typically outspend Republican candidates. In 1982, Democratic congressional candidates raised $91 million, compared to $85 million raised by their Republican opponents. Since much of the money is raised by incumbents who have relatively little need for it, the phenomenon of candidate political action committees (PACs) has emerged, providing a mechanism for members of Congress to support other members in the hope they will improve their internal struggles for leadership in the House or Senate or gain support for a presidential run. In addition, Democrats have nonmonetary and nonreportable contributions available to them through labor and other membership organizations around the country which provide important volunteer help.

The question to be addressed in the long run is whether or not the new Republican organizational strength will make a substantial difference, and if it does, just what that difference will be.

THE HISTORY

The GOP has gone through two major periods of change since the 1950s —our base period. The party we see today is very much a product of those changes in substance and in process: the conservative revolt in 1964; and the post-Watergate era of rebuilding. We will describe the two periods in this section and reserve the specifics of party activities for the next section.

THE 1964 ELECTION

The 1964 race for the presidency in which Barry Goldwater captured the nomination, but went down to defeat in a landslide to Lyndon Johnson, was in large part a challenge to the established leadership. It led to the same kind of transfer of leadership positions within the Republican party that Democrats were to experience a decade later. In the Republican case, western, middle-class activists replaced upper-class business and banking interests from the East. The schism was based more on geography and class than ideology, but it was fought out on an ideological ground. The resolution had to be found at the national level because of the distinct regional hostilities.

Following the election, Ray Bliss, a former state chairperson from Ohio, became the new chairperson of the Republican National Committee (RNC). Using the workers Goldwater brought into the party, Bliss began the process of rebuilding by focusing on national fund raising, local party structure, and a professional, full-time leadership at the top. Wary of the divisiveness on issues, Bliss avoided policy positions by deferring to the Republican congressional delegation.

Beginning in 1965, the RNC began its direct mail fund raising program based on the Goldwater lists. Until then, the national committee had been funded by assessments made on the states—yet one more reason for state dominance of the national parties which has fallen away with the redirection of the flow of funds. By the time Rogers Morton succeeded Bliss, the finance committee responsible for raising state money had all but disappeared from the RNC structure.

It is more than likely that no one in the early years, including Bliss, understood the difference between the new generation of activists and the older one. James Q. Wilson published *The Amateur Democrat* in 1962, which was about a generational shift in the Democratic party, but the Republican shift came later and scholarship often takes awhile to become accepted in any case. The new generation of Republicans, like their Democratic counterparts, were motivated more by ideological considerations and less by expectations of the material rewards that had been important to their predecessors. Over time, it led both parties to greater cohesion on issues among the activists, but at a cost to the heterogeneity of the membership. At the time, the latter half of the 1960s, the shift at the local level occurred quite rapidly, although the national leadership was not completely aware of it. The value to the party was the tremendous support it was able to provide Richard Nixon's candidacy in 1968, helped even more by the disarray among the Democrats.

THE WATERGATE ERA

The second crisis faced by the Republican party is often calculated to have occurred in 1974 when the party tried to survive the scandals of Watergate and ended up losing forty-seven incumbents. In all likelihood, however, the position of the national party reach crisis proportions in 1972 when it was completely subordinated to the White House and the Committee to Re-Elect the President. Nixon's distance from the party was partly reflected in the re-election effort aimed at achieving 60 percent of the vote. In order to achieve their targeted vote count, they would have to attract a large number of Democrats and independents, and for that reason, none of the campaign material published by the Nixon-Agnew campaign carried the word "Republican" or the elephant symbol (a tactic that actually has been employed by both sides from time to time, depending on the popularity of the party or the party's presidential nominee).

The national party was also ordered by the president's people to stay out of the re-election bids of approximately three dozen Democratic congressmen who had been supportive of Nixon. Although these House elections may not have been winnable by the GOP, the party's lack of support for Republican opponents certainly contributed to the lack of any coattail effect in Nixon's victory, which was the most overwhelming since Johnson's election in 1964.

In a study undertaken for the RNC by pollster Robert Teeter, he concluded that the Republican party bore a stronger resemblance to a minor party in the rest of the world than it did to a minority party in the American two-party system. That the GOP did not disappear entirely was, however, probably due to the two-party structure and the lack of an alternative. Most, if not all, of the Republican and conservative activists participating in politics since the Goldwater years had no place to go.

Mary Louise Smith became the RNC chairperson during the Ford presidency, and the party once again turned to rebuilding. Given the clear objective of winning back a respectable portion of voter support, there was an era of good feeling within the party until late in 1975 when Ronald Reagan announced his candidacy against President Ford. It may be that the division with the GOP in the contest for the presidency freed it from being entirely usurped by the presidential campaign of 1976, as it had been in 1972, and enabled it to address itself to other elections. For the first time, the national committee moved directly into campaigning to overcome the tremendous electoral losses of the 1974 elections.

Building on the efforts begun in 1964 to create a reasonably secure and loyal group of small donors, the RNC was probably the only party entity with a financial base, a surprising strength given the revelations about large donations to Nixon's re-election campaign and the subsequent Watergate scandals. In 1975, the RNC had approximately 300,000 on its mailing list, and the Congressional Committee had 25,000 (the Senate Committee had not yet moved to direct mail). With a gross budget of $9 million for the RNC in 1973-74, $4.5 to $5 million was directed into political activity at the congressional and gubernatorial levels. The Congressional Committee's budget was $2.3 million that year, which they cut to $1.7 million when only $200,000 had been raised in the first six months of the year.[11]

It may bear mentioning at this point that there is a major difference between Republican and Democratic party spending on behalf of their candidates. Republicans, in deference to their minority party standing, devote much of their resources to recruiting candidates and funding challengers. Democrats direct most of their resources to incumbents, not a surprising policy given the fact that it is the incumbent (not the party) who usually raises the money and does so because of his incumbency, and it is in the interest of the party to retain its numerical strength.

When William Brock succeeded Mary Louise Smith as chairperson, RNC attentions turned to state legislative as well as congressional races in preparation for the 1980 reapportionment. Although the effort was not notably successful in electoral outcomes (the Republican congressional candidates won 49.8 percent of the popular vote in the 1984 election, but picked up only 42 percent of the seats), it was an important departure for the national party and it generated and supported a cadre of professionally-trained, sophisticated campaign workers and candidates around the country. It was under Brock's leadership that the party made massive strides in income (Table 8.1).

Throughout the latter half of the 1970s, 75 percent of the income came from direct mail solicitations, at a cost to the party that declined to 19 percent by 1980.[12] As the party regained strength, and especially as it became electorally competitive in the Senate and for the White House, its large donor program also increased from 198 $10,000 donors in 1978, to 865 such donors in 1980.

The spending disparities between the two parties grew significantly in the same period: In the 1977-78 electoral period, the Republicans spent $85.9 million compared to $26.9 million by the Democrats. In 1979-80, Republican spending increased to $161.8 million, to $35 million by Democrats, and in the 1981-82 election, the Republicans spent $213.9 million to $40 million by the Democrats.[13] Although, as we have already noted, party spending is not synonymous with total election spending, and there was much more parity between the candidates, the dramatic surge in Republican fund raising was bound to have an effect on party's behavior and, possibly, on its strength in the long run.

THE CHANGES

The financial growth of the Republican National Committee required decisions about what to do with the new resources, many of them made under Brock's tenure as RNC chairperson. Some of the new activities of the party were organizational in nature, such as the creation of issue task forces, which brought together representatives from the spectrum of Re-

Table 8.1 Republican Gross Income (in Millions)

1974	1975	1976	1977	1978	1979	1980
$6.3	$8.9	$19	$10.7	$14.5	$17	$37

Source: From "Chairman's Report," 1978, 1979 (Washington, D.C.: Republican National Committee).

publican opinion and charged them with reaching a consensus. Some were technological. Not everything worked, but the party had the opportunity to learn from the experience. So, too, did the Democrats who emulated many of the Republican innovations as their candidates began calling for the same kinds of services Republican opponents were receiving. As Martin Schram noted in an article entitled "Why Can't the Democrats Be More Like the Republicans? They're Trying," published in the *Washington Post* in the spring of 1982,

> One of Brock's first GOP creations was a program to attract young community leaders to Republicanism; he called it the "Concord Program." One of Manatt's first creations was a similar program for the Democrats. He called in the "Lexington Program."
> Today the Democrats are awash in Republican-style task forces and targeting committees, strategy councils and study groups, programs for recruitment and programs for direct mail fund raising—and workshops where they tell each other how to put it all together.[14]

THE ORGANIZATIONAL CHANGES

STAFFING

The focus on participation in campaigns was not a surprising reaction given the losses sustained by the Republican party in 1974. Under Brock, the party continued to direct its resources to campaigns instead of supporting local party organizations. Proven political professionals were hired to travel the states running seminars and offering advice. The National Committee paid for professional staff positions at the state level and tried employing regional directors, responsible for a group of states. Today, the regional directors have control over a wide array of resources with supporting staff in press, communications, and politics. There are now nearly a hundred people on the RNC staff with regional responsibilities.

When Brock's chairmanship ended with the Reagan election in 1980, he was succeeded by Dick Richards, who shifted the focus from campaign support to local party building, leaving most of the campaign work to the other two national Republican committees in the House and Senate. The growth of both of these committees has reached the stage where they are able to provide all of their candidates with the maximum amount of money allowed by the law, and an extraordinary array of campaign services which do not come under federal restrictions, such as advice on PAC fund raising, research, assistance in setting up direct mail and telephone bank services, polling data, and so on.

ISSUES

One departure in the rebuilding effort under Brock was to focus on issues through the use of task forces to develop a party agenda and the publication of a quarterly journal entitled *Common Sense*, which became a vehicle for developing and exploring Republican ideas. In time, the issue research done by the party almost completely replaced much of that function in Republican campaigns. The capacity of the party to maintain records on election districts and opponents, to do sophisticated voter analyses, and to develop and present policy positions would be hard for a campaign to match. The first step in research on any given topic for a campaign issue committee would be to contact the national party. It may not be a sufficient step for some campaigns, but has become a building block.

The Republican task forces were a marked contrast in style from the Democratic issues conventions. What they may have lacked in visibility, they more than made up for in their capacity to build some measure of consensus. It is very hard, indeed, to reach a compromise with the public eye so finely focused and the constituencies back home so carefully attuned. The views developed by the party this way are not apt to meet the demands of its constituent members, but they do seem to suffice for the party.

ADVERTISING

Another departure for the national party, copied from the Conservative party in England, is what is known as "genre" advertising—media advertising that advocates the party and is not tied to a candidate. The low percentage of Republican identifiers in the post-Watergate years made such an effort especially appealing, and their ads have been among the most sophisticated and memorable in recent campaign advertising history.

The GOP began this institutional advertising in 1978, when the polls showed that any candidate for office labeled Republican started out 10 to 12 points behind in the polls automatically. The advertising campaign was designed to make Republicans feel better about being Republican, and to influence the large number of independents, particularly those in the baby boom generation, calculated to number about 75 million.

In 1980, the party spent $9 million with a series of ads running in four or five waves promoting the theme "Vote Republican. For a Change." The most effective ad depicted a Tip O'Neill look-alike in a large limousine running out of gas. The party credits the ads with an increase of 3 or 4 percentage points for their congressional candidates across the board.

In 1982, having won the White House and control of the Senate, the ads took a more defensive tone and urged voters to "Stay the Course." Again, the party credits the ads with keeping mid-term congressional losses down. the GOP lost twenty-six seats that year, instead of the forty-one or forty-two they expected to lose.

In the 1984 campaign, Mondale's pledge to raise taxes provided the theme for the party ads, and from late August on through the election, Republican party ads played on the prospect of increases taxes. The most successful ad in the series showed a group of people in an elevator with a Democratic congressman who was asked if he intended to support Mondale's tax plan. The party spent about $13 million on their genre advertising, expanding beyond television to radio and several *Reader's Digest* ads as well.[15]

Chairperson Brock noted in 1980, "There was a time just a few years ago when many people said there wasn't a dime's worth of difference between Republicans and Democratics. Our position on issues wasn't clearly defined, and most voters [who were angered or disappointed by the Republicans] felt that there was no real difference between the two parties."[16] The ads were designed to clarify the differences and to promote a positive attitude toward the GOP and a negative attitude toward the Democrats.

The Democratic party adopted the use of genre advertising as a counter measure, although it has not yet been able to put the funds into it that the three national Republican committees have to date. One Democratic ad played on a Republican ad from 1980. In the original Republican ad, a worker was shown talking about wanting a change. The Democratic follow-up showed the same worker saying that he had made a mistake and was speaking on behalf of the Democrats on his own, without getting paid for it.

CANDIDATE SUPPORT IN PRIMARIES

Under Brock, the Republican National Committee also began intervening in state primaries. It was a logical extension of the candidate recruitment program in which the party assured its prospect that it would provide as much support as possible. The national party entered into this area cautiously—and not always successfully, such as the time it supported a candidate for governor of Wisconsin who lost in the primary to Lee Sherman Dreyfus. Dreyfus went on to win the general election in 1978 and never did establish strong ties to the established Republican party. This departure into the primaries is a major step forward in recapturing control of one of a political party's most important functions: the control of its nominations.

Theoretically, it is possible for a national committee (more likely the House or Senate campaign committees) to support their own candidate, without regard to the partisan line-up in the state. It is not likely to be a common occurrence, but could, for instance, happen in a special election in the South where state law may call for a nonpartisan election.

In 1980, there was a party rules change—Rule 26 (f)—which limits the participation of the Republican National Committee to those instances approved by the state party chairperson and the national committee persons from the state. The congressional and Senate campaign committees are not affected by the limitations and continue to support candidates they believe to be most likely to win a general election. The Senate Campaign Committee, for instance, supported the moderate Elliot Richardson for the Senate nomination in Massachusetts in 1984, against a candidate who came out of the ranks of the more dominant conservative state party organization. Ray Shamie swamped Richardson in the primary election but ran far behind the Democratic nominee in the general election, as the national party committee would have predicted.

Primaries were designed to democratize the political process and eliminate the influence of party bosses as much as possible. Those who vote in primaries tend to be more active and committed party identifiers. Although federal law prohibits a party from behaving differently than a nonparty committee in primary contests for federal office (that is, for instance, contributing no more than $5,000), the legitimacy of party endorsement carries great weight among the party faithful. The non-monetary contributions the party can make can be extensive, however. In the fall of 1983, the Republican Senatorial Committee sent out staff people to oversee the research, fund raising, polling, and telephone bank efforts in a special election in the state of Washington to fill the seat held by Senator Henry Jackson. The party also helped its candidate, former governor Dan Evans, get PAC funds.

On the odd occasion when the unendorsed candidate has won, it has meant some embarrassment and required some fence mending for the party establishment, but on the whole the intention has been to assure the strongest possible candidate for the GOP in those critical elections in which it has chosen to participate.

By 1978, 46 percent of the RNC expenditures were devoted to campaign support, divided equally between candidates for federal office and candidates for state and local office. Thirteen percent of the party resources were devoted to party development, and 12 percent to communications.[17] It was not until the 1980 election that the national party began to encourage grassroots participation by volunteers; until then the emphasis had been on professionalism and centrally-based decisions on whom to support and how to do it. The organization was designed to meet those objectives.

THE TECHNOLOGICAL CHANGES

The changes we would include in this discussion include the application of computer technology in fund raising, research, communications, and general campaigning; and the growing use of electronic media for training and communication with party activists and the electorate at large.

THE COMPUTERIZATION OF POLITICS

The extraordinary changes computers have made in American life have also been felt in politics in general and in the Republican party particularly because it has had the resources to invest in the new technology. By 1984, the congressional and the Senate campaign committees were so completely computerized that employees gave up writing memos and instead communicated with each other through the computer, whether in the office or on the road.

The benefits of electronic mail in campaigns can be profound. A staff member working in a campaign in a western state can, for instance, end the day with a campaign meeting at 9:00 in the evening, send in a report with questions and problems to the national office, and come into work the next day to find the questions answered because the Washington staff has had a three hour headstart on it.

Among the most important use of computers for the party itself has been the development of a series of sophisticated data processing systems, either based in Washington and made available to Republican state parties at low user rates, or through mini and personal computers. The programs provide for accounting and reporting, political targeting and survey processing, mailing list maintenance, donor preservation and information, and correspondence and word processing.[18]

REACHING THE VOTER

Perhaps the most important inroad of computerization is the capacity it provides for refining the communication that comes from the party. Messages can be targeted according to socioeconomic status, pulling the political and census geography together in a method called "digitizing." There are now three major firms with household lists (Donnelly, Metromail, and Polk) which include every household in the country with a listed telephone. The codes can identify households by specific census tracks or block groups and correlate them with relevant political information. The California Republican party, for example, is able to send out a mailing to all the residents in precincts that voted over 60 percent for Reagan in 1984, with an average age of over forty-five, in houses costing over $100,000, who have lived there for more than five years. Other state and some county parties are expected to gain that capacity in the next several years.

Until recently, there have been two kinds of lists used in direct mail solicitations: those bought from other sources (magazine, contributors to other causes, buyers of Ruby Red Grapefruit—the most "fruitful"—and other catalogs); and lists made up of party regulars. Mailing to lists of party registrants is usually a losing proposition unless the lists are correlated with other socioeconomic status (SES) data—a possibility existing only since the 1980 census. The capacity the technology provides to reach the right person with the right message opens tremendous possibilities in party communication.

In addition to fund raising, computers have also become powerful tools in communication for direct campaign activity. Historically, campaign lists came from church memberships, members of local organizations, and so forth, but each of the lists were ad hoc in nature and fairly expensive to manipulate on a reliable basis. The files now in process of being created will give the party a master list of over 500,000 voters in New Mexico, for example, which would be accessible by election districts for state representative. Such a list would include registered Democrats in the district who, when canvassed by telephone, said they would be willing to vote Republican, at least at the top of the ticket. King County, Washington has a refined list of voting behavior for 2,300 precincts.

Personal computers will carry the technological revolution even further—possibly even beyond the party because of the capacity of computer software firms to develop programs designed specifically for politics. By 1984, there were already fourteen firms selling software for personal computer campaigns. Although we think it is unlikely such firms will every seriously challenge the capacity of the party to maintain the lists, that possibility does exist.

DIRECT MAIL

Although the use of direct mail solicitations in politics is controversial because of its application by single issue groups and the new strength it
has given them, it has come to play an important part of party building
and maintenance since it was first used in the 1964 Goldwater campaign.
The next successful use was by the Democrats in 1972 with the
McGovern campaign, and it was not until a few years after that the Republican National Committee made it the linchpin of its fund raising
strategy.

By 1978, the year the direct mail dividends really took off for the
RNC, it had a base of 511,638 contributors, 58 percent of whom gave under $25.[19] In 1981, the first year of the Reagan administration, 77 percent
of RNC funds came through the mail (with an additional 2 percent coming from telephone solicitations of those who had contributed through
the mail in the past but had fallen off recently).[20] Of course, having the
White House and the Senate also enable the party to increase its large
donor programs which amounted in 1981 to 20 percent total RNC income.[21] Still, the average contribution to the Republican party is under
$30. In 1985, the party expects to be able to send mail to one out of every
four households in the country.

Direct mail solicitations in American politics are generally based on
negative appeals: urging the donor to return the envelope because he or
she is angry about something. They are generally issue appeals, although issues can (and often do) include individuals, such as the RNC's
successful appeal opposing Carter's U.N. Ambassador Andrew Young.
Both parties (and a number of interest groups as well) made millions opposing and supporting Reagan's first Secretary of the Department of the
Interior, James Watt. Party appeals seem to be most successful when they
do not come in conflict with existing constituencies on the issues they
are opposing: The RNC made money opposing the Panama Canal
Treaty, the Democratic party did better opposing Reagan's proposed social security cuts than it did on environmental issues or the ERA (the fact
that the social security appeal went out in a brown envelope bearing a
strong resemblance to the mail which typically comes from the Social Security Administration was an interesting, albeit somewhat controversial,
element in its success in the eyes of many direct mail specialists).

Because the Republicans controlled the administration, and for a
while the Senate, the appeals require a certain amount of creativity to
convince potential donors that there is a danger. In 1983, an airmail appeal was sent on the letterhead of the Hotel George V in Paris (mailed in
England). The message was that the party leader sending the note could
almost smell the tear gas as Parisians rose up in protest against the poli-

cies of the socialist government of François Mitterand. If Republicans were not vigilant enough, the same thing could happen in America.

The most successful appeals include something besides the dire warning. Appeals for a special purpose, such as enabling the party to mount a television advertising campaign, usually work. A membership card to the party proper, or some special group within the party, is usually effective for both parties. The Republican Christmas card in 1984 included a smaller Christmas card to be mailed back to the Reagans (with a donation to help carry on the work).

COMPUTER FEEDS TO CANDIDATES

Communication to supporters through the mails has raised money and educated Republican voters to the party's positions on issues, but a more intensive program of weekly computer feeds to candidates and party leaders has gone even further in developing a party line on issues. As it gets closer to the election, the frequency of the communication increases to up to five times a week. Each feed covers one issue and presents a speech outline, a possible press release, and is designed to help Republican candidates handle critical questions about the day's events and the administration's role in them. Those candidates who are elected to office will come to Washington with a common history on positions on a wide range of issues—positions written by professional party staffers. The program began in 1982 and has been refined and increased in subsequent elections. When the GOP loses the White House, it may lead to a far more homogeneous policy position and a far more critical role of the party in defining it.

RESEARCH

Although it used to be the case that campaign research was an activity designed to occupy volunteers more than to generate important information for the campaign, the field has grown far more important in recent years with the application of market research techniques and the capacity to synthesize and communicate vast amounts of information.

One critical departure made possible by the increased funds has been the greater application of tracking (retesting of poll respondents on a frequent basis). A classic example pointed to by Republican professionals was the 1982 Senate race in Missouri. John Danforth, the Republican incumbent, planned to run a positive campaign on his record. His opponent, state Senator Harriet Woods (who herself came out of a media background), ran a surprisingly effective negative campaign against him, pointing to his being one of the richest men in the Senate. In the last few weeks of the election, the polls showed them about even. She ran out of money, however, and had to draw her ads for a week, but what the Republicans felt was the critical factor was their decision to run a more negative campaign against her—and their certainty they were right because of the tracking that showed the new campaign to be working. Danforth won re-election with one of the closest margins of victory in the country that year: 51 to 49 percent.

Data gathering has become an important role for the national party committees. The RNC monitors all newspapers, magazines, and broadcast networks, providing synopses to candidates and party leaders. The House campaign committee has the most comprehensive record of C-Span tapes (video recording of Congressional business) since the House began broadcasting. The House itself keeps tapes for only sixty days and the Library of Congress keeps audio tapes, but with the tacit agreement of both parties that the tapes will not be used. With the recent application of computer technology, the national party has also begun to maintain substantial records on opposition candidates: their votes, their speeches, any public utterance by them or about them. Its data base and retrieval systems are probably the most comprehensive in the country for a political organization.

What used to be known as "targets of opportunity," that is, examples of opponents engaging in what might be considered negative activities (voting the wrong way, and so on), have become far more sophisticated. The party can now provide information that Senator X failed to show up at a committee hearing, which consequently failed to get a quorum, which consequently failed to send out important legislation—and it was all the senator's fault.

One of the more effective advertising ploys in recent years are videotapes of opponents "shooting themselves in the foot." In 1984, Democratic Senator Carl Levin from Michigan was able to run an ad showing his opponent speaking to employees of the Toyota Company in Japan, telling them that he had a Toyota at home. The Levin campaign did not get the tape directly from the party, but it stands to reason that the permanent party organization is better able to retain and catalogue such moments than any other participant in the electoral process.

Most research expenditures are exempt from limitations imposed by the federal campaign finance law. The exception is survey research, which can be sold after fifteen days to a campaign at 50 percent of cost, and after sixty days at 5 percent of cost. Some things can be told about a campaign immediately if it is somewhat veiled: Your share of support is more than a third, but less than a half; your stand on position "X" is rated favorably by about half the voters; and so on.

Since both the House and Senate Republican Campaign Committees have now reached the stage where they can fund all of their candidates to the maximum allowed under the law—and they continue to raise additional money—the "excess" will increasingly be put into "soft" money programs such as research and genre advertising. According to staff sources, in the 1983-84 cycle, the Senate Committee raised $90 million, spent $25 million, paid off a $3.5 million debt, and after covering overhead expense, put $6 million aside for the next election period. That sort of planning is just about unheard of in American party politics.

TELEVISION

Although the Democrats now have the most sophisticated television capacity in Washington, the GOP has been exploring and expanding the use of video taping, cable, and other television vehicles to reach its own leadership around the country. Training candidates, explaining new programs, bringing selected persons into closed circuit communication with party leaders, and providing video opportunities for elected officials so that they can communicate with the voters at home are the most typical applications. The satellite facilities available to the Republicans enable them to "get the message" home almost immediately.

The power of the television medium assures it a continuing and growing role in American political life, matched only by the computer. There are, for instance, currently ten cable networks that accept local advertising, and it matters to political advertisers who watches USFL football and who watches tennis. A message about crime would be couched differently to the golf and tennis set, to those watching CPN and religious network programming, and to those who watch USFL and the Nashville network. The issue would be the same—the language and the appeal would be different.

Targeting audiences is hardly new; it has been the basis of all television advertising for many years. Political advertising has benefited from the experience and sophisticated market research of general advertisers who know, for instance, that the fans of "As the World Turns" on one channel may watch the local news on another channel. The message can be the same; it is just the rates that change.

Another wrinkle in the field of political advertising has been the development of a methodology which enables political spots to be pretested in a day or two, instead of the commercial market research method which can take as much as thirty days. Along with tracking, focus groups have been increasingly used by both sides (groups of eight or nine "real" people brought together to view an ad or discuss the campaign in depth). That capacity to learn more in depth about reactions—

reaching the point where pollsters used rheostats to sample reactions during the 1984 presidential debates—along with the refinements in market segmentation have increased the use of television and, incidentally, been a major factor in the increase of campaign costs.

The Mondale/Ferraro campaign, in order to cut some of those costs, did away with testing in the latter phase of the campaign, relying instead on their intensive polling to tell them what message would be successful —for example, the Star Wars issue which came out of the debates. In the days preceding the second debate on foreign policy, the Mondale campaign ran a series of ads focusing on the message of Reagan's weaknesses they expected to get across during the debate. Republican tracking showed them that the message was having a negative effect and was, in fact, costing Mondale support among people who did not want to see Reagan attacked.

The Reagan/Bush campaign, on the other hand, did extensive testing on an ad showing a bear wandering through the woods. The ad was beautifully photographed and very sophisticated. The test showed that only a third of those who saw it understood it was a Republican political ad before the tag line at the end identifying it as paid for by the Reagan/ Bush campaign, and then only another 20 percent understood it. In its favor, aside from pleasure the professionals took in its sophistication, it tested highest in recall and guaranteed it would be talked about for days after it was seen. It was so memorable, in fact, that Garry Trudeau did a take-off on the ad in Doonesbury three weeks after the election.

TECHNICAL SERVICES

The business of politics in the 1980s bears very little resemblance to itself in the decades before. The technological changes have been matched by the changes in law and in the expectations of the American electorate about how politics ought to be run. Federal, and often state, requirements place a tremendous emphasis on accounting. The party can and does ease the burden of campaigns by providing advice, computer programs, and computer access to handle the work. During the 1980 election, the party computer staff wrote about 700 programs, processed more than 130 surveys for candidates, plus 5 national surveys, and handled more than 20 million names and addresses for voter registration and get-out-the-vote activities. It also surveyed data from 175,000 precincts in the country, combining the analysis with other relevant electoral data for the benefit of Republican candidates.[22] The services provided in 1984 were even more extensive, particularly at the county level where the national party was focusing much of its party rebuilding efforts.

THE CASE FOR RESURGENCE

During the 1970s, three things changed in American politics: the technology; the passage of complex federal campaign finance law; and the emergence of political action committees which institutionalized interests in American politics and, to some extent, fostered the growth of significance of ideology. We will...[conclude] this chapter with an analysis of what the activities and processes we have described add up to for the party system.

THE ACTIVISTS

The active membership of both parties has changed in the past two decades. There is a new generation of actors, tuned to the values and expectations of today's political society. There will always be a need for generational change in the parties, and in politics, if the system is to remain healthy, but the characteristic that most distinguishes this generation from its predecessors is its interest in organization. Individuals within it have been touched from time to time with the passions of the years past and committed themselves to charismatic candidates and controversial issues, but they have been tempered by the disappointments of our time, and today, they tend to be more distant, more task-oriented, more professional. How much they represent the voters within their parties remains to be seen—in all probability they are (as always) more conservative or more liberal than their respective Republican and Democratic constituents—but their ideology is usually subordinate to their desire to win.

Both party staffs are better educated and more professional than those who used to fill party positions. The Republican staffs at both the national and the state levels are much larger than their Democratic counterparts, but the most important difference is not the quantitative but the qualitative difference between who is there now and who was there before.

One reason the Democratic staff appears much smaller is because it contracts out much of the work the Republicans do in-house, such as its direct mail campaigning. It is not a surprising difference given the traditional reliance Democrats have put on campaigns compared to Republican reliance on their party for campaign support. Nonetheless, the field of campaign consulting, which has grown dramatically in recent years, is just another reflection of the need of politicians to run for office with professional help. A good number of the consultants received their training in the party and then moved on to set up their own firms, helped along by party contacts and, in many cases, party urging that the candidate hire a consultant to oversee the campaign. Recently, however, the party has begun helping candidates avoid overcharging by consultants, by providing information about rates and so on.

Professionalization usually means that standards of behavior have been inculcated in the practitioner, that he or she is judged by peers, and that there is some formal process of accreditation to which the practitioner must submit himself. For our purposes, the professionalization of politics means that campaigns will become more homogenized, perhaps more nationalized. They will employ the same techniques, they will focus on those aspects of technical development which will advance the field: for example, new approaches to selling the candidate. Political scientist Larry Sabato cited former presidential candidate Milton Schapp's comment that he was "not trying to buy the election; I'm trying to sell myself!"[23] The selling will become more sophisticated, which may not be a bad thing. In itself that does not mean the candidates sold will be better or worse, but we would argue that the more candidates are selected by the professionals, the more likely they are to be worth selling because another standard by which the professionals will judge each other is the quality of the candidate and whether or not they win. This is particularly true of the professionals within the parties, as opposed to the private consultants, because they have a longer-range perspective and a closer body of supervisors.

The professionalization of the parties, and of politics in general, is a cause and effect of a different system of rewards. What distinguishes the professionals from their forbearers in party politics is a different set of rules of behavior, a different expectation of the spoils of victory. What distinguishes the professionals from the nonprofessionals is an understanding of the modern technology of campaigning and the intricacies of the law which effect the way money is raised and the distribution of campaign resources. What has not changed is the fact that each election is a choice that the voters must make based on the information the campaigns provide. Who provides the information (whether amateur or professional) is not as critical as the substance of what is said.

There is something of a cultural gulf existing between the professionals in both parties and many of the volunteers at the local level. One party worker described it as drawn between the wool vested and the polyester crowd. The fact that young people come out from Washington carrying the certainty that they know the answers, along with the fact that those they have come to counsel have often participated in politics for many years, adds up to resistance about turf, more than about questions of winning. It is the conflict of class and generation. It is the kind of conflict that has characterized the change in all organizations as they move from one era to another.

THE RESOURCES

In the two years preceding the 1984 election, the Republican party raised $225.4 million, almost four times the $57.3 raised by the Democrats in the same time period. The balance was an improvement for the Democrats who had been out-financed by five or six times in previous elections.[24] The Republicans continued to raise more money from individuals (five and a half times the Democratic proportion of individual contributions), but the Democrats raised four times the proportion of PAC funds, which are still a small, albeit growing proportion of party funding.[25]

The amount of money is phenomenal in its own right, especially if one considers that national party funds used to come entirely from the states in the form of assessments on the state committees. The amount of money is probably phenomenal for many reasons, but at the very least it is a measure of the financial strength of both parties at the national level. Money is not all that matters, even with that oft-quoted comment of California politician Jess Unruh that "money is the mother's milk of politics." It is an indication of well-being, and it is a first step toward the resurgence of party organization.

The fact that the Republicans have raised so much money has been widely noted for several years. For many political observers, the big question was whether or not the Democrats could ever catch up. David Adamany, President of Wayne State University, for instance, has argued that the base of the Democratic party will never yield the same financial results the Republican base has. According to Adamany:

> Contributing to politics is disproportionately an activity of the well educated, higher-income groups and of those who engage in other political activities as well. These groups are primarily Republican....A further complication for the Democrats is the ideological division within the party. Givers...[are] much more liberal than the Democratic electorate. Since mass-mail appeals appear to be most successful when pitched to ideological groups, the Democrats may find responses to their mass-mail fund raising largely limited to the party's liberal wing, the smallest ideological group in population....The Democrats draw the support of a vast majority of the nation's liberal activists, but the party is so diverse that it includes important groups of moderates and conservatives as well. It would therefore risk alienating important constituencies if it pitched its financial appeals to one ideological group within the party coalition.[26]

200

Only time will tell, but it should be noted that both parties have traditionally directed their fund raising to their more ideological wings: Republicans appealing to the more conservative; Democrats relying on the liberals. Even if liberals are the smallest ideological segment of the population, they are still large enough to fund a national party. As it happens, however, the party began expanding its contribution base to the rest of the Democratic constituency in 1981, reaching out to older voters on social security and prospecting many younger voters on a variety of non-ideological issues with the sophisticated technology now available. The Democrats expected to catch up by 1988; certainly the potential base is there in the population among party identifiers.

The balance of party fund raising in the 1984 election does not make our case, but it does suggest the possibility that the Democrats will catch up. The rate of financial growth within the Democratic party is tied to three factors: the kind of fund raising it relies upon; the politics of the day; and the balance of power between the parties in the elective branches of government.

The Democrats began a serious shift to direct mail fund raising only after the 1980 election. The GOP began more than a decade before that, but began to see returns only several elections later. The large donors on whom the Democrats have relied since the Kennedy administration have been seriously circumscribed by the laws, and to some extent, by the loss of powerful incumbents in the White House and Senate. The shift to small donors is probably a necessity but a process which takes time and is not dependent on holding office. The argument could be made that the party out of power does better at direct mail solicitation because it has a more identifiable need to raise money. The fact that the GOP continued to out raise the Democrats once it regained the presidency is probably due more to the greater strength and sophistication of its list than to the fact of incumbency. It will take several elections for the Democrats to refine their lists and to train their donors to give to the party instead of the campaigns. Much of the perceived imbalance, after all, is due to the Democratic tendency to give to candidates rather than to the party which does make the elections, if not the party organizations, at least, more equitable.

HISTORICAL INEVITABILITY

Cornelius Cotter and John Bibby wrote an interesting article several years ago entitled "Institutional Development of Parties and the Thesis of Party Decline."[27] Their thesis was that American political parties tend to counterorganize, a thesis originally developed by V. O. Key, but applied in this instance to the national parties and their organizational structure. The theory is that if one party in a state is strong, the other will be strong; if one party dominates, it will be broken into factions, with the minor party behaving as another faction. One of the best examples of a strong party state is Indiana, in which both parties operate with a high degree of sophistication and skill, due in large part to the 2 percent kickback to the party permitted by those receiving patronage. On the lower end of the scale, the dominance of the Democratic party in the South has usually been described as a system of factions, in which the Republican party (until recently) participates as another faction. The new organizational strength of the GOP in the South has forced Democratic state parties to make changes, to offer more to their candidates, and to try to emulate in many instances what the opponents are doing.

At the national level, Cotter and Bibby point to the history of the development of national party committees and to the support structure behind them. Typically, it is the Republicans who take the lead in organizational development with a lag of eight to twelve years (depending on when the Democrats lose the White House) before the Democrats catch up. If these political scientists are correct, the current imbalance between the Republicans and Democrats is characteristic of the lag time.

Perhaps the most important element in party balance is the nature of a two-party system. Whether the organizations are strong or weak, sophisticated or primitive, if the party out of power has a chance of replacing the party in power, it will never fall too far behind. It is the balance of power that assures equity in the equation, not the balance of structure, or even the balance of assets.

But the assets have grown, and the structure has changed accordingly. In the long run, the resurgence of the parties depends on their ability to capture the functions parties ideally possess: control of nominations; control of party resources in elections; influencing public policy; and as a vehicle for drawing individuals into the political culture.

The resources the national party can mass and distribute today cannot be matched by any other actor in the political process because of the restrictions the campaign finance law imposes, if for no other reason. It would be difficult for anyone to run for statewide or federal office as a Republican today without the support of their party. It would be surprising if the same thing would not be equally true of Democrats in a few year's time. Even today, Democratic candidates for federal office are more apt to first make a trip to Washington to see party leaders about the support they can expect from the party directly and from the network of PACs the party is capable of sending their way. In the old days, the first contact might have been more likely to go to the local party chairperson if not a private campaign consultant.

Party strength may come and go in American politics, just as the generations of political activists change and reflect the needs and values of their time, but the parties have demonstrated an endurance that challenges any institution in American history. The key to their success is their linkage to power. It may be that as power shifts the parties shift, that as interest in public power waxes and wanes, parties wax and wane.

It is unlikely the parties will disappear: too much is structured around them legally and culturally. Legislatures are organized by party representation. Voters may not see their political preferences as part of their sense of identity, but they do see political actors in terms of their parties and will vote on their estimation of how those politicians/parties behave. Morton Kondracke, a political journalist, has argued that the decline in partisan identification has encouraged the parties to work harder; like the brokerage house, they are now forced to win the old-fashioned way: "They have to earn it."

> This has made elections more competitive across the country, which has made candidates more dependent on their party organization.
> No longer can a politician in the South, for example, assume victory because he is a Democrat.
> He now has to run a more sophisticated campaign, and for assistance he must turn to the party organization, rather than, as before, simply taking advantage of the party name.
> On all levels, party aid to candidates—financial and strategic—has been growing incredibly.[28]

The changes in both parties in the past two decades have been enormous. The structures, the active participants, and the world around them have been altered. The increased financial resources at the national level in both parties (and the reversal of the flow of those resources from national to state instead of the other way around) have made many things possible. It may not be sufficient in itself to change the status of the parties in the public mind—it may not be necessary to change the status—but it is the necessary first step.

NOTES

1. David S. Broder, *The Party's Over: The Failure of American Politics* (New York: Harper & Row, 1972).

2. In 1952, a Democratic national committeeman from Texas chose to support the Republican nominee, Dwight Eisenhower. The DNC refused to seat him

and the Texas State Committee went without a representative for three years until it acceded to the national party and named a more acceptable replacement. The opposite situation occurred a few years later in 1958, when the Louisiana Democratic State Committee wanted to unseat its representative to the DNC for being "soft" on civil rights. The national committee refused the state committee the right to determine qualifications for membership to the national body. Both instances were cited in Austin Ranney, *Curing the Mischiefs of Faction: Party Reform in America* (Berkeley: U. of California Press, 1975), pp. 27, 101.

3. Byron E. Shafer, *The Quiet Revolution: The Struggle for the Democratic Party and the Shaping of Post-Reform Politics* (New York: Russell Sage Foundation, 1983), pp. 41-43. The issue of balance between reformers and regulars on the commission was critical to both sides. From the perspective of one of the reformers, the full commission was divided equally between reformers and regulars, with 70 percent of the executive committee and 100 percent of the staff drawn from the ranks of the reformers.

From the perspective of the regulars, the division was slightly different: the full executive committee was seen as 64 percent reformer to 36 percent regular; the executive committee as 80 percent reform and the staff as 100 percent reform. Either way, the tilt toward the reformers had a significant impact on the party during the following decade. It was the battle line within the party until at least 1980. (Drawn from analyses by Eli Segal, a reformer, and Al Barkan, director of COPE, AFL-CIO, a representative of the regulars. Shafer, *The Quiet Revolution*, pp. 85, 95.

4. Drawn from Austin Ranney, Byron E. Shafer, Nelson Polsby, and Aaron Wildavsky, *Presidential Elections: Strategies of American Electoral Politics*, 4th ed. (New York: Charles Scribner's Sons, 1976).

5. Carol F. Casey, "The National Democratic Party" in Gerald M. Pomper, ed., *Party Renewal in America: Theory and Practice* (New York: Praeger, 1981), p. 91.

6. Charles T. Manatt, Chairman of the Democratic National Committee, "Charge to the Commission on Presidential Nomination," mimeo, 2 July 1981.

7. Patrick Caddell, unpublished memorandum, 5 February 1982, p. 2.

8. Memorandum from Rick Stearns, Technical Advisory Committee, to the Hunt Commission, re: Rules Reflections, undated.

9. Shafer, *The Quiet Revolution*, p. 7.

10. See David S. Broder, *The Changing of the Guard: Power and Leadership in America* (New York: Penguin Books, 1980); and Xandra Kayden, *Campaign Organization* (Lexington, Mass.: D. C. Heath, 1978).

11. Interview with Wyatt Stewart, Finance Director of the Republican Congressional Committee, 14 November 1984.

12. Ibid.

13. "FEC Reports Republicans Outspent Democrats by More than 5-to-1 in '82 Elections," Press Release from the Federal Election Commission, 26 April 1983.

14. Martin Schram, *The Washington Post*, 21 March 1982, p. A-2.

15. The FEC turned back a bid by Representative Tony Coelho in 1984, which argued that the advertising represented a campaign contribution and should be counted under the party contribution limitations.

16. "Chairman's Report," Republican National Committee, Washington, D.C., 1980, p. 2.

17. "Chairman's Report," Republican National Committee, Washington, D.C., 1979, p. 23.

18. Ibid.

19. Ibid.

20. "Chairman's Report," Republican National Committee, Washington, D.C., 1982, p. 32.

21. Ibid.

22. "Chairman's Report," Republican National Committee, Washington, D.C., 1981, p. 16.

23. Sabato, *The Rise of Political Consultants*, pp. 330-31.

24. FEC Report, cited in *The Sunday Globe*, 4 November 1984.

25. Ibid.

26. David Adamany, "Political Parties in the 1980 Election" in Michael S. Malbin, ed., *Money and Politics in the United States: Financing Elections in the 1980s* (Chatham, N.J.: Chatham Press and the American Enterprise Institute, 1984).

27. Cornelius P. Cotter and John F. Bibby, "Institutional Development of Parties and the Thesis of Party Decline," *Political Science Quarterly* 95 (Spring, 1980).

28. Morton Kondracke, "CPR for Political Parties," *The Washington Times*, 22 October 1984.

Do Parties Make a Difference?
The Role of Party Organizations
in Congressional Elections

Paul S. Herrnson

The last few decades comprise an era of tremendous change for American political parties. Newly enacted campaign finance laws have served as a catalyst for the growth of vast numbers of political action committees (PACs), which now compete with parties for influence over candidates and voters. Party-initiated reforms in the nomination process have restructured the roles of party organizations in candidate recruitment and selection. The emergence of a more independent and more volatile electorate has helped to bring about changes in the tactics that candidates and parties use to garner support. Finally, technological innovations developed in the field of public relations have been adapted to the electoral arena, enabling candidates and parties to use new, more sophisticated means for contesting elections. The impact of these changes has been so overwhelming that it has sparked a debate among political scientists over the efficacy of political parties and their prospects for survival. A major issue in this debate is whether or not parties are capable of adapting to, and performing their traditional functions in, the contemporary political environment. This study brings new evidence to bear on this debate by reassessing the roles of party organizations in contemporary congressional elections.

PARTIES IN DECLINE OR PARTIES IN TRANSITION?

A number of scholars, including William Crotty and Gary Jacobson,[1] Gary Orren,[2] and several members of Harvard University's Campaign Finance Study Group,[3] view the recent developments in campaign politics with alarm, arguing that the influence of political parties has been severely reduced. They note that party organizations now play diminished roles in the candidate recruitment and nomination processes. They also indicate that parties contribute only a tiny fraction of the money that constitutes the typical candidate's campaign chest.[4] Moreover, it is believed that parties have become a less important source of information and strategic advice in contemporary elections.[5] They also appear to be less effective in mobilizing the electorate.[6] Parties, it is argued, have been unable to adapt to the changing political environment. As a result, they do not possess many of the resources needed to conduct a modern campaign.

Closely tied to the decline of parties is the rise of PACs. In many of the areas where party activity has dwindled, PAC activity has increased. PACs now play a major role in financing elections.[7] They also have become active in more traditional party functions, such as candidate recruitment, assisting candidates in developing campaign strategies, and voter mobilization.[8] In some activities, particularly in the area of campaign contributions, PACs not only have challenged the parties but have surpassed them in the amount of assistance given to congressional candidates.

An alternative interpretation emphasizes that political parties have entered a period of transition rather than a period of decline. Scholars adhering to this perspective contend that national party organizations have assumed new functions which suit the current political environment and, to some extent, compensate for those areas in which state and local party influence has diminished. They note that party organizations, especially the Republican National Committee, have taken an active role in encouraging candidates to run for Congress, as well as for state and local offices.[9] They also report that these organizations are providing candidates with increasingly larger amounts of campaign services, including training sessions, survey data, and media assistance.[10] Moreover, studies of PAC decision making have found that some PACs utilize cues provided by party organizations when deciding which candidates to support,[11] and that many PACs are aligning themselves with parties having similar philosophical or programmatic commitments.[12] Thus, the relationships among parties, PACs, and political candidates are considerably more complex than the parties-in-decline thesis suggests.

METHODOLOGY

The procedure used in conducting this study is as follows. First, personal interviews were conducted with congressional candidates and their campaign advisors, as well as executives in the Democratic and Republican National Committees and Congressional Campaign Committees. The interviews are used to establish the types of involvement that national party organizations pursue when conducting their campaign activities. They also furnish insights into the perceptions that party staffers and congressional candidates have of the roles of party organizations in campaign politics.

Second, a mail questionnaire was sent to all of the major party House candidates who faced major party opposition in the 1984 general election. The questionnaire asked each candidate to evaluate how important party organizations, unions, PACs, and other interest groups were in assisting them in four key areas of campaigning: campaign management, campaign communications, fund-raising, and electoral information and voter mobilization. More specifically, the candidates were asked to rate each organization from 1 to 5, depending on whether they considered it to have been unimportant, slightly important, moderately important, very important, or extremely important in each of ten campaign activities.

Fifty-two percent of the 734 questionnaires were completed and returned, resulting in a sample of 385 usable observations. The data are analyzed using a straightforward technique. First, the sample is divided into Republicans and Democrats, and each subgroup is divided again on the basis of the candidates' office-holding status and the competitiveness of the election.[13] Next, arithmetic means are calculated for the evaluations that each group of candidates provided for each political organization. The product is a series of tables consisting of the mean scores supplied by each of the twelve groups of candidates for each of the seven political organizations. The mean scores are used to undertake a comparative evaluation of the importance that different groups of candidates attach to the contributions made by different organizations in each area of campaigning. The statistical significance of these differences are tested using t-tests and multivariate analysis of variance (MANOVA) tests.

CONTEMPORARY NATIONAL PARTY ORGANIZATIONS

As noted earlier, some political observers have reported that party organizations have begun to adapt to some of the changes occurring in the electoral environment. The size and functions of both the Republican and Democratic National Committees (RNC and DNC) have expanded tremendously. However, of even greater significance to candidates running for the House is the recent institutionalization of the parties' congressional campaign committees. Both the National Republican Congressional Committee (NRCC) and the Democratic Congressional Campaign Committee (DCCC) are now staffed year-round by large numbers of full-time professional party workers and have become important centers of campaign activity.

The congressional campaign committees provide their candidates with a wide array of services. They maintain lists of campaign managers, media consultants, pollsters, direct-mail specialists, and other campaign professionals. These are made available to all party candidates. Moreover, the committees, particularly the NRCC, also purchase large "blocks" of campaign services from prominent campaign consultants. Some of these services are provided to a select group of candidates as "in-kind" contributions, and others are sold at well below their market value. Committee executives stress that the competitiveness of the race, the candidate's office-holding status, and the particular needs of the campaign are crucial in determining the types of services that each candidate receives and the price that he or she is charged for them.

Some services, such as media advertising and fund-raising assistance, may be furnished directly by the two congressional campaign committees. Each committee has its own center, which is capable of producing professional quality television and radio advertisements. The DCCC's media center provides its candidates with the use of its facilities and technical assistance. The candidates must provide their own ideas and script. Republican candidates, on the other hand, may receive a more complete advertising package from their party's media center. According to Director Ed Blakely, the center played a major role in designing and producing the campaign advertisements of 25 to 30 competitive Republicans during the 1984 election. Furthermore, because of its greater financial resources, the NRCC has been able to provide its candidates with mass media services at much lower rates than has the DCCC.

A similar set of developments appears to have taken place in the realm of campaign finance. The NRCC, the DCCC, and the parties' national committees are now giving their House candidates larger cash contributions than ever before, as well as making increasingly larger coordinated expenditures on their behalf. Once again, the activities of the Republican committees have far surpassed those of the Democrats.[14] Moreover, the NRCC has a much larger and far more elaborate PAC division than does its Democratic counterpart. The NRCC's PAC director maintains that his committee designed the PAC solicitation strategies of about 100 Republican contenders in the 1984 general election. The committee arranged for small meetings to take place between these candidates and leading members of the PAC community. It also helped to design the "PAC-Kits" the candidates used to solicit PAC contributions and regularly sent out campaign updates on their behalf.

The DCCC's PAC division also introduces its prime contenders to PAC officials, but due to its limited staff size it has not been able to become as involved in the intricacies of its candidates' fund-raising operations as has the NRCC. In the words of the DCCC's PAC director, "The committee has been able to direct its leading candidates to potential givers and send out campaign updates to PACs on their behalf, but it has not been able to take them by the hand and personally introduce them to all of the key PACs on Capitol Hill." Still, the DCCC has arranged luncheons and other meetings where groups of competitive candidates have been able to meet with large numbers of PAC officials. As one member of the PAC community commented, "The Democrats rely on the much larger 'Cattle Shows,' while the Republicans also use the more intimate 'Dog and Pony Show' approach." Both strategies appear to be effective, as both committees are generally credited with directing large sums of PAC money to their most competitive contestants.

This brief description of some of the recent activities of the NRCC and DCCC elaborates just a few of the ways that these committees have become involved in modern congressional elections. The NRCC and the DCCC also provide their candidates with legal advice, assistance in developing their issue positions, and help in other important areas of election decision making and campaign management. The NRCC is generally acknowledged to be the larger and more effective of the two committees, but the DCCC has been reportedly gaining ground during the last five years.

It is important to note that even though several candidates and campaign advisors have acknowledged that party committee members have played influential roles in their campaigns, neither the DCCC nor the NRCC has actually managed any of them. The executive directors and other key personnel in the congressional and national party committees consider their primary tasks to be assisting candidates with the performance of major campaign activities and facilitating contacts and agreements among candidates, campaign consultants, PACs, and other groups. They often refer to these as advisory and "brokerage" functions.

In summary, the recent developments occurring at the NRCC and the DCCC, and the other Washington party committees, provide some preliminary support for the hypothesis that parties are capable of adapting to the changing political environment. How successful this adaptation has been, and whether or not parties are currently making a difference in election campaigns, are two questions that are addressed in the remainder of this article.

PARTY ORGANIZATIONS AND HOUSE RACES: THE VIEW FROM THE CAMPAIGN

CAMPAIGN MANAGEMENT

The development of modern campaign techniques, the introduction of recent campaign finance legislation, and the erosion of traditional partisan electoral cleavages, have greatly increased the complexity of campaigning, making campaign management a more difficult task. These changes also have increased the challenges associated with assembling a viable campaign organization. As already noted, party organizations, particularly the parties' Washington committees, have attempted to ease some of the burdens these changes have imposed upon candidates and campaign managers. In this section, we assess the effectiveness of party programs in the area of campaign management by examining how the candidates evaluated the assistance they received from party organizations, unions, PACs, and other political groups in hiring campaign consultants, formulating campaign strategy, complying with campaign finance laws and other election statutes, and conducting other, more general aspects of campaign management.[15]

Table 9.1 provides a detailed breakdown of the candidate evaluations of the services rendered by the party committees and other political groups. It reveals that the vast majority of the candidates provided rather low ratings for the campaign management assistance they received from most political organizations. The abundance of mean scores falling between one and two indicates that most candidates believed that these organizations supplied them with little to no assistance in managing their campaigns. To a large extent, this finding reflects the candidate-centered nature of American electoral politics.[16] The low scores also reflect the strong tendency of candidates and campaign managers to respond "we did it ourselves" when asked about the assistance they received from parties and other groups in campaign management and other campaign functions. Hence, the figures presented in the tables somewhat underestimate the importance of the services and contributions provided by organizations that were external to the campaign organizations themselves.

In addition, the table reveals that significant variations exist in evaluations given for different organizations by different groups of candidates. It demonstrates that all six groups of Republican candidates and nearly all of the Democrats reported that their congressional campaign commit-

Table 9.1 Candidate Appraisals for Assistance Provided in Campaign Management

	Democrats					
	Incumbents		Challengers		Open seat	
	Comp.	Nonc.	Comp.	Nonc.	Comp.	Nonc.
Local party	1.26	**1.25**	1.21	1.40	**1.56**	**1.62**
State party	1.25	1.20	1.42	1.21	**1.56**	1.25
Natl. pty. cte.	1.12	**1.25**	**1.66**	1.42	**2.02**	1.45
Con. camp. cte.	**1.52**	**1.30**	**2.25**	**1.52**	1.53	**1.56**
Union	1.22	1.20	1.17	1.37	1.34	1.06
Interest groups	**1.34**	1.20	1.29	**1.46**	1.28	1.28
PACs	1.16	1.14	1.17	1.14	1.12	1.06
	N = 32	N = 61	N = 7	N = 75	N = 8	N = 8

	Republicans					
	Incumbents		Challengers		Open seat	
	Comp.	Nonc.	Comp.	Nonc.	Comp.	Nonc.
Local party	1.22	1.34	1.61	1.46	1.28	1.11
State party	1.47	1.26	1.66	**1.47**	**1.75**	1.25
Natl. pty. cte.	**1.66**	**1.42**	2.02	1.45	1.72	**1.68**
Con. camp. cte.	**3.00**	**2.00**	**3.47**	**2.15**	**3.12**	**2.46**
Union	**3.00**	**2.00**	**3.47**	**2.15**	**3.12**	**2.46**
Interest groups	1.44	1.33	1.39	1.27	1.38	1.11
PACs	1.22	1.02	1.32	1.10	1.22	1.00
	N = 9	N = 59	N = 30	N = 76	N = 8	N = 7

Total N = 380.

Note: The two largest within-column means are printed in **bold** to attract the attention of the reader.

tee provided them with significantly more assistance in campaign management than did the any other political organization (for the Republicans t = 12.30, p<.001; for the Democrats t = 2.30, p<.011). Moreover, the RNC, and particularly the NRCC, were evaluated more favorably than were their Democratic counterparts (F = 45.15, p<.001). The mean scores for the DCCC are on average under two, indicating that most Democratic candidates believed that their party's congressional campaign committee was, at best, only slightly helpful. Republican candidates, on the other hand, rated the NRCC between 2.15 and 3.47, indicating they consider it to have been slightly to moderately helpful in assisting them with managing their campaigns. Further, Republicans running in competitive districts, especially those facing a sitting incumbent, had significantly higher praise for the NRCC than did noncompetitive Republicans (t = 7.22, p<.001).

Interviews with candidates and campaign managers provided some insights into the disparities among the candidate evaluations. Although both parties' congressional campaign committees provided many of their candidates with lists of political consultants, candidate interviews revealed that only the NRCC had a tendency to become actively involved in the actual hiring of these professional campaigners. Republican campaigners from a few competitive districts reported that the NRCC strongly suggested that they purchase the services of specific consultants. In others, the NRCC went so far as to purchase the services itself and donate them to the campaign in the form of an in-kind contribution. Moreover, once the campaign was underway the NRCC did a better job of maintaining close contact with its most competitive contestants than did its rival. A number of competitive Republican candidates, and campaign managers, commented that the NRCC field director assigned to their region provided them with valuable advice and reassurance about their campaign decisions. As a campaign manager working for a competitive Midwestern challenger volunteered, "I am on the phone with [the regional director] at least four times a day, and I don't make a major campaign decision without him. . . . He's the most important person in our campaign, with the exception of [the candidate] and myself." The DCCC did not have any regional field directors during the 1984 general election, so in many cases there was no one with enough proximity to Democratic candidates to offer them detailed advice on some of the developments occurring in their campaigns.

The evidence provided by the candidate evaluations suggests a number of generalizations about the nature of party activity in the area of campaign management. First, and foremost, neither party organizations, unions, PACs, nor any other political groups dominate the management of the typical House campaign. Rather, only a few organizations, particularly the parties' congressional campaign committees, have any influence at all in this area. Furthermore, the influence of these committees varies substantially. The NRCC provides its candidates with significantly more assistance than does its Democratic counterpart. About 25% of all Republican House candidates reported that NRCC was moderately to very important in their campaign management activities, while very few Democratic candidates rated the DCCC as having been more than slightly important in the management of their campaigns. The candidate evaluations for the parties' national committees display similar patterns. The RNC seems to have been the more active of the two national committees, at least insofar as the management of congressional races is concerned. Finally, Republican party organizations in general, and especially the NRCC, appear to have been much more effective at targeting their campaign management services to competitive candidates than were the Democratic party organizations. The Republican's regional directors seem to have been largely responsible for the effectiveness of their party's resource allocation.

CAMPAIGN COMMUNICATIONS

Issue development and mass media advertising, sometimes referred to as campaign communications, represent another important area of campaigning in which national party organizations have attempted to assume a greater role. The most obvious examples of this form of activity are the "Vote Republicans for a Change," the "Stay the Course," and the "America's Back Again" advertisements that were aired on television by the RNC during the 1980, 1982, and 1984 general elections, and the "It Isn't Fair—It's Republican" television commercials that were aired by the DNC in 1982. Other, less visible forms of party activity in the realm of campaign communications involve the two congressional campaign committees. The research divisions of each of these committees compile lists of popular issue positions and themes that are mailed to all of their party's candidates. They also put together more individualized issue packages for candidates running in competitive elections. Finally, the congressional committees' media centers play a central role in the campaign advertising and image development of some of their most competitive contestants.

Table 9.2 presents the mean scores for party organizations, unions, and other political groups in the area of issue development. It demonstrates that national party organizations and other political groups do provide some candidates with significant amounts of assistance in developing their issue positions and campaign themes. Turning first to the Republicans, it is apparent that even Republican incumbents, whose issue positions often were researched by congressional staffers and typically were formulated well before the beginning of the campaign season, still found their parties' Washington committees to be somewhat helpful in setting their campaign agendas. Nonincumbent Republicans, who did not possess the organizational advantages associated with holding a congressional office, found the NRCC to have been of even greater assistance ($t = 4.32$, $p<.001$). They appraised the committee as having been moderately helpful in performing this function. They further reported

Table 9.2 Candidate Appraisals for Assistance Provided in Issue Development

	Democrats					
	Incumbents		Challengers		Open seat	
	Comp.	Nonc.	Comp.	Nonc.	Comp.	Nonc.
Local party	1.16	1.29	1.00	1.31	1.88	1.62
State party	1.16	1.22	1.14	1.27	1.38	1.25
Natl. pty. cte.	1.19	1.41	1.57	1.77	1.50	**2.25**
Con. camp. cte.	**1.53**	1.49	**2.29**	**1.96**	1.25	2.00
Unions	1.34	**1.52**	**2.00**	1.73	**2.25**	**2.25**
Interest groups	**1.56**	1.47	1.86	**1.94**	2.12	**2.50**
PACs	1.22	1.33	**2.00**	1.44	1.50	1.62
	N = 32	N = 63	N = 7	N = 75	N = 8	N = 8
	Republicans					
	Incumbents		Challengers		Open seat	
	Comp.	Nonc.	Comp.	Nonc.	Comp.	Nonc.
Local party	1.33	1.42	1.53	1.55	1.00	1.28
State party	1.33	1.37	1.47	1.59	1.38	1.28
Natl. pty. cte.	1.78	1.76	**2.10**	**1.95**	**1.88**	**1.86**
Con. camp. cte.	2.11	1.92	3.07	7.70	2.50	3.00
Unions	1.11	1.19	1.00	1.10	1.00	1.28
Interest groups	1.33	1.42	1.90	**1.70**	1.25	1.43
PACs	1.44	**1.87**	1.73	1.38	1.25	1.43
	N = 9	N = 59	N = 30	N = 76	N = 8	N = 8

Total N = 382.
Note: The two largest within-column means are printed in **bold** to attract the attention of the reader.

that the RNC also furnished them with significant amounts of assistance. As one competitive challenger stated, "The National Committee and the President set the overall agenda for the campaign, but the NRCC researched my opponent's voting record and identified his weaknesses. They then helped me put together a campaign that would hammer away at them, while displaying my strengths."

Democratic candidates generally did not evaluate either the DCCC or the DNC as favorably as Republican candidates evaluated their party's Washington committees ($F = 19.88$, $p<.001$). Few candidates considered these committees to have been more than slightly important in developing their issue agendas and campaign themes. Remarks made by a number of Democratic campaigners indicated that the DCCC either sent out too much material, failed to adequately tailor the material to meet the needs of particular candidates, and, more often than not, the materials arrived too late in the campaign to be of any use. Still, one of the competitive Democrats interviewed found the issue information and "talking points" circulated by the DCCC to be helpful in writing speeches and preparing for debates with his opponent.

One of the reasons that the DCCC may not have been as well evaluated as the NRCC in the area of issue development is that Democratic candidates may have received larger amounts of assistance from nonparty groups in this area than did those running under the GOP's standard ($F = 21.03$, $p<.001$). The data provide a modicum of support for this hypothesis. Even though only selected groups of Democrats considered the contributions made by these organizations to have been significant, those who did were either competitive challengers or candidates running in open seat races. Some of these candidates found the position papers provided by unions, nuclear freeze groups, and other interest groups to be fairly useful in preparing their issue positions. Yet, it must be emphasized that Democratic candidates did not rate these groups as highly as Republican contenders rated the NRCC; the assistance provided by nonparty interest groups does not appear to have been the equivalent of the aid which was delivered by the Republican party's congressional campaign committee.

The findings for mass media advertising provide further evidence of the growing involvement of national party organizations in the area of campaign communications (see Table 9.3). When asked how important party committees were in assisting with mass media advertising and developing the candidate's public image, competitive Republican candidates, as well as those running for open seats, typically responded that the NRCC was very important and the RNC was slightly to moderately important. The remainder of the Republicans responded that the NRCC and RNC provided them with substantial amounts of assistance in campaign advertising, even though they generally received considerably less assistance than did the more competitive Republicans ($F = 19.92$, $p<.001$).

Democratic candidates, by comparison, reported receiving slightly less help from their party's national and congressional campaign committees ($F = 34.78$, $p <.001$). Democratic incumbents and open seat candidates found the DCCC to have been only slightly helpful, while competitive Democratic challengers considered the DCCC to have been moderately important ($t = 3.37$, $p<.001$). None of the six groups of Dem-

Table 9.3 Candidate Appraisals for Assistance Provided in Mass Media Advertising

	Democrats					
	Incumbents		Challengers		Open seat	
	Comp.	Nonc.	Comp.	Nonc.	Comp.	Nonc.
Local party	1.50	1.48	1.57	1.64	1.62	**1.75**
	Do parties make a difference? 599					
State party	1.47	1.47	1.14	1.32	1.38	1.12
Natl. pty. cte.	1.53	1.29	**2.00**	1.19	1.25	1.12
Con. camp. cte.	**2.09**	1.48	3.14	1.59	**1.88**	1.50
Unions	1.81	**1.76**	1.57	**1.85**	2.12	1.38
Interest groups	**2.03**	**1.61**	1.86	**1.85**	**1.88**	**2.00**
PACs	1.81	1.47	1.29	1.47	1.50	1.12
	N = 32	N = 62	N = 7	N = 74	N = 8	N = 8

	Republicans					
	Incumbents		Challengers		Open seat	
	Comp.	Nonc.	Comp.	Nonc.	Comp.	Nonc.
Local party	1.67	**1.66**	1.87	**1.88**	1.25	1.14
	Do parties make a difference? 599					
State party	1.44	1.59	2.13	1.75	1.75	1.14
Natl. pty. cte.	**1.89**	1.63	**2.43**	1.87	**2.12**	**2.57**
Con. camp. cte.	**3.78**	**2.25**	**4.03**	**2.49**	**3.62**	**3.14**
Unions	1.00	1.19	1.03	1.08	1.00	1.28
Interest groups	**2.03**	**1.61**	1.86	**1.85**	**1.88**	**2.00**
PACs	1.44	1.25	1.57	1.28	1.38	1.71
	N = 9	N = 59	N = 30	N = 76	N = 8	N = 7

Total N = 380.

Note: The two largest within-column means are printed in **bold** to attract the attention of the reader.

ocratic candidates provided particularly favorable evaluations for the DNC's role in campaign advertising. Some of the Democrats interviewed commented that the DNC offered them no help or guidance in planning their campaign brochures or television and radio advertisements. Others found the advertising assistance provided by unions and interest groups to be more useful than that which was provided by their national party organizations. Democratic party organizations at all levels were significantly less helpful in the area of campaign communications than were their Republican opponents.

FUND-RAISING

Campaign finance has undergone greater change during the last decade than any other aspect of congressional elections. The enactment of the Federal Election Campaign Acts, the recent proliferation of PACs, and the introduction of direct-mail solicitation have vastly changed the way campaign money is raised, regulated, and expended. A major question that has emerged in this vastly transformed realm of electioneering is whether party organizations are capable of adapting to and playing a significant role in, the new cash economy of election politics.[16] Table 9.4 provides evidence that indeed they are. It indicates that many House candidates considered their party's congressional campaign committee to have been a valuable source of assistance in their fund-raising operations. Nevertheless, significant variations exist in the evaluations given by different groups of candidates to different political organizations.

The first set of important differences is partisan in nature. All of the Republican candidates considered the NRCC to have been fairly important, characterizing it as the most important outside organization in their fund-raising operations. Most Democratic candidates evaluated the DCCC less positively (t = 5.12, p<.001). In addition, the Republican candidates evaluated the RNC much more positively than the Democrats rated their party's national committee (t = 4.45, p<.001). These differences reflect the ability of the NRCC and the RNC to make larger monetary contributions and become more highly involved in the fund-raising activities of their candidates. As previously mentioned, the Republican Washington committees have much larger budgets and more highly developed PAC Divisions than do their Democratic counterparts.

The second important set of differences is concerned with candidate status and the competitiveness of the election. Both the NRCC and the DCCC, and the two national committees, appear to be extremely effective at targeting their fund-raising assistance to competitive incumbents and challengers, as well as to candidates running for open seats. Republican prime contenders typically evaluated the NRCC as having been moderately to very important in their fund-raising operations. They also evaluated the RNC as having been slightly to moderately important. Noncompetitive Republican incumbents and challengers rated these committees as having been significantly less helpful (F = 16.86, p<.001). Similarly, competitive Democratic incumbents and challengers and all

Table 9.4 Candidate Appraisals for Assistance Provided in Campaign Fund-Raising

	Democrats					
	Incumbents		Challengers		Open seat	
	Comp.	Nonc.	Comp.	Nonc.	Comp.	Nonc.
Local party	1.66	1.59	1.86	1.80	1.50	2.12
State party	1.56	1.49	1.71	1.62	1.50	1.88
Natl. pty. cte.	1.53	1.38	2.14	1.28	1.38	2.00
Con. camp. cte.	2.50	1.84	**3.57**	1.57	2.38	**3.00**
Unions	**2.68**	**2.60**	3.29	**2.53**	**2.75**	**3.00**
Interest groups	2.44	2.21	2.57	**1.96**	2.38	**3.12**
PACs	**2.81**	**2.73**	3.29	1.86	**2.50**	2.75
	N = 32	N = 63	N = 7	N = 74	N = 8	N = 8

	Republicans					
	Incumbents		Challengers		Open seat	
	Comp.	Nonc.	Comp.	Nonc.	Comp.	Nonc.
Local party	1.66	1.59	1.86	1.80	1.50	2.12
State party	1.89	1.63	2.23	1.59	2.25	2.28
Natl. pty. cte.	2.33	1.81	2.40	1.58	2.38	**2.43**
Con. camp. cte.	3.33	**2.58**	3.53	**2.11**	4.12	**3.14**
Unions	1.00	1.15	1.00	1.09	1.00	1.43
Interest groups	1.89	1.63	2.03	1.56	1.62	1.86
PACs	**2.29**	**2.20**	**2.43**	1.47	**3.38**	**2.43**
	N = 9	N = 59	N = 30	N = 76	N = 8	N = 7

Total N = 381.
Note: The two largest within-column means are printed in **bold** to attract the attention of the reader.

Democrats running in open seats evaluated the DCCC and the DNC more positively than did less competitive partisans (F = 15.85, p<.001).

Turning to the figures for unions and other nonPAC interest groups, it appears that these organizations played a much more important role in the fund-raising operations of Democratic candidates than they did in those of their Republican opponents (F = 70.70, p<.001). Democrats generally considered the assistance provided by these organizations to have been moderately important to their fund-raising activities, whereas most Republicans reported the impact of nonPAC interest group and union activity to have been negligible (F = 98.26, p<.001). PACs, however, played a fairly important role in the financial operations of both Republicans and Democrats, though the Democratic candidates had a tendency to rate the assistance provided by these committees somewhat higher (t = 2.74, p<.003). Democratic candidates have traditionally relied on the support of labor unions and other interest groups for monetary contributions and assistance in implementing their fund-raising programs. Obviously, they continue to rely rather heavily upon the largest of these organizations. Republican candidates, in contrast, have never been as dependent upon unions and nonPAC interest groups for either of these activities. They currently are receiving significant amounts of assistance in their campaign finances from their party and sympathetic PACs.

In summary, it appears that national party organizations, and particularly the congressional campaign committees, have successfully adapted to a number of features of the cash-based economy of campaign politics. Although neither of these committees has provided candidates with overwhelming sums of money, all of them supply most competitive contestants with significant amounts of seed money and in-kind contributions, which can be crucial in attracting campaign money from other sources. The committees also played an important role in helping competitive candidates design their fund-raising strategies and solicit PAC funds. Moreover, as is the case with most other aspects of House campaigning, the Republican party organizations, and particularly the NRCC, provided their candidates with more assistance than did their Democratic counterparts.

ELECTORAL INFORMATION AND VOTER MOBILIZATION

Gauging public opinion, conducting voter registration and get-out-the-vote drives, and supplying the manpower needed to carry out these campaign activities have traditionally been the responsibilities of local party committees. Tables 9.5 through 9.7 reveal that some local parties still play an active role in all three of these areas. Table 9.5 displays the results for gathering electoral information. It reveals that Republicans, especially those competing in open seat races, relied rather heavily on the assistance of the NRCC for gauging public opinion in their districts. A number of those interviewed explained that the NRCC played a prominent role in their polling activities. The committee provided them with base polls early in the election cycle and with tracking polls during the last two weeks of the campaign. Sometimes the polling was conducted by NRCC staff, and other times it was purchased by the committee from outside consultants. More often than not it was provided to the candidates in the form of an in-kind contribution. In addition, the table indi-

Table 9.5 Candidate Appraisals for Assistance Provided in Gauging Public Opinion

	Democrats					
	Incumbents		Challengers		Open seat	
	Comp.	Nonc.	Comp.	Nonc.	Comp.	Nonc.
Local party	**1.78**	2.10	1.43	1.89	**2.25**	1.75
State party	**1.78**	1.90	1.43	1.64	**1.88**	1.62
Natl. pty. cte.	1.59	1.66	1.28	1.89	1.38	**2.00**
Con. camp. cte.	**2.28**	1.94	1.43	**2.05**	1.38	**2.25**
Unions	**1.78**	1.71	1.57	1.82	1.62	
Interest groups	1.69	1.63	**2.00**	1.97	1.25	**2.00**
PACs	1.62	1.42	**1.86**	1.54	1.12	**2.00**
	N = 32	N = 62	N = 7	N = 74	N = 8	N = 8
	Republicans					
	Incumbents		Challengers		Open seat	
	Comp.	Nonc.	Comp.	Nonc.	Comp.	Nonc.
Local party	**2.78**	2.12	2.07	**2.38**	1.62	**2.43**
State party	2.56	2.14	2.73	2.24	**2.38**	2.28
Natl. pty. cte.	2.78	2.19	2.83	2.14	**2.38**	2.14
Con. camp. cte.	3.78	2.75	3.93	2.79	3.75	**2.43**
Unions	1.00	1.14	1.00	1.10	1.00	1.14
Interest groups	1.22	1.44	1.67	1.74	1.25	1.57
PACs	1.22	1.46	1.43	1.36	1.62	1.14
	N = 9	N = 59	N = 30	N = 76	N = 8	N = 7

Total N = 380.

Note: The two largest within-column means are printed in **bold** to attract the attention of the reader.

cates that the RNC, and Republican state and local party organizations, also provided many candidates with significant assistance in gauging public opinion. However, a number of candidates commented that the information received from local party committees was of a substantively different type than that which was offered by the other levels of the party organization. Local party leaders typically provided more textured information, such as reports about the political opinions of neighborhood leaders, rather than quantitative data gleaned from scientifically conducted surveys.

The figures for the Democrats indicate that they received significantly less help from all levels of their party organization in collecting electoral information than did the Republicans (F = 16.25, p<.001). The Democratic Washington and local party committees were evaluated as, at best, having been only slightly important in this area. In fact, competitive challengers and open seat candidates typically reported that the DCCC provided them with virtually no help. The Republican party organizations not only have provided their House candidates with more assistance in gauging public opinion than have the Democrats (F = 16.25, p<.001), but they also were better at delivering this assistance strategically. Republicans running in competitive districts received significantly more help than did other GOP candidates or Democratic close contenders (F = 6.32, p<.001).

The differences in the candidate evaluations of the Republicans and the Democrats can be attributed to a number of factors. The Republicans are able to invest greater sums of money in conducting public opinion surveys and carrying out studies of previous election returns. They also are able to provide candidates with the results of these studies free of charge or for well below their market value. In addition, as part of its party-building program, the RNC has provided a number of state parties with computer systems that have been used to analyze polling data and election returns. A number of Republican state party organizations, such as the one in Colorado, have used their computer systems and other informational resources to assist congressional, as well as state and local, candidates. Finally, as is the case with campaign communications and campaign finance, Democratic candidates continue to rely upon unions and other nonparty groups for assistance in this area. Still, none of these groups can be considered an adequate substitute for either the NRCC or the RNC. In short, when it comes to assessing the mood of the general public, Republican aspirants for the House are able to count on the assistance of their party, while Democratic hopefuls are largely on their own.

The candidate evaluations for voter registration and get-out-the-vote drives provide further evidence of the continuing vitality of the local organizations of both political parties. Table 9.6 indicates that all of the Republican candidates typically considered their local party committees to have been at least moderately important. Some even considered them to have been very important. Republican state party organizations and the RNC also received favorable evaluations. Yet, even though there appears to have been a high level of cooperation between Republican House candidates and various elements of the party's organizational apparatus, the same cannot be said for Republican candidates and nonparty groups. Unions, PACs, and other political committees were virtually uninvolved

Table 9.6 Candidate Appraisals for Assistance Provided in Registering
Voters and Conducting Get-Out-the-Vote Drives

	Democrats					
	Incumbents		Challengers		Open seat	
	Comp.	Nonc.	Comp.	Nonc.	Comp.	Nonc.
Local party	**2.81**	**3.11**	2.57	**2.70**	**2.62**	**2.62**
State party	1.88	2.10	2.00	1.86	2.38	1.75
Natl. pty. cte.	1.41	1.56	1.28	1.34	1.62	1.25
Con. camp. cte.	1.56	1.35	1.14	1.12	1.25	1.50
Unions	**2.72**	**2.79**	**2.86**	**2.58**	**2.75**	2.12
Interest groups	2.66	2.10	3.14	2.35	2.13	**3.13**
PACs	1.44	1.39	1.00	1.39	1.88	1.38
	N = 32	N = 62	N = 7	N = 74	N = 8	N = 8
	Republicans					
	Incumbents		Challengers		Open seat	
	Comp.	Nonc.	Comp.	Nonc.	Comp.	Nonc.
Local party	**4.33**	**3.29**	**3.27**	**3.04**	**3.00**	3.71
State party	**2.78**	**2.57**	**2.87**	**2.32**	**2.63**	**2.86**
Natl. pty. cte.	1.89	1.95	2.37	1.78	2.50	2.14
Con. camp. cte.	1.89	1.45	2.00	1.57	1.88	2.00
Unions	**1.00**	**1.24**	**1.10**	**1.13**	**1.00**	**1.28**
Interest groups	1.33	1.46	1.83	1.63	1.38	1.43
PACs	1.33	1.07	1.57	1.18	1.25	1.14
	N = 9	N = 58	N = 30	N = 76	N = 8	N = 7

Total N = 376.
Note: The two largest within-column means are printed in **bold** to attract the
attention of the reader.

in the Republicans' attempts to get their supporters into the voting
booth.

Democratic candidates typically did not evaluate their party organizations as highly as did their opponents. Even though they typically
were considered to have been moderately effective in helping congressional candidates get their supporters to the polls, Democratic local party
organizations were not evaluated nearly as highly as were Republican local party committees (t = 2.88, p<.002). Further, Democratic state parties and the DNC not only were assessed less positively than their local
affiliates, but they were rated lower than unions and other interest

groups (t = 3.44, p<.001). To a large extent these findings are indicative of the comparative weakness of Democratic party organizations and the tendency of many Democratic candidates to rely upon the assistance of labor unions and other nonparty groups when mobilizing voters. Nevertheless, they also may reflect the attempts made by some Democratic House candidates to distance themselves from an underdog presidential candidate and the get-out-the-vote drives the DNC organized in support of him.

The recruitment of volunteer campaign workers is also an activity which is generally dominated by local political organizations. The findings presented in Table 9.7 indicate that Republican candidates relied primarily on their local party organizations for assistance in this area. They assessed these organizations as having been moderately to very important, considering them to have been significantly more helpful than interest groups, such as their local chamber of commerce, which were rated second (t = 9.06, p<.001). Clearly, most Republican campaign volunteers are recruited from among the ranks of their local party and by local party activists.

Democrats, on the other hand, appear to have received slightly less assistance in recruiting volunteer workers from all four levels of their party organization. Democratic party committees generally were not nearly so good at providing their most competitive House contenders with volunteer workers as were Republican committees (F = 4.58, p.<.002). In fact, Democratic candidates had a slight tendency to rely more heavily upon labor unions and other interest groups for their volunteer workers than their local party (t = 1.31, p<.100). Still, it should be noted that most Democratic candidates believed that local party committees provided them with slight to moderate amounts of assistance in recruiting volunteer workers. They merely considered nonparty organizations as having been better sources of campaign activists. In short, it is apparent that while Republican House candidates relied almost solely on their local party committees for assistance in recruiting volunteer campaign workers, Democratic candidates received substantial help in this area from both party and nonparty organizations.

The above findings suggest that even though local party organizations no longer play a dominant role in many phases of campaign politics, they continue to make important contributions to those aspects of campaigning that require direct contact with voters. They also provide many candidates with the volunteer workers needed to conduct these and other grass-roots campaign functions. The decline of the importance of local party organizations in providing candidates with electoral information is largely a reflection of the increased reliance that many candi-

Table 9.7 Candidate Appraisals for Assistance Provided in Recruiting Volunteer Campaign Workers

| | Democrats | | | | | |
| | Incumbents | | Challengers | | Open seat | |
	Comp.	Nonc.	Comp.	Nonc.	Comp.	Nonc.
Local party	2.23	**2.49**	**2.57**	2.37	2.38	**2.88**
State party	1.32	1.43	1.29	1.28	1.62	1.88
Natl. pty. cte.	1.10	1.06	1.00	1.12	1.00	1.38
Con. camp. cte.	1.13	1.06	1.57	1.11	1.00	1.25
Unions	**2.74**	2.52	2.43	**2.51**	**2.63**	2.38
Interest groups	**3.06**	2.13	**2.86**	2.35	**2.75**	**2.50**
PACs	1.90	1.22	1.43	1.56	1.62	1.38
	N = 31	N = 63	N = 7	N = 75	N = 8	N = 8
	Republicans					
	Incumbents		Challengers		Open seat	
	Comp.	Nonc.	Comp.	Nonc.	Comp.	Nonc.
Local party	4.00	2.85	3.30	2.53	3.00	3.00
State party	1.44	1.59	1.63	1.36	1.50	1.57
Natl. pty. cte.	1.00	1.14	1.13	1.18	1.25	1.00
Con. camp. cte.	1.00	1.19	1.20	1.22	1.50	1.00
Unions	1.00	1.20	1.03	1.01	1.00	1.14
Interest groups	1.78	1.61	2.10	1.82	1.75	1.14
PACs	1.33	1.07	1.63	1.18	1.50	1.14
	N = 9	N = 59	N = 30	N = 76	N = 8	N = 7

Total N = 381.
Note: The two largest within-column means are printed in **bold** to attract the attention of the reader.

dates have on public opinion polls for voter information. Few local party committees are able to provide their candidates with polling services; thus many candidates have turned to private polling agencies, national party organizations, and a few state party organizations for assistance in this campaign activity. These findings as well as those of other studies of political parties,[17] strongly suggest that local party organizations are continuing to play an important role in mobilizing the electorate and in providing the volunteer workers who canvass election districts, stamp envelopes, and perform some of the other nuts-and-bolts tasks associated with the typical House campaign.

CONCLUSION

Congressional elections have changed tremendously in recent years and so have the roles that party organizations are playing in them. Parties are no longer dominating the electoral process, as they were believed to have done during the heyday of the old-fashioned political machine, nor are they on the periphery of it, as they were during the 1950s and 1960s. Rather, party organizations can be described as being selectively involved in contemporary campaign politics. They make important contributions in specific areas of campaigning to a limited group of House candidates, while they remain, at most, minimally involved in the election bids of many others. Party organizations occupy an important, but not dominant, position in the American political landscape.

In conclusion, this study has sought to address two questions. First, are party organizations capable of adapting to the changing environment of campaign politics? And second, do parties make a difference in contemporary House elections? The answer to the first question appears to be yes; party organizations do appear to be adapting to the changing political environment. Signs of their adaptability include the recent growth in the size and services provided by their Washington committees, and the integration of these committees into the networks of PACs and political consulting agencies that comprise the new corps of congressional campaigners. National party organizations, particularly the congressional campaign committees, now provide selected candidates with assistance in campaign management, campaign communications, fundraising, and other areas of campaigning requiring technical expertise, indepth research, or connections with other influential electoral actors. They are helping House candidates to run more professionalized and sophisticated campaigns, campaigns which are well suited to the electoral conditions of the twentieth century United States. In this way, they also are contributing to the nationalization of American politics.

However, it is important to note that significant differences exist in the amounts of progress made by the two parties. The Republican party has adapted more readily to the contemporary political environment. Republican party organizations at all levels, and particularly the NRCC, provide their candidates with significantly more services than do their Democratic rivals. The Republican Washington committees are also more adept at targeting these services to their most competitive candidates.

The Republican party's preeminence in campaign politics can be attributed to a number of factors. First, they possess greater financial resources than do the Democrats. Second, their head start in party-building has enabled them to put together a more experienced team of campaign professionals and establish more stable working relations with private political consulting agencies. Third, because Democratic party organizations are still very dependent upon the fund-raising activities of a small group of prominent party spokesmen for much of their financial resources, these party leaders continue to dominate national party decision making. This has impeded the committees from developing stable decision-making processes. As a result of their being less financially secure and less institutionalized, the Democratic committees have been unable to provide their candidates with as many campaign services as have the Republicans, nor have they been able to distribute their campaign services as strategically.

Nevertheless, it must be emphasized that both the DNC and the DCCC have substantially updated their campaign services programs since the 1970s. Their staffs have grown and become more experienced, and the quality and quantity of the campaign services they provide have improved. The two committees also are becoming more financially secure and have been purchasing computers and other pieces of modern campaign hardware. They, along with the Democratic Senatorial Campaign Committee, have recently moved into the party's new headquarters building located just a few blocks from the Capitol Building in Washington, D.C. The DCCC also plans to have regional directors out in the field working with Democratic congressional candidates. These developments indicate that Democratic party organizations are beginning to make some progress in reaching the standards established by the Republican party. A number of Democratic party officials maintain they will catch up with the Republican committees within three or four election cycles.

The answer to the second question is somewhat more involved than the answer to the first. From the perspective of those working in them, party organizations do make an important difference in contemporary House elections. Party organizations, particularly the parties' Washington committees, provide significant numbers of candidates with important campaign services. The parties also assist them in obtaining nonparty resources and services by facilitating the development of contacts and agreements between candidates, PACs, and other electoral organizations. In this sense parties function as important appendages or accessories to the candidates' regular campaign organizations.

From the perspective of PACs and other nonparty electoral groups, it has been suggested that national party organizations also might make a difference. When national party organizations designate some elections as competitive races, and make large contributions to candidates running in them, they help nonparty agencies make informed decisions about which candidates to support. That is, the activities of the parties' Washington committees enable nonparty agencies to distinguish the candidates who are competitive, and have a chance of winning, from those who are not. Hence, national party organizations have assumed a brokerage role.[18] They direct valuable resources, including money, campaign services, and endorsements, towards their competitive contestants, and they channel strategic information about these candidates to organizations that may be interested in supporting them.

From the perspective of the candidates, parties also make a difference, depending upon the group of candidates to which one is referring. Many nonincumbents have little chance of getting elected, and many incumbents possess safe seats. These groups of candidates typically receive some help from their local party organizations and small amounts of services and assistance from their parties' national and congressional campaign committees. For these candidates, parties probably do not make a very big difference. However, a select group of House candidates, approximately 25% of those running, are involved in competitive contests. Most of the candidates falling into this group, and particularly those who belong to the Republican party, receive large amounts of services and assistance from their parties' Washington committees. For these candidates, parties may make a very big difference...perhaps enough of a difference to change the course of a campaign and affect the outcome of an election.

NOTES

1. William J. Crotty and Gary C. Jacobson, *American Parties in Decline* (Boston: Little, Brown, 1980).

2. Gary R. Orren, "The Changing Styles of American Party Politics" in Joel L. Fleishman, ed., *The Future of American Political Parties* (Englewood Cliffs, N.J.: Prentice-Hall, 1982).

3. Campaign Finance Study Group, Institute of Politics, John F. Kennedy School of Government, Harvard U. *An Analysis of the Federal Election Campaign Act, 1972–1978* (Washington, D.C.: U.S. Government Printing Office, 1979).

4. Gary C. Jacobson, *The Politics of Congressional Elections* (Boston: Little, Brown, 1983), p. 53.

5. Robert Agranoff, "Introduction/The New Style of Campaigning: The Decline of Party and the Rise of Candidate Centered Technology" in Robert Agranoff, ed., *The New Style in Election Campaigns* (Boston: Holbrook, 1972); Larry J. Sabato, *The Rise of the Political Consultants: New Ways of Winning Elections* (New York: Basic Books, 1981).

6. Frank J. Sorauf, "Political Parties and Political Action Committees: Two Life Cycles," *Arizona Law Review* 22 (1980): 455–64.

7. Jacobson, *The Politics of Congressional Elections*, p. 53.

8. Lee Ann Elliot, "Political Action Committees—Precincts of the '80s, *Arizona Law Review* 22 (1980): 539–54; Edwin M. Epstein, "Business and Labor under the Federal Election Campaign Act of 1971" in Michael Malbin, ed., *Parties, Interest Groups, and Campaign Finance Laws* (Washington, D.C.: American Enterprise Institute, 1980), pp. 110–12; Larry J. Sabato, "Parties, PACs, and Independent Groups" in Thomas E. Mann and Norman Ornstein, eds., *The American Elections of 1982* (Washington, D.C.: American Enterprise Institute, 1982), pp. 86–96; Sabato, *PAC Power: Inside the World of Political Action Committees* (New York: W. W. Norton, 1984), pp. 72–121.

9. M. Margaret Conway, "Republican Political Party Nationalization, Campaign Activities, and Their Implications for the Political System," *Publius* 13 (1983): 1–17.

10. John F. Bibby, "Party Renewal in the National Republican Party" in Gerald M. Pomper, ed., *Party Renewal in America: Theory and Practice* (New York: Praeger, 1980); Cornelius P. Cotter and John F. Bibby, "Institutional Development of Parties and the Thesis of Party Decline," *Political Science Quarterly* 95 (1980): 1–27; F. Christopher Arterton, "Political Money and Party Strength" in Joel L. Fleishman, ed., *The Future of American Political Parties* (Englewood Cliffs, N.J.: Prentice-Hall, 1982); David Adamany, "Political Parties in the 1980s" in Michael Malbin, ed., *Money and Politics in the United States: Financing Elections in the 1980s* (Washington, D.C.: American Enterprise Institute, 1984), pp. 89–101; Majorie Randon Hershey, *Running for Office: The Political Education of Campaigners* (Chatham, N.J.: Chatham House, 1984), pp. 139–43; David E. Price, *Bringing Back the Parties* (Washington, D.C.: Congressional Quarterly Press, 1984), pp. 38–44.

11. Diana M. Owen and Paul S. Herrnson, "An Analysis of the Internal Decision-Making Process of Business and Trade Association Political Action Committees: A Case Study of BANKPAC." Paper presented at the annual meeting of the Midwest Political Science Association, Chicago, Illinois, 1983.

12. Adamany, "Political Parties in the 1980s," pp. 84–85, 92.

13. Competitive candidates are defined as those receiving between 43% and 57% of the vote. Twenty-five percent of the sample fell into this category, closely approximating the 27% of the underlying population (200 campaigns) that the National Republican Congressional Committee (NRCC) and the Democratic Congressional Campaign Committee (DCCC) considered to have been competitive races. The validity of these categories was checked by comparing the competitive Republican candidates in the sample with those candidates appearing on the NRCC's list of "opportunity races." (A similar list could not be obtained from the DCCC.)

14. Federal Election Commission. FEC release, 5 December 1985.

15. A separate question was asked for each of the four aspects of campaign management. The responses were then combined to form an overall campaign management index. (Cronbach's Alpha ranged from .75 to .84, with an average value of .80, for the party organizations and ranged from .66 to .76, with an average value of .71, for the other political groups.)

16. In the U.S., as opposed to many other countries (e.g., Great Britain), candidates possess their own campaign organizations, and candidates, not parties, bear the primary responsibility for running their general campaigns.

17. James L. Gibson, Cornelius P. Cotter, John F. Bibby, and Robert J. Huckshorn, "Whither the Local Parties? A Cross-Sectional and Longitudinal Analysis of the Strength of Party Organizations," *American Journal of Political Science* 29 (1985): 139–60.

18. The concept of national parties as brokers is more fully developed in Herrnson (1986).

REFERENCES

Adamany, David. 1984. "Political Parties in the 1980s." In Michael J. Malbin, ed., *Money and Politics in the United States: Financing Elections in the 1980s.* Washington, D.C.: American Enterprise Institute.

Agranoff, Robert. 1972. "Introduction/The New Style of Campaigning: The Decline of Party and the Rise of Candidate Centered Technology." In Robert Agranoff, ed., *The New Style in Election Campaigns.* Boston: Holbrook.

Arterton, F. Christopher. 1982. "Political Money and Party Strength." In Joel L. Fleishman, ed., *The Future of American Political Parties.* Englewood Cliffs, N.J.: Prentice-Hall.

Bibby, John F. 1980. "Party Renewal in the National Republican Party." In Gerald M. Pomper, ed., *Party Renewal in America: Theory and Practice.* New York: Praeger.

Campaign Finance Study Group, Institute of Politics, John F. Kennedy School of Government, Harvard U. 1979. *An Analysis of the Federal Election Campaign Act, 1972–1978.* Washington, DC: U.S. Government Printing Office.

Conway, M. Margaret. 1983. "Republican Political Party Nationalization, Campaign Activities, and Their Implications for the Political System." *Publius*, 13: 1–17.

Cotter, Cornelius P., and John F. Bibby. 1980. "Institutional Development of Parties and the Thesis of Party Decline." *Political Science Quarterly*, 95: 1–27.

Crotty, William J., and Gary C. Jacobson. 1980. *American Parties in Decline.* Boston: Little, Brown.

Elliot, Lee Ann. 1980. "Political Action Committees—Precincts of the '80s." *Arizona Law Review*, 22: 539–554.

Epstein, Edwin M. 1980. "Business and Labor under the Federal Election Campaign Act of 1971." In Michael J. Malbin, ed., *Parties, Interest Groups, and Campaign Finance Laws.* Washington, D.C.: American Enterprise Institute.

Federal Election Commission. 1985. FEC Press Release, December 5.

Gibson, James L., Cornelius P. Cotter, John F. Bibby, and Robert J. Huckshorn. 1985. "Whither the Local Parties? A Cross-Sectional and Longitudinal Analysis of the Strength of Party Organizations." *American Journal of Political Science*, 29: 139–160.

Herrnson, Paul S. 1986. "Political Party Organizations and Congressional Campaigning." Paper presented at the annual meeting of the Midwest Political Science Association, Chicago, IL.
Hershey, Marjorie Randon. 1984. *Running for Office: The Political Education of Campaigners.* Chatham, N.J.: Chatham House.
Jacobson, Gary C. 1983. *The Politics of Congressional Elections.* Boston: Little, Brown.
Orren, Gary R. 1982. The Changing Styles of American Party Politics. In Joel L. Fleishman, ed., *The Future of American Political Parties.* Englewood Cliffs, N.J.: Prentice-Hall.
Owen, Diana M., and Paul S. Herrnson. 1983. "An Analysis of the Internal Decision-Making Process of Business and Trade Association Political Action Committees: A Case Study of BANKPAC." Paper presented at the annual meeting of the Midwest Political Science Association, Chicago, IL.
Price, David E. 1984. *Bringing Back the Parties.* Washington, D.C.: Congressional Quarterly Press.
Sabato, Larry J. 1981. *The Rise of the Political Consultants: New Ways of Winning Elections.* New York: Basic Books.
_____ . 1982. Parties, PACs, and Independent Groups. In Thomas E. Mann and Norman J. Ornstein, eds., *The American Elections of 1982.* Washington, D.C.: American Enterprise Institute.
_____ . 1984. *PAC Power: Inside the World of Political Action Committees.* New York: W. W. Norton.
Sorauf, Frank J. 1980. "Political Parties and Political Action Committees: Two Life Cycles." *Arizona Law Review,* 22: 445–464.

Reading 10

STATE AND LOCAL
PARTY ORGANIZATIONS
IN AMERICAN POLITICS

James L. Gibson and Susan E. Scarrow

It is sometimes said that the United States has not a two-party system but rather a one-hundred-and-two-party system. There are not one hundred and two parties competing with each other for political power in the United States. The two major parties—the Democrats and the Republicans—are split into fifty-one different organizations. In addition to the national parties, there are party organizations in each of the fifty states. While it is hyperbole to say that the sate and national parties are completely independent of one another, there is much more to party politics in the United States than what happens within the Democratic and Republican National Committees in Washington.

Not only are the state parties relatively independent of the national parties, but they are reasonably strong, and they seem to be gaining strength and influence as well. The state parties not only have a puissant influence on local parties—and, after all, some claim that *all* politics is local—but they are increasingly influencing the recruitment and nomination of candidates for public office, the activities of party officials in the government, and the very electoral policies that shape so much partisan political activity in the United States. If one aspires to understand politics in the United States, one cannot ignore the state and local party organizations.

Party organizations are playing an important role in the transformation of the American party system. Some see this transformation as a "realignment"—a change in the basic cleavage structure of American politics (who supports which party and why?)—while others characterize contemporary politics as a "dealignment"—a period of declining relevance of the current political parties. Whatever the exact nature of changes that are unfolding, party organizations will surely shape the process. It is typical to think of parties as the institution being "realigned"; our view is that party organizations are not merely the clay that is molded by the political system, but are also active sculptors, shaping the processes of change.

Our purpose in this reading is to assess the role of state and local party organizations within American politics. We begin with a conceptualization of "political party" that separates the various organizations and structures commonly placed under the "party-system" umbrella. We then discuss how these institutions are organized in the states and localities, as well as the functions they perform. We are especially concerned with the relationships party organizations have with other institutions in the political landscape, even with institutions that compete with party organizations for political power. We are especially mindful of the ways in which parties affect, and are affected by, changes in other portions of the political system. Where appropriate, we also consider how United States parties are similar and different to their counterparts throughout the world. Our task begins with an effort to conceptualize "political party" in a rigorous fashion.

CONCEPTUALIZING PARTIES

At one level, the definition of a political party seems fairly straightforward. One study of political parties in democratic political systems chose to consider any group as a party so long as the group sought "to elect governmental office-holders under a given [party] label."[1] While such a definition provides guidance about what qualifies as a political party, it does not provide direction about how to study the multiple tasks and the multifaceted structures of the political parties themselves.

To help organize studies of parties, political scientists often accept the distinction among "the party-in-government," "the party-in-the-electorate," and "the party organizations." These are all elements of the *party system*. Each party-in-government consists of party members who hold public office. Within legislatures, for instance, there are often formal party caucuses that may influence legislative politics in many important ways.[2] In most state legislatures in the United States, the legislature itself is organized by the "parties-in-government" (although the activity and strength of these organizations vary enormously across time and across states). As in the United States Congress, party caucuses in the state legislatures determine the leadership of the institution, as well as the chairpersons of most standing committees. Although it is rare that all of a party's public officeholders act in close concert with other party officials, elected government officials play a very important role within political parties.

The party-in-the-electorate is traditionally conceptualized as consisting of ordinary citizens who are adherents of each party. We use the word "adherents" loosely since American political parties are not mass-membership parties. Unlike many political parties in other democracies, American parties have few formal, "card-carrying" members. Instead, the party-in-the-electorate consists of those who identify with one of the parties, who think of themselves as Democrats or Republicans. Though it is conventional to consider party adherents as a component of the party itself, in an era of dealignment or realignment it may be more accurate to characterize most voters as consumers whom the parties seek to attract to their candidates and positions.

The third element of political parties is the party organizations. Legally, these institutions are rightly called the political parties in the United States. The party organization is typically governed by a central committee, and central committees exist for both the Democrats and Republicans in each of the fifty states (and at the national level as well). The state party organizations have the exclusive right to call themselves the "Democratic" or "Republican" parties, and it is these organizations that conduct most of the affairs of the party itself.

"Below" the state-level party organizations, political parties in the United States are typically organized at the county (or county-equivalent) level.[3] Though it has not always been true in the past, today there are both Democratic and Republican county-level organizations in nearly all counties in the country. The county parties typically are led by a chairperson who is assisted by a county central or executive committee.

One other element of political parties does not fit so neatly into this conventional tripartite division of parties—the party activists. These are individuals, typically with strong attachments to the party, who sporadically participate in various party affairs. The most common type of activist is one who attends a party nominating caucus or convention, although volunteer activists serve in many different roles within party organizations. Most leaders of the county party organizations might rightly be termed "activist." Party activists are the "human capital" of American political parties.

These various party components interact with each other within a party system. The party system, itself a subcomponent of the larger political system, includes a set of interdependent institutions, with the tripartite division of party at the core of the system. There are a variety of institutions that function as part of the party system. These are autonomous institutions that are interdependent.

There is sufficient sovereignty among the various subcomponents to warrant distinguishing them as separate entities. When one considers the problem of change, and perhaps even the dealignment or realignment of the political parties in the United States, it is essential to consider the possibility that not all of these components are changing at the same speed, or perhaps even in the same direction. Different components of the party system have a causal impact upon each other—for instance, change in the party-in-the-electorate may cause change in the party organizations. The parts are not strongly connected to each other and the nature of their interrelationships is a key issue in the study of party system change. By placing political parties within the larger party and political systems, we are kept mindful of the fact that parties are just one of a panoply of institutional actors struggling over political power in the United States.

This reading focuses on state and local party organizations. First we will examine these organizations from the standpoint of how they are structured and what their functions are. But to understand party organizations and how they are changing, it is important to place them within the larger context of the party system. Thus, after considering both the structure and activities of these organizations we will turn to their interactions with other elements of the party and political system, and ultimately to the issues of dealignment and realignment.

THE STRUCTURES AND RESOURCES OF STATE AND LOCAL PARTY ORGANIZATIONS

As in most federal countries, the organizational tiers of the American parties parallel those of the governmental system in which they operate. Consequently, both the Democratic and Republican parties can be diagrammed as organizational pyramids. At the base of these pyramids are the party units in electoral precincts (roughly 180,000 precincts); at the next level are the party organizations in the counties (3,137 counties) and county-like units (852 county-like units; e.g., towns in New England); closer to the top of each pyramid are the fifty state parties; national party committees occupy the single spot at the top of each of these organizational pyramids.

Yet, such an organizational chart, with the National Committee at the apex of the pyramid, presents a misleading picture of the distribution of decision-making authority within the parties. American parties have never been rigidly hierarchical organizations in which orders are issued from the top and executed at the bottom. Instead, political scientists have used the word *stratarchy*—a hierarchy of strata—to describe the structure of American parties.[4] Parties have independent layers of activity and decision making within loose organizational hierarchies. At the state level, the party organizations are legally independent of the national committees; they collect and disperse most of their own funds, and they are largely accountable for their own decisions.

Perhaps also reflecting the structure of political institutions in the United States, there are only two major parties in the United States—the Democrats and the Republicans. For the past fifty years, all levels of American politics have been dominated by just two political parties. To many foreign observers, one of the most striking aspects of the American party system is how few parties there are. To a certain extent this two-party dominance is a product of structural aspects of elections in the United States—most representatives are selected from single-member districts on the basis of winner-take-all elections.[5] This kind of electoral system provides few incentives for parties that cannot even conceive of attracting a large percentage of the electorate to their positions and candidates, since parties gain no representation if their candidates do not secure at least a plurality in the electoral district. The electoral system itself is no guarantee that in the future politics throughout the United States will be dominated by the same two parties. New parties seeking to gain initial representation under such an electoral system do best if they concentrate on building strength within specific districts or regions. The rise of the New Democratic party in Canada in the 1980s and 1990s is a good illustration of how, even under single member district electoral rules, a third party can move from being a regional (provincial) player to being a national political force. Such powerful "minor" parties have not been a recurrent feature of politics in the United States.[6]

Present two-party domination means that we will focus in this reading on Republican and Democratic party organization in the states. While these are currently the only consistently successful parties in United States politics, they are certainly not the only parties that regularly nominate candidates for public office. Parties such as the Libertarians and the Socialist Workers party have at least skeletal organizations in many states, and in New York the Liberals and the Conservatives have often been viable third and fourth parties. We should emphasize that there is a myriad of alternative structures for the minor parties operating in the United States.

The organizational charts of the principle American parties do not reveal much about the characteristics or capacities of the different layers of party organization. To understand these, we need to look directly at the institutional focal points of the state and local party organizations—at the party headquarters.

STATE AND LOCAL PARTY HEADQUARTERS

To an increasingly uniform extent, American party organizations represent palpable institutional presences below the national level. Today, inquisitive citizens in search of their state's Republican or Democratic state party organization would be almost certain to end up at an actual headquarters building, at a location that is the year-round base for that state party's activities. This has not always been the case: as late as the 1950s and 1960s many state parties lacked the sort of organizational permanence which year-round headquarters provide. Until recently, the state party "headquarters" was often merely the home or office of the state party chair.[7] State parties began to establish permanent, professionally staffed headquarters as they changed their notions of what were the appropriate tasks for party organizations. This was an important step for the institutionalization of state party organizations.

After 1945, innovative techniques and sophisticated technologies began to change radically the nature of electioneering at all levels throughout the United States. Competitive candidates became increasingly reliant on opinion polling to assess their support in the electorate, and on new methods to convey their messages to the electorate (including television advertising, and direct mail and telephone targeting of likely supporters). To be able to provide these services to party candidates, the state parties needed to acquire the necessary technology, to assemble an appropriately trained staff, and to generate enough revenue to support these more sophisticated operations. By the 1980s most state parties employed, in addition to their clerical staffs, several professionals with specialized responsibility for such areas as party fundraising, budgeting, communications, opinion polling, and a panoply of "field operations." Today the year-round state party operations are usually supervised by either a full-time party chair or by an executive director (or, in some instances, both). While state party organizations are typically not large bureaucracies, they have become increasingly staffed by professionals rather than amateurs.

State parties have consumed substantial financial resources in the process of transforming themselves into permanent professional organizations. By the mid-1980s, several state parties had annual budgets in excess of $1 million. One of the richest of the state parties, the Florida Republican party, spent $6 million in 1988 for the staff and equipment of its large and active state party headquarters.[8] This example illustrates the necessary connection between successful party fundraising and the professionalization of state party organizations—indeed, maintaining the professional organization is one of the primary duties of fundraisers employed by any state party. In comparison with the parties of the 1950s, state parties have become considerably more sophisticated fundraisers. However, some aspects of fundraising did not change between these decades: in the 1980s, as in the 1950s, it was Republican state committees that tended to be most systematic and aggressive in their use of professional fundraisers, and of highly successful fundraising techniques (such as direct-mail solicitation and "large-giver" programs).

Our inquisitive citizens would be much less likely to succeed if they went out in search of their local Republican or Democratic county party headquarters. Unlike party organizations at the state level, very few county parties possess their own year-round offices or even their own listings in the telephone book. Most county parties are strictly volunteer organizations, operating out of space donated by the county party chairperson. Yet, despite this lack of physical presence, county parties are real organizations in the same way that local garden clubs or League of Women Voters chapters are real organizations. County parties usually have constitutions or bylaws, hold regular meetings of their elected officers (among them, a county party chair), and maintain lists of their regular supporters. With very few exceptions, county party organizations are not nearly as institutionalized as are their state-level counterparts.

Although most county parties are not imposing organizational entities, state and national party organizers are attaching increasing importance to the work of these local party organizations. County party organizations in electorally crucial areas are now likely to receive monetary assistance from state and national party committees, and they may well be included as partners in state or national party get-out-the-vote efforts. Although state and national party grants to county parties rarely exceed several thousand dollars, even such modest financial assistance can be crucial to the county organizations.

One study in the 1980s[9] found that state and local parties engage in a variety of joint activity (see Table 10.1). It is common for state and local party organizations to cooperate on voter registration drives, get-out-the-vote programs, and in compiling mailing lists of contributors and party members. State organizations sometimes also provide services to the local parties, but this is somewhat less common and is more likely to take place with the Republicans than the Democrats. Generally speaking, state and local party organizations are reasonably well interrelated.

The impact of this cooperation and assistance was reflected in a 1984 survey in which county party leaders throughout the United States named assistance from state and national party organizations as the most important factor in strengthening their local organizations.[10] As

Table 10.1 Local Party Relations with State Party Organizations, 1984

	Percentage of organizations engaging in activity	
	Republicans	Democrats
Joint state-local activities:		
Shares mailing lists of contributors and members	66	62
Joint fundraising programs	43	49
Cooperation in recruiting or checking patronage appointments	42	35
Joint get-out-the-vote drives	74	74
Joint registration drives	68	64
State party services to local parties:		
Assistance with financial record keeping	12	12
Legal advice	52	39
Computer services	48	38
Research	50	34
Office space	2	4
Staff	13	8
Assistance with candidate recruitment	32	22
Funds for operating expenses	7	9
Funds for campaign expenses	16	17

Source: James L. Gibson, John P. Frendreis, and Laura L. Vertz, "Party Dynamics in the 1980s: Change in County Party Organizational Strength, 1980–84," *American Journal of Political Science* 32 (1989): 77.

formal institutions—rather than the highly personalized entity of a particular party leader—both state and county parties are much more likely to exist today than in the past.

THE ACTIVITIES OF STATE AND LOCAL PARTY ORGANIZATIONS

Just what is it that these state and local party organizations do? Most party activities fall into two major categories: supporting party candidates and officeholders, and building and maintaining the party organization.

If a basic function of parties is to contest elections, then supporting the party's candidates is one of the most important activities of any party organization. Typical kinds of party support for candidates may range from monetary campaign contributions, to legal advice about campaign finances, to coordination of a single opinion poll on behalf of several party candidates (see Table 10.1). State parties have also played an increasingly active role in arranging for party candidates to pool resources when renting campaign headquarters and office equipment. County parties often play a similar role in local government elections, and it is during the election season that county parties become most visibly active, doing such things as distributing campaign literature, making monetary contributions to candidates, and conducting voter registration drives.

Outside the immediate campaign season, American parties are increasingly likely to sponsor a variety of activities generally intended to maintain or to build electoral support for the party and its candidates. Especially since the 1960s, state parties have played an increasing role in locating and contacting party supporters in the electorate as a whole. Many state parties now sponsor targeted voter registration and get-out-the-vote efforts, publish newsletters for their supporters, and conduct their own public opinion surveys during, and often between, election campaigns.[11]

A crucial party maintenance activity is fundraising for state and local party headquarters. Party organizations, like all organizations, allocate a portion of their efforts to their own sustenance. Most parties, however, have been successful at moving beyond this narrow sort of activity to work for the benefit of the entire party. Thus, many state parties' maintenance activities include off-year fundraising, polling, voter identification, and candidate recruitment and derecruitment. As one of the few institutional actors active year-round, party organizations can do much work preparatory to the campaign season.

Party organizations also act as lobbyists for the party's interests. Parties are increasingly bound by statutory restrictions, laws that limit and define many party structures and activities (see below). The permanent staffs of the party organizations are actively engaged in trying to influence legislation that affects the competitive status of the party and the health of the party system itself.

Thus, party organizations perform a myriad of tasks. Though they are not always extremely successful in achieving the goals they establish, the level of party organizational activity is in general far higher today than it was in the past, and, as a result, the effectiveness of parties is most likely increasing rather significantly.

PARTY PERSONNEL: MEMBERS AND SUPPORTERS

One of the challenges faced by contemporary American party organizations is the problem of gathering those resources that enable them to provide services to party candidates and officeholders. In this sense, political party organizations are very similar to the interest groups with which they compete for influence in the electoral process. Above all, both kinds of groups are voluntary organizations that rely primarily on nonmaterial rewards to maintain their organizational networks. Successful parties must be able to rely on a reservoir of reliable individual supporters who will contribute money, influence, expertise, and time to the party cause.

Identifying these supporters is not an easy task for either researchers or for the parties themselves. Unlike many European political parties, United States parties have never attempted to build large membership bases, bases in which locally organized members are active between elections. For United States parties, formal membership has not been an important category, and it became even less important after primary elections opened the privilege of candidate selection to nominal "members." But American parties still need the help of a core of active supporters, people who can serve as volunteer officers in the organization (for instance, county party chairpersons); people (candidates) who will carry the party banner into even hopeless electoral contests; and people who will donate labor and money to support the efforts of the party as an organization as well as to support individual party candidates.

Like other voluntary organizations, parties can offer three types of rewards to their active supporters: material, solidary, and purposive benefits.[12] Contemporary American parties, unlike their predecessors, cannot offer most of their supporters either material rewards or a privileged place in the candidate selection process. Nor are these parties cohesive, year-round, social organizations capable of providing most supporters with either a social network or a sense of political solidary. The paucity of material and solidary rewards probably explains why groups motivated by strong programmatic or ideological agendas have, in recent years, scored some spectacular victories inside the political parties. Factions with strong ideological agendas, such as right-to-life Republicans, are comparatively successful in getting their supporters to show up at county party caucuses or at primary elections. The ability of Conservative Christians to get their supporters elected as precinct delegates in the 1986 primary elections gave this faction strong leverage within the Michigan Republican party, and threatened to cost George Bush the Michigan presidential nomination in 1988, despite the support the then vice-president enjoyed from the state party's top leaders and top elected officials.

SUMMARY

State and local party organizations are increasingly visible as year-round organizations. They are organizations that are willing and able to play a role in politics that is active—not just *reactive*. Yet our account of these institutions has also shown the difficulties involved in trying to understand the simultaneously professional and voluntary nature of the party organizations within the states. On the one hand, these party organizations are professional operations—both Republican and Democratic state party organizations try to assemble similar teams of specialists to run technically similar campaign and interelection activities. On the other hand, the purposes for which these organizations will be used and the availability of resources for running the professional operations are, in greater or lesser part, determined by those for whom politics is, at most, a volunteer job. The extent to which these resources are worth assembling and controlling will become clearer in the following section.

THE POLITICAL RELEVANCE OF STATE AND LOCAL PARTY ORGANIZATIONS

It is important to understand the changing nature of state and local party organizations because the strengths and weaknesses of these organizations are directly and indirectly reflected in the outcomes of American political processes. We see the impact of these organizations on electoral outcomes and on public policies in the states. In these and other ways, party organizations are integral to many vital democratic processes in the United States.

THE ELECTORAL IMPACT OF PARTY ORGANIZATIONS

Strong party organizations influence elections through both direct and indirect pathways. The direct link between party organizations and electoral outcomes was shown most clearly in one recent study of gubernatorial elections. This study found a direct positive relationship between relative organizational strength and votes.[13] In the states in which one party held a relative advantage in party organizational strength, that party's candidate was more successful in garnering votes in gubernatorial elections. Strong parties appear to assist gubernatorial candidates by providing money, people, and organization. Though the contributions of strong state party organizations are rarely decisive in gubernatorial elections, it appears that organizational strength does make some difference in the electoral arena.

In most cases it is difficult to measure the electoral impact of strong party organizations, both because there are other variables that influence election outcomes, and because the relation between party organizational strength and electoral outcome may be indirect. Still, studies of some individual states have clearly identified the relative strength of particular state party organizations as key factors in certain election outcomes.

The Democratic party in Michigan and the Republican party in Indiana both contributed to the success of their party's candidates in the 1980s. The wealthy and well-organized Republican party in Florida helped the long-time minority Republicans to win the governorship in that state in 1986 and to win a Florida Senate seat in 1988.

At least some of the Republican party's success in the South in the last few decades—perhaps itself an element of party system realignment—is attributable to the increased activities of the Republican state party organizations. In the 1960s the Republican National Committee made a conscious decision to begin contesting elections in the historically Democratic South. The initial Republican penetration of the South was at the level of presidential elections and was inspired mainly by the Democrats' unpopular support for racial integration. The watershed period was the presidential election of 1948. But until the late 1960s, the Republicans had not been successful at parlaying success at the presidential level into control of the statehouses. Many see the success of the Republican gubernatorial candidates in the 1970s and early 1980s as a function of the development of party organizations. Concomitantly, the continuing failure of the Republicans at the local level in the South, especially in rural areas, may be due in part to the Republican failure to establish strong county party organizations. Party organizations have played a crucial role in the early stages of realignment in the South.

The impact of party organizations should not be measured merely in terms of short-term electoral gains, especially since contemporary American political parties often have set their own sights much further than the next election. The parties' growing attachment to long-term goals is one explanation for the recent development of American state party organizations as year-round professional operations. Parties' increased willingness to invest in organizational activities beyond the scope of traditional election campaigns does not mean that these parties no longer view their primary task as being to win control of political power through the election of public officeholders. Parties now pursue a variety of strategies in their quests for power—some may focus on gains in the short term, while others take a long-term orientation. Elections are won not on election day but in the months, if not years, prior to the balloting. As one of the few institutional actors active during the off-season, party organizations can have an important influence on electoral strategies. Even where the efforts of state party organizations do not contribute to immediate victories for party candidates, the emergence of a year-round organization in any particular state may be essential to that party's longer term success. Even only moderately strong party organizations may be able to provide the crucial infrastructure that allows candidates and activists to mount credible challenges to the state majority party. In recent years party organizations have taken the lead in conducting public opinion polling during the "off-years" (outside the traditional campaign period) in an effort to assist party candidates in developing issues for the next election.

Another important way in which state and local party organizations can and do act to improve party electoral chances is by playing an active role in the recruiting, and derecruiting, of candidates. Table 10.2 reports data on the involvement of state party organizations in the recruitment of candidates in the late 1970s.[14] At least as reported by the state party chairpersons, the party organizations were fairly active in candidate recruitment. Except for the U.S. Senate, a majority of state party organizations is active in recruiting candidates for the major state and federal races.

In terms of candidate nomination, parties are obviously limited by state laws about candidate selection. Yet, the establishment of primary elections as the usual route for candidate selection has not entirely removed state and local parties from the selection process. In some states parties hold their own pre-primary caucuses and issue pre-primary candidate endorsements. In all states parties may make selective promises of campaign support in order to encourage particular individuals to seek the party nomination. Party organizations have also actively sought to *discourage* certain candidates from running for office (e.g., in 1991, the Louisiana State Republican party sought to discourage the candidacy of David Duke, a former leader of the Ku Klux Klan, from seeking that state's governorship as a Republican). At the local level, parties may play a particularly important role in recruiting individuals to fill the party slate, especially for obscure offices or for contests that the party has no chance of winning.

Table 10.2 The Involvement of State Party Organizations in Candidate Recruitment, 1975–1980

Office	Percentage of state parties involved in recruiting candidates
Governor	55.2
Other state constitutional offices	58.2
U.S. House of Representatives	64.4
U.S. Senate	43.8
State legislature	79.5

Source: Cornelius P. Cotter et al., *Party Organizations and American Politics* (New York: Praeger, 1984), p. 25.

Any assessment of the electoral impact of state and local party organizations must tread a fine line between overstatement and understatement. Political party organizations can seldom be identified as the single decisive determinant of contemporary election outcomes. They are politically relevant actors that can, in the right circumstances, make crucial contributions to a winning election formula, whether by encouraging an attractive candidate to compete, or by helping candidates identify critical issues early in the campaign, or by providing technical or other campaign resources.

THE POLICY PERTINENCE OF PARTY ORGANIZATIONS

Much less is known about how party organizations affect public policy. This in part reflects a presumption made long ago that ideological activity on the part of party leaders is inimical to party success[15] and, in part, reflects the reality of nonpartisanship in many local public offices. The assumption is often that party leaders who are motivated by ideology are not sufficiently flexible to accept the compromise that is essential to politics; that they are not sufficiently committed to the party to maintain allegiance to it even when they disagree with party policy positions; and that they do not have the requisite organizational and technological skills to build and maintain party organizations. All of these attributes are captured in the term applied to these party activists—they are "amateurs."

It is highly doubtful that county party organizations have much of an ideological effect on public officeholders once they assume their positions. Mayors, county officials, and even state legislators are required to make a variety of nonideological decisions, and when ideology is important, they are much more influenced by other political actors than by county party officials. Yet, some ideologically motivated party leaders have been able to build strong county party organizations. Gibson, Frendreis, and Vertz[16] have argued that while ideology may provide the goals for the party, organization provides the means, and organizational means are not incompatible with ideological goals. To the extent that party leaders influence candidate recruitment, party nominations, and election-day activity, opportunities for getting the "right" candidates into office exist. Even though those most active in county party organizations are frequently more motivated by material and solidary incentives than by ideology, political activists could plausibly aspire to achieve certain ideological ideals through some local party organizations.

THE DEMOCRATIC RELEVANCE OF STATE AND LOCAL PARTY ORGANIZATIONS

Some observers have been eager to ascribe to party organizations a role in the democratization of politics. Within this perspective, party organizations can provide opportunities for political participation that not only give citizens a greater voice in controlling their government, but also a greater *sense* of control.

Throughout the past century there has been an ongoing debate in the United States about the role that parties, and party elites, should play in candidate selection. Those who oppose a strong role for parties have sometimes excoriated control of the party "bosses" over the nomination process as a means of depriving citizens of the right to choose their political leaders. The nomination process in most states has become more open to participation by ordinary citizens, and political participation is a crucial value in democracies. However, others have retorted that, where parties do not have at least some control over the nominating processes, it is difficult to hold parties accountable for the candidates that bear their party colors. They ask whether parties can be held responsible for their candidates if, for instance, state law allows voters who are not adherents of the party to vote in the party primary. To the extent that party organizations lose control over nominations, culpability and accountability are lost. Those in favor of giving the parties the authority to control who participates in candidate selection argue that this type of party responsibility is essential to ensuring democratic accountability. There is some tension between the opening of party processes to widespread political participation and the maintenance of any sort of responsibility of parties for their candidates and policies.

There has recently been an unprecedented level of effort by party organizations—national, state, and local—to reach out to a broad range of party supporters. The bulk of this activity is in the context of fundraising. Receiving a letter requesting a financial donation to the party may have little to do with democracy, and it would be unwise to claim too much impact from the simple act of writing a check. Nonetheless, the advent of direct mail, telephone campaigns, and so on has given the ordinary voter a much greater sense of the reality of political parties, and has provided more opportunity than ever before for citizens to participate.

SUMMARY

Attempts to gauge the political relevance of state and local party organizations in the United States are all too likely to produce an assessment that concentrates on the political *irrelevance* of these organizations. This is especially true if these organizations are being explicitly or implicitly compared with their counterparts in parliamentary democracies. There is, for example, little risk of confusing United States state parties with their state-level counterparts in the Federal Republic of Germany—a country that is frequently described as a "party democracy." In Germany the paying membership of the state parties select party candidates for the state parliaments and approve the policy programs that guide their parliamentary parties. The German state and national party organizations control most campaign resources, and German voters cast their most important votes for parties, not for candidates. Thus, this sort of cross-national perspective tends to highlight the lack of influence of the United States parties.

Yet, a different assessment of United States state and local parties emerges if one compares these organizations to their American counterparts in previous decades, instead of to their contemporary counterparts in parliamentary democracies. This comparison reveals state and local parties as organizations that have recently increased their access to those resources that allow them to contribute directly, and indirectly, to the success of party candidates. In some circumstances, ideologically motivated factions do try to use these party organizations to advance their programmatic goals. State and local parties have been playing an increasingly central role in some important aspects of election campaigns: they have become crucial conduits for campaign contributions from nonparty groups, and they have become increasingly active in efforts to help all party candidates by registering voters and by getting these voters to the polls. While the United States is far from being a "party democracy," it is a democracy in which political parties make consequential contributions.

THE ENVIRONMENT OF STATE AND
LOCAL PARTY ORGANIZATIONS

State and local political parties obviously do not operate in a vacuum. Because parties are pursuing electoral success for their candidates, party organizations must adapt to both the rules under which they compete and to competition from party and nonparty entities. But parties do not merely passively respond to their environments; instead, they often actively seek to manipulate these environments in ways intended to help the party cause. Party organizations have been particularly active in their efforts to make their legal environments more hospitable.

LEGAL REGULATIONS: THE CHANGING RULES OF THE ELECTORAL GAME

Over the past century legal changes have severely limited the power of party organizations in two crucial areas: in their control of resources, and in their control of candidate selection processes. To understand the impact legal changes have made on the scope of resources controlled by party organizations, it is helpful to glance back to the end of the nineteenth century. To many party theorists, this was the golden age of the political party "machine," a time when city and state party bosses played a major role in selecting candidates and in using patronage—the distribution of public jobs, of welfare services, and of other public monies—to ensure that chosen candidates won popular electoral support.[17] "Machine" parties were never the norm in the smaller cities and towns in America, but they do illustrate the resource-gathering possibilities some American parties once possessed.

By the middle of the twentieth century, many of the original conditions that had supported these political machines had disappeared. New social welfare programs—organized by the government, not by the political parties—replaced the services once provided by the neighborhood party apparatus. These new programs aimed to reach all "deserving" recipients, not just those who voted "correctly." Of equal importance was the progressive expansion of civil service protections (i.e., appointments on the basis of "merit," not party affiliation) to state and local jobs. These had once been strictly political appointments; civil service protections meant that employees could not be dismissed for failing to contribute to a political party, or because a new political party had gained control of city hall. Despite these changes, "traditional party organizations"—parties that could offer material incentives to their supporters—continued to thrive in a few states and cities through the 1960s.[18] While the party patronage machine may not have disappeared as quickly as was once supposed, legal attacks on the scope of patronage continued into the 1990s to undermine the ability of parties to provide material rewards to supporters.

Legal changes have also affected parties' control of campaign resources. Since the beginning of the 1970s, there have been ongoing, major changes in regulations about the ways in which parties and candidates raise and spend campaign funds. At the level of federal elective offices, the 1971 Federal Election Campaign Act, and its 1974 amendments, placed tight restrictions on the size of campaign contributions made by individuals (including candidates), interest groups, and by political parties themselves. Within the decade, all the states had adopted some type of regulation of campaign finances for state-level elections.[19] Even after a 1976 Supreme Court ruling overturned mandatory limits on campaign contributions, voluntary limits were permitted as a condition for those candidates accepting public campaign financing (see *Buckley v. Valleo*). Although the new rules tended to restrict the amount of direct financial support parties could give their candidates, by the end of the 1970s separate rules had been adopted that encouraged national and state party organizations to spend money on noncandidate specific voter registration and on turnout-boosting activities. The parties have often targeted such activities to help candidates in crucial races.[20] One recent study found that over $43 million was spent on the 1990 congressional elections by state and local party organizations in nine states.[21] If practices such as these continue to expand, party organizations will quickly become highly influential in the electoral process.

Several types of changes over the past century in the laws governing candidate nomination and election have also forced party organizations to make major changes in their own strategies and goals. In the United States, state governments have responsibility for making most of the rules pertaining to elections for public offices. State laws stipulate which parties may nominate candidates (ballot access), the procedures by which these parties must select their candidates, and even the structure and appearance of the ballots. Indeed, from a cross-national perspective one of the distinctive features of American parties is that they are not in full control of the processes by which they select *party* nominees; these processes are stipulated by laws. Election mechanics—a crucial aspect of the parties' environments—vary among the states.

Reducing the power of the party organizations was a specific goal of those late-nineteenth and early-twentieth-century reformers who successfully lobbied, state by state, for the adoption of primary elections as the means of selecting party nominees. Today, primary elections are used in every state for at least some offices. The rules about who is eligible to participate in each party's primary vary from state to state, and often vary within single states from year to year. For parties, the most consequential distinction is between so-called "closed" primaries, in which voters must register their party affiliation in advance of the election, and "open" primaries, in which any eligible voter may choose on election day to participate in either party's primary. Closed primaries not only protect parties from so-called "crossover" voting by those who will not support the party's candidates in the general elections; they also provide both major parties with lists of registered supporters. Whatever kind of primary election is used, however, parties themselves have no exclusive veto power over who may use the party label. Thus, primary elections make possible the exceptional, yet notorious, cases in which voters select candidates who are repudiated by their "own" party organization. The California State Democratic party in 1983 supported a Republican for a state Senate seat after a Ku Klux Klan leader won the Democratic nomination in a primary election.[22] In another infamous example in 1986, the Illinois Democratic candidate for governor, Adlai Stevenson III, chose to officially run as an Independent after primary voters chose a Lyndon Larouche supporter to carry the Democratic label into the race for lieutenant governor.[23] Without giving parties control of the nomination process, it is difficult to hold them accountable for the candidates who emerge.

While the introduction of primaries deprived party organizations of the possibility of a decisive role in the selection of candidates, state and local party organizations may still influence the nomination process. In several states, parties hold conventions and issue pre-primary candidate endorsements—that is, the party organization's preference among the various candidates is explicitly stated. In some cases, the winners of these endorsements gain specific advantages in the primary process, such as automatic ballot access or top position on the primary ballot.[24] Party organizations also use informal endorsements as a means of trying to influence the candidate selection process.

Although party organizations must be highly responsive to changes in their legal environments, it would be incorrect to view them as the passive captives of their environments. It is party representatives in the legislatures who make and modify most of these laws governing parties and the electoral process. Most states were using some type of closed primary by the 1980s. Before the 1990 primaries, more than half the states required voters to declare their party affiliation days, weeks, or even months before election day.[25] Beyond control over the candidate nomination process, several kinds of legislation help protect the importance of the established party organizations. To enhance the value of the Republican or Democratic party nominations, state legislatures may pass highly restrictive regulations designed to keep all but the two established parties off ballots for state and local offices. In Minnesota, there is a relatively high hurdle which ensures that a locally successful third party will not get automatic ballot access in city or county elections: in this state, a party is only eligible to nominate its candidates for any office via a primary election if the party's gubernatorial candidate received at least 5 percent of the vote in *every* county in the previous gubernatorial election; candidates for other parties are only placed on the ballot if they can prove their support by a successful petition drive ahead of the election. State legislatures may also establish programs that offer a more direct type of aid to the party organizations. In 1988 twenty-one states provided some kind of public funds for state elections (see Table 10.3). In thirteen of these states, these funds were channeled in part or exclusively through the parties, whereas in the other eight states the funds went directly to the candidates.[26]

Parties and their representatives can and do influence their legal environments in ways that contribute measurably to the strength of the party organizations. This was shown particularly clearly in one study of state party organizations that examined the relationship between public policies supportive of state parties and the strength of the state-level organizations. An index of supportive policy was derived from six areas: (1) the openness of primaries; (2) the restrictiveness of regulations governing voter party declarations; (3) whether a straight-ticket option was provided to voters; (4) whether the state had a statue requiring that independent presidential candidates and/or their electors declare they are not members of any political party at some time period prior to their nomination; (5) whether the state had a statute precluding a candidate who had lost a party primary from running as an independent for the same office in the succeeding general election (a "sore-loser" statute); and (6) whether the party had the authority to replace deceased or resigned candidates. According to this measure, the state with statutes most supportive of parties in the early 1980s was Kentucky; the least supportive state was Wyoming. More importantly, the authors demonstrated that party organizations tended to have grown stronger in those states in which public policies were more supportive.[27]

INTERPARTY COMPETITION

Another important attribute of the environment of party organizations is the level of interparty competition. There is a great variability in the

Table 10.3 State Funding of Election Campaigns, 1988*

Public funds distributed in part or in entirety to parties:

Alabama	North Carolina
California	Ohio
Idaho	Oregon
Indiana	Rhode Island
Iowa	Utah
Kentucky	Virginia
Maine	

Funds distributed to candidates only:

Hawaii	Minnesota
Maryland	Montana
Massachusetts	New Jersey
Michigan	Wisconsin

No provisions or public campaign financing:

Alaska	New Hampshire
Arizona	New Mexico
Arkansas	New York
Colorado	North Dakota
Connecticut	Oklahoma
Delaware	Pennsylvania
Florida	South Carolina
Georgia	South Dakota
Illinois	Tennessee
Kansas	Texas
Louisiana	Vermont
Mississippi	Washington
Missouri	West Virginia
Nebraska	Wyoming
Nevada	

*Funding for some or all state-level contests.
Source: The Book of the States, 1990–1991 edition, Lexington, Ky.: Council of State Governments, 1990, Table 5.8, p. 259.

American states in levels of competitiveness. In many areas of the South the Democratic party is firmly ensconced; in some areas of the Midwest and the Mountain states the Republicans have an enduring electoral advantage.

Virtually everything parties do is in part a function of their competitive status. Campaign strategies range from voter mobilization for the dominant party to voter conversion for the subordinant party. The relative balance of in-state versus out-of-state support for the party organization may also be affected by the depth of its indigenous roots. For instance, many Republican parties in the South functioned for lengthy periods of time on resources provided by national donors (including the Republican National Committee). Party organizations behave differently depending upon whether they are the majority or minority party.

Another important environmental factor is simply the activity of the opposing party organization. There is a tendency for party organizations to try to match the innovations of their competitors. As one party implements sophisticated new voter identification strategies the opposite is likely to copy the innovation. Somewhat paradoxically, one of the major factors strengthening *Democratic* party organizations throughout the country has been the rapid development of *Republican* organizations. Activity by a resurgent minority party can be especially effective at shaking dominant party organizations out of their lethargy.

NATIONAL PARTY ORGANIZATIONS

State and local parties not only learn from each other, but they also learn from the national party organizations. Since the 1960s, the Democratic and Republican National Committees have strengthened even more dramatically than have the parties' state and local organizations. Although the national party committees initially started from a weaker level of organization, it was these national committees that played important roles in bolstering their state-level counterparts. The Republican National Committee led the way in these organization-building efforts. Table 10.4 reports data from a study in the late 1970s that showed large differences in the support provided party organizations by the Republican and Democratic national committees.

In the mid-1970s, the Republican National Committee (RNC) discovered hidden treasure when it began to make systematic use of direct-mail fundraising. The national party invested much of the new riches this fundraising netted in efforts to build up the party organization both at the national level and throughout the states. The RNC not only hired its own large staff of campaign and fundraising professionals; it also paid the salaries of staff members who worked with, and sometimes within, the state party organizations. The RNC in the 1970s was not merely concerned with party victories at the national level: the national party also channeled funds into recruiting and training candidates for state legislative contests, and into providing services for state-level campaigns in target areas.[28]

Table 10.4 National Services to State Party Organizations, 1975–1980

Service	Percent receiving service	
	Democrats	Republicans
Staff	3.8	63.0
Polls and research	7.7	44.4
Voter identification	19.2	22.2
Campaign seminars	40.7	88.9
Rule enforcement	53.8	0.0
Technical assistance	22.2	22.2
Cash transfers	7.4	51.9

Source: Cotter et al., *Party Organizations*, p. 63.

The Democratic National Committee (DNC) was slower to concern itself with building up state party organizations and with providing support to state candidates (mainly because the party was deeply mired in debt), although in the early 1970s it took a strong interest in the rules under which these candidates were selected. After the 1968 Democratic National Convention, a series of national party commissions recommended the use of particular types of rules in the selection of candidates and of convention delegates. The DNC successfully persuaded and pressured Democratic delegations in state legislatures to adopt these changes, including the use of the closed primary for candidate selection. These rules became performance standards for the party organizations. It took the impressive Republican victories in 1980 to alert the DNC to the political significance of the 1970s' growth of all levels of Republican party organization. In response, by the mid-1980s the DNC was providing state and local party organizations with most of the services and support which the RNC had begun offering its affiliates in the 1970s.[29] On the other side, the Republican National Committee in the 1980s began imposing even more regulations on its constituent organizations.

By the end of 1980s, both national parties had become major contributors of money and of services to congressional campaigns. Both could compete with the Political Action Committees (see below) in terms of being important resources for serious candidates, especially in strategically important districts. To circumvent legal limits on direct party support for candidates, in the 1980s and 1990s the increasingly wealthy national parties channeled national party campaign contributions through the state party organizations—another way of closely linking the state and national organizations.[30]

Both national party committees offer at least some of their services with "strings attached." State and local parties that accept national party support are required to satisfy national party wishes. Candidates receiving campaign support may be depended on to conform to certain programmatic expectations (i.e., it is not the case that every candidate who wins the party primary automatically receives national party support). The wealth of the national parties and the services into which this wealth translates have become means of increasing levels of integration between the national and state and local party organizations.

One of the consequences of this has been the nationalization of partisan politics in the United States. State and local party organizations are increasingly involved in campaigns for national office (including congressional elections), and national resources are becoming more influential in state and local politics. If such a trend continues, it may well turn out that all politics is not "local."

CANDIDATE CAMPAIGN ORGANIZATIONS

Because of state regulations concerning campaign finance, one of the first things a candidate for any level of public office does is to form a campaign committee with, at the least, an official treasurer. Candidates, particularly candidates who must compete in party primaries, must put effort into building up their own campaign organizations—even candidates for the most local of offices cannot rely solely on the party organization. The complexity of a candidate's campaign organization, and the relation between this organization and the party organization, are determined in large part by the level of office that the candidate is seeking, by the financial resources the candidate can gather for the campaign, and by the degree of competition for that office. Incumbent candidates for statewide offices (governors, attorneys general) are the most likely to have well-financed campaigns staffed by paid political experts who are personally loyal to the candidate. Incumbents are also likely to have developed their own networks of volunteer supporters and campaign contributors. On the other hand, new candidates, and most candidates for local offices, are likely to be in greater need of the support that can be provided by state and local party organizations. This support may be especially important in the early stages of the campaign, when introductions through the party organizations may allow candidates to gather the financial support necessary to build up their independent organizations.

The actual effectiveness of party contributions to campaigns cannot be easily measured. The relatively large monetary contribution that may be given by a state party to its gubernatorial candidate may be more easily replaceable than the free legal advice given by a local party volunteer to a party's candidate for county clerk. Other kinds of services that parties may provide for candidates include financial support (contributing directly and encouraging contributions by others); technical support (providing facilities such as printing presses or telephone banks, coordinating the purchase of other services, such as opinion polls); and the mobilization of voters (e.g., assisting in voter registration drives or sponsoring advertisements endorsing all party candidates). Table 10.5 reports the levels at which state party organizations conducted such activities in the late 1970s. In deciding where to use limited party resources, both state and local parties must make choices between fairness (equal services to all candidates) and probable effectiveness (targeting services on closely contested elections).

POLITICAL ACTION COMMITTEES

As party organizations have seen their patronage resources dwindle and their direct control over nominations shrink, they have faced the challenge of maintaining their positions as essential providers of resources (organizational, financial, informational) for candidates. Nonparty groups have taken over some of the jobs once performed solely by party organizations. The most prominent of these groups are the Political Action Committees (PACs), the campaign-contributing branches of business, labor, and other interest groups.

PACs proliferated in the 1970s and 1980s as a result of new restrictions on campaign giving by groups and by individuals. Whereas in 1972 there were only 113 PACs registered with the Federal Election Commission, by 1988 there were 4,268 registered PACs.[31] The number of PACs grew because these constituted an easy way for wealthy individuals to multiply their support for favored candidates: individuals could legally contribute much higher amounts to PACs than to individual campaigns. PACs could offer favored candidates both direct (monetary) and indirect (services, advertising campaigns) support—kinds of support once provided primarily by party organizations. In the 1970s PACs became a crucial component in most campaign fundraising, and became a powerful way for groups to gain political leverage.

The increased availability of PAC support, especially for incumbents in national politics, potentially reduced some candidates' reliance on party support. In contrast, candidates for less influential political offices,

Table 10.5 Contributions of State Party Organizations to Candidates, 1975–1980

Office	Percentage of state parties contributing to candidate campaigns
Governor	41.7
Other state constitutional offices	35.9
U.S. House of Representatives	39.6
U.S. Senate	57.7
State legislature	40.6

Source: Cotter et al., *Party Organizations*, p. 23.

and candidates challenging incumbents, necessarily rely more on the resources provided by local or state party organizations than on PAC contributions.

SUMMARY

The picture we have painted in this section is one of party organizations being constantly forced to respond to a dynamic political environment. The parties must adapt to changes in voters' preferences and to changes in relevant legal regulations. The party organizations compete for political influence with other parties, with nonparty groups—and even with party-supported candidates. Yet this competition is by no means one-sided: parties do not inevitably lose out in these political struggles, and parties may well be able to find ways to turn apparent constraints to their own advantage. Thus, for instance, parties have adapted to new patterns of candidate financing by making themselves allies of would-be candidate sponsors, and by helping to ensure that campaign finance legislation puts parties in a privileged position. Contemporary party organizations operate under a wide variety of highly visible constraints in the United States—but recognition of these constraints should not obscure the fact that these party organizations are far from powerless.

PARTY ORGANIZATIONS IN A CHANGING POLITICAL WORLD

One of the great challenges in the study of party organizations is to cultivate the ability to simultaneously view parties as organizations that react to their broader legal, social, and electoral environments, and as organizations which are critically involved in shaping these environments. We now put change in parties and their environments into the broader perspective of the transformation of the United States party system.

Some observers of the American party system perceive basic change in the structure of party politics—a "dealignment" of the system. There are two basic elements of this diagnosis. First, the primary party attachments of American voters have weakened, and second, many of the essential functions of party organizations have been expropriated by nonparty organizations and groups. Some scholars have even gone so far as to argue that the demise of the traditional party organization threatens democracy because "democracy, save party, is unthinkable."

Evidence supporting such a view is not difficult to assemble. Parties are said to be no longer able to control access to the ballot, mainly due to the rise of direct primaries. Candidates and officeholders are no longer beholden to the party organization for resources, both because the resources that parties can uniquely provide (mainly people) are no longer so important for electoral politics, and because the increasing amounts of PAC money in politics have made candidates more dependent upon interest groups than on party organizations. Voters who are no longer persuaded by party-based appeals believe that state and local party organizations have become largely irrelevant to politics. The various maladies support a pessimistic assessment of the viability of parties as they have been known throughout much of American history.

At the same time that parties are buffeted by antiparty winds, new opportunities have arisen. All organizations—political and nonpolitical alike—are continually faced with changing environmental circumstances, some of which are threatening to the basic structure and function of the organization (e.g., witness the problems currently being faced by American banking institutions). Parties are no different. If we are to understand the role of party organizations in American politics we must remember that one of the most important attributes of a strong organization is its ability to adapt to changing environmental circumstances.

There is clear evidence that contemporary environmental changes have not completely undermined state and local party organizations. The party organizations are devising new strategies for coping with change. As the number of organizational players proliferates, the need for a coordinating role becomes paramount. State and especially local party organizations are well situated to perform such a function. As the cost of the campaigning skyrockets, the need to launch cooperative efforts (e.g., joint surveys on behalf of several candidates) increases. While it may be true that contemporary party organizations do not dictate state or local politics the way they once did in a few urban areas, party organizations have significant opportunities for persuasion, organization, and coordination.

Party organizations are one of the few institutional actors functioning outside the campaign season. Off-year activities such as recruitment, research, organization, and planning can be an important means of extending the influence of party organizations. Recruiting candidates and showing the party flag in hopeless elections, encouraging candidates and officeholders to switch their party affiliations, and even sponsoring legal challenges to the practices of the dominant party are all activities for which party organizations have few competitors. Some may view this as a sign of weakness—party organizations can only function well when there are few competitors—but we have argued that this is a sign of health: adaptable organizations modify their activities to function most effectively under the contemporary circumstances.

It is possible that the uncertainty of the political environment has actually contributed to the strengthening of party organizations. The weakening of party attachments in the South has provided new opportunities for Republicans. Republican organizational development in the South contributed to increasing Republican electoral success. At the same time, however, it provided a catalyst for the strengthening of *Democratic* party organizations. Especially at the early stages of party development, strong local and state organizations can make a great deal of difference, fundamentally changing the structure of party politics. Obviously, we do not contend that all changes in the party and political system have aided party organizations; nor are we certain that party organizations will be able to survive a continued onslaught of antiparty change. Party organizations are not helplessly swept along by changing tides in the party system.

Party organizations may be one of the most important and effective institutions resisting dealignment. Parties are not helpless actors, standing passively by, waiting for their funeral. As significant influences over electoral outcomes, party organizations certainly contribute to realignment in the sense of heightened competition in all areas of the country for the allegiance of voters. Party organizations are significant independent forces that themselves contribute to the transformation of the party system. This may ultimately be the most important function of state and local party organizations.

NOTES

1. Leon Epstein, *Political Parties in Western Democracies*, 2d ed. (New Brunswick, N.J.: Transaction Books, 1980), p. 9.

2. See, for example, Malcolm E. Jewell and David M. Olson, *Political Parties and Elections in American States,* 3d ed. (Chicago: Dorsey Press, 1988), p. 237.

3. In most New England states, the parties are organized at the level of the township. In Louisiana, there are parish organizations, and in some states there are organizations at the level of the state legislative (or some other) district.

4. Samuel J. Eldersveld, *Political Parties: A Behavioral Analysis* (Chicago: Rand McNally, 1964).

5. This is in contrast to multimember districts (e.g., many city councils elect several "at large" representatives) and proportional representation systems (e.g., Germany allocates seats in the subnational and national legislatures to political parties in rough proportion to the percentage of votes each party receives in the election).

6. Robert Goldstein, *Political Repression in Modern America* (Cambridge, Mass.: Schenkman, 1978), has argued that the weakness of alternative parties in the United States has been due, at least in part, to a systematic attempt of the American government to crush so-called "radical" parties.

7. Robert J. Huckshorn, *Party Leadership in the States* (Amherst, Mass.: U. of Massachusetts Press, 1976), p. 254.

8. Larry Sabato, *The Party's Just Begun: Shaping Political Parties for America's Future* (Glenview, Ill.: Scott, Foresman/Little, Brown, 1988), p. 91; James Barnes, "Reinventing the RNC," *National Journal* 14 (January 1989): 70.

9. Cornelius P. Cotter, James L. Gibson, John F. Bibby, and Robert J. Huckshorn, *Party Organizations and American Politics,* repr. 1989 (New York: Praeger, Pittsburgh, Penn.: U. of Pittsburgh Press, 1984).

10. James. L. Gibson, John P. Frendreis, and Laura L. Vertz, "Party Dynamics in the 1980s: Change in County Party Organizational Strength, 1980–84," *American Journal of Political Science* 32 (1989): 67–90.

11. Cotter et al., *Party Organizations and American Politics,* pp. 19–26.

12. James Q. Wilson, *The Amateur Democrat: Club Politics in Three Cities* (Chicago: U. of Chicago Press, 1962).

13. Cotter et al., *Party Organizations and American Politics,* pp. 100–1.

14. Ibid., p. 25.

15. For example, Wilson, *The Amateur Democrat.*

16. Gibson et al., "Party Dynamics in the 1980s."

17. We should note, however, that even if these organizations were powerful, they were highly personalized—built around a specific party leader—and therefore could not be considered to be institutionalized party organizations.

18. David Mayhew, *Placing Parties in American Politics* (Princeton, N.J.: Princeton U. Press, 1986), p. 20.

19. Stephen Frantzich, *Political Parties in the Technological Age* (New York: Longman, 1989), p. 188.

20. Ibid., p. 191.

21. Joshua Goldstein, *The $43 Million Loophole: Soft Money in the 1990 Congressional Elections* (Washington, D.C.: Center for Responsive Politics, 1991).

22. Frantzich, *Political Parties,* p. 109.

23. Malcolm E. Jewell and David M. Olson, *Political Parties and Elections in American States*, 3d ed. (Chicago: Dorsey Press, 1988), p. 142.

24. Ibid., pp. 94–104.

25. See *Almanac of State Politics*, Table 5.3, p. 236.

26. *Book of the States: 1990–1991* (Lexington, Ky.: Council of State Governments), Table 5.8, p. 259.

27. Cotter et al., *Party Organizations and American Politics*, p. 136.

28. John Bibby, "Party Renewal in the National Republican Party" in Gerald Pomper, ed., *Party Renewal in America* (New York: Praeger, 1980), pp. 107–12.

29. Frantzich, *Political Parties*, p. 89.

30. Larry Sabato, "PACs and Parties" in Margaret Latus Nugent and John R. Johannes, eds., *Money, Elections, and Democracy* (Boulder, Colo.: Westview Press, 1990), p. 192; Goldstein, The $43 Million Loophole.

31. Sabato, "PACs and Parties," p. 188.

REFERENCES

Barnes, James. 1989. "Reinventing the RNC." *National Journal*, January, 14: 67–71.

Bibby, John. 1980. "Party Renewal in the National Republican Party." In *Party Renewal in America*, Gerald Pomper, ed., New York: Praeger Publishers.

The Book of the States, 1990–1991. Lexington, Ky.: Council of State Governments.

Cotter, Cornelius P., James L. Gibson, John F. Bibby, and Robert J. Huckshorn. 1984. *Party Organizations and American Politics.* New York: Praeger. [Paperback edition, 1989. Pittsburgh, Penn.: U. of Pittsburgh Press.]

Eldersveld, Samuel J. 1964. *Political Parties: A Behavioral Analysis.* Chicago: Rand McNally.

Epstein, Leon. 1980. *Political Parties in Western Democracies*, 2d ed. New Brunswick, N.J.: Transaction Books.

Frantzich, Stephen E. 1989. *Political Parties in the Technological Age.* New York: Longman.

Gibson, James L., John P. Frendreis, and Laura L. Vertz. 1989. "Party Dynamics in the 1980s: Change in County Party Organizational Strength, 1980–84." *American Journal of Political Science* 32: 67–90.

Goldstein, Joshua. 1991. *The $43 Million Loophole: Soft Money in the 1990 Congressional Elections.* Washington, D.C.: Center for Responsive Politics.

Goldstein, Robert Justin. 1978. *Political Repression in Modern America.* Cambridge, Mass.: Schenkman.

Huckshorn, Robert J. 1976. *Party Leadership in the States.* Amherst, Mass.: U. of Massachusetts Press.

Jewell, Malcolm E., and David M. Olson. 1988. *Political Parties and Elections in American States*, 3d ed. Chicago: Dorsey Press.

Mayhew, David. 1986. *Placing Parties in American Politics.* Princeton, N.J.: Princeton U. Press, 1986.

Sabato, Larry. 1988. *The Party's Just Begun: Shaping Political Parties for America's Future.* Glenview, Ill.: Scott, Foresman/Little, Brown.

―――――. 1990. "PACs and Parties." In *Money, Elections, and Democracy,* edited by Margaret Latus Nugent and John R. Johannes. Boulder, Colo.: Westview Press.

Wilson, James Q. 1962. *The Amateur Democrat: Club Politics in Three Cities.* Chicago: U. of Chicago Press.

PART FOUR

PARTY REFORM

The most widely discussed changes in party organizations occurred in the 1970s when the two major parties (especially the Democrats) reformed their presidential nominating processes. The Democrats have restructured their nominating procedures every four years since 1972. Has this tinkering also led to a reinvigorated party system?

William Crotty, in "Party Reforms and Party Adaptability," answers with a resounding yes. Crotty traces the conflicts within the Democratic party that led to the reforms. Party regulars were more concerned with winning elections, reformers with having the parties espouse particular political philosophies. Neither side really understood the other and since the 1970s each has struggled mightily to gain the upper hand. The reformers have largely won out. Party nominations are now largely determined by primaries and caucuses; the smoke-filled rooms have completely disappeared. Yet, the regulars have been able to restore a modicum of their old power. The Republicans have followed the Democrats in many respects, but they have neither fought fierce internal battles nor implemented major shifts on their own.

While Crotty argues that "[r]eform came because it was needed," Everett Carll Ladd, in "Party Reform and the Public Interest," maintains that the reformers sought the wrong goals with the wrong methods. He finds little merit in the argument that political parties should primarily be concerned with espousing policy goals and even less in the idea that rank-and- file identifiers should have such great power over presidential nominations. He suggests a counterreform that would restore much of the power of party officials and officeholders in the nomination process.

Howard L. Reiter, in "The Limitations of Reform: Changes in the Nominating Process," suggests that both Crotty's and Ladd's analyses miss a fundamental point. The Democratic party reforms did not bring about a sea change in who contested the party's nominations, how many ballots it takes to nominate a candidate, or even who emerges as the nominee. The shifts in these and several other indicators of competitiveness at conventions began *before* the reforms were adopted in 1972; the structural changes amounted to admissions that the rules of the game had already changed. If Reiter is correct, then it doesn't matter much whether Crotty's reformers or Ladd's regulars prevail over rules fights.

PARTY REFORMS AND PARTY ADAPTABILITY

William Crotty

ASSESSMENT OF REFORM OBJECTIVES

Party reform introduced a remarkable era to American politics. More was attempted and accomplished than could truthfully be said to be envisioned in the decades since the Progressive movement of the early 1900s. And, remarkably, the reforms had been initiated and executed by the political parties themselves. In contrast to earlier attempts at political change, the intent was to strengthen and preserve an institution of incomparable value to the American political system rather than to destroy or replace it.[1]

The changes introduced were many. The traditional priorities of American party structure had been reversed. The national party units had attempted, with some success, to establish a code as to fair and decent behavior and to have it prevail in the conduct of party business. A sense of rationality had been introduced into an incredibly complex system and an aura of openness and equity had begun to prevail in the presidential nominating process especially, the most significant of the national party's duties, that appeared a threat to invade all aspects of party operations. A series of organizational structures and institutional values little changed since the formation of the political parties almost two centuries earlier were giving way to a new sense of national purpose and, hopefully, a relevancy and responsiveness to constituent pressures, a kind of responsibility neither had acquitted impressively over the years.

The political implications of what the reformers were attempting to accomplish were never far from mind.[2] The work of the reformers would effectively open the party in two regards. It would permit new groups to enter the process and make their views as to policy or candidates felt without depending on the goodwill or sponsorship of the party elders whose favor they would have had to curry. Second, it developed the foundation for establishing a permanent set of rules that would treat all with an impartiality previously unknown in party circles.

Party processes were given a new legitimacy at a time when parties had begun to appear increasingly irrelevant to the solution of the main problems besetting American life and at a juncture when both the party and the political system more broadly needed whatever support it could muster. In these terms then—and they are impressive—the reform movement, and most significantly the achievements of the McGovern-Fraser Commission within the Democratic party, had accomplished a good deal. In its own way, the reform era constituted a revolution in party operation—notable as much for its impact on traditional modes of thinking as on the structures placed in question.[3]

OVERVIEW OF THE REFORM PERIOD

Party reform began in the violence and bitterness engendered by the Democratic National Convention held in Chicago in August 1968. The police confrontations, factional disputes, Vietnam debate, and street riots resulted in the most violent national convention in either party's history. The Democratic party was torn apart, and "reform"—whether for cosmetic and face-saving purposes or to accomplish something more fundamental—became mandatory.

The national convention, in one of its least-noticed moves, passed resolutions to establish two reform bodies to assess presidential nominating procedures and to review convention operations. The two bodies were appointed in February 1969, and an era of basic change within the party system had begun.

The first two reform bodies appointed were the McGovern-Fraser Commission to review presidential nominating practices and the O'Hara Commission to modernize national convention procedures. The McGovern-Fraser Commission was by all odds the most aggressive and successful of the reform bodies. The commission's standards were enacted by the states' parties and resulted in a restructuring of the presidential nominating system.[4]

The new rules encountered strong opposition from party regulars and state party leaders that led to several noteworthy political and legal confrontations.[5] The reformers managed to enforce their rules in the 1972 national convention, although at some cost to party unity. The divisiveness of the new rules and the weak candidacy of Senator George McGovern, the man most closely associated with the reforms, assured that the battle over reform—and, not incidentally, for control of the Democratic party—would be renewed in the post-1972 period.

The Mikulski Commission (see Table 11.1) was empowered to review the McGovern-Fraser guidelines. It did so in the period 1972–1974 and while instituting some minor (but significant modifications) basically upheld the reform standards. An off-shoot of the Mikulski Commission, the Credentials Review Commission, was created in 1974 to supervise the application of the modified rules. In 1975 also, a new commission, the Winograd Commission, was established by then national chairman, Robert Strauss, to again reappraise the developments since the initial McGovern-Fraser innovations. The Winograd appointees made a serious, and partially successful, effort to close the presidential nominating processes. The commission acted out of a mix of motives that included political ideology (see below) and the need to placate significant elements within the party now in control of the national party.

The O'Hara Commission attempted to create a workable and representative convention operation. Its work was relatively uncontroversial and provided the first formal standards for Democratic conventions.[6]

The Sanford Commission (1973–74) evolved from a neglected aspect of the combined work of the McGovern-Fraser and O'Hara commissions.[7] Its objective was to attempt to achieve an open, representative, and accountable national party structure through the development and application of rules similar to those proposed by the McGovern-Fraser Commission for presidential nominations. Its most notable accomplishments were the development of the "party charter" and the institution of mid-term national conventions. The mid-term conventions appeared successful in representing grassroots sentiments and focusing these on a national party agenda. However, after the embarrassment suffered by then President Jimmy Carter at the 1978 mid-term convention from attacks directed at his policies by the more liberal side of the Democratic party, the Democrats quickly decided to abolish the mid-term meetings.

While the reform movements, and the splits they engendered in the Democratic party, were primarily over policy issues, the 1980s arguably saw the Democratic party nationally deemphasizing policy debates and a concern with voicing issue alternatives to the Reagan administration in favor of rebuilding party organizations and better funding campaign activities. During the 1980s also, the movement that had taken root with the Winograd Commission, the effort to revise and deemphasize the earlier McGovern-Fraser changes, continued. The Hunt Commission (1980–

84), led by Governor Jim Hunt of North Carolina, reassessed the rules with the intention of better representing party officeholders and organizational leaders and returning more power over nominations to the prereform coalition of labor, big city mayors, democratic governors, and party regulars that had dominated the process up until 1968.

The effort was partially successful. Many rules were relaxed; the party made it clear that it would be less unyielding in enforcing others; attempts were made to weaken the role of primaries in the process (basically unsuccessful); and a quota, or percentage of seats at the national conventions (between one-tenth and later one-fifth) was reserved for party officials. Unlike other delegates, these "superdelegates" did not have to contest for their convention seats in elective races and they did not have to formally commit themselves prior to the national convention to any candidate (or to declare officially their neutrality). The intent was to return more prominence to the national conventions, reemphasize the role and importance of elected and organizational party representatives, and provide more flexibility in the nominating process. It was partially successful. Arguably, Walter Mondale would not have been nominated on the national convention's first ballot in 1984 without the 83 percent support of the 568 "superdelegates." The Winograd and Hunt Commission rules changes also allowed the reintroduction of the winner-take-all primaries at the congressional district level, a practice that had been effectively banned since 1972.

One consequence of all of these modifications was a push for yet more changes after 1984, this time toward a more equitable distribution of national convention votes in line with candidate success at the state level (whether in primaries or state conventions). The new drive was led by the supporters of the Rev. Jesse Jackson, in particular, and led to campaigns to restudy the rules after both the 1984 and 1988 national conventions.[8]

However, the Democrats' heart was no longer in reform. Many felt the nominating system had been examined to the point of exhaustion and that it was difficult to mobilize support for any further changes in the fundamental operations of the process of presidential selection. The commissions on nominating rules established after both the 1984 and 1988 elections did little; their membership was selected by the national party chairs concerned more with minimizing conflict and building a party consensus; and the groups operated as essentially internal party committees that received little media or public attention. The explosiveness that characterized the early reform era and the anger and insistence on rollbacks the second, the postreform era had faded.

The three areas then addressed by the reform movement were (see

Table 11.1 Democratic Reform Commissions by Area of Interest

Presidential nominations	McGovern-Fraser Commission (1969–72)
	Mikulski Commission (1972–74)
	Credentials Review Commission (1974–76); (1976–78)
	Winograd Commission (1975–76) Agenda: • representation; quotas • representation; defining a Democrat inclusiveness/exclusiveness • representation; candidate strength • the debate over the purpose of a political party • restricting role of the primaries
	Hunt Commission (1980–84) Agenda: • same as Winograd Commission
	Fairness Commission (1984–88) Agenda: • to review apportionment of national convention votes; not very active (established in response to delegates of Rev. Jesse Jackson)
	Party Rules Committee (1988–92) Agenda: • to set rules for 1992 nominations • to assess the proportional representation of national convention delegate votes in stricter accordance with candidate's vote at state level; not very active (established in response to delegates of Rev. Jesse Jackson)
National Convention modernization	O'Hara Commission (1969–72) (Humphrey Commission on Vice-Presidential Selection, 1973)
Reform party structure	Sanford Commission (1973–74)

Table 11.1): presidential nominating procedures; national convention operations; and structural reform of the national party.

ISSUES IN THE REFORM CONTROVERSY

Several basic issues were involved in the reform controversy. These re-

Table 11.2   Chronology of Democratic Reform Commissions

Time frame	Reform Commission evolution
1964:	1964 National Convention, Special Equal Rights Committee
1968:	1968 National Convention, Ad Hoc Committee McGovern-Fraser Commission on delegate selection O'Hara Commission on convention reform
1972:	1972 National Convention, Vice-Presidential Selection Committee Mikulski Commission on delegate selection Sanford Commission on party structure
1974:	Credential Review Commission 1974 Mid-Term Convention
1976:	1976 National Convention
1978:	Winograd Commission
1980:	1980 National Convention, Hunt Commission
1984:	1984 National Convention, Fairness Commission
1988:	1988 National Convention, Party Rules Committee
1992:	1992 National Convention

lated to the different value positions held by the antagonists on either side of the debate over reform that called on different views of representation and different beliefs as to the purpose of a political party in a democratic society.

A review of these questions would include (1) the antagonists in the reform controversy, as they were perceived by the two camps; and (2) nominations—election year grassroots representation in presidential nominations or indirect representation through party leaders.[9]

Because the relevant controversy centered on the Democratic party, and since the most substantial of the reforms were enacted within the Democratic party, the discussion that follows is primarily restricted to the issues and cleavages associated with that party.

THE COMBATANTS AND THEIR VIEWS

It is important to understand the antagonists in the battle over reform as they saw each other. In many respects, this depiction of the two sides predicts to the views held by the opposing camps, the values they held to be important, and what they wanted the party system to represent.

On one side were the party regulars. No one held any illusions as to whom they represented or how they came to be chosen as delegates to national conventions. One of the principal concerns of the McGovern-Fraser Commission was to limit convention participation to those committed to a presidential contender and elected on their behalf to the convention. The party regulars objected to this provision. They believed their role in the national convention assured the most electable candidate in the general election. They believed they had the experience to choose the candidate most representative of the party's coalitional interests and that, in relative terms, they were the most impartial and reliable in these regards. They put the party's interest first rather than any faction's; they could be counted on to select as a presidential nominee the best and most promising of the potential candidates. Their commitment was to the party and its continued vitality and they placed a heavy emphasis on such values as party loyalty. They deemphasized any issues, candidates, or concerns that would divide or disrupt the party or limit its chances on election day.

Some party regulars believed that people holding elective or party office *deserved* to be seated in the national conventions. They should be rewarded for their service to the party by appointment to the national conventions. This would encourage them to continue working on behalf of the party in the tedious days between elections and it would allow the party to benefit from their experience and judgment in selecting a presidential nominee.

The regulars felt so strongly about this point that it represented their first amendment to the McGovern-Fraser Commission rules. By the time of the Mikulski, Winograd, and Hunt commissions, the reformers had pretty much given in on the issue, settling on 10 to 20 percent or more of a delegation to be reserved for party appointments.

Opposed to the party regulars were the reformers, who sought representation in conventions on behalf of an issue or a candidate they favored. The reformers believed that the grassroots party member should decide in an open and meaningful contest between candidates for convention seats who ran for delegate positions on behalf of the presidential contenders. Those running in this manner are akin to the familiar concept of the "amateur."[10] Alternatively, and more accurately, they could be called "grassroots activists."

The grassroots activists believed policy differences among the presidential candidates should be brought into the open and debated during the prenomination campaign and that each of the presidential candidates should have the opportunity to convince party voters that his or her stand was the most relevant and supportable. The grassroots activists did not prize party loyalty and consensus as highly as the regular.

The latter, already a member of the party hierarchy, had much to lose through controversy, put less emphasis on issues, and was most concerned with maximizing electional success. This was the perspective of professionals.

The grassroots activists strongly believed that the major of the day had to be openly aired in party contests. They were important and the party and its prospective candidates should be forced to address them. Grassroots activists were unwilling to leave national issues and their resolution to chance or to goodwill of the regulars who controlled the nominating process. They wanted to participate in the process; they wanted a voice in the issue agenda the party committed to; and they wanted a direct say in who the party's nominee would be.

The issues of paramount concern at the conception of the reform movement were Vietnam, race relations, crime, the future of cities, and, although it is not often addressed in this manner, the accountability of power, whether it is being exercised by a president, a mayor, or a political party. The coalition of individuals and groups brought together by these issues and the turmoil of the 1960s included antiwar activists, students, and militants, as well as the clergy, academics, professional people, women's groups, and liberal political leaders. The late Abbie Hoffman and Tom Hayden (later a California state legislator) came to symbolize the rhetorical and lifestyle excesses of a reform-type mentality that in its frantic and potentially destructive ways had the old order under siege. Many party regulars believed they were fighting to keep the party from being destroyed by Hoffman-like reformers. As an alternative, and for others, the embodiment of the reformer was U.S. Representative (and later Minneapolis mayor) Don Fraser, a solid, reasonable, intelligent, and experienced politician committed to a liberal agenda and to a politics of fairness and openness.

Many reformers seemed to believe they were fighting parochial, old-guard pols, regulars who would go to any length to protect their fiefdoms. They found little to admire in many of the more boisterous regulars who opposed reform. Yet, possibly a more accurate indicator of the regular position was a person like James O'Hara, a former congressman and reform commission chair and an involved and concerned proponent of a strong Democratic party. The images held by the two groups, however, did not appear to admit to many shades of gray.

The views of the two groups and the party's relation to these were in conflict. The basic question might well have been: What is a political party's role in and contribution to an advanced democratic society? Such a basic proposition was never entertained. Implicit, however, in the debates over reform were such concerns as who should the party represent and what values it should perpetuate. The regulars and antireformers generally were quite clear on these points. They placed a high value on loyalty. The reformers put less emphasis on strict loyalty and more on finding candidates they believed responsive to the pressing social concerns of the nation as they saw them. This difference in approach particularly rankled the party professionals. Worse, the regulars believed the assumptions underlying a number of the rules promulgated by the McGovern-Fraser Commission reflected the reformers' liberal and anti-professional bias.

The merits of the different approaches to politics of the regulars and the newcomers could be debated. Which forms the basis for a relevant evaluation of a political party's role in modern society? Which best served the needs of the constituent groups the Democratic party professed to represent? Which would best help the party to accommodate to a changing communications and campaign technology and an evolving social order? Such an exchange was never attempted. The debate took on emotional overtones and political implications that made any broader political assessments impossible.

The depiction of the regulars' position would be shared by, and is representative of, the regulars and party conservatives, party organization workers, and most elective officeholders, state and local party leaders, the AFL-CIO, the party's financial backers, and, in 1968 (and earlier), the majority of convention delegates.

Attitudinal, age, and lifestyle differences also existed among regulars and reformers. Their perceptions of politics differed as did the criteria they applied to judge the parties and their performance. Winning might suffice as a gauge of success for one group but not the other. For many reformers, the battle was over social change. Politics as usual, in the sense of not addressing in the earlier period the issue of the Vietnam War and the divisions that tore the society, was unacceptable. The political parties, and especially the dominant Democratic party, were the vehicles of change. The strong issue component to those pressuring for reform was never understood by the old-line regulars. And, in fact, it was resented. The regulars had put in their time working for the party's success and their own advancement, and they had every intention of claiming their rewards. Vietnam, student demonstrations, riots, and the general social disruptions that characterized the years from 1965 to 1968 seemed to them considerations somewhat outside the normal bounds of a national party and a national convention. They failed to make the connection with such issues and the presidency of Lyndon Johnson or the candidacy in 1968 of his vice-president, Hubert Humphrey.

The United States was a nation in turmoil during the 1960s. The values of the country and the perceptions of government authority were changing drastically. Meanwhile, the operations and presumptions concerning the party system changed little. For many, the old ways seemed irrelevant to addressing the social turmoil in which the nation found itself. This point more than any other marks the reformers from the antireformers. The regulars would not concede such a position. For reformers, the basic question would be whether the party could do enough in time to halt the erosion of its influence in the society. *Change came because it was needed.* The political party was out of touch with the times, with the problems faced by the social order, and with its own everbroadening coalition.

The party loyalists reacted strongly because the comfortable political world they knew was about to explode. With the default of the old order went their positions and the powers they had invested lifetimes accumulating. The newer elements within the Democratic coalition that would test them were less committed to a party structure they found outdated and unresponsive. They refused to offer unquestioned allegiance to forms and policies few understood or could influence. When they attempted to play the game by the old rules, the system had rebuffed them. The reformers had tried during the primaries and caucuses of the 1968 election in particular to force the party to recognize their legitimate needs by running campaigns for delegate seats in support of candidates they believed offered reasonable alternatives on the major issues of the day. In the process, they discovered just how undemocratic the party would be and how outdated its procedures had become.[11]

The regulars did not quarrel with the charges made by the insurgents. Their rejoinder was that the system worked well. It recognized and institutionalized other values (loyalty; experience; power, whether elective or party-based; governability; and electoral success). It had performed admirably in the past as it would in the future. The present difficulties were simply short-term disruptions in an otherwise well-functioning process.

Quite obviously, there was little room for compromise in such diametrically opposed perceptions. The emotional overtones of the debate would continue long after the specific issues in question (quotas or nonquotas, participant-oriented structures, due process party standards) had been settled. The fundamental nature of the attack launched by the reformers, and the emotion that surrounded the battle, explains the unwillingness of regulars to ever quite give up the struggle. For two decades, the bickering, and changes in rules, would continue to engage the Democrats.

The depiction of the insurgents by the party regulars was harsh but not necessarily inaccurate. The ad hoc coalition that supported reform sprang from the social problems of the 1960s and the political difficulties encountered in 1968 in particular. This much is clear. The reform coalition included middle-class professionals, blacks, young activists, and suburban housewives among others. Its adherents tended not to live for politics or off it (i.e., make their living from it), as did professionals. The reform coalition also counted among its members a goodly number of party moderates and centrists as well as elective and party officeholders who quietly supported the movement as it advanced. The reformers worked within the system. Eventually, it responded to them.

NOMINATIONS: ELECTION YEAR REPRESENTATION IN PRESIDENTIAL NOMINATIONS OR INDIRECT REPRESENTATION THROUGH PARTY REGULARS

The position of reformers and regulars on the issue of what could be called election year representation (or grassroots influence on the presidential nomination) as against professional party representation is easily sketched. The issue involved the controversy over whether the party should systematize its procedures to reflect candidate strength and issue feelings during the presidential election year (the reformer's contention) or whether it should retain the relatively closed institutions of the past with power in the hands of the party's leadership. The emphasis in the latter case would be on trusting the wisdom of the party's elders to do what was best for both the party and the country (the loyalists' position).

REPRESENTATION: THE QUOTAS

A second broad problem area of representation involved the quotas. Should blacks, women, and youth be given special privileges, even mandatory guaranteed representation, to compensate for alleged past iniquities? Would such mandatory representation better promote the interests of the affected groups? The reformers answered yes to both questions. The regulars objected. They felt more adequate representation would not be assured by such proposals and that the party's leaders were at least as likely to advance the cause of the groups specified as any delegates elected from the ranks under a forced quota requirement. As to the argument that the regulars had not done well in this area in the past, party professionals offered several defenses. First came repeated contentions that social equity in the form of categoric representation is not the function of a political party of a national convention and that it would weaken the party electorally.[12] Second, the party professionals contended that the party was moving in the direction of greater representation of minority groups and women.

Another approach of the opponents to quotas was to reduce the proposition to absurdity. Why not quotas for ethnics (e.g., Lithuanians, Poles, Czechs, Mexican-Americans, Indians), the poor, the elderly, the handicapped, and so on? This was the most popular response and it received the greatest media attention. It might have had appeal if the party could identify its key support groups within the electorate. However, this was not the intention and it was never seriously considered. The argument was put forth simply to question why the groups chosen had been marked for preferential treatment rather than others and to place the reforms in as questionable, even ridiculous, a light as possible.

The problem was a political one, and it was decided on that basis. The groups specified in the quotas pushed for inclusion at a time when the party and the reformers were susceptible. These groups were organized and they were able to achieve what they sought. There was little of democratic ideology or competitive fairness for all party factions or a new concept of party involvement.

The other side of the argument was seldom mentioned. The party's leaders and federated labor wished to retain the "quota" representation they had. The ex officio or automatic delegate seats assured many regulars of a convention position. The party leaders chose the vast majority of delegates from their states. The delegates thus selected could be expected to be loyal to their sponsors and to reflect their sentiments. They had weak ties to the party's base or even to the candidates for nomination.

When the party regulars were pressed, they would admit to being beneficiaries of procedures under the old rules that ensured their control of presidential selection processes. They justified this as being best for that party and the nation. They felt that the professionals who had a long-run interest in the party and its affairs and were those most knowledgeable and experienced in political matters should make the decisions. The Mikulski Commission modifications that weakened the quota idea increased the number of appointments set aside for party leaders and later the Winograd and Hunt commissions' emphasis on superdelegates alleviated much of the criticism.

The question of democratic theory and its application to the reform assumptions received an especially vigorous workout in the quota battle. Democratic theory does not constitute a coherent and systematically interrelated body of ideas. Many of these theories, like the changes in party operations considered by the Democrats, grew out of the justification for increasingly more open and broadly controlled deliberative processes. They were a response to demands of a given time and grew out of a need to rationalize and justify an emerging political order. One can argue from different assumptions as to, for example, representation, depending on what values one chooses to maximize and what theorists one finds particularly persuasive.[13]

Finding a common ground for debate is not the only problem. Democratic theory contains paradoxes that are irreconcilable. One must make a choice, or a series of choices, based on other criteria (in the reform context, this might be maximizing political advantage). The most notable paradox in democratic thought is between the rights of the minority and the will of the majority.[14] In a pure sense, it is not possible to have both. They represent competing values. One must choose where and how one set of objectives leaves off and another begins and how the two should relate to each other. The reformers made their choice; the regulars theirs.

REPRESENTATION: DEFINING A DEMOCRAT-INCLUSIVENESS/EXCLUSIVENESS

The respective arguments on this question are predictable given the debates on the preceding points. What is a Democrat? Who should be eligible to participate in party decision making?

Reformers generally favored relaxed definitions that would be inclusive of nominal Democrats and that might even help attract to party affairs a portion of the 40 percent of the electorate that refuses to affiliate formally with either of the major parties. As a consequence, they pushed for limited registration (thirty days, for example) in primaries and a general opening of caucuses to all concerned Democrats or those willing to identify as Democrats. Consistent with their view of who should be represented, the regulars wanted restrictive standards of registration and identification and a more closed party system (e.g., prior registration as a party member for a specified term as a precondition to participation in a primary or party caucus).

By the time of the Mikulski (1972-1974) and Winograd commissions (1975-1978), the two groups had pretty much come together on these issues. The old procedures were redesigned and in the process their requirements considerably relaxed. At the same time, the regulars' argument for a prior commitment to the party before taking part in its delegate selection process had been accepted. The concept of the "open" primary, for example, in states like Wisconsin (which required no previous test of party loyalty) was outlawed. With the emerging consensus, these particular issues faded as points of dispute between the two camps.

REPRESENTATION: CANDIDATE STRENGTH

The basic differences between the opposing groups are predictable. An important concern of the reform movement was the effort of the reformers to rewarded delegate votes in proportion to a candidate's strength at each level of the nominating process. The outcome would be a proportionally distributed and representative convention, closely conforming to the contenders' strength within the states.

Proportional representation is an interesting conception. Hanna Pitkin, in *The Concept of Representation*, traces the various usages and meanings of the term representation and quotes Carl Frederich to the effect that the " 'fundamental principle' of proportional representation is the attempt to 'secure a representative assembly reflecting with more or less mathematical exactness the various divisions in the electorate.' "[15] This explanation constitutes a fair description of what the reformers intended.

Proportional representation and descriptive representation in the form of demographic quotas are logically incompatible. The problem is not as difficult as it may sound. The reform commissions responded to political realities and made their choices based on the alternatives placed before them. They did not ask fundamental questions as to who should be represented or how. The lack of any general conceptual orientation is in fact one of the major failings in the O'Hara Commission's (1969–72) work on convention reform and modernization and helps explain some of its omissions. It might have been more beneficial in the long run if the reform commissions had debated broader questions of representation. They could have then gone on to mold a system that best realized the values they felt most important. Bits and pieces of such concern did arise on occasion, sometimes by indirection, when a particular reform body evaluated a specific proposal. Anything more would be too much to expect from the practical orientation that characterized the politicians and power brokers who made up the bulk of the reform commissions' membership.

It is not surprising that inconsistencies in assumptions underlie many of the specific rules endorsed by the reform groups. In the case of provisions on the minority quotas and the "fair reflection," or proportional representation, of a candidate's electoral strength, the conflict is not serious. The quotas accomplished their purpose, forcing a fuller recognition of blacks and women (youth constitute a considerably less homogenous and politically important group) in national conventions and party deliberations more generally. The "quotas" were quickly dropped in the post-1972 period, but they and their "affirmative action" successors kept the pressure on the state parties to include a representative number of blacks and females (although not youth) on their slates.

The proportional representation of candidate strength is another matter. *Implementing this concept is basic to what the reformers hoped to achieve,* and it, more than the highly publicized quotas, was to be a continuing issue of contention within the party. Each of the reform commissions through the 1970s and 1980s dealt with the problem in some manner. The generally accepted compromise was to settle on a 10 to 15 percent floor (a candidate would need this level of support or more in a caucus or primary before receiving a proportionate share of the delegate vote). In the Winograd Commission, one fight came over the attempts of the Carter administration representatives to increase the 15 percent base to as high as 25 percent (depending on when the primary or caucus was held; the later the event, the higher the proportionate vote needed to qualify for delegate support). The intention was to discourage potential competitors from challenging the incumbent (especially in the later primaries), thus helping to ensure Carter's renomination.[16] The problem reemerged in the push by Jackson delegates in both 1984 and 1988 for a more accurate representation in national convention of a candidate's strength at the state level. The conflict over this issue goes to the heart of the reform concern.

REPRESENTATIONS: DIFFERING ROLE INTERPRETATIONS

Austin Ranney has made one of his many contributions to the reform debate by calling attention to the differing perspectives on the role of the party representative and the national convention delegate.[17] The contrasting interpretations relate to the perceptions the reformer and the regular had of what their role in the process of party decision making should be.

The reformers favored the "agent" conception of the national delegate role, believing it would result in more responsible and accountable convention representatives. The agent theory of the delegate position (as developed by Pitkin)[18] emphasizes that the persons chosen (in this case) by the party voters should be bound to the extent possible by those that select them and that they should be required to reflect their preferences in their convention voting. The party regulars (although it is unlikely either group would have expressed it in such terms) sided with Edmund Burke's conception of delegated authority; the convention delegates would use their best judgment as to what was needed. They were responsible to their constituents only to the extent of their success, or lack of it, in promoting objectives they presumably shared (e.g., winning office).

The beliefs of the professionals as to the way in which the convention operated prevailed prior to 1972. Until then, the primaries, for example, were viewed in a more advisory role. They helped the party's leadership ascertain which of the presidential contenders could campaign effectively and the extent of their support among various segments of the electorate. Delegates elected in primaries were not necessarily pledged to support the primary winner in the national convention. Whatever voice the nominating institutions at the state level presumed to give, the party's rank-and-file in the choice of a presidential nominee was mostly indirect. The real decision was left to the party leaders.

This practice was one of the chief evils, as they saw it, that the reformers had set out to correct. The reformers were prepared to argue that the "agent" theory of a delegate's role was more democratic in that power was effectively dispersed among those with a stake in the nomination; control would be shifted from a few at the top to the many at the base of the party who had made the effort to participate in the nominating process. Whether this kind of procedure would be more accountable or responsible, of course, would be challenged by the loyalists and is dependent on the objectives one believes each approach best serves.

The argument over the various role conceptions has important practical ramifications. First, it illustrates the gulf between reformers and antireformers in both values favored and behavior expected. Second, the O'Hara Commission mandated, and the national convention accepted, a freedom-of-conscience rule for delegates. A delegate could not be bound (or instructed) to vote at the national convention by any state law or party resolution. The convention was denied the power to enforce any such sanctions. As a consequence, a state law (or for that party regulations) can and does require an elected delegate to vote at the national convention for the presidential contender whom he or she pledged to support at the state level and on whose slate he or she ran. Once at the convention, however, the delegate was free to follow his or her own instincts.

There probably is no strictly legalistic solution to this problem that would be acceptable to the party. The issue cuts across several areas of concern and what would be a gain in one would constitute a loss in another. The reform guidelines carried the message that the participants in the state caucuses and primaries were, in effect, choosing the party's presidential nominee. They were, in this sense, casting a "meaningful" ballot and the system employed in delegate selection from the precinct to the national convention would do its best to reflect accurately their wishes. This objective became generally understood and accepted.

THE PURPOSE OF A POLITICAL PARTY

Unfortunately, no one, and least of all the reform commissions, dealt explicitly with this question. The party regulars made their position repeatedly clear: the purpose of a political party is to win elections and the purpose of a national convention is to pick a nominee who would win. They pointed with pride to their record in selecting nominees and they drew on it as a justification of the practices in effect prior to 1972.

Reformers would have a more difficult time than regulars in describing a political party's purpose. They would not reject the regulars' belief in the need to field a winning ticket but they would argue that this is not the only objective of a political party or a national convention. For a reformer, a political party, and a national convention and its deliberations as well as the process leading up to it (a most important point for the reformer; a lesser one for the loyalist), should reflect as closely as possible the views of the party membership. Implicitly, this would mean that in choosing a nominee and in drafting a platform, the party would have to deal in some manner with interests expressed by those who participated in the various stages of the nomination process. If a political party refuses to address the social concerns of the electorate, it calls into question (at least for the reformers) the very purpose of having political parties at all. Winning office is not an acceptable goal in itself.

Both loyalist and reformers could probably agree that the assertions and motivations underlying the reform initiative was forcibly put in the McGovern-Fraser Commission's *Mandate for Change:*

> If we are not an open party; if we do not represent the demands of change, then the danger is not that people will go to the Republican Party; it is that there will no longer be a way for people committed to orderly change to fulfill their needs and desires within our traditional political system.[19]

The threat is clear: If the political parties do not meet this need, the electoral system will have been found wanting. The citizenry in turn will find other outlets (such alternatives as third parties, demonstrations, violence, withdrawal from political activity, or the like). Probably the most basic, single factor distinguishing the reformer from the antireformer was that the reformer believed that the party system did not meet the needs of the country and was incapable of doing so in its present form. The antireformers believed the party system worked quite well and that it possibly required some tinkering, but no substantial change. This fundamental difference between the two groups was irreconcilable. The reformers' creed was best expressed in the conclusion to the McGovern-Fraser Commission report: "We believe that popular control of the Democratic Party is necessary for its survival."[20]

A NOTE ON REPUBLICAN PARTY REFORM

The Republican party did not undergo substantial reform in its procedures during the period from 1968 on.[21] There are several reasons for this. First, and unlike the Democrats, the Republicans had clear rules regulating their national conventions in particular. The problems that arose in the management of the 1968 Democratic National Convention were unlikely to occur at a Republican National Convention.

Second, much of the reform movement arose over frustration with the Vietnam War policies during the decade of the 1960s and the inability of those seeking change to affect Democratic policies in any fundamental way. The Republicans were not in office during this period and did not become associated with the prosecution of the war until the Nixon administration took office in 1969. By that time, the reform movement was well launched within the Democratic party. Alternatively, there was little dissatisfaction within Republican ranks with the prosecution of the war.

Third, the Republican party's coalition was much smaller and more homogeneous than the Democrats'. There were not the tensions—racial, youth, and feminist divisions, lifestyle and generation conflicts and ideological polarization—that plagued the broader, more heterogeneous, and more divided Democratic alliance.

Finally, there was no constituency for reform within the Republican party. Republicans were generally satisfied with their party, the way in which it operated, and what it stood for. While there were divisions within Republican ranks, they were not strong or unhappy enough with its procedures to fuel any broadscale attack on its operations.

Yet, the Republicans did empower two reform commissions to assess its rules. In large part, these were in response to the highly publicized efforts of the Democrats. Although the second of its committees dealt with a problem that has long bothered Republican party strategists—the inability of the party to broaden and diversify its coalitional lines—neither party committee had much impact. The two commissions—the DO (Delegates and Organization Committee, 1969–72) and the Rule 29 Committee (1972–75)—recommended (and the operative word is "recommended"; the Democrats enforced their rule changes) such practices as the national convention system be retained, that *Robert's Rules of Order* be used for national convention proceedings, and that the party "encourage the broadest possible participation of all voters in the Republican Party activities at all levels."[22] The recommendations essentially emphasized practices already in place or goals the party might aspire to.

Nonetheless, the Republican party was affected by reform. When one party makes fundamental changes in the American system, the other, whether it chose to or not, is influenced. The need to change state statutes that, for example, set the dates and conditions for primary elections, the qualifications of potential delegates or candidates, and the obligations the delegate has to voters that elected him or her in many cases affected the operations of both parties. The reform era left its mark on both political parties through the opening of the nominating system; the increased reliance on primaries; the willingness of contenders to challenge the party establishment, frontrunners, and even incumbent presidents of the same party (the Reagan race against Ford in 1976); the belief that a candidate must participate in the primary selection process to legitimate his or her claim to the nomination; the expectation that the party's voters, working through state party structures, will decide the outcome; and, while not necessarily intended by reformers, the importance in the process assumed by the media along with the public funding of candidacies. Quietly, maybe even unintentionally, the Republican party has undergone its own subtle reform process.

RAMIFICATIONS OF THE REFORM MOVEMENT

The reform movement accomplished a great deal in a very short period of time. It managed to breathe new life into moribund party structures and to center debate on the operation and representative capacities of these agencies, in itself no small contribution. Political parties are seldom the focus of public concern. They have grown episodically over the generations to fill political needs. They are of concern quadrennially when the various presidential contenders and their supporters attempt to bend them to their will. Between presidential elections, a short-run interest is replaced by a more customary apathy. It could be argued that during the interim the national party only fitfully at best serves any function of consequence to the electorate. The reform movement attempted to resurrect an interest in party activities per se and to revitalize party structures and adapt them to modern concerns.

Two final questions then are: Why at this particular point in time did the reform movement arise? And how successful in actuality was it?

The first question is relatively easy to answer; the second more difficult. Political parties had changed little in form or activity since their inception. One factor, however, had become increasingly clear: they had become organizationally outdated and functionally they appeared to be increasingly less relevant to the operation of a modern democracy.[23] The parties responded more to organized pressures and financial strength than they did to the mass of their membership. Party supporters were an inconvenience to be suffered and catered to only during national election campaigns.

Such foreboding might never have arisen above the level of irrelevant speculation had it not been for the events of 1968. The fury unleashed, the clear abuse of official party machinery, and the picture of party operations that resulted convinced most people within and without the Democratic party that change was overdue. The forces that would propel reform had been set in motion and the events of that election year proved the catalyst to create the necessary reform constituency; and people were available. The results overall constitute the most vital series of changes to be introduced into the modern party structure since the Progressive Era.

How successful has the movement been? Some notable results have emerged. It is unlikely that these can be reversed to a significant extent. The real question in this regard centers less on the substance of the reforms or the answers as to who got what and why. Rather, the criteria should be the extent to which the parties have been made equal to the present-day demands made upon them. To what extent does a political party now reflect its base in the citizenry? What measure of control do party supporters exercise over party actions? How effective has the party become as a representative instrument in advancing the needs of its constituents? In what measure does it compliment and strengthen the operation of other democratic structures? While the answers to such questions are unclear, obviously both political parties have a long way to go in these regards.

The reform movement of the recent years constitutes but a beginning. Where the parties go from here and what their future contribution will be to a democratic nation sorely in need of their services depends on them.

NOTES

1. See in relation to this William Crotty, *Decision for the Democrats* (Baltimore: Johns Hopkins U. Press, 1978); and Crotty, *Party Reform* (New York: Longman, 1983). For different perspectives, consult: Nelson W. Polsby, *Consequences of Party Reform* (Oxford: Oxford U. Press, 1983); James W. Ceaser, *Presidential Selection: Theory and Development* (Princeton, N.J.: Princeton U. Press, 1979); J. W. Ceaser, *Reforming the Reforms* (Cambridge, Mass.: Bollinger, 1982); Jeane Kirkpatrick, *Dismantling the Parties* (Washington, D.C.: American Enterprise In-

stitute, 1976); Byron E. Shafer, *Quiet Revolution: The Struggle for the Democratic Party and the Shaping of Post-Reform Politics* (New York: Russell Sage Foundation, 1983); B. E. Shafer, *Bifurcated Politics: Evolution and Reform in the National Party Convention* (Cambridge, Mass.: Harvard U. Press, 1988); Alexander Heard, *Made in America: Improving the Nomination and Election of Presidents* (New York: Harper-Collins, 1991); Alexander Heard and Michael Nelson, eds., *Presidential Selection* (Durham, N.C.: Duke U. Press, 1987); Howard L. Reiter, *Selecting the President: The Nomination Process in Transition* (Philadelphia: U. of Pennsylvania Press, 1985); Robert E. DiClerico and Eric M. Uslaner, *Few Are Chosen: Problems in Presidential Selection* (New York: McGraw-Hill, 1984); Crotty, "Party Reform, Nominating Processes, and Democratic Ends" (pp. 63–86) and Austin Ranney, "Farewell to Reform—Almost" (pp. 87–111), both in Kay L. Schlozman, ed., *Elections in America* (Boston: Allen & Unwin, 1987); David E. Price, *Bringing Back the Parties* (Washington, D.C.: Congressional Quarterly Press, 1984); and William Crotty and John S. Jackson III, *Presidential Primaries and Nominations* (Washington, D.C.: Congressional Quarterly Press, 1985).

2. See Judith A. Center, "1972 Democratic Convention Reforms and Party Democracy," *Political Science Quarterly* 89 (June 1974): 325–50, for examples of the conventional rejoinders and, in answer to these, Jeffrey L. Pressman and Denis G. Sullivan, "Convention Reform and Conventional Wisdom: An Empirical Assessment of Democratic Party Reforms," *Political Science Quarterly* 89 (Fall 1974): 539–62.

3. See Austin Ranney, *Curbing the Mischief of Faction* (Berkeley: U. of California Press, 1975); Ranney, "Changing the Rules of the Nominating Game" in James David Barber, ed., *Choosing the President* (Englewood Cliffs, N.J.: Prentice-Hall, 1974), pp. 71–93; Ranney, "The Democratic Party's Delegate Selection Reforms, 1968–1976" in Allan P. Sindler, ed., *America in the Seventies: Problems, Policies, and Politics* (Boston: Little, Brown, 1977), pp. 160–206; Crotty, *Party Reform*; and Crotty, *Decision for the Democrats*.

4. See William Crotty, *Political Reform and the American Experiment* (New York: Thomas Y. Crowell, 1977), pp. 193–237; and Crotty, *Decision for the Democrats*.

5. For an elaboration of the most significant, legally and politically, of these encounters, see W. Crotty, "Anatomy of a Challenge: The Chicago Delegation to the Democratic National Convention" in R. Peabody, ed., *Cases in American Politics* (New York: Praeger, 1976), pp. 111–58.

6. Crotty, *Decision for the Democrats*, pp. 148–221.

7. Crotty, *Party Reform*, pp. 110–17.

8. See W. Crotty, "Jesse Jackson's Campaign: Constituency Attitudes and Political Outcomes" in Lucius J. Barker and Ronald W. Walters, eds., *Jesse Jackson's 1984 Presidential Campaign: Challenge and Change in American Politics* (Urbana, Ill.: U. of Illinois Press, 1989), pp. 57–95.

9. Particularly helpful in setting out some of the main issues in the reform controversy, and as a guide to this discussion, was Ranney, "The Democratic Party's Delegate Selection Reforms, 1968–76" in Sindler, ibid., pp. 170–82.

10. The original conception, although it has gone through a number of permutations, can be found in James Q. Wilson, *The Amateur Democrat* (Chicago: U. of Chicago Press, 1962).

11. Crotty, *Decision for the Democrats.*

12. For an elaboration of this argument, see Jeane J. Kirkpatrick, "Representation in American National Conventions: The Case of 1972," *British Journal of Political Science* 5 (July 1975): 265–332.

13. See Hanna F. Pitkin, *The Concept of Representation* (Berkeley: U. of California Press, 1972); and Carole Pateman, *Participation and Democratic Theory* (Cambridge: Cambridge U. Press, 1970).

14. The point is made in Robert A. Dahl, *A Preface to Democratic Theory* (Chicago: U. of Chicago Press, 1956).

15. Pitkin, *The Concept of Representation,* p. 61.

16. See Rhodes Cook, "Democrats to Adopt Final Rules for 1980," *Congressional Quarterly* (3 June 1978): 1392–96; Cook, "DNC Panel Reviews Delegate Selection Rules," *Congressional Quarterly* (13 May 1978): 1217; Cook, "Democrats Adopt New Rules for Picking Nominee in 1980," *Congressional Quarterly* (17 June 1978): 1571; and Cook, "White House Is a Winner on Rules Changes," *Congressional Quarterly* (28 January 1978): 199–200.

17. Ranney, "The Democratic Party's Delegate Selection Reforms, 1968–1976," pp. 179–81.

18. Pitkin, *The Concept of Representation.*

19. Commission on Party Structure and Delegate Selection, *Mandate for Reform,* Washington, D.C.: Democratic National Committee (1970), p. 49.

20. Ibid. Ranney illustrates how the reformers' rationale for change would differ from that of the regulars' in this regard, in "The Democratic Party's Delegate Selection Reforms, 1968–1976," pp. 181–82.

21. Crotty, *Party Reform,* pp. 205–32.

22. Quoted in ibid., p. 228.

23. There are a number of good critiques on political parties available although they do not all agree on the problems besetting the parties or the cure. These include: Austin Ranney, "Are Political Parties Necessary?" Midwest Political Science Association, 1977; James L. Sundquist, *Dynamics of the Party System* (Washington, D.C.: The Brookings Institution, 1973); John G. Stewart, *One Last Chance* (New York: Thomas Y. Crowell, 1974), pp. 193–264; Walter Dean Burnham, *Critical Elections and the Mainsprings of American Politics* (New York: Norton, 1970); W. D. Burnham, "The End of American Party Politics," *Trans-Action* (December 1969): 12–22; W. D. Burnham "Elections as Democratic Institutions" in K. L. Schlozman, ed., pp. 27–60; Reiter, *Selecting the President;* and W. Crotty, "Political Parties Research: Issues and Trends" in W. Crotty, ed., *Political Science: Looking to the Future* (Evanston, Ill.: Northwestern U. Press, 1991), pp. 137–201.

Reading 12

PARTY REFORM AND THE PUBLIC INTEREST

Everett Carll Ladd

The way the United States chooses its political leadership—especially the way it picks its presidents—the condition of its political parties, and the parties' place in the governing process have long been the object of critical attention. Arguments on the imperative of "reform" are being raised today much as they have been over the past century. Is the American system of parties and elections in fact failing the country? Does this system need fixing to enable it to better advance what are variously called common, public, and national interests?

SERVING THE NATIONAL INTEREST

Before exploring this question, I should note that American political science has had a terrible time grappling with the idea of the public interest. Glendon Schubert argued in a 1960 study that the concept "makes no operational sense, notwithstanding the efforts of a generation of capable scholars. . . . Political scientists might better spend their time nurturing concepts that offer greater promise of becoming useful tools in the scientific study of political responsibility."[1] Frank Sorauf nominated the term "public interest" as a leading candidate for inclusion in "a list of ambiguous words and phrases 'which never would be missed.'"[2] Robert Dahl and Charles Lindblom have insisted that in most instances the meaning of the national or public interest is "left totally undefined. . . . Often enough a precise examination would show that it can mean nothing more than whatever happens to be the speaker's own view as to a desirable public policy."[3] According to Howard Reiter, radical political scientists (in whose company he places himself) "argue that in any society dominated by class interests, like the United States, there can be no general interest that unites all classes, and the concept of a 'public interest' is a sham intended to fool the lower classes into supporting the interests of the upper class."[4]

Other scholars have found the concept of public or national interests highly meaningful, of course, and I put myself in their ranks.[5] In discussing their political aspirations most people seem to find the concept natural and essential. Probably this is because, as Daniel Bell and Irving Kristol argued in introducing their magazine, *The Public Interest*, "there has never been a society which was not, in some way, and to some extent guided by this ideal...."[6]

I content myself with a few basic distinctions. Most people seem able to distinguish between interests that are broadly shared and those that are quite narrow. Obtaining a system that provides high quality public education on its face reflects a broader constellation of interests than does a special tax write-off for Uptight Motors, Inc. Furthermore, some interests are fundamental and enduring; pursuit of immediate goals that threaten basic long-term objectives is counter to the national interest. For Americans, their national interest includes their country's security and the maintenance of an environment conducive to national hopes for the extension of liberty and democracy around the world. It includes, too, a healthy, growing economy that extends economic opportunity. And surely, most Americans see it in the national interest that successful popular governance be obtained. Does the American party and electoral system do as much as any other we can specify to serve such broad, enduring ends? Or does it sacrifice them by being too responsive to claims that are narrow, particularistic, special, short-sighted and short-term?

THE CASE THAT THE SYSTEM PROVIDES GOVERNMENT TOO INATTENTIVE TO THE NATIONAL INTEREST

Specific criticisms of the parties and the electoral system for insufficiently serving the pursuit of broad public interests cannot really be separated from more general criticisms of the entire American system of widely dispersed and decentralized governmental authority. Most arguments that have been advanced throughout this century for strengthening political parties in their control over nominations and the policy process stem from one underlying assumption: the separation of powers and all its ramifications—whether seen as a serious deficiency that must be lived with or as an overall strength that has its downside—need mitigation through the intermediary of relatively disciplined and integrated parties.

In *Congressional Government*, first published in 1885, Woodrow Wilson stated forcefully the argument that the American system and its extreme dispersion of authority frustrate the achievement of national interests. "As at present constituted," he wrote, "the federal government lacks strength because its powers are divided, lacks promptness because its authorities are multiplied, lacks wieldiness because its processes are roundabout, lacks efficiency because its responsibility is indistinct and its actions without competent direction....Nobody stands sponsor for the policy of the government. A dozen men originate it; a dozen compromises twist and alter it; a dozen offices whose names are scarcely known outside of Washington put it into execution."[7]

In this view, the system hampers pursuit of the national interest first by making it virtually impossible for government to frame the kind of coherent, integrated approaches to complex policies that are required. The policy incoherence bred of separation of powers was one thing in 1793, when the federal government did very little and could take a long time doing it. It was already something quite different, Wilson thought, by the late nineteenth century when, he observed, "the sphere and influence of national administration and national legislation are widening rapidly...and populations...growing at such a rate that one's reckoning staggers at counting...."[8] Wilson was then a strong advocate of responsible party leadership and an admirer of the British system of cabinet government. He stopped short of advocating its application in America as a remedy for the ills he observed, but throughout *Congressional Government* he lamented the weakness of the American "committee system of government" with its ineffectual parties and extolled the virtues of the British parliamentary system with its disciplined parties and responsible ministries.

Wilson's early advocacy of responsible party government was modified considerably by the turn of the century. In writing the preface of the fifteenth printing of *Congressional Government* in 1900 he argued that the nation's plunge into international politics had produced "greatly increased power and opportunity for constructive statesmanship given the President...[and that as a result] the Executive...will have very far-reaching effect upon our whole method of government." Those views were fully developed in *Constitutional Government*, first published in 1908.[9] Wilson did not, of course, abandon his commitment to the goal of more coherent national leadership. Presidential leadership would replace party leadership in linking all the power centers of our constitutionally separated government.

The prevailing view in American political science since World War II has been that presidential leadership is insufficient in the absence of disciplined parties. In 1950, for example, the Committee on Political Parties of the American Political Science Association (APSA) issued its call for a system of stronger parties able to meet the national need "for more effective formulation of general policies and programs and for better integration of all of the far-flung activities of modern government.[10]

The American system's dispersion of authority has often been faulted for retarding political accountability and popular control. Giving the public effective means of control over a big, complex government is difficult—yet a vital national interest in any country that takes democracy seriously. A century ago, Wilson lamented that "the average citizen may be excused for esteeming government at best but a haphazard affair upon which his vote and all his influence can have but little effect. How is his choice of a representative in Congress to affect the policy of the country as regards the questions in which he is most interested...? It seems almost a thing of despair to get any assurance that any vote he may cast will even in an infinitesimal degree affect the essential course of administration...."[11]

Contemporary American political science for the most part sees the strengthening of parties as essential for extending popular control over government and insuring greater responsiveness of public institutions to popular wishes. Only strong parties can so organize issues that the public can speak effectively on them. If they make elected officials in some sense collectively, rather than individually, responsible to the electorate, parties greatly expand the public's capacity to reward and punish.

Similarly, stronger and more disciplined parties have been seen as an important potential antidote—though one very difficult to come by—to extreme congressional individualism and the opening it offers the swarm of special interests. The 1950 APSA report made this case. "The value of special-interest groups in a diversified society...should be obvious," its authors argued. "But organized interest groups cannot do the job of the parties. Indeed, it is only when a working formula of the public interest in its general character is made manifest by the parties in terms of coherent programs that the claims of interest groups can be adjusted on the basis of political responsibility.... It must be obvious... that the whole development [the proliferation of interest groups and the extension of their sway] makes necessary a reinforced party system that can cope with the multiplied organized pressure."[12]

Strong parties are needed to curb special-interest influence by forcing these interests "to pick on people their own size"—through requiring that they take their case to central party leadership that is charged with balancing a great variety of conflicting demands. Strong parties are also needed to help the underorganized many have their proper say in competition with the highly organized few. E. E. Schattschneider gave classic statement to the argument that the system of organized special interests has a pronounced bias in favor of the well-heeled and otherwise well-positioned: "The flaw in the pluralist heaven is that the heavenly chorus sings with a strong upper-class accent."[13]

AN IMPRESSIVE IF INCOMPLETE ANALYSIS

If one stays within the body of theory and political argument I have been reviewing, one is hard put to quarrel with it. Surely, the American governmental system, built upon federalism and separation of powers, does greatly divide and disperse political authority. Indeed, in the parliamentary sense of the term, the United States really does not have a *government* at all: The president has significant authority, of course, but he and his executive subordinates are rightly called the *administration*, not the *government*; Congress's role is so great that it would have to be part of the government for there to be a government. In our dispersed and decentralized scheme, barriers aplenty are erected to coherent, centrally-developed policies. And interest groups are indeed presented with multiple points of access at all levels. The system is very messy, and presidents invariably find it frustrating.

The American governmental order has dictated a special type of party system. Given federalism, the parties historically were organized on state lines, and even when individual state parties were robust and disciplined, the national party system remained fragmented. Given separation of powers, the case for party discipline evident in parliamentary systems could never be made, and party factions were given a variety of bases from which to maintain their independence. Given the extreme individualism that has always distinguished American political culture, claims for greater collective party authority have rarely struck a responsive chord among the public; and succeeding waves of "reform" have had the principal result of further extending political individualism. The reforms of the 1960s and early 1970s in Congress, for example, left individual members more advantaged than they had been vis-à-vis more central elements of House and Senate leadership.

All in all, today's parties-elections systems does not reduce the effects of the constitutionally dictated separation of powers: rather it reflects them, and in so doing, in a very real sense magnifies them. American political parties are not well equipped at all for developing comprehensive policy positions, presenting them to the electorate, and seeing them through into legislated programs that might be voted up or down in the next election.

THE CASE THAT THE PROPOSED CHANGES WOULD NOT IN FACT ADVANCE THE PUBLIC INTEREST

No one who pays close attention to politics would reject out of hand every call for change in our parties and elections systems. I do maintain, however, that the more substantial changes that have been proposed fail to show real promise of making things better by such national-interest standards as more responsive democratic government and wiser long-term policies. I should acknowledge that my current judgment in this regard differs to some extent from that of times past. I have always been skeptical about claims that changes proposed for one area or another of the parties and elections system should be readily recognized as reforms. Often the changes have not in fact made things better, and within a few years of their enactment the cry has been raised loudly that the reforms must themselves be reformed. The literature on past reforms is filled with references to unforeseen and unintended consequences. Nonetheless, I did at one time accept much of the argument that stronger parties would likely advance the public interest. At one time, too, I could not resist the enthusiasm that afflicted so many others for seeking ways to improve the presidential nomination process. I offered my own elegant blueprint for change, which included a bigger role for party and elected officials, in conjunction with a single, nationwide presidential primary.[14] While I remain comfortable with much of the earlier analysis, I think I yielded too readily to the underlying notion that successful institutional tinkering is easily conceived.

TINKERING

Proposed changes occupy different levels of reach or comprehensiveness. Some are potentially far-reaching, such as arguments for strengthening the national parties. Others are much more limited, such as proposals for altering the schedule of presidential primaries. My concern with the latter sort of proposals is in part the familiar one about unintended consequences—that they in fact often result in two steps forward and two steps backward, or sometimes two-and-a-half steps back. They advocate change that has merit but also disadvantages.

The continuing discussion of the scheduling of presidential primaries is a good case in point. Concern has been voiced about the implications of small states (Iowa and New Hampshire) leading the parade of caucuses and primaries and permitting their Republican and Democratic electorates, which are far from national microcosms, to receive undue weight. Intense press coverage of these early contests is followed by the obligatory *Time* and *Newsweek* cover photos of "the big winners." Infinite effort goes into establishing the "expected" showing for each candidate, which is then set against actual achievement to determine the "real" victor. In 1968 Lyndon Johnson got a majority of the Democratic vote in the New Hampshire primary, but Eugene McCarthy was seen doing better than expected and this "spin" came to be imposed on the entire campaign. It is hard not to find annoying the hype that surrounds the early contests. For 1988 southern states have taken things in their own hands by scheduling an early regional primary on March 8. This balloting follows the Iowa caucuses and the New Hampshire primary, which are held in February; but its huge jackpot of delegates means that it, too, will attract an enormous amount of early press coverage. The southern electorate is already being dissected by elaborate public opinion surveys.

Are there unfortunate implications in giving one state or region, whose social and political outlook differs from the other sections, so much weight in establishing early momentum? All manner of suggestions have been made to cope with such scheduling problems. For example, some have argued for a series of four primary dates, with all states holding primaries assigned to one or another so that no region dominates any date. This has some merit. New Hampshire and Iowa would get less attention, and a more "representative" collection of states would lead things off. But there are drawbacks: candidates would be forced to campaign simultaneously in four scattered sections of the country, putting enormous burdens on them, especially on those who start with less funding and organizational resources. By leading off, manageable little Iowa and New Hampshire enable less well-known and well-heeled candidates to gain attention through presenting their wares to real people in real election settings. If a candidate with modest resources and previously lacking a national reputation manages to impress a fair number of voters in these small states, isn't this laboratory experience of some considerable interest to the country?

In offering in 1980 "a better way to pick our presidents," I argued that we would improve things if we managed to combine in the selection system large doses of two differing, even conflicting, elements: peer review by party leaders and a strong voice for rank-and-file voters. The former would be achieved by providing that one-third of all national convention delegates be chosen wholly outside the primaries, in their capacities as party officials and officeholders. The remaining two-thirds would be chosen in state delegate-selection primaries held in every state on a single day—for example, the third Tuesday in June. Each state's delegates would be divided among the candidates in proportion to the candidates' respective shares of the state's total vote, with perhaps a threshold of 10 percent of the vote required before one gets any delegates.

Under this system a candidate who ran strongly in the national primary would almost surely add enough support from party leaders to be nominated on the first ballot. If he received 60 percent of the primary vote, for example, across the fifty states, he would go to the convention assured of roughly 40 percent of the first-round convention ballots—that is, 60 percent of the two-thirds of the delegates chosen through the primary. It would be surprising if the candidate couldn't pick up another 10 percent from the party officials. Otherwise, the convention would go on to further balloting, with no delegate bound but all aware of voter preferences. Bargaining and negotiation would finally produce the nominee.

These arguments still seem sound to me in 1987. I am less inclined to argue confidently on behalf of their implementation today, however, than I was in 1980—for two different sorts of reasons. First I am now more skeptical about the desirability of imposing upon the states and parties any national reform of presidential nominee selection, even assuming the political readiness in Congress to legislate such change. Respect for the federal character of presidential selection and for the private associational nature of the national parties require that Congress should not presume to tell the states and the parties that delegate-selection primaries must be held on a given date and delegates chosen according to one particular, nationally-set standard. It is entirely appropriate, of course, to try to educate and persuade the parties to consider certain approaches, like those that build a greater measure of peer review into the selection process. And here, it should be noted, recent developments give us reason to be modestly satisfied. I refer, in particular, to the Democrats' decisions to increase the numbers of party leaders and officeholders selected ex officio as convention delegates. Such gradual change, based on the lessons of experience, is wholly consistent with the modest Burkean approach to reform to which I think we should commit ourselves.

My second reason for quarreling with the position I took around 1980 is related but still distinct. We should be careful lest our laudable enthusiasm for making things better lead us to urge the parties to constantly tinker with their procedures. This argument is something more than insisting we need to be sensitive to "the unintended consequences of purposive social action." It is also more than insisting upon the need to recognize that every system of presidential selection must have its own weaknesses and biases. It involves, especially, the judgment that there is a vital national interest in achieving order, stability, and predictability in election machinery. Electoral reform should be approached from a perspective that recognizes how important it is in this area to settle on something and stick with it.

I have made this same argument with regard to the endless stream of proposals for improving campaign finance. Like Michael Malbin, I have concluded that our present arrangements for funding elections don't work badly and certainly aren't guilty, as is so often charged, of giving certain special interests a corrupting financial influence.[15] Some of the changes made in the 1970s through the Federal Election Campaign Act (FECA) and its amendments do seem to have improved things, as in providing for a far more complete accounting to the public of who receives how much in campaign contributions from whom; and undoubtedly some further improvements can be made. The greatest improvement we can now make would come from securing bipartisan agreement on an election finance scheme which, while not perfect, would meet a few basic objectives, thereby bringing to an end the long period of partisan skirmishing.

If the United States does not resist the urge to tinker with campaign finance every few years, this area may become for us what election laws for France were during the 1946–1958 Fourth Republic—subject to regular change guided by nothing more substantial than immediate partisan advantage. (Electoral law skirmishing resumed in France in the mid-1980s, when the Socialists put through changes designed to reduce expected losses.) Before every election during the Fourth Republic, a key battle was fought on what election law would prevail in the balloting: several variants of proportional representation were used, for example, each differing substantially in its implications for how votes would get translated into seats in the French National Assembly. If this comes to pass in American campaign finance law, popular confidence is bound to suffer. People in a democracy need to have confidence that the basic rules governing the way they choose their leaders have a durability that reflects an underlying propriety and legitimacy. Constant change suggests that rulemaking is a shallow, cynical, political game.

Changes sometimes have to be made, and interested parties and groups will inevitably differ as to where their interests lie. But stability in electoral rules and procedures is in the national interest. The proper goal of reform is to remove *electoral machinery* as far as possible from partisan debate and endless tinkering. The U.S. single-member district, simple majority system seems to me to offer the model. It certainly has its biases, but both parties have learned to live with it; and the American electorate has come to see it as involving generally fair, justifiably permanent rules of the game.

MAJOR SURGERY: IS MORE CENTRALLY INTEGRATED POLICY MAKING IN THE NATIONAL INTEREST?

The American system in its entirety—which includes the separation of powers and the decentralized, undisciplined party system established within it—undoubtedly makes more difficult enactment of programs that reflect some centrally inspired coherence. Even when a president wins a handsome public endorsement, he must immediately grapple with a fiercely independent Congress in which members of his own party as well as the opposition oppose him at critical junctures. Compared to parliamentary systems with relatively disciplined parties, our presidential/congressional system with undisciplined parties is surely disjointed and at times even incoherent.

Given the record of party factions that in other systems have gained working control of the government and managed to enact their programs with less compromise and adjustment than is typically required in the United States, we must question whether the biases of the American system should be seen as disadvantageous. Historian Arthur Schlesinger, Jr. argues that the key problem evident in the making of public policy in the United States isn't that we have at hand a set of elegant programs that we can't enact because of the fracturings attendant our system of dispersed authority. "Our problem—let's face it—is that we don't know what to do. . . . If we don't know what ought to be done, efficient enactment of poor programs is a dubious accomplishment—as the experience of 1981 demonstrates. (Schlesinger was critical of various economic proposals that the Reagan administration advanced, including the Economic Recovery Tax Act, and that Congress did in fact enact.) What is the great advantage of acting with decision and dispatch when you don't know what you are doing?"[16]

Schlesinger points out that as early as a century ago foreign visitors to the United States were leveling much the same criticisms of the American system of separation of powers, party indiscipline, and the absence of party accountability as we encounter today. In *The American Commonwealth*, Lord Bryce summarized the British view that these elements of the American system made it virtually impossible for it to settle major national questions. "An Englishman is disposed to ascribe these failures to the fact that as there are no leaders, there is no one responsible for the neglect of business, the miscarriage of bills, the unwise appropriation of public funds. 'In England,' he says, 'the ministry of the day bears the blame of whatever goes wrong in the House of Commons. Having a majority, it ought to be able to do what it desires.'"[17]

Bryce also reported the response that he encountered among American political leaders. They insisted that Congress had not settled a number of major national questions not because of defects in institutional structure "but because the division of opinion in the country regarding them has been faithfully reflected in Congress. The majority has not been strong enough to get its way; and this has happened, not only because abundant opportunities for resistance arise from the method of doing business, but still more because no distinct impulse or mandate toward any particular settlement of these questions has been received from the country. It is not for Congress to go faster than the people. When the country knows and speaks its mind, Congress will not fail to act." Schlesinger endorses this general argument. *"When the country is not sure what ought to be done, it may be that delay, debate and further consideration are not a bad idea. And if our leadership is sure what to do, it must in our democracy educate the rest—and that is not a bad idea either."* [18]

Admittedly, the argument that the national interest is well served by programmatic approaches that involve delay, debate, and compromise when the country is divided and uncertain as to what should be done, has a large subjective component. This argument is distrustful of the notion that an ascendent political faction is likely to be the repository of special wisdom and insight on what programs will best advance certain ends. Schlesinger seems to have come to this perspective with some encouragement from Reagan administration policies of 1981 and 1982—policies with which he strongly disagreed. I find a recurring experience: the record of a great many ascendant factions in many different governmental contexts has demonstrated that the probability of error is so great that barriers to any faction's being able to gain clear control of the government and see its ideas through are generally conducive to sound long-term policy in the national interest.

When reasonably broad agreement is reached on a course of action, the American system seems perfectly capable of coherent and expeditious responses, even on complex policy questions. The Tax Reform Act of 1986 is a case in point. We had been told repeatedly prior to its enactment that it presented precisely the kind of question where the special interests inevitably dominate—that our hyperindividualistic Congress is wholly incapable of fending off special interest pleas given the complexity, and hence invisibility to the general public, of detailed tax code provisions. Yet no such thing happened. When substantial agreement was reached (intellectually among economists and politically among Democrats and Republicans) on the wisdom of a general course of change in tax policy, that change was swiftly and coherently established. Whether we will live to regret it is, of course, another matter.

Any governmental or electoral system can at times yield policy that passes muster by standards of enduring national interests; and similarly any can fail to do so. Our judgments as to the adequacy of a particular system are inevitably colored by our views on their recent yield. A case in point is the criticism of the British system advanced by some American political scientists, notably Pendleton Herring and Don K. Price, at the end of the 1930s. Leon Epstein notes that both Herring and Price "thought that Britain's disciplined party leadership had produced bad policy results during the 1930s, at the very time that American presidential leadership appeared to have been relatively successful."[19]

Herring's observations are worth considering as we contemplate whether our own system needs more party discipline and centralization. In Britain, Herring argued, "it is the whole tendency of the system that distinctive parties govern the nation in accordance with the class basis upon which their strength is organized. . . . [T]he isolation of classes into separate parties prevents that modification of extreme points of view that is possible when different elements join in compromise. The results of the British Conservative Party in encouraging German armament because of a fear of communism are now apparent. Parliamentary government does not provide a place in policy formulation for all of the parties at interest. One party machine rules while the opposition elements stand aside and hope for mistakes that will oust those in power."[20] Such a system, Herring argued, is poorly suited to advancing the national interest. Herring found the American presidential system with its weak parties and dispersed power rather more attractive. "The chief executive is forced to seek middle ground. He cannot depend on his own party following. His measures are often supported by minority party members. The separation of executive and legislative branches gives both Congress and the president an opportunity to appeal to the voters."

Epstein suggests that American political science has suffered from its infatuation through much of this century with its idealized picture of a British "responsible-party" system.[21] Shaken from their attraction to some degree by developments in the 1930s and again by recent British experience in formulating public policy, political scientists still have not sufficiently examined questions of the institutional capacity of the British system for encouraging sound, broad-based policies. My own limited examination suggests that every party system in the advanced industrial democracies—Britain and the U.S. included—is a complex mix that reflects both the strengths and the weaknesses of the larger political-institutional system of which it is a part. Cross-national borrowing is a dubious venture.

MAJOR SURGERY: DOES THE U.S. SYSTEM NOTABLY ADVANTAGE SPECIAL INTERESTS?

The United States has a plethora of interest groups intruding into the governmental process at all levels. Moreover, the number of groups operating at the national level has burgeoned over the last quarter-century. From these developments it has been easy to reach the conclusion that the American system of dispersed governmental power, organizationally weak parties, and a hyperindividualistic legislature has given special interests a unique and excessive opportunity to shape policy. Jack L. Walker, a leading student of American interest groups, challenges the view, however, that the explosion of interest-group activity has anything at all to do with the characteristics of the American parties and elections system. The factors he cites for the expansion of group activity nationally are: long-term increases in the level of education of the population, which provides a large pool of skills on which various citizen movements can draw; development of methods of communication that are relatively inexpensive yet sophisticated; a period of social protest beginning with the civil rights demonstrations of the early 1960s, which called many established practices into question and provided a strong stimulus for change; the creation of massive new governmental programs; the subsequent response by governmental agencies and foundations of encouraging links among the service providers and consumers of the new programs; and the defensive response by groups that felt threatened by new regulatory legislation in areas like consumer protection, occupational health and safety, and environmentalism.[22]

A great number of developments outside the parties and elections system have encouraged groups to organize, set up Washington offices, and try to bend programs and policies more to their wishes. It might still be, of course, that the American electoral system gives unusual opportunities to special interests; but upon examination this claim, too, appears unsubstantiated. The experience of Western democracies indicates that different electoral and governmental systems stimulate different forms of interest-group intervention; it does not establish that more centralized systems fare better in resisting special interests.

In France, notes Frank L. Wilson, "with deputies voting *en bloc* according to their parties' decisions, interest groups might be expected to redirect their pressure from the individual members to the party, but there is no evidence that this shift took place. Rather, they redirected their activities toward influencing governmental agencies directly."[23] Over half of the interest-group leaders Wilson interviewed said that their groups rarely or never contacted the parties as such. These officials described contacts with ministers and civil servants as by far their most effective means of action; parliamentary lobbying ranked at the bottom of the list. Interest-group interventions in France look different from those in the United States, but are not less influential.

In Britain, decision making is highly centralized in the government and in the parties. As a result, parliamentary lobbying is relatively limited compared to the United States, though far from nonexistent. When, however, interest groups form strong bonds with tightly disciplined parties in this centralized decision-making environment, the influence of these special interests over the totality of government policy may dwarf that achieved by their counterparts in the United States. No interest group or collection of groups has influence over the Democratic or Republican parties comparable to what the labor movement has over the Labour party in Britain. The British system may have an especially difficult time responding to more general interests because of the strength of group ties to established party decision makers.

Elected officials of both parties in the United States routinely do business with a great variety of different interest groups. The reverse is also true: most groups consider it in their interest to maintain access to people on both sides of the aisle and in the various sectors where decisions are made, reflecting the dispersion of power that is the hallmark of the American system. The main result seems to be that groups rarely dominate any broad sector of national policy, although they may exercise great influence in narrower policy sectors where "iron triangle" relationships (involving agency bureau chiefs, congressional subcommittees, and well-organized interest groups) apply.

MAJOR SURGERY: DOES THE SYSTEM DIMINISH PUBLIC CONTROL?

Calls for "reform" aimed at more disciplined and "responsible" parties have typically assumed that the public is frustrated by the wide dispersion of power in which no faction is able to gain clear control of the government and see its programs comprehensively enacted. The exact opposite seems to be the case, however. When public opinion polls ask Americans what they think about a system in which Republicans control the presidency and the Democrats, Congress, they invariably indicate their satisfaction. In the last half-century, the United States has had much experience with divided control over the presidency and Congress; and repeatedly, surveys show approval of split control rather than frustration with it.

Examining public opinion on many of the large contemporary issues, one gets a better sense of why divided control may not appear to Americans as either confusing or threatening. Again and again one finds a public that is highly ambivalent—torn between the contending partisan positions. For example, *Public Opinion* magazine has reviewed the opinions of Americans on various "role of government" questions. Over the last two decades the public has been continuously pulled in two directions. On the one hand, Americans make expansive claims for services of all sorts—many of which they expect government to provide. On the other hand, they see government as intrusive, clumsy, and problem-causing. Those who have wanted to cut back on domestic government have naturally chosen to emphasize the public's dissatisfaction with government's size and scope; those who want more government intervention stress the public's appetite for services. The fact is, though, that both dimensions have been prominent in American thinking over the last two decades; the tensions between the two viewpoints, not their resolution left or right, Democratic or Republican, is the story.

Given these ambivalent feelings, fractured party control may be seen as a highly effective vehicle of popular control. If the public hasn't made up its mind what direction it wants to go, or more precisely, has decided it doesn't want to go consistently in any direction, what better vehicle than a system in which a loosely disciplined Democratic majority pushes one way through the Congress and a loosely disciplined Republican coalition often pushes the other way through the executive?[24] The policy control of an ambivalent public is enhanced by a system of dispersed authority. Frustration seems to reside more with certain party elites than with the general public.

CONCLUSIONS

The relationship of a party system to the promotion of broad national interests will never be demonstrated with the final precision of the Pythagorean theorem. It involves too many slippery concepts and too many sources of variation in end result. Nonetheless, it is striking that over the past century, in which the American system of dispersed authority has been so much lamented, so little real evidence has been accumulated supporting the argument that party discipline and centralization in policy making actually serve the national interest. Special interests don't appear less influential in parliamentary systems with disciplined parties.

Centralized systems of policy making show no signs of being able to regularly produce sounder results. The American public shows satisfaction, not frustration, with the system in which no party faction can dominate the course of public policy. The basic case for extensive reform of the American party system simply has not been established.

NOTES

1. Glendon Schubert, *The Public Interest* (New York: Free Press, 1960), p. 224.

2. Frank Sorauf, "The Conceptual Muddle" in Carl J. Friedrich, ed., *The Public Interest* (New York: Atherton Press, 1962), p. 190.

3. Robert A. Dahl and Charles E. Lindblom, *Politics, Economics and Welfare* (New York: Harper, 1963), p. 501.

4. Howard L. Reiter, *Parties and Elections in Corporate America* (New York: St. Martins Press, 1987), p. 63.

5. See, among recent writers, Virginia Held, *The Public Interest and Individual Interests* (New York: Basic Books, 1970); and Richard E. Flathman, *The Public Interest: An Essay Concerning the Normative Discourse of Politics* (New York: John Wiley, 1966).

6. Daniel Bell and Irving Kristol, "What is the Public Interest?" *The Public Interest* 1 (Fall 1965): 5.

7. Woodrow Wilson, *Congressional Government: A Study in American Politics* (Baltimore: Johns Hopkins U. Press, 1981), pp. 206–7.

8. Ibid., p. 206

9. Woodrow Wilson, *Constitutional Government in the United States* (New York: Columbia U. Press, 1908).

10. American Political Science Association, "Toward a More Responsible Two-Party System," A Report of the Committee on Political Parties, *The American Political Science Review* 44 (September 1950).

11. Wilson, *Congressional Government*, pp. 331–32.

12. American Political Science Association, "Toward a More Responsible Two-Party System," p. 19.

13. E. E. Schattschneider, *The Semisovereign People: A Realist's View of Democracy in America* (New York: Holt, Rinehart, and Winston, 1960), p. 35.

14. Everett Ladd, "A Better Way to Pick Our Presidents," *Fortune*, 5 May 1980, pp. 132-42.

15. See, for example, Michael Malbin, "Looking Back at the Future of Campaign Finance Reform: Interest Groups and American Elections" in Malbin, ed., *Money and Politics in the United States* (Chatham, N.J.: Chatham House, 1984), pp. 232-76; and Everett Ladd, "Campaign Spending And Democracy," *Ladd Report #4* (New York: Norton, 1986).

16. Arthur Schlesinger, Jr., "Leave the Constitution Alone" in Donald L. Robinson, ed., *Reforming American Government* (Boulder, Colo.: Westview Press, 1985), p. 53.

17. James Bryce, *The American Commonwealth* (New York: Macmillan, 1918), vol. 1, pp. 153–54.

18. Schlesinger, "Leave the Constitution Alone," p. 54 (emphasis added).

19. Leon D. Epstein, "What Happened to the British Party Model?" *The American Political Science Review* 74 (March 1980): 10; Don K. Price, "The Parliamentary and Presidential System," *Public Administration Review* 3 (Autumn 1943): 317–34; and Pendleton Herring, *Presidential Leadership* (New York: Farrar and Rinehart, 1940), esp. pp. 128–46.

20. Herring, *Presidential Leadership*, pp. 129–30.

21. Epstein, "What Happened to the British Party Model?"

22. Jack L. Walker, "The Origins and Maintenance of Interest Groups in America," *The American Political Science Review* 77 (June 1983): 397.

23. Frank L. Wilson, "French Interest Group Politics: Pluralist or Neo-Corporatist?" *The American Political Science Review* 77 (December 1983): 905.

24. For data on the public's conflicting views of government, see *Public Opinion*, March-April 1987, pp. 21–33.

Reading 13

THE LIMITATIONS OF REFORM: CHANGES IN THE NOMINATING PROCESS

Howard L. Reiter

For more than two decades, a debate has been raging among American political activists, journalists and scholars about the numerous rules changes enacted by the Democratic party since its tumultuous 1968 national convention, and the various legal changes at the state and federal levels that have also affected the Presidential nominating process. The rules changes have included the introduction of fairer practices such as written state party rules for delegate selection; proportional representation of candidates' supporters in the delegations; increased representation of women, racial minorities and young people at the convention; and measures to require nominees to respond in writing to the party platform. The legal changes include the proliferation of delegate selection primaries and the Federal Election Campaign Act of 1971 and its various subsequent amendments.[1] The debate has centered around the desirability of these changes, which will here be referred to generically as "the reforms," with no normative connotation intended.

Perhaps the most prolific group of political scientists are those who condemn the rules for overturning a decent nominating system that combined the openness of a small number of primaries with the deliberative wisdom of party elites at the convention itself. In its place there has emerged a wide open system in which party organization is rendered impotent, and inexperienced candidates can win nominations by securing pluralities among the small number of people who vote in primaries and caucuses. A McGovern can thus defeat a Humphrey, a Carter can overturn a Henry Jackson, a Hart can very nearly upset a Mondale. There is no question in the minds of these critics that the reforms bear the major responsibility for this apparently grievous state of affairs.

Austin Ranney, a member of the first post-1968 reform commission, has perhaps been most prolific in assailing "the most radical changes (made by the Democratic party) in procedures for choosing its presidential nominees since the 1820s...a major change in the nature of presidential politics and therefore in our whole political system."[2] Another disaffected Democrat, Jeane Kirkpatrick, called the reforms the most important cause of "party decomposition," and Nelson Polsby devoted an entire book to what he claimed were "the consequences of party reform."[3] These included everything from Democratic losses in Presidential elections to wrongheaded Presidential behavior. To Byron Shafer, the reforms were a "quiet revolution" that produced "the diminution, the constriction, at times the elimination, of the regular party in the politics of presidential selection."[4] Two Democratic activists, Penn Kemble and Josh Muravchik, claimed that "the reforms have left one of the major institutions of American democracy in a shambles."[5]

On the other side of the ideological divide are those who applaud the reforms for replacing a closed and often corrupt system of power brokerage with one that is more open and involves the participation of many more activists than before. These authors defend the impact of the reforms in terms reminiscent of the language of the critics. A leading academic exponent of reform, William Crotty, writes, "The reforms introduced a remarkable era to American politics. More was attempted, and accomplished, than can truthfully be said to have been envisioned in the decades since the Progressive movement of the early 1900s." It was, he concluded, "a revolution in party operations."[6] Both Crotty and Austin Ranney agree that Jimmy Carter's nomination in 1976 would have been impossible without the reforms.[7]

The purpose of this article is to join neither the critics nor the advocates of the reforms. Rather, it is to take issue with both sides, and demonstrate that both have vastly exaggerated the consequences of those reforms. Indeed, it is possible that the basic contours of the present nominating process would look approximately as they do even if the rules had not been changed at all. Some of the authors cited above occasionally qualify their position by indicating that the role of the reforms was more limited than the passages quoted above indicate, but each has spent so much time criticizing or defending the reforms and attributing so many consequences to them that the qualifying statements pale in significance.

In order to argue for the limited significance of the reforms, one must either maintain that the system has not changed in the direction that both sides of the debate agree that it has, or establish that changes have occurred but that the system was evolving in that direction anyway. This article takes the second approach. The data to be presented below demonstrate that change has indeed occurred, but that much of it antedated the first meeting of the first reform commission in 1969. In some respects, the reforms seem to have accelerated some trends that had been under way for years; in others, the reforms seem to have had virtually no impact.

If the formal rules did not change the nominating process, then what did? Although appropriate data are lacking to prove this claim, this paper's argument is that the secular decline in strength of state and local party organization was primarily responsible for the devolution of the Presidential nominating process (the party decline hypothesis).[8] In the past, state and local party leaders would control their delegations to the national convention by the traditional instruments of party cohesion—control over patronage and other government benefits. As the power of those machines was eroded, delegates were freed from the control of the leaders of the delegations. Delegates increasingly enjoyed the option of supporting whatever candidate they wanted, and were increasingly susceptible to the influence of bodies other than party leaders, such as interest groups and constituencies based on demographic characteristics such as race. This was an evolutionary process that began to reach fruition in the late 1960s.

In order to substantiate this argument, at each juncture empirical indicators of the phenomenon under consideration will be examined. Only by viewing the changes in those indicators over time can one pinpoint when the transition to the new system began to occur, and in most cases that will be before 1972, the first year in which the impact of the reforms could be felt. In order to provide a sufficiently long lead time, whenever possible data from the beginning of the twentieth century will be used.

NOMINATING PATTERNS: AN OVERVIEW

In the heyday of "boss" control over nominating conventions, party leaders had a number of resources at their disposal.[9] To understand how the local boss functioned, one must understand his goals, which were primarily to nominate a candidate who would be an asset to the ticket and who would co-operate with the boss on patronage. This made it necessary to establish a good relationship with the candidate who would be the nominee, preferably by making the candidate beholden to oneself by providing delegate votes at a critical moment. That "moment" might be early in the campaign—the legendary "For Roosevelt Before Chicago" group of 1932—or at the convention climax—the famous Vice-Presidential "deal" between Roosevelt and Garner that year.

Given such goals, it was in the party leaders' interest to maintain maximum flexibility so that if an unforeseen nominee began to emerge at the convention, a savvy boss could jump on his bandwagon at a strategic juncture. This meant that in the absence of a consensual nominee, who by definition would not find it necessary to bargain with anyone, the nomination should be kept from the winner as long as possible. Moreover, it meant that each boss's delegation should refrain from committing itself too early and too strongly to a candidate, and that its votes be available for horse-trading by the leader. These considerations resulted in a number of features of conventions familiar to students of political lore. One was the large number of uncommitted delegates, whom the bosses could use as bargaining chips. A variation of this was the "favorite son" candidacy, in which the delegation would support a local notable who had little apparent chance to be nominated. This was a convenient way of keeping one's delegates from other candidates until the bargaining began, while giving recognition to a local hero who might even, with some luck, end up as the nominee. Another feature of the older conventions was the length of the nominating process, which could be considerable if enough leaders held on to their delegates, waiting for the best bargaining opportunity. This meant several or even dozens of ballots, with numerous candidates placed in nomination. It also encouraged late entries and the emergence of legendary dark horses, the James K. Polks and Warren G. Hardings. And the atmosphere of uncertainty put a special premium on pre-nominating roll-call ballots to test the strength of the leading candidates and provide clues as to who might win.

In this article, each of the features noted in the preceding paragraph will be considered.

THE DECLINE OF THE UNCOMMITTED

Two Democratic activists, each representing a different portion of the ideological spectrum, have asserted that the new rules tend to decrease the proportion of uncommitted delegates. Rick Stearns of the 1972 McGovern campaign argued that the rule requiring that delegates running in primaries indicate their Presidential preferences had the effect of diminishing the uncommitted bloc.[10] Anti-reform leader Penn Kemble subsequently maintained that the proportional representation rules would have the same effect.[11] Nelson Polsby has argued that primary electorates in general prefer not to vote for uncommitted delegates.[12] But Denis Sullivan and his colleagues, arguing the party-decline thesis, assert that a number of trends since 1945, including the rules, have resulted in fewer uncommitted delegates.[13]

Who is right? Journalists' delegate counts from the weekends before each contested convention since 1952 have been compiled; here, a "con-

Table 13.1 Percentage of Delegates Who Were Uncommitted the Weekend Before Each Contested Convention, 1952–1988

Year	Percentage	Source
		A. Democrats
1952	29.3	*The New York Times*, 20 July 1952, sec. 1, p. 34
1956	27.8	*The New York Times*, 13 August 1956, p. 13
1960	24.2	*Washington Post*, 10 July 1960, p. A6
1968	11.9	*The New York Times*, 25 August 1968, sec. 1, p. 1
1972	7.3	*Washington Post*, 9 July 1972, p. A2
1976	*	
1980	3.1	*Washington Post*, 10 August 1980, p. C5
1984	5.8	*Washington Post*, 15 July 1984, p. A15
1988	*	
		B. Republicans
1952	9.8	*The New York Times*, 6 July 1952, sec. 1, p. 36
1964	15.4	*The New York Times*, 12 July 1964, sec. 1, p. 57
1968	3.8	*The New York Times*, 4 August 1968, sec. 1, p. 1
1976	4.7	*The New York Times*, 15 August 1976, sec. 1, p. 24

*No count available, as nomination was not in doubt.

tested convention" is one in which more than one candidate receives more than 10 per cent of the votes.[14] There was no count for the cut-and-dried Democratic convention of 1976, when the media did not bother to count after Carter secured the nomination in early June. No precise counts could be found from before 1952. Table 13.1 shows a monotonic drop among Democratic uncommitteds from 1952 through to 1980, with the greatest decline occurring not in 1972 or 1976, but in 1968. Had Robert Kennedy not been assassinated, the figure for 1968 would probably have been lower still. Similarly, the chief Republican drop occurred between 1964 and 1968. Of course, these data are dependent on many factors, notably the number of serious candidates left by the time of the convention and how far ahead the front-runner is, but clearly the rules did not cause a major decline in the uncommitted bloc. And equally clearly, the decline was occurring before 1972.

FEWER FAVORITE SONS

One of the reform commissions established in the wake of the 1968 Democratic convention, the Commission on Rules or O'Hara Commission, stipulated that nominating speeches could only be made for candidates who could secure at least fifty delegates' signatures.[15] As twenty delegations to the party's 1972 convention had at least fifty votes, this was not a draconian rule. Nevertheless, those who wish to stress the impact of the reforms could argue that it might have undercut favorite son candidacies. Another rule with potentially the same effect was cited by Rick Stearns above—that would-be delegates express a Presidential preference in the primaries; primary voters might be unwilling to vote for a delegate whose preference was not for a major candidate. Indeed, this was part of Nelson Polsby's argument, cited above.

Has there been a decline in favorite sons, and if so, when did it begin? Table 13.2 shows for each contested convention since 1900 the proportion of first-ballot votes that were won by candidates receiving less than 10 per cent. Not surprisingly, the Democrats' abolition in 1936 of the requirement that nominees receive two-thirds of the vote seems to have had an impact, for shortening the balloting probably discouraged longshot candidacies. However, after 1960 there was a further drop-off. The 1900–32 mean was 24.8, and the 1948–60 mean 15.1, and the 1968–88 mean 6.2. Without a rules change in 1936, the Republicans have also had a clear and almost monotonic drop-off since the zenith in 1916. The post-1948 conventions are clearly different form earlier ones. Here again, the party decline hypothesis is most convincing, with the rules change in 1936 apparently important for the Democrats.

NUMBER OF BALLOTS

It has been decades since either party has taken more than one ballot to nominate a President; the most recent multi-ballot conventions were in 1948 for the Republicans and in 1952 for the Democrats. As many have pointed out, this means that conventions no longer decide nominations; instead, the nominee arrives at the convention with enough delegates to secure a victory. In the words of Max Frankel, the delegates "come to the convention simply to be unwrapped and counted."[16] Or as a Republican politician said in 1980, "You could have these conventions by mail."[17]

Indeed, every contested convention since 1952 has been a game of "Try to Stop the Front-Runner," and the front-runner has won every time. Other candidates have resorted to platform fights (the Republicans in 1964), credentials challenges (the Democrats in 1972), and rules battles (the Republicans in 1976 and the Democrats in 1980), but all to no avail. Skeptics will say that Kennedy could have been stopped in 1960 (he had only 45 votes more than a majority), Nixon in 1968 (25 votes), McGovern in 1972 (109.28 votes on the crucial California credentials vote), and Ford

Table 13.2 Percentage of Votes on First Ballots of Contested Conventions Going to Candidates Who Individually Received Less Than 10 Per Cent of the Vote, 1900–1988

Year	Democratic	Republican
1904	14.2	—
1912	5.9	6.2*
1916	—	53.2
1920	40.2	35.7
1924	38.8	—
1932	24.8	—
1940	—	34.6
1948	3.4	25.5
1952	18.3	9.2
1956	18.7	—
1960	20.1	—
1964	—	16.1
1968	10.0	13.7
1972	12.6	—
1976	11.9	0.1
1980	1.7	—
1984	0.7	—
1988	0.2	—

*Not including vote for Theodore Roosevelt or abstentions.

in 1976 (57 votes). But clearly there is a bandwagon effect, and as the old saw has it, there are always enough delegates with aspirations for a US Attorneyship to put any candidate with close to 50 per cent over the top.

Nelson Polsby has implied that this trend dates from "the transformation of 1968–72,"[18] but if anything this trend seems to confirm the impact of the decline of party. There was a long-term decline in the frequency of multi-ballot conventions until they disappeared in the 1950s. The Democrats had laboured under the two-thirds rule until 1936, so the Republicans will provide the most useful longitudinal data, uninterrupted by relevant rules changes. Because of the well-known ability of incumbents to win nomination on the first ballot, the only data presented are from conventions that did not nominate incumbents, divided by party system eras. In the 1856–92 period, five of the seven such Republican conventions were multi-ballot (71 per cent); from 1896 through 1924, two out of four (50 per cent); and from 1928 through 1948 two out of five (40 per cent). The numbers here are small, but nevertheless the trend is in the direction predicted by the party decline thesis. This is especially so when we add the years from 1952 to 1988, when none of the six such conventions lasted longer than one ballot.

Some have predicted that the post-1968 rules changes would result in more multi-ballot conventions, including Ohio's former Governor, John Gilligan; William Keech and Donald Matthews; Jeane Kirkpatrick; Judith Parris; and Nelson Polsby and Aaron Wildavsky.[19] This is a plausible argument, for it is based on the expectation that proportional representation, as mandated by the Democrats from 1968 onwards, would enable so many candidates to win delegates in so many states that nobody would be able to win a majority of convention delegates. Moreover, the provision of federal matching funds and spending ceilings, also beginning in 1976, would seem to encourage the participation of more candidates than ever, thereby dividing the pie further.

There are problems in testing the hypothesis that more candidates are entering the race nowadays than before. For one thing, many a candidate in the past waited in the wings, hoping to be regarded as a latter-day Cincinnatus and plucked from his plough. Conversely, there are literally hundreds of announced candidates, especially now that the Federal Election Commission requires a statement of candidacy before one can collect contributions. Even when a recognized political figure announces, how serious is his (Reubin Askew's) or her (Shirley Chisholm's) candidacy?[20]

But one *can* say that all of the conventions under these new rules have been decided in one ballot. The prediction might still be borne out in the future, but clearly it has not been an immediate consequence of the rules. Why not? Paul David and James Ceaser suggest that proportional representation may aid prominent candidates by guaranteeing them a large bloc of delegates.[21] This was not borne out by the results of the open contests of 1976, 1980 and 1984, when such lesser-known candidates as Jimmy Carter, Morris Udall, George Bush, John Anderson and Gary Hart outpolled such big names as George Wallace, Birch Bayh, John Connally, Howard Baker and John Glenn. Perhaps the one-ballot convention has survived because the costs of campaigning have had the effect of destroying the candidacies of anyone who did not accumulate an early share of delegates. A Bayh or a Baker might hope to hobble to the convention with a potentially critical 10 per cent of the vote, but the cost of getting through the primaries on a shrinking base of contributions is prohibitive. This is another hypothesis that does not lend itself conveniently to empirical analysis, although if true it could be one of the most significant effects of the proliferation of primaries. In short, campaign costs, despite the equalizing effects of the legal changes, override the fragmentizing effects of proportional representation to guarantee more single-ballot conventions.

PROLIFERATION OF CANDIDATES

Despite these reservations about our ability to test empirically the proposition that more candidates are participating in the race, those who argue that the rules encourage such participation deserve more of a hearing.[22] If indeed more candidates are entering the race, then even though modern conventions are decided on the first ballot, more candidates should be sharing the vote.

How can we determine whether a greater number of serious candidates are entering the fray? In other words, how can we factor out those candidates who receive only a trace of the vote? A cut-off of 1 per cent seems to divide the favorite sons and daughters from the idiosyncratic candidates who are backed by only a small handful of delegates. Has the number of candidates who receive at least 1 per cent of the vote at contested conventions increased in recent years? It is important to distinguish between single-ballot and multi-ballot conventions here, because the latter will naturally tend to draw more candidates than the former, and the former type of convention has been the rule in recent decades. Therefore Table 13.3 displays the single-ballot, contested conventions since 1900 and the number of candidates receiving at least 1 per cent at each of them. By this measure, there has been no proliferation of candidates, and perhaps it would be safest to say that no clear trend emerges.

Table 13.3 is not an altogether satisfactory test of the proposition, however, given the tendency of a number of serious candidates to withdraw from the race entirely after losing one or two primaries. There were five such Democrats in 1984. Therefore another test of whether a race is attracting more candidates is the number of serious entrants into the primaries. Here "serious" is defined as garnering at least 10 per cent of the vote in any primary. This will count not only those who lasted until the convention, but also those who made a reasonably strong early showing but dropped out and released their delegates before the convention. Unfortunately it also includes local favorite sons and daughters and stalking horses for major candidates, but their inclusion should not seriously affect the long-term trend.

Table 13.4 shows the results, and it is difficult to credit the rules with drawing more candidates into the contest. On the Democratic side there was a surge from 1952 to 1976, but the number has declined since then. As for the Republicans, there appears to be little trend there, and certainly no longitudinal increase in the number of candidates.[23]

Table 13.3 Number of Candidates Receiving at Least 1 Per Cent of the Vote at Single-Ballot, Contested Conventions, Both Major Parties, 1900–1988

Year	Democratic	Republican
1904	6	—
1912	—	4
1948	3	—
1952	—	4
1956	8	—
1960	8	—
1964	—	6
1968	4	9
1972	7	—
1976	3	2
1980	2	—
1984	3	—
1988	2	—

Table 13.4 Number of Candidates Winning at Least 10 Per Cent of the Vote in at Least One Primary, Contested Conventions, 1912–1988

Year	Democratic	Republican
1912	4	3
1916	—	12
1920	6	8
1924	5	—
1932	5	—
1940	—	7
1948	3	9
1952	10	5
1956	3	—
1960	9	—
1964	—	9
1968	8	5
1972	9	—
1976	11	2
1980	3	—
1984	5	—
1988	5	—

LONGER NOMINATING RACES

If party leaders no longer control the process, then nominations go to those who campaign hard for them. No longer can a candidate like Adlai Stevenson in 1952 sit back and wait for party leaders to nominate him without so much as declaring his candidacy. This seems to be reflected in the background of nominees. The current nominating process is biased against candidates with time-consuming jobs (besides the Presidency itself), such as governors and Congressional leaders.

Several authors have argued that a number of recent changes in the rules have lengthened the process. The proliferation of primaries, they say, forces candidates to organize those states early, proportional representation encourages them to contest many primaries, and the Federal Election Campaign Act requires them to declare their candidacies early in order to get publicity and qualify for matching funds from the government.[24] On the contrary, argue Kenneth Bode and Carol Casey, early starts have long been an asset, as John Kennedy showed in 1960 and Richard Nixon demonstrated in 1968.[25]

It is almost impossible to measure when a campaign begins. A candidate's decision to run is usually an evolutionary process, and there is often an unofficial drive by his or her supporters even before the decision is made. Once the die is cast, the candidate usually waits until the time seems ripe before making a formal announcement, often working quietly or even not so quietly for the nomination in the meantime. Even the definite step of the formal announcement was often not taken in an earlier age when the myth of Cincinnatus had more potency. Indeed, it is virtually impossible to identify announcement dates for many major candidates before 1932.

Nevertheless, the formal announcement dates will be used as an index of when a campaign begins, for two pragmatic reasons: there is no alternative, and what is of interest is trends over time. Even if the dates themselves are not wholly meaningful, announcement dates should get earlier over time if campaigns are indeed getting longer. In other words, the announcement date is assumed to be positively correlated with the date the campaign "really" began, however the reader wishes to define it.

For each major candidate at each contested convention since 1932, the number of days between his announcement and the opening of the convention has been calculated. These are presented in Table 13.5. The data for the Democrats in 1952 and 1968 must be regarded with some caution, for in both cases an incumbent President dropped out of the race after the New Hampshire primary, encouraging other entrants (par-

Table 13.5 Number of Days Before the Convention Opened That Major Candidates in Contested Conventions Formally Announced Their Candidacies, 1932–1988

Year	Nominee	Others	Mean
A. Democrats			
1932	156	141	148.5
1948	126	0	63.0
1952	0	90,144,180	103.5
1956	272	91	181.5
1960	191	6	98.5
1968	121	270	195.5
1972	539	179,234	317.3
1976	582	597	589.5
1980	251	279	265.0
1984	511	256,515	427.3
1988	446	282	364.0
B. Republicans			
1940	44	326,540	303.3
1948	157	242,552	317.0
1952	183	265	224.0
1964	192	31	111.5
1968	185	0,97	94.0
1976	405	270	337.5

ticularly those friendly to the President) to announce later than they otherwise might have.

In general, campaigns in recent years have been longer than those of the past, which suggests that the rules did have a major impact. McGovern, Ford, Carter and Mondale established a modern record for nominees by announcing well over a year before the convention. While the 1980 Republican convention was uncontested, candidates' announcements followed the trend. The nominee, Ronald Reagan, announced 244 days before the convention, and his two closest competitors, George Bush and John Anderson, announced respectively 440 and 402 days prior to the opening gavel. For 1988, George Bush announced 308 days ahead. On the other hand, the data also show a gradual upward trend for nominees. Democratic nominees in 1956 and 1960 announced earlier than those of 1932 and 1944, and Republicans show an almost monotonic trend from 1940 to 1976. Complicating these trends is the fact that when *all* major candidates are observed (the last column of Table 13.5), the Democratic trend is similar to that for nominees but the Republican data are quite different. The 1976 Republican average is not much higher than those of the 1940s, and until 1976 there was a trend towards *shorter* campaigns!

Perhaps the must judicious conclusion to draw from these murky data is that while nominees' campaigns have been getting longer over the years, the rate of increase has accelerated since 1968.

THE EXTINCT DARK HORSE

Polsby and Wildavsky argue (for reasons unspecified) that the recent rules changes have prevented candidates from coming from behind to win.[26] This is of course a corollary of the fact that recent conventions have all been decided on the first ballot. The argument in this article can only be repeated: it has been *many* years since a dark horse won, and the reforms therefore did not create that phenomenon. The last time a Republican front-runner was stopped was in 1940, and the last time for a Democrat was in 1952. The last nominees who started with less than 10 per cent on the first ballot—true dark horses—were Warren G. Harding in 1920 and John W. Davis in 1924.

If "dark horse" is understood instead to mean someone who started out behind the pre-primary polls, Polsby and Wildavsky have an argument consistent with their first one: the reforms give the advantage to well-known politicians, because financial restrictions place a special burden on obscure candidates who have a harder time raising money.[27] To test this, a list of the front-runners in Gallup polls at the beginning of each election has been compiled in Table 13.6. Democratic dark-horse nominations were frequent before 1972 and frequent thereafter, with about half the nominees in each period overtaking the winter front-runner. Republicans have usually nominated the front-runner. The uncontested 1980 convention fits the pattern, as Reagan was both the early front-runner and the nominee. The same was true for Bush in 1988. Either definition of dark horse leads to the conclusion that little or no change seems to have occurred over time.

PRE-NOMINATION ROLL-CALL VOTES

Has the nature of test votes that deal with rules, credentials or the platform changed in recent years, and have the new rules affected those changes? Christopher Arterton writes:

Table 13.6 Front-runners in Gallup Poll, January or February of Years of Contested Conventions, and Nominees, 1940–1988

Year	Early front-runner	Nominee
A. Democrats		
1948	Harry S. Truman	Harry S. Truman
1952	Harry S. Truman (C. Estes Kefauver after Truman's withdrawal)	Adlai E. Stevenson
1956	Adlai E. Stevenson	Adlai E. Stevenson
1960	John F. Kennedy	John F. Kennedy
1968	Lyndon B. Johnson (Eugene J. McCarthy after Johnson's withdrawal)	Hubert H. Humphrey
1972	Edmund S. Muskie	George S. McGovern
1976	Edward M. Kennedy (Hubert H. Humphrey with Kennedy's name removed)	Jimmy Carter
1980	Jimmy Carter	Jimmy Carter
1984	Walter F. Mondale	Walter F. Mondale
1988	Gary W. Hart	Michael S. Dukakis
B. Republicans		
1940	Thomas E. Dewey	Wendell L. Willkie
1948	Thomas E. Dewey	Thomas E. Dewey
1952	Dwight D. Eisenhower and Robert A. Taft (tie)	Dwight D. Eisenhower
1964	Richard M. Nixon	Barry M. Goldwater
1968	Richard M. Nixon	Richard M. Nixon
1976	Gerald R. Ford, Jr.	Gerald R. Ford, Jr.

Sources: Gallup Opinion Index, Nos. 32, 125, 127, 129, 174, 175, 224, and press release dated 28 January 1988.

> Formerly national conventions were the highest decision-making bodies on a range of questions besides the presidential nominations. Delegates currently arrive at conventions due to their relationship to a political candidate; other matters tend to become compressed along that dimension of conflict.[28]

Arterton's assertion is surely in keeping with arguments that candidate organizations have become the loci of power at national conventions, and that delegates are more candidate-bound than ever. The only problem is that no real change in this area has occurred over the years. More than twenty years ago, Richard Bain demonstrated over many conventions the close link between non-nominating roll-call votes and the division on the nominating ballots(s).[29] Has the incidence of pre-nominating votes increased? Table 13.7 shows an increase on the Democratic side that apparently began in 1968, and a paucity of such votes on the Republican side since 1912, with no trend. If the subject matter of the Democratic votes is any indication, the increase in the incidence of such votes reflects the ideological divisions of American politics since the 1960s, including the Vietnam war, abortion, affirmative action and national health insurance as well as some votes on reforms.

Are these votes more likely today than in the past to be correlated with the fight for the Presidential nomination? Table 13.8 lists Pearson's correlation coefficients between pre-nominating roll-call votes and peak votes for major Presidential candidates. For each convention, Table 13.8 shows the highest such correlation, whether it involved the nominee or not, on the ground that the vote for a compromise candidate might not have reflected the main factional split at the convention. It is worth noting that all the coefficients in Table 13.8 are rather high. Democratic coefficients have generally been higher since 1932 than earlier, and Republican coefficients have consistently been remarkably high.

The role of pre-nominating roll-call votes has not been affected by rules changes, either in their incidence or in their correlation with candidacies.

SUMMARY

Nominating races are very different today from at any time in the past, as most of the indicators in this article reveal. There are fewer uncommitted delegates as conventions open; fewer votes go to favorite sons and daughters; Presidential nominations are decided on the first ballot; and major candidates enter the race earlier. On several measures, there has been little change over the years, including the number of candidates running, the chances of nominating the early front-runner, and the role of pre-nominating roll-call votes.

What caused the trends noted above? Changes in the rules were not responsible, for most of the trends—in uncommitted delegates, in favorite sons and daughters, and in the number of nominating ballots—clearly began before 1972. Only one development, earlier entries, appears to have begun in the 1970s, and even here there are signs of earlier change.

If the rules did not cause these changes, what did? The party decline thesis seems a more plausible explanation, for as state and local party

Table 13.7 Number of Pre-nomination Roll-Call Votes, Contested Conventions, 1900–1988

Year	Democratic	Republican
1904	1	—
1912	4	7
1916	—	0
1920	3	0
1924	3	—
1932	5	—
1940	—	0
1948	2	0
1952	2	3
1956	0	—
1960	0	—
1964	—	1
1968	7	0
1972	7	—
1976	1	1
1980	6	—
1984	4	—
1988	2	—

Table 13.8 Maximum Pearson's Correlation Coefficient Between a Pre-nominating Roll-Call Vote and the Vote for a Major Candidate, Contested Conventions, 1900–1988

Year	Pre-nominating vote	Candidate	Pearson's r
A. Democrats			
1904	Illinois credentials	Parker*	0.748
1912	South Dakota credentials	Wilson*	0.744
1920	Byran prohibition plank	Cox*	0.442
1924	First adjournment vote	McAdoo	0.744
1932	Minnesota credentials	Roosevelt*	0.953
1948	Moody civil rights platform plank	Truman*	0.972
1952	Adjournment	Kefauver	0.707
1968	Vietnam platform plank	Humphrey*	0.924
1972	First California credentials vote	McGovern*	0.858
1976	Platform	Carter*	0.635
1980	Release delegates from pledges	Carter*	0.909
1984	No first use of nuclear weapons	Mondale*	0.583
1988	Progressive taxation	Jackson	0.919
B. Republicans			
1912	California credentials	W. H. Taft*	0.989
1952	Georgia credentials	R. A. Taft	0.973
1964	Civil rights platform	Goldwater*	0.916
1976	Naming running-mate	Ford*	0.942

*Nominee.

leaders began to lose their grip on local political activists, they became unable to keep them from supporting major Presidential candidates. Delegates saw no advantage in being uncommitted or in backing a local favorite, and their party leaders could not compel them to do so by withholding patronage or by other obsolete practices. If a candidate seemed to have a real shot at the nomination, he could win delegates in droves, and one such candidate would win enough to secure nomination on the first ballot. The old practices of party leaders—keeping their delegates away from the leading candidates, waiting for the opportune moment, bargaining, striking a deal—gradually became extinct well before the parties began to change their convention rules in any significant way.

Under these circumstances it was to a candidate's advantage to get into the race early and win all those delegates who were up for grabs. This is perhaps why campaigns gradually lengthened. However, that process seems to have accelerated after 1968. Two of the reforms singled out by those regarding the rules changes as significant probably did have some impact on this matter. The proliferation of primaries necessitated a more public entry into the race at an earlier moment than had previously been necessary, and the 1974 amendments to the Federal Election Campaign Act encouraged early announcements in order to qualify for matching funds. But it is important to stress that even this trend began earlier.

CONCLUSION

This article demonstrates that in its basic contours the Presidential nominating process began to evolve into its current form long before the changes in laws and party rules that took effect in the 1970s. This has two implications that are worth underscoring. First, the significance of the reforms was not, as their champions and critics would have us believe, that they brought about the new system. Instead, they seem to have routinized and legitimized the system that was evolving. Under the old system, authority and a kind of moral accountability were easily located at national conventions in the party leaders who controlled them. It may be an overstatement to say that these leaders were vested with legitimacy, because anti-bossism has long been an important strain in the American political culture, but at least they were tolerated as controllers of the nominating process, and only sporadic attempts to increase the number of primaries challenged their authority. When that authority began to wane, for reasons that had little to do with the Presidential nominating process, newer and less easily identifiable groups began to displace them. Candidate cadres, adherents of incumbents, constituency groups and ideological factions became more important, but there were no routinized patterns of access to convention power, nor were these disparate groups vested with formal legitimacy.

The reforms have provided such routinization and legitimacy. New primaries and caucuses, each with carefully defined rules guaranteeing access for any well-organized group, rules for dividing delegations fairly among the claimants, and new agencies of appeal and review all provided routinized access to the convention. They also conferred legitimacy on whoever made best use of these access routes. Austin Ranney has often pointed out that the proliferation of primaries was an *unintended* consequence of the reforms,[30] but the present argument suggests one reason why primaries proliferated: because they fit Americans' populistic notions of legitimacy so well, they were the most logical way to legitimize the new system. By 1980, even the caucuses were treated as quasi-primaries, with returns reported in the media as though they were primaries. In 1976 and 1980, the Iowa caucuses began to equal the New Hampshire primary in psychological impact.

Legitimacy was also conferred in other ways, most notably by provisions that delegates declare their Presidential preferences early (thereby legitimizing candidate cadres) and the affirmative action rules (which legitimized the mobilization of the affected groups). Not only did affirmative action legitimize the increased presence at the convention of these groups, but it also helped to legitimize the new convention as a whole. While representation takes many forms,[31] one that is notably salient in politics is the physical representation of key groups in numbers roughly equivalent to their proportion of the total population. Since many Americans regard representation as a major element of legitimacy, this increased actual representation can serve to increase the legitimacy of the convention and hence the nominating process.

Finally, it is striking that the American political system's chief institution for conferring legitimacy, the Federal judiciary, has ratified the rules whenever possible. It has upheld both parties' delegate apportionment formulas, approved with relatively peripheral modifications the Federal Election Campaign Act, and permitted national party rules to override state law. Moreover, the Supreme Court indirectly ratified longer campaigns by requiring television stations to grant advertising time to candidates regardless of when the station deems the campaign to have begun.[32] While it would be wrong to imply that the courts have been in cahoots with party elites, their stamp of approval strengthens the legitimacy of the rules and therefore the process.

Indeed, by 1980 even William F. Buckley, Jr., cited the "rule" that primaries have been the determining factor in the nominating process as "a stabilizing factor in American politics," and as a self-styled conservative he approved of this function.[33]

The second implication is that if the reforms did not produce the current system, then other reforms will not undo it. Many of the reforms that took effect in 1980 and 1984 were intended to roll back many of the trends depicted here, and they have been ineffective. For example, the Hunt Commission stipulated that at least one-seventh of the delegates to the 1984 Democratic national convention be party officials and public officials. This was done to restore to such people some of their lost power, and to restore to the convention an element of cautious deliberation. If it was intended to produce a nominating process in 1984 markedly different from that of recent years, it was a failure. Although the party did end up nominating the hero of the party establishment, Walter Mondale, the primaries very nearly deprived Mondale of the nomination after a series of victories by Gary Hart. Hart was exactly the sort of candidate who has done well under the new system: relatively unknown at first (like John Kennedy, Eugene McCarthy, George McGovern and Jimmy Carter), not close to party leaders, yet able to mount, for a time, an effective campaign in the primaries. Indeed, he won more of them than Mondale did, although Mondale received more votes than Hart. Moreover, the campaign of Jesse Jackson demonstrated how a candidate who would never have been a factor in a bygone era was able to influence the race by appealing to a particular constituency in the primaries. The convention itself was typical of those recent years, decided in one ballot with a minimum of mystery as to its outcome. Furthermore, a CBS News survey of the delegates found that when the uncommitted and unpledged were removed, there was virtually no difference on candidate preference between those delegates who were party or elected officials and those who were not.[34] There could be no more dramatic illustration of the innocuous nature of the Hunt Commission reforms than their endorsement by the father of the original reform movement, George McGovern.[35]

Why were these "anti-reform reforms" unsuccessful? They were apparently based on a failure of analysis, for they assumed that the main reason for the decline in the power of the party leaders at conventions was the earlier reform cycle, which had kept some of the leaders away from the convention. Put the leaders back, went the reasoning, and their earlier position of power will be restored. This line of reasoning ignored the fact that the power of the leaders had declined because of long-term factors such as the advent of the electronic media, civil service reforms which undercut the patronage system, the rise of the educated middle class and assimilation of immigrants, government social welfare programs, new campaign techniques, and the nationalization of politics; these longitudinal developments, and not the reforms of the 1970s, were the culprit. Putting party leaders back in the convention was like bringing back knights in armour in an age of gunpowder.

For the time being the new age of Presidential nominations is irreversible by human will. While some of the features of the process, such as the number of primaries and the demographic composition of delegations, are manipulable, the basic power structure is not. Something resembling the earlier kind of nomination, as desirable as it might be, would only be possible if American political parties in general were rejuvenated. That does not appear to be in the offing very soon.

NOTES

1. On Democratic rules changes, see William Crotty, *Party Reform* (New York: Longman, 1983). On financial rules changes, see Michael Malbin, ed., *Parties, Interest Groups, and Campaign Finance Laws* (Washington, D.C.: American Enterprise Institute, 1980), and Elizabeth Drew, *Politics and Money* (Washington, D.C.: Macmillan, 1983).

2. Austin Ranney, "The Democratic Party's Delegate Selection Reforms, 1968–76" in Allan P. Sindler, ed., *America in the Seventies* (Boston: Little, Brown, 1977), p. 163.

3. Jeane Jordan Kirkpatrick, *Dismantling the Parties* (Washington, D.C.: American Enterprise Institute, 1978), p. 2; and Nelson W. Polsby, *Consequences of Party Reform* (New York: Oxford U. Press, 1983).

4. Byron E. Shafer, *Quiet Revolution* (New York: Russell Sage Foundation, 1983), p. 525.

5. Penn Kemble and Josh Muravchik, "The New Politics and the Democrats," *Commentary*, December 1972, p. 78.

6. William J. Crotty, *Decision for the Democrats* (Baltimore: Johns Hopkins U. Press, 1978), pp. 254–5.

7. Ranney is quoted in "Primaries '80: Once Again the System Worked, Sort Of," *The New York Times*, 8 June 1980, sec. 4, p. E5; Crotty's comments is in William J. Crotty, *Political Reform and the American Experiment* (New York: Thomas Y. Corwell, 1977), pp. 272–3.

8. On party decline in general, see Walter Dean Burnham, *Critical Elections and the Mainsprings of American Politics* (New York: W. W. Norton, 1970); William J. Crotty and Gary C. Jacobson, *American Parties in Decline* (Boston: Little, Brown, 1980); and Martin P. Wattenberg, *The Decline of American Political Parties, 1952–1980* (Cambridge, Mass.: Harvard U. Press, 1984).

9. This discussion owes much to Nelson W. Polsby, "Decision-Making at the National Conventions," *Western Political Quarterly* XIII (1960), pp. 609–19.

10. Quoted in Ernest R. May and Janet Fraser, eds., *Campaign '72: The Managers Speak* (Cambridge, Mass.: Harvard U. Press, 1973), pp. 106–7.

11. Quoted in Paul T. David and James W. Ceaser, *Proportional Representation in Presidential Nominating Politics* (Charlottesville: U. Press of Virginia, 1980), p. 111.

12. Polsby, *Consequences of Party Reform*, p. 71.

13. Denis G. Sullivan, Jeffrey L. Pressman and F. Christopher Arterton, *Explorations in Convention Decision Making* (San Francisco: W. H. Freeman, 1976), pp. 19–20.

14. There is one slight exception to this rule, the 1912 Republican national convention. William H. Taft was the only candidate to exceed 10 per cent, but he received only 51.6 per cent. Theodore Roosevelt ran second, garnering 9.9 per cent, and nearly a third of the delegates abstained. The vote of even one of the 348 abstainers would have given Roosevelt more than 10 per cent, so this is designated a contested convention.

15. See the Commission's report, *Call to Order...*, published by the Democratic National Committee, p. 56.

16. Max Frankel, "Ho Hum, Another Last Hurrah," *The New York Times Magazine*, 11 July 1976, p. 10.

17. Quoted in Adam Clymer, "Gauging the Delegate Count as the Nominations Approach," *The New York Times*, 17 May 1980, p. 10. This development makes ludicrous Tom Wicker's lament that if the Carter forces won their rules fight with the Kennedy supporters in 1980, "a delegate would become not a real representative of those who elected him, acting on their behalf and accepting the responsibility for his or her actions, but an automatic vote cast in a predetermined manner"—as if delegates had been anything but that for decades. See Wicker, "What Is a Delegate?" *The New York Times*, 11 July 1980, p. A25.

18. Polsby, *Consequence of Party Reform*, p. 77.

19. Gilligan is quoted in David and Ceaser, *Proportional Representation*, p. 10. See also William R. Keech and Donald R. Matthews, *Party's Choice* (Washington, D.C.: The Brookings Institution, 1976), p. 234; Jeane Kirkpatrick, *The New Presidential Elite* (New York: Russell Sage Foundation and the Twentieth Century Fund, 1976), p. 365; Judith H. Parris, *The Convention Problem* (Washington, D.C.: The Brookings Institution, 1972), pp. 84–5; and Nelson W. Polsby and Aaron Wildavsky, *Presidential Elections*, 5th ed. (New York: Charles Scribner's Sons, 1980), pp. 230–1.

20. Later in this article, the hypothesis that more candidates are *receiving votes* than ever before will be tested.

21. David and Ceaser, *Proportional Representation*, p. 111.

22. They include Keech and Matthews, *Party's Choice*, p. 87; Kirkpatrick, *Dismantling the Parties*, p. 23; Polsby and Wildavsky, *Presidential Elections*, p. 150; Gerald M. Pomper et al., *The Election of 1976* (New York: David McKay, 1977), pp. 3–4; and Ranney, "The Democratic Party's Delegate Selection Reforms," p. 195.

23. The 1980 Republican nomination, which by the present definition was uncontested and hence does not appear in the table, drew five candidates who each received at least 10 per cent of the vote in one primary.

24. See Herbert B. Asher, *Presidential Elections and American Politics*, rev. ed. (Homewood, Ill.: The Dorsey Press, 1980), p. 285; John Kessel, *Presidential Campaign Politics* (Homewood, Ill.: The Dorsey Press, 1980), pp. 251–3; Polsby, *Consequences*, pp. 59–62; Polsby and Wildavsky, *Presidential Elections*, pp. 81, 84; and the remarks of Jessica Tuchman of Morris Udall's 1976 staff in Jonathan Moore and Janet Fraser, eds., *Campaign for President* (Cambridge, Mass.: Ballinger, 1977), p. 152.

25. Kenneth A. Bode and Carol F. Casey, "Party Reform: Revisionism Revisited" in Robert A. Goldwin, ed., *Political Parties in the Eighties* (Washington, D.C. and Gambier, Ohio: American Enterprise Institute and Kenyon College, 1980), p. 18.

26. Polsby and Wildavsky, *Presidential Elections*, p. 115.

27. Polsby and Wildavsky, *Presidential Elections*, pp. 80–1. See also Donald M. Fraser, "Democratizing the Democratic Party" in Goldwin, ed., *Parties in the Eighties*, p. 125.

28. F. Christopher Arterton, "Recent Rules Changes Within the National Democratic Party," paper presented to the annual meeting of the Social Science History Association, Columbus, Ohio, 1978, p. 22.

29. Richard C. Bain, *Convention Decisions and Voting Records* (Washington, D.C.: The Brookings Institution, 1960).

30. See, for example, Austin Ranney, "Changing the Rules of the Nominating Game" in James David Barber, ed., *Choosing the President* (Englewood Cliffs, N.J.: Prentice-Hall, Inc., 1974), pp. 73–4.

31. A comprehensive treatment of the subject is Hanna Fenichel Pitkin, *The Concept of Representation* (Berkeley: U. of California Press, 1967).

32. *Bode v. National Democratic Party*, 452 F.2d 1302 (D.C. Cir. 1971); *Georgia v. National Democratic Party*, 447 F.2d, 1271, 1275 (D.C.Cir. 1971); *Ripon Society, Inc. v. National Republican Party*, 525 F.2d 548, 567 (D.C. Cir. 1975); *Buckley v. Valeo*, 424 U.S. 1 (1976); *O'Brien v. Brown*, 409 U.S. 1 (1972); *Cousins v. Wigoda*, 419 U.S. 477 (1975); *National Democratic Party v. LaFollette*, 450 U.S. 107 (1981); and *Columbia Broadcasting System v. Federal Communications Commission*, 453 U.S. 367 (1981).

33. William F. Buckley, Jr., "His Unbiased Analysis," *Norwich Bulletin* (Connecticut), 7 August 1980, p. 6.

34. Data graciously provided by Carey Funk of CBS News.

35. George McGovern, "The Democrats Change the Rules," *The Nation*, 15 May 1982, pp. 580–2.

PART FIVE

PARTIES AND REPRESENTATION

If people fight over party reform, they believe that whom the party represents matters. Parties provide a key linkage between voters and their elected officials. What is this relationship and how does it vary between the parties?

Warren E. Miller, in "A New Context for Presidential Politics: The Reagan Legacy," examines representation in the context of the 1984 presidential election. If Ronald Reagan's 1980 and 1984 elections constituted a realignment in American politics, then voters should have moved to the right so that they would be closer to Republican than Democratic elites. Contrary to conventional wisdom, Miller finds little support of a general shift toward conservatism among voters—or of a bolt to the right among the younger voters who identify with the Republicans. Delegates to the Democratic and Republican conventions—Miller's elite group—had policy preferences that diverged from both Democratic and Republican party identifiers. Yet, in 1980 and especially 1984, Democratic elites were considerably closer to both their own identifiers and to *Republican* identifiers in the electorate than GOP delegates were. Americans apparently voted for Reagan despite disagreement with the policies that both he and his core supporters favored.

If convention delegates are out of step with the electorate, is the primary election system the culprit? Because voters in primaries are wealthier, more educated, and more ideologically extreme than the entire electorate, we tend to blame the primary system brought into effect by party reforms of the 1970s. Yet, John G. Geer, in "Assessing the Representativeness of Electorates in Presidential Primaries," disputes the unrepresentativeness of primary elections. If we consider "party followers" as potential supporters of the party in general elections, the differences between the primary electorate and the party following are small.

Each party may faithfully represent its own following, but the constituencies of the Democrats and Republicans differ profoundly. Jo Freeman, in "The Political Culture of the Democratic and Republican Parties," maintains that the Democrats are a loose coalition of groups, bound together more by a participatory ethic than a coherent political philosophy. The Republicans, in contrast, have a more consistent political philosophy and a more "corporate" organizational structure. The two parties represent different groups and different philosophies of organization.

If the new environment is one of interest groups jousting for positions within each party, then the relationship between parties and interest groups must remain uneasy. Allan J. Cigler, in "Political Parties and Interest Groups: Competitors, Collaborators, and Uneasy Allies," agrees with Salisbury (first section) that parties and interest groups are more than competitors in American politics. Cigler sees parties as both competitors and collaborators. Parties seek broad coalitions, interest groups narrow goals. Yet, each needs the other. Groups without financial resources may depend upon linkages with parties to achieve success. Wealthier groups may find that contributions to campaigns help them obtain additional support for their goals. The proliferation of groups has complicated the situation, forcing the parties to act more like interest groups in an increasingly candidate-centered politics.

A NEW CONTEXT FOR PRESIDENTIAL POLITICS: THE REAGAN LEGACY

Warren E. Miller

Due to the 22nd amendment and to the elections that saw McGovern, Carter, and Mondale swept aside, American presidential politics is certain to move into the late 20th century under new party leadership. Due to changes wrought during the incumbency of President Reagan, the new leaders will inherit a changed and still changing electoral context. The changes are not necessarily all that either Democrats or Republicans would prefer, and they are not all changes that conventional wisdom among party activists has, as yet, recognized. Nor is it clear that the unconventional wisdom of the academic research community understands exactly what is going on. Nevertheless, research focused on both political masses and political elites has now divined enough of what has changed, and not changed, to make a review of the current state of affairs useful.

A NEW CONSERVATIVE UNITED STATES?

First let me take up the challenge to the conventional perspective which understands the national electorate to have moved sharply to the right. It is true that in 1972 George McGovern overestimated the extent to which national sentiments had moved to the left with increased popular support for the civil rights movement, growing opposition to the war in Viet Nam, and the rise of the antiestablishment counterculture. It is also true that four years later a markedly more conservative Democratic Jimmy Carter restored the Democrats to power in the White House. And, finally, it is true that an even more conservative Ronald Reagan defeated Carter in 1980 and then trounced the left-of-center Democrat Walter Mondale in 1984.

Nevertheless, the succession of electoral decisions does not constitute a good indication of changes taking place in the ideological predispositions of the voting public or in their preferences for public policy. This is true, in part, simply because election results are so heavily influenced by so many other considerations. In line with this truism, the relative stability of popular policy preferences over the last twenty years has been documented, for at least some of the central election issues, by various indicators, including the Michigan National Election Studies series. Table 14.1 depicts some of the changes that have occurred through recent time, and it includes the evidence of a clear drift to the *left*, not to the right, between 1980 and 1984. This array of data does not document any *sea change* in national ideological or policy preferences, but does suggest that whatever changes occurred in ideology-tinged policy preferences between 1980 and 1984, the nation moved in a liberal direction rather than in the direction of increased support for conservative policies.

The aggregate or net drift of national policy preferences does not, of course, constitute definitive evidence that the votes for conservative presidential candidates were not increasingly buttressed by conservative ideological inclinations of the voters. In fact, two relatively elaborate and detailed probings into this question have disclosed somewhat different configurations in the elections of 1980 and 1984. In an analysis of the 1980 election, Merrill Shanks and I concluded that preferences for policy change were only somewhat less powerful predictors of voting decisions than were evaluations of presidential and governmental performance.[1] We also concluded that voters' policy preferences summed to a national preference for *conservative* changes in governmental policy, and those preferences made a positive contribution to the margin of Reagan's first national victory. Four years later, however, the latter conclusion was reversed. According to our analysis of the 1984 election, preferences for policy change were again significant predictors of individual behavior, but the preferences in 1984 favored the Mondale candidacy. An overall national preference for a change to somewhat more *liberal* policies contributed even more to limiting the magnitude of the Reagan victory margin than the Democratic plurality in party identification.[2]

Yet a third perspective on the reconciliation of recent election results with public sentiment on policy questions can be provided by attacking the problem from a quite different direction. This line of attack not only helps to explain why elections cannot necessarily be interpreted as mandates for public policy; but it will also prove extremely helpful in the subsequent analysis of national changes in party identification. The line of attack consists quite simply of examining the division of the vote within two quite different strata of voters. The strata are defined in terms of the relative richness and structuring of the "systems of beliefs" and evaluations employed by citizens in their assessments of the national political

Table 14.1 Summaries of Ideological Attitudes, Preferences, and Perceptions, 1964–1984

	1964	1966	1968	1970	1972	1974	1976	1978	1980	1982	1984
Liberal-conservative self-placement (a)					−08	−05	−09	−08	−11	−13	−11
Perceived power of natl. govt. (b)	+06	−12	−11	+02	−14		−29	−29	−33		−10
Government support for jobs & good standard of living (c)					−12	−12	−15		−15	−16	−08
Government aid to minorities (d)					−07	−09	−08	−18	−23	−18	−05
Evaluation of civil rights movements (e)	−58	−60	−56	−44	−38	−39	−31		−20		−18
Attitudes towards abortion (f)					+13		+15	+16	+17	+22	+22
Egalitarian role for women in society (g)					+18	+22	+26	+34	+40	+40	+39
Preferences for changes in govt. services and spending (h)									−15		+18
Preferences for change in defense spending (i)									−53		+38

Note: Scores were obtained by subtracting the proportion of "conservative" responses from the proportions of "liberal" responses. A negative sign, therefore, indicates a plurality of "conservative" responses.

parties and their presidential candidates. The assignment of voters to strata is made according to the rules established for defining different "levels of conceptualization" in citizens' responses to questions asking them to specify what they like and what they dislike about each of the major parties and each of the parties' candidates.

Individuals in the first of our two strata evaluate one or more of the two parties or one or more of the two presidential candidates in terms of abstractions, such as liberal or conservative and make references to policies or programs; or they talk in terms of group conflict or group interest. For them the Democratic party may be liberal, or it may be the party that is for the working class, or the party that helps blacks, or they may like the Republican candidate because of his farm policy or because he is a conservative, and dislike the Democratic candidate because he is in favor of the labor unions. Where the more elaborate and sophisticated responses of the first stratum may include mentions of particular policies, our second stratum of responses relevant to matters of policy is usually represented by, at best, broad generalizations reflecting observations on the nature of the times. For example, in 1980 it was common to have individuals note the hostages in Iran, or inflation or unemployment, with no elaboration that had particular policy implications. In 1984 a comparable response might be the unelaborated reaction, "He just makes me proud to be an American." This second stratum is also populated by citizens who have absolutely nothing to say about either party or either candidate, or, when they do express some partisan sentiment it is likely to be of the "Me and my family have always been Democrats" or "I don't know why, I just like Ike" variety.[3]

Given the assignment of citizens to one or the other of the two strata, we can then proceed to examine and compare vote decisions they made in 1980 and 1984. Even with only a simple dichotomy separating the more sophisticated, more politicized), voters from the less sophisticated, the difference in vote preferences between the groups, presented in Table 14.2, is astounding. Among the 60% of the voters who were classified as the more verbally sophisticated (or, perhaps, more politicized), changes in the aggregate division of the vote between 1980 and 1984 produced an *increase* of some 10 percentage points in the Democratic vote, with virtually no change in the Republican proportion.[4] Within the 40% of the electorate who are classified as exhibiting lesser degrees of complexity or sophistication in their descriptions of the parties and the candidates, the picture was dramatically different. Between 1980 and 1984 the Democratic vote *declined* by three percentage points while the Republican proportion increased by 14 points. The Republican triumph of 1984 rested

Table 14.2 Change in Vote, 1950–84, by Party Identification and Ideology, within Differently Politicized Strata of Voters

	Democrats	Independents	Republicans	Total
	A. The more politicized			
Liberals	+14[a]	+33	+22	+21
	(82)	(120)	(35)	(237)
Moderates	+22	+32	−6	+6
	(39)	(63)	(63)	(165)
Conservatives	—	−14	−6	−6
	(7)	(26)	(105)	(138)
	B. The less politicized			
Liberals	−15	−9	−33	−9
	(19)	(81)	(29)	(129)
Moderates	−19	−4	−2	−3
	(15)	(83)	(25)	(133)
Conservatives	—	+1	−11	−5
	(9)	(61)	(36)	(106)

[a]Entries are net percentage point gains for Democrats between 1980 and 1984; a negative sign reflects a net Republican vote gain. Numbers of cases in 1980 (the smaller national sample) are enclosed in parentheses.

entirely on the votes of the less sophisticated; Mondale actually "won" the vote in the more sophisticated sector by a narrow 52–48 margin.

This dramatic depiction of differences in vote preferences between 1980 and 1984 adds to our earlier analytic explanations of the antecedents of the vote decisions in those years as it dramatizes the extent to which different sectors of the electorate may have very different things in mind when they go to the polls. In both years the more sophisticated among the voters voted *both* their party preferences and their ideological predispositions. The change in their vote divisions between the two elections increased the match with their standing ideological preferences and reflected patterns of interrelationships among perceptions and opinions worthy of designation as political belief systems. In the process, Mondale and the Democrats benefitted more than did Reagan and the Republicans.

Among the less sophisticated, vote preferences in 1980 were virtually unrelated to ideological predispositions, although they were strongly colored by the standing partisanship of party identifiers. Four years later, the changes in their level of support for Reagan occurred virtually without regard for either ideological or partisan predisposition.

The uniformity with which the less sophisticated increased their vote support for Mr. Reagan without regard to their partisanship or their ideology argues very strongly against the presumption that they were somehow voting in favor of more conservative Republican governmental policies as a consequence of the evaluations provided by their political belief systems.

PARTY REALIGNMENT

If it is possible to misinterpret the ideological implications of a series of national elections—and the foregoing argument was clearly intended to demonstrate such a possibility— it is even less surprising to discover that the conventional wisdom has thus far missed the significance of the widely documented decline in the Democratic plurality among party identifiers. Although the various public opinion polls and academic surveys of American political opinion and behavior often differ in their gross results, such is not the case, at least not in the large, where recent shifts in party identification are concerned. The CBS/*New York Times* poll, the Yankelovich, Skelly, and White Poll reported by *Time* magazine, the Gallup Poll, and the Michigan National Election Studies are in substantial agreement in mapping a rise in Republican fortunes and a decline in Democratic strength between 1980 and 1984. Although the various findings differ in detail, they all suggest that the Democratic plurality of party identification was cut roughly in half in that four year interval.[5] Given the coincidence of this reduction with the Reagan landslide in the election of 1984, the reasonable if superficial conclusion has tended to portray party realignment—along with the election outcome—as a response to the conservative Republican leadership of the Reagan administration.

A full analysis of the many nuances involved in the changing of partisanship goes beyond the limits of our present argument. The major conclusions are, however, an important addition to our description of the political context provided for the elections of the late 1980s. The essential message of a more complex analysis can be presented with a simultaneous consideration of the impact of age, ideology, and levels of conceptualization on changes in the party identification of the citizenry. In this presentation, age is crudely dichotomized to separate the younger quarter of the electorate from the older three-quarters. Ideological predispositions are those which citizens assign to themselves when asked to identify themselves as liberals, moderates, or conservatives. And, as with the foregoing analysis of vote choice, levels of conceptualization are represented by a dichotomy distinguishing the more politicized from the less politicized among rank and file citizens. Finally, party identification is reflected (for each of the resulting 24 subgroups) in the simple arithmetic which subtracts the proportion of Republicans from the proportion of Democrats within any group. The resulting data are presented in Table 14.3.

Our overall task is to explain a 7 percentage point reduction in the Democratic plurality of party identifications. In 1980 Democrats outnumbered Republicans by a margin of 40% to 23%. Four years later the Democratic figure had been reduced to 37% while the Republican figure had grown to 27%. A 17 point margin (also 17 points in 1976 and 18 points in 1972) had been reduced to a 10 point plurality by 1984. A first consequence of our separation of the electorate into four quadrants defined by age and levels of conceptualization is to expose the different patterns and magnitudes of change among our four subgroups, differences concealed by the overall national totals. As Table 14.3 makes clear, the more sophisticated, more politicized younger citizens actually moved against the national tide between 1980 and 1984 and become more predominantly Democratic in their partisanship. This move was countered among the less sophisticated young, by the total disappearance of their 1980 Democratic margin of 15 points. As one can properly infer, the pro-Democratic movement and the pro-Republican movement virtually offset each other; within the full set of younger cohorts there was only a very limited net movement away from the Democrats or toward the Republicans.

That portion of the electorate made up of the older citizenry was the prime source of the Democratic decline and the burgeoning of Republican support, with the less politicized making almost twice the contribution of the more sophisticated. Indeed, although not visible in Table 14.3, the net Republican gains among the less politicized of the older citizens were, in fact, concentrated entirely among the least sophisticated, those reflecting absolutely no discernible issue- or policy-relevant content in their 1984 assessments of the parties and their candidates. Within this subset, Republican gains and Democratic losses of party identification totaled over 20 percentage points: 25 points among liberals, 20 points among moderates, and 27 points among conservatives. A very large portion of the Republican gains and the Democratic losses in party support between 1980 and 1984 thus came from segments of the electorate least attuned to the ideological struggles within and between the parties.

For the more politicized of the older cadres, the absence of any significant shift in the net balance of partisan identification meant that a high level of ideological polarization separating partisans was simply maintained in both years (reflected in tau beta correlations of + .38 and + .40). In 1984 they remained, as in 1980, a heavily Democratic but ideo-

Table 14.3 Changes in Partisanship, 1980–1984, by Ideological
Predisposition of Younger and Older Citizens, Categorized by
Levels of Conceptualization

	Young: Entered electorate 1976–1984					
	Liberals	Moderates	Conservatives	Total	Tau B	Cases
More politicized						
1980	+14	+35	−32	+7	+.20	100
1984	+49	+44	−40	+21	+.36	204
Change	+35	+0	−8	+14	+.16	
Less politicized						
1980	+6	+16	+16	+15	−.03	163
1984	+3	+7	−25	0	+.12	339
Change	−3	−9	−41	−15	+.15	

	Old: Entered electorate prior to 1976					
	Liberals	Moderates	Conservatives	Total	Tau B	Cases
More politicized						
1980	+63	+53	−23	+29	+.38	707
1984	+60	+48	−30	+24	+.40	803
Change	−3	−5	−7	−5	+.02	
Less politicized						
1980	+33	+9	−10	−7	+.14	598
1984	+15	+5	−25	−2	+.16	899
Change	−18	−4	−15	−9	+.02	

Note: Each entry (other than the tau b) is derived by subtracting the proportion of Republican identifiers (Rs + Rw) from the proportion of Democratic identifiers (Ds + Dw) within the group, i.e., More Politicized Young Liberals in 1980 (+14), or Less Politicized Older Moderates in 1964 (+5). The tau b entries summarize the correlations between party identification and ideological predisposition; a positive sign associates Democrat with Liberal and Republican with Conservative. As of 1984, the More Politicized Young made up about 10% of the total electorate; the Less Politicized Young, some 15%; the More Politicized Old, 35%; and the Less Politicized Old, 40%.

logically polarized third of the electorate. Appropriately, among the less politicized, ideological lines were not sharply associated with partisan differences in either year (correlations of +.14 and +.16), and their across-the-board move to the Republican party neither strengthened nor weakened the ideological alignment of partisans.

Turning back to the patterns of change among the young, it should also be noted that the sharpening of the ideological lines associated with the changes in partisanship produced, by 1984, a level of ideological polarization between the more politicized young Democrats and Republicans quite comparable to the level observed among the more sophisticated voters of the older generations (a tau beta correlation of + .36 compared to the + .40 among old citizens). The increase in ideological polarization among the *less* politicized young (-.03 to + .12) left that group no more ideological in its partisan differences than the least politicized of the older cohorts, but the pattern of changing party identifications clearly reflected their standing ideological predispositions as the Republican gains were almost entirely limited to self described conservatives in the group. Had the sheer numbers of less sophisticated, young conservatives been greater (they were only 3% of the electorate in 1984), their contribution to the change in national party parameters would have been commensurately more notable. As it is, or was, it seems evident that prior ideological predispositions among the younger citizens contributed heavily to changes in party identification between 1980 and 1984, but made only a marginal contribution to the net decline in the Democratic plurality. By 1984 the more politicized citizenry among both young and old had attained a high degree of ideological polarization in their partisanship, but this occurred without serious disadvantage to the Democrats among the older citizens (a 5 percentage point loss) and to the clear advantage and benefit of the Democratic party among the younger citizens (with a 14 point gain). Among the less politicized the Democrats had lost a full 15 points within the ranks of the young and a substantial 9 points in the much larger group of older citizens.

PARTY REALIGNMENT AND POLICY PREFERENCES

The thesis that most of the Republican gains in party identification during the first term of the Reagan administration *did not* originate in the growth of support for conservative causes, nor in response to the increased saliency of ideology and ideological polarization, is further supported by direct evidence concerning changes in citizens' policy preferences and evaluations of the Reagan administration's performance. A reduction in the plurality of Democratic party supporters had, in fact, been anticipated and forecast for some time, and after four years of the Reagan presidency it actually took place. Nevertheless, the full configuration of changes in party identification that apparently occurred between 1980 and 1984 does not fit a simple straight extrapolation from the new success of a conservative Republican party. Instead, changes in partisanship seem to have been of two distinct types, one "distributional" and one "relational." Each was characteristic of a different segment of the electorate, and each has quite different implications for the future of American politics.

The "distributional" shift, favoring the Republicans as it diminished the Democratic national plurality, occurred among citizens who are not disposed to think of politics—parties or candidates—in abstract terms or in ways that systematically tie performance to policy, policy to ideology, or ideology to party or to candidate. The gains were not supported by commensurate shifts in policy preferences; they more often occurred in the face of changes in preferences that actually gave increased support to liberal (Democratic) alternatives. The changes in party identification were seldom a systematic function of the citizens' own ideological predispositions. Except for the less sophisticated among the young, self-proclaimed liberals were as likely to have increased their Republicanism as were conservatives. The most dominant "reason" for the growth of Republican strength appears to have resided in perceptions of the personal attributes of Ronald Reagan who, in this sector of the electorate, was ever more visible as a competent, moral, knowledgeable, inspiring leader.

PRESIDENTIAL LEADERSHIP AND CHANGES IN PARTY IDENTIFICATION

If there were a more fully developed body of relevant theory, this stage of the inquiry could be introduced with a theoretical exegesis on the role of political leadership in the formation of partisan identifications. Such a theme is certainly not out of keeping with the emerging restatement of the dynamics of the 1930s that created the last major change in the alignment of the American electorate. Nonetheless, it would be less than accurate to suggest that our understanding of the nature of American electoral behavior includes a well defined thesis concerning the role of presidential leadership. Consequently, our current analysis can do little more than point the way to future research that may, or may not, document a larger and more precise role for presidential leadership in future accounts of the generic processes shaping American presidential politics.

My concluding argument concerning distributional shifts of party identification is congruent with the conclusion that performance evaluations, at least in 1984, were more important as determinants of the election outcome than were voters' considerations of issues and ideologically defined policy questions. However, the argument goes on to specify that the relative importance of different contributions to mass politics varies across different strata of the electorate, as in the present instance when the focus of analytic attention is on changes in party identification. The evidence on this point is sufficiently dramatic to add weight to the questioning of methods that seek the best "average" explanation for political behavior without taking explicit account of categorical differences among citizens.

As Table 14.4 indicates, presidential approval ratings not only varied with citizens' levels of political sophistication in both 1980 and 1984, but the pattern of change between the years was dramatically different for the more and the less politicized members of the electorate.[6] Between 1980 and 1984, the more politicized citizens, young and old alike, moved sharply away from their strongly anti-Democratic (anti-Carter) views of 1980 and gave Reagan little more than an even break in their appraisals four years later. Surprisingly, conservatives in 1984 were only about as "pro-Reagan" as they had been "anti-Carter" in 1980; liberals and moderates, on the other hand, moved from having been evenly divided or mildly anti-Carter in 1980 to being sharply anti-Reagan in 1984. Liberals, in particular, were almost as uniformly disapproving of the Reagan performance in 1984 as the conservatives were united in their approval.

Among both young and old within the more sophisticated stratum of the electorate, the shifts in presidential approval ratings between 1980 and 1984 were very clearly a function of individual ideological predispositions. By 1984 the ideological polarization of presidential approval ratings produced quite impressive correlations indeed. The net result of the first Reagan term for these citizens was, therefore, a sharp polarizing movement favoring the Democrats—virtually eliminating the 1980 Republican advantage—as liberals and conservatives agreed to disagree in their appraisals of presidential performance.

Among the less politicized the story was strikingly different in most major respects. First of all, the conservatives—who were the big contributors to the new distributional bulge in Republican party identifications—moved from positions of ambivalence in 1980 to overwhelming approval for Reagan in 1984. They at least matched if they did not exceed the levels of approval for Reagan expressed by their more politicized conservative age peers.

The second, and still more striking, set of interyear differences concerns the less sophisticated liberals and moderates. They shared in the strong pro-Reagan movement of the conservatives—shifting some 20 to 30 points in his favor—despite the fact that their more sophisticated counterparts moved 12, 20, 47, and 53 points in the *opposite* partisan direction in the same time interval. The sharply pro-Reagan movement of these unsophisticated liberal and moderate judgments more than

Table 14.4 Changes in Presidential Approval Ratings, 1980–1984, by Ideological Predisposition of Younger and Older Citizens Categorized by Levels of Conceptualization

	Young: Entered electorate 1976–1984				
	Liberals	Moderates	Conservatives	Total	Tau B
More politicized					
1980	−11	−12	−58	−26	+ .18
1984	+ 42	+ 8	−60	−3	+ .37
Change	+ 53	+ 20	−2	+ 23	+ .19
Less politicized					
1980	+ 6	−7	+ 9	−3	−.03
1984	−30	−28	−66	−36	+ .12
Change	−36	−21	−75	−33	+ .15
	Old: Entered electorate prior to 1976				
	Liberals	Moderates	Conservatives	Total	Tau B
More politicized					
1980	0	+ 6	−61	−18	+ .26
1984	+ 47	+ 18	−63	−4	+ .42
Change	+ 47	+ 12	−2	+ 14	+ .16
Less politicized					
1980	0	−15	−41	−19	+ .13
1984	−18	−39	−70	−45	+ .18
Change	−18	−24	−29	−26	+ .05

Note: Each entry is the difference between the proportions who "approve the job (the President) is doing" and the proportions who disapprove. As with the other tabular presentations, the scoring in both years indicates a pro-Democratic, or anti-Republican, plurality as positive (+) and an anti-Democratic, or pro-Republican, plurality as minus (–).

matched their pro-Republican shifts in party identifications between 1980 and 1984. (In combination with the sharp changes of sentiment on the part of the less sophisticated conservatives, this presumably provided the attitudinal support necessary to produce the electoral support which the entire stratum accorded the Reagan bid for reelection, as noted in the discussion of Table 14.2.) In the more sophisticated half of the electorate, the positive regard for Mr. Reagan was limited, and the changes in presidential approval that had taken place over the four year interval were, as with party identification, a direct function of ideological predispositions.

Although neither policy preferences nor perceptions of policy outcome matched the strong patterns of changing party identification among the less politicized voters, changing assessments of presidential performance did provide a dramatic match, one that single handedly *could* have determined their changes in partisanship. The increase in positive regard for Reagan is clearly dominant in the same groups in which the Republican party found increased favor.

Citizen appraisals of Reagan as an "inspiring," "moral," or "knowledgeable" leader also produced patterns virtually identical with those pertaining to the presidential "job ratings." All of our measures of citizens' perceptions of personal traits and response to Reagan's personal leadership qualities match the patterns of stability and change in party identification in all four of our analytic quadrants. The data are as consistent with the thesis that recent changes benefitting the Republican party are a direct tribute to Reagan's political leadership as they are inconsistent with the thesis that we have finally seen the long awaited growth in conservative Republican partisanship.

THE IDEOLOGICAL POLARIZATION OF PRESIDENTIAL POLITICS

"Relational" shifts in party identification occurred largely among those in the more politicized or verbally sophisticated sector of the electorate who were possibly young enough in 1980 to still be malleable and changeable as far as their political perceptions and preferences were concerned. Between 1980 and 1984, Democratic pluralities increased in this stratum among self-proclaimed young liberals, while Republican pluralities increased among young conservatives.

Contrary to the patterns associated with "distributional" change, the relational changes among the politicized young *were* supported by commensurate changes in policy preferences; by 1984 young liberals more often preferred liberal policy alternatives, and young conservatives increased their support for conservative policy alternatives. In like manner, changing views of both national and personal economic circumstances fit personal ideological proclivities, as did changing perceptions of personal traits related to Reagan's role as a political leader. However, the politicized young actually shifted their party identifications to give slightly *greater* support to the *Democratic*—not the Republican—party; they did not share in the growth of optimism about economic conditions; they were restrained in their appraisals of Reagan; and, by 1984 they were consistently the most liberal of all groups in their policy preferences. In every respect their patterns of change shaped them more and more in the image of their comparably politicized older counterparts. The patterns of interyear change among the younger sophisticates are readily understandable as reflections of developing and evolving systems of political belief that were being shaped by dramatic events of political change.

The politicized among the older generations were, in turn, apparently largely unaffected by the changes in political circumstance that produced such marked reactions elsewhere in the electorate between 1980 and 1984. Their partisanship, their policy preferences, their economic perspectives and their appraisals of Reagan remained virtually unchanged as clear and strong correlates of their ideological predispositions. The only major changes within the group were associated with their evaluations of presidential leadership, short term responses heavily influenced by their standing ideological predispositions. The volatility in the party identification of the less politicized, both young and old, takes on added meaning when contrasted with the stability of party identification within this group.

Even without further study, it would seem reasonable to conclude that the changes in party identification among the politicized young were not capricious. Insofar as the changes brought both party voting and party identification into line with ideology as a part of a general ideological clarification of political attitudes and beliefs—including policy preferences, economic outlook, and evaluations of leaders—it would seem reasonable to expect the change in party identification to endure as central elements in the belief system of these younger citizens. If so, the years of the Reagan administration could make a lasting contribution to American politics by shaping evolving systems of political beliefs to produce an increase in the ideological polarization of partisans in the electorate. A prediction of increased ideological polarization among the informed young need not be an alarmist prediction. In most of the instances we have documented, the younger of the politicized have simply approached the levels of ideological polarization among their older counterparts, albeit very swiftly in the brief interval between 1980 and 1984. In no instance have they appeared to be more ideological than their elders, but in their growing proportions they, in combination with their elders, may well redefine the terms of partisan conflict in the years ahead.

LEADERSHIP AND CHANGE

It is difficult to be equally elaborate and confident in predicting the future for the shifts in party identification that so strongly advantaged the

Republican party in the less politicized half of the electorate. The dispro-portionate concentration of the incidence of change among those exhibit-ing lower levels of political sophistication resembles the findings reported in the very first presentation of research exploring the conse-quences of variations in the complexity of the structure of citizens' modes of political thought. Some 30 years ago, following the reelection of Eisenhower in 1956, the authors of *The American Voter* devoted a num-ber of pages to the discussion of "Differences in Conceptualization and the Interpretation of Partisan Change." Carefully discounting the evi-dence, saying, "we must remember that positive findings may be bound to peculiarities of this period," they went on to demonstrate and discuss "the conclusion that in the Eisenhower period partisan change was most visible at the lower levels [of sophistication in individual belief sys-tems]."[7] The present analysis differs substantially from that reported in *The American Voter*. In the absence of subsequent research elaborating the theoretical implications that flow from differences in levels of concep-tualization, I am reluctant to extrapolate from an analysis which, as the events of late 1986 suggest, may be similarly time and period bound.

Nonetheless, the fact that in 1984 distributional changes in partisan-ship were primarily associated with an increase in positive regard for Reagan does accord with the broad thesis that those with relatively im-poverished, less complex systems of belief concerning contemporary politics are more susceptible, in general, to the influences of volatile short term factors. At this point it is tempting to draw the conclusion that their responses, including changes in party identification, are probably as volatile and subject to change as are the causative factors.

It is true that changes in party identification among the less politi-cized were not accompanied by, and therefore inferentially not rein-forced by, changes in policy preferences or even in policy related performance evaluations. It is also true, however, that among the young the changes in partisanship produced a slight increase in the modest congruence of their party identifications and their presumably prior ideological predispositions. The strengthening of the party ideology bond did not produce reinforcing patterns at all equivalent to the indica-tors of ideologically structured belief systems to be found among the more highly politicized citizenry; nevertheless, there was no evidence that their new identifications were in greater conflict with other relevant attitudes or preferences and therefore more susceptible to future change.

In like manner, although we may be satisfied that the changes we noted between 1980 and 1984 were apparently the consequences of re-sponses to the first term of the Reagan presidency, we do not know how durable such response may be. Thus far, no reconstruction of the party realignment associated with the period of the New Deal has even attempted to separate such causal determinants as perceived party policies, performance evaluations of the Hoover and Roosevelt administrations, and personal regard for Roosevelt. The thesis that the realignment which resulted in the Roosevelt coalition was produced by mobilization of new partisans and not the conversion of old would be consonant with the corollary that change then, as now, was concentrated among the less politicized; but we simply don't know whether the new partisanships of the 1930s were primarily a response to personal presidential leadership, or to less ephemeral stimuli such as the continuing appeal of social welfare policies.

Nor do we know that the certain end to Reagan's role as presidential leader will restore the *status quo ante* as rapidly as did the disappearances of Presidents Eisenhower and Johnson at the end of other eras that held some promise of enduring party realignments. But if it is true that changeable, short term factors, such as the relative attractiveness of an incumbent president, can dislodge sentiments of party attachment, the national surge of Republicanism which was visible in 1984 seems to have been very fragile. Taken together, the potential fragility of the distributional shift and the intensity of the ideological polarization among very different strata of the electorate add a theme of intellectual excitement to the political tensions that will build to a climax in 1988.

CHANGING PARTY ELITES

Thus far we have offered a series of amendments to contemporary conventional political wisdom, wisdom that is always born *post hoc* to explain electoral victory or justify electoral defeat. As both parties launch a search for new leadership for 1988, it seems likely they both may be swayed if not governed by the same misconceptions that have led the conventionally wise astray in their interpretations of the Reagan electoral victories and the declining levels of Democratic partisanship.

It is not surprising that Republican party elites have sought to extend their electoral triumphs with the claim of a popular mandate to transform their own issue preferences into public policy. It *is* perhaps surprising that the continuous assertion of mandate has not, in fact, produced at least a minor drift to the right given the limited resistance to the thesis by Democratic leadership. Particularly in 1980 it seemed that Democratic liberals joined in a public outpouring of guilt evoked by the presumption of public rejection of "excessively" liberal policies. Although the Mondale candidacy represented some resurgence of the old Democratic, moderate left, neither his campaign of 1984 nor the subsequent leadership from the Democratic side of the aisles in House or Senate carried the liberal fervor of the Democratic left of years gone by. The Democratic party at midterm was clearly very much in the process of trying to decide in what direction and in whose favor the national ideological winds will blow in 1988. The Republicans, on the other hand, do not seem beset by comparable doubts. The conservative wing of the party is not simply in the ascendancy in Washington; it is firmly in control of the administration. Although George Bush could lay legitimate claim to the moderate (or "Eastern Liberal," "Me Too") lineage that once dominated Republican presidential politics, even he seems properly persuaded that within the party, might is on the right.

With the search for the winning ideological posture so salient to political leaders in both parties, it is useful as a last exercise in our portrayal of the contemporary context for presidential politics to examine the relationship between the ideological preferences of party elites and party followers in the recent past. To accomplish this I turn to work recently completed in cooperation with M. Kent Jennings. Our work consists of a study of delegates to the Democratic and Republican national nominating conventions of 1972, 1976, and 1980. It is not a study of the delegates in their role as nominators, but a study of their participation in presidential campaign politics before, during, and subsequent to their activities in the convention halls. Using these delegates as exemplars for the larger population of midlevel party elites and party activists, we have pursued a number of curiosities about recent changes in party leadership. One of these interests has centered on the extent to which the policy preferences of delegates match those of their parties' supporters in the electorate.[8]

We employ four different indicators of ideological positioning. One, an index of policy preferences, rests on five contemporary policy questions touching on the domains of social welfare, race, moral, and social questions. A second indicator rests on evaluations of politically salient groups in the society. A third is based on evaluations of contemporary political leaders of both parties. And a fourth measure involves individuals' self-classifications as liberals, moderates, and conservatives. For present purposes I will use only one of these, the index of policy preferences, although the results I shall report are essentially the same for all measures.

Again, the purpose is to measure the relative level of agreement or disagreement, congruity or discontinuity, between two status groups in each party. The delegate campaigners constitute one status group; rank and file party identifiers from the national citizenry constitute the second. As a measure of difference between the two groups, I will use a

Table 14.5 Differences between Convention Delegates and Identifiers, by Partisan Combinations

	(1)	(2)	(3)	(4)
Delegates:	Democratic	Republican	Democratic	Republican
Identifiers:	Democratic	Republican	Republican	Democratic
Issue index	.29	.38	.43	.57

Note: Entries are product moment correlations (r) and indicate the relationship between party status (identifiers v. delegates) and attitude. The larger the score, the greater the difference between delegates and identifiers. The data are a subset from Table 9.1 in Miller and Jennings, *Parties in Transition*.

simple product moment correlation which will vary from zero, where the two status groups do not differ and have identical distributions, to a theoretical maximum of 1.00, where the groups are maximally different, concentrated at opposing ends of an ideological continuum. (Although I am using the product moment correlation, as is often done in other assessments of dyadic representation, the interpretation is, of course, dramatically different. For most of the traditional dyadic assessments one is correlating attitude with attitude, and the greater the similarity the higher the correlation. Here I am correlating status differences with attitudes, and the greater the similarity the lower the correlation.)

This is, of course, not the first time such an inquiry has been pursued, and the results of other similar inquiries have born results as different as the times and contexts that have been studied.[9] The classic study by McClosky described a situation in which Republican elites of 1956 had gone astray and were much less representative of their own followers than were even the Democratic elites. For a later era, the sequel to the McClosky study was provided by Kirkpatrick (1976), who demonstrated that in 1972 the tables had been thoroughly turned with the Democratic elites now quite out of touch with their own followers, to say nothing of Republican rank and file supporters. Eight years later our own research found a situation more like that depicted by McClosky.

As Table 14.5 indicates, Democratic elites in 1980 were more like Democratic identifiers in their issue preferences than Republican elites were like Republican identifiers, to say nothing of the differences between Republican elites and Democratic masses. Democratic elite preferences were about as different from those of the Republican rank and file as were Republican elite preferences, and the Democratic elite/

Republican mass differences were substantially less than those in the pairing representing Republican delegates and Democratic identifiers. The Miller-Jennings analysis of the circumstances producing such a dramatic change since 1972 emphasizes the contributions of the circulation of elites as they are mobilized by, and disengage from, presidential politics. Our conclusion is that elite circulation makes a real difference in the degree to which a given elite represents the relatively stable preferences of the citizenry. And the ascendancy of the Republican right wing produced a massive decline in the representative nature of the Republican party leadership in 1980.

More generally, global comparisons between national populations of party elites and national populations of party followers conceal a number of sharp differences among the various factions in each party, and some of the differences carry with them monumental ironies involving the sequence of presidential elections with which we introduced this essay. For example, within the Republican hierarchy, there are few nationally visible representatives of the old "Eastern" (Dewey-Rockefeller-Romney-Scranton) faction that once dominated the party and nominated its candidates. In 1980 their ranks were further thinned as John Anderson bolted the party on his own behalf. At the same time, George Bush and Howard Baker, representing the old Center, if not the liberal Eastern contingent, made modest attempts to prevent the stampede toward Reagan and were, of course, unsuccessful. Their failure found the moderate wing of the Republican party virtually divested of power, even though those delegates favoring some choice other than Reagan in the 1980 convention were ideologically very closely attuned to the issue positions of the national Republican party rank and file. While the measure of difference in issue preferences produced the overall rating of .38 for the entire Republican elite compared with all rank and file Republicans, it produced a score of only .08 for the limited differences between "moderate" delegates and rank and file Republican party identifiers.

This near identity of issue preferences stood in clear contrast to differences created by the faction of the leadership which had consistently supported Reagan for nomination, including the contest against Ford in 1976. The difference score between these "consistent" conservatives and the national population of Republican party identifiers was a resounding .58. Leaders of the newly dominant wing of the party were every bit as distant from their own national party constituency as the total set of Republican activists were from the national population of Democratic identifiers. Although much has been made of the discontinuity between the Democratic masses and elites in 1972, 1980 thus produced even greater discontinuity between the conservative leaders of the Republican party and rank and file preferences of their followers. In contrast to the lessons drawn from the Democrats' plight in 1972, electoral victory in 1980 was clearly not dependent on a high degree of congruence between the issue preferences of Reagan supporters among party leaders and Reagan supporters in the citizenry.

The first systematic examination of comparable data for 1984 indicates that the renomination and reelection of Reagan in that year were accompanied by an extension of these discontinuities in leader-follower agreement on questions of policy preference. We already know that by 1984 the national electorate had moved slightly to the left of their 1980 positions. There is little reason to expect that those who nominated Reagan for the second time were any more moderate than those responsible for his initial victories.

The Democrats, on the other hand, have provided a perversely parallel lesson in the utility, or nonutility, of developing rapport between leaders and followers. The Democratic elite who supported Carter in 1976 and 1980, *or* who dropped out of the national presidential politics by 1980, were very much in tune with the issue preferences of the Democratic national rank and file. The measure of difference between the policy preferences of the ordinary Democratic partisans was a statistically insignificant .06 (to match the .08 for Republican moderate elites and ordinary Republican partisans). At the other extreme, the leaders of the persistent liberal opposition to the Carter nominations, led by Kennedy in 1980, were as out of touch with the Democratic rank and file as were Reaganites with their Republican followers. Democratic party activists who represented the party's McGovern-Udall-Kennedy wing in 1980 differed from Democratic identifiers by a score of .59.

Nineteen-eighty-four may, of course, have been a different year for the Democratic party. If Mondale supporters were indeed more like those of the traditional Humphrey-Muskie faction, they would have been much closer to the Democratic rank and file because those elite activists who represented the traditional left-of-center leadership in 1980 were very similar to mass Democratic identifiers, as indicated by a difference score of only .14. The irony is complete, nevertheless, as the Democratic elite factions whose candidates were defeated in the 1980 and 1984 elections were demonstrably more representative of national policy preferences, including both Republicans and Democrats, than were the successful Republican elites. Once again we have come full circle with another demonstration that electoral majorities may be very poor indicators of the policy preferences of a national electorate.

CONCLUSIONS

The discontinuity between expectations borne of conventional wisdom and the evidence we have reviewed in this discussion make any prediction for the near future a dangerous gamble indeed. If, miraculously, the interpretations of electoral context that I have presented were to become the new conventional wisdom for leaders of both parties, it would indeed be difficult to prophesy what the future would hold. The optimism of the most conservative Republicans would be shattered, while the pessimism of traditional Democrats might well be replaced by euphoria. If the Democratic left created sufficient ideological space between itself and the nation's voters to permit Republican victories in the 1970s, so the Republican move to the right in the early 1980s may have opened the way for an immediate resurgence of Democratic strength en route to the White House in 1988.

On the other hand, the world of politics has changed. It would be reasonable to expect, political catastrophe or natural disaster aside, that there would be fewer Democrats and more Republicans in the electorate in 1988 than there have been in the prior 40 years of modern political history. At the same time, a well balanced system for partisan competition may be threatened with a divisiveness born of ideological polarization, for which our system of checks and balances through the separation of governmental powers is ill suited. The New Deal Coalition, shaped and exploited by Democratic presidents stretching from Roosevelt through Lyndon Johnson, has been reshaped and reduced in size. But, if Mr. Stockman is right, the conservative aspirations that created the national debt are themselves doomed to continued political failure. With new leadership yet to be chosen by both national parties, the future of American politics is uncertain indeed.

NOTES

1. W. E. Miller and J. M. Shanks, "Policy Directions and Presidential Leadership: Alternative Interpretations of the 1980 Presidential Election," *British Journal of Political Science* 12 (July 1982): 299–356.

2. J. M. Shanks and W. E. Miller, "Policy Direction and Performance Evaluation: Complementary Explanations of the Reagan Elections." APSA annual meetings, New Orleans, 1985.

3. P. R. Hagner and J. C. Pierce, "Correlative Characteristics of Levels of Conceptualization in the American Public," *Journal of Politics* 44 (1982): 779–807. Our measures follow from the original work on political belief systems by Converse and are derived from direct coding of the original interview protocols. They actually were constructed by Paul Hagner, or under his supervision, for each of

the presidential election years through 1980. Hagner and Professor Kathleen Knight coded the 1984 NES materials. In the interim a number of provocative and informative analyses have appeared in the professional literature. They reflect the growing importance attached to this particular aspect of the original "Belief Systems" argument. Special attention should be given to Cassel (1984), Hagner and Pierce (1982), Klingemann and Wright (1973), and the two influential discussions by Knight (1984, 1985).

4. This is possible, of course, because of the presence of the Anderson candidacy in 1980 but not in 1984. The inference that the Anderson candidacy cost Carter some 10% of the 1980 vote among the sophisticated is only an inference at this stage, but certainly one that bears further investigation.

5. Shanks and Miller, "Policy Direction and Performance Evaluation."

6. One should not make too much of the similarities in the absolute values in Tables 14.3 and 14.4 measuring partisan balance and regard for Reagan. The measures cannot be compared to determine whether Reagan was more or less popular than his party. This does not interfere with comparing each measure's relationship with ideological predisposition nor with comparing the various patterns of change between 1980 and 1984.

7. A. Campbell, P. E. Converse, W. E. Miller, and D. E. Stokes, *The American Voter* (New York: Wiley, 1960)

8. W. E. Miller and M. K. Jennings, *Parties in Transition: A Longitudinal Study of Party Elites and Party Supporters* (New York: Russell Sage, 1986), chaps. 8–10.

9. Similar findings are reported in H. McClosky, P. J. Hoffman, and R. O'Hara, "Issue Conflict and Consensus Among Party Leaders," *American Political Science Review* 54 (June 1960): 406–27; R. S. Mountjoy, W. R. Shafer, and R. E. Weber, "Policy Preferences of Party Elites and Masses: Conflict or Consensus?" *American Politics Quarterly* 8 (July 1980): 329–43; J. S. Jackson III, B. Leavitt, and D. Bositis, "Herbert McClosky and Friends Revisited: 1980 Democratic and Republican Party Elites Compared to the Mass Public," *American Politics Quarterly* 10 (April 1982): 158–79.

REFERENCES

Campbell, A., Converse, P. E., Miller, W. E., and Stokes, D. E. (1960). *The American Voter*, pp. 256–65. New York: Wiley.

Cassell, C. A. (1984). "Issues in Measurement: The 'Levels of Conceptualization' Index of Ideological Sophistication." *American Journal of Political Science* 28: 617–45.

Hagner, P. R., and Pierce, J. C. (1982). "Correlative Characteristics of Levels of Conceptualization in the American Public: 1956–1976." *Journal of Politics* 44: 779–807.

Jackson, J. S., III, Leavitt, B., and Bositis, D. (1982). "Herbert McClosky and Friends Revisited: 1980 Democratic and Republican Party Elites Compared to the Mass Public." *American Politics Quarterly* 10 (April): 158–79.

Kirkpatrick, Jeane (1976). *The New Presidential Elite*. New York: Russell Sage Foundation and Twentieth Century Fund.

Klingemann, H. D., and W. E. Wright (1973). "Models of Conceptualization and the Organization of Issue Beliefs." Paper presented at the World Congress of the International Political Science Association.

Knight, K. (1984). "The Dimensionality of Partisan and Ideological Affect." *American Politics Quarterly* 12: 305–34.

Knight, K. (1985). "Ideology in the 1980 Election: Ideological Sophistication Does Matter." *Journal of Politics* 41(3): 828–53.

McClosky, H., Hoffman, P. J., and O'Hara, R. (1960). "Issue Conflict and Consensus Among Party Leaders." *American Political Science Review* 54 (June): 406–27.

Miller, W. E., and Jennings, M. K. (1986). *Parties in Transition: A Longitudinal Study of Party Elites and Party Supporters*, chaps. 8-10. New York: Russell Sage.

Miller, W. E., and Levitin, T. E. (1976). *Leadership and Change*, chap. 1. Cambridge, Mass.: Winthrop.

Miller, W. E., and Shanks, J. M. (1982). "Policy Directions and Presidential Leadership: Alternative Interpretations of the 1980 Presidential Election." *British Journal of Political Science* 12 (July): 299–356.

Mountjoy, R. S., Shaffer, W. R., and Weber, R. E. (1980). Policy Preferences of Party Elites and Masses: Conflict or Consensus? *American Politics Quarterly* 8 (July): 329–43.

Shanks, J. M., and Miller, W. E. (1985). "Policy Direction and Performance Evaluation: Complementary Explanations of the Reagan Elections." APSA annual meetings, New Orleans.

ASSESSING THE REPRESENTATIVENESS OF ELECTORATES IN PRESIDENTIAL PRIMARIES

John G. Geer

The most democratic system for nominating presidents that the United States has ever had is currently under attack for being, in effect, "undemocratic." One of the charges critics have made is that certain kinds of voters are underrepresented in primary electorates, leading to the nomination of candidates who are unrepresentative of the concerns of rank-and-file voters (Lengle, 1981; Marshall, 1981; Ceasar, 1982; Polsby, 1983.) This paper disputes this view. First, the biases associated with primary electorates are the opposite of what they have conventionally been thought to be. Second, these biases are small enough to be essentially inconsequential. These conclusions emerge quite clearly if one accepts my normative assumption that the main objective of parties is to win elections.

BACKGROUND

V. O. Key was the first to voice a concern about the unrepresentativeness of primary electorates, arguing that "the effective primary constituency ...may come to consist predominantly of the people of certain sections of a state, of persons of specific national origin or religious affiliation, of people especially responsive to certain styles of political leadership or shades of ideology, or of groups markedly unrepresentative in one way or another of the party following."[1] Other scholars have since found that voters who participate in the state primaries are better educated, better paid, and more ideologically extreme than the party following (Ranney, 1972; Lengle, 1981; Polsby, 1983; Keeter and Zukin, 1983; Crotty and Jackson, 1985).

If these critics are correct, it raises serious questions about the use of primaries to nominate presidential candidates. If voters, for instance, are more ideologically extreme in their orientation to politics than the party following, the candidates chosen by primary electorates may reflect this ideological bias (Lengle, 1981). Such nominees could have a difficult time winning general elections, since they would have limited success in appealing to the moderate voters who are essential to a victory in November. These kinds of outcomes would be troublesome, given that a major objective of any political party is to win elections. A further implication of these claims is that if ideologically extreme elements of each party dominate the nominating process, there is a chance that the political discussion would become "polarized," alienating the more moderate elements in the electorate. Key (1956) feared that such scenarios might result in a realignment of the party system.

Before we consider the adequacy of these complaints, it should be noted that every system of presidential nominations since the adoption of the Constitution has been attacked as "unrepresentative." Opponents of the Congressional Caucus criticized that method "mainly on the ground that it was unrepresentative and undemocratic" (Ranney, 1975). Some scholars argued that the National Convention by the late 1800s was simply a tool of the party leadership, unresponsive to the wishes of the party following (Bryce, 1891; Sait, 1927; Ostrogorski, 1921). The "mixed" system also had its share of detractors. For instance, the written report of the McGovern-Fraser Commission (1970), *Mandate for Reform*, questioned the representativeness of that system because all Democrats did not have a "full, meaningful, and timely opportunity to participate" in the selection of nominees.

While the accuracy of all these complaints is uncertain, it is clear that they have often been motivated by partisan considerations. Progressives, such as Robert LaFollette and Woodrow Wilson, attacked the national convention as "unrepresentative," in large part, because it did not represent their views very well. Likewise, attacks against the current system may well reflect a frustration of many politicians and scholars that voters in primaries rather than party leaders are receiving "representation." In short, whether a system is representative depends, in large part, on one's views of who should be represented. As Austin Ranney correctly notes, "Just about every conflict over making the parties more representative...turns on the basic question of who should be treated as party members."[2]

In this paper, I shall present a new definition of the party following, which is based on the normative assumption that the major purpose of parties is to win elections. Relying on this new definition of the party following, I shall show, contrary to past research, that the party following, not voters in primaries, are the better paid, better educated, and more ideologically extreme group.

A DEFINITION OF THE "PARTY FOLLOWING"

Previous studies have used a variety of conceptions of the party following. Comparisons have been drawn between primary voters and those who did not vote in the primaries (Ranney and Epstein, 1966; Ranney, 1968, 1972), primary voters and party identifiers (Kritzer, 1977; Lengle, 1981), and primary voters and voters in general elections (DiNitto and Smithers, 1972; Kritzer, 1977; Rubin, 1980; Winograd, 1978). Many of these comparisons, however, are misleading, since they often include people who never vote for the party in the general election. Any good definition of the party following should constitute those individuals who are likely to turn out in the general election and are potential supporters of the party in that election. Otherwise, the party risks representing those individuals who have no intention of voting for the party in the November contest. Some studies, for instance, compare all primary voters to all general election voters (Rubin 1980; DiNitto and Smithers, 1972). Such a comparison makes little effort to identify the "followers" of either party, since supporters of both parties are lumped together. James Lengle criticizes using only nonvoters as the base of comparison: "The important empirical question, as originally posed by Key, is whether the primary electorate consists of groups markedly unrepresentative of the party following. The answer is found, not by comparing two mutually exclusive parts, that is, primary voters with nonvoters, but by comparing the part with the whole, that is, the primary electorate (voters) with the entire party membership."[3] His argument is important because it points to the fact that nonvoters may or may not be members of the party.

On the basis of this reasoning, Lengle uses party identification as a proxy for the party following. Though this approach is superior to many previous efforts, there are still problems with this conception of the party following. One should, for instance, expect primary voters to be unrepresentative of party identifiers, since the latter group includes large numbers of habitual nonvoters. Nonvoters, of course, tend to be from lower socioeconomic groups than voters. Consequently, by including these nonvoters in the "party following," one would automatically increase the proportion of the less well-off. This increase would, in turn, affect the ideological composition of the party following, since the less well-off tend to be less ideologically extreme than the better-off. So the findings of Lengle (1981) and other that primary electorates are more ideologically extreme than the "party following" may, in part, be a result of the definition used.[4]

There is another, more important, problem in using party identifiers as a proxy for the party following. It does not provide a clear idea about those who generally support the party in the general election. Votes in the general election, not identification with a party, is the important issue for parties when trying to win general elections. The leaders of the parties want to represent, and hence consider, the views of a potentially winning coalition in the general election. And since neither party constitutes a majority of the electorate, as measured by self-identification, the party leadership needs to consider the views of other potential party voters when choosing a candidate. In short, by using party identifiers, previous studies have not examined directly the behavior that is central to a party's effort to win in November.

A good proxy, then, for the followers of a party can be found in those who vote in general elections. Specifically, the following should be made up of those who usually vote for the party's candidates; those who lean toward the party, yet do not always vote for its candidates; and those independents and opposing partisans who occasionally support the party in the general election. This line of argument has long been recognized by political scientists. As Key once argued, if the party is to win the general election, it "must maintain the loyalty of its own standpatters; it must also concern itself with the great block of voters uncommitted to either party as well as those who may be weaned away from the opposition."[5] Given these guidelines for a successful coalition, a good proxy for the party following would be the general election voters who identify with the party and those who voted for the party but do not identify with the party. The party following, therefore, would consist of two parts. The first part would be all identifiers of the party who turned out, regardless of the party they voted for. While this group would include some individuals who "defected" from the party, presumably their self-identification indicates a general tendency to support the party in the general election. To use Key's terms, this group would be the "standpatters." The second component of the party following would be independents and members of the opposition who supported the party in that general election. These people are the "potential" party supporters.

This definition has a number of advantages. First, the party following consists of a potential winning coalition in the general election.[6] This aspect of the definition is very attractive, since it gets at the central concern of most politicians: winning elections. A second, and related, advantage of the definition is that independents and wavering partisans of the other party are included among the party followers, provided they support the party in that general election. Struggles over these voters are where elections are won and lost.[7] A third advantage is that by comparing two sets of voters, I avoid the built-in bias that exists when including nonvoters in one's definition of the party following.[8]

Underlying these "pragmatic" reasons for adopting this definition is a normative ideal: parties should seek to represent those people who turn out and are potential supporters of the party in the general election. It strikes me as perverse to represent those who do not support the party in the general election, either because they do not vote at all or always vote for the opposing party. Yet this is exactly what occurs under the other definitions. This outcome is ironic, since many scholars who advocated these alternative proxies for the party following probably did in fact seek to represent those who generally vote for the party in the general election.

Although this definition has much appeal, there is at least one drawback to it. In deciding whether voters in primaries are representative of the party following, I shall only be able to examine the demographic characteristics and ideological composition of both groups. I cannot assess voters' and followers' attitudes on issues or preferences for candidates because the campaign differs in primaries and in general elections, preventing any meaningful comparison. In 1980, for example, 55.6 percent of voters in Democratic primaries favored some increase in defense spending. Among Democratic voters in the general election, the proportion jumped to 76.5 percent. Was this increase the result of Reagan's call in the general election for a military build-up or because the two electorates differed on that issue? One cannot tell.[9] The same problem exists for assessing the electorate's preferences for candidates, since preferences measured during the heat of a primary campaign may well change by the time the general election rolls around.[10]

Inability to compare preferences for candidates poses perhaps the most serious problem for my definition because agreement between voters and party followers in this matter is probably the most important consideration when assessing the representativeness of a nominating system.[11] Yet even if one uses self-identification or nonvoters as a proxy for the party following, there is a potential problem with comparing the choice of voters to the preferences of identifiers and nonvoters. At the outset of most contested presidential primary campaigns, a large proportion of the electorate either have weak preferences or no preference at all, making these preferences highly volatile.[12] Consequently, the results of each contest greatly influence the preferences of voters, party identifiers, and nonvoters. As Bartels (1985) and others have shown, "momentum" shapes voters' preferences. Thus, one should *expect* there to be some convergence between the choice that voters make in primaries and the preferences of self-identified partisans and nonvoters—as the primary season progresses. And in fact, if one examines the 1980 CPS Panel Study, there is general agreement between primary voters and party identifiers immediately following the primary season.[13] But this agreement is not clear evidence of the representativeness of primary electorates; it may simply demonstrate the influence of the campaign on voters' and followers' preferences for candidates. In short, an accurate reading of preferential representation is exceedingly difficult to obtain because of the confounding effects resulting from the sequence of presidential primaries.

Nonetheless, by focusing only on the demographic characteristics and the ideological composition of primary electorates and their respective party following, I shall still be able to address, at least in part, the question of representativeness. First, much of the criticism leveled against primary electorates centers on their demographic and ideological composition (see Lengle, 1981). Second, it is likely that demographic characteristics and ideological position are related to preferences for candidates. A "liberal" voter, for instance, would have been more likely to favor Senator Kennedy over President Carter in 1980, or Vice-President Mondale over Senator Glenn in 1984.

DATA

In assessing the representativeness of primary electorates, I shall use data from CBS/*New York Times* and ABC/*Washington Post* exit polls of voters in presidential primaries and in the general elections of 1976 and 1980. I shall examine seven Democratic primaries and five Republican primaries.[14] These data should serve my purposes very well, since exit polls provide reliable estimates of who voted in primaries and in general elections (Levy, 1983). By surveying only voters, they avoid the overestimation of turnout that plagues surveys relying on self-reported votes.[15] James DeNardo, for instance, reports that "self-reported rates of turnout in the SRC/CPS surveys consistently exceed official figures by 13 to 20 percentage points," suggesting that surveys may "provide a badly distorted picture of the actual voting electorates."[16] My data avoid this kind of bias.

There is another important advantage of these data. Previous studies generally have examined only one of two elections (Ranney, 1968, 1972; Lengle, 1981). Yet a single election may have certain features that encourage unrepresentativeness. If a black (such as Jesse Jackson) runs in a primary, blacks may be more likely to vote. If blacks turn out at a higher rate than normal, the results could suggest overrepresentation or mask underrepresentation that occurs for blacks in the absence of such a candidacy. Campaign issues could also promote unrepresentativeness in a given election. If an issue in a campaign, such as gun control or abortion, is very salient to a particular group, its members may turn out at a higher rate than normal. Therefore, an accurate test of representativeness requires using a wide range of cases so as to avoid the idiosyncratic factors associated with any one race. Fortunately, I have a number of data points to study this problem—a luxury most previous studies have not enjoyed.

THE RESULTS

Table 15.1 presents the demographic differences between voters in primaries and party followers. In stark contrast to the findings of previous works, the Democratic following is *better* educated and *better* paid than voters in Democratic primaries.[17] While this pattern was not completely consistent, the differences were often sizable. On average, eight percentage points more of the party following had a college education than did voters in Democratic primaries. Much the same pattern exists for differences in income between the two groups. The Republicans are no different. The voters in Republican primaries were also generally less well paid and has less formal education than their party following. Among the college educated, there was more than a four-percentage-point gap between voters in Republican primaries and their followers. Although the gap in education among the Democrats was larger, there still could be sizable differences. In Illinois (1980), for instance, 47 percent of the Republican following had completed college compared to about 35 percent of the primary voters.

Another consistent difference between primary electorates and the following of both parties is that the former is older than the latter. On average, voters in Democratic primaries overrepresented the 60 and over age-group by eight percentage points. Among Republicans the comparable difference was 10 percentage points. When examining other demographic categories, such as race, sex, and union membership, there were few consistent differences between voters and followers of both parties.[18] Blacks, for instance, seem to be slightly overrepresented in Democratic primary electorates. Women, on the other hand, appear to be well represented in Democratic primaries but slightly underrepresented in Republican primaries. In neither party were the differences in union membership consistent, suggesting that misrepresentation is not a problem. In general, the differences in these categories tend to be small and inconsistent.

Table 15.2 reports the ideological affiliations of primary voters and party followers. As one can see, Democratic followers are *more* liberal than voters in Democratic primaries in five of the six cases studied. In Pennsylvania (1980), for instance, 32 percent of the Democratic following labeled themselves liberal, while only 22 percent of voters in Democratic primaries did so. On the Republican side of the ledger, the differences are not as great, but it appears that followers are slightly more conservative than voters in primaries. Of the five cases, only voters in California's Republican primary were more conservative than the party following.[19]

AN EXPLANATION

The results in Tables 15.1 and 15.2 show that voters in primaries are less educated, less well paid, and more moderate in the ideological views than the party following—results that run directly counter to the conventional wisdom on the subject. In explaining these findings, skeptics, of course, might point to the proxy I am using for the party following. I did try other ways to define the "party following" to see if my particular definition was accounting for the findings presented. In each case, however, the data point to similar conclusions: voters in primaries are not from higher socioeconomic groups than these other followings.[20] Some scholars might also question whether the data employed could account for these surprising findings. Exit polls, however, should provide good estimates of who votes in both primaries and general elections. As Mark Levy writes, "The exit polls... appear to have been conducted with a degree of meticulousness which compares favorably to the highest standards of commercial and academic research."[21]

What other explanations might account for these surprising findings? Certainly, comparing primary voters to a subset of those who vote in general elections accounts for some of the differences between voters and followers. Nonetheless, these critics would still not expect the party following, that is, voters in general elections, to be better educated, better paid, and more ideologically extreme than voters in primaries. The accepted view of scholars is that "low stimulus" primary elections would tend to attract voters who are more ideologically extreme and generally better off than those in the "high stimulus" general election. The expla-

Table 15.1 Difference between Primary Voters and the "Party Following"

	Democrats		Republicans	
	Mean difference[a]	Percentage of times consistent[b]	Mean difference[a]	Percentage of times consistent[b]
Sex				
Female	−.4	50.0	−2.9	80.0
Race				
Black	2.0	70.0	.7	50.0
White	−3.1	70.0	−.2	50.0
Age				
18–29	−8.0	100.0	−4.6	80.0
30–59	−.3	43.0	−5.7	80.0
60+	8.3	83.0	10.3	100.0
Education				
> High sch.	6.6	100.0	1.2	50.0
High sch.	2.7	80.0	1.1	50.0
> College	−1.3	60.0	2.2	75.0
College	−8.2	100.0	−4.4	75.0
Religion				
Protestant	−2.7	50.0	10.4	100.0
Catholic	−3.0	43.0	−9.2	100.0
Income[c]				
Low	3.8	70.0	2.4	67.0
Middle	1.5	70.0	1.9	80.0
High	−5.3	80.0	−4.3	80.0
Union member				
Union mem.	2.1	67.0	−3.8	60.0
Number of samples	7		5	

Note: [a]The "mean difference" is the average difference between the proportion of voters and followers in a given demographic category across the various samples. A negative value indicates that primary electorates underrepresent the party following.

[b]The proportion of "times consistent" indicates whether all samples agreed with the general pattern of representation for that particular category. A value of 67 percent, for example, means that one-third of the surveys disagree with the direction of the "mean difference." If the difference between the primary electorate and the party following was less than one percentage point, I counted this case as a draw, that is, it was neither consistent nor inconsistent.

[c]Income was coded differently in 1976 and 1980. In 1980 the "high" group earned over $15,000, while in 1976 that figure was $12,000. I have treated these two categories as the same. These figures may not strike one as "high" income, but due to differences in coding this was the only breakdown that was possible without throwing away cases. The "middle" figure is $8,000 to $12,000 in 1976 and $10,000 to $15,000 in 1980. The "low" figure is below $8,000 in 1976 and below $10,000 in 1980.

Source: CBS/NYT and ABC/WP Exit Polls.

Table 15.2 A Comparison of the Ideological Affiliations of Primary Voters and the "Party Following" (in Percentages)

Voters	Liberal	Moderate	Conservative	N
Republicans:				
California, 1976				
Primary	9.6	46.4	44.0	919
The following	10.0	46.7	43.3	4,244
California, 1980				
Primary	7.7	38.8	53.7	801
The following	8.9	47.9	43.2	993
Illinois, 1980				
Primary	11.9	37.7	50.3	605
The following	16.0	29.8	54.3	298
Pennsylvania, 1980				
Primary	9.5	54.7	35.8	721
The following	14.1	35.3	50.6	372
Ohio, 1980				
Primary	9.6	44.4	46.0	527
The following	7.0	42.0	51.0	255
Democrats[a]:				
California, 1976				
Primary	35.9	49.5	14.6	1,490
The following	34.4	50.6	15.0	4,571
California, 1980				
Primary	24.2	57.8	18.0	1,131
The following	35.2	51.5	13.3	876
Illinois, 1980				
Primary	32.9	49.9	17.2	605
The following	44.8	35.2	19.9	282
New York, 1980				
Primary	30.6	55.4	14.0	547
The following	35.9	51.7	12.3	718
Pennsylvania, 1980				
Primary	21.7	56.3	22.0	949
The following	31.6	41.4	27.0	261
Ohio, 1980				
Primary	22.2	55.6	22.2	884
The following	32.4	42.5	25.1	273

Notes: In each of these surveys the liberal-conservative question was coded and worded the same. The question lacked a "don't know" category, however. The absence of such a category greatly inflates the proportion of "ideological" respondents, since those individuals who do not think in liberal-conservative terms could not say so. This omission should not, however, pose a problem, since my objective is to compare the two groups not to assess how ideological a particular electorate is.

[a] I did not include the results from New York's 1976 primary and general election because of coding differences between the two surveys.

nation for these findings lies in the relationship between age and turnout in primaries and in general elections.

As Table 15.1 demonstrated, voters over 60 years old make up a larger proportion of primary electorates than of the party following. These older voters tend to have less education, less income, and a more moderate orientation to politics—which may account for at least part of the differences between voters and followers.[22] Older voters turn out in disproportionate numbers in primaries, I suspect, because they tend to be more partisan than younger voters (Campbell, Converse, Miller, and Stokes, 1960; Price, 1983). For instance, according to the 1980 National Election Study only about 8 percent of those citizens over 60 were self-identified independents, while about 19 percent of those citizens under 29 years old labeled themselves independent. As one might expect, partisans tend to be more interested in the prenomination campaign than independents.[23] With greater interest, partisans will be more likely to participate in primaries, accounting for the high rate of turnout among this oldest cohort.[24] In addition, some states require that an individual register as a member of that party in order to participate—something that a partisan is more likely to do. Thus, legal barriers help prevent the less partisan from voting. In short, a consequence of the dwindling partisanship among younger voters may be that older, more partisan, voters have a disproportionate influence in primaries.

A useful way to think about why older voters turn out in greater numbers in primaries is to borrow Campbell's famous distinction between "core" and "peripheral" voters. "Core" voters consist "of people whose level of political interest is sufficiently high to take them to the polls in all national elections, even those in which the level of political stimulation is relatively weak."[25] "Peripheral" voters, on the other hand, are those voters ''whose level of political interest is lower but whose motivation to vote has been sufficiently increased by the stimulation of the election situation to carry them to the polls."[26] Since presidential primaries are "low stimulus" events in comparison with presidential elections, the former should have a higher proportion of "core" voters than the latter. In most elections "interest" is strongly related to socioeconomic status: the better-off tend to be more interested in the campaign than the less well-off (Verba and Nie, 1972). In a partisan affair, such as a primary, "interest" is *also* a function of one's partisanship. Consequently, the "core" does participate in large numbers in primaries, as Campbell's theory would suggest, but this "core" is made up of the less well-off, but more partisan, elements of society.

CONCLUSION

It turns out that Key's original argument is correct: voters in primaries are unrepresentative of the party following. Key himself was unsure of how this unrepresentativeness would influence outcomes, arguing that "the exact form of these consequences would. . .be a product of the facts of the situation as they existed in a particular state at a particular time."[27] The belief that voters in primaries are better paid, better educated, and more ideologically extreme than the party following came from scholars who sought to test Key's idea. By not thinking of the "party following" as those individuals who turn out and are possible supporters of the party, they drew vastly different conclusions from mine. One, of course, could contend that my results are misleading because my definition of the party following is suspect. Such an argument might have merit, especially if one does not believe that the major purpose of parties is to win elections, and, therefore, the "party following" should not consist of a potentially winning coalition. But many of these scholars share my normative assumption that parties should strive to win elections, suggesting that my definition should have much appeal to them.[28]

Even though I have questioned previous work in this area, voters in primaries are still unrepresentative of the party following. The consequences of this unrepresentativeness, however, are less severe for parties than they would be if primary electorates were more ideologically extreme. The chances of a "polarized debate" declines, since voters in primaries are more moderate in their orientation to politics. This change may affect the realignment scenario outlined briefly in the introduction. No longer would disenchanted moderate voters be the focus of attention; rather the more ideologically extreme voters would be the frustrated contingent and perhaps assume the "reigns" of realignment.

The more immediate, and probably more important, implication involves the parties' chances for victory in November. When scholars believed that voters in primaries were more ideologically extreme than the party following, there was concern that the nominees might reflect this bias and hence be less "electable." But my evidence suggest that voters in primaries are more moderate than the party following, which should ease such concerns. In fact, if general elections are a struggle for the "middle" of the ideological spectrum, primary electorates may be especially able to produce nominees capable of competing successfully in them.

While there have been only a handful of candidates nominated under the current system, we can crudely test to see if the system tends to produce "moderate" or "extreme" nominees. George McGovern would certainly be labeled as a "noncentrist" by most observers, but the other nominees have tended to be "moderate." In fact, moderate candidates have often defeated more "extreme" challengers for the nomination: Carter in 1976 and 1980, Ford in 1976, and Mondale in 1984.[29] One might point to Reagan as an "ideologically extreme" nominee, but he did go on to victory in November, suggesting that he was not so "extreme" as to alienate over 50 percent of the voters. In short, while the evidence is not overwhelming, the nominees selected under this arrangement have tended to be somewhat moderate in their orientation to politics—a finding that is consistent with the results presented in this paper.

Actually, the kinds of differences reported in Tables 15.1 and 15.2 are unlikely to have much effect on who is nominated. For instance, even if we assume that moderates are overrepresented by 15 percent in primary electorates (almost twice the amount actually shown in Table 15.2 for the Democrats and four times for Republicans), and even if we further assume that moderates differ in their preferences from liberals by 25 percentage points (an unusually large difference, according to my data), the effect on the share of the two-candidate vote is less than two percentage points.[30] In a three-candidate race with only one moderate contender, the potential bias is only about three percentage points.[31] The only time such biases might make a difference would be in very close elections. Yet even in close elections, the effect will generally be modest, since many states currently use some form of proportional representation to allocate delegates in presidential primaries. If delegates were distributed, however, on a "winner-take-all" basis, then there might be more cause for concern, since in a close race such a bias might tip the scales to one of the candidates. But even so, this kind of bias is not a major concern when trying to pick an "electable" candidate, since a moderate contender generally would have more success in general elections than more "extreme" challengers. Actually, the amount of bias may decline even further in the future, as generational replacement reduces the differences in partisanship among the old and the young.[32]

An important implication of the findings in this paper involves our assessment of presidential primaries. In general, one can say that they are under attack by many leading scholars of political parties (see Ceasar, 1979, 1982; Polsby, 1983; Ranney, 1975). A major reason for their unfavorable assessments is the belief that primaries are unduly influenced by the ideologically extreme elements of the parties. The evidence presented here should ease these concerns. Or at the very least, scholars should consider other features of primaries that may be fostering these perceived weaknesses. Of course, any changes in assessment would still depend on one's answer to the question raised at the outset: Who should be represented in primaries? But if óne believes that presidential primaries should represent those most likely to bring the party a victory in November, then perhaps we should be less critical of them.

NOTES

1. V. O. Key, *American State Politics: An Introduction* (New York: Knopf, 1956), p. 153.

2. Austin Ranney, *Curing the Mischiefs of Faction: Party Reform in America* (Berkeley, Calif.: U. of California Press, 1975), p. 145.

3. James Lengle, *Representation and Presidential Primaries* (Westport, Conn.: Greenwood, 1981), pp. 11–12.

4. As evidence of how Lengle's definition may create artificial bias, I compared voters in general elections to all party identifiers. As I expected, voters tended to be better educated and better paid than party identifiers. For instance, 20 percent of voters had less than a high school education, while 25 percent of identifiers failed to complete high school. The five-percentage-point gap supports my contention that party identifiers include a number of nonvoters, which lowers the socioeconomic standing of the whole group.

5. V. O. Key, *Politics, Parties, and Pressure Groups*, 5th ed. (New York: Cromwell, 1964), p. 220.

6. In each case examined later, the party following constituted over 50 percent of those who voted in the general election. It is possible, however, that my definition would not always yield a majority of voters. For instance, in Utah it would be difficult to forge a winning Democratic coalition given this state's strong Republican leanings. This kind of incident would not, however, be common.

7. As one may have noticed, "defectors" are counted in each party's following. That is, Democratic identifiers who vote Republican are included both as members of the Democratic and Republican following. This double counting is a strength of the definition, since both parties covet the support of these voters in November.

8. By excluding nonvoters from my definition, I do not intend to suggest that nonvoters are unimportant to the election process. "Get out the vote drives" have been at the heart of efforts by both parties to increase their proportion of the vote. Though my definition ignores nonvoters, any successful effort at increasing the turnout of a particular group in the general election would immediately influence the composition of the party following. In fact, my definition would respond quicker to changes in turnout than relying on party identification as a proxy for the party following, because to be counted as a follower all one has to do is to vote for the party—one need not have developed a partisan label.

9. Actually, a panel study would be able to answer this question, but the data I use are not from that kind of survey.

10. To complicate matters further, as the election year progresses the electorate becomes better informed (Patterson, 1980). This additional information results in a decrease in "don't know" responses, which may affect the distribu-

tion of opinion on these matters and also may lead to changes in position on them.

11. Lengle (1981), for example, states, "A strong argument could be made that demographic unrepresentativeness, its severity and pervasiveness notwithstanding, is irrelevant as long as ideology, issue concerns, and *more importantly*, candidate preferences are unrelated to, or independent of, the socio-economic status of Democrats" (p. 25).

12. For instance, among Democratic party identifiers in Erie, Pennsylvania (1976), 27 percent did not have a preference for any of the contenders for their party's nomination. For Republicans in Erie, over 30 percent of identifiers responded "don't know" to the question about preferences. The rapid rise of contenders, such as Gary Hart, George Bush, and Jimmy Carter, point in the same direction. Hart, for instance, rose from having 3 percent of Democratic identifiers supporting him in the Gallup Poll to 33 percent in less than two weeks. Such large and rapid shifts in support indicate that many citizens have weakly held preferences.

13. Specifically, about 61 percent of Democratic primary voters cast their ballots for Carter, while over 58 percent of Democratic identifiers supported the incumbent president for renomination. On the Republican side, 54 percent of the primary electorate voted for Reagan, and 55 percent of Republican identifiers supported the former governor.

14. The Republican primaries were held in the following states: California (1976, 1980), Pennsylvania (1980), Illinois (1980), and Ohio (1980). On the Democratic side, the states were: New York (1976, 1980), California (1976, 1980), Pennsylvania (1980), Illinois (1980), and Ohio (1980).

15. David Moore and Richard C. Hofstetter (1973) argue that overestimation of turnout in the Ohio primary was 30 percent.

16. James DeNardo, "The Architecture of Partisan Electorates." Photocopy, U. of California at Los Angeles.

17. These results contradict the findings of the Winograd commission. This Democratic party commission found that primary voters were better educated and better paid than Democratic voters in general elections (Commission on Presidential Nomination and Party Structure, Morley Winograd, Chairman [1978] *Openness, Participation, and Party Building: Reforms for a Stronger Democratic Party* [Washington, D.C.: Democratic National Committee], pp. 11–13). My data support the opposite conclusion. What accounts for these differences? First, the Winograd study uses only Democratic voters, rather than Democratic voters and identifiers as I have. When I excluded party identifiers from my data, however, the results still contradict those in the Winograd study. The answer may lie in how the Winograd commission defined Democratic voters. They based their estimates on samples of *likely* voters. Relying on such data may greatly inflate the number of respondents who are treated as voters. The exit polls, on the other hand, survey only voters.

18. There is one other consistent difference. Republican followers are much more likely to be Roman Catholic than are voters in Republican primaries. This

difference is probably attributable to the number of Roman Catholics who "defect" to the Republican party in general elections.

19. In general, voters in the primaries of both parties were more moderate than their respective following. For Democrats, moderates, on average, were overrepresented in primary electorates by about nine percentage points. While in the Republican camp, moderates in primary electorates out-numbered moderates in the following by about four percentage points.

20. One alternative conception included only those respondents who were both Democratic voters *and* identifiers as a proxy for the Democratic following. Another possible way to define the party following is to use all voters in the general election who identify with the party, regardless of how they voted in the general election. While neither of these other definitions offer the advantages mine does, they do not, as stated above, alter the general direction of the findings.

21. One might still have doubts about exit polls. In an effort to ease possible concerns, I tried to compare my results to other available data. While the data are far from ideal because of a small sample size and being a national survey, I examined voters in primaries from the Center of Political Studies' panel in June 1980. While the results do not confirm all the findings in Tables 15.1 and 15.2, it was quite clear that voters in primaries were not consistently richer, better educated, and more ideologically extreme than the "party following." For instance, 56 percent of the Republican primary electorate from June's wave of the panel study labeled themselves either slightly liberal, moderate, or slightly conservative. Among the "party following," the equivalent proportion was 47.4. This eight-percentage-point gap supports the notion that the moderate elements are more common in primaries than in the party following—evidence that is consistent with my findings. The Democrats tell a similar story.

Finally, even if one remains suspicious of exit polls, the evidence presented here does not purport to argue *how* well paid or ideological the electorates are, but instead seeks to *compare* the demographic and ideological makeup of primary electorates to that of the party following. Thus, even if the data are suspect, the problems confronting exit polls should be the same for both primaries and general election—suggesting that a comparison should provide the needed leverage to study the problem.

22. The reasons for these differences between older and younger voters are understandable. While having a high school education is now commonplace among younger citizens, it was uncommon for those who are currently over 60 years old to have completed twelve years of school. Even among those who turned out in Pennsylvania's Democratic primary (1980), 46 percent of those participants over 60 years old had less than a high school education, while only 3 percent of the 18 to 29 year olds had not completed high school. This pattern is similar for all the state studies. With less education, these citizens probably did not make as much money as they would have with a better education. Moreover, a good proportion of this group are retired and probably live on a fixed income. Such individuals will tend to have lower incomes than those who are still work-

ing nine-to-five jobs. Consequently, it should be no surprise that in Ohio's Republican primary (1980) about 26 percent of those over 60 earned less than $10,000, while only 18 percent of those between 18 and 29 years old had a similar income. Since older voters are generally not as well-off or as well educated as other parts of the electorate, they will tend to be more moderate in their ideological orientation to politics. For instance, in California's Democratic primary (1980), about 66 percent of voters over 60 years old labeled themselves moderates while approximately 47 percent of voters between 18 and 29 did so. In short, these demographic differences between the "young" and the "old" coupled with the fact that the 60-and-over cohort constitutes a higher proportion of the electorate in primaries than in general elections probably explain much of the differences between voters and followers found in Tables 15.1 and 15.2.

23. In January 1980, 30 percent of independents were "not much interested" in the campaign. This figure stands in contrast to only 19 percent of Democratic identifiers and 15 percent of Republican identifiers who were "not much interested" in the campaign.

24. Data from the 1980 CPS National Election Study further confirms that older voters are more likely to turn out in primaries than in general elections when compared to the younger cohort. Specifically the data indicate that the 60-and-over age-group has a two and a half times greater participation rate in primaries than the 18-to-29 cohort, while in the general election this figure declines to less than one and a half times.

25. Angus Campbell, "Surge and Decline: The Study of Electoral Change," *Public Opinion Quarterly* 24 (1960): 399.

26. Ibid.

27. Key, *American State Politics*, p. 153.

28. Lengle, *Representation*, p. 9; Nelson Polsby, *Consequences of Party Reform* (Cambridge: Oxford U., 1983), pp. 85–88.

29. Mondale's nomination does not really fit in with the other cases mentioned, since he and his main challenger Hart were very close on the so-called ideological spectrum. Mondale (and Hart) did, however, fend off liberal challenges by Cranston, Jackson, and McGovern.

30. I arrive at this figure as follows. Assume a two-candidate race in which moderates prefer one candidate to another by 75 percent to 25 percent; liberals split their vote 50—50 between the two candidates; and conservatives split 80 percent to 20 percent in their preferences. In addition, the moderates constitute 50 percent of the following and 65 percent of the voters. The rest of the electorate in both cases are split evenly among liberals and conservatives.

Even in Lengle's (1981) study of California's 1972 Democratic primary, he found only a bias of three-to-five percentage points in McGovern's share of the vote attributable to "unrepresentativeness" he uncovered. The magnitude of this bias is small, pointing to the fact that even when there appears to be much unrepresentativeness the effects are rarely very large. As a side note, California was a very unusual case. Not only was California the last primary in a hotly contested nomination, but the winner, McGovern, received all the delegates in this large state because of the "winner-take-all" rule. The combination of these factors exaggerated the effect of this perceived bias that Lengle reports.

31. I have made a number of assumptions to arrive at this figure. First, there are three candidates in the race: one liberal, one moderate, and one conservative contender. The "liberal" vote is divided among the contenders as follows: the liberal candidate receives 50 percent, the moderate candidate 30 percent, and the conservative candidate 20 percent. The "moderate" vote is divided in a similar fashion: the liberal candidate receives 30 percent, the moderate candidate 50 percent, and the conservative candidate 20 percent. The "conservative" vote is split in the following manner: the liberal candidate receives 20 percent, the moderate candidate 30 percent, and the conservative candidate 50 percent.

The final set of assumptions concerns the makeup of the electorate. I assumed the following distribution in the electorate:

	Percentage of voters	Percentage of "followers"
Liberals	25	30
Moderates	50	40
Conservatives	25	30

As one can see, the moderates are overrepresented by 10 percent. Of course, one could adjust these assumptions and uncover different "biases," but the point is that there is not much effect on the outcome of presidential primaries.

32. If a realignment took place, a new "core" might emerge, changing radically who votes in primaries. Such a change could also alter many of my findings.

REFERENCES

Bartels, Larry. 1985. "Expectations and Preferences in Presidential Nominating Campaigns." *American Political Science Review* 79:804–15.

Bryce, James. 1891. *The American Commonwealth*. Vol. 2, 2d ed. New York: Macmillan.

Campbell, Angus. 1960. "Surge and Decline: The Study of Electoral Change." *Public Opinion Quarterly* 24:397–418.

Campbell, Angus, Philip Converse, Warren Miller, and Donald Stokes. 1960. *The American Voter*. New York: Wiley.

Ceasar, James W. 1979. *Presidential Selection: Theory and Development*. Princeton: Princeton U. Press.

———. 1982. *Reforming the Reforms*. Cambridge, Mass.: Ballinger.

Crotty, William, and John S. Jackson III. 1985. *Presidential Primaries and Nominations*. Washington, D.C.: Congressional Quarterly Press.

DeNardo James. 1986. "The Architecture of Partisan Electorates." Photocopy, U. of California at Los Angeles.

DiNitto, Andrew, and William Smithers. 1972. "The Representativeness of the Direct Primary: A Further Test of V. O. Key's Thesis." *Polity* 4:209–24.

Keeter, Scott, and Cliff Zukin. 1983. *Uninformed Choice*. New York: Praegar.

Key, V. O. 1956. *American State Politics: An Introduction*. New York: Knopf.
———. 1964. *Politics, Parties, and Pressure Groups*. 5th ed. New York: Cromwell.
Kritzer, Herbert. 1977. The Representativeness of the 1972 Presidential Primaries." *Polity* 10:121–29.
Lengle, James. 1981. *Representatives and Presidential Primaries*. Westport, Conn.: Greenwood.
Levy, Mark R. 1983. "The Methodology and Performance of Election Day Polls." *Public Opinion Quarterly* 47:54–67.
Marshall, Thomas. 1981. *Presidential Nominations in a Reform Age*. New York: Praeger.
McGovern, George, and Donald Fraser. 1970. Commission on Party Structure and Delegate Selection. *Mandate for Reform*. Washington, D.C.: Democratic National Committee.
Moore, David, and Richard C. Hofstetter. 1973. "The Representativeness of Primary Elections: Ohio." *Polity* 6:197–212.
Ostrogorski, M. 1921. *Democracy and the Party System*. New York: Macmillan.
Patterson, Thomas E. 1980. *The Mass Media Election*. New York: Praeger.
Polsby, Nelson. 1983. *Consequences of Party Reform*. Cambridge: Oxford U. Press.
Price, David. 1983. *Bringing Back the Parties*. Washington, D.C.: Congressional Quarterly Press.
Ranney, Austin. 1968. Representativeness of Primary Electorates. *Midwest Journal of Political Science* 12:224–38.
———. 1972. "Turnout and Representation in American Presidential Elections." *American Political Science Review* 66:21–37.
———. 1975. *Curing the Mischiefs of Faction: Party Reform in America*. Berkeley: U. of California Press.
Ranney, Austin, and Leon Epstein. 1966. The Two Electorates: Voters and Non-voters in a Wisconsin Primary." *Journal of Politics* 28:598–616.
Rubin, Richard. 1980. "Presidential Primaries: Continuities, Dimensions of Change, and Political Implications." In William Crotty, ed., *The Party Symbol*. San Francisco: Freeman.
Sait, Edward M. 1927. *American Parties and Elections*. New York: Century.
Verba, Sidney, and Norman H. Nie. 1972. *Participation in America: Political Democracy and Social Equality*. New York: Harper and Row.
Winograd, Morley. 1978. "Commission on Presidential Nomination and Party Structure." *Openness, Participation, and Party Building: Reforms for a Stronger Democratic Party*. Washington, D.C.: Democratic National Committee.

THE POLITICAL CULTURE OF THE DEMOCRATIC AND REPUBLICAN PARTIES

Jo Freeman

Although political parties have been a pervasive part of American politics, studies of their internal organization and style have not received a great deal of attention. Some commentators have noted that "despite their deceptively similar governing forms" the two major parties are "distinctively separate entities,"[1] and others have observed that "the two parties are different not only in name, program, and coalitional components but also in type," yet no one has attempted any systematic comparison.[2] It is the contention of this article that despite the similarities in governing forms, and even policy outcomes, there is nonetheless a fundamental difference between the national Democratic and Republican parties. That difference can be seen not so much in outcomes, which must pass through the filter of political reality, as in the mode by which internal politics is conducted. The difference is not one of purpose, but of political culture.

I am relying on the definition of political culture in the *International Encyclopedia of the Social Sciences:*

> ...the set of attitudes, beliefs and sentiments which give order and meaning to a political process and which provide the underlying assumptions and rules that govern behavior in the political system. It encompasses both the political ideals and operating norms of a polity. Political culture is thus the manifestation in aggregate form of the psychological and subjective dimensions of politics. A political culture is the product of both the collective history of a political system and the life histories of the members of the system and thus it is rooted equally in public events and private experience.[3]

This is a study of national party elites in the party system created by the New Deal realignment.[4] The subjects include holders of public and party office and activists in national party affairs (party and presidential campaign staff, delegates to national conventions). The data for this article derive primarily from interviews with these officials and activists, from observations made by me at the 1976, 1980, and 1984 national conventions of the Republican party, and at every national nominating convention of the Democratic party since 1964. I also briefly attended the 1960 Democratic and 1964 Republican national conventions. In addition, I conducted numerous interviews with insightful participants in both parties on the national level in the fall of 1984 and read newspaper accounts, party platforms, speeches, and other key documents.

Both parties are currently undergoing major transformations, which are strengthening their national organizations in different ways. These transformations have been molded, but not caused, by the fundamental characteristics of each party's distinctive culture and do not represent a change in the culture itself.[5] While the parties may also be undergoing a change in their electoral base,[6] it is well established in the literature that party elites and party masses (the voters) do not always think alike. Therefore, no attempt is made to ground the description of each party's culture in their electorates. However, if the ideas posited in this article have explanatory value, they should be generally applicable to the state parties; reference will be made to them where appropriate.

There are two fundamental differences between the parties in which all others are rooted. The first one is structural: in the Democratic party power flows upward and in the Republican party power flows downward. The second is attitudinal: Republicans perceive themselves as insiders even when they are out of power, and Democrats perceive themselves as outsiders even when they are in power.

PARTY STRUCTURE AND THE FLOW OF POWER

In Ronald Reagan's acceptance speech at the 1984 Republican convention he declared that the Democrats' "government sees people only as members of groups. Ours serves all the people of America as individuals." Although this characterization was intended as a stinging criticism of the Democrats, and they would decry it as inaccurate, it does capture an essential difference between the two parties (though not necessarily their governments). Essentially, the Democratic party is pluralistic and polycentric. It has multiple power centers that compete for membership support in order to make demands on, as well as determine, the leaders. The Republicans have a unitary party in which great deference is paid to the leadership, activists are expected to be "good soldiers," and competing loyalties are frowned upon. These differences are a direct consequence of the different direction in the flow of power. In a collectivity in which power flows downward, separate and distinct internal groups are potentially dangerous; they provide loci for the development of competing loyalties and competing leadership. But when power flows upward, it must do so through some mechanism. Unorganized individuals without institutional authority or financial resources cannot exercise power. They must organize into groups in order to develop an agenda and act collectively in order to effect that agenda. Organization is the creator of collective power; it is the means by which followers influence leaders.

The post New Deal Democratic party has long been viewed as composed of constituencies. But while the party's distinct components could be identified in the electorate, they were not directly represented in the national organization. Organizationally the Democratic party was a collection of state and local organizations, with only organized labor, through the AFL-CIO's Committee on Political Education, having direct influence on the very weak national party. Insofar as the interests of the different constituency groups were represented it was through the state and local party organizations, by whatever means and to the extent that those organizations permitted. Thus while Democratic party leaders were often assumed to put together slates of candidates with an eye to group representation, major voting blocks would often be ignored. For example Mayor Richard Daley's Chicago machine was regularly observed to slate persons identified as Irish, Polish, and Jewish for each of the top city offices, but never a black though blacks significantly increased their importance in the electorate during the Daley era. In effect the organizational components of the national party were geographic, even though the electoral constituencies were identified by religion and ethnicity as well as region.

The transformation of the Democratic party during the last twenty years has not changed its basic nature as a coalitional, pluralistic party.[7] But the nature of the coalition and the manner in which the party's constituency groups make their concerns felt is changing. As the national party has strengthened itself, groups that were previously unorganized or whose organizations could not make their influence felt on state and local parties have sought to directly influence the national organization. Some of these groups are also demanding representation on the local level, but their success has not been as noticeable as it has on the national level.

These new constituencies are ones who identify themselves as having a salient characteristic, creating a common agenda that they feel the party must respond to. Virtually all of these groups exist in organized form independent of the party and seek to act on the elected officials of both parties. They are recognized by Democratic party officials as representing the interest of important blocks of voters, which the party must respond to as a party. Some groups have been recognized parts of the Democratic electoral coalition since the New Deal (blacks and labor); others are relatively new (women and gays). Still others who participated in state and local Democratic politics when those were the only significant party units have not been active as organized groups in the party on the national level (ethnics).

Between 28 May 1982 and 13 July 1983, seven of these constituencies were recognized as official caucuses of the Democratic National Committee (DNC). Five represented demographic groups (women, blacks, hispanics, Asians, and gays) and two ideational ones (liberals and business/professional). In May 1985 the DNC Executive Committee revoked official recognition of these caucuses to deflect attacks on the party as being run by "special interests."[8] The caucuses still exist, but they no longer receive support services from the DNC. Until May 1985 some of them had staff members of the Democratic National Committee identified as their liaisons. In addition, in the last few years an informal understanding has arisen that one of each of the three vice-chairs will be a member of and represent women, blacks, and hispanics. These groups still have their vice-chairs, as well as ex-officio membership on the DNC Executive Committee. The largest and most important constituency—labor—never had a staff liaison, for union leaders feel they should deal directly with the party chair without benefit of an intermediary. Instead, a majority of the twenty-five at-large seats on the DNC, as well as seats on the executive committee and the rules and credentials committees at the conventions, are reserved for union representatives.

Party constituencies generally meet as separate caucuses at the national conventions. While caucuses are usually open to anyone, the people who attend, not all of whom are delegates, are generally those for whom that constituency is a primary reference group—a group with which they identify and which gives them a sense of purpose. Thus it is the most committed or identified constituency members who set the tone of the caucus. Not unexpectedly, most of those attending the women's caucus are committed feminists. Virtually all black delegates attend the black caucus, but not all union members go to the labor caucus. When forced to choose between conflicting meetings of the black and women's caucuses during the 1984 convention, black women went to the former. They also held their own separate caucus for the first time, as did Asians and the handicapped.

Although the leaders of these caucuses are rarely chosen by the participants, they nonetheless feel compelled to have their decisions ratified by them through debate and votes in the caucuses. With an occasional exception the power of group leaders derives from their ability to articulate the interests of constituency members to the party leaders. Ratification is the means by which their right to lead is renewed. The fact that the votes usually go the way the leaders direct and that caucus attendees may not perfectly reflect the interests of the constituency is usually overlooked. But when there is a conflict between claimants to leadership, those who do not have caucus support will dismiss it as unrepresentative.

The Republican party also has relevant components, but they are not as important as the Democratic party's constituent groups, because they are not mechanisms for exercising power and they are not primary reference groups.[9] The basic components of the Republican party are geographic units and ideological factions. Unlike the Democratic groups, these entities exist only as internal party mechanisms. At the quadrennial conventions the geographic units—state and local parties—are primarily channels for mobilizing support and distributing information on what the party leaders want. They are not separate and distinct levels of operation.

Ideological factions are also not power centers independent of their relationship to party leaders. Unlike Democratic caucus leaders, Republican faction leaders do not feel themselves accountable to their followers.[10] Sometimes there are not identifiable followers. Although faction leaders hold press conferences at the national conventions, they rarely have meetings. When they do, they too use them to mobilize support and distribute information, not debate the issues. The purpose of ideological factions—at least those that are organized—is to generate new ideas and test their appeal. The leaders' concept of success is not winning benefits, symbolic or otherwise, for their group, so much as being able to provide overall direction to the party.[11]

The Republican party does have several demographic groups within it, such as the National Federation of Republican Women, the National Black Republican Council, and the Jewish Coalition; but they are auxiliaries, not constituencies. Their purpose is to recruit and organize group members into the Republican party as workers and contributors, not to represent the views of these groups to the party. They carry the party's message outward, not the group's message inward. Democratic constituency group members generally have a primary identification with their group, and only a secondary one with the party. The primary identification of Republican activists is with the Republican party. They view other strong group attachments as disloyal and unnecessary.

CONVENTION ACTIVITIES

The difference in the flow of power can be seen in the operation of the national conventions. When not in session, the time of delegates attending the Democratic convention is largely occupied with caucus meetings. In addition to state caucus meetings, there are caucus meetings for any group that wishes to call one. Generally, the DNC makes space available for these meetings; but occasionally it declines when it feels the group making the request is clearly operating contrary to the interest of an incumbent president. Virtually all of these caucuses are open to whomever cares to attend, including nonmembers. Competing candidates for the presidential nominations acknowledge the importance of the group by speaking to its caucus. Indeed the importance of a particular group within the Democratic party can be ascertained by the number and status of the party leaders who seek to address it.

Republicans do not attend caucuses apart from those of their states. They go to receptions. These receptions are usually by invitation only. Invitations may not always be hard to obtain, but they are required. Receptions are privately sponsored, with each group responsible for getting its own space. There may be some speeches, but they are perfunctory ones and no debate is asked for or expected.

Republican receptions do have one major characteristic in common with Democratic caucuses; they are both places for demonstrating the status of the group and individuals within it. Status at caucuses is conveyed to those individuals invited to sit at the speakers' platform, as well as to the group by those who agree to speak. Status at receptions is conveyed to those introduced or acknowledged by the occasional speaker and to the sponsoring group by the prominent people attending the reception who are not also sponsors.

The kind of interaction between delegates at caucuses is very different from that at receptions. Caucuses have many speeches and frequently have debates. Occasionally votes will be taken, if only to give the "sense of the meeting." Caucus meetings are places for the groups' leadership to listen as well as to speak, though some leaders listen better than others. Discussion is public, and it's quite permissible to be loud and demanding in one's behavior—as long as one doesn't interfere with others' ability to listen to the speaker. Caucuses are supposed to be places where delegates debate, discuss, and decide on the relevant issues before the convention. Thus, even when the outcome of a particular question is forgone or there are no decisions to make, the illusion of participatory decision making is maintained. One exception to this is the labor caucus, which is less frequent and less vocal. Participants come to get their marching orders and find out who their floor leaders are, not to debate issues. Since the leaders of this caucus are established union leaders, their right to lead doesn't need to be ratified.

Despite the occasional speech at Republican receptions, discussion is largely private. Consequently, people usually talk to those they already know and who most likely agree with them. Even when participants of different views encounter each other, the exchange is expected to be very civil in keeping with the rules of polite society. Receptions are not places to exercise group influence. They are places to network, to be seen, and to get information. If one wishes to exercise influence, it is best to arrange an introduction to a recognized leader by a mutual friend.

LEGITIMACY

The different direction in the flow of power also creates different conceptions of legitimacy. In the Democratic party legitimacy is determined by who you represent, and in the Republican party by whom you know and who you are. It is this difference that makes the Democratic party so much more responsive to demands for reform within it and the Republican party so much more responsive to changes in leadership.

Reform within the Democratic party is usually traced to the 1968 Chicago convention, which was marked by external strife and turmoil. Although few delegates and no leaders joined the demonstrators outside, reform Democrats nonetheless used these demonstrations to argue that the nominating system was closed to dissent and unrepresentative of popular opinion. The fact that there were seventeen credentials challenges involving fifteen states, some of which were successful, reinforced their claims.[12] In the decade before the 1968 convention many local Democratic clubs had been taken over by reformers who believed that "management of the affairs of the party ought to be widespread and in accord with strictly democratic procedures."[13] At the 1964 convention the Mississippi Freedom Democratic party (MFDP) had heightened the contradiction between the national party's claim to be the party of civil rights and its traditional deference to state parties in the governance of their affairs by challenging the right of the regular Mississippi party to seat an all-white delegation.[14] Although the resulting compromise pleased no one (two MFDP delegates were seated as at-large delegates and the regulars were required to sign a loyalty oath) it opened Pandora's box. The implicit threat of numerous credentials challenges at future conventions added force to the demands of reformers that the party open up.

Party leaders were sensitive to these demands, because they were quite conscious that the Democratic party is a coalition party and that maintaining and broadening the coalition has been its primary political strategy. Claims that it was unrepresentative of a relevant bloc of voters was a serious challenge to the party's legitimacy. But it was a challenge that could be met only by reforming the structures of representation to an extent that has been characterized as revolutionary.[15] For years party leaders had automatically assumed that geographic representation would sufficiently reflect the interests of its many voting blocs in party affairs. The MFDP undermined this assumption by demonstrating the obvious: a southern state party did not represent southern black Democrats. They made it clear that another means of representation than a strictly geographic one was necessary for all members of the coalition to feel adequately represented. These demands were amplified in 1968 when antiwar protestors, most of them young enough to be drafted, marched in the streets during the convention and the Democratic candidate narrowly lost in November. The party responded to the recommendations that it open up the system and involve more groups in party decision making by agreeing to a reform commission. By the time it made its report women had been added to minorities and youth as publicly vocal demographic groups who felt unrepresented by geographic organization. Thus, a key feature of the reforms was an attempt to impose requirements for demographic representation on the loose geographic structure of the party. However, these changes did not result in a consensus. Consequently, a new reform commission is appointed after every convention.

Legitimacy within the Republican party is dependent on having a personal connection to the leadership. Consequently, supporting the wrong candidate can have disastrous effects on one's ability to influence decisions. Republican presidents exercise a monolithic power over their party that Democratic presidents do not have. With the nomination of Ronald Reagan, many life long Republicans active on the national level who had supported Gerald Ford or George Bush and did not immediately change their views to conform to those of the winner found themselves completely cut off. Others immediately flocked to the Reagan banner, curbing any dissenting views in order to do so. Mavericks, who do not have any personal attachments to identified leaders, may be able to operate as gadflies, but can rarely build an independent power base. Since legitimacy in the Democratic party is based on the existence of just such a power base, real or imagined, one does not lose all of one's influence within the party with a change in leaders as long as one can credibly argue that one represents a legitimate group.

While the importance of personal connections works against those Republicans who have the wrong connections, it rewards those who spend years toiling in the fields for the party and its candidates. The longer one spends in any organization, the more personal connections one has an opportunity to make. These aren't lost when one's party or leaders are out of power, and thus can be "banked" for future use. Occasionally a dedicated party worker can develop sufficient ties, even to competing leaders, to assure continued access, if not always influence, regardless of who's in power. Those Democrats whose legitimacy derives from leadership of a coalition group find it is quite transitory when they can no longer credibly represent the group. The greater willingness of the Republican party to reward loyalty and dedication to the party in preference to any other group makes it easier for the party to discourage extraparty attachments.

The operation of these different forms of legitimacy can readily be seen in the activities of feminists at the 1976 conventions. A group of women including DNC members, prominent feminists, and elected officials met with the Carter campaign to negotiate whether there would be a floor fight on the minority report to the Rules Committee that future conventions should require that half of all delegates be female. These women felt it necessary to call and report to meetings of women delegates (and whatever non-delegates cared to attend) on the progress of the negotiations every day. When they finished, all women attending, including non-delegates, took to the floor to express their own opinions on what should happen. After agreement was reached in the negotiations, the women's caucus leadership asked the participants to vote on the agreement. Since Jimmy Carter packed the meeting with delegates committed to him, the outcome was forseeable, but no one suggested that the process was irrelevant. The daily reports, debate, and ratification were all essential parts of the legitimation process. They gave the largely self-selected leadership of the women's caucus their claim to represent a key constituency.[16]

At the Republican convention, four women with close personal ties to the Ford campaign, but operating as the Republican Women's Task Force (RWTF) of the National Women's Political Caucus, quietly lobbied to keep the Equal Rights Amendment (ERA) in the platform. They called one meeting, the Sunday before the convention, which was poorly attended. There they passed on information on what they intended to do and what kind of volunteer help they could use. There was no debate or discussion, no votes, and no further meetings. Furthermore, they focused strictly on the ERA, leaving abortion to others, because ERA was the only issue Ford supported. They said that reelecting Ford was the single most important thing they could do for women.

The 1980 GOP convention had few former Ford supporters. The women who represented the RWTF had no influence at the convention, which saw the ERA removed from the platform by an overwhelming vote, because they had no access to the Reagan campaign, which had complete control of the proceedings. Mary Louise Smith, former chair of the Republican National Committee (RNC), finally intervened with Reagan on their behalf. She was able to secure a meeting, but no influence, because she too had supported the wrong candidate.[17]

CAREER PATHS

The different structure of the parties has different consequences for the fate of activists. Since the Democratic party is composed of groups, the success of individuals whose group identification is highly salient, such as blacks and women, is tied to that of the group as a whole. They succeed as the group succeeds.

That is not the case within the Republican party. It officially ignores group characteristics, though it is obvious that it does pay attention to them when it feels the need to cater to the interest of the voting public in a particular group. In 1984 women were showcased as they had never been before, though both black and hispanic speakers addressed the convention. Generally, individuals succeed insofar as the leaders with whom they are connected succeed. Another means of getting access is through sponsorship. If persons who are already accepted pass favorably on someone new, it is a lot easier for the latter to obtain recognition than if they must make it on their own. Many of the influential women within the Republican party are related to influential men. These men are their sponsors.

WORLD VIEW

New York Governor Mario Cuomo in his keynote address to the Democratic convention accused the Republican party of having policies that "divide the nation—into the lucky and the left-out, into the royalty and the rabble." Whether the party's policies are divisive is certainly debatable, but Cuomo did articulate a difference in perspective by the parties that shapes their way of dealing with the world. It has been argued that society as a whole has a cultural and structural "center" about which most members of the society are more or less "peripheral."[18] Republicans see themselves as representing the center, while Democrats view society from the periphery.

The Republican center does not include the state, that is, the major organs of the national government. Republicans have always felt a tension between the state and society, and have viewed the former with suspicion even when in power. Since Republicans as individuals control most of the major private institutions, particularly economic ones, a strong central government is seen as a threat to their power. The Democratic periphery feels a strong government is necessary in order to counterbalance private economic domination. Indeed, they feel that the state's primary function *ought* to be a check on private economic power. Nonetheless, Democrats, like typical outsiders, are ambivalent toward the state. Their ambivalence derives not from a suspicion of strength, but from concern that the state will not act as they feel it should. Indeed, until Reagan began to redirect the national government, most Democrats did not appreciate how valuable the federal government was to them or even how thoroughly they had captured its main components.

Although Republicans do not want to increase state power, they nonetheless feel that what they are and their conception of the American dream is inherently desirable. They are insiders who represent the core of American society and are the carriers of its fundamental values. What they have achieved in life, and wish to achieve, is what every true American wishes to achieve. The traditions they represent are what has worked for America, and the policies they pursue are ones that ultimately will be best for everyone. They argue that the Republican party and Republican policies represent the national interest, unlike the Democrats, who only serve the "special interests" that are powerful within it. Their concept of representation is as a trustee who pursues the long-range best interests of the represented.

The Democrats have a very different world view and a different concept of the meaning of representation. To them, representation does not mean the articulation of a single coherent program for the betterment of the nation but the inclusion of all relevant groups and viewpoints. Their concept of representation is delegatory, in which accurate reflection of the parts is necessary to the welfare of the whole. Ironically, this requires a free market view of the political arena as one in which the most collective good comes from maximizing properly represented individual goods. Because there is no common agenda, there is no common conception of a national interest independent of the total interests of the parts. Instead, groups seek to maximize what each gets through bargaining and building coalitions on the assumption that everyone should get something.[19] This expectation lay behind Jesse Jackson's statement to the Black Caucus at the 1984 Democratic convention that blacks had received nothing from the Democrats, unlike women and Southerners, who had.[20] Thus blacks had a legitimate reason to be angry and Democrats should not expect their undivided loyalty without giving them something in return. The Republican attitude is more one of "to the victor go the spoils."

Guided by a more unitary conception of representation as meaning the correct articulation of the national interest, Republicans feel the needs of minorities will be met best by improving the economy. They believe that that which most benefits the whole will most benefit each part. Although the party sometimes does offer discrete programs or benefits to discrete groups, it does so reluctantly and only because it must meet Democratic criticisms that it is ignoring the needs of such groups.[21] Complaints such as Jackson's might be voiced privately, but never publicly. To do so would be disloyal, for it would call into question the universal desirability of the Republican program.

Democrats do not have an integrated conception of a national interest, in part because they do not view themselves as the center of society. The party's components think of themselves as outsiders pounding on the door seeking programs that will facilitate entry into the mainstream.[22] Thus, the party is very responsive to any groups, including such social pariahs as gays and lesbians, that claim to be left out.

Insofar as the Republican idea of a national interest can be summed up in a single phrase, it would be the promotion of "individual success." Insiders generally view their achievements as due to their own merit and efforts rather than to aspects of the social structure or plain luck. Success is its own justification. Thus what's worked for them, or what they acknowledge as having worked for them, should work for everyone. For government to interfere, other than to remove barriers to individual action, is undesirable.

The word that would most aptly characterize what Democrats want is "fairness."[23] This is a common goal of outsiders who do not accept their fate as being caused by their own failures. They are rather skeptical that there is a linear relationship between individual effort, ability, and reward and feel that a major function of government is to make life more fair. Exactly what is fair, however, is rarely debated. Thus, potential conflicts between groups that might have contradictory goals are avoided.

ORGANIZATIONAL STYLE

It has often been noted that Democratic party politics are open, loud, and confrontational, while those of the Republican party are closed, quiet, and consensual. These contrasting characteristics are consequences of the structural and attitudinal differences discussed earlier. They result in different styles of party organization, even though there is a superficial similarity in the formal structure of both parties and they have the same ultimate goal of winning elections.

These contrasting styles were exemplified by a description of the battles over replacing the Massachusetts state party chairs in 1956.

> ...in the Democratic party the affair could best be called a brawl all the way—at least as the press reported it, no doubt with some gleeful exaggeration. Statements and counter-statements to the press, accusations of falsehood mutually tossed back and forth, gave the dispute most of the elements of an Irish donnybrook, minus only the swinging of fists. There were threats of that too. While the Democrats were having their fracas, the heir apparent for the Republican nomination was carrying on a quiet war against the incumbent Republican chairman, but with a very different tone and with very different procedures. A dispatch to the *New York Times* illustrated the differences of approach. It noted that the Democrats had allowed the reporters in to hear their showdown on replacing their chairman; it then went on to describe the Republican methods: "Following a brief exchange of statements in the newspapers, a characteristic hush fell over the Republican headquarters. It has been the experience of political reporters in Massachusetts for years that the Republicans promote publicity, and hire press agents to carry out the program so long as it is favorable. Anything unfavorable is carefully thrashed out behind closed doors of private social and dining clubs. The participants then walk out smiling at each other, each trying to ignore political knife handles protruding from their backs. So it was Tuesday night....Reporters were barred from the meeting until after the balloting was finished. They were admitted in time to hear [the defeated chairman] make his valedictory."[24]

The Republican party sees itself as an organic whole whose parts are interdependent. Republican activists are expected to be good soldiers who respect leadership and whose only important political commitment is to the Republican party. Since direction comes from the top, the manner by which one effects policy is by quietly building a consensus among key individuals, and then pleading one's case to the leadership as furthering the basic values of the party. Maneuvering is acceptable. Challenging is not. This approach acknowledges the leadership's right to make final decisions and reassures them that those preferring different policies do not have competing allegiances. On the other hand, open challenges or admissions of fundamental disagreements indicate that one might be too independent to be a reliable soldier who will always put the interests of the party first. This cuts off access to the leadership and thus is quite risky—unless the leadership changes to people more amenable to the challengers. While not risky like an open challenge, quietly building an internal consensus is nonetheless costly of one's political resources. Activists learn early to conserve their resources by only contesting issues of great importance to them.

Liberals in the Republican Party (former supporters of Nelson Rockefeller and William Scranton), who have repeatedly challenged the Reagan administration, have been virtually read out of the party. On the right, Representative Newt Gingrich's (Ga.) attack on David Stockman for betraying the supply side "revolution" (not a Republican word) incurred very angry responses from the Republican leadership, who dismissed his arguments as "ego-gratification."[25] However, Gingrich has been more successful at being listened to than the liberals, who no longer even use the word "liberal," having retreated to "moderate" after Reagan came to power. His success and that of other vocal challengers from the right is based on their ability to demonstrate a public following. If Gingrich can translate this following into winning campaigns, whether for himself or people who support him, he will continue to be listened to and eventually join the leadership. If not, he not only won't join the leadership, he won't even have access to it. Reagan was not accepted by the Republican establishment until his electoral successes gave them no choice.

Liberal Republicans have largely failed to demonstrate a following and thus have lost power as their leaders have ceased to occupy major roles within the party. They argue that the "yuppies" who voted for Gary Hart ought to look favorably upon Republicans like them who have liberal social agendas and conservative economic policies.[26] Unfortunately, as demonstrated by the Ripon Society and more recently the Mainstream Republican Committee, they know how to talk but don't know how to organize. Thus their potential following is not really aware that they exist. Apart from the unlikely event of a spontaneous public uprising in their favor, their position within the party will continue to atrophy as individuals learn that the price of access to conservative leadership is keeping quiet.

In the Democratic party, keeping quiet is the cause of atrophy and speaking out is a means of access. As the type and importance of powerful groups within it has changed over time, there has been a great deal of conflict. Former participants resist declining influence (for example, the South, Chicago's Mayor Richard Daley) while newer ones jockey for position (women and blacks). Successfully picking fights is the primary way by which groups acquire clout within the party.

Since the purpose of most of the conflict is to achieve acceptance and eventually power, it does not matter whether the issues that are fought over are substantive or only symbolic. In the 1950s and 1960s these fights were usually over credentials as southern delegations were challenged because of their refusal to declare their loyalty to the national ticket and their inadequate representation of blacks. In the 1970s and 1980s, the fights have usually been over platform planks, but some have concerned rules changes or designations of status. In 1976 women's groups fought over the equal-division rule to require that half of all delegates be women. Although they lost, they had to find another issue in 1980 because the DNC decided to adopt "50–50" in 1978. That year they focused on minority planks on abortion and denying party support to opponents of the ERA. In 1984 the issue would have been a woman vice presidential candidate, but this was preempted by Walter Mondale's selection of Geraldine Ferraro as his running mate, so there was nothing to fight over.

Jesse Jackson's entire campaign was a way for a new generation of black leaders to establish clout both within the party and within the black community. The means by which blacks have exercised power in the party has been less through organizations than through elected officials and their individual followings. As there is no internal mechanism for selecting leaders among the many contenders, those blacks who have exercised power within the party have usually been those whom white party leaders chose to listen to. Jackson's candidacy challenged both the current black political leadership and the right of whites to decide which blacks were legitimate leaders. By showing that black voters would unite behind his candidacy in the primaries, Jackson established his legitimacy as a national black spokesperson independent of white approval. This gave him a claim to dictate the black agenda in the party, even though he had not previously been a party activist, and there were many competent black leaders within the party who were not supportive of this upstart.

Because Jackson represented a generational split within the black community, his demands for recognition presented the Mondale campaign with problems not presented by feminists. Among feminists, elected officials and organizational leaders were united on wanting a woman vice presidential candidate and even agreed on a particular individual. Since blacks were not united, any recognition of Jackson and his followers threatened the position of established black elected officials to speak for the black community. If Jackson had subsequently refused to campaign for Mondale, his legitimacy as a *party* leader, though not as a *black* leader, would have been seriously undermined. Since he chose to play by the rules, he's still a contender.

Fights do not have to be won in order for those picking them to be successful. They are opportunities for demonstrating political skills and establishing territory. Feminist leaders didn't win the equal division fight in 1976, and everyone knew that had it gone to a floor vote, they would have lost. What they won was recognition. The Carter campaign negotiated with them, because they showed that there were a substantial number of women willing and able to fight on the issue. This established the right of women to be recognized as an important group within the party. However, Carter refused to negotiate with feminists in 1980, largely because he perceived them as surrogates for his rival, Ted Kennedy, and not important in and of themselves. This was changed by their success in getting the convention to adopt two minority planks that the Carter administration opposed. By showing that they were both politically skilled and persistent, feminists successfully claimed the right to represent women within the party.

The Jackson campaign did for a new generation of black leaders what the equal-division fight did for feminists. They are now recognized as contenders, but are not yet players. Many party leaders, both black and white, still hope they will go away. Thus Jackson and his followers cannot take any concessions for granted. It will be necessary to organize for 1988 in order to demonstrate continuity.

The open confrontations that occur in the Democratic party do not take place within the Republican party, because it is a very different kind of organization. If one were to place the many different forms of collectivities on a spectrum, the Democratic and Republican parties would not occupy the same point. At one end would be groups exhibiting a great deal of spontaneity that are easy to join and have minimal structure, such as fads and crowds. At the other would be formal organizations that have well developed divisions of labor, hierarchical layers of authority, are selective in their membership, and are relatively impervious to spontaneous impulses, such as corporations or at the extreme end, military bodies. In the middle are most social movements, which, however diverse they may be, exhibit both noticeable spontaneity and a describable structure. Parties and campaigns lie on the more organized end of the spectrum, but because they must mobilize voters, raise money from contributors rather than by selling a product, and recruit volunteers to accomplish their goals, they exhibit many properties of social movements.

Republican party organizations have more characteristics of the corporate style and fewer typical of social movements than do Democratic party organizations. This has been a continuing attribute; the semi-organized chaos seen in the Democratic party today is not a consequence of contemporary reforms. Cornelius P. Cotter and Bernard C. Hennessy wrote in their book on the national party committees in the early 1960s that the

> ...Democrats are relatively undisturbed by—and often seem to thrive
> on—the *ad hoc*ness of politics. Republicans embrace order; they try to im-
> press it on the anarchy of politics. Democrats resist order or accept it only
> as a last resort. This difference may be, in part, no more than the prodi-
> gality of the majority party willing and able to waste some of its margin,
> and the frugality of the minority party aware that organization may com-
> pensate for numbers. Or it may be, as some have suggested, a psychologi-
> cal and temperamental difference between those who are attracted to one
> party and those attracted to the other.[27]

Evidence that minority status is not the cause is given by Duane
Lockard's description of the Massachusetts parties in the late 1950s,
when the Republican party was dominant in that state. He wrote that the
parties responded very differently to challenges by ethnics to advance
within them.

> The Republicans lay down the line in the pre-primary convention to as-
> sert some control over those who would disrupt the party organization in
> a primary. In the Democratic party the non-Irish, non-Boston candidate
> comes to the fore by using the free-for-all tactics of the primary; in the Re-
> publican party the leadership arranges to put some ethnic representative
> on the ticket.[28]

Data to test the psychological theory are not available. A simpler explanation is found by looking at the different resources of the parties.
Like corporations, or well-established interest groups, Republican party
organizations rely heavily on money and professional expertise. Like social movements and volunteer organizations, Democratic party organizations rely more on donations of time and commitment.[29] The RNC has
had a larger staff for decades, while the DNC has always relied heavily
on volunteers to fulfill its functions.[30] One function of the Democrats'
constituency groups, especially organized labor, is to recruit volunteers
for local campaigns.

This resource analysis was used by James Q. Wilson to explain some
of the differences he found between amateur Democratic and Republican
clubs in the 1950s. He found that Democratic clubs were mass based and
stressed intraparty democracy and participation, while Republican
groups were "leadership-oriented organizations." While he found some
explanation for this in the different political philosophies and profes-
sions of the typical Republican and Democratic amateur activist, he also
noted that

> the chief resource the conservative brings to civic—or to political—action
> is economic: money, corporate power, and the personal contacts flowing
> from business position. The liberal, lacking money, brings numbers and

personal contributions of time and effort. The conservative organization, to the extent that it is successful in mobilizing money and prestige, incapacitates itself for direct political action insofar as the people it recruits are successful in business or their careers; personal success leaves them little time for or interest in personal participation. The contributors are at a point where political action can offer little in status or recognition— indeed some action is more likely to be considered harmful. This lack of personal involvement may produce an indifference to organizational forms and procedures and an emphasis on organizational goals. To say the same thing another way, whatever incentives a conservative club can offer will derive from its stated goals; direct participation itself is not an important reward to the member, and internal democracy is therefore not of crucial significance to him.[31]

Nationally the Republican party supports its larger permanent staff and its numerous services for candidates by raising and spending several times the amount of money that the Democrats do. The attitude toward money raising of the 1950s and 1960s is still true today. The Republican party approaches "the problem of national party financing with businesslike matter-of-factness. . . . The Democratic national finance machinery is decentralized, with each committee doing what it damned well pleases. . . . In general, money-raising procedures at the Democratic National Committee remain informal and largely oral."[32]

The greater financial resources of the Republican party are somewhat illusory, though their greater centralization is not. The party organizations outspend their Democratic rivals, but Democratic candidates often have more money than Republican ones. The evidence is that Democrats are more likely to donate money to candidates than to the party, which may partially explain why the national committees of the minority party have so many more contributors than the majority party, as well as more money to spend.[33] This also appears to be true on the state level. Lockard's data on Massachusetts in the early-1950s showed that not only did the Republican party raise and spend more money, but it was spent by the state committee; Democratic money was raised and spent by the candidate organizations. Even non-campaign money was raised centrally and passed down to the town committees for local use. Democratic money was raised locally and spent locally.[34]

The nature of the Democratic resource base requires it to devote more time and energy to organizational maintenance—keeping the troops satisfied. Thus it has less available for external programs. This places a greater burden on the staff of the Democratic National Committee compared to the RNC. Senior staff of both, especially the chairs, must be good managers, but DNC officials in addition bear responsibility for creating and keeping a consensus among the party's many constituencies.

This pattern is not necessarily repeated on the local level where party organizations are much more diverse. Indeed of all party organizations, past and present, few have been more hierarchical, exclusive, and hostile to spontaneity than the big city Democratic machines. However, these machines relied on patronage, not volunteers. Where state civil service acts undermined the material basis of their power, they became vulnerable to challenge by reformist volunteers whose political commitment was greater than theirs.

Even where staff and money are plentiful, many party functions are accessible to or require volunteers, and groups that can mobilize volunteers can be very influential. These groups are often dedicated to specific causes, and like social movements, they rely on the time and commitment of their members to attain their goals. In particular the delegate selection processes of both parties are vulnerable to adherents of specific causes (sometimes called special interests), who can engage in intensive short-term efforts. This is especially true in caucus states, because so few people are willing to attend and participate for the hours or even days necessary to elect delegates. However, even in primary states the voters usually only determine how many delegates a given candidate will get. Other mechanisms determine who these delegates are. Ideological groups whose members see being a delegate as a way to pursue their issue concerns can frequently have an impact far greater than their proportion of the voters would warrant. Observers of the last three Republican conventions have noted that the delegates were disproportionately to the right of typical Republican activists. As one disgruntled Ford supporter explained his near loss at the 1976 Convention, "They're willing to get up at 6:00 A.M. and go to caucus meetings and we're not."

Groups operating on the social-movement model can also be very effective in campaigns, at least those for which heavy media attention is not key. If group members are geographically concentrated and willing to contribute large amounts of time and energy to a particular campaign, they can be very important to its success and consequently very influential. Right-wing organizations have found this approach more appealing than those on the left, who are usually either poorly organized on the local level or disdainful of electoral politics. An exception to this are gay Democratic clubs, which have used heavy campaign activity to win support from many public officials who might not otherwise favor their cause.

The Democrats are trying to strengthen the financial base of the national party though they remain behind the Republicans.[35] But even if the party were to have the same financial resources it would still be a very different party with a different organizational style. Any organization that is polycentric, pluralistic, and in which power flows upward will require greater attention to internal matters and be more contentious than one which is hierarchical, unitary and in which power flows downward. The latter will be able to use more of its resources for attaining its goals and direct them more efficiently.

Nonetheless, it does not follow that the Democratic style lacks any advantages over that of the Republicans. In the short run it appears disruptive, but in the long run it is more stable. Once a consensus develops about the desirability of a particular course of action, whether it be programmatic or procedural, it is accepted as right and proper and is not easily thwarted by party leaders, even when one of them is the president. Except for its core values, the Republican party is more likely to change directions when it changes leaders. If it were to change directions too drastically, it could undermine both its credibility and its programs. Thus the contest for the 1988 Republican nomination for president may send reverberations throughout the party, while that for the Democratic nomination will reflect in part what has happened in the party.

DISSENT AND DISLOYALTY

One of the most common observations of the Democratic party is how much more fractious it is than the Republican party. Although there are bounds on dissent, one can say things about the Democratic party leaders and candidates, publicly, that in the Republican party would be deemed disloyal. Only the Republican party has an eleventh commandment—thou shalt not criticize a fellow Republican. Thus during the 1984 conventions, such Republican adversaries as liberal Senator Lowell Weicker (Conn.) and conservative Representative Trent Lott (Miss.) curbed their criticism of each other in public while leading figures in the Democratic party, whose mutual disagreements were comparatively minor, let their complaints be constantly quoted in the press. Republicans do fight, sometimes viciously, but by and large their fights are not public, and even in private take place on more limited terrain. When they do occur, the ill feelings they create last a lot longer. Democratic sparring partners are more willing to kiss and make up.

The difference in the bounds of dissent can be seen in the different ways the parties have treated those who had fundamental disagreements with their party's presidential candidates. In 1980 the National Organization for Women (NOW) voted not to endorse Jimmy Carter and at the convention led a floor fight for a minority plank strongly disliked by the candidate. Despite this opposition in an election year and the fact that no one thought NOW would possibly defect to the Republicans, NOW President Ellie Smeal was invited to meet with President Carter that fall and was subsequently (after Carter's defeat) hired as a consultant to the DNC. Indeed, refusal to toe the line and leadership of a successful floor fight strengthened NOW within the party because it had demonstrated clout.

In the Republican party many, though certainly not all, prominent Ford supporters, found themselves eased out after Reagan was elected, including ones who professed loyalty to the President but disagreed with some aspects of his program. Feminists who criticized Reagan for his opposition to the ERA have been virtually read out of the Republican party. Although George Bush was selected to be Reagan's running mate despite many well known disagreements, it was a practical decision that was not completely accepted by Reagan's own supporters. The opposition to Bush was much greater and runs much deeper than that of Democrats to Lyndon B. Johnson as John F. Kennedy's running mate or to Hubert Humphrey as Johnson's. Even after several years of total subservience to Reagan policies, Bush is still viewed with great suspicion by hard-core Reaganites.

This exclusionary attitude is not restricted to the Reagan administration. After Barry Goldwater's devastating defeat in 1964, he and his supporters were ostracized to the point that Goldwater was no longer wanted as a speaker in even conservative areas and his former staff members could not get jobs with any Republican officials.[36] In contrast, although George McGovern's supporters were blamed for the Democrats' 1972 loss, and there was some retrenchment in the delegate selection rules that made his nomination possible, they were not cut out. Several got jobs in the Carter administration, though no one thought of Carter as an heir to McGovern's policies or people.

Another illustration is the attitude toward delegates in 1984 who voted for someone other than the expected victors for president and vice president. The delegate who refused to vote for Reagan and the two who refused to vote for Bush were treated by their own delegations as apostates, even though there was no crisis mandating a loyalty test. Illinois delegate Susan Catania, a former state senator, was asked by liberal Governor Jim Thompson to give up her vote to an alternate rather than vote an abstention in the nomination tally. In contrast, the Democrats don't expect all their delegates to vote for the expected winner, as long as it doesn't deprive the candidate of a first ballot victory. Even Jesse Jackson's appeal to his supporters to deny Mondale a first ballot victory was tolerated, if not appreciated. Nor is the vice presidential vote the loyalty test it is for the Republicans; rather it is an opportunity for delegates to express themselves. At the 1972 Democratic convention over seventy people, six of whom were formally nominated, received vice presidential votes (including three for Mao Zedong).[37]

The extensive contentiousness of the Democrats can be traced to their different structure. Coalitions are inevitably more conflict-ridden than unitary organizations, because group leaders are accountable to their members as much or even more than to the coalition. Furthermore, the more people who can legitimately claim consideration of their views, the more legitimate viewpoints there are. This in turn legitimates expression of different views, even by participants who are not powerful enough to merit consideration on their own. This situation is exacerbated for the Democrats, because they tend to value change and experimentation in and of themselves. Thus each new idea has to be discussed and fought out on every level and in every power center of the party until a consensus is finally achieved. As a party more enamored of tradition then change, the Republican party would have fewer issues to fight over even if it had as many places in which to fight them.

The self-perception of the Democrats' constituency groups as perennial outsiders adds another twist. Winners are expected to concern themselves with the welfare of the losers. Republicans have more of a winner-take-all attitude. If you support the wrong candidate, you have no claim on the spoils. Access to the leaders, appointments, or other indicia of inclusion are commodities whose value is increased through scarcity. The Democrats view access as much more of a right to which everyone, including the losers, are entitled. Leaders should represent and listen to all the people in the party, not just those who supported them.

This attitude makes it more difficult for Democratic party leaders to punish those who disagree. Since coalitions generally involve shifting alliances, the relatively powerless may combine with others to become relatively powerful at some future date. Thus it is unwise to completely shut anyone off, or out. Even party leaders who would like to ignore those whose opinions they find obnoxious rarely find it worthwhile to do so. Since legitimate power flows upward, personal connections with and access to the leadership don't have the same value they have in the Republican party. Severing access doesn't so much punish dissidents as it portrays the leaders who do so as unwilling to listen. Those subunits of the Democratic party that have had bosses like the Chicago Democratic party under Mayor Daley have not been noted for their tolerant attitude toward dissidents. Local Democratic party leaders who are powerful enough to command obedience, generally do so.

Another consequence of the coalition structure is that multiple loyalties are normal. While many Democrats are party people first and foremost, many others are not. The idea that one should juggle competing loyalties is unexceptional, as is the possibility that one might seek to re-solve conflicting agendas by getting the party to adopt the positions of nonparty groups. The Republican party frowns on multiple loyalties. In-deed it looks with great suspicion on anyone susceptible to conflicting agendas as potentially disloyal. A major reason Republican feminists have had so much more trouble rehabilitating themselves into the Reagan party than others who did not initially support him is because they are assumed to have a major or even primary loyalty to feminism and feminist organizations. Even in 1976, when Republican feminists were aligned with party leaders, one organizer commented that because the GOP is not "an interest group party...the RWTF is viewed with skepticism. Party regulars have a hard time adjusting to the presence of an organized interest."[38] The current leadership views feminist organiza-tions as Democratic party front groups. Thus it is virtually impossible to be both an accepted Republican activist and an outspoken supporter of feminist goals. Since the party discourages people from identifying themselves as members of a group with a group agenda, it minimizes the possibility of multiple loyalties. But should the Republicans succeed in recruiting substantial numbers of potential party activists from other groups that do have specific agendas (for example, Jews), both will expe-rience some discomfort.

The party's emphasis on being a team player does not mean that there can be no debate. When the party is out of power, different factions or different candidates with different visions to sell will back their vi-sions vigorously. Even when it is in power, not all issues are decided by the president and his staff. But he and other party leaders have the power to decide them if he chooses. This has been clearly evident in the three Congresses with which Reagan has dealt, even though legislators are not as compliant in their public official roles as they are in their party roles. Not all issues have required party line votes. But on those for which Reagan has asked for support, it has been remarkably uniform. In December 1985 Reagan initially lost the vote on his tax reform bill due to Republican defections,[39] but he was able to turn that around within one week. Minority whip Trent Lott (R.-Miss.), a critic of tax reform, apolo-gized with tears in his eyes. "Mr. President," he said emotionally, "I wouldn't hurt you."[40]

Conversely, room for disagreement in the Democratic party is not unlimited. Indeed, there are certain issues and attitudes that constitute a party line. These protected issues are ones that are important to power-ful groups within the party. Once a group has been accepted as a legiti-mate player, it acquires a certain amount of sovereignty over a policy territory and can usually designate those issues and positions within it that are to be part of the party line. If there is disagreement within a group, or there is no recognized group representing a particular issue, a subject can be debated within the party. But otherwise a recognized group has sovereignty over issues within its territory.

This does not give a group sovereignty over issues outside its territory. For example, women's organizations would not be able to dictate the party's position on the nuclear freeze; establishing a party line on this issue would require a consensus of all concerned groups. Sometimes there are disputes between groups over territory. Disagreements between blacks and Jews over the party's positions on affirmative action and the Mideast are in this category. The argument is as much over which group has the right to determine party policy on these issues as it is over what that policy should be.

COHESION AND COMMITMENT

Since dissent does exist in both parties, albeit to a different extent, there must also be some glue to hold them together. Obviously one source of cohesion is the desire to win, but this by itself is not sufficient to hold either party together between campaigns or after divisive primaries. Although the desire to win is mutual, the primary sources of cohesion are peculiar to each party.

Different factions of the Republican party are held together by their common ideology, but this is not what holds the party as a whole together. The fact that the party is not ideologically homogenous is a potential source of fragmentation. Instead the party is held together by social homogeneity.[41] Party activists share membership in common social strata, with common rules of behavior and a common definition of who is acceptable. These rules of behavior or acceptability create an informal language and style that is hard for outsiders to learn and thus operates as a barrier to their assimilation. Some aspects of this homogeneity are easily visible. A crowd of traditional Republicans can be identified by their common dress and their unspoken understanding that someone who dresses differently is not one of them. A crowd of Democrats cannot be identified by a common appearance; indeed they are so diverse that a few Republicans in their midst would not even be noticed.[42]

While Republicans have much in common, their style and the rules of social acceptability vary somewhat by geography. An "Eastern Establishment" Republican is not the same as a "Midwestern Mainstreet" or

"Western conservative" Republican. Thus an active Republican in one part of the country who relocates can have trouble being accepted as an active Republican in another, as illustrated by George Bush's constant battle to be viewed as a Texan rather than a scion of Connecticut.

Similarly, entire groups seeking to become Republican activists who do not share the common style find acceptance difficult because their presence threatens the social homogeneity that holds the party together. A frequent reaction by traditional Republicans to the New Right supporters of Reagan is to assert that they are "not real Republicans" and thus do not deserve to exercise power within the party. This claim was first made at the 1976 convention. When Reagan delegates dominated the 1980 convention it was muted, but still there. Reagan's political success curbed the expression of this sentiment, but not its existence. The 1984 convention saw many traditional Republicans present as Reagan delegates, but in eight years their opinion of the newcomers there with them had not really changed. One reporter described the women delegates as coming "in two main flavors: Ultrasuede and polyester."

> The Ultrasuedes...look down on the polyesters....Some Ultrasuedes are feeling outnumbered by the polyesters this year as though their party has been taken over by people they would never allow to join the country club. Not the right sort....As though someone had let some tacky girls into a Kappa chapter.
>
> I guess it is a simple class distinction, but along with having more money, the Ultrasuedes tend to be more sophisticated and also more liberal on social issues than the polyesters. They are frankly embarrassed, if not mortified, by the party's Jerry Falwell connection, but only in a social sense.[43]

Democrats would not seriously accuse someone of not being a real Democrat, because a Democrat is anyone who claims to be one. Mondale tried it during the 1984 primary in an attack on Hart, but reaction to this charge was so negative it was quickly dropped. As a party with neither a common ideology nor a common social base, there is no real basis for erecting standards. Indeed, an essential characteristic of the Democratic party is its heterogeneity.

The greater sense of boundaries that Republicans have, of knowing who's acceptable and who's not, serves an important social function. It facilitates trust. People normally trust those who are like them to think like them and do what they would do. People understand others who are like themselves. Organizations or communities whose members trust each other function more smoothly and take direction more willingly than those where trust is more limited. Republicans trust their party and their leaders to do what they think is right more than Democrats do, because they are socially homogenous.

Heterogeneity facilitates misunderstanding. People with different backgrounds, different values, different styles, and different modes of expression interpret the world differently and often misinterpret each other. A great deal of communication, clarification, and reassurance is necessary to maintain working relationships among diverse allies. In a highly heterogeneous organization people with one group identity are reluctant to trust those with another to act as their leaders or adequately represent their interests. Instead they demand consultation, representation, and participation. The heterogenous nature of the Democratic party requires that time and energy be devoted to intraparty relationships and that identifiable groups feel they have as much say as they want.

The glue that holds the Democratic party together is pluralism. The fundamental principles of pluralist theory were spelled out by James Madison in *Federalist No. 10*. He argued that a large and diverse republic would best check majority passions and "factious combinations." Although Madison was more concerned with curbing power than with creating unity, diversity is the secret to cohesion under certain conditions. These conditions occur when individuals are members of many groups, no combination of which encompasses all of their members' primary interests. When there are many cross-cutting memberships, each of which have a claim on individual loyalties, the urge to put one issue or group ahead of all others at any cost is restrained. Face-to-face discussions and the need to ally with different people in one group or on one issue tempers the tendency to view people as "enemies" because there is disagreement.

The caucus structure of the Democratic party facilitates pluralism. A delegate to the conventions will attend numerous state caucuses, candidate caucuses, and often one or more group caucuses. The three biennial miniconventions increased the opportunities for these kinds of contacts.[44] The opportunity to both listen to and talk with different people from different parts of the country, who are members of different groups, increases awareness and understanding of diverse positions. The need to work with other people to achieve common goals increases receptivity to their particular concerns. Some political commentators have often marveled that a party so fractious, heterogeneous, and seemingly disorganized can remain intact. As long as a particular group does not become insular, with its members having no participation in or concern for other caucuses, the diversity of the Democratic party is its strength, not its weakness.

DOES DIFFERENCE MAKE ANY DIFFERENCE?

This article has argued that there are significant differences in the political culture of the major political parties—differences that manifest themselves in different organizations, styles, attitudes, and approaches. These differences have been commented on only in passing by students of political parties. Instead, the literature has viewed the parties as possessing the common goal of putting together a winning coalition by being "all things to all people."[45] There has been an implicit assumption, untested by field studies, that this common goal requires similar political strategies by similar political organizations. Although it has never been explicitly stated, the model behind this assumption appears to be the Democratic party, because the descriptions in the literature of how a political party operates "fit" the Democratic party. Until the Republican party scored significant successes in the 1980 elections, it was assumed to be merely a pale imitation of the majority party, striving unsuccessfully to put together a winning coalition. Since then, there has been a tendency to view the operating style and approaches of the Republican party as "the party of the future."[46]

I would argue that the Republican party is *not* a poor imitation of a normal coalition-building party, but a different type of political organization that does things in different ways. The differences in its political culture have put the Republican party at a disadvantage in its competition with the Democratic party for most of the New Deal era. However, the roads to political success have been changing rather rapidly in the last fifteen years, and the new roads are ones that the Republican party is well equipped to travel. Thus, their strategies are now becoming the new model, which is not necessarily an appropriate one for the Democratic party. Before asking what these changes portend for either party, let us first look at how the political cultures of the parties have molded their responses to the pressures of the last two decades.

NATIONALIZATION

For several years political scientists have been bemoaning the decline of political parties and trying to analyze why this has occurred.[47] A few years ago some began to notice that while parties were supposedly declining, the national party committees were asserting more control over state and local parties both by changing the structure of the party and by increasing the services the national committees have to offer candidates and party organizations.[48] Indeed, the most recent work argues that even state and local party organizations are no weaker, and are possibly stronger, than they used to be.[49] It now appears that the fabled and much-analyzed party decline is restricted to party identification of the electorate. Both parties have been strengthening their national organizations in the last ten years, and neither has completed this task. But they have gone about it very differently.

The Republican party has drawn upon modern technology to create a highly sophisticated direct mail operation and uses the money raised to implement candidate recruitment and training programs and provide resources to campaigns. It also channels money and staff to the state party organizations to develop voter registration efforts, a solid financial base, and a permanent staff. However the money is not given away. The RNC analyzes what local party projects can best meet its long-term goals and restricts its largesse to those. Its resources have enabled the RNC to build up the state parties and solidify their loyalty, while the Democrats are still wrestling with a collection of independent and diverse entities.[50]

The Democratic party's drive toward nationalization has focused inwardly. Although it has developed some support programs for local parties and candidates, much of its energy and money has gone into reform commissions to rewrite the party rules, compliance review commissions to implement them, and midterm conferences (abolished in May of 1985) to facilitate internal debate.

The different approach by the Democrats to pressures for nationalization was partially a consequence of being the majority party and of having fewer financial resources than did the Republicans. But it also reflected the party's different political culture. This difference was summarized by DNC Chair John R. White when he told one interviewer that "politics is an emotional experience" and campaigns are not merely a matter of polls and organizations. "Timing is the most important thing in politics. Everything else is just a tool to get a wave going or to catch the wave."[51]

PROFESSIONALIZATION

Despite its laissez-faire ideology, the Republican party has much more central control than the Democratic party has ever contemplated. A spin-off of its efforts has been the creation of a community of professional political managers who rotate among state party staff positions, national party staff positions, campaigns, and other political jobs. People in this community generally know each other and rely on their mutual connections through the national party to promote their careers. They have developed a cosmopolitan attitude and a loyalty to the national Republican party greater than to any state organization. This in turn makes those in this community who are in state staff jobs more amenable to national party direction. As this community becomes self-sustaining, the strings the national party attaches to its state aid become less important, because the state staffs in effect become agents of the national party.

Although the Democrats also have many professional political organizers, they aren't part of a self-identified community and don't look to national party networks for job assistance. Each state has its own cadre of political activists, and there is very little exchange between them except during presidential campaigns, which are separate from party work. Campaign and party work is less likely to be a career than an occasional diversion. Those for whom it is a career often work their way up to a position in Washington, but once no longer employed by a national party or campaign organization, return to their own states, obtain jobs in Congress, or occasionally become political consultants or political directors of interest groups. The consequence is a more parochial attitude in which staffs are the agents of their employers and not the national party.

Renewal

In order to survive and flourish, both parties must constantly renew themselves. They must recruit new supporters while retaining the loyalty of old ones. In the last few decades the political landscape has changed considerably. New groups, who identify their interests by their common demographic characteristics, have organized. The influence of older ones has altered. Federal campaign laws have made it relatively easier for national party committees to raise and spend money and harder for local ones to do so.[52] Mass media bring the message of parties and candidates directly to the voters and organized interest groups bring the message of the voters to public officials. Technological developments have altered the kinds of political expertise necessary to win elections.[53]

The Democratic and Republican parties have different recruiting styles. The Democratic party has always co-opted groups. Theodore H. White wrote of the prereform party that "the old power brokers understood what gave the Democratic party its unique power—its ability to absorb new groups."[54] This understanding had not changed by the time John R. White became chair during the Carter administration. He too felt that a primary purpose of the Democratic party was to "absorb new movements" and bring people into the party.

> That is why the Democrats continue to be the majority party. The Democrats spent money for ERA and to develop women's issues. The women's equality issue is the new issue which brings people, men and women,

into the Democratic party. This is like civil rights was in the 1950s. The party needs to be continually reborn by bringing new people in.[55]

Republicans seek to recruit new people on a one-to-one basis, rather than through groups, and primarily by the force of ideas, rather than by supporting programs with specific benefits. At the end of his book on the 1972 campaign, White recounts an interview with President Nixon in which he said he "wasn't putting groups together in a coalition the way Roosevelt had—he was trying to cut across groups, binding people in every group who had the same ideas."[56] Current RNC chair Frank Fahrenkopf has expressed similar sentiments. "[W]here we seek to build coalitions, we build them on a commonality of interests which is greater than a belief in special benefits legislated for special interests. Whether we talk to white collar workers, Blacks, Hispanics, bank presidents, spot welders or astronauts...we concentrate on points in common rather than *why* they, as a distinct group, should feel different and in need of different treatment."[57]

These different recruiting styles have both advantages and disadvantages in the shifting political sands. The Democratic strategy of recruiting groups is advantageous when there are identifiable groups to recruit whose members have specific interests and can be mobilized by their leaders. Such groups have been growing on the national level, though their ability to mobilize their members for campaign work and to influence their vote has yet to be established.

The Republican strategy for renewal is more expensive but less problematical. As students of social movements know, individual recruiting is more costly than bloc recruiting. The latter can utilize pre-existing networks of like-minded people, who reinforce each others' changing beliefs. Individual recruiting requires a heavy expenditure of time and energy both to get and keep each recruit. Most incipient social movements don't have the resources to do this, but the Republican party does. It has invested a great deal of money in developing mailing lists of potential contributors of money and votes. However, impersonal recruitment is most effective when what is wanted is not actual participation but superficial indexes of support such as money and voting. That is currently what the party wants from its followers. As long as the party can recruit and market attractive candidates, it should increase its base.

However, the Republican party will face problems should its new recruits want to do more than just contribute money and votes. The social homogeneity of the party's primary base has served as a barrier to full participation by people from other social strata. The we/they attitude of traditional Republicans toward the New Right reflects a tension in the party that may seriously divide it in 1988. Since social homogeneity is the basis for cohesion, it is extremely difficult for the party to absorb a large group of newcomers sufficiently different from the traditional party activists without threatening homogeneity. The newcomers in turn pick up this hostility and reflect it back. The Republican party by and large is not receptive to new groups. It may work with them, albeit uncomfortably, and it may even assimilate them. But the price of assimilation is similarity, and that is hard to achieve.

Should the Republican party strengthen itself to the point of becoming the majority party it will attract many newcomers, including organized groups who have not previously thought it worth their time to join. It will discover that the price of success is that everyone wants a share, even when they have not made a contribution. Coping with increased demands, rapid expansion, and inadequate assimilation has destroyed many developing organizations. Styles and approaches to problems that are compatible with being a minority faction or underdog are not appropriate to being a majority party. Whether the party can anticipate and prepare for these problems sufficiently to preclude them, remains to be seen.

As the majority party the Democrats face different prospects. The reformation of the coalition from one of independent state and local parties, each with its own ethnic balance, to a national coalition of constituency groups has created constant turmoil and diverted resources from technological modernization. Furthermore, party activists who do not clearly fit into one of those groups feel left out.

Both parties, and the political scientists who study them, should reconsider the assumption that there is only one route to political success, and the party that loses an election must adopt the other as a model to follow in the future. Each party, for reasons peculiar to its own tradition and the social base from which it draws, has a different organizational style uniquely adapted to its particular circumstances. While each party must bend with the political winds, particularly in times of rapid change, an attempt to deny their differences will deprive them of the opportunity to recognize and build upon their strengths.*

* The author would especially like to thank Aaron Wildavsky and James Reichley for their assistance and encouragement in the preparation of this paper and the Brookings Institution and the Brooklyn Public Library for use of their facilities. In addition, thanks are extended to the following people for useful comments made on an earlier draft of this manuscript: David Reisman, Mark Cohen, Carol Koch, Norma Zane Chaplain.

NOTES

1. William Crotty, *Party Reform* (New York: Longman, 1983), pp. 205–6.

2. David Nexon, "Asymmetry in the Political System: Occasional Activists in the Republican and Democratic Parties, 1956–1964," *American Political Science Review* 65 (September 1971): 717; see also passing comments in the special section on the 1976 Republican Convention in *Political Science Quarterly* 92 (Winter 1977–78); and repeated but brief references in Theodore White's popular histories of *The Making of the President* for 1960, 1964, 1968, and 1972 (New York: Atheneum, 1961, 1965, 1969, 1973).

3. *International Encyclopedia of the Social Sciences*, vol. 12 (New York: Macmillan, 1968), p. 218.

4. See Walter Dean Burnham, *Critical Elections and the Mainsprings of American Politics* (New York: Norton, 1970) for an analysis of party systems.

5. Republican Party Chair Frank Fahrenkopf claimed in "Campaign 84: The Contest for National Leadership," *Presidential Studies Quarterly* 14 (Spring 1984): 176, that while the Democratic party is still that of the New Deal, the Republican party "is, ideologically, a new party." Even if this new ideology should not prove transitory, it does not necessarily mean the party has a new political culture.

6. John R. Petrocik, *Party Coalitions: Realignments and the Decline of the New Deal Party System* (Chicago: U. of Chicago Press, 1981).

7. Everett Carll Ladd and Charles D. Hadley, 2d ed., *Transformations of the American Party System* (New York: Norton, 1978).

8. Since the 1984 election, the accusation that the Democratic party is a "captive of the special interests" has become a sufficient public relations problem that party leaders bemoan it in public and several Democratic governors and senators have set up an independent Democratic Leadership Council with the goal of recapturing the loyalty of Democrats who supposedly left the party because of this capture. *Congressional Quarterly Weekly Report*, 9 March 1985, pp. 457–59. Although official recognition of the caucuses was withdrawn, there is no evidence that the party intends to institute a major revolution in its structure or outlook, and the main Democratic "special interest," organized labor, is not among those groups whose supposed influence is under internal attack.

9. Fahrenkopf, "Campaign 84," described the GOP as "clearly the homogenous political party" compared to the "unhomogenized" Democrats.

10. When conservatives sought to start a third party after Reagan wasn't nominated in 1976, they held meetings among themselves at the convention but made no effort to contact delegates. Jeffrey L. Pressman, "Groups and Group Caucuses," *Political Science Quarterly* 92 (Winter 1977–78): 680.

11. This is less true of the New Right, some prominent members of which have occasionally threatened to form a new party. However, their efforts have been strongly opposed by traditional Republicans such as Barry Goldwater, who refused to join in the 1976 third party effort. See William Rusher, *The Rise of the Right* (New York: William Morrow, 1984), chap. 11. Others, such as the Reverend Jerry Falwell at the 1984 convention, threatened to sit the election out if the platform was not to their liking.

12. Crotty, *Party Reform*, chap. 3.

13. James Q. Wilson, *The Amateur Democrat* (Chicago: U. of Chicago Press, 1962, 1966), pp. vii–viii.

14. *National Party Conventions 1831–1976* (Washington, D.C.: Congressional Quarterly, 1979), p. 105.

15. Barry Shafer, *The Quiet Revolution: Party Reform and the Shaping of Post Reform Politics* (New York: Basic Books, 1984).

16. Jo Freeman, "Something DID Happen at the Democratic Convention," *Ms.*, October 1976, pp. 74–76, 113–115.

17. *In These Times*, 30 July–12 August 1980.

18. Edward Shils, "Center and Periphery," *Selected Essays* (Chicago: Center for Social Organization Studies, U. of Chicago, 1970).

19. White, *Making of the President—1964*, pp. 59, 62.

20. "Women got what they want in Geraldine Ferraro. The South got what it wants in Burt Lance. What did you get? You ain't got nothing." Quoted in *Time*, 19 November 1984, p. 72.

21. White, *Making of the President—1964*, p. 62, summed up the difference between the parties' beliefs by saying the "Republicans are for virtue, the Democrats for Santa Claus."

22. White, *Making of the President—1968*, pp. 62–64.

23. See "The Democratic Party Credo" in Section 17, Article 11 of the *Charter of the Democratic Party*. "At the heart of our party lies a fundamental conviction that Americans must not only be free, but they must live in a fair society." The Charter was adopted in 1974, and the Credo was added in 1984. In 1965 Theodore White wrote that the most hallowed word among Democrats was "humanitarian"; among Republicans it was "principles," p. 138. This word reflects a similar outlook as "fair," but is less of an outsider's term. The language of the Charter probably reflects the influence of insurgent Democrats who were only recently outsiders but nonetheless share the basic vision of regular Democrats.

24. *New York Times*, 27 May 1956; quoted in Duane Lockard, *New England State Politics* (Princeton, N.J.: Princeton U. Press, 1959), pp. 138–39.

25. Helen Dewar, "Republicans Wage Verbal Civil War," *Washington Post*, 19 November 1984.

26. This was the message of Representative Jim Leach (R.-Iowa) in a press conference at the 1984 Republican convention. He is chair of the Ripon Society and co-chair and chief spokesperson for the Republican Mainstream Committee (RMC). Leach asserted that the RMC would hold a membership drive, but later in an interview stated that this would be done through "networking" with other organizations. There is no evidence that the RMC has attempted to organize Republican activists since the convention.

27. Cornelius P. Cotter and Bernard C. Hennessy, *Politics Without Power: The National Party Committees* (New York: Atherton, 1964), p. 183.

28. Lockard, *New England State Politics*, p. 147.

29. See Jo Freeman, "A Model for Analyzing the Strategic Options of Social Movement Organizations" in Jo Freeman, ed., *Social Movements of the Sixties and*

Seventies (New York: Longman, 1983), for an analysis of how resources effect organizational structure and style.

30. Cornelius P. Cotter and John F. Bibby, "Institutional Development of Parties and the Thesis of Party Decline," *Political Science Quarterly* 95 (Spring 1980): 1.

31. Wilson, *Amateur Democrat*, pp. 186–88; see also Hugh A. Bone, "New Party Associations in the West," *American Political Science Review (APSR)* 45 (December 1951): 1115–25; and Frank J. Sorauf, "Extra-Legal Political Parties in Wisconsin," *APSR* 48 (September 1954): 692–704.

32. Cotter and Hennessy, *Politics Without Power*, pp. 177–79.

33. Gary Jacobson, "Party Organization and Campaign Resources in 1982," *Political Science Quarterly* 100 (Winter 1985–86): 612; Xandra Kayden, "The Nationalizing of the Party System" in Michael J. Malbin, ed., *Parties, Interest Groups and Campaign Finance Laws* (Washington, D.C.: American Enterprise Institute, 1980), pp. 263, 268.

34. Lockard, *New England State Politics*, pp. 137–38.

35. In the 1983–84 election cycle the Democrats raised $98.5 million and the Republicans $297.9. This was up from $26.4 and $84.5 respectively in the 1977–78 cycle. Federal Election Commission press release of 5 December 1985, p. 2.

36. White, *Making of the President—1968*, pp. 31–32.

37. White, *Making of the President—1972*, p. 185.

38. Pressman, "Groups and Caucuses," p. 680.

39. According to the *New York Times* this was because House Republicans felt they had been taken for granted and left out of the negotiations between the White House and Democratic Ways and Means Committee Chairman Dan Rostenkowski (D.-Ill.). "Not only did Reagan not ask nicely," the *Times* quoted an unidentified first-term Republican as explaining, "he didn't ask at all, and I really resented that." *New York Times*, 22 December 1985.

40. *Newsweek*, 30 December 1985, p. 16.

41. Analyses of convention delegates and party officials have shown that the Republican party elite is heavily white, Protestant, and of English or northern European stock. See Charles W. Wiggins and William L. Turk, "State Party Chairman: A Profile," *Western Political Quarterly* 23 (1970): 332; Jeane Kirkpatrick, *The New Presidential Elite: Men and Women in National Politics* (New York: Russell Sage Foundation and the Twentieth Century Fund, 1976), chap. 3.

42. Despite this proclivity for sartorial conformity, Republican convention delegations show much more originality and creativity than Democrats when indulging in the personal expressionism that the convention atmosphere permits. Delegates to both conventions often wear costumes and/or hats decorated with political paraphernalia. Those worn by Republican delegates are considerably more numerous and picturesque.

43. Molly Ivins, "The Fabrics that Define Republican Women," *Dallas Times Herald*, 27 August 1984.

44. It was abolished by the DNC Executive Committee in May 1985. *Congressional Quarterly Weekly Report*, 29 June 1985, p. 1287.

45. Ladd and Hadley, *Transformations*, p. 305.

46. Kayden, "Nationalizing of the Party System," p. 263; Larry Sabato, "Parties, PACs, and Independent Groups" in Thomas E. Mann and Norman J. Ornstein, eds., *The American Elections of 1982* (Washington, D.C.: American Enterprise Institute, 1983), pp. 73–74.

47. The better known analyses include Burnham, *Critical Elections*; Jeane Kirkpatrick, *Dismantling the Parties: Reflections on Party Reform and Party Decomposition* (Washington, D.C.: American Enterprise Institute, 1978); William J. Crotty and Gary C. Jacobson, *American Parties in Decline* (Boston: Little, Brown, 1980).

48. Kayden, "Nationalizing of the Party System"; Cotter and Bibby, "Institutional Development"; Austin Ranney, *Curing the Mischiefs of Faction: Party Reform in America* (Berkeley, Calif.: U. of California Press, 1975).

49. Cornelius P. Cotter, James L. Gibson, John F. Bibby and Robert J. Huckshorn, *Party Organizations in American Politics* (New York: Praeger, 1984).

50. Sabato, "Parties, PACs, and Independent Groups," pp. 73–82; David Adamany, "Political Parties in the 1980s" in Michael J. Malbin, ed., *Money and Politics in the United States* (Chatham, N.J.: Chatham House, 1984), pp. 78–85; Gary D. Wekkin, "The New Federal Party Organizations: Intergovernmental Consequences of Party Renewal," paper given at the 1985 meeting of the American Political Science Association.

51. Adamany, "Political Parties," pp. 87–88.

52. Jo Freeman, "Political Party Expenditures Under the Federal Election Campaign Act: Anomalies and Unfinished Business," *Pace Law Review* 4 (Winter 1984): 267.

53. Kayden, "Nationalizing of the Party System," pp. 265–67.

54. White, *Making of the President—1972*, p. 158.

55. Quoted in Adamany, "Political Parties," p. 88.

56. White, *Making of the President—1972*, chap. 12.

57. Fahrenkopf, "Campaign 84," p. 174.

POLITICAL PARTIES AND INTEREST GROUPS: COMPETITORS, COLLABORATORS, AND UNEASY ALLIES

Allan J. Cigler

In the modern democratic state, where direct citizen representation seems impractical, political parties and interest groups have emerged as the major mediating institutions linking citizens to their governments. In some countries, such as those in Western Europe, parties and interest groups are intertwined organizationally and financially, making it often difficult to consider them separate institutions. In the United States, however, parties and interest groups are typically viewed as distinct entities that engage in quite different political activities.

American interest groups are most often exclusive, private organizations, largely unregulated by the government. Composed of individuals (or other organizations) who unite because of some common characteristic or concern, interest groups desire to advance favored policy positions in the political arena. Parties, in contrast, seek control of government power, which they attempt to achieve through selecting candidates for public office, and mobilizing voters to support them. Parties are broadly based, inclusive, quasipublic organizations, regulated chiefly by state law. They seek to staff the government and reap rewards such as patronage, status, and influence. Interest groups have dominated the politics of policy making and parties have reigned supreme in the electoral sphere.

Scholarly observers have not been equally appreciative of the two institutions.[1] Interest groups are often viewed ambivalently. Recognized as inevitable in a free, heterogeneous and complex environment, they are troublesome because of their impact. Many seem to pursue narrow and selfish interests, and research suggests that the group universe is skewed in a conservative, pro-business direction, despite the growth in the number of public interest groups in the past quarter of a century.[2] Even public interest groups are suspect on representational grounds because of their higher educated, upper- and middle-class composition, and typically undemocratic internal decision-making style.[3]

The proliferation of interest groups in recent decades has raised "governability" concerns as well. Some believe that there is a danger that the policy process has been "destabilized," as ever larger numbers of interest-group claimants make demands on decision makers.[4] In such an environment, priorities are difficult for decision-makers to discern. Many demands may be ambiguous and majorities necessary for policy closure are difficult to build.[5]

Parties, in contrast, are viewed in a much more positive vein. Many would agree with E. E. Schattschneider's conclusion that "political parties created democracy and that modern democracy is unthinkable save in terms of party."[6] Seen as the glue that unites separate elements within American politics, parties are regarded as uniquely suited to reconcile diversity with majority rule in both the electoral and policy processes through coalition-building. Unlike interest groups, parties offer broad policy direction, reduce fragmentation, and provide for the representation of the many elements of society that are vulnerable and unorganized. Parties offer the potential of providing a counterweight to excessive interest-group influence.

THE PARTY/INTEREST GROUP CONNECTION

A common view among students of American politics is that party and interest group strength are inversely related. When parties are weak, a political vacuum is created, which is allegedly filled by interest groups. In states with strong, viable political parties, interest groups appear to be less influential in the public arena than in states where political parties are weak.[7] In the contemporary period, characterized by a vibrant interest-group system and parties with a lessened capacity to influence voters and elected officials, some have even suggested a causal link between the two institutions; interest-group activities, such as the development of political action committees (PACs), hasten the demise of parties.[8]

It makes more sense to treat the relationship between political parties and interest groups as *competitive, yet symbiotic.* As potential competitors there can be no doubt. Both "make claims on society on behalf of the shared attitudes and interests of their members."[9] Both seek access to and the attention of public decision makers.

The basis of the competition is found in the desires of elected officials to win reelection and their willingness to grant access to those who can reduce electoral uncertainty.[10] Officials are often unclear about constituent concerns, including their policy preferences. Cooperation and consultation with mediating institutions become a strategy for dealing with such uncertainty. Besides contributing tangible campaign resources such as money or personnel, both interest groups and parties operate as agents of "political intelligence" for officials seeking to efficiently gather information about voters.[11]

Compared to parties, which approach voters only during campaigns, interest groups may be more reliable agents of political intelligence for risk-averse officials. Parties are decentralized organizations indirectly representing heterogeneous population elements. Interest groups are typically specialized, thus offering a more direct communication route to well-defined, homogeneous groups of constituents. They may be better able than parties to inform officials about likely voter behavior on a continuing basis.[12] Their knowledge of constituent-issue positions and their rationales may be invaluable to legislators, as is their ability to influence constituents on the lawmaker's behalf. When group perspectives dominate elections, "close working relationships" are encouraged with interest groups, often at the expense of parties.[13]

The inherent competition between political parties and interest groups should not cloud the fact that much of the party/interest group relationship may be symbiotic, more cooperative than hostile, since party and interest group goals may not necessarily conflict. Striving to build coalitions of broad interests for electoral purposes, parties are well aware that specific groups often claim to represent such interests and that a close relationship is advantageous. Interest groups also provide the resources necessary for the party to achieve its electoral aims, from funding party organization and its candidates to registration drives that target likely party voters. Parties often court interest groups.

Parties can also be vehicles for interest groups to achieve their goals. Groups may seek to introduce their policy goals into party platforms; this contributes to the perceived legitimacy of their aims and incorporates them into the broader political agenda. When party and group interests coincide, as in the case of electing candidates preferred by the group, cooperation and the sharing of resources will often occur. Participation in party affairs can be crucial for groups that lack financial resources or insider access to decision makers, since taking part in party activities may represent one of their few routes to policy influence. The political gains made by women and gay rights activists as a consequence of their internal Democratic party activities, and by evangelicals in the Republican party, are illustrative.

The long-standing relationship between parties and interest groups in electoral politics has been altered in recent decades. Traditionally aggregating agencies, parties appear to have developed some of the policy advocating characteristics typically associated with more narrow interest groups. On occasion, especially in the Democratic party, this has compromised the party's fundamental goal of winning elections. Although the vast majority of interest groups in American politics do not engage in electoral activities, several interest groups have become involved in traditional party activities, from recruiting candidates for public office to funding campaigns to mobilizing voters. The distinctions between the two mediating agencies seem far less clear than just two decades ago.

PARTY/INTEREST GROUP RELATIONS BEFORE THE 1970s

Parties and interest groups in the United States emerged separately as institutions. Parties, as active mobilizers of the mass public in elections, began to develop in the 1830s, and reached the height of their influence from roughly 1865 until the Progressive Reform Movement started to take its toll around the turn of the century.

During this period, called by historian Arthur Schlesinger, Jr., the "golden age" of parties, local party organizations were especially powerful. They mobilized the masses in almost militialike fashion.[14] "The price of mass participation was organization," with the result being the rise of the professional party politician, who received compensation in the form of either patronage positions or money or both.[15] Interested individuals and a few groups contributed money, at times large amounts, to the parties and their candidates. Raising money and the disbursement of funds was coordinated by party officials. The resources of politics, money, and manpower came overwhelmingly from public employees, and parties had a virtual monopoly over the electoral process. Several loosely organized political movements influenced party business, but interest groups did not ordinarily involve themselves in party affairs.

The development of interest groups as formal organizations parallels the rise of parties. Sustained interaction between the two institutions did not occur early on. In the early history of the nation, before the industrial revolution, while interests were latent, organizations reflecting the interests were not needed. Farmers had no political or economic reason to organize when they worked for their families; nor did workers, who were often laboring in small family enterprises. Local guilds often existed to train apprentices and to protect jobs.

In the early 1830s the first national organizations representing groups of individuals with common interests, such as the Elks, came into being, often for social reasons. Several "cause" groups, such as the abolitionists, did have major effects upon the parties. Group-based attempts to influence the nomination process and the general election campaign during this period were relatively rare, however, and when they did occur it was through the parties.

Group formation "tends to occur in waves" and is greater in some periods than in others.[16] The period after the Civil War saw the rise of large numbers of interest groups with strong interests in government policy (e.g., agriculture, labor, business). Not only did improvements in communications and transportation make national organizations viable, a number of societal forces, such as increasing social and economic complexity, had the effect of creating new interests and redefining old ones. Coupled with the growing government involvement in business affairs, these forces encouraged a mushrooming of interests with incentives to organize formally.[17] Group proliferation accelerated during the periods 1900 to 1920 and 1945 to the present. A variety of "disturbances" upset the economic or social equilibrium, which helped or hurt certain interests, and acted as a catalyst for individuals to form groups as counterweights to the new perceptions of inequality.[18]

Most interest groups have not attempted to encroach on the party's domination of the electoral process. Advantaged groups have preferred to work directly within the policy process, while disadvantaged groups often found the party too entrenched for meaningful change and have sought to create alternatives such as third parties.

In the case of farmers, the first encompassing political organization, the National Grange (1867), was initially quite influential. It shaped banking and railroad legislation, but eschewed direct involvement in elections.[19] With the waning of the Grange movement in the 1870s, farmers turned to the electoral process for the first time. They formed various political parties, such as the Greenback-Labor party in the 1870s and 1880s and the Populist party a decade later. Not until the middle 1890s did farm interests work within a major party, helping to nominate their candidate William Jennings Bryan as the Democratic standard bearer and imposing their platform on the party. The relationship of farm groups to the Democratic party at the turn of the century represents the most prominent example of a successful attempt by organized interests to capture a major political party in the national electoral arena. Cooperation for mutual advantage was not the farmers' goal.

The New Deal Democratic party's relationship to organized labor perhaps best represents the competitive, yet symbiotic relationship of interest groups and parties. Long involved in electoral politics, labor usually worked independent from the major party organizations. It focused at the local level. In 1828, Philadelphia labor leaders formed the Workingman's Labor party; by 1834 local labor parties could be found in fifteen states.[20] The first major success of labor groups in national electoral politics occurred in 1878, when the Greenback-Labor party elected fourteen candidates to Congress and garnered more than a million votes.

Samuel Gompers moved organized labor into Democratic campaign politics as early as the first decade of the twentieth century. Not until the 1930s did labor develop a close relationship to a major party, making the transition "from a pluralist, if often pro-Democratic, voluntarism to an intimate partisan alliance" with the Democratic party.[21] While not monolithic in its attachment to the Democratic party, and with serious internal divisions, the labor movement still proved to be a core element of the New Deal coalition.

The relationship between organized labor and the Democratic party evolved because of mutual self-interest. Labor's principal goal since the 1880s had been organizational security, including the right to organize freely, bargain collectively, and select its own representatives without company interference. Until the early 1930s, organized labor had largely fought its own battles, typically facing business interests allied with government, but various New Deal policies bore witness to Roosevelt's personal support for unionism. Regulations found in such legislation as the National Industrial Recovery Act (NIRA) and the Fair Labor Standards Act of 1938 recognized fundamental union organizational rights. The Wagner Act in 1935 created the National Labor Relations Board (NLRB), with the power of enforcement to guarantee such rights. Indebted to the Roosevelt administration, and believing that the Democratic party's policy thrusts were compatible with working class interests, labor "took the party's interest in winning elections as its own."[22]

By the late 1930s, much of organized labor had become avidly partisan: active in mobilizing its own members on behalf of most Democratic candidates, and in furnishing the party what it needed most, the money and manpower to energize the working class ethnic voters crucial to the New Deal coalition. By the mid-1940s, the CIO had formed the first political action committee, the Committee on Political Education (COPE). It not only raised funds for pro-labor, Democratic candidates, but also engaged in such partylike activities as registration drives, distributing pro-Democratic literature, and conducting get-out-the-vote programs on election day. Organized labor, with its endorsement of a candidate, also acted as a cue for other liberal groups, such as the National Association for the Advancement of Colored People (NAACP), Americans for Democratic Action (ADA), and the American Civil Liberties Union (ACLU).[23]

While it is difficult to access precisely the resource contribution of organized labor to the Democratic party, fragmentary evidence is provided by several researchers. Alexander Heard concludes that in 1952 and 1956 "one-seventh of the direct expenses of national-level pro-Democratic committees were met with labor money."[24] In 1960, when unions across the country were active in support of Kennedy, Nicholas Masters reported a number of instances in which the union contribution was substantial; 407 unionists in Missouri registered more than 85,000 new voters in just one day.[25] Labor, in conjunction with other groups, added 100,000 new registrants to the voting rolls in Spanish-speaking parts of southern California. As the party often lacked the patronage to build a strong organization and attract party workers and money, it welcomed labor's contribution.

The party did not welcome attempts by organized labor to take over the party structure or infringe on the party's traditional role in the nomination process. In areas such as Detroit, COPE was so strong that it functioned as the party organization, at times aggressively seeking to control the candidate selection process.[26] In Detroit, the UAW operated powerful congressional district COPE organizations, which functioned as "standing political caucuses" within the regular Democratic party. One study found that over three-fourths of the party officials in Wayne County (Detroit) were union members.[27] For all intents and purposes, even at the precinct level, much of the party organization was the union organization. Greenstone noted that in Los Angeles and Chicago, as well as in Detroit, the interest group and party roles often were reversed; the party sought access to the labor organization to "exert pressure on the pressure group," in order to protect the organizational interests of nonlabor party leaders.[28]

In general, unions "had a difficult time influencing nomination processes in environments supporting traditional party organizations,"[29] in spite of their great contributions of manpower and money to the party and its candidates. Even exceptionally strong labor organizations deferred to nonlabor party officials by recognizing that party and interest-group roles were distinct, and that labor's "particular economic interests limited its aggregating role" in the electoral process.[30]

In the presidential nomination process, while union officials were often "recognized" by receiving a national convention delegate position, selection was made by party officials.[31] In 1948 labor union representatives constituted only 2.1 percent of the delegates to the national convention, and in 1952 "around 200 unionists" were either convention delegates or alternates.[32] Party regulars still controlled the presidential nomination process.

Prior to the 1970s, the Republican party situation was similar. Businesses and their executives, usually on an individual basis, were important in providing financial resources to the party, but attempts to duplicate labor's efforts at mobilizing members as party workers and campaign operatives were largely unsuccessful.[33] Like the Democrats, Republican operatives dominated electoral politics.

PARTY REFORM: ALTERING PARTY/INTEREST GROUP RELATIONS

While most observers believe that the decline of American political parties represents a long-term, secular trend that began around the turn of the century, a series of party and campaign reforms that occurred in the early 1970s fundamentally altered party/interest group relations. These changes weakened the party's ability to be a force in electoral politics and expanded the role played by interest groups in areas traditionally dominated by parties. By the mid-1970s, interest groups were participating in elections in an increasingly direct fashion, at times supplanting party officials in the candidate selection process and bypassing the party organization by providing campaign operatives and financial resources to individual candidates.

The complex configuration of forces that led to such changes is difficult to summarize in any causal fashion.[34] Parties, strongest at local and state levels, proved incapable of addressing national needs and aspirations that were reflected in a new political agenda. Parties seemed unable or unwilling to accommodate the aspirations of newly "entitled" social groups such as women, youth, and nonwhite minorities. They failed to address the matrix of economic, social, and cultural issues that had emerged by the late 1960s, as American society moved from an industrial to a postindustrial society.[35]

Prior to the 1970s' reforms, party organizations had already lost much of their influence in performing electoral functions, not to interest groups, but to the individuals seeking office, as campaigning had increasingly become candidate-centered rather than party-based. The Progressive reforms, especially the introduction of the direct primary as a nominating device for most public offices, diminished party control of recruitment and nomination processes. The decline of patronage eroded the parties' personnel and financial base. By the late 1960s, the dominant influence of the mass media in political life and the existence of increasingly educated and individualistic voters were further creating a context hostile to partisanship. Political campaigning was becoming the domain of independent professionals—campaign consultants, pollsters, and advertising specialists.

The new reforms altered the relationship between the national parties and their state and local affiliates and provided an opening for interest groups to play a greater role in electoral politics. Prior to the 1970s, the two major parties were distinctly confederal organizations, with weak national party central committees. The national party was essentially the quadrennial meeting of party delegates to select the presidential nominee. The Democratic party was "an amalgam of urban machines in the North, volunteer activist branches scattered through the country and old courthouse rings in the South," supplemented in places by organized labor and civil rights organizations.[36] The Republican party was likewise decentralized. While issue activists were active in presidential nomination politics as early as the 1950s, organized business interests commonly associated with the party did not play the role that labor and civil rights groups did in the Democratic party in providing funds and other resources.[37]

The catalyst for party reform was the race for the 1968 Democratic nomination. Delegates at the Chicago convention nominated Hubert Humphrey, in the face of a challenge by New Left, reformist elements that had arisen to challenge the old New Deal liberalism characteristic of most party regulars, elected officials, and their organized labor allies. While the central issue of the 1968 nomination contest was the Vietnam War, the split in the party extended to include cultural and economic issues. Differences arose over lifestyles, the meaning of equality, concern about the environment, and the role of women and youth in the political process. Interest groups involved in the challenge, such as the Vietnam Moratorium Committee, were not traditional membership organizations based on occupation or economic activity. They were loosely organized issue or cause groups, often without any formal organizational structure or financial resources, whose decisions were often the prerogative of a small number of intense activists. Protest was often their major political resource.

While failing to deny Humphrey the nomination, New Left elements did successfully pressure the Democratic party to reexamine its presidential nomination process. The process continued as the lone bastion of meaningful party influence, since party officials remained the dominant force in the outcome. Humphrey accumulated convention delegates and won the nomination without ever having entered a primary. Even where primaries existed, contests were most often popularity or "beauty" contests, unrelated to delegate selection. In 1968 only sixteen states had some form of presidential primary; only nine held a presidential preference poll and only three of these were binding.[38] Most delegates to the convention were either party officials or individuals chosen by party officials, usually as a reward for faithful party service. State conventions and caucuses, where most delegates were chosen, were typically closed to outsiders. The key to gaining the nomination lay in constructing a grand coalition of state party delegations, which encouraged contenders to court governors and other top party officials who could deliver state majorities.

To outsiders the system appeared to be closed, undemocratic, and unrepresentative of the party rank-and-file. The intention of the reformers was to open up the party to all those who wanted to participate. The 1968 convention mandated the creation of a commission to address the party structure and delegate selection process. The resulting McGovern-Fraser Commission (1968–72) was originally supposed to represent a broad range of "groups" in its composition, including various demographic categories, party officials, and interest groups such as organized labor and civil rights groups.[39] The final composition had a strong reform bias, with reformers outnumbering party regulars nearly two to one.[40] Organized labor, which believed that it had been underrepresented in the selection process, eventually opted out of commission deliberations.

Labor's sense of being slighted was understandable, given its long-standing relationship to the party. The AFL-CIO and COPE leadership believed union efforts after the divisive Chicago convention (which the unions blamed on the reform elements) had nearly salvaged a Humphrey victory. Theodore White describes the effort:

> The dimension of the AFL/CIO effort, unprecedented in American history, can be caught only by its final summary figures; the ultimate registration, by labor's efforts, of 4.6 million voters; the printing and distribution of 55 million pamphlets and leaflets out of Washington and 60 million more from local unions; telephone banks in 638 localities, using 8,055 telephones, manned by 24,511 union men and women and their families; some 72,255 house-to-house canvassers; and, on election day, 94,457 volunteers serving as car-poolers, materials distributors, baby-sitters, poll-watchers, telephoners.[41]

Reform forces emerged triumphant from the McGovern-Fraser Commission. Sweeping changes governed the 1972 convention, including new rules for state parties that would be enforced through a strengthened national committee. The state and local party organizations' control over delegate selection and behavior was broken. Major requirements included delegate selection through either primaries or open meetings (caucuses), the virtual elimination of delegate selection by state central committees, incentives for selection at the local level, and the establishment of representation quotas on the basis of race, gender, and age. While the Republican party did not formally follow suit, it became more sensitive to representative issues because state Republicans frequently found themselves under the same laws mandating primaries or open caucus systems. As the more middle-class, homogeneous party, Republicans did not find themselves under as much pressure from groups as did the Democrats.

The new delegate selection rules altered presidential aspirant nomination strategies. "The official party as a formal structure was no longer the effective framework through which delegates were selected; the official party as an extended organization was no longer—and probably could no longer be—the effective means by which nominating campaigns were mounted."[42] In its place, candidates seeking to put together a winning nomination coalition had to focus on constructing a coalition of issue publics. The new strategy "produced a political arena crowded with interest groups and issue organizations, seeking and being sought, demanding rewards and offering support, while both presidential aspirants and interested partisans tried to secure the maximum benefit from these negotiations."[43] The new system involved direct candidate negotiation with group leaders, "compelling them to court group support with a promiscuity that often appears excessive."[44]

Among interest groups, blue-collar unions seemed initially to be big losers in the process. Rather than the "automatic" appointment of labor officials by party officials to delegate positions, labor representatives would now have to win their positions through a much more open process. Certain groups of white-collar professionals, on the other hand, seemed to have distinct advantages under the reform rules. While basically inactive in partisan politics before the mid-1970s, the nation's largest teacher organization quickly became a force in nomination politics starting in 1976.

A total of 172 National Education Association members attended the 1976 convention. In 1980 the group was larger than all but the California delegation, with 302 delegates, 269 committed to Carter's renomination. They represented nearly 8 percent of all delegates and almost 16 percent of the number needed to win the nomination. The group was highly organized at the 1980 convention, communicating with its affiliated delegates by means of an elaborate whip system, powerful enough to win platform planks opposed by the Carter campaign.[45]

Groups composed of relatively small numbers of intense issue activists were also advantaged, and wielded influence far in excess of their size or their financial resources in the new, permeable presidential nomination process. In 1980 Gay Vote '80, with a budget of about $100,000, aggressively sought to activate gays to participate in and become delegates to the Democratic National Convention. It also lobbied candidates to put gays on the platform committee.[46] The group was so successful that the number of openly gay delegates or alternates increased from four in 1976 to seventy-seven in 1980, with six represented on the platform committee. This resulted in some major policy successes, including the first pro-gay rights plank in history.

During the 1970s, several other groups had major impacts on the business of the national parties. They included the antinuclear campaign for Safe Energy and the National Welfare Rights Organization in the Democratic party to the Pro-Life Impact Committee and the Moral Majority in the Republican party. The new process encouraged group formation to influence a party's political agenda. The National Women's Political Caucus (NWPC), an organization made up of elected women political officials and other prominent women interested in expanding the role of women in both political parties, was created in September 1971. It was founded by reform-minded women Democratic officials in order to push the party to translate the party's new demographic representation guidelines for women into formal representation rules.[47] The NWPC later played a major role in Republican convention politics as well.[48]

The changes in the nomination process broadened the scope of interest-group involvement to the detriment of the traditional political party organization. By the 1970s in states such as Iowa, home of the first major battle for convention delegates, activist farmers, teachers, pro- and antiabortion advocates, evangelicals, as well as organized labor, were actively courted and worked for candidates eager to accumulate convention delegates, and group participation in each of the party's platform proceedings took on new meaning. Group political endorsements were crucial to a candidate's success.[49] In an era of candidate-centered politics, it appeared that interest groups had become key elements in politicians' strategies to secure their party's presidential nomination.

PARTY/INTEREST GROUP RELATIONS AND CAMPAIGN FINANCE REFORM

As parties struggled to reform their processes, public concern over rising campaign costs, expenditures, and "excessive" individual contributions was leading to overhaul of federal campaign laws, the first major change since the Corrupt Practices Act of 1925. The Federal Campaign Act of 1971, and its 1974, 1976, and 1979 amendments, like the internal party reforms, had a major effect on party/interest group relations. The law had several very specific provisions, ranging from federal funding of presidential elections to limitations on campaign contributions in House and Senate races to elaborate campaign committee reporting requirements.

Its overall impact was to alter the balance between parties and interest groups in funding and organizing campaigns in both presidential and congressional contests.[50]

Party/interest group relations have been most affected by provisions that encouraged the development of political action committees (PACs), which are "either the separate, segregated campaign fund of a sponsoring labor, business or trade organization, or the campaign fund of a group formed primarily or solely for the purpose of giving money to candidates."[51] PACs did exist well before the 1970s. The Congress of Industrial Organizations (CIO) is usually credited with creating the first PAC in 1943, and when the union merged with the American Federation of Labor (AFL) in 1955, the AFL-CIO's PAC (COPE) quickly became the largest interest group contributor to elections prior to campaign reform. Business PACs, such as AMPAC, formed in 1962 by the American Medical Association, and BIPAC, formed in 1963 by the National Association of Manufacturers, later became major players in campaign finance with a conservative, pro-Republican bias. Federal statutes legalizing and defining PACs, coupled with limitations on individual contributions (no more than $1,000 per election, with an overall limit of $25,000 to all federal election candidates in a given year), created an even greater incentive for organized and coordinated giving through PACs, and they proliferated in the late 1970s.

Aside from encouraging PAC formation, the reform legislation had the inadvertent effect of decreasing the party role in providing campaign resources to candidates. Prior to the enactment of the law, parties were unmentioned in federal statute; now their role in elections was clearly delineated. James Ceaser concludes:

> [The federal campaign act] has had the effect of defining, and fixing in law the party's status relative to the candidate's. It recognizes the individual candidate's organization as the responsible legal agent of the campaign and limits how much a party can spend to promote its candidates. The legal position of the parties is thus at odds with their actual role during much of American history, when they often contributed most of the relevant resources needed to run congressional campaigns.[52]

The party had been defined by the new law as an interest group, albeit a special one. Parties retain some advantages. While both parties and PACs are limited to $5,000 per candidate in each campaign (or $10,000 each election cycle), parties may contribute "coordinated" expenditures (such as advertisements, polling, mass mailings) to the efforts of their House and senatorial candidates (up to 10,000 per House race, and two cents times the voting age population in a state or $20,000, whichever is greater, for a Senate race). Inflation is taken into account in determining maximum coordinated expenditures, but not for individual or group contributions. This reached $23,053 for House races in 1988.[53] Still, parties were formally limited in their campaign activities, while PACs, if they decided to spend money "independently," had no such limitation.

Although individuals remain the main source of campaign funds, the number of PACs mushroomed, and their proportional contribution to campaigns rapidly increased after the 1974 amendments gave precise guidelines for PAC operation. The number of federally registered PACs went from 608 in 1974 to nearly 4,200 by 1990. In the 1989–1990 election cycle PACs provided more than 40 percent of the campaign funds received by House candidates and about one-fourth of those received by candidates for the Senate.[54] Incumbents of both parties were even more reliant upon PAC contributions; while in 1978 House incumbents received less than one-third of their campaign funds from PACs, by 1988 it was nearly half; Senate incumbents have increased the proportion of funding from PACs during the same period from 15 percent to 29 percent of their campaign totals.[55]

Ironically, because of the FEC limitations on party committee cash contributions to candidates, the proportion of candidates' total receipts from party committees actually declined in House races from 1978 to 1988 (from 7 percent to 4 percent), and only modestly increased for senatorial candidates (from 6 percent to 9 percent).[56] It seems reasonable to conclude that candidates have increasingly turned to PACs, not parties, for campaign funds, and the "more money a member of Congress can attract from PACs, the more the member can be independent of the party."[57]

The competition between PACs and parties went beyond merely fundraising from a limited pool of givers and providing alternative sources of funding and support for candidates. By the early 1980s PACs had exceeded parties in terms of amounts "expended on direct efforts to influence voter choices among candidates." They competed with parties in such traditional campaign activities as voter registration and get-out-the-vote drives, which are excluded from FEC regulation due to their "nonpartisan" nature.[58] Especially threatening were the nonconnected, independent PACs, those not tied to a particular group or institution such as a corporation. Some of the new PACs were aggressively anti-party. Most noteworthy was the behavior of the National Conservative Political Action Committee (NCPAC) and its leader Terry Dolan, who while mostly supportive of Republicans, had a disdain for both parties. In 1982 NCPAC even considered becoming a political party.[59] It not only contributed to candidates who agreed with its agenda, but also ran negative campaigns against candidates from both major parties.

The proliferation of PACs and their increasing importance in providing campaign resources not only had the effect of making parties less important in elections, but also appeared to increase the electoral vulnerability of incumbents. The defeat of a large number of prominent incumbents in 1978 and 1980 reinforced the perception that powerful interest groups, especially the independent, more ideological PACs, were increasing electoral risk for officeholders. Talk among many political insiders now turned to efforts to strengthen political parties.

THE PARTY FIGHTS BACK

By the early 1980s the competitive threat to parties by groups appeared overwhelming. The extraordinary role played by New Right elements in the nomination of Ronald Reagan as the Republican standard bearer in 1980, the influence of organized labor in the selection of Walter Mondale as the Democratic nominee in 1984, and an apparent "deal" with the National Organization for Women in the selection of Geraldine Ferraro as the vice-presidential candidate, combined to suggest group domination of the presidential nomination process. In congressional elections, scholars worried not only about the potential impact of growing PAC funding, but attempts by some PACs "to usurp functions of the two parties and establish themselves as substitutes by recruiting and training candidates and creating pseudo-party organizations of their own."[60]

Viewed from the temporal distance of the early 1990s, the interest-group threat to parties did not fully materialize. A strong case can be made that party and campaign reform forced both major parties to come to terms with the social as well as technological changes that have characterized the late twentieth century; in the end, these reactions saved the political parties as players in electoral politics, although with diminished roles. Arthur Schlesinger, Jr., has argued that the party reform removed the nomination process from effective control by state and local party elites. Yet, the changes were designed "to tame the new social energies and incorporate them into the party process," which kept parties from becoming totally meaningless institutional entities in an era of rising expectations and democratic fervor.[61]

The interest-group threat forced both major political parties to adapt organizationally to survive. During the 1980s, the Democrats in particular made a number of attempts to "re-reform" the presidential nomination process in order to increase the possibility of "peer review" by party officials and officeholders. The Hunt Commission (1980–84) increased the role of party regulars in the process by designating a certain percentage of national convention delegates to be "superdelegates," drawn from a pool of party and public officials (state chairs, governors, U.S. representatives, and so on). The rationale for this effort was not just the self-interest of party professionals, but the expectation that their experience and moderate orientation would counterbalance claims of issue and group activists and enhance ties between the party and its officeholders. The pro-party reformers hope was that the superdelegates would remain largely uncommitted throughout much of the nomination process, and perhaps play a compromising role at the national convention.[62]

The addition of party "peers" to the process appears not to have had its intended effects. Given the realities of a contemporary presidential selection process dominated by the media and candidate organizations, a great deal of pressure has been put on the superdelegates to commit early to give various candidates a momentum advantage in the media's coverage of the nomination "horse race." In 1984 most superdelegates committed to Walter Mondale early, well before the Iowa and New Hampshire contests. His selection looked "bossed" to some. In 1988 the clear preferences of the superdelegates for established political figures so angered insurgent candidate Jesse Jackson that the procedures were modified. Like so many reforms to strengthen the party in the nomination process, such efforts seem undemocratic in the contemporary era, and are overwhelmed by other campaign factors. As Howard Reiter has asserted, "increasing the number of party 'leaders' at the convention is like bringing back knights in armor in the age of gunpowder."[63] The contemporary nomination process simply recognizes the expansion of players in American politics, ranging from more traditional party leaders, such as county and state chairpersons, to members of the press, to campaign operatives, financial contributors, and group representatives and issues activists.[64]

While the nomination process is still as "open" as it was in the late 1970s and early 1980s, and group domination remains possible, it appears that group impact has been reduced. The energy apparent in the "movement politics" of the late 1960s, 1970s, and early 1980s may have run its cyclical course. The mobilization of cause activists is more difficult once some of their basic political aims have been achieved. Even "establishment" groups like the NEA appear to be less involved in presidential elections today, since their high-priority desire for the establishment of a Department of Education became reality during the Carter presidency. For other groups, such as the independent PACs, organizational resources and funds are now more difficult to attain, due at least in part to the greater competition in raising funds by mail.[65] NCPAC has ceased operations because of financial difficulty. Intense issues such as abortion seem destined to be settled in the judicial rather than legislative or executive arenas, or at the state level. The attention of the issue activists seems less focused on the national electoral arena. State and local party activists and traditional group allies such as organized labor have re-emerged as important elements in presidential nomination politics.

Parties as national institutions also seem enhanced organizationally compared to their nadir in the 1970s. The threat to elected politicians of an interest group–dominated campaign process, particularly one helping challengers, proved to be a major incentive for risk-averse officials to re-vamp the national party organization to counter the threat.[66] At the national level, each of the two major parties is currently really three parties: a national committee, and Senate and House party campaign committees. All six committees have become well-funded, professional organizations, with large staffs and budgets.[67] While it has become fashionable in recent years for several party scholars to applaud the "resurgence" of the national parties, and how they have adapted to the new features of American politics, it is important that those interested in representational questions understand the role played by contemporary national parties.

The national parties have adapted by becoming special interest groups of their own: less voter-mobilizing agencies and coalition-building vehicles in the traditional party sense, than "service-vendor" organizations dedicated primarily to the reelection of legislators who have a party label, largely unrelated to how they vote on legislative issues.[68] Parties have proven to be surprisingly capable of adjusting to an environment dominated by campaign resources candidates must purchase, while interest groups and their PACs have been largely unable to go beyond channeling cash to candidates. They remain "a far cry from the electoral organizations that political parties are."[69]

Both national parties currently perform a variety of services for their incumbent members of Congress and serious challengers, ranging from coordination of fundraising efforts to providing polling services to designing candidate campaign strategies and doing research on the opposition.[70] They have become effective at raising funds and targeting funds to incumbents and serious challengers.[71] Parties, in terms of the total amount of funds given by the party committees to candidates, contribute far less than the amount given by individuals and groups. Yet, much of the money is more cost effective in campaigns, as the parties apply a "needs" test to the incumbents, shunting funds to where it is of most use.[72]

The party committees since the mid-1980s appear to have turned the potential PAC threat to their advantage. While parties and PACs competed vigorously for campaign funds in the early years of PAC proliferation, "the institutionalization of the national parties...transformed the hostility that surround early party-PAC...relations into a less conflictual and, in many ways, highly cooperative set of relationships."[73] Although Republicans remain ahead of Democrats, both national party organizations have formed loose fundraising alliances with some prominent PACs. In their emerging role as brokers, national parties regularly assist PACs in directing contributions to particular campaigns and aid candidates by soliciting funds from potential donor PACs.[74] Parties have even been involved in new PAC creation.[75] The party committees have learned to use some interest groups as electoral allies in novel ways; at times the party is a patron to an interest group trying to nominate one of its own for public office.[76] Contemporary PAC contributors are not necessarily antiparty (as early speculation suggested). Even ideological and single-issue PACs have not altered American politics in fundamental ways.[77] The business-labor division among PACs roughly follows the New Deal divisions that continue to differentiate the parties.

Parties have also turned a loophole in the campaign financing laws to their own advantage, magnifying their real contribution to party candidates by "arranging" for individual or PAC money to go for a variety of nonpartisan activities that do not count toward contribution maximums at the federal level.

The upsurge of party activity designed to utilize PAC resources, reflecting party/PAC alliances and cooperation, has not eliminated party/PAC tensions. Some PACs jealously guard their independence. Others, such as BIPAC, formed by the National Association of Manufacturers, directly compete with the national parties as cue-givers to PACs, helping them raise funds, and evaluate candidates and make contribution decisions.

Even the interest groups and PACs closely aligned with each of the two major parties have an uneasy relationship with the formal party structure. The relationship between organized labor and the Democratic party is so close that fifteen seats on the DNC Executive Committee are reserved for labor representatives. Labor contributes almost exclusively to Democratic candidates; it is the largest contributor to the party organization as well, consistently giving more than $1 million a year. Yet, worried about its own influence within the party, organized labor often resists strengthening local parties, which it views as a competitor.[78]

The tension between parties and their interest-group allies is greatest in situations when a party's desire to attract a diverse population of voters through an optimal electoral message clashes with the desires of its more narrowly oriented interest-group supporters. This is particularly a problem for the Democratic party, whose associated constituent groups such as labor, gays, and feminists often expect the party to act in their interests even if general public support seems to be lacking.

While both parties continue to actively court interest groups and issue activists, party officials and officeholders have come to understand that making the party a forum for interest-group demands can have negative consequences. During the 1970s, the Democrats officially recognized and encouraged several special-interest caucuses to become active in Democratic National Committee meetings, including a Women's Caucus, Black Caucus, Asian-Pacific Caucus, Hispanic Caucus, Liberal/Progressive Caucus, Business and Professional Caucus, and a Lesbian and Gay Caucus. In 1985, under the leadership of Chairman Paul Kirk, who was convinced that "the prominence of the caucuses was conveying an image of the party as a collection of special interests," the party withdrew official caucus recognition.[79] Presently, while the black, women's, and Hispanic caucuses retain ex officio DNC Executive Committee representation, the role of the now informal caucuses is much less visible and influential.

During the 1970s and early 1980s, the Democrats also held a number of party mid-term conferences in which party issues were debated. But because of "fear of their own constituency groups," they have yielded to pressure from their congressional leaders, who believed that "any party forum would be seized by activists as a vehicle promoting their own agendas."[80] The last meaningful Democratic party forum was held in Philadelphia in 1982. Likewise Republicans, not anxious to call attention to the cultural conservatives and antiabortion stances of their right-wing, have recently avoided party-sponsored policy forums.

What contemporary parties, dominated by their officeholders, want is interest-group resources, particularly money, without the baggage of internal disputes that create the impression that interest groups and issue activists dominate party decision making.

CONCLUSION: REPRESENTATIONAL CONCERNS

The threat to the major parties posed by interest groups appears much diminished compared to even ten years ago. Political scientists now write of "party resurgence," and interest groups are seen as having less clout and influence on decision makers than previously thought.[81] In the electoral process, largely because of the decline of movement politics and efforts by the party leadership to temper the excesses of group influence, party operatives again are playing a central role. The national party committees, especially the four Hill committees, have turned the PAC threat into a positive force for the parties' officeholders, and have evolved into highly professional organizations providing valuable campaign resources.

From a representational perspective, a variety of concerns can be raised. Contemporary national parties look suspiciously like special interest groups of their own, whose major concern is to raise campaign resources for their parties' officeholders seeking reelection. When incumbents are threatened, both national parties may even cooperate with each other, as they did in 1987 in the face of a public outcry over congressional pay raises (the party chairmen agreed not to financially support challengers to incumbents who had voted for the pay raise). Because neither of the two parties is anxious to involve their group supporters in policy debates or their internal organizational business, policy issues go unexplored.

An electoral system based largely upon the ability of parties and their candidates to raise financial resources from special interests inevitably clashes with the notion that parties are aggregators of broad interests, potential counterweights to the excessive demands of special interests. In spite of heightened tension and rhetoric between Democrats and Republicans that characterizes contemporary Washington politics, especially on largely symbolic cultural issues, moneyed interests appear to have the upper hand, as both parties compete for funds. The Democratic party, traditionally the representative of the most vulnerable in society, has been perhaps most affected.

The notion that parties are in the midst of a resurgence begs many of the important representation questions that must be central to any analysis of party/interest group relations. Parties, as organizations devoted to incumbent safety with little if any regard to officeholder policy positions, not only don't control the excesses of special interest politics, but likely contribute to the problem as well.

NOTES

1. Leon D. Epstein, "The Scholarly Commitment to Parties" in Ada W. Finifter, ed., *Political Science: State of the Discipline* (Washington, D.C.: American Political Science Association, 1983); Allan J. Cigler, "Interest Groups: A Subfield in Search of an Identity" in William Crotty, ed., *Political Science: Looking to the Future,* vol. 4 (Evanston, Ill.: Northwestern U. Press, 1991).

2. Kay Lehman Schlozman, "What Accent and Heavenly Chorus? Political Equality and the American Political System," *Journal of Politics* 46 (1984): 1006–32;

Schlozman and John Tierney, *Organized Interests and American Democracy* (New York: Harper & Row, 1986).

3. Michael T. Hayes, "Interest Groups or Mass Society" in Allan J. Cigler and Burdett A. Loomis, eds., *Interest Group Politics*, 1st ed. (Washington, D.C.: Congressional Quarterly Press, 1983).

4. Thomas L. Gais, Mark W. Peterson, Jack L. Walker, "Interest Groups, Iron Triangles and Representative Institutions in American National Politics," *British Journal of Political Science* 14 (1984): 1611–85.

5. Burdett Loomis and Allan J. Cigler, "Introduction: The Changing Nature of Interest Group Politics" in Allan J. Cigler and Burdett A. Loomis, eds., *Interest Group Politics*, 3d ed. (Washington, D.C.: Congressional Quarterly Press, 1991).

6. E. E. Schattschneider, *Semisovereign People* (New York: Holt, Rinehart and Winston, 1960).

7. Belle Zeller, *American State Legislatures* (New York: Thomas Y. Crowell, 1954), pp. 190–93.

8. Larry J. Sabato, *PAC Power* (New York: Norton, 1985).

9. Carol S. Greenwald, *Group Power* (New York: Praeger, 1977), p. 211.

10. John Mark Hansen, *Gaining Access* (Chicago: U. of Chicago Press, 1991).

11. Ibid., p. 16.

12. Ibid.

13. Ibid., p. 17.

14. Arthur M. Schlesinger, *The Cycles of American History* (Boston: Houghton Mifflin, 1986), p. 264.

15. Jasper B. Shannon, *Money and Politics* (New York: Random House, 1959), p. 24.

16. David E. Truman, *The Governmental Process* (New York: Knopf, 1971), p. 17.

17. Robert H. Salisbury, "An Exchange Theory of Interest Groups," *Midwest Journal of Political Science* 13 (1969): 1–32.

18. Truman, *The Governmental Process*; James O. Wilson, *Political Organizations* (New York: Basic Books, 1973); Jack L. Walker, "The Origins and Maintenance of Interest Groups," *American Political Science Review* (1983): 390–406.

19. William P. Browne and Allan J. Cigler, "Introduction: Agricultural Interests" in William P. Browne and Allan J. Cigler, eds., *Agricultural Groups* (Westport, Conn.: Greenwood Press, 1990), p. xxiv.

20. Robert F. Bonitati, "Labor Political Clout in the 80s," *Campaigns and Elections* 1 (1980): 58.

21. David J. Greenstone, *Labor in American Politics* (New York: Alfred A. Knopf, 1969), p. 39.

22. Ibid., p. 48.

23. Harry M. Scoble, "Organized Labor in Electoral Politics," *Western Political Quarterly* 14 (1963): 666–85.

24. Alexander Heard, *The Costs of Politics* (Chapel Hill, N.C.: U. of North Carolina Press, 1960).

25. Nicholas A. Masters, "Organized Labor Bureaucracy as a Base of Support for the Democratic Party," *Law and Contemporary Problems* 27 (1962): 252–65.

26. Greenstone, *Labor in American Politics,* pp. 289–310.

27. Samuel J. Eldersveld, *Political Parties: A Behavioral Analysis* (Chicago: Rand McNally, 1964), p. 156.

28. Greenstone, *Labor in American Politics.*

29. David R. Mayhew, *Placing Parties in American Politics* (Princeton, N.J.: Princeton U. Press, 1986), p. 242.

30. Greenstone, *Labor in American Politics,* pp. 200–9.

31. V. O. Key, *Politics, Parties, and Pressure Groups* (New York: Thomas Y. Crowell, 1958), p. 73.

32. Ibid.

33. Hacker and Aberbach, 1962.

34. Martin Wattenberg, *The Decline of American Politics* (Cambridge, Mass.: Harvard U. Press, 1984); Everett Carll Ladd, *Where Have All the Voters Gone?* (New York: Norton, 1977); Stephen E. Frantzich, *Political Parties in the Technological Age* (White Plains, N.Y.: Longman, 1989).

35. Ladd, *Where Have All the Voters Gone?;* Ladd and Charles D. Hadley, *Transformation of the American Party System* (New York: Norton, 1975).

36. Byron Shafer, "The Notion of an Electoral Order: The Structure of Electoral Politics at the Accession of George Bush" in Byron Shafer, ed., *The End of Realignment?* (Madison, Wis.: U. of Wisconsin Press, 1991), p. 46.

37. Michael D. Reagan, "The Seven Fallacies of Business in Politics," *Harvard Business Review* 38 (1960): 60–68.

38. Elaine Ciulia Kamarack, "Structure as Strategy: Presidential Nominating Politics in the Post-Reform Era" in L. Sandy Maisel, ed., *The Parties Respond* (Boulder, Colo.: Westview Press, 1990).

39. Byron Shafer, *Quiet Revolution* (New York: Russell Sage Foundation, 1983), pp. 3–40.

40. Ibid., p. 95.

41. Theodore H. White, *The Making of the President, 1968* (New York: Pocket Books, 1970).

42. Byron Shafer, *Bifurcated Politics* (Cambridge, Mass.: Harvard U. Press, 1988), p. 108.

43. Ibid., p. 110.

44. James W. Ceaser, "Political Parties—Declining, Stabilizing or Resurging" in Anthony King, ed., *The New American Political System,* 2d ed. (Washington, D.C.: AEI Press, 1990), p. 110.

45. Michael J. Malbin, "The Conventions, Platforms, and Issue Activists" in Austin Ranney, ed., *The American Elections of 1980* (Washington, D.C.: American Enterprise Institute, 1981).

46. Ibid.

47. Shafer, *Quiet Revolution,* pp. 460–90.

48. Malbin, "The Conventions, Platforms, and Issue Activists," pp. 105–7.

49. Ronald Rapoport, Walter J. Stone, and Alan I. Abramowitz, "Do Endorsements Matter? Group Influence in the 1984 Democratic Caucuses," *American Political Science Review* 85 (1991): 193–203.

50. Austin Ranney, 1979.

51. Sabato, *PAC Power*, p. 7.

52. Ceaser, "Political Parties," p. 120.

53. David B. Magleby and Candice J. Nelson, *The Money Chase* (Washington, D.C.: The Brookings Institution, 1990), p. 103.

54. Harold W. Stanley and Richard G. Niemi, *Vital Statistics on American Politics*, 2d ed. (Washington, D.C.: Congressional Quarterly Press, 1991).

55. Magleby and Nelson, *The Money Chase*, p. 81.

56. Ibid., p. 102.

57. Ross K. Baker, *The New Fat Cats* (New York: Priority Press, 1989), p. 12.

58. David Adamany, "Political Parties in the 1980s" in Michael Malbin, ed., *Money and Politics in the United States* (Chatham, N.J.: Chatham House, 1984), pp. 101–2.

59. Sabato, *PAC Power*, pp. 150–51.

60. Ibid., p. 151.

61. Schlesinger, *The Cycles of American History*, p. 267.

62. Frantzich, *Political Parties*.

63. Howard L. Reiter, *Parties and Elections in Corporate America* (New York: St. Martin's Press, 1987), p. 230.

64. Everett Carll Ladd, "Misstating the Problems," *Public Opinion* 11 (1988): 2–4, 59.

65. R. Kenneth Godwin, *One Billion Dollars of Influence* (Chatham, N.J.: Chatham House, 1989).

66. Joseph Schlesinger, "The New American Political Party," *American Political Science Review* 79 (1985): 1151–69; Paul S. Herrnson and David Menefee-Libey, "The Dynamics of Party Organizational Development," *The Midsouth Political Science Journal* 11 (1990): 3–30.

67. Herrnson, *Party Campaigning in the 1980s* (Cambridge, Mass.: Harvard U. Press, 1988); Xandra Kayden, "Alive and Well and Living in Washington: The American Political Parties" in Michael Margolis and Gary Mauser, eds., *Manipulating Public Opinion* (Pacific Grove, Calif.: Brooks/Cole, 1989).

68. Frantzich, *Political Parties*.

69. Frank J. Sorauf, "PACs and Parties in American Politics" in Allan J. Cigler and Burdett A. Loomis, eds., *Interest Group Politics*, 3d ed. (Washington, D.C.: Congressional Quarterly Press, 1991), p. 230.

70. Herrnson, *Party Campaigning in the 1980s*.

71. Magleby and Nelson, *The Money Chase*.

72. Sorauf, "PACs and Parties."

73. Paul S. Herrnson, "National Party Organization and Congressional Campaigns." Paper presented at the annual meeting of the Midwest Political Science Association. Chicago, Illinois, 1985, p. 7.

74. Sabato, *PAC Power*; Sorauf, "PACs and Parties"; Herrnson, *Party Campaigning in the 1980s*; Jackson, 1988.

75. Frantzich, *Political Parties*.

76. Cigler, "Interest Groups: A Subfield," pp. 96–97.

77. John C. Green and James L. Guth, "Interest Group Politics and Interest Group Activists in American Politics" in Allan J. Cigler and Burdett Loomis, eds., *Interest Group Politics*, 2d ed. (Washington, D.C.: Congressional Quarterly Press, 1986).
78. Robert Kuttner, *The Life of the Party* (New York: Viking, 1988), p. 106
79. John Bibby, 1987, p. 87.
80. David S. Broder, "Democrats Showing Inability to Set, Sell a National Policy," *Washington Post*, 18 September 1991.
81. Slisbury, "An Exchange Theory."

REFERENCES

Adamany, David. 1984. "Political Parties in the 1980s." In Michael Malbin, ed., *Money and Politics in the United States.* Chatham, N.J.: Chatham House Press.

Baker, Ross K. 1989. *The New Fat Cats.* New York: Priority Press.

Bonitati, Robert F. 1980. "Labor Political Clout in the '80s." *Campaigns and Election* 1:57–64.

Broder, David S. 1991. "Democrats Showing Inability to Set, Sell a National Policy." *Washington Post.* September 18.

Browne, William P., and Allan J. Cigler. 1990. "Introduction: Agricultural Interests." In William P. Browne and Allan J. Cigler, eds., *Agricultural Groups.* Westport, Conn.: Greenwood Press.

Ceaser, James W. 1987. "Improving the Nomination Process." In A. James Reichley, ed., *Elections American Style.* Washington, D.C.: The Brookings Institution.

———. 1990. "Political Parties—Declining, Stabilizing or Resurging." In Anthony King, ed., *The New American Political System.* 2nd ver. Washington, D.C.: AEI Press.

Cigler, Allan J. 1991. "Interest Groups: A Subfield in Search of an Identity." In William Crotty, ed., *Political Science: Looking to the Future,* vol. 4. Evanston, Ill.: Northwestern U. Press.

Eldersveld, Samuel J. 1964. *Political Parties: A Behavioral Analysis.* Chicago: Rand McNally.

Epstein, Leon D. 1983. "The Scholarly Commitment to Parties." In Ada W. Finifter, ed., *Political Science: State of the Discipline.* Washington, D.C.: American Political Science Association.

Frantzich, Stephen E. 1989. *Political Parties in the Technological Age.* White Plains, N.Y.: Longman.

Gais, Thomas L., Mark W. Peterson, and Jack L. Walker. 1984. "Interest Groups, Iron Triangles and Representative Institutions in American National Politics." *British Journal of Political Science* 14:161–85.

Godwin, R. Kenneth. 1988. *One Billion Dollars of Influence.* Chatham, N.J.: Chatham House.

Green, John C., and James L. Guth. 1986. "Interest Group Politics and Interest Group Activists in American Politics." In Allan J. Cigler and Burdett Loomis, eds., *Interest Group Politics*, 2d ed. Washington, D.C.: Congressional Quarterly Press.

Greenstone, David J. 1969. *Labor in American Politics.* New York: Alfred A. Knopf.

Greenwald, Carol S. 1977. *Group Power.* New York: Praeger.

Hacker, Andrew, and Joel D. Aberbach. 1962. "Businessmen in Politics." *Law and Contemporary Problems* 27:266–79.

Hansen, John Mark. 1991. *Gaining Access.* Chicago: U. of Chicago Press.

Hayes, Michael T. 1983. "Interest Groups or Mass Society." In Allan J. Cigler and Burdett A. Loomis, eds., *Interest Group Politics*, 1st ed. Washington, D.C.: Congressional Quarterly Press.

Heard, Alexander. 1960. *The Costs of Politics.* Chapel Hill, N.C.: U. of North Carolina Press.

Herrnson, Paul S. 1985. "National Party Organization and Congressional Campaigns." Paper presented at the annual meeting of the Midwest Political Science Association, Chicago.

_____ . 1988. *Party Campaigning in the 1980s.* Cambridge, Mass.: Harvard U. Press.

_____ , and David Menefee-Libey. 1990. "The Dynamics of Party Organizational Development." *The Midsouth Political Science Journal* 11:3–30.

Kamarck, Elaine Ciulia. 1990. "Structure as Strategy: Presidential Nominating Politics in the Post-Reform Era." In L. Sandy Maisel, ed., *The Parties Respond.* Boulder, Colo.: Westview Press.

Kayden, Xandra. 1989. "Alive and Well and Living in Washington: The American Political Parties." In Michael Margolis and Gary Mauser, eds., *Manipulating Public Opinion.* Pacific Grove, Calif.: Brooks/Cole.

Key, V. O., Jr., 1958. *Politics, Parties, and Pressure Groups.* New York: Thomas Y. Crowell.

Kuttner, Robert. 1988. *The Life of the Party.* New York: Viking.

Ladd, Everett Carll, 1977. *Where Have All the Voters Gone?* New York: Norton.

_____ . 1988. "Misstating the Problems." *Public Opinion* 11:2–4, 59.

_____ with Charles D. Hadley. 1975. *Transformation of the American Party System.* New York: Norton.

Loomis, Burdett A., and Allan J. Cigler. 1991. "Introduction: The Changing Nature of Interest Group Politics." In Allan J. Cigler and Burdett A. Loomis, eds., *Interest Group Politics*, 3d ed. Washington, D.C.: Congressional Quarterly Press.

Magleby, David B., and Candice J. Nelson. 1990. *The Money Chase.* Washington, D.C.: The Brookings Institution.

Malbin, Michael J. 1981. The Conventions, Platforms, and Issue Activists. In Austin Ranney, ed., *The American Elections of 1980.* Washington, D.C.: American Enterprize Institute.

Masters, Nicholas A. "Organized Labor Bureaucracy as a Base of Support for the Democratic Party." *Law and Contemporary Problems* 27:252–65.

Mayhew, David R. 1986. *Placing Parties in American Politics*. Princeton, N.J.: Princeton U. Press.

Rapoport, Ronald, Walter J. Stone, and Alan I. Abramowitz. 1991. "Do Endorsements Matter? Group Influence in the 1984 Democratic Caucuses." *American Political Science Review* 84:193–203.

Reagan, Michael D. 1960. "The Seven Fallacies of Business in Politics." *Harvard Business Review* 38:60–68.

Reiter, Howard L. 1987. *Parties and Elections in Corporate America*. New York: St. Martin's Press.

Sabato, Larry J. 1984. *PAC Power*. New York: Norton.

Salisbury, Robert H. 1969. "An Exchange Theory of Interest Groups." *Midwest Journal of Political Science* 13:1–32.

_____ . 1990. "The Paradox of Interest Groups in Washington—More Groups, Less Clout." In Anthony King, ed., *The New American Political System*, 2d ver. Washington, D.C.: AEI Press.

Schattschneider, E. E. 1960. *The Semisovereign People*. New York: Holt, Reinehart and Winston.

Schlesinger, Arthur M., Jr. 1986. *The Cycles of American History*. Boston: Houghton Mifflin.

Schlesinger, Joseph. 1985. "The New American Political Party." *American Political Science Review* 79:1151–69.

Schlozman, Kay Lehman. 1984. "What Accent and Heavenly Chorus? Political Equality and the American Political System." *Journal of Politics* 46:1006–32.

_____ , and John Tierney. 1986. *Organized Interests and American Democracy*. New York: Harper and Row.

Scoble, Harry M. 1963. "Organized Labor in Electoral Politics." *Western Political Quarterly* 14:666–85.

Shafer, Byron. 1983. *Quiet Revolution*. New York: Russell Sage Foundation.

_____ . 1988. *Bifurcated Politics*. Cambridge, Mass.: Harvard U. Press.

_____ . 1991. "The Notion of an Electoral Order: The Structure of Electoral Politics at the Accession of George Bush." In Byron Shafer, ed., *The End of Realignment?* Madison, Wis.: U. of Wisconsin Press, 1991.

Shannon, Jasper B. 1959. *Money and Politics*. New York: Random House.

Sorauf, Frank J. 1988. *Money in American Elections*. Glenview, Ill.: Scott Foresman.

_____ . 1991. "PACs and Parties in American Politics." In Allan J. Cigler and Burdett A. Loomis, eds., *Interest Group Politics*, 3d ed. Washington, D.C.: Congressional Quarterly Press.

Stanley, Harold W., and Richard G. Niemi. 1990. *Vital Statistics on American Politics*, 2d ed. Washington, D.C.: Congressional Quarterly Press.

Truman, David B. 1951. *The Governmental Process*. New York: Knopf.

Walker, Jack L. 1983. "The Origins and Maintenance of Interest Groups." *American Political Science Review* 390–406.

Wattenberg, Martin. 1984. *The Decline of American Political Parties.* Cambridge, Mass.: Harvard U. Press.

White, Theodore H. 1970. *The Making of the President, 1968.* New York: Pocket Books.

Wilson, James Q. 1973. *Political Organizations.* New York: Basic Books.

Zeller, Belle. 1954. *American State Legislatures.* New York: Thomas Y. Crowell.

PART SIX

PARTIES IN THE GOVERNMENT

Parties do more than nominate candidates for office and help them campaign. They govern—or at least the men and women who get elected on party labels govern. If parties are representative institutions, then it clearly matters how our elected leaders relate to their parties.

Most modern presidents, from Franklin D. Roosevelt onward, have found party organizations too preoccupied with state and local concerns to be of much assistance in getting their programs enacted, according to Sidney M. Milkis in "The Presidency and Political Parties." Several presidents have attempted to centralize power in the federal bureaucracy and the White House, working around the party apparatus. Yet, Ronald Reagan and George Bush have tried to reinvigorate national party organizations.

David T. Canon, in "The Institutionalization of Leadership in the U.S. Congress," examines the evolution of party leadership in the House and the Senate. He finds that both the Democratic and Republican parties in the House of Representatives have established clear lines of succession in their party leadership ranks, although each has greatly expanded the number of leadership positions available to rank-and-file members. Senate Democrats have clearer lines of succession in their leadership structure than do Republicans. The more volatile pattern of party control of the Senate hinders the development of a highly institutionalized system of leadership succession.

What about the representational role of party elites in the government? Convention delegates are to the left (Democrats) or the right (Republicans) of the rank-and-file (see Miller, "A New Context for Presidential Politics" in the "Parties and Representation" section). If a realignment took place in the 1980s, Patricia A. Hurley argues in "Partisan Representation and the Failure of Realignment in the 1980s," the emerging dominant party (the Republicans) should better represent both its own partisans and independents. Comparing public opinion data with roll call voting by members of the House of Representatives between 1980 and 1984, Hurley finds that congressional Democrats represented their partisan followers better than Republicans in the House did theirs. Congressional Republicans remained far away from independents and did not moderate their policy views to woo these voters. At the elite level, no realignment took place.

Reading 18

THE PRESIDENCY AND POLITICAL PARTIES

Sidney M. Milkis

The relationship between the presidency and the American party system has always been a difficult one. The architects of the Constitution established a nonpartisan president who, with the support of the judiciary, was intended to play the leading institutional role in checking and controlling the "violence of faction" that the framers feared would destroy the fabric of representative democracy. Even after the presidency became a more partisan office during the early part of the nineteenth century, its authority continued to depend on an ability to transcend party politics. The president is nominated by a party but, unlike the British prime minister, is not elected by it.

The inherent tension between the presidency and the party system reached a critical point during the 1930s. The creation of the modern presidency, arguably the most significant institutional legacy of Franklin D. Roosevelt's New Deal, ruptured severely the limited, albeit significant, bond that linked presidents to their parties.[1] In fact, the modern presidency was crafted with the intention of reducing the influence of the party system on American politics. In this sense Roosevelt's extraordinary party leadership contributed to the decline of the American party system. This decline continued—even accelerated—under the administrations of subsequent presidents, notably Lyndon B. Johnson and Richard M. Nixon. Under Ronald Reagan, however, the party system showed at least some signs of transformation and renewal.

NEW DEAL PARTY POLITICS, PRESIDENTIAL REFORM, AND THE DECLINE OF THE AMERICAN PARTY SYSTEM

The New Deal seriously questioned the adequacy of the traditional natural rights liberalism of John Locke and the framers, which emphasized the need to constitutionally limit the scope of government's responsibilities.[2] The modern liberalism that became the public philosophy of the New Deal entailed a fundamental reappraisal of the concept of rights. As Roosevelt first indicated in his 1932 campaign speech at the Commonwealth Club in San Francisco, effective political reform would require, at minimum, the development of "an economic declaration of rights, an economic constitutional order," grounded in a commitment to guarantee a decent level of economic welfare for the American people. Although equality of opportunity had traditionally been promoted by limited government interference in society, certain economic and social changes in society, such as the closing of the frontiers and the growth of industrial combinations, demanded that America now recognize "the new terms of the old social contract."

The establishment of such a new constitutional order would require a reordering of the political process. The traditional patterns of American politics, characterized by constitutional mechanisms that impeded collective action, would have to give way to a more centralized and administrative governmental order. As Roosevelt put it, "The day of enlightened administration has come."[3]

The concerns expressed in the Commonwealth Club speech are an important guide to understanding the New Deal and its effects on the party system. The pursuit of an economic constitutional order presupposed a fundamental change in the relationship between the presidency and the party system. In Roosevelt's view, the party system, which was essentially based on state and local organizations and interests and was thus suited to congressional primacy, would have to be transformed into a national, executive-oriented system organized on the basis of public issues.

In this understanding Roosevelt was no doubt influenced by the thought of Woodrow Wilson. The reform of parties, Wilson believed, depended on extending the influence of the presidency. The limits on partisanship inherent in American constitutional government notwithstanding, the president represented his party's "vital link of connection" with the nation: "He can dominate his party by being spokesman for the real sentiment and purpose of the country, by giving the country at once the information and statements of policy which will enable it to form its judgments alike of parties and men."[4]

Wilson's words spoke louder than his actions; like all presidents after 1800, he reconciled himself to the strong fissures within his party.[5] Roosevelt, however, was less committed to working through existing partisan channels, and, more important, the New Deal represented a more fundamental departure than did Wilsonian progressivism from tra-

ditional Democratic policies of individual autonomy, limited government, and states' rights.

As president-elect, Roosevelt began preparations to modify the partisan practices of previous administrations. For example, feeling that
Wilson's adherence to traditional partisan politics in staffing the federal
government was unfortunate, Roosevelt expressed to Attorney General
Homer S. Cummings his desire to proceed along somewhat different
lines, with a view, according to the latter's diary, "to building up a national organization rather than allowing patronage to be used merely to
build Senatorial and Congressional machines."[6] Roosevelt followed traditional patronage practices during his first term, allowing Democratic
Chairman James Farley to coordinate appointments in response to local
organizations and Democratic senators, but the recommendations of organization people were not followed as closely after his reelection. Beginning in 1938 especially, as Ed Flynn, who became Democratic
chairman in 1940, indicated in his memoirs, "the President turned more
and more frequently to the so-called New Dealers," so that "many of the
appointments in Washington went to men who were supporters of the
President and believed in what he was trying to do, but who were not
Democrats in many instances, and in all instances were not organization
Democrats."[7]

Moreover, whereas Wilson took care to consult with legislative party
leaders in the development of his policy program, Roosevelt relegated
his party in Congress to a decidedly subordinate status. He offended legislators by his use of press conferences to announce important decisions
and, again unlike Wilson, eschewed the use of the party caucus in Congress. Roosevelt rejected as impractical, for example, the suggestion of
Rep. Alfred Phillips, Jr., "that those sharing the burden of responsibility
of party government should regularly and often be called into caucus
and that such caucuses should evolve party policies and choice of party
leaders."[8]

The most dramatic aspect of Roosevelt's attempt to remake the Democratic party was his twelve-state effort, involving one gubernatorial and
several congressional primary campaigns, to unseat conservative Democrats in 1938. Such intervention was not unprecedented; in particular,
William H. Taft and Wilson had made limited efforts to remove recalcitrant members from their parties. Yet Roosevelt's campaign took place on
an unprecedentedly large scale and, unlike previous efforts, made no attempt to work through the regular party organization. The degree to
which his action was viewed as a shocking departure from the norm is
indicated by the press's labeling of it as "the purge," a term associated

with Adolf Hitler's attempt to weed out dissension in Germany's National Socialism party and Joseph Stalin's elimination of "disloyal" party members from the Soviet Communist party.

Finally, in 1936 the Roosevelt administration successfully pushed for the abolition of the rule for Democratic national conventions that required support from two-thirds of the delegates for the nomination of president and vice president. This rule had been defended in the past because it guarded the most loyal Democratic section—the South— against the imposition of an unwanted ticket by the less habitually Democratic North, East, and West.[9] To eliminate it, therefore, both weakened the influence of southern democracy (which the journalist Thomas Stokes described as "the ball and chain which hobbled the Party's forward march") and facilitated the adoption of a national reform program.[10]

After the 1938 purge campaign, the columnist Raymond Clapper noted that "no President ever has gone as far as Mr. Roosevelt in striving to stamp his policies upon his party."[11] This massive partisan effort began a process whereby the party system was eventually transformed from local to national and programmatic party organizations. At the same time, the New Deal made partisanship less important. Roosevelt's partisan leadership, although it did effect important changes in the Democratic party organization, ultimately envisioned a personal link with the public that would better enable him to make use of his position as leader of the nation, not just of the party governing the nation.[12] For example, in all but one of the 1938 primary campaigns in which he personally participated, Roosevelt chose to make a direct appeal to public opinion rather than attempt to work through or reform the regular party apparatus. This strategy was encouraged by earlier reforms, especially the direct primary, which had begun to greatly weaken the grip of party organizations on the voters. Radio broadcasting also had made direct presidential appeals an enticing strategy, especially for as popular a president with as fine a radio presence as Roosevelt. After his close associate Felix Frankfurter urged him to go to the country in August 1937 to explain the issues that gave rise to the bitter Court-packing controversy, Roosevelt, perhaps in anticipation of the purge campaign, responded: "You are absolutely right about the radio. I feel like saying to the country—'You will hear from me soon and often. This is not a threat but a promise.' "[13]

In the final analysis, the "benign dictatorship" that Roosevelt sought to impose on the Democratic party was more conducive to corroding the American party system than to reforming it. Wilson's prescription for party reform—extraordinary presidential leadership—posed a serious, if not intractable, dilemma: on the one hand, the decentralized character of politics in the United States can be modified only by strong presidential leadership; on the other, a president determined to fundamentally alter the connection between the executive and his party eventually will shatter party unity.[14]

Roosevelt, in fact, was always aware that the extent to which his purposes could be achieved by party leadership was limited. He felt that a full revamping of partisan politics was impractical, given the obstacles to party government that are so deeply ingrained in the American political experience. The immense failure of the purge campaign reinforced this view.[15] Moreover, New Dealers did not view the welfare state as a partisan issue. The reform program of the 1930s was conceived as a "second bill of rights" that should be established as much as possible in permanent programs beyond the vagaries of public opinion and elections.[16]

Thus, the most significant institutional reforms of the New Deal did not promote party government but fostered instead a program that would help the president govern in the absence of party government. This program, as embodied in the 1937 executive reorganization bill, would have greatly extended presidential authority over the executive branch, including the independent regulatory commissions. The president and the executive agencies would also be delegated extensive authority to govern, making unnecessary the constant cooperation of party members in Congress. As the *Report of the President's Committee on Administrative Management* put it, with administrative reform the "brief exultant commitment" to progressive government that was expressed in the elections of 1932 and, especially, 1936 would now be more firmly established in "persistent, determined, competent, day by day administration of what the Nation has decided to do."[17]

Interestingly, the administrative reform program, which was directed to making politics less necessary, became, at Roosevelt's urging, a party government-style "vote of confidence" in the administration. Roosevelt initially lost this vote in 1938 when the reorganization bill was defeated in the House, but he did manage, through the purge campaign and other partisan actions, to keep administrative reform sufficiently prominent in party councils that a compromise measure passed in 1939. Although considerably weaker than Roosevelt's original proposal, the 1939 Executive Reorganization Act was a significant measure, which provided authority for the creation of the White House Office and the Executive Office of the President, and enhanced the president's control over bureaucratic agencies. As such, the 1939 administrative reform program represents the genesis of the institutional presidency, which was better equipped to govern independently of the regular political process.

The civil service reform carried out by the Roosevelt administration was another important part of the effort to displace partisan politics with executive administration. The original reorganization proposals of 1937 contained provisions to make the administration of the civil service more effective and to extend the merit system. The reorganization bill passed in 1939 was shorn of this controversial feature; but Roosevelt found it possible to accomplish extensive civil service reform by executive order. Although the purpose of administrative reform ostensibly was to strengthen the presidency, the extension of the merit system "upward, outward and downward" gave government machinery an especially New Deal hue. This entailed extending merit protection beginning in June 1938 to the personnel appointed by the Roosevelt administration during its first term, four-fifths of whom had been brought into government outside of regular merit channels.[18] Patronage appointments had traditionally been used to nourish the regular party apparatus, whereas the New Deal–initiated personnel practices were developed to orient the executive department toward expanding liberal programs. But, as the administrative historian Paul Van Riper has noted, the new practices created another kind of patronage, "a sort of intellectual and ideological patronage rather than the more traditional partisan type."[19]

Roosevelt's leadership and the administrative reform program of the New Deal transformed the Democratic party into a way station on the road to administrative government. As the presidency developed into an elaborate and ubiquitous institution, it preempted party leaders in many of their limited, but significant, duties: providing a link to interest groups, staffing the executive department, contributing to policy development, and organizing campaign support. Moreover, New Deal administrative reform was directed not to creating presidential government per se but to imbedding Progressive principles (considered tantamount to political rights) in a bureaucratic structure that would insulate reform and reformers from electoral change.

LYNDON JOHNSON'S GREAT SOCIETY AND THE TRANSCENDENCE OF PARTISAN POLITICS

Presidential leadership during the New Deal helped to set the tone when the party resumed its decline after 1950. It prepared the executive branch to be a government unto itself and established the presidency rather than the party as the locus of political responsibility. But the modern presidency was created to chart the course for, and direct the voyage to, a more liberal America. Roosevelt's pronouncement of a "second bill of rights" proclaimed and began this task, but it fell to Johnson, as one journalist noted, to "codify the New Deal vision of a good society."[20]

Johnson's attempt to create the Great Society marked a significant extension of programmatic liberalism and also accelerated the effort to transcend partisan politics. Roosevelt's ill-fated efforts to guide the affairs of his party were well remembered by Johnson, who came to Congress in 1937 in a special House election as an enthusiastic supporter of the New Deal. He took Roosevelt's experience to be the best example of the generally ephemeral nature of party government in the United States, and he fully expected the cohesive Democratic support he received from Congress after the 1964 elections to be temporary.[21] Thus Johnson, like Roosevelt, looked beyond the party system toward the politics of "enlightened administration."

Although Johnson avoided any sort of purge campaign and worked closely with Democratic congressional leaders, he took strong action to deemphasize the role of the traditional party organization. For example, the Johnson administration undertook a ruthless attack on the Democratic National Committee (DNC) beginning in late 1965, slashing its budget to the bone and eliminating several of its important programs, such as the highly successful voter registration division. The president also ignored the pleas of several advisers to replace the amiable but ineffective John Bailey as DNC chairman. Instead, he humiliated Bailey, keeping him on but turning over control of the scaled-back committee activities to the White House political liaison, Marvin Watson.[22]

Journalists and scholars have generally explained Johnson's lack of support for the regular party organization by referring to his political background and personality. Some have suggested that Johnson was afraid the DNC might be built into a power center capable of challenging his authority in behalf of the Kennedy wing of the party.[23] Others have pointed to Johnson's roots in the one-party system in Texas, an experience that inclined him to emphasize a consensus style of politics, based on support from diverse elements of the electorate that spanned traditional party lines.[24]

These explanations are surely not without merit. Yet to view Johnson's failures as a party leader in purely personal terms is to ignore the imperative of policy reform that also influenced his administration. Like Roosevelt, Johnson "had always regarded political parties, strongly rooted in states and localities, capable of holding him accountable, as intruders on the business of government."[25] Moreover, from the beginning of his presidency Johnson envisioned the creation of an ambitious program that would leave its mark on history in the areas of government organization, conservation, education, and urban affairs. Such efforts to advance not only the New Deal goal of economic security but also the "quality of American life" necessarily brought Johnson into sharp conflict with the still unreconstructed Democratic party.[26] As one Johnson aide put it, "Because of the ambitious reforms [LBJ] pushed, it was necessary to move well beyond, to suspend attention to, the party."[27]

There is considerable evidence of the Johnson administration's lack of confidence in the ability of the Democratic party to act as an intermediary between the White House and the American people. For example, an aide to Vice President Hubert Humphrey wrote Marvin Watson that "out in the country most Democrats at the State and local level are not intellectually equipped to help on such critical issues as Vietnam and the riots." After a meeting with Queens, New York, district leaders, the White House domestic adviser Joseph Califano reported that "they were . . . totally unfamiliar with the dramatic increases in the poverty, health, education and manpower training areas."[28] The uneasy relationship between the Johnson presidency and the Democratic party was particularly aggravated by the administration's aggressive commitment to civil rights, which created considerable friction with local party organizations, especially, but not exclusively, in the South. It is little wonder, then, that when trouble erupted in the cities, the president had his special assistants spend time in the ghettos around the country, instead of relying on the reports of local party leaders.[29]

Lack of trust in the Democratic party encouraged the Johnson administration to renew the New Deal pattern of institutional reform. In the area of policy development, one of the most significant innovations of the Johnson administration was to create several task forces under the supervision of the White House Office and the Bureau of the Budget to establish the basic blueprint of the Great Society. These working groups were made up of leading academics throughout the country who prepared reports during the Johnson presidency in virtually all areas of public policy. The specific proposals that came out of these groups, such as the Education Task Force's elementary-education proposal, formed the heart of the Great Society program. The administration took great care to protect the task forces from political pressures, even keeping them secret. Moreover, members were told to pay no attention to political considerations; they were not to worry about whether their recommendations would be acceptable to Congress and party leaders.[30]

The deemphasis of partisan politics that marked the creation of the Great Society was also apparent in the personnel policy of the Johnson presidency. As his main talent scout, Johnson chose not a political adviser but John Macy, who was also chairman of the Civil Service Commission. Macy worked closely with the White House staff, but, especially during the earlier days of the administration, he was responsible for making recommendations directly to the president. As the White House staff rather grudgingly admitted, Macy's "wheel ground exceedingly slow but exceedingly fine."[31] Candidates with impressive credentials and experience were uncovered after careful national searches.

The strong commitment to merit in the Johnson administration greatly disturbed certain advisers who were responsible for maintaining the president's political support. James Rowe, who was Johnson's campaign director in both 1964 and 1968, constantly hounded Macy, without success, to consider political loyalists more carefully. Rowe believed Johnson's personnel policy was gratuitously inattentive to political exigencies. At one point he ended a memo to Macy by saying, "Perhaps you can train some of those career men to run the political campaign in 1968. (It ain't as easy as you government people appear to think it is.)" Macy never responded, but the president called the next day to defend the policies of his personnel director and to give Rowe hell for seeking to interfere in the appointment process."[32]

The rupture between the presidency and the party made it difficult to sustain political enthusiasm and organizational support for the Great Society. The Democrats' very poor showing in the 1966 congressional elections precipitated a firestorm of criticism about the president's inattention to party politics, criticism that continued until Johnson withdrew from the 1968 campaign. Yet Johnson and most of his advisers felt this deemphasis on partisanship was necessary if the administration were to achieve programmatic reform and coordinate the increasingly unwieldy activities of government. During the early days of the Johnson presidency, one of his more thoughtful aides, Horace Busby, wrote Johnson a long memo in which he stressed the importance of establishing an institutional basis for the Great Society. About a year later, that same aide expressed great satisfaction that the Johnson presidency had confounded its critics in achieving notable institutional changes. In fact, these changes seemed to mark the full triumph of the Democrats as the party to end party politics:

> Most startling is that while all recognize Johnson as a great politician his appointments have been the most consistently free of politics of any President—in the Cabinet or at lower levels.
>
> On record, history will remember this as the most important era of non-partisanship since the "Era of Good Feeling" more than a century ago at the start of the nineteenth century. Absence of politics and partisanship is one reason the GOP is having a hard time mounting any respectable defense against either Johnson or his program.[33]

As in the case of the New Deal, however, the institutional innovations of the Great Society did not truly eliminate "politics" from the activities of the executive branch. Rather, the Great Society extended the
merging of politics and administration that had characterized executive
reform during the 1930s. For example, in order to improve his use of the
appointment process as a tool of political administration, Johnson issued
an executive order to create a new category of positions, called Noncareer
Executive Assignments (NEAs). In recognition of their direct involvement in policy making, NEAs were exempted from the usual civil service
requirements.

To be sure, NEAs gave Johnson a stronger foothold in the agencies.[34]
But the criteria his administration used to fill these positions emphasized
loyalty to Johnson's program rather than a more narrow, personal commitment to the president. Consequently, Johnson's active role as manager of the federal service, which John Macy considered unprecedented
for a "modern-day Chief Executive," helped to revive the high morale
and programmatic commitment that had characterized the bureaucracy
during the 1930s.[35] As White House aide Bill Moyers urged in a memo to
the newly created Department of Housing and Urban Development, the
goal of the Great Society was to renew "some of the zeal—coupled with
sound, tough executive management of the New Deal days."[36]

The attempt to marry programmatic commitment with technical
competence also characterized the work of the Johnson task forces. Each
of the outside task forces generated proposals that conformed with Johnson's vision of a Great Society. Moreover, each included both government officials and professors in order to provide an umbilical cord
connecting campus and Washington. Finally, all task force proposals as
well as all appointments were carefully imbued with the political concerns of the executive office of the president so that Johnson could put
forth a reasonably comprehensive program that established his political
identity.[37]

The legacy of Johnson's assault on party politics was apparent in the
1968 election. By 1966 Democratic leaders no longer felt they were part of
a national coalition. As 1968 approached the Johnson administration was
preparing a campaign task force that would work independently of the
regular party apparatus.[38] These actions greatly accelerated the breakdown of the state and local Democratic machinery, placing organizations
in acute distress in nearly every large state.[39] By the time Johnson withdrew from the election in March 1968, the Democratic party was already
in the midst of a lengthy period of decay that was accentuated, but not
really caused, by the conflict over the Vietnam War.

Thus, the tumultuous 1968 Democratic convention and the party re-forms that followed in the wake of those events should be viewed as the culmination of longstanding efforts to free the presidency from tradi-tional partisan influences. In many respects, the expansion of presiden-tial primaries and other changes in nomination politics initiated by the McGovern-Fraser Commission were a logical extension of the modern presidency. The very "quietness" of the "revolution" in party rules that took place during the 1970s is evidence in itself that the party system was forlorn by the end of the Johnson era. These changes could not have been accomplished over the opposition of alert and vigorous party lead-ership.[40]

Johnson was well aware that forces were in place for the collapse of the regular party apparatus by 1968. From 1966 on his aides virtually bombarded him with memos warning him of the disarray in the Demo-cratic party organization. Johnson was also informed that reform forces in the states were creating "a new ball game with new rules." These memos indicated that the exploitation of a weakened party apparatus by insurgents would allow someone with as little national prominence as antiwar senator Eugene McCarthy to mount a head-on challenge, which could not be easily fended off by the power of incumbency.[41] The presi-dent expressed his own recognition of the decline of party politics in a private meeting he had with Humphrey on April 3, 1968, a few days after announcing his decision not to run for reelection. Although indicating an intention to remain publicly neutral, Johnson wished his vice presi-dent well. But he expressed concern about Humphrey's ability to win the support of the party organization: "This the president cannot assure the Vice President because he could not assure it for himself."[42] Like Roosevelt, Johnson had greatly diminished his political capital in pursuit of programmatic innovation.

RICHARD NIXON, NONPARTISANSHIP, AND THE DEMISE OF THE MODERN PRESIDENCY

Considering that the New Deal and Great Society were established through a strategy to replace traditional party politics with administra-tion, it is not surprising that when a conservative challenge to liberal re-form emerged, it entailed the development of a conservative "administrative presidency."[43] This further contributed to the decline of partisan politics.

Until the 1960s opponents of the welfare state were generally op-posed to the modern presidency, which had served as a fulcrum of liberal reform. Nevertheless, by the end of the Johnson administration, it became clear that a strong conservative movement would require an activist program of retrenchment in order to counteract the enduring effects of the New Deal and Great Society. Once the opponents of liberal public policy, primarily housed in the Republican party, recognized this, they looked to the possibility that the modern presidency could be a two-edged sword. Fred Greenstein argues that even Dwight D. Eisenhower, who talked of "restoring the balance," quickly became a defender of the accrued responsibilities of the modern presidency.[44]

With the Nixon administration especially, conservatives began to use the presidency as a lever to effect fundamental policy change in a rightward direction. Nixon emphasized a legislative strategy to achieve policy goals during the first two years of his presidency. But, faced with few legislative achievements, he later attempted to carry out his policies by executive administration. Nixon intensified his efforts to strengthen executive administration after 1972, reflecting the more conservative and pessimistic position on domestic issues that characterized his presidency during the second term. The administrative actions of the Nixon presidency were, of course, a logical extension of the practices of Roosevelt and Johnson. The centralization of authority in the White House and the reduction of the regular Republican organization to perfunctory status during the Nixon years was hardly new.[45] The complete autonomy of the committee for the Re-Election of the President (CREEP) from the regular Republican organization in the 1972 campaign was but the final stage of a long process of White House preemption of the national committee's political responsibilities. And the administrative reform program that was pursued after Nixon's reelection, in which executive authority was concentrated in the hands of White House operatives and four cabinet "supersecretaries," was the culmination of a longstanding tendency in the modern presidency to reconstitute the executive branch as a more formidable and independent instrument of government.[46]

Thus, just as Roosevelt's presidency anticipated the Great Society, Johnson's presidency anticipated the administrative presidency of Richard Nixon. Ironically, the strategy of pursuing policy goals through administrative capacities that had been created for the most part by Democratic presidents was considered especially suitable by a minority Republican president who faced a hostile Congress and bureaucracy intent on preserving those presidents' programs. Nixon, actually, surpassed previous modern presidents in viewing the party system as an obstacle to effective governance.

In many respects, however, the conservative administrative presidency was ill-conceived. The centralization of responsibility within the presidency had originally been instituted to build a more liberal America. As a program of the Democratic party, the modern presidency depended on broad agreement among Congress, the bureaucracy, and eventually the courts to expand the welfare state; a formidable politics of executive administration depended, then, upon a consensus that powers should be delegated to the executive. Once such a system was in place, any conservative assault on the welfare state, such as that intended by Nixon, needed to be more intense and calculated than those of the earlier, liberal presidents. Yet, mainly because of Watergate, Nixon's presidency had the effect of strengthening opposition to the unilateral use of presidential power, while further attenuating the bonds that linked presidents to the party system. The evolution of the modern presidency now left it in complete political isolation.

This isolation continued during the Ford and Carter years, so much so that by the end of the 1970s statesmen and scholars were lamenting the demise of the presidency as well as of the party system. The ability of the political parties to facilitate consensus and redirect policy seemed to be a thing of the past. The modern presidency, which was developed to alleviate the need for parties in the political process, now seemed overburdened with responsibilities and a lack of organizational support. Although in the past critical realignments had restored the vigor of democratic politics in the United States and provided opportunities for extraordinary presidential leadership, American government now seemed stricken by a "dealignment"; the disintegration rather than the renewal of the polity.[47]

THE REAGAN PRESIDENCY AND THE REVITALIZATION OF PARTY POLITICS

Although the traditional party system was severely weakened by the emergence of the modern presidency, a phoenix may yet emerge from the ashes. The erosion of old-style partisan politics has opened up the possibility for the development of a more national and issue-oriented party system, which may provide the foundation for closer ties between presidents and their parties.

The Republican party, in particular, has developed a strong organizational apparatus that displays unprecedented strength, for an American party, at the national level. Since 1976 the Republican National Committee (RNC) and the other two national Republican campaign organizations, the National Republican Senatorial Committee and the National Republican Congressional Committee, have greatly expanded their efforts to raise funds and provide services for party candidates. Moreover, these efforts have carried the national party into activities, such as the publication of public policy journals and the distribution of comprehensive briefing books for candidates, that demonstrate its interest in generating programmatic proposals that might be politically useful. The Democrats have lagged behind in party-building efforts, but the losses they suffered in the 1980 elections encouraged them to modernize the national party machinery, openly imitating some of the devices employed by the Republicans.[48] As a result, the traditional party apparatus, based on patronage and state and local organizations, has given way to a more programmatic party politics based on the national organization. These developments have led some to suggest that there is not simply a revitalization but a reconstruction of political parties as more formidable organizations.[49] Perhaps, therefore, a party system has finally evolved that is compatible with the national polity forged on the anvil of the New Deal.

The revival of the Republican party as a force against executive administration may complete the development of a new American party system. The nomination and election of Ronald Reagan, a far more ideological conservative than Nixon, galvanized the Republican commitment to programs, such as "regulatory relief" and "new federalism," that severely challenged the institutional legacy of the New Deal. If such a trend continues, the circumvention of the regular political process by administrative action may be displaced by the sort of full-scale debate about political questions usually associated with political realignments.

It is also significant that the Reagan administration made a concerted effort to strengthen the Republican party.[50] In order to enhance cooperation among the White House, the national committee, and the congressional campaign organizations, Reagan chose his close friend, Sen. Paul Laxalt, R-Nev., to fill a newly created position—general party chairman. Laxalt's close associate Frank Fahrenkopf former chairman of the Nevada Republican party, was given the traditional post of the Republican National Committee chair. The White House, with Laxalt's support, then actively intervened to replace the head of the National Republican Senatorial Committee, Sen. Robert Packwood of Oregon, a frequent Reagan critic, with a more reliable political ally, Sen. Richard Lugar of Indiana.[51] These developments enabled the Reagan administration to improve the coordination of campaigns and policy development within the party without undermining Republican organizational strength. Reagan himself surprised even his own political director with his "total readiness" to shoulder such partisan responsibilities as making numerous fund-raising appearances for the party and its candidates.[52] Apparently, after having spent the first fifty years of his life as a Democrat, Reagan brought the enthusiasm of a convert to Republican activities.

Future presidents may lack Reagan's political skill or motivation to support their parties, which will mean a decline of party politics. Yet the recent institutionalization of the national committees and the strengthening of the campaign committees in Congress have created the foundation for a national party organization that is no longer exclusively absorbed in presidential politics.[53] This may increase the distance between the regular party apparatus and the presidency in one sense, but it also makes possible a strengthened alliance. Because the reconstitution of the party system has been associated with issues and sophisticated fund-raising techniques rather than with the patronage that served as the lifeblood of traditional party politics, it may pose less of an obstacle than did the traditional apparatus to the personal and programmatic ambitions of presidents. For example, leading members of the modern party organization are likely to be more sensitive than were traditional party operatives to exigencies of governance that prevent presidents from being strict partisans. As William Greener, the former deputy chief of staff for political operations at the RNC, put it:

> It is unreasonable to expect a President to be a partisan in all respects. Maybe twenty years ago complete partisanship made sense. But the scope of what government undertakes now is much greater. You could not strictly speaking use the party as a spoils system.[54]

The experience of the Reagan administration suggests how the relationship between the president and the party can be mutually beneficial. Republican party strength provided Reagan with the support of a formidable institution, solidifying his personal popularity and facilitating the support of his program in Congress. As a result, the Reagan presidency was able to suspend the paralysis that seemed to afflict American government in the 1970s, even though the Republicans never attained control of the House of Representatives. In turn, Reagan's popularity served the party by strengthening its fund-raising efforts and promoting a shift in voters' party loyalties, placing the Republicans by 1985 in a position of virtual parity with the Democrats for the first time since the 1940s.[55] It may be, then, that the 1980s marked the watershed both for a new political era and for a renewed link between presidents and the party system.

Nevertheless, the separation of political institutions in the United States provides a precarious setting for comprehensive party programs. The Reagan White House, intent on a conservative revolution, fought to impose a program of reform that necessarily looked beyond the limited

451

agreements that could be worked out in the fragmented structure of American party politics. It is unlikely that the emergence of national parties will fundamentally alter these processes. The intractable fragmentation that governs party politics in the United States will thus continue to encourage modern presidents—particularly those intent on ambitious policy reform—to emphasize popular appeals and administrative action rather than collective responsibility. It is not surprising, therefore, that the Reagan presidency frequently pursued its program with acts of administrative discretion that short-circuited the legislative process and weakened efforts to carry out broad-based party policies. The Iran-*contra* scandal, for example, was not simply a matter of the president being asleep on his watch. Rather, it revealed the Reagan administration's determination to assume a more forceful anti-Communist posture in Central America in the face of a recalcitrant bureaucracy and Congress.[56]

Sen. Richard Lugar, who as chair of the Foreign Relations Committee from 1985 to 1987 acted as Reagan's Senate floor leader in matters of foreign policy, considers the Iran-*contra* affair to have been a "glaring exception" to Reagan's general willingness to consult with Congress and to work closely with the Republican leadership. The irony, according to Lugar, is that this uncharacteristic inattention to "partisan" responsibility made possible the president's "most signal policy failure."[57]

Yet a close examination of policy making during the Reagan years provides other examples of the administration resorting to unilateral executive action when it anticipated or was confronted with resistance within the party councils. A wide range of deregulation policies were pursued not through legislative change but by administration inaction, delay, and repeal. President Reagan's executive orders 12,291 and 12,498, which mandated a comprehensive review of existing and proposed agency regulations by the Office of Management and Budget (OMB), demonstrated quite clearly the emphasis he placed on *administrative* regulatory relief.[58] In this light, the Iran-*contra* scandal may be seen not as an aberration but as an extreme example of how the Reagan administration reacted when its proposals were resisted by Congress.

The importance of presidential politics and executive administration in the Reagan presidency may actually have weakened the prospects for a Republican realignment. The journalist Sidney Blumenthal has argued that Reagan "did not reinvent the Republican party so much as transcend it. His primary political instrument was the conservative movement, which inhabited the party out of convenience."[59] Blumenthal is only partly correct—Reagan's commitment to strengthen his party was sincere and, in many respects, effective. Nevertheless, his administration's devotion to certain tenets of conservative ideology led it to rely on unilateral executive action and on the mobilization of conservative citizen groups in ways that ultimately compromised the president's support for the Republican party. To some extent, at least, Republican leaders were justified in blaming Reagan's personalistic leadership style for the failure to convert his personal popularity into Republican control of the government.[60] Reagan's landslide reelection in 1984 did not prevent the Democrats from maintaining control of the House of Representatives; nor did his plea to the voters during the 1986 congressional campaigns to elect Republican majorities prevent the Democrats from recapturing control of the Senate.

As such, Reagan did not transform Washington. He managed to strengthen the Republican beachhead in the nation's capital, solidifying his party's longstanding dominance of the presidency and providing better opportunities for conservatives to become part of the Washington community. But the Democrats' control of Congress remained as solid as ever when Reagan retired to his ranch in California.

THE ACCESSION OF GEORGE BUSH

The 1988 election seemed to indicate that a "split-level" realignment had become an enduring characteristic of American politics. Certainly Vice President George Bush's election as president was a triumph for Ronald Reagan. The Bush campaign took its shape from the Reagan legacy: in the final analysis, Bush's nomination by the Republican party and his victory by a substantial margin over his Democratic opponent, Massachusetts governor Michael Dukakis, were expressions of the voters' approval of the Reagan administration.[61] Yet the 1988 election also revealed the limits of the Reagan revolution, reflecting in its outcome the underlying pattern that has characterized American politics since 1968: Republican dominance of the White House, Democratic ascendancy almost everywhere else. In fact, the 1988 election represented an extreme manifestation of this pattern. Never before had a president been elected while the other party gained ground in the House, the Senate, the state legislatures, and the state governorships. Never before had voters given a newly elected president fewer fellow partisans in Congress than they gave Bush.[62]

Bush's first year as president revealed both his skill as a political conciliator and the continuing obstacles to the restoration of partisanship in the presidency. Facing a Democratic Congress and lacking his predecessor's rhetorical ability to appeal directly to the electorate, Bush had little choice but to reach across party lines to accomplish his goals. His "kinder, gentler" approach to Congress was often reciprocated during his first year. After intensive negotiations, Bush managed to reach agreements with Congress on two of the most troubling issues he faced upon taking office—aid to the *contra* rebels in Nicaragua and the crisis of the savings and loan industry. The president won high marks from many legislators for his give-and-take approach to domestic and foreign policy, as well as for the personal attention he paid to the political needs of Democrats and Republicans alike. But several Republicans, especially the party's more conservative members, grew restless at Bush's disinclination to lead in a partisan style. Jeffrey A. Eisenach, who advised the 1988 presidential campaign of Delaware governor Pierre S. duPont, expressed the widespread fear of conservatives that the Republican party would not gain control of Congress in the 1990s should Bush "submerge the difference between the parties so it's impossible to create a set of issues to distinguish Republicans from Democrats."[63]

In many ways, however, Bush's conciliatory approach camouflaged an aggressive partisanship aimed at extending the political effects of the Reagan revolution beyond the presidency. Having served as a Republican county chair in Texas during the 1960s and as chair of the RNC during the Watergate scandal, Bush, more than any other recent president, came to the White House with a zeal for his partisan duties. He not only continued the Reagan practice of campaigning for fellow Republicans and of raising funds for the regular party apparatus, but he also gave his party's national organization an unprecedentedly high profile in the era of the modern presidency. Significantly, Bush placed his principal political adviser, Lee Atwater, not in the White House (the usual custom of modern presidents), but in the national party chair.[64]

Atwater, with the president's approval, has not confined himself to the customary responsibility of the party chair to preside over the party's institutions. Instead, he has transformed the RNC into an aggressive political organization that seeks to highlight the differences between the Democrats and Republicans on economic, social, and foreign policy issues at every level of the political system. As such, Atwater's aggressive partisanship has provided balance to a presidency that otherwise favors consultation and compromise over confrontation.

It remains to be seen whether Bush's dual approach to presidential and party governance will extend the reach of the Reagan revolution. The public certainly approved of the way Bush was handling his job during his first year in office. Polls in January 1990 recorded that three of four Americans approved of Bush's performance as president, a level rarely achieved by presidents since World War II and especially since the crises of political confidence brought on by the Vietnam War and Watergate. None of the four presidents before Bush—Nixon, Ford, Carter, or Reagan—stood that tall with the public after a year in office.[65]

Bush's popularity, however, did not immediately redress the Republican party's weakness below the presidential level. The party's candidates did badly in a series of elections in 1989, suffering especially important defeats in the Virginia and New Jersey gubernatorial races. In addition, Atwater's style of hard-edged partisanship suffered a setback in 1989 when an RNC memo, ostensibly intended to attack the liberal politics of the new Democratic Speaker, Thomas Foley, was widely perceived to have implied that Foley might be a homosexual. Although Atwater insisted he had nothing to do with the memo, and the Republican official who released it resigned immediately, the incident turned into a three-week media storm and tarnished the image of the vaunted new Republican machine.[66]

Thus, the closer ties that the Reagan and Bush administrations have tried to forge between the modern presidency and the Republican party have yet to alter the unprecedented partisan and electoral divisions that characterize the recent era of "split-level" realignment. Furthermore, the persistence of divided government itself retards the restoration of partisanship to the presidency.

The disassembling of the partisan and presidential realms in American politics is reinforced by the modern nominating process, a legacy of the McGovern-Fraser reforms. These reforms established the conditions for a candidate-centered system of presidential selection that discourages close cooperation between presidential candidates and their fellow partisans during the course of the general election campaign.

There have been important efforts to "reform the reforms," and the decline of party caused by its loss of control over nominations has been ameliorated by the strengthening of the financial and organizational capacity of the national and congressional committees. Yet the process of selecting presidential candidates by a series of state primaries and caucuses is so permeable that it may be virtually impossible to sustain any substantial spirit of partisan community.

The modern nominating process has created especially difficult problems for the Democrats, who are more divided than Republicans on most issues and are therefore less able to develop a strategically unified national party organization.[67] The fragility of Democratic party-building efforts was revealed all too clearly during the 1988 campaign. The 1988 Convention Rules Committee was controlled by Michael Dukakis, who was eager to placate his chief rival for the nomination, Jesse Jackson. The committee agreed to changes in the nomination rules for 1992 that subordinated the interests of the party to the short-term tactical considerations of the leading candidates. These changes—one tied the selection of Democratic delegates more closely to each candidate's share of the primary or caucus vote, and another sharply reduced the number of "superdelegates" (party and elected officials with guaranteed seats as uncommitted delegates) at the 1992 convention—were a retreat from the efforts made by Democratic officials since 1980 to strengthen the role of party leaders in the nominating process. Rep. David Price, D-N.C., a leader in the effort to reform the reforms, observed with dismay: "It's a familiar path we see. Candidates meet their short-term needs but sell out the long-term interests of the party."[68]

Finally, it must be recognized that the revival of partisanship may require presidents who are committed to lessening White House influence to favor shared responsibility with the diverse elements of the party. As we have seen, during his first year in office George Bush displayed an unusual disposition to use, and to delegate responsibility to, his party, despite his bipartisan style of dealing with Congress. Even if such leadership makes sense politically, however, it remains to be seen whether future presidents will recognize its wisdom. As Alexis de Tocqueville noted about the forces tending toward centralization in a democracy, "The only public men in democracies who favor decentralization are, almost invariably, either very disinterested or extremely mediocre; the former are scarce and the latter are powerless."[69]

NOTES

1. Elizabeth Sanders has argued that "Woodrow Wilson was the first clearly 'modern' president, the first to recognize the full institutional implications of the distinction between his and his party's electoral constituencies." Sanders, "The Institutional Conditions of an Instrumentalist Presidency: Contrasting Threads of Reform in American Political Development." (Paper delivered to the 1989 annual meeting of the American Political Science Association, Atlanta, Georgia, August 31.)

To be sure, Wilson, building on Theodore Roosevelt's innovative "stewardship" of the nation, inaugurated a new theory and practice of executive power that strengthened the presidency and established its independence from the regular party organizations. Nevertheless, it fell to Franklin D. Roosevelt to institutionalize these changes in the executive office. Unlike Theodore Roosevelt and Wilson, FDR presided over a realignment, the first in American history to focus national attention on the potential of the presidency to expand the political capability of the American people. None of the pre–New Deal realignments had elevated the executive to preeminent leadership status.

2. For a more detailed treatment of the issues discussed in this chapter, see Sidney M. Milkis, *The Modern Presidency and the Transformation of the American Party System* (New York: Oxford U. Press, forthcoming).

3. Franklin D. Roosevelt, *Public Papers and Addresses*, 13 vols. (New York: Random House, 1938–1950), 1: 751–52.

4. Woodrow Wilson, *Constitutional Government in the United States* (New York: Columbia U. Press, 1908), pp. 68–69.

5. Arthur S. Link, "Woodrow Wilson and the Democratic Party," *Review of Politics* 18 (April 1956): 146–56. Wilson effectively established himself as the principal spokesman for the Democratic party. But he accepted traditional partisan practices concerning legislative deliberations and appointments in order to gain support for his program in Congress, thus failing to strengthen the Democratic party's organization or its fundamental commitment to Progressive principles.

6. Personal and Political Diary of Homer Cummings, 5 January 1933, box 234, No. 2, 90, Homer Cummings Papers (no. 9973), Manuscripts Department, U. of Virginia Library, Charlottesville, Virginia.

7. Edward J. Flynn, *You're the Boss* (New York: Viking, 1947), p. 153.

8. Alfred Phillips, Jr., to Franklin D. Roosevelt, 9 June 1937; and Roosevelt to Phillips, 16 June 1937, President's Personal File, 2666, Franklin D. Roosevelt Library, Hyde Park, New York.

9. Franklin Clarkin, "Two-Thirds Rule Facing Abolition," *New York Times*, 5 January 1936, sec. 4, 10.

10. Thomas Stokes, *Chip Off My Shoulder* (Princeton: Princeton U. Press, 1940), p. 503. For an assessment of Roosevelt's role in the abolition of the two-thirds rule that also addresses the significance of this party reform, see Harold F. Bass, Jr., "Presidential Party Leadership and Party Reform: Franklin D. Roosevelt and the Abrogation of the Two-Thirds Rule." (Paper delivered to the 1985 annual meeting of the Southern Political Science Association, Nashville, Tennessee, November 7–9.)

11. Raymond Clapper, "Roosevelt Tries the Primaries," *Current History* (October 1938): 16.

12. Morton Frisch, *Franklin D. Roosevelt: The Contribution of the New Deal to American Political Thought and Practice* (Boston: St. Wayne, 1975), p. 79.

13. Frankfurter to Roosevelt, 9 August 1937, box 210, The Papers of Thomas G. Corcoran; Roosevelt to Frankfurter, 12 August 1937, reel 60, Felix Frankfurter Papers; both in Manuscript Division, Library of Congress, Washington, D.C.

14. Herbert Croly, a fellow Progressive, criticized Wilson's concept of presidential party leadership along these lines. Although he shared Wilson's view that executive power needed to be strengthened, Croly argued that the "necessity of such leadership [was] itself an evidence of the decrepitude of the two-party system." A strong executive would not reform parties, but instead would establish the conditions in which partisan responsibility would decline and a more direct and palpable link between the president and public opinion would be created. The emergence of a modern executive and the destruction of the two-party system, Croly wrote, "was an indispensable condition of the success of progressive democracy." See *Progressive Democracy* (New York: Macmillan, 1914), pp. 345–48.

15. In the dozen states where the president acted against entrenched incumbents, he was successful in only two—Oregon and New York. Moreover, the purge campaign galvanized opposition throughout the nation, apparently contributing to the heavy losses the Democrats sustained in the 1938 general elections.

16. The term "second bill of rights" comes from Roosevelt's 1944 State of the Union message, which reaffirmed the New Deal's commitment to an economic constitutional order. Roosevelt, *Public Papers and Addresses*, 13:40.

17. *Report of the President's Committee on Administrative Management* (Washington, D.C.: U.S. Government Printing Office, 1937), p. 53. The President's Committee on Administrative Management, headed by Louis Brownlow, played a central role in the planning and politics of executive reorganization from 1936 to 1940. For a full analysis of the committee, see Barry Karl, *Executive Reorganization and Reform in the New Deal* (Cambridge, Mass.: Harvard U. Press, 1963).

18. Richard Polenberg, *Reorganizing Roosevelt's Government* (Cambridge, Mass.: Harvard U. Press, 1966), pp. 22–23, 184. The merging of politics and administration took an interesting course as a result of the passage of the Hatch Act in 1939. Until the passage of this bill, which barred most federal employees from participating in campaigns, the Roosevelt administration was making use of the growing army of federal workers in state and local political activity, including some of the purge campaigns. The Hatch Act demolished the national Roosevelt political machine as distinct from the regular Democratic organization. Yet Roosevelt was more interested in orienting the executive branch as an instrument of programmatic reform than he was in developing a national political machine, and the insulation of federal officials from party politics was not incompatible with such a task. This explains why Roosevelt, although he fought against passage of the Hatch bill, decided to sign it.

19. Paul Van Riper, *History of the United States Civil Service* (Evanston, Ill.: Row, Peterson, 1958), p. 327.

20. Richard A. Rovere, "A Man for This Age Too," *New York Times Magazine*, 11 April 1965, 118. For an account of the influence of Roosevelt and the New Deal on Johnson's presidency, see William E. Leuchtenburg, *In the Shadow of FDR: From Harry Truman to Ronald Reagan*, rev. ed. (Ithaca: Cornell U. Press, 1985), chap. 4.

21. Lyndon Baines Johnson, *The Vantage Point: Perspectives of the Presidency, 1963–1969* (New York: Holt, Rinehart and Winston, 1971), p. 323.

22. Theodore White, *The Making of a President, 1968* (New York: Atheneum, 1969), p. 107.

23. Rowland Evans and Robert Novak, "Too Late for LBJ," *Boston Globe*, 21 December 1966, p. 27.

24. David Broder, "Consensus Politics: End of an Experience," *Atlantic Monthly*, October 1966, p. 62.

25. Doris Kearns, *Lyndon Johnson and the American Dream* (New York: New American Library, 1976), p. 256.

26. Larry O'Brien, Johnson's chief legislative aide, gives an interesting report on one of the early strategy sessions that led to the Great Society in a November 1964 memo, which expressed concern about the acute political problems he an-

ticipated would result from such an ambitious program. Memorandum, Larry O'Brien to Henry Wilson, 24 November 1964, Henry Wilson Papers, box 4, Lyndon Baines Johnson Library, Austin, Texas.

27. Interview with Horace Busby, 25 June 1987.

28. Memorandum, William Connel to Marvin Watson, 27 August 1967, Marvin Watson Files, box 31; Memorandum, Joe Califano to the president, 27 March 1968, Office Files of the President (Dorothy Territo), box 10; both in Johnson Library.

29. Memorandum, Harry C. McPherson, Jr., and Clifford L. Alexander to the president, 11 February 1967, Office Files of Harry McPherson; Sherwin J. Markman, Oral History, by Dorothy Pierce McSweeny, tape 1, 21 May 1969, pp. 24–36; both in Johnson Library. Many local Democrats felt threatened by the community action program with its provision for "maximum feasible participation." See Daniel P. Moynihan, *Maximum Feasible Misunderstanding* (New York: Free Press, 1970), pp. 144–45.

30. William E. Leuchtenberg, "The Genesis of the Great Society," *Reporter*, 21 April 1966, p. 38.

31. Memorandum, Hayes Redmon to Bill Moyers, 5 May 1966, box 12, Office Files of Bill Moyers, Johnson Library. For an excellent book-length treatment of Johnson's personnel policy, see Richard L. Schott and Dagmar S. Hamilton, *People, Positions and Power: The Political Appointments of Lyndon Johnson* (Chicago: U. of Chicago Press, 1983).

32. Memorandum, James Rowe for John W. Macy, Jr., 28 April 1965, John Macy Papers, box 504; James H. Rowe, Oral History, by Joe B. Frantz, interview 2, 16 September 1969, pp. 46–47; both in Johnson Library. Rowe's battles with Macy are noteworthy and ironic, for as a charter member of the White House Office he performed Macy's role for the Roosevelt administration, upholding the principle of merit against the patronage requests of DNC chairman James Farley and his successor, Ed Flynn.

33. Draft memorandum, Horace Busby to Mr. Johnson, n.d., box 52, folder of memos to Mr. Johnson, June 1964; Memorandum, Horace Busby for the president, 21 September 1965, box 51, Office Files of Horace Busby, Johnson Library.

34. Terry Moe, "The Politicized Presidency" in John E. Chubb and Paul E. Peterson, eds., *The New Direction in American Politics* (Washington, D.C.: The Brookings Institution, 1985), p. 254.

35. Memorandum, Horace Busby to the president, 21 April 1965, and attached letter from John Macy (17 April 1965), box 51, Office Files of Horace Busby, Johnson Library; Joseph Young, "Johnson Boost to Career People Called Strongest by a President," *Washington Post*, 16 May 1965; Eugene Patterson, "The Johnson Brand," *Atlanta Constitution*, 30 April 1965; and Raymond P. Brandt, "Johnson Inspires the Civil Service by Appointing His Top Aides from among Career Officials," *St. Louis Dispatch*, 2 May 1965. For a comprehensive treatment of Johnson's management of the bureaucracy, see James A. Anderson, "Presidential Management of the Bureaucracy and the Johnson Presidency: A Preliminary Exploration," *Congress and the President* 1 (Autumn 1984): 137–63.

36. Memorandum, Bill Moyers to the president, 11 December 1965, box 11, Office Files of Bill Moyers, Johnson Library.

37. Leuchtenburg, "Genesis of the Great Society," pp. 37–38.

38. James Rowe became quite concerned upon hearing of the task force proposal. He warned the White House staff that this might further weaken the regular party apparatus, which was "already suffering from shellshock both in Washington and around the country because of its impotent status." James Rowe, "A White Paper for the President on the 1968 Presidential Campaign," n.d., Marvin Watson Files, box 20, Folder of Rowe, O'Brien, Cooke, Griswell Operation, Johnson Library.

39. Allan Otten, "The Incumbent's Edge," *Wall Street Journal*, 28 December 1967.

40. Byron E. Shafer, *Quiet Revolution: The Struggle for the Democratic Party and the Shaping of Post-Reform Politics* (New York: Russell Sage Foundation, 1983). For a discussion of the long-term forces underlying the McGovern-Fraser reforms, see David B. Truman, "Party Reform, Party Atrophy and Constitutional Change," *Political Science Quarterly* 99 (Winter 1984–85): 637–55.

41. Memorandum, John P. Roche for the president, 4 December 1967, White House Central Files, folder of PL (Political Affairs); Memorandum, Ben Wattenberg for the president, 13 December 1967, Marvin Watson Files, box 10; Memorandum, Ben Wattenberg for the president, 13 March 1968, Marvin Watson Files, box 11; all in Johnson Library.

42. Memorandum of conversation, 5 April 1968, White House Famous Names, box 6, Folder of Robert F. Kennedy, 1968 Campaign, Johnson Library.

43. Richard Nathan, *The Administrative Presidency* (New York: John Wiley and Sons, 1983).

44. Fred I. Greenstein, "Nine Presidents in Search of a Modern Presidency" in Greenstein, ed., *Leadership in the Modern Presidency* (Cambridge, Mass.: Harvard U. Press, 1988), p. 309.

45. On Nixon's party leadership as president, see the Ripon Society and Clifford Brown, *Jaws of Victory* (Boston: Little, Brown, 1973), pp. 226–42.

46. Nathan, *Administrative Presidency*, pp. 43–56. Toward the end of the Johnson presidency, the administration gave attention to the need to consolidate further the president's power over the activities of the executive branch. As an aide to LBJ's domestic policy adviser Joseph Califano indicated in a 1969 interview, the concerns expressed by Johnson administration officials at that time anticipated many of the measures that were later pursued by the Nixon administration:

> I think in the long run we probably have to be thinking about super departments on the domestic side, one on human resources holding together most of the activities of HEW and OEO and Labor and others, probably one on natural resources holding together many of the activities of Agriculture and Interior.

Apparently, during the last few years of the Johnson presidency, Califano had been pulling together all of the pet interests of the heads of the domestic departments to formulate a comprehensive approach to urban problems. James

Gaither, Oral History Interview, by Larry Temple, tape 4, 17 January 1969, p. 6, Johnson Library.

47. Walter Dean Burnham, *Critical Elections and the Mainsprings of American Politics* (New York: W. W. Norton, 1970); Everett Carll Ladd, *Transformations of the American Party System*, 2d ed. (New York: W. W. Norton, 1978).

48. A. James Reichly, "The Rise of National Parties" in *The New Direction in American Politics*, pp. 191–95.

49. Ibid., pp. 195–200; Cornelius P. Cotter and John F. Bibby, "Institutionalization of Parties and the Thesis of Party Decline," *Political Science Quarterly* 95 (Spring 1980): pp. 1–27; Joseph A. Schlesinger, "The New American Party System," *American Political Science Review* 79 (December 1985): 1152–69; Michael Nelson, "The Case for the Current Nominating Process" in George Grassmuck, ed., *Before Nomination* (Washington, D.C.: American Enterprise Institute, 1985); and Larry Sabato, *The Party's Just Begun* (Glenview, Ill.: Scott, Foresman, 1988).

50. Rhodes Cook, "Reagan Nurtures His Adopted Party to Strength," *Congressional Quarterly Weekly Report*, 28 September 1985, 1927–30.

51. Howell Raines, "Laxalt and Political Ally Chosen for G.O.P. Posts," *New York Times*, 9 January 1983, p. 10; and Steven V. Roberts, "Packwood Loses Party Job in Senate," *New York Times*, 3 December 1982, p. 19.

52. David S. Broder, "A Party Leader Who Works at It," *Boston Globe*, 21 October 1985, p. 14; and personal interview with Mitchell Daniels, assistant to the president for political and governmental affairs, 5 June 1986.

53. Cotter and Bibby, "Institutionalization of Parties," 25; and Leon Epstein, *Political Parties in the American Mold* (Madison, Wis.: U. of Wisconsin Press, 1986), pp. 208–25.

54. Personal interview with William Greener III, 4 June 1986.

55. Thomas E. Cavanaugh and James L. Sundquist, "The New Two-Party System" in John E. Chubb and Paul E. Peterson, eds., *The New Direction in American Politics*, p. 254.

56. The president, in fact, played a much greater role in funding the *contras* than was reported by his appointed review board, the Tower Commission. Not only did Reagan take an active and involved part in setting up a network of suport for Nicaraguan rebels when Congress refused his request for aid (he authorized the solicitation of funds from third countries and private individuals), but he also governed on the presumption that a 1985 congressional ban on aid to the *contras* did not apply to the National Security Council or the national security adviser. This presumption directly contradicted White House statements to Congress in 1985 about how the administration was complying with the Boland amendment. Stuart Taylor, Jr., "A New Stand over Contras," *New York Times*, 25 May 1987, pp. 1, 5; *Report of the Congressional Committees Investigating the Iran-Contra Affair*, 100th Congress, 1st sess., House Report 100-433, Senate Report 100-216 (Washington, D.C.: U.S. Government Printing Office, 1987), pp. 501–2.

57. Interview with Sen. Richard Lugar, 7 August 1987.

58. For an examination of Reagan's regulatory program that addresses the question of realignment, see Richard A. Harris and Sidney M. Milkis, *The Politics of Regulatory Change: A Tale of Two Agencies* (New York: Oxford U. Press, 1989).

59. Sidney Blumenthal, *The Rise of the Counter-Establishment: From Conservative Ideology to Political Power* (New York: Times Books), p. 9.

60. The following comments on Reagan's party leadership by William Brock, who as RNC chair from 1977 to 1981 played the leading role in the revitalization of the Republican party apparatus, were echoed by many GOP officials during several interviews carried out between 1985 and 1989:

> The president's strength as party leader has been his public commitment to the Republican program and what the GOP stands for. He also has worked tirelessly for our candidates, even showing a willingness to go into congressional districts and fight for Republican candidates who had little chance to win. This kind of commitment means something to a party. Yet too many of those around him seem to have a sense of party that begins and ends in the Oval Office. The White House really does not have an appreciation of the party's institutions and its professional cadres. Too many really don't understand what it means to link the White House to the party in a way that creates an alliance between the presidency, the House, and the Senate, or between the national party and officials at the state and local level. Under the Reagan administration, party building has gone on in fits and starts; but this kind of activity needs to be supported every day to keep the weeds out—to maintain the strength of the regular party apparatus.

Interview with William E. Brock, 12 August 1987.

61. On election day Bush won the support of at least 80 percent of the voters who approved of Reagan's performance, while losing the votes of the 40 percent of those who disapproved of Reagan by a margin of nine to one. Michael Nelson, "Constitutional Aspects of the Elections" in Michael Nelson, ed., *The Elections of 1988* (Washington, D.C.: Congressional Quarterly Press, 1989), p. 192.

62. Ibid., p. 195.

63. Jeffrey A. Eisenach is quoted in Burt Solomon, "Bush's Zeal for Partisan Duties Tempered by His Bipartisan Style," *National Journal*, 28 October 1989, p. 2651.

64. Solomon, "Bush's Zeal," p. 2651.

65. Michael Oreskes, "Approval of Bush, Bolstered by Panama, Soars in Poll," *New York Times*, 19 January 1990, p. A20.

66. Michael Oreskes, "Atwater's Long Year's Journey as the Republican National Chairman," *New York Times*, 29 December 1989, p. A16.

67. Robert Kuttner, *The Life of the Party: Democratic Prospects in 1988 and Beyond* (New York: Viking, 1987), pp. 72–88.

68. Representative Price as quoted in Rhodes Cook, "Pressed by Jackson Demands, Dukakis Yields on Party Rules," *Congressional Quarterly Weekly Report*, 2 July 1988, p. 179. In September 1989 the Democratic National Committee voted to rescind the part of the Jackson-Dukakis agreement concerning the cutback in "superdelegate" seats; but the proportional requirement was retained. See Rhodes Cook, "Democratic Party Rules Changes Readied for '92 Campaign," *Congressional Quarterly Weekly Report*, 17 March 1990, pp. 847–49.

69. Alexis de Tocqueville, *Democracy in America*, ed. J. P. Mayer (New York: Doubleday, 1969), p. 735. A few months after this essay was written, the Bush administration apparently moved the center of political operations to the White House. In March 1990, Lee Atwater was found to have a brain tumor, minimizing his role in fashioning political strategy. Atwater's absence returned the center of political strategy to the West Wing, leaving chief of staff John Sununu as Bush's chief political adviser. Burt Solomon, "In Atwater's Absence, Sununu Is Bush's Top Political Adviser," *National Journal*, 23 June 1990, pp. 1154–55.

THE INSTITUTIONALIZATION OF LEADERSHIP IN THE U.S. CONGRESS

David T. Canon

Leadership in the U.S. Congress is constantly evolving. In the past century, "Czarist" Speakers, a "King Caucus," and powerful committee chairmen ruled the House, and autocratic leaders, committee barons, and collegial leaders led the Senate. Since the mid-1970s, leadership has responded to increased individualism and decentralization in the House and Senate by becoming more inclusive and service-oriented but also more institutionalized. This essay will examine the dimensions of institutionalization and ask the more general question, "How and why do leadership institutions change?"

The theory of institutionalization employed by Polsby (1968), Hibbing (1988), and others provide an excellent basis for answering the "how" part of the question. It also permits a focus on changes in leadership institutions that transcend the importance of any given leader. Most leadership studies are reluctant to generalize because of the perceived importance of leadership style and personality (Mackaman and Sachs 1988, 16–17, 38–39). The theory does not fare as well in explaining why institutions change (Hibbing 1988, 707–10). Gradual historical forces, such as increased societal complexity, cannot explain the evolution of institutions, nor do they recognize the tensions between different aspects of change.

The central part of this article addresses the question of how leadership institutions change, with a focus on the 1970s and 1980s. Changes in House and Senate leadership before this period are well documented (Ripley 1967; Peabody 1976) and therefore will be discussed only to place them within the framework of institutionalization theory. Differences between the two institutions are discussed throughout. In the conclusion, I speculate about the consequences of institutionalization and present a theory of why leadership institutions change.

COMPONENTS OF THE INSTITUTIONALIZATION OF LEADERSHIP

The institutionalization of leadership in the House and Senate is indicated by four vaguely hierarchical characteristics. The first, durability, is the most fundamental; institutions must survive in order to develop. The second and third—internal complexity and boundedness—evolve together during the second stage; as institutions become more complex they are more well bounded and autonomous. The fourth, the universal norms and rules employed by the leadership, are the last to develop because they tend to undermine strong leadership. I will discuss each in turn.

INSTITUTIONAL DURABILITY

The only constitutionally prescribed officers of Congress are the Speaker of the House, the vice-president (who serves as president of the Senate), and the president pro tempore of the Senate. The other leadership positions in the House and Senate survive by custom, inertia, and institutional need. Therefore, durability is not a foregone conclusion.

To be characterized as durable, leadership institutions must meet two conditions: first, clearly defined leadership offices must persist over time and, second, powers and duties must have institutional rather than personal definition. Evidence for the first condition is easily obtained, but distinguishing between institutional and personal power is more complicated. Dramatic changes in the patterns of leadership associated with leadership turnover would indicate personal, rather than institutional, leadership. Evidence presented in this section indicates that House leadership is highly institutionalized, while Senate leadership is less stable and more personalized, especially in the Republican party.

DURABILITY OF HOUSE LEADERSHIP

Both parties in the House have met the first condition of durability for more than a half century. The top three leadership positions have existed continuously since the turn of the century.[1] The next level of leadership—the whip system, the party caucuses (or Conference, for the Republicans), the Rules committees, and policy committees—have undergone changes in the twentieth century, but they too have had a continuous existence. However, until the 1970s, patterns of leadership often changed dramatically as a result of leadership turnover, thus violating the second condition of durability. Sam Rayburn did not use the whip system in the 1950s, breaking with past practices. Barbara Sinclair reports that the whip, Carl Albert, had nothing to do, and Hale Boggs, the deputy whip, had "double nothing to do" (1983, 55). The Republicans' whip system was more stable (Leslie Arends was whip from 1943 to 1974), but the role of their other party institutions, the Republican Conference and the Policy Committee, varied greatly. John Byrnes transformed the Policy Committee into a vital part of the leadership from 1959 to 1965, after which time the Conference became more central (Jones 1970, 153–60).

Since the early 1970s, Democratic leadership has met the second condition for durability, exhibiting continuity through several leadership changes. The whip system was greatly expanded and activated by Tip O'Neill, but the trend continued under John Brademas, Tom Foley, and Tony Coelho. The Speaker's task forces, used by O'Neill to promote an inclusive leadership style, have been expanded under the leadership of Jim Wright. Similarly, the Democratic Congressional Campaign Committee (DCCC) was transformed into a moneymaking machine under Coelho and the committee's practices were institutionalized by Beryl Anthony.

Leadership in the minority party tends to be volatile, responding more dramatically than majority party leadership to external events, such as changes in the party of the president and electoral disasters. However, the Republican leadership in the House has been more durable in the 1970s and 1980s. The whip system was strengthened under Trent Lott, and in the early days of the 101st Congress it appeared that Dick Cheney would carry on his practices.[2] William Connelly concludes that the Policy Committee "has not changed fundamentally" in the past 20 years, despite membership and leadership change (1988, 26). The leadership of Robert Michel has also contributed to continuity; in the 101st Congress, he will become the minority leader with the longest continuous service.

The increased durability of the Democratic and Republican party leadership in the House does not mean that institutionalization obliterates the inprint of individual leaders. Jim Wright is more involved in policy than Tip O'Neill was, and Tony Coelho has a style different from Tom Foley's. However, leadership discretion is constrained in an institutionalized setting (Smith 1985, 228). As leadership institutions become durable, as I define that quality here, they develop inertia and expectations among the rank and file that are difficult to change.

DURABILITY OF SENATE LEADERSHIP

Senate leadership is not as durable as leadership in the House, especially in the Republican party. Party offices have fallen into disuse in various periods, and positions are defined by the skills and style of given leaders, rather than by the institution. There are several reasons for this lack of durability, each of which I will discuss in turn. First, there is not a long tradition of strong formal leadership in the Senate. While the House had a Speaker in the First Congress, the first floor leader in the Senate was elected in 1911 (Peabody 1976, 325–29). The first Senate whip was elected in 1913, but did not play much of a role until the 1950s. Lacking clearly defined purposes, lower party offices have been unstable. Second, Senate leadership changes readily in response to changing external conditions (primarily, changes in which party controls the presidency). Third, given its size the Senate has always been more disposed to personal leadership.

The first condition of durability has not been met by either party during the twentieth century. While parties have continuously elected majority and minority leaders in this period, stability in the lower leadership offices is less evident. Peabody reports that Republicans did not even bother to elect a whip between 1935 and 1944, and some whips, such as Lister Hill (Democratic whip from 1941 to 1947), "voluntarily gave up the job because they did not feel the position was worth the effort" (1976, 331). A deputy whip and assistant whips were appointed by the Democrats in 1937 but were soon discarded (Oleszek 1985, 9). More recently, the Republicans abolished their whip system, which had grown to 16 assistant whips by the 96th Congress. This incident deserves brief discussion because it illustrates the instability of Senate leadership and the importance of external conditions in dictating change.

In 1981, when the Republicans took control of the Senate for the first time in 20 years, they disbanded their whip system. This move is counterintuitive: the responsibilities of being in the majority and having to pass an ambitious presidential agenda should create a greater need for a whip system. But a top leadership aide explained that the principal service provided by the whip system was floor coverage, and the presiding officer of the Senate, who was now a Republican, could play that role.[3] The other two important functions of the whip system, whip counts and the dissemination of information, are done through other channels. Howard Green, the party secretary, handles whip counts, and the Policy Committee serves as the primary source of agenda and policy information. The Republicans abolished their whip system in part because the division of labor broke down. The system was underutilized, because the whips did not know what they were supposed to do. "Functions were fairly ill-defined," the aide said. "There was not a clear sense of getting anything done, so the assistant whips did not feel they were having an impact. More basically, there just was not that much for them to do."[4]

The second condition, that leadership be institutionally defined, is less likely to hold in the Senate than in the House. For example, the roles of the Republican Policy Committee and the Democratic Conference have depended greatly on who led those groups. When Robert Taft or Styles Bridges chaired the Policy Committee, it was an important arm of the leadership. However, because the leadership was not institutionally defined, the committee's role changed greatly under the guidance of Bourke Hickenlooper and John Tower. Similarly, Robert Byrd as secretary of the Democratic Conference transformed it into a valuable service organization, but he was unique in that regard. For others, there is an initial period of adjustment, before they put their own imprint on the office. Robert Dole, for example, initially exhibited institutionalized leadership by following past practices: "Not having served as Party leader of the Senate, Senator Dole concluded that instead of trying out some new procedures immediately, he would utilize selected established processes until he had more time to examine and study the existing procedures" (Riddick 1985, 20). Within a few months, Dole had implemented his own brand of leadership, with his "quorum government" allowing him to be at the center of most negotiation (Deering 1986). This pattern typifies personalized leadership and is less likely to happen in an institutionalized system.

Another way of understanding the same point is that leadership institutions in the Senate are not strong enough to compel a reluctant to lead. Two successive Democratic Whips, Russell Long (1965–69) and Edward Kennedy (1969–71), were not willing to make the personal sacrifices that are required of Senate leaders. Long complained that the whip's position is "a grueling, day-to-day, thankless, time-consuming job of being around when nobody else cares to be" (quoted in Peabody 1976, 366). Kennedy, who defeated Long in 1969, found that he did not enjoy the duties of the position any more than his predecessor.

Robert Byrd's actions as whip and floor leader are further evidence of the personal rather than institutional, nature of leadership in the Senate. Byrd transformed the whip's office, becoming very active in scheduling and in the formation of complex unanimous consent agreements. But when he was elected majority leader, he continued to play the same role. Steven Smith and Marcus Flathman (1989) show...that in the 92d Congress (Byrd's first year as whip) the majority whip sponsored 66 complex unanimous consent agreements on key-vote measures, while the majority leader sponsored only 37. By contrast, in the 88th Congress, the majority leader had sponsored 23 of the 24 complex unanimous consent agreements formed by the leadership. When Byrd became majority leader, he sponsored all 71 of the agreements formed by the leadership, while Cranston was relegated to a much smaller role as whip. In a durable leadership system, the tasks would have remained in the whip's domain, once they had been defined as tasks performed by that office.

INSTITUTIONAL BOUNDARIES

Polsby defines a well-bounded institution as one that is "differentiated from its environment" (1968, 145). Well-bounded leadership systems are not permeable; they have career structures that promote leaders from within. Other defining characteristics include long apprenticeships before top leadership positions are attained, lengthy tenure in leadership, and careers that finish in leadership positions (Polsby 1968, 148–52). By these measures, the top level of leadership in the House was well bounded by 1900.[5] Institutionalization is well documented for the House Democratic leadership (Hinckley 1970; Sinclair 1983; Brown and Peabody 1987), but relatively little attention has been directed to leadership career paths in the other three legislative parties, where leadership boundaries have been less distinct, or to careers in the extended leadership systems. I will show that boundaries have become more clearly defined for Senate Democrats and House Republicans and that additional evidence of institutionalization may be gained from examining career patterns below the top leadership in all of the legislative parties.

When positions below the top leadership are examined, it is evident that a well-bounded leadership system emerges in four stages. In the first stage, newly formed leadership positions are not the objects of intense competition; the leadership is permeable and turnover is high. In the second stage of development, as the number of leadership positions expands, top positions will be hotly contested but lower-level positions will not. In the third stage, there is competition at all levels of the leadership structure, and lower positions emerge as stepping stones to high party office; apprenticeship in the institution becomes a requirement for movement into the leadership. Voluntary retirement from the leadership system is relatively rare, and careers in leadership tend to be long. Finally, in a fully institutionalized system, competition continues at lower levels in the structure, but the top position will be uncontested as the heir apparent reaches the top of the ladder. The ladder extends deeper into the structure as the leadership becomes more institutionalized (in the 100th Congress, neither Tom Foley nor Jim Wright was challenged for the top position in his party in the House).[6]

ESTABLISHING BOUNDARIES IN HOUSE LEADERSHIP

The House Democratic party is the most institutionalized of the legislative parties. Having held majority status continuously for 36 years, the House Democrats have developed long-term career expectations and stable institutions. Though the pattern of succession is not written in stone, recent experience indicates it has solidified for the top three positions (whip to majority leader to Speaker). This ladder is unlikely to be challenged in the near future. With the top leadership progression firmly in place, most career decisions are made lower in the system. Little is known, however, about career patterns in the extended leadership.

The whip system is now the training ground and incubator for aspiring leaders. The top three Democratic leaders in the 101st Congress—Jim Wright (TX), Tom Foley (WA), and Tony Coelho (CA)—all served in lower leadership positions. Other prominent Democrats who have competed for access to the leadership ladder have also been weaned in the whip system, including Norman Mineta (CA), Bill Alexander (AR), Dan Rostenkowski (IL), and Charles Rangel (NY). However, all leaders do not attempt to climb the ladder.[7] Three distinct career types were identified in an examination of the leadership structure from 1973 to 1988: dabblers, whippers, and ladder climbers. Examining the careers of these three types will provide a picture of the boundedness of the leadership system. More institutionalized systems should have a larger proportion of ladder climbers and fewer members who voluntarily leave the system.

Dabblers are those who serve in the leadership for one or two terms and then leave. More than half of the 40 Democratic dabblers remained in the House after leaving the whip system (57.5%), the others retired or were defeated (27.5%), or sought higher office (15%). Despite the relatively large number of members in this category, careers in the extended leadership do not resemble the revolving door of the nineteenth-century leadership (Polsby [1968] mentions Henry Clay's wild career as being indicative of the fluid congressional careers in that period). Only 4 of the 122 Democrats and 1 of the 70 Republicans in this 14-year period reentered the leadership structure after leaving.

Whippers are the relative few who continue as at-large or regional whips year after year (the coding rule was three terms or more). Some, such as John P. Murtha (PA) and Tom Bevill (AL), seem to enjoy the cajoling and persuading, while others perform the whipping function out of a sense of duty or loyalty to the party. These members do not aspire to move beyond this limited but valuable role, and often they are heavily involved in committee work and other legislative concerns. Democratic whippers are loyal; only 5 of the 43 (11.6%) left the leadership voluntarily and only 2 were defeated.

Ladder climbers aspire to the speakership. Generally they move from regional whip to at-large whip to deputy whip and wait their turn to compete for the top positions (occasionally the intermediate level is skipped).[8] Members are included in this group if they have served at least three terms in the whip system and have climbed at least one level. Of the 39 in this category, 21 can be considered "super ladder climbers," by virtue of having progressed at least to the level of deputy whip. None of the ladder climbers voluntarily left the leadership system, indicating their commitment to a leadership career and their intense ambition. Two—McFall and Alexander—dropped out of the leadership after being defeated for a higher party office, and five were defeated in reelection attempts, including Whip John Brademas in 1980.

For most of the twentieth century, the leadership of the House Republicans has not been as well bounded as the Democratic leadership. Republicans were much quicker to turn their leaders out of office when the times got tough, and they did not establish clear patterns of succession. House Republicans revolted four times in the twentieth century against incumbent floor leaders or heirs apparent to the top position (1919, 1931, 1959, and 1965).

The absence of well-defined boundaries is further illustrated by the different paths to the top of Republican leadership. In contrast to the House Democrats, the Republicans do not use the whip system extensively as a stepping stone. Instead, they use the six positions below the floor leader as outlets for leadership ambitions. Trent Lott was elected whip in 1981 from the Rules Committee and Research Committee, and neither Rhodes nor Ford served in the whip system. Ford used the Conference and Rhodes used the Policy Committee as stepping stones to the top.

This career pattern undermines the incentive to serve in the whip system. If there is no long-term payoff of a high leadership position, ambitious members may not be willing to commit the time and energy to serve in the whip system. Consequently, Republicans are far more likely to leave the system voluntarily than are their Democratic counterparts, perhaps seeing little value in the ultimate prizes. More than a third of all "whippers" (those who serve for three terms or more as a whip) voluntarily left the leadership between 1973 and 1988 (11 of 30), but only 14.7% of the Democratic whippers did so. Only 18.6% of those in the Republican leadership can be classified as ladder climbers, but 32% of the Democrats can be so classified. Even fewer stay in the leadership long enough to climb several levels.

It is too early for conclusive statements, but the 1980s may indicate that Republicans are creating a more bounded leadership system. The top four Republican positions in the House were held by the same people from 1980 until Jack Kemp stepped down as conference chairman in June 1987. The Republicans resisted their tendency to change leaders in the face of electoral defeat in 1982, and the 1987 and 1989 successions were chapters from the Democratic escalator.[9] Despite the recent election of Newt Gingrich to the whip position, the patterns of Republican leadership in the 1980s seem to contradict Peabody's hypothesis that "the longer the period of minority status, the more prone the minority party is to leadership change through revolt" (1976, 297).

Recent patterns of leadership succession in the House indicate that both parties have reached the fourth stage of the establishment of leadership boundaries. Top leadership positions are filled by heirs apparent in smooth transitions; the competition occurs lower in the leadership structure. The whip system is the vehicle for ambition in the Democratic leadership, while for the Republicans the outlet is the plethora of lower-level leadership positions. The stages of development are most clear for the Republicans. In the period from 1955 to 1974, the three successions to minority leader occasioned two successful revolts against an incumbent and one defeat of an heir apparent. In this same period, there was little competition for lower leadership positions. In the next three elections (1975–79), there were no challenges to the minority leader, and competition increased for lower offices. Stepping stones began to emerge in lower offices: Bob Michel moved from campaign chair to whip in 1975; two Research Committee chairs, Louis Frey and Bill Frenzel, attempted to move to Policy in 1977 and 1979; and Samuel Devine moved from conference vice-chair to conference chair in 1979. Between 1981 and 1989 the Republicans reached the fourth stage. Michel moved unopposed from whip to minority leader in 1981, and the regular patterns of succession described above emerged in the lower offices.

ESTABLISHING BOUNDARIES IN SENATE LEADERSHIP

Peabody begins his chapter on Senate leadership by wondering, "why do so few Senators gravitate toward elected party leadership, while the vast majority choose to make their mark on public policy primarily through legislative specialization?" (1976, 321). The primary reason is that the legislative process is more open and the leadership more fluid than in the House. Senators do not have to be in the formal leadership to help shape legislation. Though informal leaders and "leaders without portfolio" have recently played a more prominent role in the House (Calmes and Gurwitt 1987; Hammond 1988), these players have always been central in the Senate. As a consequence, leadership ladders have not developed fully and the leadership is very permeable, especially in the Republican party.

The measures used by Polsby in his seminal work—the number of years in Congress before succeeding to a top leadership position, the number of years in the leadership, and the length of time out of Congress after retirement from the leadership—indicate that the boundaries have not become better defined for either the Democratic or Republican leadership in the post-World-War-II period (see Table 19.1). The mean years of prior service in the Senate have increased for Democratic leaders but have fallen dramatically for Republicans. The length of time in the leadership has increased for Democratic floor leaders and Republican assistant leaders but stayed about the same for Republican leaders and Democratic whips.[10] The most significant change is that Democratic and Republican floor leaders are much less likely to finish their careers in the Senate.

Although the traditional measures of well-boundedness do not provide clear evidence, the Democratic leadership is more institutionalized on several other dimensions of well-boundedness: membership is more stable for the Democrats, succession at top levels is more structured, and, until recently, patterns of contesting leadership positions indicated a higher level of development.

From 1977 to 1989, the same three individuals occupied the top positions in the elected Democratic leadership. This degree of stability was unprecedented in the Senate. The Republicans, during the same period, had two different floor leaders, two whips, four conference chairs, three conference secretaries, and two policy committee chairs. The pattern holds in lower leadership positions. Almost 40% of the Republican membership held an assistant whip position in the 96th Congress; according to a top leadership aide, anybody who wanted the title of assistant whip could have it. Less than 20% of the Democratic membership is generally in the whip system, and the current figure is one in six. As might be expected, the less bounded system also has greater turnover. In its last year, the Republican whip system had a 50% turnover, whereas the Democratic system's membership remained unchanged from the 97th through the 99th Congresses, except for the loss of Walter Huddleston (KY) through electoral defeat in 1984. Such stability is not observed even in the highly institutionalized Democratic whip system in the House. The average tenure of Republican whips in the last year of their system was 1.9 years; for Democrats in the 99th Congress it was 7.8 years.[11]

Both the Democrats and Republicans have gone through the first two stages of career ladder development in fits and starts. The cyclical low interest in leadership positions that was typical before World War II has now given way to generally intense competition for the top leadership positions. Neither party has evolved to the final stage, in which top positions are not contested, but the Democrats have come closer than Republicans to reaching the third stage, characterized by competition at all levels, with stepping stones emerging. Since 1949, the whip position has become a regular stepping stone to majority leader for Democrats. Before 1949, six of the seven incumbent whips who had an opportunity to become floor leader when there was a vacancy were passed over (Peabody

Table 19.1 The Establishment of Boundaries in the Senate: The Careers of
Floor Leaders and Party Whips, 1911–89 (in Numbers of Years)

Position	Period	In Senate before election		In leadership[a]		After leadership until death		(N)
		Mean	Median	Mean	Median	Mean	Median	
Democrats								
Floor								
leaders	1911–49	8.5	7.5	6.3	4.0	3.5	1.5	(6)
	1949–89	10.0	10.0	8.0	8.0	18.0	14.5	(5)
Party whips	1913–49	5.6	4.0[b]	5.1	6.0			(7)
	1949–89	7.3	8.0	4.4	4.0			(9)
Republicans								
Floor								
leaders	1911–49	18.9	16.0	5.6	5.0	3.8	1.0	(7)
	1949–89	11.0	10.5	5.0	5.0	5.6	4.0	(8)
Party whips	1915–49	5.7	6.0	4.2	4.0			(6)
	1949–89	6.0	6.0	6.2	7.5			(7)

Sources: Peabody 1976, Tables 11–1 and 11–2; Riddick 1985, Table II; various
editions of *Congressional Quarterly Weekly Report, Politics in America,* and *The Almanac
of American Politics.*

[a]Includes leadership in the 100th Congress.

[b]J. Hamilton Lewis served two nonconsecutive terms (1913–19, 1933–39) and served
all 12 years as whip. Thus Lewis is counted twice: the first time with zero years of prior
experience in the Senate, the second time with six years.

1976, 330–32). Between 1949 and 1988, all four incumbent Democratic
whips who had an opportunity were elected floor leader. This pattern
was broken in the 101st Congress, when Alan Cranston did not run for
majority leader.[12] Republicans also had established a pattern, with three
whips out of four succeeding to floor leader between 1947 and 1976;
however, in 1976 Howard Baker was elected over whip Robert Griffin,
and in 1984 Robert Dole won over whip Ted Stevens.[13]

Since the revolts against incumbent whips in 1969 and 1971, the contests for Democratic leadership positions have been relatively peaceful.
Frank Moss was unopposed in 1971 to fill Byrd's position as conference
secretary, which he held for three uncontested terms. The next change in
leadership was 1977, when Byrd moved up to majority leader with a

brief challenge from Hubert Humphrey. Cranston and Inouye were un-opposed for the number two and three positions. The only challenge to the leadership in the next 12 years was Lawton Chiles's race for majority leader in 1984, in which he gained only 11 supporters. In 1989, Wendell Ford challenged Cranston, winning 12 votes, but in general it seems the Democrats have moved away from their more rebellious days. A true leadership ladder has not emerged, but the system is not as permeable as the Republican leadership.

Senate Republicans exhibit a pattern of contesting leadership posi-tions that does not fit neatly into the theory of stages of development presented above. Between 1955 and 1969, the Republican leadership was in a classic stage two: elections for the top three positions were all con-tested (seven successions), and there was little interest in the lower of-fices of conference chair and conference secretary. Milton Young was the only secretary through the 1950s and 1960s, and only three people occu-pied the conference chair between 1948 and 1972 (Milliken, Saltonstall, and Smith). In the 1970s and 1980s, competition for the top positions abated slightly (four of six successions contested), and the lower posi-tions were hotly contested. In 10 elections, Republicans elected 6 differ-ent conference chairs (4 contested) and 6 different conference secretaries (3 contested). This pattern would be consistent with third stage develop-ment if lower positions became stepping stones to higher office, but the opposite happened. The tentative first step on the ladder that began to emerge in the 1960s and early 1970s (whip to floor leader) disappeared with the defeats of Griffin and Stevens, and lower offices did not develop patterns of succession.

AUTONOMY

Thus far, I have defined the boundedness of leadership by the patterns of careers within the leadership. Congressional leadership is also differ-entiated from its environment by the degree of which congressional par-ties are autonomous or distinct from national parties. Until recently, congressional parties had little autonomy in one important area: fund-raising. For example, John F. Kennedy used his considerable fund-raising power to help the congressional committees, but the cost to congressio-nal leadership was a merger of the Democratic National Committee (DNC) and the DCCC and a complete loss of control. This relationship remained intact until 1968, though Lyndon B. Johnson exerted less con-trol over the congressional committees than Kennedy had (Menefee-Libey, forthcoming). Recently, congressional parties have strengthened their fund-raising committees to gain autonomy.

Figure 19.1 Campaign funds raised by the legislative party campaign committees as a percentage of total party receipts, 1976–88.

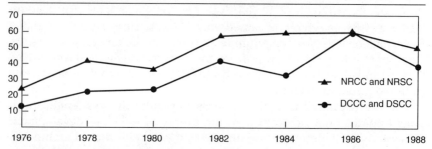

Source: *Vital Statistics on Congress,* 1987, Table 3–13 (Washington, D.C.: Congressional Quarterly Press). Reprinted in Federal Election Commission Press Release, 3 November 1988, 2–3.

Note: For each party, the total party receipts are the sum of funds raised by the national party committee (the DNC or RNC) and by the Senate and House campaign committees (the DCCC and DSCC or the NRCC and NRSC). The points plotted are for two-year election cycles.

In the early 1980s, the Republican congressional campaign committees surpassed the Republican National Committee (RNC) in total receipts, and the Democratic committees pulled even with the DNC, surpassing it in 1986 (see Figure 19.1). The increases are stunning, not only in relative terms but also in absolute terms. The Democratic Senate and House campaign committees raised their revenues from just under $2 million in 1976 to $25.7 million in 1986, while Republicans increased their totals from nearly $13 million to almost $126 million (Ornstein, Mann, and Malbin 1987, 99–101; FEC Press Release, 3 November 1988).

Increased financial power has allowed the congressional committees to become organizationally independent of the national party committees (Menefee-Libey, forthcoming), and it has influenced leadership ladders. Tony Coelho used his position as DCCC chairman to win the first election for Democratic whip in the House, and George Mitchell's chairmanship of the Democratic Senatorial Campaign Committee (DSCC) put him in good standing with the 1986 freshman class, who contributed to his election as majority leader of the Senate in December 1988. "Money, whether we like it or not, is a pretty powerful tool," commented W. G. Hefner, one of Coelho's opponents in the whip race. "He was the man who signed the checks," noted Charles B. Rangel, the other defeated candidate (Hook 1986, 3068).

Others who aspire to leadership positions recognize the power of money. "Member PACs" have become an increasingly popular tool for gaining favor with colleagues. Party leaders use PACs to solidify their position within the leadership and to strengthen party leadership generally. Others use PACs to win support in leadership races (Baker 1989). Lyndon Johnson was the first to systematically raise and distribute campaign funds within Congress for personal gain (though his activities were nominally under the auspices of the DCCC). In 1940, he became a "one-man national committee for congressmen" when he raised many thousands of dollars for marginal congressmen in desperate need of money (Caro 1982, 606–64). In the 1980s, there have been 111 PACs "associated with recognized individuals," ranging from Jerry Falwell's "I Love America Committee" to William Buckley's "BuckPAC" and Jim Wright's "Majority Congress Committee."[14] Seventy-six of these were still active at the end of the 1987–88 campaign cycle, and 31 are leadership PACs (those associated with congressional leaders or members who were campaigning for a leadership position). In 1980, there were only five leadership PACs, and these raised a total of $563,061 (for O'Neill, Wright, Rhodes, Dole, and Tower). In 1986, 26 leadership PACs raised $13.3 million; in 1988, 26 leadership PACs raised $10.1 million. The proliferation of leadership PACs indicates the attractiveness of leadership positions. Members would not be willing to spend so much time and money to be part of a leadership organization that was not well bounded.[15]

INTERNAL COMPLEXITY

As leadership institutions become more highly developed, they delegate responsibility to lower party offices, devote more resources to the organization, and regularize patterns of communication and behavior. The degree of integration within the leadership—that is, the extent to which the various offices of the party structure are coordinated and utilized—is a new indicator of complexity that will be addressed here.

INTERNAL COMPLEXITY IN HOUSE LEADERSHIP

Democratic leadership in the House has become more internally complex. This development is most evident in the whip system, which has evolved slowly throughout the twentieth century. The first whips worked alone, but the Republicans greatly expanded their whip system in 1931, and in 1933 the Democrats expanded theirs. However, growth was not continuous. As Speaker, Sam Rayburn did not make much use of the whip system and instead "ran the whole thing out of his back pocket" (Sinclair 1983, 55). John McCormack moved toward institutionalized leadership by expanding the powers of the whip system in 1962 (Ripley 1967, 102), but he did not use the system extensively either (Ripley 1967, 212). In 1969, the leadership used the whip system more aggressively because the president's liaison office was no longer in friendly hands.

The transition to a fully institutionalized House leadership system occurred between the 91st and the 94th Congresses. In the 92d Congress the leadership disseminated whip packets, which contain the floor schedule, information on bills up for consideration, and copies of bills. Also, the division of labor became increasingly well defined: elected regional whips were responsible for headcounts and at-large whips for persuasion (Dodd and Sullivan 1983). In the 93d Congress the leadership circulated whip advisories, which detailed the party's position on important legislation. The use of whip counts increased from 17 counts in 1962–63, to 53 in the 93d Congress (Dodd 1979, 37) to 80 in the 95th and in the 96th Congresses (Sinclair 1983, 56).

The Democratic whip system has also expanded. The number of at-large whips doubled from the 96th to the 98th Congresses and then doubled again in the next four years; the number of deputy whips tripled in that period (there were 81 members in the Democratic whip system in the 100th Congress). The system was originally expanded to give more balance to the party leadership, but more recently appointive whips have been used as an arm of the top leadership and the leadership team has been better integrated.

Republican leadership in the House is not as internally complex as Democratic leadership. Charles Halleck attempted to activate the Policy Committee and to make extensive use of the whip system, but members complained of his leadership style, claiming there was too much whipping (Ripley 1967, 108). Under Gerald Ford, the Policy Committee was downgraded and there was not as much use of the whip system, but a hierarchical chain of command was implemented in the leadership. The goal, to develop policy alternatives to majority party proposals, met with some success. (The new breed of Republican activists in the House today has a colorful acronym for this minority strategy: CRAP—Constructive Republican Alternative Policies.)

John Rhodes and his successor, current minority leader Robert Michel, moved to integrate the leadership system and create a more active whip system. Trent Lott, the minority whip from 1980 to 1988, was a key player in this process. Under his active leadership, the Republican whip system evolved into an effective machine that rivals the Democrats in its ability to disseminate information, count heads, and build coalitions. He also integrated the whip system with the rest of the leadership through weekly whip meetings and good communication with Michel (personal interview). Recently, the Research Committee has become more important through the leadership of Jerry Lewis, Mickey Edwards, and Duncan Hunter. Most important, policy task forces, mimicking the Democratic counterpart, are now run from the Research Committee office.

A summary, albeit somewhat crude, measure of these various trends toward greater internal complexity is the allocation of resources to the leadership. The Reports of the Clerk of the House and the Reports of the Secretary of the Senate are the best available documents, but information is incomplete. As Polsby noted, "Reliable figures, past or present, on personnel assigned to the House are impossible to come by" (1968, 158). For example, through the 1960s, the minority party in the House had no separate authorization for its Conference, Policy Committee, or Research Committee, but it did shift funds from individual members' staff allotments (Jones 1970, 177). Bearing these limitations in mind, the Clerk's Reports show that funds allocated to the leadership have increased greatly: from $47,825 in 1955, to $482,850 in 1968, to $2,343,225 in 1974, to $6,755,468 in 1986. This 141-fold increase is dramatically larger than the 21-fold increase in total legislative branch appropriations (both in nominal dollars), the tripling in the size of personal staff, and the 6-fold increase in the size of committee staff over this same period.[16]

INTERNAL COMPLEXITY IN SENATE LEADERSHIP

Leadership is not as internally complex in the Senate as in the House, primarily because the Senate's smaller size makes institutions less necessary. The Senate is not easier to lead than the house; to the contrary, the highly fragmented and individualized nature of the body makes leading the Senate like "trying to push a wet noodle," according to a frustrated Howard Baker (Granat 1984, 3024). Cognizant of the difficulty of pushing wet noodles, the Senate has steadily increased its appropriations to the leadership: from $79,172 in 1956, to $388,064 in 1966, to $750,318 in 1974, to approximately $7 million in 1986. This 88-fold increase outpaced the growth in legislative branch appropriations reported above, the doubling of personal staff, and the tripling of committee staff during the same period. Thus, by this most simple indicator, Senate leadership has become more institutionalized.

Other measures of complexity—the division of labor, integration, and regular patterns of communication—reveal a mixed picture of institutionalization in Senate leadership. The division of labor appears to be more institutionalized in the Republican leadership because their secondary party positions—the chairs of the Republican Conference, the

Policy Committee, and the Committee on Committees—are all held by different people. By contrast, the Democratic floor leader had also been chair of the Democratic Conference, the Policy Committee, and the Steering Committee through the 100th Congress. Two factors caution against drawing any conclusion from these divisions of labor. First, the Democrats dispersed power in the 101st Congress by making Daniel Inouye chair of the Steering Committee and Tom Daschle cochair of the Policy Committee. Second, the lesser party positions have never been well integrated into the leadership in either party. Only the Republican policy chair and the Democratic conference secretary have ever assumed any importance (Peabody 1976, 332-33).

The number two leader in the Senate, the whip (or assistant leader, as the Republicans call him), gained a more prominent place on the leadership ladder but has generally not played a central role in leadership activities. The relatively weak position of the Republican whip is highlighted by the fact that Assistant Leader Alan Simpson is not authorized to conduct a whip count. That order must come from Minority Leader Dole. The previous Republican whip, Ted Stevens, also played a limited role in floor activity. One aide said that Baker was afraid to leave the Senate in Stevens's control because "he might get into fisticuffs with Metzenbaum or into some godawful parliamentary situation. He was always fighting with Metzenbaum."[17] Until recently, Cranston has not fared much better. According to two aides in the Republican Senate leadership, Alan Cranston's reputation as an integral player in the Democratic leadership[18] is exaggerated. One said, "Byrd likes to build him up in public, but Cranston is not the one who makes things run on the other side of the aisle. We never worked much with him, I'll tell you that much. Byrd runs the show." Integration is also a problem with the Democrats: Byrd and Cranston have never worked closely. Richard Cohen says, "There is not nearly so close a working relationship between Byrd and Minority Whip Alan Cranston of California, who has preferred to maintain his independence from Byrd and has been given few responsibilities. Their aides do not meet on an organized basis" (Cohen 1982, 1547).

The new majority leader, George Mitchell, has vowed to change all this. He says, "I want to try to get the whip and chief deputy whip involved and have them undertake meaningful assignments....I've said I do not intend to be a one-man band, and I've meant it" (*Congressional Quarterly Weekly Report* 3 December 1988, 3423). The whip systems have shown some signs of increased internal complexity since the 1960s, especially on the Democratic side. In 1966, Majority Leader Mike Mansfield appointed four assistant whips, and Minority Leader Hugh Scott in 1969–70 nominated six regional whips (Oleszek 1985, 9–11). By 1981, the Democrats had eight regional whips and a chief deputy whip. Today there is another layer of four regional deputy whips in the system, with an assistant deputy whip under each of them. As was noted above, by 1979 almost 40% of Republicans were in the whip system (16 of 41), but the following year all assistant whip positions were abolished. Whip notices, which alert members to pending floor action and the timing of votes, have been used more frequently in recent years, expanding the visibility and importance of the office.

Another area in which patterns of behavior have become more institutionalized is the negotiation of complex unanimous consent agreements. With their increased use in the 1960s, Steven Smith and Marcus Flathman (1989) note...that senators began to demand a more institutionalized mechanism for receiving advance notice of unanimous consent requests. The informal procedure for informing the leadership of holds (objections to unanimous consent agreements) became institutionalized by Byrd's practice of circulating objection forms. This practice made scheduling easier and routinized the procedure for accommodating senators' desires.

UNIVERSALISTIC PRACTICES

The tendency in institutionalized organizations to replace discretionary behavior with universalistic rules and norms undermines strong leadership. The seniority system (the main evidence of universalism in Polsby's account) constrains leaders' ability to promote sympathetic members to committee chairs, and the routinization of committee assignments precludes the aggressive use of assignments as a tool. Only rarely may leaders provide a prize assignment as a favor, strip a member of their assignments (e.g., Phil Gramm in 1982), or deny an assignment (Loomis 1984). The most important norm limiting the power of leadership is that of allowing members to "vote their district," even when their vote conflicts with the interests of the party.

On a very mundane level, some universalistic or regularized patterns of behavior are evident: weekly leadership meetings, strengthened channels of communication, and a strategy of inclusiveness on important policy concerns. On the other hand, leadership naturally tends to resist universalistic practices, because strong leadership inherently involves the strategic and discretionary uses of power. Members obviously resist discretionary uses of power, so a compromise has been struck.

Leaders maintain some discretionary power and adopt some universalistic practices, but both tend to support individual members' goals as the means to a collective goal of institutional maintenance.

The current use of party money in congressional elections is a good example: the collective goal is to maintain or expand the party's base in Congress, but the goal is achieved by supporting individual members' campaigns. A discretionary use of funds based on levels of party support would not be supported by the rank and file. Examples of discretionary uses of power that serve members' needs are the aggressive use of modified rules in the Rules Committee, the use of complex unanimous consent agreements in the Senate, Robert Byrd's masterful use of parliamentary tactics, and strategic use of multireferrals in the House and Senate.[19] In all of these instances, the commonly assumed tradeoff between individual and collective interests is avoided. Members' interests are served, but the leadership is permitted to set the ground rules and make important decisions.

CONSEQUENCES OF THE INSTITUTIONALIZATION OF LEADERSHIP

Though Polsby does not examine the point in detail, he argues that "along with the more obvious effects of institutionalization, the process has also served to increase the power of the House within the political system" (1968, 166). It is not so clear that the institutionalization of leadership has increased the power of leaders in Congress.[20] Powerful leadership is typically defined as the ability to pass a legislative agenda, an ability which is primarily shaped by external conditions (the presidency and the party system) and internal conditions (the partisan split in the legislature and the personal skills of the leaders). Powerful leaders have been those who have exerted personal control, independent of constraining institutions. Therefore, institutionalization may seem marginally significant or even inimical to effective leadership. However, given the modern context of individualism and a weak party system, the institutionalization of leadership reveals that leadership is adaptive and can make the best of a difficult situation. Individual leaders are not as dominant in an institutionalized system, since the division of labor disperses authority, but the leadership team gains capacity to lead.

The institutionalization of leadership has also had an impact on the composition of leadership. A leadership structure that is well bounded and promotes from within is more likely to recruit ambitious, high-quality members than one that is open to outside challenges, because the thankless tasks of party whipping or floor coverage may have some payoff. A Howard Baker or a Robert Dole who is elected majority leader without "serving time" in a lower leadership position undermines members' incentive to sacrifice other options for a position that has no power and little prestige. Internally complex institutions will also be better able to recruit better members for low-level leadership positions because the tasks will be more meaningful and better defined. Ripley supports this conclusion: "These 36 men and women have made a commitment of time—which members of the House must necessarily hoard—to work for their respective parties within the House. Unless they felt that party work was worth doing, a sufficient number of commitments, of a desirable caliber, might not be forthcoming" (1964, 575). A top Senate leadership aide concurred: "The lack of clearly delineated lines to higher office undermined the attractiveness of assistant whip position [in the Republican system]. In the most highly developed whip system, that of the Democrats in the House, there is an expectation that you get a bit of a leg up in moving up the leadership system. This is clearly an incentive that didn't exist in our whip system, and this influences the type of member who is looking to serve in that position."

Well-bounded systems are also more likely to produce members who have shown their commitment to the party and to institutional maintenance. Speaker Jim Wright argues that leadership ladders produce "people who understand the institution and the problems, and who have seen Congress grapple with things, succeed and fail" (Calmes 1987, 6). Valuable skills are gained by serving an apprenticeship in the leadership. Furthermore, the automatic escalator avoids potentially divisive leadership contests. Though he expresses some reservations about the escalator, Peabody acknowledges that "it allows the House to get on with business" (Calmes 1987, 6). From an organizational standpoint, smooth leadership transitions are preferable to palace coups.

A THEORY OF LEADERSHIP INSTITUTIONALIZATION

This paper has shown that leadership in the House is highly institutionalized on all dimensions. Both parties have established patterns of succession and autonomy in campaign finance. House Democrats now have membership on demand in the Speaker's task forces (Loomis 1988), a Rules Committee that services committee chairs (Smith and Bach 1988), an ever expanding whip system, and flexible scheduling. House Republicans obviously do not play a central role in many of these leadership tasks, but they too have expanded their whip system and have an inclusive leadership style. Both parties in the House now have institutions that outlive the tenure of any single member.

The picture of the Senate is mixed. Senate Democrats have developed some boundedness in leadership careers and have increased autonomy in campaign finances, but personal leadership has limited the development of complex and durable institutions. Republican leadership in the Senate is the least institutionalized among the four legislative parties. In this concluding section, I will explain why leadership systems develop at different paces in the two chambers and offer a more general theory of leadership institutionalization.

The large size of the House creates logistical problems for leadership in coalition building and communication. The decentralization of the House over the last two decades renders a Rayburn-style approach to these tasks impossible, so the leadership has adapted accordingly. The Senate, on the other hand, can survive with personalized leadership; indeed, members expect it. If the past is the best indicator, personal leadership is more effective than institutionalized leadership in the Senate. The three most effective Republican leaders in the post-World-War-II period—Dirksen, Baker, and Dole—and the best Democratic leader, Lyndon Johnson, all had highly personalized leadership styles. Existing leadership institutions were largely ignored, and new institutions were established to meet their needs. Elaborate institutional structures only get in the way in the Senate. As one aide put it, "Senators want direct access to the top. They don't want to deal with some regional whip."

A theory of institutionalization must do more than explain interchamber differences; it must explain why institutions develop. Four sets of factors must be considered: the stability in the partisan control of the chamber, external conditions, member goals, and the skills of individual leaders, primarily their ability to utilize existing institutions.

PARTISAN STABILITY

Democrats have controlled the House since 1954. This stability promotes the institutionalization in both parties, as uncertainty about the future control of the chamber is reduced. This assertion runs counter to existing theory, according to which increasing frustration in the minority party could break down leadership institutions (Peabody 1976). The more volatile nature of partisan control and the size of party margins in the Senate make it more difficult to establish durable institutions.

EXTERNAL CONDITIONS

Two factors are central here: the party of the president and the nature of the party system. First, the president has some impact on the institutionalization of leadership. If the president is relatively popular, the leaders' job of passing his agenda is aided by lobbying from the president and pressure from public opinion. Therefore, the need for strong leadership institutions may be more acute for the party that does not control the presidency. A more important factor is the weak party system, which requires each member of Congress to operate as an independent entrepreneur (Cooper and Brady 1981a). When members' electoral fortunes are only loosely tied to the party, the task of leadership is greatly complicated. Without control over the ultimate sanction, the party is unable to prevent each member from padding his or her own political canoe in the legislature.

MEMBER GOALS

Members place individual and collective demands on the leadership. They want to vote as they wish, to go home when they wish, and to help form the legislative agenda when they have strong policy interests. Collectively, they want leadership that can mobilize coalitions to pass important legislation. Most aspects of today's service-based leadership meet these needs. The only component of institutionalized leadership that does not fit this picture is the leadership ladder, which forces members to sacrifice future career options.

Members are willing to support the ladder if the leadership is satisfying their current needs and if there is a reasonable expectation that collective goals will be met. Forming these expectations is not easy—information about the future behavior of candidates is at a premium in any election. Well-developed leadership institutions reduce information costs by allowing the rank and file to gain a clear picture of the leadership style of the candidate who is attempting to climb the ladder. In these cases, promoting from within becomes the low-risk alternative. Past leadership behavior allows members to make judgments about an "insider" candidate that may not be possible for an insurgent who has not served in the leadership. Edward Madigan's strong showing in the recent House Republican whip's race supports this observation. This decision context helps create leadership ladders.

UTILIZATION

The skills and desires of individual leaders have a significant impact on the shape of leadership institutions; their actions determine whether institutions endure or fade away. When institutions become durable and highly complex, they develop a life of their own, but the process of evolution is highly unstable. Whether leaders maintain and develop existing institutions also has an impact on the emergence of leadership ladders. This link between durability, internal complexity, and the boundedness of leadership can be presented as a hypothesis: leaders are promoted if they maintain and develop their previous position. If a leader is ineffective in using the current office, it is not likely to become a springboard for higher office. Though a systematic test of this hypothesis is beyond the scope of this paper, anecdotal evidence supports the idea. Tip O'Neill, Tony Coelho, and Dick Cheney in the House and Robert Byrd, Lyndon Johnson, Robert Taft, and George Mitchell in the Senate all met this condition and climbed the leadership ladder. Ted Kennedy, Russell Long, Ted Stevens, and John McFall did not, and they were bumped off (though in McFall's case, personal scandal played a dominant role). Those who fall between these two extremes, such as Mansfield and Griffin in the Senate and Charles Halleck and Carl Albert in the House, may or may not succeed or remain in office. In these cases, members who have already assumed a place on the career ladder will benefit from the institution building of his or her predecessors and be elected to the next rung on the ladder. If there is no ladder, other factors that are traditionally referred to—such as ideological diversity within the party, electoral losses, and personality—will predominate.

The theory describes tensions between individual and collective goals in Congress and the importance of external conditions: representatives pursuing individual goals, without a strong party system as an anchor, will continually press toward service-oriented, weak leadership. At the same time, leadership must be allowed to play an integrative role, to prevent legislative paralysis. If a balance is struck, institutionalized leadership can serve both individual and collective needs—a recipe for institutional stability. If a compromise is not reached, institutional drift, or even chaos, may reign.

NOTES

I thank John Aldrich, William Bianco, and Chuck Jones for their comments on an earlier version of this paper. I extend special thanks to John Hibbing for hosting the Hendricks Symposium on the Senate and for providing very useful comments on the paper. I also thank Jim Granato and Patrick Sellers for their help in collecting data. This research was supported by a grant from the Duke University Research Council.

1. The defeated candidate for Speaker has been recognized as the minority leader since 1883; the majority leader has been a distinct office since 1899 (prior

to that, the Ways and Means Committee chair was considered the floor leader). The Republicans elected their first whip in 1897, the Democrats elected theirs in 1900 (Ripley 1967, 24–38).

2. Since this article was written, Dick Cheney became Secretary of Defense and Newt Gingrich was elected by a narrow 87–85 margin over Edward Madigan. This election appears to undermine my arguments that Republican leadership in the House has become more durable and, as I argue below, more well-bounded. As a self-proclaimed "bomb thrower," Gingrich clearly intends to change the whip's duties, changes which would violate the second condition of durability. His lack of experience in lower leadership positions also violates the newly emerging boundedness of Republican leadership, which had observed rigid leadership ladders in the 1980s.

However, three factors reveal the highly idiosyncratic nature of this move. First, many Republicans believed they needed a strong spokesman to exploit the opportunities presented by Speaker Jim Wright's difficulties. As the initiator of the Wright investigation, Gingrich was the logical choice. Second, the Republicans had just gone through a leadership shuffle following Whip Trent Lott's election to the Senate. The newly elected conference chair, Jerry Lewis (CA), was urged by Bob Michel and others not to run, in order to minimize intraparty strife. "If he had, it would have set off another competition to succeed him and likely a chain reaction of lower-level leadership races. 'We would have spent the next two months rearranging the chairs of our leadership and not moving forward on our programs,' Lewis said" (*Congressional Quarterly Weekly Report* 18 March, 563). Many insiders indicated to me that Lewis would have won had he run. Finally, some Republicans were not willing to vote for Madigan because of a regional imbalance (he and Michel are both from Illinois). That Madigan lost by only two votes is strong testimony to the institutionalization of leadership among House Republicans.

3. In July 1988, I conducted interviews with 12 top-level staffers and former staffers in the House and Senate leadership. Ten interviews were conducted in person and two over the phone; they ranged in length from 25 to 55 minutes. Unattributed quotes used in this article are from these interviews.

4. The whip system was reinstituted briefly in 1987 when the Republicans were back in the minority. A leadership aide said that each senator who volunteered (nine in all) became a regional whip. Once again, their duty was primarily floor coverage, but the system did not work because the regional whips were never there when Whip Alan Simpson needed them. The aide said, "When I would call the senators' offices to get them onto the floor for their four hour shift, their administrative assistant would often say, 'Oh, I didn't know he was a regional whip.' They didn't take the job too seriously."

5. Leadership in the nineteenth-century House was permeable, unstable, and transitory. There was no identifiable leadership ladder, and prospective leaders did not serve long apprenticeships, to say nothing about training in lower leadership positions.

6. Development is not always linear. A leadership system may show signs of reaching the third stage only to sink back to the second (as with the Senate Republicans in the mid-1970s). For example, leadership positions become less desired as a party moves from being relatively competitive in the institution to being a small minority. On the other hand, the value of minority leadership increases when the president is of the same party.

7. With the expanded size of the whip system, only a small percentage of those who serve in the system win top positions. Of the 122 Democrats and 70 Republicans who served in the leadership from 1973 to 1988, fewer than a dozen held the positions of whip, floor leader, or Speaker.

8. The move from regional whip to at-large whip is clearly a step up the leadership ladder. In the past decade, 10 have made the move in this direction and only 1 has made the opposite move.

9. In 1987, Dick Cheney moved without opposition from the number four (Policy Committee chair) to the number three position (Conference Committee chair), and Jerry Lewis, the "insider" candidate, moved from the number five position (Research Committee chair) to the number four position. The two top contenders for the Research Committee chair were ladder climbers from the whip system: Steven Bartlett of Texas, who had moved up from regional whip to deputy whip, and the winner, Mickey Edwards, who had moved up from regional whip to head regional whip of the Western and Plains states. The "new stability" was supported again in the leadership shuffle following Whip Lott's election to the Senate in 1988. Michel and Cheney were unopposed for the top two spots and Lewis and Edwards both moved up one notch (in the race for conference chair, Lewis defeated Lynn Martin, the former vice-chair of the conference, 85–82; Edwards was unopposed for Policy Committee chair (*Congressional Quarterly Weekly Report*, 10 December 1988, 3474–75).

10. Although there is almost no difference in the length of time that members hold the top leadership positions in the House and in the Senate, there is large difference in the average length of apprenticeship for House and Senate leaders. Since 1900, House Democrats had served an average of 25.9 years before being elected Speaker and 18.9 years before being elected floor leader; for the Republicans, the averages were 22.4 and 16.8 years for those top two positions. The apprenticeship in the Senate is approximately half as long: Democrats had served an average of 9.2 years before being elected floor leader and 6.5 years before being elected whip; Republicans, 14.7 and 5.9 years.

11. The stability of the Democratic whip system changed in the 100th Congress, with only three whips carried over from the 99th Congress and five new whips appointed. The dramatic difference in the tenure of Democratic and Republican whips can be explained by the practice in the Republican system of assigning all freshman senators to the whip system.

12. Nonetheless, the two top contenders for majority leader in the 101st Congress, Inouye and Mitchell, were third and fourth in the leadership hierarchy in the 100th Congress, respectively. At lower levels there is some indication of an es-

calator; for example, Inouye moved to the number three position, secretary of the conference, after serving several terms as an assistant whip. Byrd moved from conference secretary to whip and, in 1989, Alan Dixon was elected chief deputy whip after serving in the whip system since 1981.

13. Baker was a surprise winner over Griffin in 1976; he did not even announce his campaign until a day and a half before the election, according to one aide. Stevens, on the other hand, was not expected to win. An aide said, "We were as surprised as hell that he did as well as he did." Dole won the final tally 28–25 on the fourth ballot in a tight five-way race (*Congressional Quarterly Weekly Report* 1 December 1984, 3025).

14. This information comes from an internal document of the Federal Election Commission that my research assistant, Patrick Sellers, acquired through great persistence. The dollar figures reported here were tabulated from the FEC's figures for PAC receipts, disbursements, and cash on hand.

15. Of the total receipts from 1984 to 1988, 56.1% were from Dole's, Kemp's, and Gephardt's PACs; most of this money probably went for their presidential campaigns rather than congressional leadership activities. On the other hand, support for colleagues' campaigns by aspiring leaders is understated by the data on leadership PACs reported here. Some aspiring leaders do not establish separate PACs for these purposes. For example, in his campaign for chair of the Policy Committee in 1987, Duncan Hunter contributed $60,000 from his own campaign funds and campaigned for at least 20 members, activity that would not be reported in this FEC data (Hook 1987, 962; also see Sorauf 1988, 174–81).

16. Data collected by the author for the leadership; other figures from Tables 5–9, 5–2, and 5–5 in Ornstein, Mann, and Malbin 1987. I am not entirely confident that the figures in the Clerk's Report and the Secretary's Report cover all the money appropriated to the leadership. For example, appropriations for the minority and majority leaders in the Senate appear to have been included in the conference monies before 1973, at which point they become a separate line item. The accounting is further complicated by changes from annual to biannual to quarterly reporting.

17. The aide pointed out that Stevens's more important role was behind the scenes, especially in negotiations with the Republican committee chairs and the Democratic minority. He said, "Stevens is one of, if not the only, person who can talk to Robert C. Byrd and get him to understand something that he doesn't want to understand or cut a deal with him." He also played a central role in improving communication with the Republican party in the House.

18. Robert Byrd called Cranston the "best nose counter in the Senate" (*Wall Street Journal* 15 March 1977); also see Byrd's favorable comments in the *Congressional Record* S4496 (May 2, 1980), and Robert Lindsay's piece, "Dark Horse from California," in the *New York Times Magazine*, 4 December 1983.

19. As Roger Davidson demonstrates in his article (1989)..., Senate leadership is far less likely to initiate multiple referrals and is more likely to ratify agreements already reached by committee chairs. On the other hand, the practice

increased the powers of leadership in the House by "strengthening their role in centralizing and coordinating the House's workload." In both instances, a balance is struck between member and collective interests.

20. Others have also contested this assertion as it relates to the House as a whole (Cooper and Brady 1981a; Schmidhauser 1973).

REFERENCES

Baker, Ross K. 1989. "Growth and Development of Leadership PACs in Congress." Presented at the annual meeting of the Midwest Political Science Association, Chicago.

Brown, Lynne P., and Robert L. Peabody. 1987. "Patterns of Succession in the House Democratic Leadership: The Choices of Wright, Foley, Coelho, 1986." Presented at the annual meeting of the American Political Science Association, Chicago.

Calmes, Jacqueline. 1987. "The Hill Leaders: Their Places on the Ladder." *Congressional Quarterly Report*, 3 January.

Calmes, Jacqueline, and Rob Gurwitt. 1987. "Profiles in Power: Leaders Without Portfolio." *Congressional Quarterly Weekly Report*, 3 January.

Caro, Robert A. 1982. *The Path to Power: The Years of Lyndon Johnson*. New York: Knopf.

Cohen, Richard E. 1982. "Nearly Anonymous Insiders Play Key Roles as Aides to Congress's Leaders." *National Journal*, 11 September.

Connelly, William F. 1988. "The House Republican Policy Committee: Then and Now." Presented at the annual meeting of the American Political Science Association, Washington, D.C.

Cooper, Joseph, and David W. Brady. 1981a. "Institutional Context and Leadership Style: The House from Cannon to Rayburn." *American Political Science Review* 75:411–25.

Cooper, Joseph, and David W. Brady. 1981b. "Toward a Diachronic Analysis of Congress." *American Political Science Review* 75:988–1006.

Davidson, Roger H. 1989. "Multiple Referral of Legislation in the U.S. Senate." *Legislative Studies Quarterly* 14:375–92.

Deering, Christopher J. 1986. "Leadership in the Slow Lane." *PS* 19:37–42.

Dodd, Lawrence C. 1979. "The Expanded Roles of the House Democratic Whip System: The 93rd and 94th Congresses." *Congressional Studies* 7:27–56.

Dodd, Lawrence C., and Terry Sullivan. 1983. "Majority Party Leadership and Partisan Vote Gathering: The House Democratic Whip System." In *Understanding Congressional Leadership*, ed. Frank H. Mackaman. Washington, D.C.: Congressional Quarterly Press.

Ehrenhalt, Alan. 1987. "Influence on the Hill: Having It and Using It." *Congressional Quarterly Weekly Report*, 3 January.

Granat, Diane. 1984. "Dole Elected Majority Leader; Simpson Wins GOP Whip Job." *Congressional Quarterly Weekly Report*, 1 December.

Hammond, Susan Webb. 1988. "Committee and Informal Leaders in the House of Representatives." Presented at the annual meeting of the Midwest Political Science Association, Chicago.

Hibbing, John R. 1988. "Legislative Institutionalization with Illustrations from the British House of Commons." *American Journal of Political Science* 32:681–712.

Hinkley, Barbara. 1970. "Congressional Leadership Selection and Support: A Comparative Analysis." *Journal of Politics* 32:268–87.

Hook, Janet. 1986. "House Leadership Elections: Wright Era Begins." *Congressional Quarterly Weekly Report,* 13 December.

Hook, Janet. 1987. "House Prepares for Leadership Shuffle." *Congressional Quarterly Weekly Report,* 16 May.

Jones, Charles O. 1970. *The Minority Party in Congress.* Boston: Little, Brown.

Loomis, Burdett A. 1984. "Congressional Careers and Party Leadership in the Contemporary House of Representatives." *American Journal of Political Science* 28:180–202.

Loomis, Burdett A. 1988. "Political Skills and Proximate Goals: Career Development in the House of Representatives." Presented at the annual meeting of the American Political Science Association, Washington, D.C.

Mackaman, Frank H., and Richard C. Sachs, 1988. "The Congressional Leadership Research Project: A Status Report." Presented at the annual meeting of the Midwest Political Science Association, Chicago.

Menefee-Libey, David. Forthcoming. "The Politics of Party Organization: The Democrats from 1968–1986." Ph.D. dissertation, U. of Chicago.

Nelson, Garrison. 1977. "Partisan Patterns of House Leadership Change, 1789–1977." *American Political Science Review* 71:918–39.

Oleszek, Walter J. 1985. "History and Development of the Party Whip System in the U.S. Senate." Senate Document 98–45. Washington, D.C.: U.S. Government Printing Office.

Ornstein, Norman J., Thomas E. Mann, and Michael J. Malbin, 1987. *Vital Statistics on Congress, 1987–1988.* Washington, D.C.: Congressional Quarterly Press.

Peabody, Robert L. 1976. *Leadership in Congress: Stability, Succession, and Change.* Boston: Little, Brown.

Polsby, Nelson W. 1968. "The Institutionalization of the House of Representatives." *American Political Science Review* 62:144–68.

Riddick, Floyd M. 1985. "Majority and Minority Leaders of the Senate: History and Development of the Offices of Floor Leaders." Senate Document 99–3. Washington, D.C.: U.S. Government Printing Office.

Ripley, Randall B. 1964. "The Party Whip Organization in the United States House of Representatives." *American Political Science Review* 58:561–76.

Ripley, Randall B. 1967. *Party Leaders in the House of Representatives.* Washington, D.C.: The Brookings Institution.

Schmidhauser, John R. 1973. "An Exploratory Analysis of the Institutionalization of Legislatures and Judiciaries." In *Legislatures in Comparative Perspective,* ed. Allan Kornberg. New York: David McKay.

Sinclair, Barbara. 1983. *Majority Leadership in the U.S. House.* Baltimore: Johns Hopkins U. Press.

Smith, Steven S. 1985. "New Patterns of Decisionmaking in Congress." In *The New Directions in American Politics,* ed. John E. Chubb and Paul E. Peterson. Washington, D.C.: The Brookings Institution.

Smith, Steven S., and Stanley Bach. 1988. "Craftsmanship on Capitol Hill: The Pattern of Diversity in Special Rules." Presented at the annual meeting of the Midwest Political Science Association, Chicago.

Smith, Steven S., and Marcus Fathman. 1989. "Managing the Senate Floor: Complex Unanimous Consent Agreements Since the 1950s." *Legislative Studies Quarterly* 14:349–74.

Sorauf, Frank J. 1988. *Money in American Elections.* Glenview, Ill.: Scott, Foresman.

Reading 20

PARTISAN REPRESENTATION AND THE FAILURE OF REALIGNMENT IN THE 1980s

Patricia A. Hurley

Contemporary prospects for realignment and dealignment have been debated at length by political scientists and journalists for the past 20 years. When V. O. Key, Jr. (1955), first introduced the notion of critical elections, he emphasized the importance of new and durable patterns of voting behavior. Since then a number of scholars have extended and clarified the concept. Burnham (1970) argues that realignments "arise from emergent tensions in society which, not adequately controlled by the organization of party politics as usual, escalate to a flashpoint; they are issue-oriented phenomena—centrally associated with these tensions and more or less leading to resolution adjustments; they result in significant transformations in the general shape of policy and they have relatively profound after effects on the roles played by institutional elites."[1]

Realignments then involve two distinct but interrelated phenomena: persistent new electoral alignments and new directions in public policy. By far the larger portion of research on realignments has been devoted to the study of the former, particularly at the presidential level.

Recent research on realignments, however, suggests the pivotal role played by the Congress. Specifically, the major redirections in public policy that result from realignments must be enacted by Congress.[2] Scholars working in this area have directed their attention to the behavior of parties in the House of Representatives. Brady (1978, 1982, with Stewart) has noted the importance of switched seat members and increased levels of party voting to the process of policy change that follows realignment. Sinclair (1977, 1982) has examined the emergence and evolution of issue dimensions in House voting patterns during periods of realignment and stability. For the realignment of the 1930s, she found the behavior of returning members of the Democratic party as well as new House Democrats supportive of New Deal policies. This literature implies that the

493

representatives of the emerging majority party respond to constituency signals for change and do so in accord with constituency preferences, which during realignments are relatively uniform across districts (Brady, 1978). Since the realignments studied took place prior to the advent of modern-day opinion surveys, the true extent of opinion-policy congruence during realignments remains a matter of inference.

Yet the extent of opinion-policy congruence between parties in the electorate and parties in government is likely to be a fundamental factor in transforming short-term electoral change into durable new patterns of voting and partisan preference. In a major study of realignment which ties together much previous work on this topic, Clubb, Flanigan, and Zingale suggest that, while the electorate creates the conditions for realignment, it can only be realized if the advantaged partisan elite pursues policies "that can win the long term support of newly eligible, weakly identified or unidentified, and formerly apolitical members of the electorate."[3]

In other words, realignments are both "bottom up" and "top down" phenomena: the arrows connecting opinion to policy should run in both directions during a realigning sequence. The electorate, dissatisfied with politics as usual, votes into Congress large numbers of switched seat members, which may result in a new majority or a greatly reduced margin of control for the existing majority. In such times a realignment is possible, but its success or failure will turn on the ability of the advantaged party to continue to represent successfully its existing identifiers, as well as provide the independents in the mass public with more policy satisfaction than does the disadvantaged party. Representation occurs as the advantaged party responds to opinions within its ranks, but is also facilitated if rank-and-file party opinion responds favorably to and hence moves in the direction of the policy action taken by the advantaged party.[4] This should be a key factor in distinguishing short-lived changes in voting behavior that have the initial appearances of realignment, such as 1912 or 1964, from more enduring changes, such as those of the 1890s or 1930s. Thus, a process that I shall call partisan representation should be essential to the culmination of a realignment.

Partisan representation is a variant of the notion of collective representation suggested by Weissberg (1978).[5] Collective representation suggests that institutions may represent the mass public more accurately than legislators represent districts. Partisan representation shifts the focus away from how well institutions represent the public or how well legislators represent districts to how well the parties in Congress represent their rank-and-file identifiers. An individual legislator may not be able to represent accurately the opinions of a district that is heterogeneous, but the parties in Congress can and may respond to the distribution of opinion among their identifiers in the electorate. In this way district minorities receive representation. A Democrat living in a district represented by a Republican may find himself or herself at frequent odds with the district's own representative, but may have his or her views taken by the majority of the Democrats in the institution. Partisan representation should play an important role in bringing about opinion-policy congruence if the parties in government respond to the parties in the electorate. Partisan representation can also occur if rank-and-file partisans bring their opinions into line with the party in government's actions. This is most likely if those actions are perceived as steps in the right direction, and this change of opinion by rank-and-file partisans would also promote opinion-policy congruence.

Partisan representation is not the only factor contributing to a realignment. Mobilization or conversion of a sizable segment of the mass public into the advantaged party is necessary. Widespread attachments to a popular leader, such as Franklin Roosevelt, and general perceptions of policy progress and success in areas germane to the realigning issues are also vital to the process. In reality, all these factors are probably closely interwined. Each is necessary to a realignment, but none alone is both necessary and sufficient. The simultaneous occurrence and mutually reinforcing effects of all these factors consolidate the realignment. Keeping in mind the importance of other factors, I shall consider in this paper only the role of partisan representation in the realignment process.

The above discussion suggests specific hypotheses about the patterns of partisan representation that should hold for the advantaged party during a realigning sequence. The congressional elite of this party should be especially representative of its own followers and should stay representative of them over a period of several Congresses. The partisan preferences of the mass of this group, and especially those of any recent converts to it, need positive policy reinforcement. The advantaged party should also be closer than the opposition to the policy preferences of the independents and remain closer to them over the period of electoral flux. Some large portion of these independents is presumably voting for candidates of the advantaged party. They need to be mobilized into active identification with it, again through a process of positive policy reinforcement.

This puts the advantaged party in a delicate situation. As the party in the electorate grows larger, it may become more heterogeneous and thus more difficult to represent. Ultimately this will always be a problem for the majority party. Yet it should not be a problem close in time to the realignment. Indeed, to prevent this problem from occurring, the advantaged party may need to bring opinion within its rank and file into line with the policy positions of the party. Opinion persuasion by a popular president would be one important mechanism for bringing this about; perceived substantive policy success would be another. Thus, during a realignment, the process of partisan representation should be reciprocal: opinion-policy congruence results both from the party in government responding to the party in the electorate and from the party in the electorate moving toward the party in government because its policy efforts are viewed favorably in retrospect. Public opinion and elite policy behavior must go through several iterations until, at the culmination of the realigning sequence, the two converge.

Two scenarios are possible for the relationship of the elite members of the disadvantaged party to its rank-and-file identifiers. At the beginning of the sequence, this elite should be less representative of its followers than is the advantaged party of its respective identifiers. Some of these followers are defecting as a result. By the end of the sequence, the disadvantaged party elite and mass may be more congruent than they were at the outset, but that group of followers will be smaller. Or, the disadvantaged party elite may remain disconnected from the party mass as it fails to adapt to changing times. The scenario for the relationship of the disadvantaged party to the independents is easier to construct: it should be further from the preferences of the independents than the advantaged party over the period of the realigning sequence. The disadvantaged party neither represents the existing concerns of the independents nor persuades them to its point of view.

A critical factor, then, in transforming short-term electoral change into durable new patterns of party identification and voting is improved partisan representation by the emerging majority party. The advantaged party must remain responsive to its followers—the core group whose support must be retained; and it must satisfy the independents—the peripheral group which must be mobilized.

The level of conflict and consensus between party leaders and followers has been examined at various points in time by a variety of researchers (McClosky, Hoffman, and O'Hara, 1960; Kirkpatrick, 1976; Montjoy, Shaffer, and Weber, 1980; and Jackson, Brown, and Bositis, 1982). While this literature has a number of important findings, only Jackson and his colleagues explicitly connect the topic to the process of realignment: "If the 1980 election comes to be viewed as the start of one of those historic realigning eras in American politics, it will be because the Republicans are successful in capturing the pervasive mood of the American public and articulating it into programs and policies that the public will support. If those programs and policies are successful, the public will identify with the Republican party and a new majority will be born."[6]

Note that Jackson, Brown, and Bositis also imply a reciprocal relationship between opinion and policy: a pervasive mood must be caught, but the policies produced in its wake must gain approval after the fact. Most research in this tradition has focused on party organizational elites. Yet if one wishes to speak of party elites who implement programs and policies, it is more appropriate to examine that portion of the party elite which is actually in the government. While Backstrom (1977) has done this for the 92nd Congress, the cross-sectional nature of his analysis and the time period (1970) mean his results do not apply to a realigning or potentially realigning period.

The ideal test of these hypotheses about the role of partisan representation in promoting or inhibiting realignment requires public opinion data on issues from a period which scholars agree was one of realignment. Unfortunately, no such data exist.[7] Yet, one can approach the test from another angle: examining realignments that might have been, or short-term periods of electoral change that did not become permanent. The "potential" realignments should fail because the apparently advantaged party does not continue to provide good partisan representation to its followers while simultaneously representing the independents more accurately than the opposition party elite.

The 1980s provide a good test case of this latter sort. The 1980 presidential and congressional elections displayed many of the characteristics of a realignment. Yet the 1982, 1984, and 1986 congressional elections failed to sustain the process. Most observers are now in agreement that no electoral realignment in American politics has occurred in the 1980s, even though policy changes followed the 1980 election. Based on the foregoing arguments, one can hypothesize that the Republican congressional party did not represent and satisfy its followers and the independents in the manner necessary to capitalize on short-term change.

While a case can be made for examining partisan representation in the Senate, a better case can be made for examining the House. First, the principal work on the role of Congress in realignments has focused on the House. Second, biennial elections of the entire membership tie that body more closely than the Senate to the electorate. Finally, if the 1980s were to become a realigning period, the Republicans needed to capture control of the House. Their failure to do so, even in the context of the 1984 Reagan landslide, may have resulted from their inability to provide sufficient partisan representation. With the expectation that the Republican congressional elite will not display the pattern of partisan representation necessary to bring about realignment in the 1980s, I will address the 1980–84 period as a test case. This test represents a first cut at examining the role of partisan representation in inhibiting or promoting realignments. If the House results conform to the expectations developed here, they should also be validated by examining the Senate.

DATA

Data on public opinion were taken from the 1980, 1982, and 1984 National Election Studies (NES) conducted by the Center for Political Studies (CPS) at the University of Michigan. Several questions were repeated in each of these studies. Respondents were asked to place themselves on seven-point scales for ideology, defense spending, general government services and spending, government aid to minorities, women's roles, and government guaranteed jobs and standards of living. In the 1980 and 1984 surveys, respondents placed themselves on a seven-point scale for busing. In 1982 and 1984 respondents were asked whether they preferred government spending for a variety of policy areas to remain at current levels, be increased, or be decreased. In 1984 respondents were also asked to place themselves on a seven-point scale ranging from less to more involvement in Central America. While this question was not repeated over time, it is used in the present analysis because of the salience of this issue. The distributions of preferences on these issues were calculated for Republicans, Democrats, and independents.[8] The seven-point scales were recoded into three-point scales by grouping scales points one, two, and three; and five, six, and seven. Scale point four was left alone as a middle of the road position. This recoding scheme should minimize any reliability problems inherent in the seven-point scales. Respondents' self-positioning may not be stable over time, but they are unlikely to cross the midpoint of the scale unless their views have undergone true change.

Data for the party elite consist of roll call votes taken in the House of Representatives during the 97th and 98th Congresses, elected in 1980 and 1982, respectively. All roll calls were examined, and those with content that most closely matched the public opinion questions were selected for analysis. Unanimous and near unanimous (fewer than 10 percent dissenting) votes as well as roll calls that were obvious instances of strategic voting were avoided. Strategic voting was indicated by extremely irregular voting patterns (such as all northern Democrats voting the apparently conservative position), or obviously ridiculous content (such as measures to cut spending for widely popular programs by 67 percent or to prohibit spending if it would lead the federal government to engage in deficit spending). This resulted in a total of 332 usable roll calls: 133 in the 97th Congress and 199 in the 98th Congress.[9]

For each roll call, the number of each party voting for and against, and the conservative position (yea or nay) was determined. The determination of conservative position was relative rather than absolute: if the decision was to reduce funding, for example, for the Environmental Protection Agency 2 percent or 5 percent, the 5 percent decrease was counted as the conservative alternative. Roll calls were then grouped into policy areas, and the mean percentage of the party taking the conservative position was calculated for each policy area for the two Congresses under study.

Some readers will object that the data for the parties in Congress are not comparable to the data for the public because the actual content of the roll calls does not match exactly the question wording of the CPS items. While it is true that "question wording" varies from general opinion items to specific roll call votes, this is exactly analogous to the representational dilemma faced by members of Congress on a daily basis. A legislator may wish to provide the constituency with the best delegated representation possible. Yet even the most diligent representative can only know the opinion of the constituency in general terms for most policy areas. Roll call votes present the representative with a specific set of alternatives. Those specific alternatives must be weighed against the member's knowledge of the general direction of opinion in the constituency and what it will support. This is true regardless of whether the constituency is defined as the member's partisans in the district, all residents of the district, or all identifiers with the member's party nationwide. It would be impossible for the representative to assess constituency opinion for every specific roll call voting situation; therefore, knowledge of general public opinion must always structure specific behavior for those representatives who wish to act as delegates (Hurley, 1982; Stone, 1979).[10]

CORRESPONDENCE BETWEEN MASS PREFERENCES AND ELITE VOTING

The analysis will proceed by examining the percentage of the partisan mass public holding a conservative opinion on various issues and comparing those figures to the mean percentage of the party elite voting conservatively on those issues. Two types of comparisons can be made. The first is to assess representation by calculating "difference scores," which are computed by subtracting the percentage of the party elite voting conservatively from the percentage of the party rank and file holding conservative opinions. Negative figures indicate that a larger portion of the elite was conservative relative to the public; positive figures indicate the liberal contingent in the elite is larger. For example, if 60 percent of the Republican mass public preferred to raise defense spending, but 70 percent of the Republican House members voted to do so, the difference score would be –10.

More important, however, is the question of whether majorities are on the same or opposite sides of the issues. In this example, majorities of the Republican mass and elite were on the same side of the defense spending question. Let us assume that 55 percent of the Democratic public wished defense spending to be raised, but only 45 percent of the House Democrats voted for increases. The difference score of + 10 is identical in absolute value to that for the Republicans, but for the Democratic party the centers of gravity in the mass and the elite are on opposite sides of the issue. Thus, the second method for assessing representation will be to determine the number of issues for which majorities of the public and the party elite are on the same or opposite sides. Three sets of comparisons will be made. Opinions of the Republican and Democratic mass public will be compared to their respective elites, and the opinions of independents will be compared to both party elites.

Tables 20.1 and 20.2 display the results for Republicans and Democrats, respectively. The top of Table 20.1 shows the percentage of the Republican rank and file with conservative opinions for 1980, 1982, and 1984. On two issues we see a sizable change in opinion: defense spending and minority aid. By 1984 a considerably smaller percentage of the Republican party expressed conservative opinions on these matters. Because changes in national policy had altered the context of these questions, this movement of opinion is not surprising. That is, federal spending on defense had increased greatly between 1980 and 1984, and programs benefiting minorities had been cut. Context had also changed for the question regarding government services, but the opinion data show a less clear pattern there. The Republican public became more conservative in 1982 on government services, but then became much less so between 1982 and 1984. All the other issues show only trivial opinion changes, but they move to the left by 1984.

The bottom portion of the table shows the mean percentage of Republican House members who voted the conservative position on these issues in the 97th and 98th Congresses. The ideology score for the party elite was calculated by averaging the conservative percentage for all votes in the policy areas examined. Because each policy area contains a different number of roll calls, this amounts to a weighted average. The differ-

Table 20.1 Republican Public and Elite, Percentage Conservative

Issue	Mass public			
	1980	1982	1984	Net change (1980–84)
Defense spending	81.1	46.4	46.5	34.6
Government services	53.4	60.2	50.3	3.1
Minority aid	60.7	57.0	48.6	12.1
Women's equality	22.2	23.3	18.2	4.0
Jobs and standards of living	65.4	65.5	59.1	6.3
Busing	92.3	—	90.1	2.2
Central America	—[a]	—	32.5	—
Ideology	67.1	66.9	63.3	3.8

Issue	House members					
	97th Congress 1981–82		98th Congress 1983–84		Net change (97th–98th)	
Defense spending	79.6	(1.5)[b]	80.0	(−33.5)[c]	−0.4	
Government services	75.6	(−22.2)	68.9	(−18.6)	6.7	
Minority aid	67.7	(−7.0)	61.0	(−12.4)	6.7	
Women's equality	—	—	66.0	(−47.8)	—	
Jobs and standards of living	61.3	(4.1)	69.2	(−10.1)	−7.9	
Busing	85.5	(6.8)	—		—	
Central America	—	—	86.5	(−54.0)	—	
Ideology	72.6	(−5.5)	72.4	(−9.1)	0.2	
Mean abs. value of differences on issues	8.3		(29.4)			

Note: [a]A dash indicates that question was not asked or no votes were taken on that issue in that Congress.

[b]Difference from the public in 1980.

[c]Difference from the public in 1984. Negative figures indicate a larger portion of the elite conservative.

Source: Calculated from the U.S. National Election Studies supplied by the Inter-University Consortium for Social and Political Research and from *Congressional Quarterly Almanac,* 1981–84.

ence scores appear in parentheses following the conservative scores for each issue. Scores for the 97th Congress were obtained by subtracting from public opinion in 1980; figures for the 98th Congress were calculated by subtracting from public opinion data for 1984. Differences from

1980 and 1984 were selected because these dates should bound the period in which realignment might have occurred. Because the hypothesis predicts congruence between partisan public opinion and the policy behavior of the respective partisan elite by the end of a realigning sequence, opinion in 1984 is compared to roll call voting in the 98th Congress. Moreover, while NES surveys are taken only in election years, members of Congress have access to numerous other public and private polls during the course of a term. This should allow them ample opportunity to adjust their behavior to public opinion or to work on bringing public opinion into line with their behavior. Two additional difference scores could be generated by comparing roll call votes in each Congress with the 1982 opinion data, but this would clutter the analysis unnecessarily without altering the substantive findings.

Recall that because realignment was not realized in the 1980s the expectation is that the relationship between the Republican elite and mass should not become more congruent between 1980 and 1984. Difference scores for the Republicans indicate generally good correspondence between elite and mass in the 97th Congress. A slightly larger portion of the Republican elite was conservative on minority aid, but a slightly smaller portion was conservative relative to the rank and file on defense spending, jobs and standards of living, and busing. The only difference score of notable magnitude at all was on the issue of general government services. An overall assessment of representation may be made by averaging the absolute values of the differences scores for the specific issue areas, which yields a value of 8.3 for this Congress.

The picture changed distinctly, however, in the 98th Congress. On the six issues examined, a larger portion of the Republican elite was conservative relative to the portion in the rank and file—in some cases by quite large margins. The average of the absolute value of the difference scores for this Congress is 29.4. More important, majorities of the elite and of the rank and file were on opposite sides of the issues of defense spending, aid to minorities, women's equality, and the Central American question. This situation arose because the Republican rank and file became generally less conservative, but the Republican House members showed little change in their voting patterns. This can be seen more clearly by examining the right-hand column of Table 20.1, which displays simple aggregate differences between public opinion in 1980 and 1984 and differences in Republican roll call voting in the 97th and 98th Congresses. The largest shift in public opinion was on defense spending, yet Republican House voting on defense spending remained nearly constant. On jobs and standards of living, the Republican public became less conservative, while a greater portion of House members voted con-

Table 20.2 Democratic Public and Elite, Percentage Conservative

Issue	Mass public			
	1980	1982	1984	Net change (1980–84)
Defense spending	64.5	25.1	26.2	38.3
Government services	21.6	26.9	18.4	3.2
Minority aid	41.0	37.8	27.1	13.9
Women's equality	19.5	17.3	15.0	4.5
Jobs and standards of living	36.0	36.6	32.3	3.7
Busing	78.1	—	79.1	−1.0
Central America	—[a]	—	19.9	—
Ideology	28.0	25.6	22.2	5.8

Issue	House members				
	97th Congress 1981–82		98th Congress 1983–84		Net change (97th–98th)
Defense spending	48.6	(15.9)[b]	39.7	(−13.5)[c]	8.9
Government services	27.4	(−5.8)	16.7	(−1.7)	10.7
Minority aid	22.1	(18.9)	5.3	(21.8)	16.8
Women's equality	—	—	6.3	(8.7)	—
Jobs and standards of living	13.2	(22.8)	14.5	(17.7)	−1.3
Busing	49.0	(29.1)	—	—	—
Central America	—	—	18.7	(1.2)	—
Ideology	28.6	(−0.6)	19.3	(2.9)	9.3
Mean abs. value of differences on issues	18.5		10.7		

Note: See Table 20.1 for [a], [b], and [c].
Source: Calculated from the U.S. National Election Studies supplied by the Inter-University Consortium for Social and Political Research and from *Congressional Quarterly Almanac,* 1981–84.

servatively on this issue. The public shift on aid to minorities resulted in 12 percent fewer Republicans holding a conservative position on this issue, while the shift among House Republicans was only half this magnitude. On the question of general government services, there was slightly greater movement to the left on the part of House Republicans than the public. The representational relationship between the Republican elite and mass not only supports the null hypothesis of no improvement but declines in several specific issue areas.

Alternatively, representation remains fairly good for the GOP if we consider ideology alone. In 1980, 67.1 percent of the Republicans in the public identified themselves as conservative, and the average percentage of Republican House members voting conservatively on the issues studied in the 97th Congress was 72.6 percent. In the 98th Congress the average percentage of Republicans voting conservatively was 72.4, and the percentage of self-described conservatives in the mass public declined only slightly to 63.3 percent. From this general ideological perspective only, the Republican elite and mass remained in relatively close agreement.

Turning to Table 20.2 for the Democrats, we observe a pattern of changes in the distribution of rank-and-file Democratic opinion very similar to that shown by the Republicans. On defense spending and aid to minorities the Democratic rank and file were significantly less conservative by 1984 than they had been in 1980, although, as one would expect, they were far more liberal than the Republicans in both years. Attitudes on government services show the same pattern as exhibited by the Republicans as well—more conservative in 1982 but a 1984 level of conservatism below that observed in 1980. On all the other issues, changes in public opinion are minor, but with the exception of busing, they always moved in a liberal direction by 1984.

The bottom portion of Table 20.2 shows the percentage of Democratic House members voting the conservative position on these issues, as well as the difference scores obtained by comparing House voting to public opinion among rank-and-file Democrats. These scores indicate that, in general, a greater portion of the Democratic elite was liberal than was true of the party rank and file. On government services in the 97th Congress and defense spending in the 98th, a somewhat larger portion of Democratic House members than rank-and-file followers was conservative.

Averaging the absolute values of difference scores for all issue areas (five in the 97th, six in the 98th) suggests that the Democratic public was more accurately represented by its elite in the 98th Congress than in the 97th; the average declines from 18.5 to 10.7. This improvement came about in part because of the addition of the Central American issue, an issue on which the party elite and the rank and file were in close agreement. It is also somewhat inflated by the absence of votes on busing in the latter Congress. The Democratic public and elite conservative percentages converged on the issue of government services and were fairly close for women's equality. For minority aid and jobs, the relative differ-

Table 20.3 Independent Percentage Conservative and Difference from Both Partisan Elites

Issue	Mass public			Net change (1980–84)
	1980	1982	1984	
Defense spending	68.7	28.7	35.9	32.8
Government services	33.8	45.7	37.0	−3.2
Minority aid	47.9	48.0	38.5	9.4
Women's equality	19.4	18.4	18.2	1.2
Jobs and standards of living	56.8	50.8	41.4	15.4
Busing	86.1	—	81.2	4.9
Central America	—	—	22.4	—
Ideology	40.8	43.6	31.9	8.9

Issue	Difference from Dem. elite		Difference from Rep. elite	
	1980–97th	1984–98th	1980–97th	1984–98th
Defense spending	20.1	3.8	−10.9	−44.1
Government services	6.4	20.3	−41.8	−31.9
Minority aid	25.8	33.2	−19.8	−22.5
Women's equality	—	11.9	—	−47.8
Jobs and standards of living	43.6	26.9	−4.5	−27.8
Busing	37.1	—	0.6	—
Central America	—	3.7	—	−63.7
Ideology	12.2	12.6	−31.8	−40.5
Mean abs. value of differences on issues	26.6	16.6	15.5	39.6

Source: Calculated from the U.S. National Election Studies supplied by the Inter-University Consortium for Social and Political Research and from data in Tables 1 and 2.

ences in the percentage of the elite and mass who described themselves as conservative remained roughly constant.

Assessing representation by considering the number of instances in which the balance of opinion in the party elite versus the rank and file put them on opposite sides on an issue or on ideology in general also shows improvements in representation for the Democratic party. In the 97th Congress, majorities were at odds on only two issues: busing and defense spending. In the 98th Congress, the majority of the Democratic elite and public were on the same side of all the issues under consideration.[11] The change scores indicate that the House Democrats' shift in voting behavior between the 97th and 98th Congress was somewhat more comparable in size and direction to the shift in public opinion than was the change in House Republican voting. Furthermore, for both Congresses the difference scores for ideology indicate a fairly close fit between party elite and identifiers: –0.6 points in the 97th and 2.9 points in the 98th Congress. A greater portion of both the public and the House members was liberal in 1984.

Table 20.3 displays public opinion data for the independents in the mass public from 1980 through 1984. Independents underwent changes on several issues fairly similar to those exhibited by both groups of partisan identifiers: large declines in support for more defense spending (although the decline is not linear) and increased support for government aid to minorities. Independents were also far less likely to take a conservative position on the issue of government guaranteed jobs and standard of living in 1984 than in 1980, again as a result of the changed context of the question. Support for a reduction of government services went up in 1982 and declined in 1984. Women's equality and busing show small changes within the bounds of sampling error. A marginally larger percentage was conservative on general ideology in 1982, but this percentage declined greatly by 1984. Net change scores summarize the difference in independent opinion between 1980 and 1984.

The bottom portion of Table 20.3 displays difference scores for the independents relative to both the Democratic and Republican elites. In both Congresses the Democratic House members were more liberal than the independents on all issues. Yet the average of the absolute value of the difference scores declined from 26.6 to 16.6. Omitting busing and Central America from the averages, which bias the test toward improvement, the average score declined from 24 to 19.2. More important, in the 97th Congress majorities of Democratic House members and independents were on opposite sides of the questions of defense spending and guaranteed jobs. By the 98th Congress, majorities were on the same sides of all six issues, even though a greater proportion of the Democratic elite was liberal.

Looking at the difference between the independents and the Republican elite, we see almost a mirror image of the pattern for the Democratic elite. In the 97th House, a greater portion of Republican members were conservative relative to the independents on all issues save busing. This conservatism put them on opposing sides from the majority of independents on government services and aid to minorities. By the 98th Congress the portion of the Republican elite who were conservative relative to the independents had increased on the four issues for which direct comparisons are possible. The gap between the two groups was extremely large on the women's equality and Central American questions as well. The majority of the Republican elite was in opposition to the majority of independents on all issues. The average of the absolute value of the difference scores goes from 15.5 to 39.6. If the busing and Central American questions are omitted from the calculations, the mean difference scores are 19.3 and 34.8 for the 97th and 98th Congresses, respectively. Thus, Republicans provided better representation to independents in the 97th Congress than they did in the 98th. The scores for ideology show the same pattern, going from −31.8 to −40.5, indicating a sizable increase in the proportion of the Republican elite who took conservative positions relative to the proportion of self-described conservatives among the independents. The representational relationship between the Republican elite and the independents, as expected, supports the null hypothesis, which posits no improvement in representation.

COMPARISON OF MASS AND ELITE SPENDING PREFERENCES

Whenever possible, House votes on these issues were coded to indicate the specific program area to which they applied, such as food stamps or social security. These votes can then be compared to the responses to the 1982 and 1984 battery of questions asking whether respondents preferred to raise, maintain, or reduce federal spending on specific policies. Table 20.4 displays the percentage of Democrats, Republicans, and independents preferring less federal spending for various program areas, as well as the percentage of Democratic and Republican House members voting for cutbacks, or the lower of two possible appropriations, in these program areas. Public attitudes for 1982 are presented with voting patterns for the 97th Congress, while public attitudes in 1984 are displayed with the voting figures for the 98th.

When presented with specific program areas, none of the three groups in the mass public was very supportive of spending cuts except in the food stamps program.[12] Further, the percentage wanting lower spending in these areas declined from 1982 to 1984 with one exception: Republicans in 1984 were more supportive of cuts in federal spending on blacks than they had been in 1982. Presumably, these declines indicate that most of the public felt the first several rounds of spending cuts during the Reagan administration were sufficient. While partisan differences remain (and are in the expected direction), even Republican

Table 20.4 Public and Elite on Spending Reductions (Percentage Preferring Less)

Program area	97th Congress and public opinion in 1982				
	Dem. reps	Dem. public	Indep. public	Rep. public	Rep. reps
Environment	34.1	8.6	13.9	16.5	73.6
Health, Medicare	18.3	3.6	6.7	11.4	52.3
Crime	30.0	4.2	10.6	7.3	67.7
Educ., public schools	6.0	5.4	10.6	11.2	39.0
Blacks	55.0	16.3	24.8	23.3	86.0
Social Security	19.0	9.9	12.3	19.4	4.0
Food stamps	11.1	44.2	56.7	68.6	77.4
Unemployment	13.3	13.1	18.8	30.0	65.1

Program area	98th Congress and public opinion in 1984				
	Dem. reps	Dem. public	Indep. public	Rep. public	Rep. reps
Environment	14.1	7.5	6.5	9.5	55.6
Health, Medicare	9.7	2.7	1.5	8.2	76.5
Crime	2.0	4.0	7.7	4.7	24.0
Educ., public schools	14.9	2.9	4.6	9.4	62.9
Blacks	7.0	13.1	19.0	30.4	63.0
Social Security	34.2	2.0	3.5	5.3	67.3
Food stamps	9.0	22.3	26.6	46.6	80.3
Unemployment	7.9	7.9	13.0	22.3	60.1

Source: Calculated from the U.S. National Election Studies supplied by the Inter-University Consortium for Social and Political Research and from *Congressional Quarterly Almanac*, 1981–84.

identifiers were less willing to support further reductions. Yet a substantial number of Republican representatives continued to vote for cuts and lower spending alternatives in the 98th Congress. The Democratic representatives, as one would expect, were much less supportive of cuts in these domestic programs than their Republican colleagues. As a result, their voting patterns were more representative of public preferences by time of the 98th Congress.

SUMMARY AND IMPLICATIONS

Both parties' elites provided their followers with good representation if we only compare elite behavior to generalized expressions of ideology by the rank and file. Some two-thirds of the Republicans in the public did identify themselves as conservative, and an average of slightly more than two-thirds of the House Republicans took the conservative position on all votes studied. Most Democrats did not describe themselves as conservative, and Democratic House members generally did not vote for the conservative alternative. Yet issue specific correspondence is rarely as close as it is on this general measure. Further, if we consider whether majorities of the party elite and public are on the same or opposing sides of issues, we find that issue specific representation worsens for the Republicans and improves for the Democrats during the 1980–84 period. The Republican elite was not at odds with the majority of its followers on any issue in the 97th, but was at odds on four issues by the 98th Congress. The Democratic mass and elite were at odds on two of five issues in the 97th Congress, but on none of six issues in the 98th.

On the ideological measures, fewer independents described themselves as conservative in 1984 than in 1980 or 1982. This moved them further away from the Republican elite by 1984 than they had been earlier. The majority of independents were on opposite sides of two of five issues when compared to the Democratic elite in the 97th and also were at odds with the Republican elite on two issues. By the 98th Congress, however, the majority of independents were at odds with the Republican elite on all of the six issues and at odds with the Democratic elite on none.

Thus, the expectation that the Republican congressional elite would fail to provide a level of partisan representation sufficient to effectuate a realignment is supported by this analysis. Rather, the Republican elite exhibits a pattern of partisan representation which is precisely the reverse of that hypothesized for the advantaged party during a realigning sequence. Their representational relationship to their own identifiers as well as to the independents declines over the period studied. While the relationship between the Democratic elite and the rank and file is consistent with one of two alternative scenarios suggested above, the relationship between this elite and the independents is counter to that expected for the disadvantaged party during a realigning sequence.

These results have further implications for any near future prospects of a Republican realignment if considered in conjunction with changes in the aggregate distribution of partisan preference from 1980 to 1984, displayed in Table 20.5.

Table 20.5 Changing Aggregate Distribution of Partisan Preferences
(in Percentages)

Party	1980	1984
Democrats[a]	53.4	48.7
Independents	13.2	11.1
Republicans	33.4	40.2
N	1,577	2,198

Note: [a]Independent leaners grouped with partisans.
Source: Calculated from the U.S. National Election Studies supplied by the Inter-University Consortium for Social and Political Research.

Between 1980 and 1984, the Democratic party in the electorate declined in size by nearly five percentage points. The size of the pure independents declined as well, by two percentage points. The Republican party was the beneficiary of these losses, picking up nearly seven percentage points by 1984. Panel data would reveal much about the dynamics of individual changes, but such data are unavailable for this time span. Thus, we are limited by the available cross-sectional data, but can nonetheless speculate about the partisan migration patterns that produced this net change in the aggregate distribution of party identification.

It is highly unlikely that many of the defecting Democrats moved directly into the Republican party. Rather, dissatisfied Democrats (presumably the more conservative element of the party) moved to the position of independents. At the same time, the more conservative portion of those calling themselves independents probably moved into the Republican party. These migration patterns can be illustrated graphically:

Democrats → independents
                independents → Republicans

The actual number of people changing is probably twice as large as the net gain to the Republican party of 6.8 percentage points.

Thus, by 1984 the composition of the two partisan groups in the mass public, as well as of the independents, should have changed in predictable ways. Specifically, the loss of the more conservative members of the Democratic party means that the remaining Democrats were more liberal and more homogeneous as a group, but smaller. The defecting Democrats who moved into the independent ranks were probably more liberal than the existing group of independents had been. This latter shift, coupled with movement of the more conservative independents into the Republican party, should have resulted in a more liberal group of independents by 1984. While the Republican party benefited from this migration, the impact should have been to lower the level of conservatism and depress homogeneity of opinion within the party's ranks. The most conservative of the independents moved into the Republican party, but these people were probably not as conservative as the existing group of Republicans had been, nor were they persuaded to a more conservative position by the Republican policy actions.

If this explanation of the change in the aggregate distribution of party preference is correct, it accounts neatly for a large part of the changes in policy preference and ideological self-placement of these three groups observed in Tables 20.1 through 20.3. All three groups, but especially the Democrats and independents, were less likely to hold conservative opinions in 1984 than they had been in 1980. While some of this shift can be attributed to the changed direction of federal policy, some change may be attributed to the altered composition of these three groups in the mass public.

The results presented in this paper are tentative, but suggest that the realignment potential of the early 1980s failed for policy-based reasons. Ironically, policy realignment in this case prevented rather than consolidated electoral realignment. New Republican initiatives in policy failed to gain high levels of support among the Republican or independent public, and Republican House members failed to modify their behavior (and hence policy) to respond to movements in public opinion after 1982.

Some would argue that electoral behavior and party identification have little policy basis in the contemporary era. The current "high-tech" politics of polling, direct mail, and media consultants emphasizes the merchandising of candidates at the expense of issues. In the short run, parties and policy may be relatively unimportant as voters respond to image-based presidential campaigns featuring charismatic candidates, and congressional incumbents, especially in the House, enjoy substantial advantages over challengers. Yet party identification remains a good predictor of voter choice. Wright and Berkman (1986) have argued that policy positions of candidates may play a greater role than other recent research on congressional elections has suggested and Macdonald and Rabinowitz (1987) have demonstrated the linkages between congressional roll call voting, presidential voting, and partisanship in a realignment context. In the long run, conversion or mobilization of members of the electorate must rest on more than attachments to a popular or charismatic president. Policy-based partisan conversions can be sustained; candidate-based conversions lack depth and are unlikely to last beyond the short term. Policy satisfaction reached through the process of partisan representation could provide support for conversions that were initially candidate based.

The gains in Republican party identification may or may not persist beyond 1984 into 1988. Currently, any policy-based mobilization of independents appears to have approached an upper limit. In the issue space of 1984 these independents were positioned closer to the Democratic rather than the Republican elite, although post-1984 opinion and roll call data would be necessary to ascertain if they remain there. As indicated in Table 20.5, this leaves the Republicans in a more competitive position than they had been, but still a minority party. Realignment has not occurred. If, however, the Republican identification gains can survive the Iran-Contra scandal and the loss of Ronald Reagan at the head of the ticket, the Reagan elections may be considered analogues to Pomper's (1967) notion of converting elections. A converting election is distinguished from a realigning one in that realignments involve both a change in majority party as well as in the distribution of party identification that underlies the normal vote. Converting elections maintain the existing majority but with an altered support coalition and a new normal vote. In Pomper's analysis, all converting elections were won by the existing majority party at the presidential level and also boosted that majority's share of the normal vote. Yet the concept of a converting election seems equally applicable to a change in the normal vote that benefits the minority party but is insufficient to elevate it to majority party status. The old majority is maintained, but the electoral coalitions of both parties are altered. Alternatively, if the 1984 Republican gains are ephemeral and the distribution of party identification returns to pre-1980 levels by 1988, the 1980 and 1984 elections will be classified as deviating, their realignment potential stymied in part by the decline in the level of partisan representation within the Republican party.

APPENDIX

This Appendix contains a list of House roll call votes used in the analysis. All vote data and descriptions were obtained from the *Congressional Quarterly Almanacs* for 1981, 1982, 1983, and 1984. The numbers refer to the *Congressional Quarterly* roll call number. A more detailed list describing each vote is available from the author on request.

The roll calls were collected by the author by consulting the *Congressional Quarterly Almanacs* for 1981 through 1984. Each vote was considered on the basis of its policy content and whether or not a conservative or liberal position could unambiguously be determined. Whenever the brief information printed with the roll calls was insufficient to code the vote, additional information was obtained to make a judgment. If the policy content of a bill was ambiguous because too many different issues were being addressed in the same vote, it was not included in the analysis.

Because the congressional party as a group rather than the individual House member is the unit of analysis, it is impossible to validate statistically these votes as forming "policy dimensions" through procedures such as factor analysis or Guttman scaling. In all probability such a procedure would produce fewer factors that there are issue areas in this analysis because voting in the 97th Congress appeared to be highly ideological although not necessarily partisan, while voting in the 98th Congress was simultaneously ideological and partisan. This is consistent with recent research which suggests that congressional voting is unidimensional (Poole and Daniels, 1985). Moreover, if a vote fails to scale, possibly because some representatives are voting for pork barrel reasons or to please PACs, that has implications for representation and such votes should be retained for analysis.

Once a vote was selected, several pieces of information about it were coded: the percentage of Democrats and Republicans voting yea and nay, respectively; the conservative position; and the primary policy area to which the bill applied (defense spending, aid to minorities, etc.). When applicable, each vote also received a secondary policy code according to the specific program area for which spending would be cut or raised. For example, a vote to increase funding for the Environmental Protection Agency is included in the general government services and spending category, but its secondary policy code is environment. Every effort was made to include as many votes as possible. The larger the number of votes, the smaller the probability that the sample is biased, or that any single vote will bias the results of the analysis. In some areas, however, only a few roll calls were taken in Congress and hence the number of votes is limited by availability. The numbers of votes within policy areas are: 97th Congress, defense: 30; government services: 60; aid to minorities: 7; jobs and standards of living: 34; busing: 2; 98th Congress, defense spending: 27; government services: 60; aid to minorities: 3; women's equality: 3; jobs and standards of living: 44; Central America: 24. A complete list of all votes used in the analysis is presented below.

Defense Spending
97th Congress, 1981: 34, 55, 56, 86, 109, 110, 119, 126, 298, 299, 300, 301, 302
97th Congress, 1982: 103, 105, 183, 186, 188, 191, 193, 195, 196, 197, 198, 215, 216, 217, 219, 220, 398
98th Congress, 1983: 180, 181, 182, 184, 185, 187, 192, 248, 391, 393, 408, 409, 471
98th Congress, 1984: 133, 134, 135, 136, 137, 147, 148, 149, 171, 177, 178, 179, 183, 254

General Government Services and Spending
97th Congress, 1981: 21, 27, 28, 30, 31, 44, 65, 82, 83, 87, 95, 96, 97, 98, 102, 104, 134, 135, 137, 160, 182, 185, 187, 208, 233, 234, 285, 330, 333
97th Congress, 1982: 6, 59, 72, 76, 78, 79, 81, 91, 92, 94, 97, 107, 108, 115, 116, 118, 166, 170, 253, 270, 277, 289, 311, 312, 313, 321, 359, 375, 380, 382, 403
98th Congress, 1983: 12, 38, 42, 88, 100, 101, 103, 106, 129, 131, 134, 135, 139, 141, 159, 164, 165, 198, 201, 204, 210, 211, 212, 220, 290, 291, 292, 294, 310, 313, 316, 317, 362, 364, 382, 387, 389, 396, 427, 428, 429, 430, 431, 434, 435, 436, 451, 489
98th Congress, 1984: 11, 27, 36, 38, 45, 66, 70, 80, 81, 88, 89, 90, 93, 94, 102, 140, 167, 175, 196, 201, 258, 275, 277, 278, 279, 290, 292, 297, 298, 300, 308, 310, 313, 314, 320, 323, 327, 338, 346, 347, 348, 360, 365, 368, 380, 393, 394, 395

Aid to Minorities
97th Congress, 1981: 172, 180, 201, 224, 225, 226, 227
98th Congress, 1983: 162, 289, 307

Women's Equality
98th Congress, 1983: 469
98th Congress, 1984: 233, 236

Busing
97th Congress, 1981: 62
97th Congress, 1982: 402

Jobs and Standards of Living
97th Congress, 1981: 49, 177, 260, 263, 264
97th Congress, 1982: 4, 7, 37, 63, 68, 110, 111, 127, 140, 165, 209, 231, 233, 242, 244, 245, 246, 262, 263, 316, 319, 345, 365, 391, 392, 394, 407, 425, 435

98th Congress, 1983: 8, 14, 15, 16, 18, 20, 21, 22, 23, 39, 43, 94, 96, 97, 98, 176, 223, 235, 260, 285, 298, 299, 300, 327, 329, 332, 333, 335, 345, 415, 416, 417, 432, 433, 445
98th Congress, 1984: 5, 6, 46, 50, 187, 302, 303, 397

Central America
98th Congress, 1983: 256, 258, 264, 265, 266, 267, 268, 269, 270, 375, 377, 378, 379
98th Congress, 1984: 76, 77, 78, 124, 125, 126, 156, 161, 162, 163, 306

NOTES

1. Walter D. Burnham, *Critical Elections and the Mainsprings of American Politics* (New York: Norton, 1970), p. 10.

2. The Supreme Court also plays an important policymaking role during re-aligning eras. See Gates (1984) for a review and critique of the literature on the role of the Court.

3. Jerome M. Clubb, William H. Flanigan, and Nancy H. Zingale, *Partisan Re-alignment* (Beverly Hills, Calif.: Sage, 1980), p. 268.

4. The notion that opinion follows policy during realignments is consistent with Clubb, Flanigan, and Zingale's (1980) articulation of the realignment per-spective. In their view, the role of the electorate is entirely a responsive one: re-alignment occurs because the new majority party is able to garner retrospective approval of its policies (Clubb, Flanigan, and Zingale, 1980, esp. ch. 8). The view presented in this paper differs in that the role of the electorate is not considered entirely passive. The electorate signals not only a demand for change but a gen-eral direction for change as well. The specific policies produced as a result are evaluated retrospectively.

5. Numerous scholars have examined representation from a dyadic perspec-tive (see, among others, Miller and Stokes, 1963; Kuklinski, 1977, 1978; Kuklinski with Elling, 1977; McCrone and Kuklinski, 1979; Erikson, 1978, 1981; Stone, 1982; Page et al., 1984). This literature has richly enhanced understanding of the representational relationship between districts and representatives, despite occa-sional methodological shortcomings (Achen, 1977, 1978; Weissberg, 1979). Yet, these studies do not address the role of representation in realignments, so the findings are not of direct relevance to the present inquiry. Scholars examining the correspondence between aggregate opinion and policy (Weissberg, 1976; Mon-roe, 1979; Page and Shapiro, 1983; Brooks, 1985) have also contributed to our un-derstanding of the linkage between opinion and policy, but again the results are of limited utility in the context of the present paper.

6. John S. Jackson III, Barbara Leavitt Brown, and David Bositis, "Herbert McClosky and Friends Revisited: 1980 Democratic and Republican Party Elites Compared to the Mass Public," *American Politics Quarterly* 10 (1982): 177.

7. The surveys conducted by the ill-fated *Literary Digest* have been reanalyzed by some, but they did not contain questions about the specific issue positions of respondents.

8. Independent leaners were coded with the partisan, while pure independents were left alone.

9. See Appendix.

10. Even the classic study of representation by Miller and Stokes (1963) did not present the members of Congress and their constituents with identical questions. Subsequent reanalyses of their data, and there have been many, have the same problem. Others have used demographic variables to simulate district opinion, which also poses problems of comparability (see, e.g., Erikson, 1978). The various studies by Kuklinski (see n. 5) compare roll call voting in the California Assembly and Senate with public opinion measured by voting in statewide referenda. Even here, roll call votes were chosen that were similar to the referenda items, but not necessarily identical.

11. If busing votes had been taken in the 98th Congress, Democratic mass and elite probably would have been on opposite sides of the issue.

12. Large portions of the public did support spending cuts in some program areas, but the same questions, or even substantially similar questions, were not repeated in both surveys. The public particularly wanted lower spending for foreign aid.

REFERENCES

Achen, Christopher. 1977. "Measuring Representation: Perils of the Correlation Coefficient." *American Journal of Political Science* 21:805–15.

————. 1978. "Measuring Representation." *American Journal of Political Science* 22:475–510.

Backstrom, Charles H. 1977. "Congress and the Public: How Representative Is One of the Other?" *American Politics Quarterly* 5:411–36.

Brady, David W. 1978. "Critical Elections, Congressional Parties, and Clusters of Policy Changes." *British Journal of Political Science* 8:79–99.

Brady, David W., and Joseph Stewart. 1982. "Congressional Party Realignment and the Transformation of Public Policy in Three Realigning Eras." *American Journal of Political Science* 26:333–60.

Brooks, Joel E. 1985. "Democratic Frustration in the Anglo American Polities: A Quantification of Inconsistency Between Mass Public Opinion and Public Policy." *Western Political Quarterly* 38:250–61.

Burnham, Walter D. 1970. *Critical Elections and the Mainsprings of American Politics*. New York: Norton.

Clubb, Jerome M., William H. Flanigan, and Nancy H. Zingale. 1980. *Partisan Realignment*. Beverly Hills: Sage.

Erikson, Robert S. 1978. "Constituency Opinion and Congressional Behavior:

A Reexamination of the Miller-Stokes Representation Data." *American Journal of Political Science* 22:511–35.

———. 1981. Measuring Constituency Opinion: The 1978 U.S. Congressional Election Survey. *Legislative Studies Quarterly* 6:235–46.

Gates, John B. 1984. "The American Supreme Court and Electoral Realignment: A Critical Review." *Social Science History* 8:267–90.

Hurley, Patricia A. 1982. "Collective Representation Reappraised." *Legislative Studies Quarterly* 7:119–36.

Jackson, John S., III, Barbara Leavitt Brown, and David Bositis. 1982. "Herbert McClosky and Friends Revisited: 1980 Democratic and Republican Party Elites Compared to the Mass Public." *American Politics Quarterly* 10:158–80.

Key, V. O., Jr. 1955. "A Theory of Critical Elections." *Journal of Politics* 17:3–18.

Kirkpatrick, Jeane J. 1976. *The New Presidential Elite.* New York: Russell Sage Foundation.

Kuklinski, James H. 1977. "District Competitiveness and Legislative Roll Call Behavior: A Reassessment of the Marginality Hypothesis." *American Journal of Political Science* 20:627–38.

———. 1978. "Representatives and Elections: A Policy Analysis. *American Political Science Review* 72:165–77.

Kuklinski, James H., with Richard C. Elling. 1977. "Representational Role, Constituency Opinion, and Legislative Behavior." *American Journal of Political Science* 21:135–47.

Macdonald, Stuart Elaine, and George Rabinowitz. 1987. "The Dynamics of Structural Realignment." *American Political Science Review* 81:775–96.

McClosky, Herbert E., Paul J. Hoffman, and Rosemary O'Hara. 1960. "Issue Conflict and Consensus among Party Leaders and Followers." *American Political Science Review* 56:406–29.

McCrone, Donald J., and James H. Kuklinski. 1979. "The Delegate Theory of Representation." *American Journal of Political Science* 23:278–300.

Miller, Warren E., and Donald E. Stokes. 1963. "Constituency Influence in Congress." *American Political Science Review* 57:45–56.

Monroe, Alan D. 1979. "Consistency Between Public Preferences and National Policy Decisions." *American Politics Quarterly* 7:3–19.

Montjoy, Robert S., William R. Shaffer, and Ronald E. Weber. 1980. "Policy Preferences of Party Elites and Masses: Conflict or Consensus?" *American Politics Quarterly* 8:319–44.

Page, Benjamin I., and Robert Y. Shapiro. 1983. "Effects of Public Opinion on Policy." *American Political Science Review* 77:175–90.

Page, Benjamin I., Robert Y. Shapiro, Paul W. Gronke, and Robert M. Rosenberg. 1984. "Constituency, Party, and Representation in Congress." *Public Opinion Quarterly* 48:741–56.

Poole, Keith T., and R. Steven Daniels. 1985. "Ideology, Party, and Voting in the U.S. Congress, 1959–1980." *American Political Science Review* 79:373–99.

Sinclair, Barbara D. 1977. "Party Realignment and the Transformation of the

Political Agenda: The House of Representatives, 1925–1938." *American Political Science Review* 71:940–53.

_____ . 1982. *Congressional Realignment, 1925–1978.* Austin: U. of Texas Press.

Stone, Walter J. 1979. "Measuring Constituency-Representative Linkages: Problems and Prospects." *Legislative Studies Quarterly* 4:623–39.

_____ . 1982. "Electoral Change and Policy Representation in Congress: Domestic Welfare Issues from 1956–1972." *British Journal of Political Science* 12:95–115.

Weissberg, Robert. 1976. *Public Opinion and Popular Government.* Englewood Cliffs, N.J.: Prentice-Hall.

_____ . 1978. "Collective vs. Dyadic Representation in Congress." *American Political Science Review* 72:535–47.

_____ . 1979. "Assessing Legislator-Constituency Policy Agreement." *Legislative Studies Quarterly* 4:605–22.

Wright, Gerald C., and Michael B. Berkman. 1986. "Candidates and Policy in United States Senate Elections." *American Political Science Review* 80:567–88.

PART SEVEN

CAMPAIGN FINANCE REFORM

Is there too much money or too little in politics? As Americans become more cynical about their government, the role of money in politics once again occupies center stage in the debate. Both Democrats and Republicans have offered campaign finance reform proposals. The Democrats believe that there is too much money in politics and seek limitations on the amount of money a candidate for office can spend. Private funding would be replaced by publicly financed campaigns. The Republicans argue that the problem is not too much money, but who has the cash and who gives it. Contributions from political action committees taint campaigns, since they must come with strings attached. Representative Barney Frank (D.-Mass.) said: "Politicians are the only people to whom perfect strangers give money and expect nothing in return." But Republicans also argue that incumbent politicians, with all of the advantages of their offices, have overwhelming financial advantages as well. The problem, they insist, is that challengers have *too little* money.

Both of these views are self-serving. The Republican party has enormous financial advantages over the Democrats (see the essays in the "Party Organization" section), so they seek to limit those funding sources that help the Democrats (political action committees). The Democrats, with more meager party financing, seek to restrict the Republican advantage in overall spending. Is there an alternative proposal that might strike a happy medium? Norman Ornstein, a Democrat, and Bernadette A. Budde, a Republican, offer alternatives.

Ornstein, in "A Modest Proposal for Campaign Finance Reform," reviews the changes in statutes since the first burst of reform in 1974. He charges that the Democratic proposals would weaken political parties and that the Republican ideas would not solve the issue of how candidates could raise enough money to compete. Ornstein suggests a tax credit for small, in-state contributions with matching funds provided by the federal government. He would also limit political action committee contributions to $2,000 rather than the present $5,000 and increase the amount individuals could contribute from $5,000 to $10,000. Finally, radio and television stations would be required to provide the lowest-cost commercial rates for political advertising.

Budde, in "Campaign Finance Revision: A Framework for the Discussion," also attacks both Democratic and Republican proposals. Both party and political action committee money have legitimate places in elections, she argues. Budde also opposes limitations on the amounts any contributor can give. Further regulations on who can give how much are not the answer. Better disclosure and clearer statements of which expenditures are legitimate—and which are not—can go a long way in resolving our problems.

A MODEST PROPOSAL FOR CAMPAIGN FINANCE REFORM

Norman Ornstein

No democracy, it is safe to say, tries to regulate the flow of money into and out of its parties and political candidates more than the United States. Volumes of laws, rules, and regulations—the accumulation of a series of campaign finance reform laws enacted through the twentieth century—set requirements for who can contribute, how much and to which entities, how contributions are disclosed, how and where candidates and parties can spend political money, and how the campaign laws are enforced. An independent regulatory commission, the Federal Election Commission, is charged with the task of overseeing the campaign laws for national parties and candidates, for the presidency, the House, and the Senate. In addition, each of the fifty states has its own laws and regulations for state and local candidates.

All these laws and regulations, dos and don'ts, are an impressive testament to Americans' desire to control political money and keep it from corrupting politics. But the result has not been satisfying. More, in this case, is not better. Indeed, the more we regulate, the more unhappy we are with our campaign system—and the more impetus to reform it yet again.

The complexities and intricacies surrounding the financing of American political parties and elections manage to keep hundreds of Washington lawyers comfortably employed. Nonetheless, the ABCs of the process can still be outlined in a comprehensible fashion.

WHO CAN GIVE

Basically, any American citizen can contribute to political parties and candidates for office. Foreign nationals, except for those with permanent resident status, cannot. Neither can corporations, labor unions, or banks (they have been barred from contributing since 1907). But there *is* a way in which corporations and unions can get involved in the political money

521

game. It is called PACs—political action committees. In 1943, the first political action committee was created by the Congress of Industrial Organizations, the forerunner of the AFL-CIO. Voluntary contributions from individual union members were pooled into a committee to give contributions to candidates, under a union label. The practice was not specifically allowed under the law—but neither was it specifically prohibited. When Congress enacted major campaign finance reform in post-Watergate 1974, PACs were specifically sanctioned, and since have mushroomed in number, for corporations as well as unions.

How Much Can They Give

Individuals can give a maximum of $1,000 to any candidate for any election, primary or general. Individuals can also give up to $20,000 to any national party committee in a calendar year, and up to $5,000 per year to a PAC or other political committee. But individuals cannot give more than $25,000 total to national parties and candidates in any calendar year. Political action committees have more leeway. They can give up to $5,000 per candidate per election, up to $15,000 to any national party committee, and up to $5,000 to another PAC, and they have no limit on how much they can give overall.

How Are Contributions Disclosed

All candidates for federal office, along with the parties and the PACs, have to file regular reports with the Federal Election Commission, giving the details of both the income and the expenditures of their campaigns and political activities. Candidates have to list the name, address, occupation, and employer of every contributor who gives more than $200, and itemize PAC and party contributions. Cash contributions of more than $100 are prohibited, and anonymous donations are limited to $50. PACs also have to give the FEC the details of all their contributors and contributions, as do the parties.

How Much Money Is Involved

In the 1988 election cycle, the Democratic party raised $128 million and spent $122 million. The Republicans raised $263 million and spent $258 million. Sixty-eight percent of the Democratic party's money came from individuals, 8 percent from PACs, the rest from other sources of revenue and party transfers. Eight-seven percent of the Republican party's money came from individuals, and only 1 percent from PACs. The 48,000 political action committees contributed $160 million to congressional candidates, who spent $458 million in all. Presidential candidates raised $198 million in primary campaigns to win party nominations; $133 million came from individual contributions, $59 million from federal matching funds given for small individual donations. In the general election, Bush and Dukakis each spent $46 million in federal funds (only in presidential elections are public funds involved).

Those are the basics. Then there are the major loopholes. One is called *soft money*. Federal election laws do not regulate the states and thus do not control the state and local parties. Contributions to them are not limited or disclosed—and big givers, the so-called "fat cats" of American politics, have made their big contributions here. In 1988 at least one contribution exceeded $500,000. That went by way of state parties to the Republican party. In 1986 Joan Kroc, the widow of the founder of the McDonald's hamburger franchise, gave $1,000,000 in soft money to the Democratic party. In all, fundraisers for both presidential candidates in 1988 raised around $25 million each in soft money. The money to state and local parties is ostensibly for state and local purposes. But get-out-the-vote and voter registration drives, polling efforts, and party advertisements are all ways in which this money can be used to benefit federal candidates—congressmen, senators, and presidential hopefuls—at the same time. The soft money loophole is also one that enables corporations, unions, and foreign nationals to contribute in many states, usually without any extensive disclosure.

REFORM PROPOSALS

Many would-be reformers argue that the focus of campaign finance reform should be on eliminating, or at least restricting, the use of soft money. Current campaign finance laws were designed to limit the size of individual donations to prevent individuals from buying access or influence. However, the soft money loophole has enabled the parties to solicit millions of dollars from wealthy individuals and powerful interests. Senate reformers are willing to limit soft-money contributions, while House members have been reluctant to do so. This may be due in part to the fact that House members, because they run for office more frequently, have more to gain from coordinated campaigns run by the state party and designed to benefit the entire party ticket. As it stands now the laws vary from state to state and are on the whole extremely lenient.

There is a dilemma inherent in the debate over soft money. Any serious limitations on this kind of fundraising would likely have the effect of weakening parties on every level. What many critics of soft money do not realize is that most of the money flowing into parties these days comes from the unlimited contributions made at the state and local level. Those who advocate the elimination of soft money would also like to see the parties strengthened. The former is not likely to lead to the latter.

Independent expenditures are another way in which limits on campaign contributions are avoided. The Supreme Court has ruled that political money is a form of speech thus allowing individuals and PACs to spend as much as they would like, if it is independent of a campaign's efforts, to get their views across. In 1988 nearly $14 million was spent independently by groups and individuals to support or oppose presidential candidates; another $7 million went independently for or against candidates for Congress. A recent reform proposal in the House would lift spending limits for any candidate whose opponent benefitted from $60,000 in independent expenditures on his behalf. Under the same theory of free speech, incidentally, candidates themselves are not limited in what they can give to their own campaigns. In 1984 John D. Rockefeller IV spent $12 million of his own money to win a Senate seat from West Virginia.

A third major loophole in the campaign finance system is a technique called *bundling*. Bundling is yet another way of getting around limitations on campaign contributions. Bundling involves an intermediary, usually an individual associated with some specific interest or cause, who solicits contributions from individuals and presents them collectively to a particular candidate. In essence the smaller contributions are "bundled" into one, although they are reported to the FEC as having come from the individuals who signed each check. The bundled amounts can range from $5,000 up to $1 million, thus surpassing the amount any single individual could give to a candidate or a PAC.

Bundling can be done on behalf of special interests, single interest groups, corporations, and others. Oftentimes the intermediary, if he is good at what he does, can gain both access and influence within the political system. Bundlers are sometimes rewarded for their efforts on behalf of political candidates with special treatment and special favors. Critics say bundling is just another means by which power and influence are bought and sold in Washington.

These loopholes are controversial, to say the least. The *New York Times* calls soft money "sewer money" in its editorials calling for more campaign finance reform because of the lack of limits and disclosure. Candidates and reformers have decried the "hit-and-run" negative tactics of independent expenditure groups; the infamous Willie Horton ad from the 1988 presidential campaign was done by an independent group, not the Bush campaign. Common Cause has described one well-known bundler as an expert in "the rights of mutual backscratching in political relationships."

THE REAL PROBLEM

These various loopholes aside, it is the core of the campaign system that truly is at the heart of public and political discontent. While real reform has remained elusive there is general consensus on the major deficiencies of the system. First, campaigns have become outrageously expensive. As a result, politicians have become obsessed with money. Without money challengers cannot run effectively and incumbents cannot be assured of keeping their seats. Today, politicians spend enormous amounts of time raising money for campaigns, plotting ways to raise money, and thinking about how much money they need to raise. This time would surely be better spent tending to constituents needs or working on public policy.

Another major problem with the system is that special interests have gained an inordinate amount of influence. The general public is particularly sensitive about this issue; people feel that they have been squeezed out by monied interests and no longer have access to their representatives in Congress. Washington is awash in lobbyists, and the most observable, reportable, and quantifiable evidence of their influence is campaign contributions. These donations may be legal, but their growing size and role in campaigns have led to an overwhelming desire to change the laws, to reduce this special interest presence.

Finally, there is general agreement that in a world of big-money campaigns, challengers are left out, and incumbents have unfair advantages. Few challengers have the wherewithal or the access to resources to raise anywhere near the amount of money needed to wage a competitive campaign these days. Incumbents increasingly have monopolized PAC contributions, thus worsening the financing problems of challengers. In addition incumbents have built-in advantages, such as mailing privileges and staff, which only add to the obstacles faced by challengers. All of this helps to explain the 98-percent reelection rates for incumbent members of Congress in 1986 and 1988.

Real reform can be achieved by taking moderate steps to improve the system from within, without starving incumbents and challengers and undermining the public discourse. Nearly everyone connected with the political process understands the shortcomings of the current system. But most move from them to a fatal misconception about their roots and to faulty assumptions about what would cure them.

The fatal misconception is that the problem is too much money. The most common solution offered by reformers is to remove as much money as possible from the system. Some would accomplish this by eliminating PACs; others by putting spending caps on campaigns. Each solution solves the wrong problem and creates a bigger one.

In a vast and heterogeneous society like the United States, elections are expensive. We have a lot of voters spread out over huge geographical expanses. Candidates need to raise great amounts of money to run effective campaigns—campaigns that adequately reach voters.

Unfortunately, the current system, designed in considerable part by the same reformers who decry it, makes raising money in any form especially difficult. For example, the single largest reason for the sharp growth in PACs has been previous "reforms" that cut the amount of money in campaigns and made it more difficult for candidates to raise money from small individual donors. For candidates needing to raise the $400,000 or so required for an average competitive House campaign, or the several million necessary for a Senate race, PACs—easily accessible in Washington, in business specifically to give money, and with much higher limits than individuals—have become increasingly attractive.

Eliminating or sharply reducing the role of PACs may well be desirable, given our concern with special interest influence. But to eliminate PACs without freeing up other sources of money would create a bigger problem, without solving the old one. All candidates, not just incumbents, would have an increased burden raising the large sums of money needed to communicate effectively with voters. Either they would become even more preoccupied with raising money, spending more time and energy on it than they do now, or they would raise and spend less money, narrowing the ability of candidates to reach voters.

Neither would eliminating PACs erase special interest influence. Long before the creation of PACs interests had access and influence in Washington, indeed, much greater influence than they have now. But that was in a prereform era, before disclosure of contributions enabled us to detail systematically and quantitatively their cash contributions to Washington. Even if PACs were eliminated, special interests would continue to exert their influence. As James Madison noted in *Federalist* 10, special interests are a part of American democracy's genetic code.

We should not simply throw up our hands and accept any system of overt influence peddling. Since we cannot erase the influence or role of special interests in our democracy, reforms must be designed with a different goal in mind. We need to channel that influence in a more balanced way, creating more avenues for rank-and-file voters and broader interests to tilt the playing field away from an overreliance on narrow special interests and their money.

But simply eliminating PACs without creating compensating changes to loosen restrictions on other kinds of money will be counterproductive. The compelling need candidates have for campaign resources would increase, not abate.

Rather than eliminating PACs, some reformers would prefer to place caps on campaign spending. Advocates of this approach believe it would reduce the obsession with money, give challengers more opportunity by reducing the huge leads of well-off incumbents, and trim special interest influence by cutting the overall money in the process.

A cap on spending might reduce a candidate's ability to communicate with voters, but it would not reduce special interest influence, merely rechannel it. And it would have the opposite effect of its intentions on incumbents and challengers. The problem for most challengers has not been how much an incumbent has, but rather how little the challenger can raise to overcome the overwhelming threshold of name recognition and issue communication required to reach a huge constituency.

WHAT KINDS OF MONEY?

How then can we achieve genuine campaign finance reform that would reduce special interest influence, reduce the intense preoccupation with raising money, and open the doors to quality challengers to make elections more competitive?

What we need to do is provide easier paths to the "right" kind of money (the kind that no reasonable person would call tainted) for all candidates, easier access to "seed money" for new candidates to get a congressional campaign under way, and methods to reduce the cost burdens of campaigns without restricting the communications vital to democratic elections. The plan outlined below would achieve all of those goals with a few simple steps.

First, a full tax credit for small, in-state contributions should be enacted. The best kind of money to have in campaigns is small contributions from individual citizens from a candidate's state. A 100-percent tax credit for in-state contributions of $200 or less would make it easy for candidates to solicit money from average citizens and add considerably to the incentive for citizens to contribute to campaigns—a nice way to get them involved in democracy.

In addition to enacting a tax credit, a matching-fund process should be established for these in-state contributions. This would serve as a major incentive for candidates to raise "good" money. A threshold could be set, perhaps $25,000, to weed out nonserious candidates. Once over that limit, candidates would get federal matching funds for every contribution of this sort.

With these two reforms, congressional candidates would have a major incentive to raise money in small individual contributions from their own state's voters, tilting the playing field sharply away from PACs and toward "average" people.

A third element of the plan would be to cut allowable PAC contributions. PACs can currently contribute up to $5,000 per election (primary or general) to a candidate. Cutting the limit to $2,000 would greatly alter incentives for candidates and open up a major new flow of funds into campaigns.

Reducing PAC contributions to individual campaigns would not eliminate PAC influence; no doubt, many interests would try to find other ways to enhance their clout in politics, perhaps through the soft money or bundling approaches mentioned earlier. But enhanced disclosure would help to counter that tendency, as would a beefed-up enforcement arm for the now toothless Federal Election Commission. More importantly, keeping PACs alive but reducing their clout would keep most interest involvement in campaigns channeled into observable and legitimate routes, but routes with a much lower volume of traffic.

The fourth component of the plan would be to install a "seed money" mechanism. This would be accomplished by raising individual contribution limits to $10,000, with some restrictions, and allowing candidates to raise up to $100,000 in early contributions of $1,000 or more. One of the goals of campaign finance reform has to be to enable challengers to "get over the hump" to raise start-up funds to create an organization, do polling and advertising, and build momentum. That is very hard to do without a seed-money mechanism.

Under current law, individuals are limited to $1,000 contributions. Candidates have been unable to finance more than a small portion of their campaigns with $1,000 individual contributions. Realistically, few individuals have the means to write $1,000 checks to political candidates (and most who do could easily add an extra zero). Sharply raising the limit would enable challengers, especially, to turn to a small number of well-heeled individuals to get campaigns under way.

This change could only be effected with several safeguards. The overall sum that a candidate could raise in this fashion would be limited, to keep the seed-money principle in place. Every contribution of more than $1,000 would be accompanied by extensive disclosure from the donor, including name, address, job positions, corporate and other board memberships, and any direct legislative interests, released within forty-eight hours of the contribution to both the Federal Election Commission and to major journalistic organizations in the state. Furthermore, to prevent a candidate from sandbagging an opponent, contributions over $1,000 would be restricted to the early stages of a campaign.

There is a danger here, of course, in letting a cadre of wealthy people have overweening influence on campaigns. But with the limits in place and with the extensive publicity the disclosure provisions would ensure, the public would have full opportunity to weigh the appropriateness and impact of the contributions during the campaign. In fact, these contributions would have the ironic benefit of providing nonwealthy candidates with a counter to the unlimited spending allowed by independently wealthy candidates.

Finally, the plan includes a provision that would require television and radio stations to provide the lowest-cost commercial rates for political advertisements of at least one minute in length for qualified congressional candidates. The largest and fastest growing expense in House and Senate campaigns is television advertising. This is one area where we can find a reform to reduce the costs of campaigning for candidates and parties. Doing so simply by requiring free time would be a mistake. Deciding how to allocate television time to thousands of congressional candidates would become a bureaucratic nightmare. Consider what the implications would be in areas like New York, where television stations reach as many as thirty or forty congressional districts in three states. Would every candidate get free time—all districts, every party—in equal amounts, even for seats that are uncontested or barely contested? Who would watch hour after hour of political commercials, and how would confused voters sort out their own candidates' messages from the hundreds being broadcast? Under what authority would cable stations, unlicensed by the federal government, be required to give time? If cable stations are left alone, what is the rationale for the competitive damage done to commercial broadcast stations vis-à-vis their cable competitors? These and other questions, including the role of the parties and of the candidates, cannot be answered without one realizing the Pandora's box created by the concept of free time for congressional campaigns.

However, there is no reason why stations, granted valuable licenses by the government to dominate public airwaves, should be able to take advantage of democracy by charging higher prices to candidates than they do to commercial advertisers. At the same time, by targeting the lowest rates to commercials of one minute or more, we would discourage campaigns from relying ever more heavily on the fifteen- or thirty-second "hit-and-run" spots that have become so popular—and so negative.

A HEALTHIER PROCESS

This series of reforms would improve the lot of candidates and generally create a healthier political and campaign process. It does not address the role and health of the political parties. There have been proposals to inject more life into the parties by making them the conduits for money and the allocators of television time into congressional campaigns. Given the widely disparate strength and sophistication of local parties around the country, this would have uneven and perhaps destructive effects. The campaign finance system cannot turn a system with weak and decentralized parties into one with strong, vibrant, and unified parties, and it would be a mistake to try to use reform as a vehicle to accomplish that goal.

At the same time, it would be an equal mistake to rush to reform soft money out of existence, without considering the unintended consequences of such a change for the parties. If we are interested in keeping our parties from going out of existence altogether, more prudent reforms in this area, including some limits on contributions, some changes in the definition of coordinated campaign activities between local and congressional parties and candidates, and fuller disclosure of soft money contributions, makes more sense than the wholesale change recommended by the *New York Times* and Common Cause.

Enacting this series of reforms would address each of the major concerns we now have about the campaign finance system. We would tilt the system away from an increasingly heavy reliance on special interest money, restoring more balance to the policy process and more of a role for rank-and-file voters. We would make it easier for politicians, incumbents and challengers alike, to raise the money necessary to run effective campaigns in our large and diverse democracy, without having to demean or prostitute themselves in the process, or to turn their attention unduly away from policy-making concerns.

In addition, we would break the logjam of noncompetitiveness in campaigns, by giving solid and promising challengers more opportunities to raise the money necessary to get their messages across but still avoiding the creation of the kinds of restrictions on incumbents that are unrealistic or counterproductive.

Of course, all of this would require a good deal of public money, perhaps as much as $150 million to $300 million a year. This seems a small price to pay for cleaning up the campaign mess, especially when we consider that $150 million constitutes a mere one-seventy-fifth of 1 percent of the federal budget. Nonetheless, given today's fiscal environment and the current public mood, finding any public money will be more difficult now than ever.

The task before us then is to find realistic and reasonable sources of funds that will pay for real and positive reform without enraging the public. Two sources come to mind. The first would be a tax on PACs. Instead of abolishing PACs, why not make the special interests they represent pay for improving the campaign system? The procedure would be simple and straightforward. For every contribution a PAC makes to a House or Senate candidate, it would be required to make an equal contribution to the U.S. Treasury, earmarked for a campaign finance trust fund. The trust fund would reimburse the Treasury for revenues lost by giving tax credits for small, individual, in-state contributions.

How much money might this generate? PAC contributions to congressional candidates in the 1990 election cycle were $150 million. Assuming some dropoff in contributions caused by the tax, it is still reasonable to expect that a 100-percent tax on PAC donations could raise $100 to $120 million. That in and of itself would pay for a $50 to $100 tax credit per American and might even make it politically feasible to have a $200 credit.

Of course, PACs won't welcome such a proposal, nor will campaign reform purists, who would prefer to see PACs eliminated altogether. PACs may try to scuttle any efforts at campaign finance reform. However, given the current pressure for reform, from inside and outside of Congress, PACs would be better off accepting this kind of compromise than risking their total demise.

A second source of money could come from a user fee on television advertising. Television advertising represents the single biggest and fastest rising cost of campaigning today. Television stations and outlets have garnered huge sums of revenue from political campaigns. Recently many observers have suggested that television stations be required to provide free time to candidates and parties. Obviously, forcing the stations and networks to allocate time to thousands of candidates in hundreds of districts would be a bureaucratic mess.

However, there is a better way to tap into the resources of television stations for the good of the campaign process. A "user" fee based on advertising revenues would raise tens of thousands of dollars that could then be put into a trust fund to help pay for the proposed tax credit. The fee could be charged once every five years, when television stations are required to apply to the FCC for license renewal. In 1991, total revenues for spot and local television advertising are projected at over $16 billion. A fee of one-half of 1 percent of a year's advertising revenue would raise perhaps $75 million per election cycle.

Of course, broadcasters would resist any such measure. They have already voiced their total opposition to any license fee, and are now feeling the effects of the recession on their ad revenues. Nonetheless, the idea of having those who benefit from the current campaign funding system pay some realistic and reasonable price for making it better ought to have enough logic and momentum to overcome these objections. And, if we can find a way, acceptable to the public, to create a new and viable source of funds for campaigns, change that is reform, not just change for the sake of change, will become a real possibility.

Reading 22

CAMPAIGN FINANCE REVISION: A FRAMEWORK FOR THE DISCUSSION

Bernadette A. Budde

Congress has struggled with campaign finance revision since the last major legislative overhaul of the early 1970s. Solutions are not easy, because nearly all forces in the debate hold different standards for evaluation. The tests for acceptance include: is the reform constitutional, will the reform work, can the revision be implemented fairly? For others, practical politics is more important: does a package have majority support in Congress and will the president sign it?

Most of the participants in the political arena have vested interests, not all of them venal. Compromise is acceptable, but the collision of "goods" has contributed to a stalemate. Solutions are probably easiest for those who are the most detached from the day-to-day campaign business. For that reason, political scientists and theorists are tempted to question the motivation of the practitioners, while the strategists sneer at the academic approach.

THE WORLD OF PRACTICAL POLITICS

Critics can argue that campaigns have become too professional or that consultants make all the decisions, but most races function with scores of volunteers or first-time staffers. It behooves the reformers, therefore, to make certain that they construct a law that makes sense for the folks on the frontlines. Their worries are not about a right of free speech as much as the basics of their operation. What about the phones or ads, how can the candidate travel, who pays for the poll, can someone donate food for the announcement ceremony, and so on. These are not frivolous worries, but they can be passed over by those who want to handle the big picture and work out the details later.

On the other hand, some of the things candidates would like that would relieve their fundraisers of headaches pose constitutional questions. Free broadcast time would help the aspirants in suitable media markets, but is it fair to confiscate the airwaves or to set standards for communication to the voters?

Voluntary spending limits with incentives to cooperate sound like a good idea to some, but experienced campaign managers may fear that an opponent would cheat in the closing days of a heated campaign. Proponents of spending limits contend that they have worked at the presidential level, yet the Federal Election Commission regularly requests that Congress do away with the state-by-state spending limits for primary candidates. For the 1992 cycle a relaxed definition of state-by-state expenditures has been adopted. Each cycle, the presidential audits (conducted long after the race has been concluded, it should be noted) reveal that violations have occurred, with the fines imposed after the winner is inaugurated. Can this system really be transferred to the hundreds of congressional campaigns?

With all these serious and not-so-serious topics to explore, it is no wonder that Congress has reached an impasse. A further factor in delay is that the longer the matter is unresolved, the more attention is given to the reform of Congress itself—not just campaigns. Institutional reform may not trigger an interest from outsiders, but the members of Congress could be reluctant to take on this task before reformulating campaign rules. Outsiders have pressed for the harshest of structural change by working at the state initiative level for term limits. When such sweeping proposals are on the agenda, a mere tinkering with campaign finance rules doesn't seem so revolutionary.

Meanwhile, the 1992 campaigns are in progress under the old rules. The modern Senate campaign has become a full, six-year undertaking, with fundraising conducted on an annual basis. For revisions to have any uniform effect, Congress must take into account a lag time in implementing anything that is enacted. It has been nearly two decades and still the Federal Election Commission is refining the regulations. If the old laws are still so murky in their application to specific situations, how can something that topples this system become standard practice quickly enough to be perceived as equitable to all players? The typical House member, uneasy about redistricting in 1992, is not about to disrupt campaign rules just as he or she is getting settled in a reconfigured congressional district.

THE OBJECTIVES OF THE REFORM-MINDED

The stated goal of most reformers outside of Congress is to make campaigns more competitive. Insiders often talk of the need to break the lock of the so-called special interests and to restore faith to the system. Spoken more often now than a decade ago is another objective—relieve the member of having to raise money. Political action committees, proudly stating that they were the reform created by the last attempt to rewrite the laws, want to remain a part of the electoral process. Political parties expect to restore discipline to the Congress by reasserting their unique role as election vehicles. Party operatives see campaign finance as a legitimate function they perform. They also recognize that the party system is not monolithic; the states feel independent from and not beholden to the national party committees for funding. State legislatures regulate how nonfederal races are conducted, and they may be unwilling to accommodate a federal law that creates confusion for local affairs. Granted, each of the above elements will imagine the worst case scenario as a consequence of reform, but no statute or legislative deliberation ever identifies all the potential downsides to change.

All of the groups who claim a stake in the outcome see different villains. It was convenient in the earlier reform debates of the 1980s to tag money as the evil and the PAC as the personification of it. In that sense, PAC replaced the fat cat of the 1970s as the bearer of ill will. Challengers see incumbents as the obstacles to a level playing field, the favorite phrase of those who think the deck is stacked before the race begins. PACs perhaps are coconspirators, they will say, but the incumbents have all the advantages of office before they raise the first dollar. Incumbents often act as if the broadcast industry is the source of the problem. Surely, much of the testimony at congressional hearings has been about the cost of advertising, including the price of consultants who produce the ads. Voters, who knows? If the pollsters are to be believed, the public may not distinguish between incumbents and challengers—they are all just politicians saying anything to get elected. The source of campaign funds may be irrelevant if the message or the messenger is held in low regard. Republicans tend to blame divided government for legislative inaction—Democrats control Congress and they stymie the administration.

Reshuffling how campaigns are financed won't necessarily do anything to ensure competitive races. A broader pool of candidates may not be available if it is something other than money that keeps prospective challengers from running. Some suspect it is the congressional life-style in a press-crazed city that keeps individuals from putting themselves, families, business partners, former college roommates, clients, and so on, through the ordeal of a race where everything and everyone will be considered public record. Fixing how Congress functions or establishing liveable ethics guidelines could be of greater help in enlarging the field of officeseekers. Equalized campaign spending cannot compensate for a district that is drawn to the specifications of one party. Nor can finance rules guarantee that candidates will be equal in organizing or targeting how they spend money.

A ROLE FOR THE PACs

Removing PACs from the system is not realistic, and serious reform proposals recognize the constitutional implications of defining too narrowly the rights of speech or assembly. Consensus within Congress would be easier to achieve if PACs existed alongside other givers, balance as to the amount and the ratio they provided in relationship to other givers (primarily the party or individuals, if not the candidate's personal treasury). One school of thought is that PACs used to be good but they turned bad when they collaborated with incumbents to rig the system against the challengers. Admonish the PACs, but don't kill them. Another school of thought is that they are desirable and should be encouraged within certain frameworks to continue to be more responsible players within campaigns. Another theory could be that they are neutral forces that are victims of the out-of-control money chase and they need to be unburdened, along with the candidates.

The good-PAC-gone-astray argument would call for leaving most of the laws alone but using the persuasion of political or other PAC leaders to encourage greater involvement with nonincumbents. Pointing out the futility of heaping money on overly funded incumbents, the PACs would free up more resources for competitive races. PACs would argue, as they have, that they abide by the rules and are highly regulated. The area where things are out of hand is on the side of the requesters, not the givers. Write a rule and then enforce it which says no member of Congress can mention fundraising in the course of a plant visit. Forbid members of Congress from making phone calls from their offices requesting checks. Keep members of Congress from asking the Washington lobbyist to serve on a steering committee for a fundraiser, or better yet, prohibit anyone from soliciting or accepting contributions within fifty miles of the U.S. Capitol unless his or her district is located within those boundaries. In other words, don't cast aspersions against the PAC when a few modest behavioral changes can take care of the problems that result from aggressive incumbents—or their hired guns who get a percentage of all PAC money raised.

Before Congress concluded its work before adjournment in 1991, the House passed a proposal that would maintain private funding of congressional elections and add an element of taxpayer financing. No mechanism was in the final bill to pay for the public financing portion of the equation. The failure to fund this provision proves how nervous even the

Democrats are about asking the average person to pick up the cost of campaigning for Congress. The bill would restrict the amount of aggregate PAC dollars and the amount of aggregate individual dollars that a candidate could accept. A spending limit was set at $600,000, more if the candidate had a competitive primary. Certain costs, such as fundraising expenses and accounting/legal fees, were exempted from these limits. According to the formula, one-third of the limit could come from individuals, one-third from PACs, and one-third from taxpayer subsidies in the form of matching grants for individual contributions or direct payments, depending on the circumstances of the race.

PACs have mixed views on this approach. Many larger PACs are pleased that the House bill did not reduce the amount that a PAC could contribute to a candidate. Leaving the ceiling at $5,000 means that the wealthy PACs could still give the maximum, as long as they gave early in the cycle before the candidate had "used up" the aggregate figure of $200,000 from PAC sources. PACs with fewer dollars feel that the "big guys" will give early, closing out those whose contributions are more modest or who wait until later in the cycle to donate. With the $200,000 overall limit, twenty PACs could freeze out all the others by giving the candidate $5,000 in the primary election and another $5,000 for the general election. Under this formula, incumbents could become even more beholden to special interests than they are now. At the very least, incumbents would be able to alienate huge segments of their district-related PACs because they need only a handful of PACs to fully fund that portion of the campaign. Most PACs want the formulas to be fair, allowing those who wish to give an equal chance to do so, regardless of their resources.

The Senate version eliminated PACs and set spending limits based on voting-age population of the state. The Senate bill also avoided a mechanism for paying the cost of the government's share of the campaigns.

President Bush has said that he will not sign a campaign finance measure unless the same rules apply to both the House and the Senate. The current versions treat only one of the bodies, and as in the case of the PACs, the right to participate is not the same. The White House has also said it will veto anything containing public financing or spending limits. As a consequence, the deadlock remains, even in the reform-minded atmosphere of 1992.

The get-rid-of-the-PACs proponents may mean well, believing that they are not committing constitutional heresy or stomping on the rights of individuals. One can still vote, they claim, or lobby, or volunteer, or give as an individual. Maybe they are right and this is the way to get the public off the backs of Congress. Few of the old hands believe this. The old-timers tell tales of black bags, cash, bogus bookkeeping entries, and arm-twisting. Exaggerated as the folklore of pre-Watergate might be, very few fundraisers think that the demand for money will go down, no matter what the legislation says. It is far better for the funds to be given through regulated and restricted political action committees than through individuals whose identities are harder to trace (Just exactly what does self-employed mean, or who are all those housewives and retired persons on FEC reports?) and whose objectives in giving are harder to determine. Granted, fear of unleashing bad actors is no excuse for avoiding campaign finance revision, but realists should recognize the potential for abuse.

THE IMPORTANCE OF OPTIONS

Setting aside for purposes of this discussion whether there is too much money, not enough money, or the right amount of money in the system, let's look at two overriding factors that any legislation should address. They are choice and reality. The debate already has enough philosophers haggling over the Constitution or the American way of life. Congress has heard from endless witnesses, so this may not add much to the debate, but it is a way of narrowing down the shouting match.

Choice should be preserved for both the candidates and the givers. No candidate should be forced to accept funds from sources that he or she finds unacceptable. The system should not be so punitive that those who refuse PAC funds or public-treasury dollars are unable to compete because they can't raise money. A candidate should be able to fund a race from individuals alone if that is considered a prudent strategy. The voters should be the ones to decide if the person who receives 100 percent PAC funds is wrapped in the strings of special interests. If a candidate wants to accept only contributions from certain PACs in specified amounts, that ought to be the prerogative of the candidate. Rejecting taxpayer financing or subsidies should be an option, without denying the candidate the opportunity to make up for those funds elsewhere. Unfair as it seems, an individual candidate should be able to spend whatever he or she wants from personal sources. If the law must equalize this advantage of the rich, that could be worked into the formula.

None of the current proposals meets this test of choice for the candidate if they include inflexible formulas of x from PACs, x from individuals, and an equivalent of x from the federal treasury. Suggestions that candidates have to raise half of their individual funds from within a state or district don't quite meet this test either. Lowering the limits on what an individual can give may also infringe on this freedom of choice for the candidate. It is fair for candidates to attack each other for the composition of their campaign treasury, but it doesn't make sense to establish a yardstick that would work for candidates of both parties in all regions of the country.

Freedom of choice for the candidates also involves the judgment about how resources are used. Providing postal subsidies or reduced broadcast rates assumes that all campaigns want to make use of these tactics. Senate candidates may make more use of television than House candidates, regardless of how cheap or expensive that purchase might be. Mailing could be a universal campaign tool, but candidates might prefer help in paying for phone banks or subsidies for rent on headquarters. Television and mail are the most indirect forms of candidate communication, yet they are the only ones the proposals contemplate providing vouchers to use. Might it not make more sense to give candidates from Alaska or Montana a voucher for airfare? How about a voucher for rent in the most prominent section of downtown? Why not a voucher for billboards or yardsigns? Why not free coffee and danish for the neighborhood block parties? Yes, the argument can't be made that the government owns the delivery system as it can claim for the post office or for the airwaves, but the mail and the television may not deliver the message as effectively as some other commodity.

Freedom of choice for the giver means selecting a vehicle for participation that makes most effective use of limited dollars. For some that is direct contribution to candidates, for others the political party represents all that they care about in public policy. Respected or not as an institution, PACs have motivated hundreds of thousands of individuals to make political contributions who would never pick a candidate on their own and have limited interest in funding the overhead of a political party. The PAC offers a specific focus and in nearly all cases a guarantee that the majority of the money will end up in the hands of the candidates. Remove the PAC, and the small giver is virtually out of politics, or those who remain are forced to give to someone they have heard about—most likely an incumbent. Checking off a box on a federal income tax return is not the same as preserving choice for the individual giver. Individuals must retain the right to direct their donations through entities which have earned their confidence and support their ideas.

THE NEED FOR REAL-LIFE SOLUTIONS

Campaign finance rules must recognize reality in all of its forms, for the participants as well as the situations within campaigns. We are a diverse society with multiple interests spanning at least three generations. We are a nation of joiners. This reality won't go away when we turn to elections. Environmentalists care about who serves in office, just as those who are worried about living on Social Security care about who wins. Even if these groups don't form PACs, the avenue must be available for interests to coordinate giving or at the very least share advice on who is a worthy candidate for financial assistance. Unless all private funds are outlawed, individuals will continue to give. Reality says they will continue to work together. Far better for them to be operating under recognized rules for political action than to fend for themselves without restrictions or disclosure. If all the supporters of gun control get together to support a candidate, aren't we better off knowing that they are gun-ban advocates than thinking they have no collective objective in supporting a candidate?

The concerns about how the system will function should not be dismissed, especially if those concerns involve enforcement and disclosure. Asking volunteers and campaign managers for advice on revising the system makes more sense than asking the incumbents, who are generally more remote from the daily decisions than outsiders realize. The campaign staffers could have better suggestions than editorial writers or academics because they have been on the ground when decisions had to be made. Those who are to comply with the rules have to believe the system will function, or the regulators will go crazy trying to second-guess the field operatives who are reacting to imagined violations from the opposing camp.

Disclosure is in itself a form of regulation, and adequate reporting of receipts and expenditures may do more to revive faith in the system than a wholesale disruption of the current rules. Most of the major PACs file monthly reports with the FEC, typewritten and accurate. Candidates file quarterly during the election cycle, often in handwriting that is unreadable, with vague descriptions of expenditures and only the slightest information on the occupation/place of business of the givers.

Another element of reality that should be examined, before the reformers get carried away in restricting what kind of money can be received in what volumes, would be to look at what constitutes legitimate campaign use. Should candidates put relatives on the payroll? What is a personal expenditure? Can nonincumbents take a salary or stipend from the campaign treasury? Should the candidate be allowed to make mortgage payments on a residence? What if it is used as a holding area for campaign papers? Is it proper to rent or lease or buy a car or van—and put a phone in it? Is a building that is purchased the same as a campaign headquarters that is rented? Are ads in high school sports programs or gifts to the local Boy Scout troop dinner the same as campaign ads on television? If the candidate helps to bury a constituent, are the payments of funeral expenses as corrupting as buying flowers for the living? How should contributions to charity be treated if they come from the candidate's campaign fund? And, should one member of Congress be able to give to a colleague? Is the situation different if the recipient of the funds is not an incumbent? A complete review of where the money goes is in order, with at least the same detailed scrutiny that has been given to the sources of campaign money.

EXPECTATIONS FOR THE FUTURE

There are no easy answers, and there may be no good answers. If the reformers realize that there are no perfect answers, maybe the deadlock in Congress can be broken. No member of Congress shares the same experience with any other, and their exposure to the PAC world is also limited. Congress may not be the institution to come up with the questions or the answers. Bipartisan commissions have looked at the whole subject in the past, but their suggestions haven't made much headway either. If the system needs a good jolt, perhaps 1992 will provide it. A combination of the antiincumbent mood and redistricting could topple incumbents in the House in ways that a new campaign finance law could never envision.

PART EIGHT

THE FUTURE OF
THE PARTIES

Where should our parties be headed? This section contains two essays, one by a pair of Democrats and the second by a pair of Republicans, assessing where the parties are and where they should be.

The Democrats are William Galston and Elaine Ciulla Kamarck, both affiliated with the Progressive Policy Institute, a moderate Democratic research organization. Galston and Kamarck examine survey evidence in recent elections in "The Politics of Evasion: Democrats and the Presidency." They conclude that their party's troubles arise not because it has foresaken traditional liberalism, nor because the Republicans have ridden a crest of good economic times, nor because the Democrats have failed to mobilized enough nonvoters, nor because the Democrats have failed to win just enough votes to carry California's mother lode of electoral votes. Instead, the Democrats have failed to attract the middle class. They have been so concerned with wooing policy activists that they have forgotten the base that made them dominant in national politics for so long. If they fail to take more moderate positions on foreign policy and moral values, the Democrats could ultimately lose the Congress as well as the White House. The Democrats took the authors' advice in 1992, won the presidential election, and took Galston on board as a White House domestic policy adviser.

Republican analysts Eddie Mahe and Jim Weber of the Eddie Mahe Company, a GOP consulting firm, highlight Americans' loss of confidence in political institutions in their essay, "The Road to Nowhere? Political Parties in the Next Millennium." People are turning away from political parties and toward interest groups and direct action at the local level. Parties have become irrelevant to many Americans, especially those born after World War II. Mahe and Weber argue that the increased salience of interest groups and local organizations is traceable to their focus on issues. Political parties have become "ideologically neutered." They believe, in contrast to Galston and Kamarck, that the path to revitalization lies in greater emphasis on ideology. Only if the parties take distinctly different positions on issues will Americans believe that the central questions of our time can be resolved by these venerable institutions.

Reading 23

THE POLITICS OF EVASION: DEMOCRATS AND THE PRESIDENCY

William Galston and Elaine Ciulla Kamarck

The Democratic Party's 1988 presidential defeat demonstrated that the party's problems would not disappear, as many had hoped, once Ronald Reagan left the White House. Without a charismatic president to blame for their ills, Democrats must now come face to face with reality: too many Americans have come to see the party as inattentive to their economic interests, indifferent if not hostile to their moral sentiments and ineffective in defense of their national security. Nor have matters improved for Democrats since the presidential election. On a variety of measures, from party identification to confidence in dealing with the economy and national security, the Democratic Party has experienced a dramatic loss of confidence among voters; only 57 percent of Democrats had a favorable image of their own party in 1989.[1]

Democrats ignored their fundamental problems. Instead of facing reality they have embraced the politics of evasion. They have focused on fundraising and technology, media and momentum, personality and tactics. Worse, they have manufactured excuses for their presidential disasters—excuses built on faulty data and false assumptions, excuses designed to avoid tough questions.

This paper is an exploration of three pervasive themes in the politics of evasion. The first is the belief that Democrats have failed because they have strayed from the true and pure faith of their ancestors—we call this the myth of Liberal Fundamentalism. The second is the belief that Democrats need not alter public perceptions of their party but can regain the presidency by getting current nonparticipants to vote—we call this the Myth of Mobilization. The third is the belief that there is nothing fundamentally wrong with the Democratic Party: there is no realignment going on, and the proof is that Democrats still control the majority of offices below the presidency. We call this the Myth of the Congressional Bastion.

THE MYTH OF LIBERAL FUNDAMENTALISM

The oldest of these myths is that Democrats have lost presidential elections because they have strayed from traditional liberal orthodoxy. Liberal fundamentalists argue that the party's presidential problems stem from insufficiently liberal Democratic candidates who have failed to rally the party's faithful. The facts, however, do not sustain this allegation. Losing candidates Michael Dukakis and Walter Mondale were very successful, in fact in most instances more successful, than 1976 winner Jimmy Carter, in winning over the ideological (and racial) base of the Democratic Party. According to CBS/*New York Times* exit polls, Dukakis got 82 percent of the liberal vote and 89 percent of the black vote. This is better than Carter, who received 74 percent of the liberal vote and 83 percent of the black vote in 1976. Mondale's loss was so big that he did less well than Carter in most groups, but he still received 71 percent of the liberal vote and fully 91 percent of the black vote.

The real problem is not insufficient liberalism on the part of the Democratic nominees; it is rather the fact that during the last two decades, most Democratic nominees have come to be seen as unacceptably liberal. Fully 36 percent of the electorate told ABC exit pollers that Dukakis' views were "more liberal" than their own. In contrast, just 22 percent thought George Bush's views were more conservative than their own. In 1976, CBS/NYT exit polls showed that Carter was able to win the support of 30 percent of the self-identified conservatives and 48 percent of the independent voters. Dukakis won over only 19 percent of self-identified conservatives and 43 percent of independents and Mondale won only 18 percent of conservatives and 36 percent of independents. Because there have consistently been many more conservative identifiers than liberal identifiers in the electorate, the perception that recent Democratic nominees are "too liberal" has worked to the advantage of the Republicans.[2] The drop in conservative support accounts for more than half of the five-point decline in overall support from Carter's 50 percent to Dukakis' 45 percent.

In the past two decades, liberalism has been transformed. The politics of innovation has been replaced by programmatic rigidity; the politics of inclusion has been superseded by ideological litmus tests. It is this transformed liberalism that we call "liberal fundamentalism," on which the electorate has rendered a series of negative judgments. Since the late 1960s, the public has come to associate liberalism with tax and spending policies that contradict the interests of average families; with welfare policies that foster dependence rather than self-reliance; with softness toward the perpetrators of crime and indifference toward its victims; with ambivalence toward the assertion of American values and interests abroad; and with an adversarial stance toward mainstream moral and cultural values.

The campaign of 1988 was waged squarely within this framework, and it dramatically confirmed continued public antipathy to liberal fundamentalism. According to ABC exit polls, nearly one-quarter of the voters felt defense and foreign affairs were important in making their choice; Bush won them 88–12. Bush held a 4–1 margin among voters who stressed the Pledge of Allegiance. On taxes and crime, Bush won 72–27 and 73–27 respectively. Of the 27 percent who named the death penalty as important, 75 percent backed Bush as opposed to only 24 percent for Dukakis.

Liberal fundamentalism refuses to adjust to changing circumstances by adopting new means to achieve traditional ends. Instead, it enshrines the policies of the past two decades as sacrosanct and greets proposals for change with moral outrage. During its heyday, the liberal governing coalition brought together white working-class voters and minorities with a smattering of professionals and reformers. Over the past two decades, however, liberal fundamentalism has meant a coalition increasingly dominated by minority groups and white elites—a coalition viewed by the middle class as unsympathetic to its interests and its values. The national Democratic Party is losing touch with the middle class, without whose solid support it cannot hope to rebuild a presidential majority. Jimmy Carter forged his 1976 victory with the help of a majority of middle-income voters, while Michael Dukakis was able to win only 43 percent of this vital group.

Liberal fundamentalism dominates two important, defining arenas for the Democrats: the institutional party and the presidential nominating process. In every presidential election this decade, the losing Democratic nominee has been charged by his intraparty foes with insufficient liberalism. Senator Ted Kennedy's 1980 campaign to unseat a Democratic president crystallized liberal fundamentalism as the party's reigning dogma, enforced through ideological litmus tests. Jesse Jackson's 1984 and 1988 campaigns—which featured vigorous critiques of Mondale and Dukakis—were the purest version of liberal fundamentalism. These attacks persisted in spite of the fact that the nominees were unwilling or unable to separate themselves adequately from liberal fundamentalism. The politics of evasion has meant that Democratic nominees have been

Table 23.1 The Mystery of the Vanishing Democrats*

Family income*	Percent of voters in Democratic primaries					Turnout change	Primary type
	Below $12,500	$12,500–24,999	$25,000–34,999	$35,000–50,000	$50,000 +		
Alabama							
1984	34%	24%	18%	10%	5%		
1988	22	21	17	17	12	−22,641	Open
Georgia							
1984	23%	26%	19%	15%	9%		
1988	13	22	21	20	18	−61,789	Open
Illinois							
1984	26%	27%	21%	12%	5%		
1988	15	20	17	22	15	−158,497	Open
Indiana							
1984	25%	32%	19%	9%	3%		
1988	18	25	20	22	8	−71,247	Open
Maryland							
1984	14%	23%	21%	22%	13%		
1988	9	18	21	24	24	+3,084	Closed

Table 23.1 continued

Family income*	Percent of voters in Democratic primaries					Turnout change	Primary type
	Below $12,500	$12,500–24,999	$25,000–34,999	$35,000–50,000	$50,000 +		
Massachusetts							
1984	12%	26%	23%	21%	9%		Democrats,
1988	10	15	16	26	24	+81,893	independents
New York							
1984	19%	27%	19%	16%	12%		
1988	10	19	17	17	28	+187,236	Closed
North Carolina							
1984	24%	27%	19%	13%	9%		
1988	13	25	24	18	13	−280,899	Closed
Ohio							
1984	23%	30%	20%	12%	5%		
1988	14	26	20	18	12	−70,384	Open
Pennsylvania							
1984	25%	30%	20%	10%	3%		
1988	17	26	19	14	10	−140,947	Closed

*Income in year before election; because some voters declined to state income, percentages do not add up to 100. Copyright 1988, *National Journal*. Reprinted by permission.

unable to break clearly with liberal fundamentalism because they and their advisers continue to embrace myths about the electorate that cannot withstand either empirical analysis or political combat.

LIBERAL FUNDAMENTALISM AND THE NOMINATING PROCESS

Liberal fundamentalism is reinforced by the dynamics of the nomination process. Primary and caucus goers are a small portion of the electorate in both parties, but they tend to be the true believers. This is a big problem for the Democrats who, as their national fortunes have faltered, have attracted fewer and fewer participants in their nominating contests, leaving the liberal wing of the party even more in control in some critical states. 1988 ABC exit polls show a pattern: in many states, liberals have increased as a percentage of total primary participants while the conservative share has diminished.

The prime engine for this shift has been a decline in overall Democratic primary participation. In Florida, 20.2 percent of the voting-age population participated in the 1976 Democratic primary won by Jimmy Carter, who also carried Florida in the general election. By 1988, only 13.2 percent of the voting-age population participated in a primary won by Dukakis. Similar declines in Democratic presidential primary turnouts have been at work throughout the South and elsewhere. Georgia had an 11 percent drop in turnout between 1984 and 1988; during that same period Alabama had a 13 percent drop, North Carolina had a 29 percent drop and Illinois had a 10 percent drop.[3] Based on CBS-*New York Times* exit polls from recent primaries, the data in Table 23.1 show that lower middle-class voters participated in the Democratic primary process in far smaller numbers in 1988 than they did in 1984. Given that the candidacy of Jesse Jackson assured continuing high rates of black primary participation, the most plausible explanation for the large decline in lower-income voter participation between 1984 and 1988 is that working-class whites were deserting the Democratic nomination process in droves. During this same period, the percentage of Democratic primary participants with incomes of $50,000 or more doubled in a number of key states.

There is a vicious circle at work here. As the increasing role of upscale liberals in the nominating process reinforces the party's emphasis on the kinds of issues that tend to antagonize working-class voters, these voters fall out of the party's nominating process, making it even more likely that Democrats will nominate a candidate without significant appeal to the demographic and political center. The failure of "Super Tuesday," an attempt by Southern elected officials to move Democratic presidential candidates in a more moderate direction by forcing them to spend time in the South, lay in their failure to anticipate that the Southern primary electorate would be as small and unrepresentative of the general election electorate as it ultimately was.

THE MYTH OF MOBILIZATION

The second pervasive theme in the politics of evasion is the Myth of Mobilization. The argument goes as follows: the Democratic Party need not alter its program or message, because it can regain the presidency by getting current nonparticipants to vote.

The most general form of this argument is that higher turnout across the board is the solution. The facts do not support this contention. According to a poll of nonvoters taken shortly after the 1988 election, if everyone had voted Bush would still have won—by a larger margin.[5] There are three reasons why general mobilization will not do the job. First, the large lead in party identification that Democrats have enjoyed since the New Deal has nearly disappeared. In 1976, the last time the Democrats won the presidency, they enjoyed a 15-point advantage over Republicans among those who identified with a political party. By 1988, 37 percent of the voters identified themselves as Democrats and 35 percent identified themselves as Republicans, leaving the Democrats with a mere two-point advantage.[6] Had party identification been the same in 1988 as it was in 1976, the percentages of Democrats, Republicans, and Independents that Dukakis actually won would have been enough to give him the presidency.[7]

The second reason why general mobilization will not work for Democrats is rooted in the changing nature of "peripheral" voters—persons whose attachment to the political process is relatively weak and who tend to vote in only high-intensity elections. During the heyday of the New Deal coalition, these voters tended to be Democrats, and it was a truism of party politics that higher turnout tended to be correlated with Democratic successes.

During the past decade, however, evidence began to mount that peripheral voters were not necessarily Democrats, a thesis urged by James De Nardo.[8] The elections of 1986 had the lowest midterm turnout since 1942, with only 33.4 percent of the voting-age population participating.[9] Nevertheless, Democrats prevailed in nearly all the closely contested races and regained control of the Senate. Two years later, with a more strongly ideological contest and the higher turnout characteristic of presidential contests, George Bush achieved a victory almost as stunning as Reagan's 1984 triumph.

The third reason why general mobilization by itself cannot get the job done lies in the changing voting patterns in the heart of the electorate. The heart of the electorate (40 percent of the total) is made up of middle-class voters with family incomes between $20,000 and $50,000 per year. In 1976 Jimmy Carter carried this group with 51 percent of the vote—by no coincidence his overall national margin. In 1988 Michael Dukakis received only 43 percent of their vote. Bush beat Dukakis 55–44 among lower middle-class white voters with annual family incomes between $10,000 and $20,000. If only voters with family incomes of under $50,000 per year had participated in the 1988 election, George Bush still would have won.

The Democrats' "disappearing middle" can be documented along dimensions other than income. For example, ABC exit polls indicate that the Democratic presidential vote now comes from the most and the least educated strata of the electorate, while Republicans claim everything in between. Voters with less than a high school education (7 percent of the total) went for Dukakis 60–40, while voters with postgraduate education (15 percent of the electorate) supported Dukakis 50–49. Everyone else (78 percent of the electorate) went for Bush 56–44.

Religion is another key dimension in the decline of the Democratic middle. The collapse of support for national Democrats among white evangelical Protestants is well known. Equally critical, however, is the erosion of the former bedrock of the New Deal coalition outside the South: ethnic Catholics of the Northeast and Midwest. Jimmy Carter (notoriously Protestant and evangelical) received 55 percent of the Catholic vote in 1976. But Michael Dukakis, son of immigrants and Greek Orthodox, received only 47 percent of the Catholic vote. Since 1976 the erosion of Democratic support among Catholics has been more pronounced than among white Protestants—by some measures twice as large. According to an ABC analysis, it was Dukakis's failure to do better among ethnic Catholics that doomed his chances in key Midwestern and Northeastern states.[10]

SELECTIVE MOBILIZATION

A very popular variant of the politics of evasion argues that selective mobilization of groups that strongly support Democratic candidates, especially minorities and the poor, would get the job done for Democratic presidential candidates.

Table 23.2 How Increases in Black Voter Turnout Would Affect the 1988
Presidential Election, by State

States moving from Bush to Dukakis if blacks had voted at a turnout rate of 52% of VAP*	=	Illinois Maryland
States moving from Bush to Dukakis if blacks had voted at a turnout rate of 62% of VAP	=	Illinois Maryland
States moving from Bush to Dukakis if blacks had voted at a turnout rate of 68% of VAP	=	Illinois Louisiana Maryland

*Voting-age population.

Ruy Teixeira demonstrated that even if black and Hispanic turnout had exceeded white turnout by 10 percentage points, Dukakis still would have lost the election by 2.5 million votes. If turnout among adults in families making less than $12,500 a year had exceeded turnout among wealthy Americans by 10 percent, Dukakis would have lost the election by more than 3.3 million votes. And even if these race- and class-based voting upsurges had occurred simultaneously, they would not have been enough to close the gap with Bush. Teixeira's overall conclusion is irresistible: Democrats lost the presidential election "because they didn't have enough support in the nation as a whole, not because enough of their people failed to show up at the polls."[11]

The selective mobilization thesis, which fails so dismally at the national aggregate level, fares no better at the state level. Table 23.2 shows the states that would shift into the Dukakis column under three scenarios: black turnout at national white turnout levels (52 percent), black turnout 10 percent above white levels (62 percent), and black turnout at 68 percent.[12] The increase in black votes is not enough to put many new states in the Democratic column. The mobilization argument is made for Hispanics as well as for blacks. Hispanic turnout is a small percentage of voting-age population (15 percent in California and 21 percent in Texas, according to ABC exit polls) because many Hispanics are not yet United States citizens and are therefore unable to vote. In California, increasing Hispanic turnout from 15 percent to 52 percent would have put that state in the Dukakis column. But in Texas, even that large an increase in turnout would not have given the state to Dukakis.[13]

Much of the support for the mobilization thesis originated with a study from The Joint Center for Political Studies which was then widely quoted by Jesse Jackson. This study gives Dukakis 146 more electoral votes by assuming a turnout rate among blacks of 68 percent—18 percent higher than the population as a whole, by assuming that 100 percent of these newly mobilized voters would cast their ballots for Dukakis, and by assuming that these events have no impact on white turnout.[14] But in practice, it doesn't work that way. In state after state, especially in the South, mobilization among black voters has been at least matched by mobilization among white voters.[15]

The myth of selective mobilization gained its greatest currency after the midterm elections of 1986 when (it was alleged) massive minority turnout was responsible for the return of the Senate to Democratic control. Again, this thesis does not survive empirical examination. In the three states for which exit polls are available, Walter Mondale did as well or better among black voters in his 1984 loss than did the winning Senate candidates two years later. The difference in each case was that the Senate candidate ran significantly better than Mondale among white voters.[16] Successful Senate candidates prevailed by holding onto strong black support and bringing a substantial percentage of white voters back into the fold—precisely the kind of biracial coalition that wins for Democrats outside the South as well. In 1984 Michigan's Carl Levin and Illinois' Paul Simon ran about even with Mondale among the black voters of their states, but they retained their seats in spite of the Reagan tidal wave because they were able to run far ahead of Mondale among white voters.

The other argument that is made to buttress the selective mobilization thesis is that women as a Democratic voting bloc—the famous gender gap—can bring Democratic candidates to victory. But contrary to conventional belief, the gender gap has not worked in favor of Democratic presidential nominees. Dukakis was supported by a slightly lower percentage of women than was Carter in 1976.[17] By contrast, Dukakis' support among men was fully nine points lower than Carter's (42 percent versus 51 percent). The gender gap that has opened up in the past twelve years is not the product of a surge of Democratic support among women, but rather the erosion of Democratic support among men.[18]

Yes, intensified mobilization among groups that have stood loyally with the Democratic Party is politically and morally essential. But the gains from such an effort cannot by themselves compensate for the broad erosion of support the party has experienced in other sectors of the electorate. There is no alternative: if the Democratic Party wants to rebuild a presidential majority, it must regain competitiveness among voters it has lost.

THE CALIFORNIA DREAM

One final element of the myth of mobilization is what we call "The California Dream." The thesis is that rising strength in the West can counterbalance the collapse of Southern support for the party's presidential candidates and that Democrats therefore don't have to work hard at regaining competitiveness in the South. This exercise in the politics of evasion fails the test of basic arithmetic. Non-Southern gains cannot fully compensate for a Southern wipeout. If Dukakis had prevailed in all the Western states where he had a chance, carried the heartland states he narrowly lost, and won all the Eastern states within reach, he still would not have assembled enough electoral votes to win.

The underlying logic of the electoral college shows why. There are 155 electoral votes in the Southern and border states, 41 in the Plains and Rocky Mountain states with impregnable Republican majorities, and 23 more in reliably Republican states of the Midwest and Northeast. If the South is conceded to the Republican presidential nominee, he begins with a base of 219 electoral votes and needs only 51 more. Michigan, Ohio and New Jersey are enough to put him over the top—and George Bush carried them handily with margins of 8 to 14 points. The electoral college arithmetic only gets worse in 1992. Reapportionment will net the states in the Republican base more than 10 additional electoral votes. If Democrats are only competitive in states with 310 electoral votes, the odds against their nominee attaining 270 are dauntingly high. The Republican nominee will start with two pairs while his Democratic opponent would have to draw to an inside straight.[19]

Just as Democrats must regain competitiveness with large segments of the electorate that they have lost, they must also regain competitiveness in every region of the country. The biggest surprise of 1988 was not that Dukakis was trounced in Dixie, but that he failed to prevail in the heartland states such as Illinois, Pennsylvania and Michigan where the costs of Reaganomics have been high and where class and ethnic identification should have worked in his favor. The Democratic Party has more than a Southern problem, and it needs a truly national remedy.

THE MYTH OF THE CONGRESSIONAL BASTION

The final element in the politics of evasion is what we call the Myth of the Congressional Bastion. It goes like this: there's nothing fundamentally wrong with the Democratic Party; there's no realignment going on; the proof is that Democrats still control Congress and a majority of state and local offices as well.

This line of reasoning stems from the 1932 experience in which changes occurred simultaneously in the presidency, both houses of Congress, and hundreds of state and local offices. Ever since, we have discounted the existence of realignment unless it is as dramatic and comprehensive as in 1932. Political scientists have invented phrases such as "split-level realignment" in an effort to characterize alleged voter preference for divided government. The notion of split-level realignment as an enduring feature of the American political landscape is blind to the underlying dynamics of contemporary politics. It also defies common sense. We are witnessing instead a slow-motion, trickle-down realignment in which, over time, Republican presidential strength is inexorably eroding Democratic congressional, state, and local strength.

A key leading indicator of voting behavior is party identification. Here a strong Republican tide is running. The 15-point Democratic edge in national party identification at the beginning of this decade shrank to only two points by the 1988 elections. This tide can be seen most clearly in the South, which is now a bastion of Republican presidential strength. In the 1988 election Bush retained more of Reagan's 1984 strength in the South than in any other region. Nearly as many Southern voters called themselves Republicans (40 percent) as Democrats (41 percent), an improvement over four years ago when Democrats still enjoyed a five point edge and a big improvement over 1980 when Democrats held a 25-point lead. The trend is most pronounced in Florida, where Republican voters outnumber Democrats.

The Republican surge is not confined to the South. ABC exit polls show that in Ohio a 15-point Democratic edge in 1980 was cut to only two points by 1988. During this same period, an 11-point Democratic advantage in Michigan was transformed into a one point Republican edge, and a 14-point Democratic advantage in Illinois turned into a similar one point Republican edge. In New Jersey, a surge in Republican Party identification between 1984 and 1988 turned a four point Democratic lead into a three point Republican advantage. A county-by-county survey by the Institute for Southern Studies showed that higher turnout was positively correlated with higher Bush majorities, and that the Bush counties are growing twice as fast as the counties carried by Dukakis.[20]

While realignment at the presidential level has been dramatic, it has been slower at other levels. The South is the strongest region for Republican presidential candidates but it is also the basis for Democratic congressional power. In the 12 Southern states, Democrats still held 16 of 24 U.S. Senate seats, 78 out of 120 House seats and most state and local offices in 1989. But one aspect of American politics since the 1932 realignment that is relatively new and very powerful is the ability of members of Congress and other incumbents to protect themselves from national ideological trends. Incumbency thus guarantees that the dramatic re-alignment at the presidential level will be slow to appear at other levels.[21] In 1988, despite the Republican presidential sweep, a staggering 98 per-cent of incumbents gained re-election to the House, emphasizing the fact that in modern politics, incumbency is a far more powerful force than party.

Incumbency is in fact the chief obstacle to realignment in the South and in other parts of the country. Earl and Merle Black, leading experts on Southern politics, point out that "Democratic incumbency con-strained Republican senatorial gains between 1966 and 1984. The irony of nonpresidential southern Republicanism is that the setting most condu-cive to Republican gains has appeared more often in the office that is comparatively isolated from national political influences [Governor-ships], while the office that is more susceptible to pro-Republican na-tional influence has frequently been immunized through Democratic incumbency."[22]

But there is evidence, both empirical and anecdotal, to the effect that once incumbency is taken into account, slow, trickle-down realignment is taking place. Nevertheless, this trend makes barely a ripple in the overall congressional alignment because of the relatively few seats that change hands even when aggregated over a decade.[23] Republicans have embarked on a determined effort to nationalize House races along the same kinds of ideological lines that have proven effective for their party in other arenas. They have embraced campaign finance reform and PAC reform because they realized that current laws help Democratic incum-bents much more than they help Republican challengers.[24] Recent events in Congress will place Congress under pressure to enact ethics laws trim-ming back electoral advantages enjoyed by current office-holders.

The Democratic grip on the Senate, where individual results are linked more closely to national trends and where the power of incum-bency is weakened somewhat by the ability of challengers to attract free media, is less secure. The 1986 mid-term election swept away most of the Reagan Senate class of 1980. But with weakness once again at the top of the Democratic ticket, 1992 could easily be a rerun of 1980. In 1992 Dem-ocrats will defend 20 of the 34 seats up, 11 of which are held by senators elected for the first time in 1986. Ten of the new senators won with 55 percent or less of the popular vote, eight with under 52 percent and four squeaked by with only 50 percent. Of the 11 freshman, 10 are from the South and West where the damage done by the presidential party to the congressional party tends to be most severe.[25]

The effects of trickle-down realignment are evident in two other ways: attitudes of young people towards the Republican Party, and the related erosion of Democratic strength among youth. According to ABC exit polls, Reagan won the 18 to 24 year-old age group by only one percentage point in 1980; four years later he won that same age group by 19 points. While less attractive to the youngest voters than Reagan, Bush still prevailed among them by five percentage points.

By some measures, the tendency for the young to identify with the Republican Party is actually growing. In a 1982 survey Gallup asked 13 to 17 year olds which political party they were more likely to vote for; 45 percent said Democrats versus 33 percent who named the Republicans. Five years later, the same survey found the numbers practically reversed; among 13 to 17 year olds 33 percent were likely to vote Democratic and 48 percent Republican.[26] Finally, a recent *New York Times* poll showed that among 18 to 29 year olds, Republicans led 52 to 38 percent, a change of 10 percentage points in less than a decade, a finding echoed by a recent Gallup poll which shows the GOP with a significant edge among those under 30 years of age on all measures of party strength.[27]

The data on age and party is best summed up in a quote from the Republican pollster Bob Teeter, who [says]...the following: "The bad news is that there are still more Democrats in the electorate, the good news is that they're dying off." Indeed, if Democratic voting strength is concentrated increasingly in the older age cohorts and Republican strength among young people continues to rise, a realignment cannot be postponed indefinitely.

The other place where evidence of realignment is prevalent is among those young people who are involved in politics and from whose ranks future talented candidates are likely to arise. In the post-1988 election period, Republicans have been the beneficiaries of an epidemic of party switching by state and local officials.[28] Few of these switches have occurred at the congressional level (after all, there are real and powerful advantages to being in the majority party in Congress). More worrisome to Democrats in the long run, however, is that these switches have occurred at the state legislative and county levels among those elected officials who are most likely to become congressional candidates.[29]

Among an even younger group of elites—politically active college students—it is clear that there has been a resurgence of political activism among Republicans while Democrats have been all but moribund. A comment by a Louisiana State University senior spells real trouble for Democrats if it is, as some think, widely held. "Democrats," according to Rod Dreher, "seem to be too bound to the solutions of the past. All the creative thinking—for better and for worse—is coming from the right."[30]

Eventually, the massive political realignment at the top of the ticket will affect races at the bottom of the ticket. Southern politicians know this better than anyone and they are worried. In their lifetimes they have seen a Republican Party that could not even fill their slots on the ballot turn into a party where presidential successes have contributed to renewed enthusiasm and competition at the grass roots level.[31] But this will affect Democrats in other places as well. A resurgence of Republican strength in two bastions of Democratic liberalism—New York City and Massachusetts—could very well scare Democrats out of their complacency. Whatever else happens, unless Democrats can regain credibility with entry-level voters, the passage of time and the movement of young people who now lean Republican into the electorate will assure the completion of this trickle-down realignment.

CONSEQUENCES OF THE POLITICS OF EVASION

The set of myths which constitute the core of the politics of evasion lulls Democrats into a false complacency. It prevents them from engaging in the kind of comprehensive, thematic and policy review that could revitalize the party. Statistical evidence confirms what political experience suggests: that presidential voters are moved by three broad "baskets" of concerns—the economy, defense and foreign policy, and social issues. Each of these baskets, moreover, is framed by basic values that provide context and meaning for specific policy issues.

The politics of evasion allows the Democratic Party establishment to sidestep these essential facts. Instead of facing up to the need for fundamental re-examination, these Democrats explain their failures in two ways that serve to stifle debate and avoid change. The first is a tendency towards economic reductionism. It can be summed up in the proposition "It's all economics," and it radically downplays the disastrous impact of the party's stance on national defense and social issues. The second is a tendency towards racial reductionism ("It's all race"). It works to thwart re-evaluation of Democratic positions on serious issues that have racial dimensions.

The first excuse goes as follows: Democrats encountered economic bad luck in the 1970s, and a Republican Party willing to purchase unsustainable prosperity with hot checks in the 1980s. But this cannot last indefinitely. Some combination of hard times and a refurbished economic message that takes on the Republican tilt towards the wealthy would be enough to restore Democratic presidential dominance. Other issues (social policy, crime, national security) that bulk so large in campaign rhetoric are in fact negligible in their effect.

This thesis allows Democrats to avoid confronting the fact that they have lost the economic base that they once enjoyed among people who work for a living. (See the Myth of Mobilization.) Voters have lost confidence in the Democrats' ability to manage the economy, a traditional strength dating back to the days of the New Deal. In addition, this thesis overlooks the profound impact of noneconomic issues on presidential elections. To be sure, there is a substantial body of data supporting the common-sense view that economic conditions, coupled with public perception of the party's economic competence, are very important in determining the outcome of presidential races.[32] Still, the manner in which the economy affects presidential races varies with specific economic circumstances. Postwar history suggests that if the economy has been growing vigorously (3 percent or more: 1964 and 1984), the incumbent party has a powerful advantage; that if the economy has been sluggish or recessionary (2 percent growth or less: 1960 and 1980), that challenger has the edge; and that if the economy has just muddled along in the 2 to 3 percent range (as frequently happens), the impact of economic factors will be roughly neutral and the election will be decided by noneconomic considerations.[33] The 1988 election fell into this last category. A recent review of presidential election forecasting models concluded that, considered in isolation, 1988 economic conditions would have been translated into a vote of just 50.4 percent for Bush.[34]

From this standpoint (and from others as well), the Bush campaign acted prudently in promoting crime, national strength, and patriotic values to at least a coequal status with economic issues. Bush beat Dukakis by only 5 percentage points among the 41 percent of the electorate that felt economic issues were most important. But Bush won 88 percent of those who felt that defense and foreign policy issues were among the most important issues in the race, while Dukakis won only 12 percent of that group.[35]

Among voters who stressed values questions such as the Pledge of Allegiance, Bush's margins were massive.[36] And on one of the central social issues of our time—drugs and violent crime—the situation was no brighter for Democrats. Nearly one-third of the voters listed the death penalty as a very important issue in choosing their candidate; Bush won 75 percent of those voters to 24 percent for Dukakis. The July 26, 1989 Gallup poll found that among those who felt that drugs are the most important problem, Republicans had a 40 percent to 28 percent advantage as the party better able to deal with the issue.

Democratic Party vulnerability on social issues goes far beyond crime: 73 percent thought that the United States had experienced a severe breakdown in moral standards over the past 20 years; only 22 percent disagreed.[37] But for many Americans whose support is essential, Democrats are part of the problem, not the solution. In their eyes, Democrats have become the party of individual rights but not individual responsibility; the party of self-expression but not moral accountability.

"It's all economics" is thus a very powerful tactic in the politics of evasion. It allows Democrats to avoid dealing with problems of vulnerability on national defense and social issues—especially crime—issues that assume a greater importance when the economic picture is neither dramatically bad nor good.

The second excuse used to avoid confronting the need for a comprehensive review of the policies of the Democratic Party is "It's all race." According to this thesis, the major themes of the past two decades, which Republicans have exploited so effectively, are all products of—and codes for—racial divisions. Whatever the ostensible issue—crime, public safety, the death penalty, jobs—the real issue is race. Because the Democratic Party has embraced the right but unpopular positions on racial justice, it has paid a heavy price among voters who do not share this view.

No one should doubt the continuing power of racial conflict in American politics. In the South, erosion of the Democratic Party began with the Dixiecrat revolt against Hubert Humphrey's 1948 convention speech and accelerated with Lyndon Johnson's focus on civil rights. Controversy over busing, affirmative action, and the general principle of race-based entitlements further exacerbated white flight from the party during the past two decades.[38] But it is one thing to say that race matters, and quite another to say that it dominates everything. A white Willie Horton may not have struck the same degree of terror as did a black Willie Horton—but violent rapists are frightening regardless of color. By concentrating on race alone, Democrats avoid confronting the fact that for years they have been perceived as the party that is weaker on crime and more concerned about criminals than about victims.

The institutional tendency of the Democratic Party to be out of sync with mainstream values exists on other issues as well. For example, according to the ABC exit poll, Bush won about as much support for his stand on the Pledge of Allegiance as for his emphasis on prison furloughs. Whatever the racial content of the Willie Horton issue, the Pledge was surely not a racial issue. It was a values issue. It played on voters' doubts about the Democratic Party's patriotism—doubts tracing back to the 1968 and 1972 conventions.

The emphasis on racial reductionism masks an equally serious problem, the post 1968 intraparty conflict between lower middle-class voters and the white liberal elites who increasingly dominate national party and presidential politics. This clash, beginning with the influx of upscale anti-war activists into the "reformed" 1972 convention and continuing to this day, has been in many ways as pervasive and significant as the clash between whites and blacks.[39] The shrinking influence of lower middle-class Democrats and the concomitant rise of higher socioeconomic status Democrats who hold liberal views on social issues is a continuing source of unresolved conflicts in the party.[40]

If the white working-class felt morally and culturally isolated from those who took over the party in the early seventies, they were to feel economically isolated when white elites turned to no-growth policies in the mid-seventies just as the economy was beginning to grind to a halt. This new economic isolation was reflected in the popular culture by items such as bumper stickers that read "If you're out of work and hungry, eat an environmentalist." It was reflected in the tax rebellion—a result of the non-indexed income tax during a period of soaring inflation that pushed average families into higher marginal brackets while their real incomes stagnated. It was also reflected in the inability of organized labor to deliver substantial proportions of their membership for the Democratic ticket and in the rise of "Reagan Democrats," working-class voters who abandoned the Democratic Party for the cultural and moral affinity provided by Ronald Reagan.[41]

The overall effect of racial reductionism is to chill honest discussion of key issues within the Democratic Party—that is, to thwart sober reflection on the relation between means and ends. The Democratic Party's commitment to racial justice is—and should be—unswerving. It does not follow, however, that every policy adopted during the past quarter-century to promote this goal need be preserved unchanged, let alone transformed into a litmus test of moral purity.

Affirmative action is a good example. Christopher Edley Jr. and Gene Sperling have made an eloquent plea for flexibility and innovation—and for an end to dogmatism, litmus-testing, and finger-pointing that have dominated discussion of this issue.[42] And yet examinations such as those by Edley and Sperling are all too rare. It is hard to escape the conclusion that Democrats are afraid even to probe questions such as affirmative action, crime, and policies to alleviate poverty. After the 1984 presidential election, the Democratic National Committee commissioned a poll that delineated the problems the party faced among white middle-class voters. Once completed, however, the poll was suppressed on the ground that it was too controversial.[43]

Reluctance to examine the established orthodoxies of the Democratic Party has reinforced the power of litmus tests on a wide range of issues. For example, among Democratic identifiers as a whole there is a profound division on the abortion question. Nevertheless, it is virtually unthinkable that a serious candidate for the Democratic presidential nomination would deviate far from the strict pro-choice position.

The most serious effect of the politics of evasion, however, is that it tends to repress the consideration of new ideas. Walter Mondale began his quest for the presidency with a highly public commitment to rethink established orthodoxy. But the dynamic of the nominating process (coupled with the deep 1981–1982 recession, which rekindled the classic Democratic desire to rerun the campaign against Herbert Hoover) led Mondale to reaffirm most aspects of the conventional wisdom—and to use Gary Hart's mild and occasional deviations from it as evidence of unacceptable heresy. Even today, suggestions that the traditional Democratic goals—for example, improving the well-being of the working poor—may require untraditional means are greeted with moral outrage.

CONCLUSION: THE ROAD AHEAD

What is to be done? The Democratic Party must choose between two basic strategies. The first is to hunker down, change nothing, and wait for some catastrophe—deep recession, failed war, or a breach of the Constitution—to deliver victory. This strategy has the disadvantage of placing the party entirely at the mercy of events. It puts the party in the position of tacitly hoping for bad news—a stance the electorate can smell and doesn't like. And it is a formula for purposeless, ineffective governance.

The other strategy, active rather than passive, is to address the party's weaknesses directly. Thus the party's nominee must be fully credible as commander-in-chief of our armed forces and as the prime steward of our foreign policy; he must squarely reflect the moral sentiments of average Americans; and he must offer a progressive economic message, based on the values of upward mobility and individual effort, that can unite the interests of those already in the middle class with those struggling to get there. Finally, he must recast the basic commitments of the Democratic Party in themes and programs that can bring support from a sustainable majority.

There is almost certainly a powerful constituency for such a message. A wealth of data suggests that the American people are uneasy about the place of our economy in the world, that they favor a diverse and tolerant society, that they are troubled by the consequences of the increasing gap between the most and least advantaged sectors of our population, and that they believe our strength abroad depends on economic and social progress at home. They want leadership that addresses real challenges and meets real needs.

But all too often the American people do not respond to a progressive economic message, even when Democrats try to offer it, because the party's presidential candidates fail to win their confidence in other key areas such as defense, foreign policy, and social values. Credibility on these issues is the ticket that will get Democratic candidates in the door to make their affirmative economic case. But if they don't hold that ticket, they won't even get a hearing.

Above all, the Democratic nominee must convey a clear understanding of, and identification with, the social values and moral sentiments of average Americans. The firm embrace of programs, such as national service, that link rights to responsibilities and effort to reward, would be a good start. The consistent use of middle-class values—individual responsibility, hard work, equal opportunity—rather than the language of compensation would also help. And finally, the American people overwhelmingly believe that the central purpose of criminal punishment is to punish—to express our moral outrage against acts that injure our community. The next Democratic nominee cannot appear indifferent to the victims of violent crime.

This is not a hopeless task. The Republicans have not solidified their hold on a governing majority. For all their successes at the presidential level, success at other levels is coming only gradually. For all the positive opinions that voters have of Republicans, they are still perceived as the party of the rich. For all the gains they have made in party identification, there are still large numbers of independent voters in the electorate. The Democratic Party can recapture the middle without losing its soul.

Republicans are beset with their own ideological purists—arch conservatives whose instincts and policies are not popular with most of the electorate. But in recent years the Republican Party and Republican nominees have been better able to put party fights and party rhetoric behind them and craft a message that appeals to a majority of the electorate. In contrast, the leadership of the Democratic Party has proven unable to shake the images formed by its liberal fundamentalist wing and has been prone to take the rhetoric of the primaries into the general election, with the predictable negative results. The politics of evasion contributes significantly to this failure by leading its proponents to believe things about the electorate that do not stand up to empirical tests.

How can the Democratic Party recapture the center? The British Labour Party decided that it was tired of losing, dumped some of its extreme left stance, and moved towards the political center. In the summer of 1989, the Japanese Socialist Party took a similar step. But American political parties are loose federations that cannot change course through a centrally designated body. The process of change in the Democratic Party must be as decentralized as the party system itself. Political leaders at all levels must take a new interest in the party and its nomination process. Influential Democrats, including candidates for the party's presidential nomination, must have the courage to challenge entrenched orthodoxies and to articulate new visions.

This will require an end to litmus tests that have for so long throttled debate. And most importantly, it will require an end to the conspiracy of silence, to the perpetuation of myths that have so weakened the Democratic Party. Only conflict and controversy over basic economic, social, and defense issues are likely to attract the attention needed to convince the public that the party still has something to offer the great middle of the American electorate. The restrained pace of political realignment indicates that many voters do not want to call themselves Republicans yet; Democrats need to give them a reason to retain (or re-establish) their traditional affiliation. The Republican Party was transformed into a governing party during the 1970s because it was willing to endure a frank internal debate on political fundamentals. If Democrats hope to turn around their fortunes in the 1990s, they must set aside the politics of evasion and embark upon a comparable course.

NOTES

1. Tubby Harrison's analysis, released 11 June 1989, of data from a survey commissioned by Democrats for the 90's also found that voters held more positive views of the GOP than of the Democratic Party: that 43% trust the Republican Party to lead the country versus only 34% who trust the Democratic Party; that the Republican edge includes the economy as well as national defense; and that the electorate connects a range of traditional values—family, religion and the rule of law—more often with Republicans than with Democrats.

Similarly, a 26 July 1989 Gallup poll found that on all three barometers of party image—peace, prosperity and handling of the nation's problems—Americans viewed Republicans as more capable than Democrats. The poll also showed a continued steady increase in the number of Americans who think of themselves as Republicans (34%) and Democratic affiliation at only 38%—a 31 year low reached in 1985 as well.

2. The ideological makeup of the electorate has not changed very much during the last twelve years. According to CBS/*New York Times* exit polls, 20% of the 1976 electorate called themselves liberals, 16% of the 1984 electorate called themselves liberals and 18% of the 1988 electorate called themselves liberals. There has been similar stability among conservatives, who constituted 31% of the electorate in 1976, 33% of the electorate in 1984 and 33% of the electorate in 1988. Using a somewhat different question, a more recent Democrats for the 90's poll (see Note #1) found the same relative strength of liberals versus conservatives; liberals constituted 27% of the electorate and conservatives 42%.

3. See Elaine Ciulla Kamarck, "Where Have All the Voters Gone?" *Newsday*, 12 September 1988.

4. This chart originally appeared in the *National Journal* Convention Preview, 20 June 1988.

5. See E. J. Dionne Jr., "If Nonvoters Had Voted: Same Winner, But Bigger," *New York Times*, 21 November 1989.

6. Data taken from CBS/*New York Times* exit polls. The difference is that in 1976 only 22% identified themselves as Republicans and 41% as independents. By 1988 the number identifying themselves as Republicans had increased to 35% and the number of independents had decreased to 26%.

7. According to CBS/*New York Times* exit polls, Bush won with 92% of Republicans and 57% of independents.

8. See James De Nardo, "Turnout and the Vote: The Joke's on the Democrats," *American Political Science Review* 74:406–20.

9. Norman Ornstein, Thomas E. Mann, and Michael J. Malbin, *Vital Statistics on Congress, 1987–1988* (Washington, D.C.: American Enterprise Institute/Congressional Quarterly, 1987), p. 46.

10. In Pennsylvania, Ohio, Michigan, and Illinois, Bush took half of this traditionally Democratic bloc; in New Jersey Bush won 61% of the Catholics. (Data from exit polls in ABC News, The '88 Vote.)

11. Ruy Teixeira, "Registration and Turnout," *Public Opinion*, January–February, 1989.

12. To confirm our results, we performed the same analysis using an alternative source of data, the November 1988 Current Population Survey (U.S. Bureau of the Census), which has larger state level sample sizes than exit polls. We found that using Census data did not change the results; in fact, it made them stronger. Fewer states with fewer electoral votes go to Dukakis when this data source is used.

13. Increasing Hispanic turnout in California to 52% of the Hispanic voting-age population and assuming that 64% of the Hispanics voted for Dukakis (ABC exit poll) gives Dukakis a net increase of 1,067,731 votes, enough to win the state. In Texas increasing Hispanic turnout to 52% (assuming a 75% Democratic vote) gives Dukakis only 602,643 extra votes, not enough to beat Bush. Ruy Teixeira has performed a similar analysis of state level selective mobilization using slightly different data (*The New Republic*, 3 April 1989). He looked at every state Bush won and calculated the effects of up to 20 percentage point increases in not only black and Hispanic turnout, but also turnout among the white poor. His results are very consistent with ours—only a small number of states go for Dukakis, far short of enough to swing the election.

14. See Dr. Linda F. Williams, "'88 Election Results: Problems and Prospects for Black Politics," Joint Center for Political Studies, Washington, D.C., p. 11.

15. Louisiana is a good example. Democratic registration among blacks in that state increased by 77,779 voters in the eight years of the Reagan presidency but Democratic registration among white voters decreased by 161,230—more than twice as much—while Republican registration increased by 176,477.

16. According to ABC exit polls, in Florida, Senate winner Bob Graham ran worse among blacks than did Mondale but ran 24 points ahead of Mondale

among whites, who made up 92% of the electorate in 1986 and 91% in 1984. In North Carolina, losing 1984 Senate candidate Jim Hunt (who ran far ahead of Mondale) and winning 1986 Senate candidate Terry Sanford ran equally strongly among black voters, but Sanford ran a critical 4% better among whites, who comprised 86% of the electorate in both years. In Alabama, according to CBS exit polls, black turnout was higher in 1984 than in 1986 (24% and 21%, respectively), and Mondale won a higher percentage of the black vote (93%) than did the 1986 Senate winner, Richard Shelby (88%). But Shelby ran 17 points better than Mondale among whites and eked out a close victory.

17. CBS/*New York Times* and ABC exit polls show Dukakis with 49% of women's votes. In 1976, according to CBS/*New York Times* exit polls, Carter received 51% of women's votes.

18. It is of course possible that remobilization of support around the abortion issue will change the dynamics of gender politics in ways that are hard to predict, conceivably to the Democrats' advantage. But a recent CBS/*New York Times* poll casts some doubt on the ability of the abortion issue to mobilize large segments of the population. See E. J. Dionne Jr., "Poll Finds Ambivalence on Abortion Persists in U.S.," *New York Times*, 3 August 1989. See also James A. Barnes, "Politics After Webster," *National Journal*, 12 August 1989, pp. 2044–48, and Jack W. Germond and Jules Whitcover, "Abortion Issue Giving Democrats Big Opening," *National Journal*, 12 August 1989, p. 2056.

19. The daunting mathematical problems faced by Democrats as they look at the electoral college and the advantages of the Republicans are described in Jack W. Germond and Jules Whitcover, *Whose Broad Stripes and Bright Stars?* (New York: Warner Books, 1989), especially Chapter 29, "The Dukakis Surge."

20. Bob Hall and Barry Yeoman, "What Happened November 8th," *Southern Exposure*, Spring 1989.

21. For a very good explanation of the phenomena of incumbency at the congressional level, see Thomas Mann, *Unsafe at any Margin: Interpreting Congressional Elections* (Washington, D.C.: American Enterprise Institute, 1978). In their book *Politics and Society in the South* (Cambridge: Harvard U. Press, 1987), p. 285, Earl and Merle Black point out that the recent trend towards allowing Southern governors to serve two consecutive terms (nine states changed their laws on this in the last two decades) has inhibited Republican gains by increasing the number of incumbents.

22. Ibid., p. 285.

23. In the entire decade of the 1970s there were only 76 open congressional seats and 84 incumbent seats that changed party. Of these only 37% moved from previously Democratic to Republican. In the 1980s there were 132 House seats that changed party. 59% of these seats moved from previously Democratic to Republican—a not inconsequential increase from the previous decade.

24. See Elaine Ciulla Kamarck, "Cutting in on Campaign Cash," *Newsday*, 12 February 1989, Ideas Section, p. 1.

25. Governor Jim Hunt in North Carolina in 1984 and Congressman Buddy McKay in Florida in 1988 are two examples of strong Senate candidates who were

adversely affected by the presidential candidate at the top of the ticket. Buddy McKay ran 22 points ahead of Michael Dukakis in Florida and still lost, although narrowly.

26. *Public Opinion,* "Opinion Roundup, Gallup Youth Survey," p. 22.

27. R. W. Apple Jr., "Public Rates Bush Highly But Sees Mostly Style," *New York Times,* 20 April 1989, p. B12. See 26 July 1989 Gallup poll, "Republican Party's Image at a High Point," by Andrew Kohut and Larry Hugick.

28. See Thomas Edsall, "Racial Forces Battering Southern Democrats," *Washington Post,* 25 June 1989, p. A6; James A. Barnes, "Florida Snowball," *National Journal,* 29 July 1989, p. 1959; Dave Maraniss, "In Wright's Texas Alliances Are Shifting," *Washington Post,* 10 August 1989, p. A3.

29. Between Bush's inauguration in January 1989 and August 1989, 130 elected officials—most of them from the South—had switched from the Democratic to the Republican Party. See Elaine Ciulla Kamarck, "Pols Who'd Rather Switch Than Fight," *Newsday,* 21 August 1989. See also James M. Perry, "Republican Campaign Is Paying Off as Conservative Democrats Make Switch in South," *Wall Street Journal,* 14 August 1989, p. A10.

30. Susan Feeney, "Hostile Student Views at LSU Have Two Top Demos Rattled," *New Orleans Times Picayune,* 9 March 1989.

31. For example, when Democratic Congressman Bill Nelson announced that he would leave to run for Governor of Florida, no fewer than fourteen candidates began jockeying for the Republican nomination.

32. See Steven Rosenstone, *Forecasting Presidential Elections* (New Haven, Conn.: Yale U. Press, 1983), and Steven Rosenstone, "Explaining the 1984 Presidential Election," *Brookings Review,* Winter 1985, pp. 25–32.

33. Rosenstone, "Explaining the 1984 Election," Table #4.

34. See Robert S. Erikson, "Economic Conditions and the Presidential Vote," *American Political Science Review,* 82–83 (June 1989), 567–73.

35. Those who felt defense and foreign affairs were most important accounted for 22% of the electorate according to ABC exit polls. The post-election survey of Americans Talk Security Project, Boston, Massachusetts, December 1988, Numbers 10 and 11, corroborates these findings. On election day, 67% of the voters thought Bush would deal with the Soviets better than Dukakis would; on arms control negotiations, it was Bush 64, Dukakis 22; maintaining a strong defense, 66 to 22; fighting terrorists, 57 to 26. Even in keeping the country out of war, a traditional Democratic advantage, Bush held a 47–36 edge. More than a third of the electorate (37%) had reached the conclusion that Dukakis would actually weaken our national security, while only 8% thought Bush would.

36. ABC News, The '88 Vote, p. 22.

37. The poll cited in Note #1 showed that Republicans have a comfortable lead over Democrats on a series of values questions having to do with belief in God, pride in the country and respect for the flag. The CBS/*New York Times* poll mentioned here is cited and discussed in Samuel L. Popkin, "Outlook on the Future and Presidential Voting," prepared for delivery at the 1988 meeting of the American Political Science Association, Washington, D.C.

38. For a good review of this history see Michael Oreskes, "Civil Rights Act Leaves Deep Mark on the American Political Landscape," *New York Times*, 2 July 1989.

39. The first exposition of this can be found in Jeane J. Kirkpatrick, *The New Presidential Elite* (New York: Russell Sage Foundation, 1976). Anthony Lukas's *Common Ground* (New York: Knopf, 1985) and Jonathan Rieder's *Canarsie* (Cambridge: Harvard U. Press, 1985) offer vivid depictions of the growing tensions between white working-class Democrats, blacks and white elites.

40. For an explanation of the phenomenon of upper income and educational groups shifting to the Democratic Party, see Everett Carll Ladd Jr., *Where Have All the Voters Gone?* 2d ed. (New York: Norton, 1982).

41. Ever since the 1980 election, the Republican Party has managed to win nearly half of the union vote in spite of very large and expensive union campaigns on behalf of the Democratic nominees. According to CBS/*New York Times* exit polls, Carter won 62% of union households in 1976; in 1980 he won only 48% of union households. Mondale managed to get 54% of the union household vote in 1984, and Dukakis received 57% in 1988.

42. Christopher Edley Jr. and Gene Sperling, "Have We Really 'Done Enough' for Civil Rights?" *Washington Post*, 25 June 1989, p. B1.

43. Peter A. Brown, "Democrats Concealed Study of How to Win White Votes," Scripps-Howard News Service, 17 April 1989.

THE ROAD TO NOWHERE? POLITICAL PARTIES IN THE NEXT MILLENNIUM

Eddie Mahe, Jr., and Jim Weber

If you want to know where something is going, look at where it's been. It's easy to understand why people and the organizations they run tend to cling to a success formula well after the formula has played out. Perhaps no institution in America displays this tendency to a greater degree than the wreckage we call our political parties.

Nonetheless, nearly seven in ten American voters continue to call themselves Democrats or Republicans.

Why? What is the pull? Is it a simple need to belong, or the belief that some deeper ideological principle still remains the driving force in party politics? Or is it simply force of habit?

While these questions may be difficult or impossible to answer with any real certainty, they are keys to what the parties will or can become in the next century. In examining the role parties are likely to play in the future, three main factors are important to consider. First and most important is the coming demographic composition of the American electorate as the massive World War II generation ages and dies. Second is the rise in civic activism—its reasons, roots, and probable effects on political parties. And third is the ideological component of political party membership and the challenges posed to parties by increasingly well-organized and well-funded interest groups.

But before examining the future, it might be useful to take a look at the present state of the parties in general, and the Republican party, with which we are much more familiar, in particular.

To say that the parties have collapsed together may be an understatement. Only a few years ago, Democrats engaged in a public debate of whether and how to become more like Republicans. Liberal became (and may remain) a negative word and the party moved to mute the voice of its delegates. In an act of supreme self-flagellation, Jimmy Carter was nominated as a middle-of-the-road Democrat. Not only did the Carter nomination represent an incredible squandering of opportunity for Democrats, but it also served to further confuse an already thoroughly disoriented party. Carter won. By collapsing toward the center, Democrats had achieved success. Or had they? In truth, one could easily make the case that nearly any Democrat could have, indeed would have, won the 1976 Watergate election. By allowing themselves to be moved by an artificial need to be centrist, Democrats were robbed of the opportunity to restore liberal leadership to the presidency, if even for only one or two terms.

Hamstrung by their own process and victims of their own success, 1980 saw no potential for the Democratic left to reassert itself at the presidential level. The abortive and strategically flawed 1984 campaign of Walter Mondale only served to reinforce arguments against liberal standardbearers, and the national party entered into an era of slow or no financial growth. Today, despite the fact that they control both houses of Congress and have aggressive and talented leaders in each, Democrats continue the self-recrimination and talk of failure simply because they do not control the presidency.

Republicans, on the other hand, were stalled in their rush to the center by the success of Ronald Reagan. As the right asserted itself in the party nominating process and delegate ranks, more establishment-type party leaders took a back seat to await the next opportunity to purge the conservatives. That opportunity began with Reagan's selection of George Bush as his running mate, and culminated with the nomination and election of Bush in 1988. Under the control of Bush operatives, party platforms have arguably become substantially less meaningful if for no other reason than that the president pays little attention to them. And organizational techniques during this same period took a decided turn to the middle with the mythical "Southern Realignment" and disastrous "Big Umbrella" edicts of the Republican National Committee (RNC).

For Republicans, Big Umbrella means little more than the loss of ideological meaning and power, replacing it instead with white-bread politics designed more to avoid alienation than to attract support. For Democrats, acceptance of liberalism as a negative in the political marketplace has similar consequences, forcing the real power of the party to silent partner status.

The apparent willingness of both national party organizations to sacrifice ideology in an attempt to broaden appeal should be viewed as a disturbing circumstance, both in terms of what it means for the future of the parties, and how it effects the attitudes and, accordingly, actions of officeholders who already feel little need to consider party platforms in the legislative process. Not everyone should be a Republican or a Democrat. There should be centers of ideas, power, and drive in each party that attract some, and repel others. But the attraction should be based upon ideas, innovation, and the energy that winning public support requires.

Instead, the ideologically neutered parties of today attract their own version of political technocrats who prioritize tactics over ideas, gimmicks over substance.

The consequence of this is the clearly visible stagnation of both major parties. There can be little argument that technology was the driving force in the dramatic financial growth of the parties which occurred during the 1970s and 1980s, but once played out, this fact has left behind little room to grow and innovate, and stubborn bureaucracies loath to change for fear of loss.

THE CREATIONS OF INERTIA

Clinging to a formula after its useful life may have ended has permitted the national parties to become largely governed and run by force of inertia. The effect can be seen today in the highly centralized nature of national parties. Much of this centralization is the result of the concentration of financial support national committees have achieved in recent years. Access to technology earlier, and more forceful application at the national level, has had the effect of bleeding once-flourishing state parties. As the national party revenues have grown, state parties have come under increasing financial pressure, with most even losing revenues when compared with financial performance a decade ago.

The collapse to the center by the parties has arguably had another effect. As issues have played a less prominent role in party activities and communications, new challenges have arisen in the form of increasingly powerful and well-funded interest groups. These groups, formed on the left and right, attract the loyalty and financial support of tens of millions of Americans precisely because they do what the parties do not: pursue specific agendas built around group interest or ideology. Just how much interest-group support represents a real loss to the parties cannot be easily determined, but the simple fact that these groups have proliferated and become financially viable is an indication of the enormous size of the issues and ideology markets that have been rejected by parties.

For the millions of people who support interest groups, membership in these groups represents the addition of necessary components of individual political activism which are not served by the major parties. Furthermore, while it is true that the major parties are the largest affiliate organizations in our nation today when expressed in terms of self-identification, it is not true that formal membership to the parties exceeds that of membership in interest groups.

THE TRADING OF VALUES FOR STABILITY

In building fundraising bases around the loosely defined goal of electing more partisans to office, the parties have essentially replaced the pursuit of values with the pursuit of stability. This puts the parties in stark contrast to issue groups and issue-driven candidates where rising and falling fortunes as a function of the political marketplace are the order of the day.

But, while the pursuit of stability may have near term appeal, it doesn't necessarily mean cycles are avoided entirely. And that is precisely what the parties are facing today—movement into a downward cycle in which response to party direct mail is falling and, along with it, revenues. In short, the parties may not have traded values for stability at all. Rather, they may well have simply opted for a longer business cycle.

In any case, the parties will experience increasing difficulties in coming years owing to three main factors: (1) increased competition from interest groups as more precisely targeted lists become available; (2) falling public confidence in government and politicians; and (3) the increasing tendency of voters to support organizations that attack problems, rather than institutions which simply exist to support other institutions.

INCREASED INTEREST-GROUP COMPETITION

Whatever edge in technology and tactical prowess centralized party organizations once held has been largely surrendered to the interest-group community. The reasons are many, but mainly relate to the freedom with which interest groups can organize and raise resources, and the easily understandable focus upon which resources are raised. As mass fundraising has matured as a technology and an industry, the cost-effectiveness advantage once held by parties has been lost. In essence, interest groups are now able to raise funds as efficiently or more efficiently than parties, owing to the precision with which the appeal can be targeted. Where parties solicit "identifiers," urging them to contribute to "the cause," interest groups solicit known donors to like causes thus enabling a greater return from fewer initial solicitations.

Most important is what interest groups do with those contributors and members, as opposed to what political parties do with their identifiers. At the heart of it, people need to belong. But belong to what? Belonging to the Republican or Democratic party frequently involves defending policies or politicians you don't like. It means being a member of a club with people you like and don't like. As a member of a political party, you may well be asked to work for the advancement of its policies, politicians, or people simply because you're a club member. You never get close to policy, never get close to government, and in the minds of many, never get close to achievement of any real goal.

Interest-group members, on the other hand, not only belong, but they work to achieve the things parties don't talk about. The focus and intensity are such that members become engaged, and work toward the goal of actually changing either a behavior or public policy. They are relatively unfettered by the constraints that generality imposes upon the parties, and can accordingly pursue their objectives with much greater intensity and zeal. By adding the element of action toward accomplishment to the mix, interest groups satisfy more than just the need to belong. They help satisfy the need to achieve, to do good.

In the coming years, parties will continue to feel pressure and competition from interest groups as these groups mature. Already, established groups such as the American Association of Retired Persons in some respects may be viewed as quasi-parties. They are dedicated to a focused purpose but expand that focus as they enlarge membership and act as interlopers within and between the parties. At what point do interest groups actually stop the flow of funds to political parties?

PUBLIC ATTITUDES AGAINST POLITICIANS

A second and increasingly powerful factor affecting the ability of the major parties to raise resources is the dissatisfaction voters feel with politicians and government. While it is easy to see public disgust with the current Congress arising from both policy failure and an avalanche of "scandals," it would be wrong to interpret current public attitudes as representative of a long-term trend.

Rather, it is important to look at longer-term trends and interpret these attitudes without the distortions caused by current events. According to published survey data, public disapproval of Congress in March 1992 had risen to 76 percent—higher than at any time since 1974.

Perhaps more important, and more ominous for officeholders, is the accompanying decline in public opinion of individual representatives. For years, officeholders could take solace in the fact that, while voters disliked Congress, they generally thought well of "our congressman." That ability to differentiate between the institution and the individual resulted in reelection rates for members of the House of Representatives of nearly 98 percent in recent years.

But individual members of Congress appear to have lost their immunity from public outrage over government. Currently, according to nationally published data, favorable voter opinions about individual members of Congress has fallen to below 50 percent—a modern-day low.

For political parties, this loss of confidence in government and legislators should be viewed with near alarm. In this country, political parties have traditionally not been held in high esteem by voters. But they represented a thesis of government that could serve as a basis from which to actively support one's individual views and beliefs. To the extent that the American public has pronounced government ineffective, it is possible that, by extension, they are moving toward a rejection of political parties as either agents of change or the keepers of workable theses of government and society.

Signs of this change in public regard for parties is evidenced not only by the increasing difficulty parties are experiencing in raising funds, but in the movement of individuals to support interest groups when real action is needed.

SUPPORT FOR ACTIONS, NOT INSTITUTIONS

A third factor in the retrenchment of parties in America relates to the growing public desire for visible action by government where problems of society are concerned. While specific studies are hard to come by, it can be said that civic activism is once again on the rise in America. This is a symptom of the greater issue of public lack of confidence in institutions. Historically, when government leadership is clear and strong, society is content to allow leaders to do just that—lead. But when issues go unresolved, Americans reluctantly but forcefully exercise their ability to influence policy through civic activism.

Perhaps the most easily observed recent instances of this are the race riots of the late 1960s and the war protest movement of the 1970s. In both of these instances, unaddressed public grievances against government and social policy were forced to the forefront through confrontation and activism.

But there is a key difference between those eras of activism and that of today. In the examples cited above, the activism was limited demographically, highly focused, and intense. In these respects, it mimicked the kind of activism now practiced by organized interest groups.

Today civic activism has taken a decided turn away from highly emotional and focused issues and has moved more toward activism directed toward solving a wider variety of social and public policy issues.

This is an important distinction because it means that people have come to view civic activism as a means of governing, not just as a way to pursue focused and specific objectives. If this is the case, then public confidence in parties as the repository of an acceptable working thesis of government has eroded significantly, further increasing the importance of interest groups, at least in the minds of voters.

This should be viewed by the parties with considerable alarm, not because it represents an immediate threat, but because it is yet another channel by which financial and political support is directed away from organized politics, and toward achievement of specific objectives.

TAPPING THE FUTURE: PEOPLE, ACTIVISM, AND IDEOLOGY AS KEYS TO SUCCESS

As stated above, three main factors will drive the success or failure of parties in the future. Those factors are changes in the demographic composition of the American electorate, long-term considerations arising from the rise in civic activism, and the power and meaning of ideology. Two of these factors—ideology and civic activism—are already heavily influencing the political marketplace and the success prospects of the parties. In the near term, demographic changes are less discernable and less destabilizing to partisan environments. In the long term, however, nothing is more important, or should be more a source of concern to organized political parties.

For the past thirty years, one generation has controlled politics and the presidency in America. That's a longer tenure for a single generation than ever before. It has been made possible by the entry of this generation into national leadership, en masse, at very early ages. World War II is the reason, and George Bush is very likely the last of his kind.

The control this generation of builders and civic-doers has exercised over American public life has, for years, made the very thought of widespread civic activism unnecessary. The same people who won the war controlled the government and ran American business. Institutions were created because problems had to be solved. Infrastructure was built because progress and quality of life depended upon it. Nothing could wait, victory was incomplete until it had been brought to the doorstep of every American family. In short, things were "taken care of," and in the process, Americans became a kept people.

Democrats seized on this uniquely American brand of collectivism and transformed it into sweeping public policy. The New Deal built a way of life for millions of Americans and provided a previously unknown element of security. However it was contemplated, this thesis of government existed frozen in demographic time. And as the World War II generation leaves the work force and eventually dies, so goes the Democratic party's hold on that entire controlling generation.

Today, simply managing those institutions and meeting those commitments is a staggering task. It's also expensive, so expensive that Americans from the Baby Boom on have had to face a hard reality: They alone can be counted on to provide for the future. The permanence that so resonated in New Deal politics is gone from everyday life in America. American business can no longer offer long-term employment security. And American financial institutions can no longer be counted on to honor commitments made to investors and pensioners.

Perhaps most significant is the loss of permanence Americans feel about government. Mountains of public debt and financial crisis after financial crisis have caused younger Americans to conclude that government can no longer honor the commitments made by their fathers. Because of this, the Baby Boom and post–Baby Boom generations demonstrate and value independence to a greater degree. They are less likely to belong to a political party and are more likely to express conservative economic views and libertarian social views.

But they are one more thing. They are the key to success for the political parties and they should be viewed as more likely to benefit the Republican party than the Democratic party for two reasons. First, generational politics built the Democratic party and relegated the Republicans to near-permanent minority status. Democrats represented the people. Republicans represented bits and pieces—economic interests mainly.

As the commitments made to millions by Democrats have become increasingly painful and difficult to meet, so-called Republican economic interests have gained new importance and new acceptance among broader sectors of the American public. Generational politics as practiced by the Democrats depended heavily on the establishment and acceptance of a "redistribution ethic" as an American economic principle. As long as it worked, this ethic could be counted on to form the foundations from which more conservative economic principles could be attacked and kept at bay.

Today, however, with the arrival of an essentially unfundable federal responsibility and with the imminent departure of the World War II generation from the leadership ranks of American politics, a new economic ethic has begun to emerge—a "growth ethic." The realization that resources, even in America, are finite has forced public attention to focus on growth, rather than simply on how to spend the by-products of the post–World War II economic boom times. With that focus on growth has come an entirely new set of priorities based more on opportunity than on collective security. And that, more than anything else at work today, represents an assault on the foundations of the New Deal and the Democratic coalition.

Opportunity, independence, and competitive ability have become the new bywords of American politics and economic thought. They are responses to what the public knows but that which government has yet to adapt. Massive cultural and economic change is taking place all over the globe and U.S. leadership into the next century depends upon our ability to understand this change and adapt. In the contemporary political history of this nation, the individual attributes needed to meet this challenge have never been valued by the Democratic party because they violate the redistribution ethic and, accordingly, threaten core Democratic constituencies.

Second, Republicans, long used to the politics of coalition building, would appear better suited to attract the next generation of leaders. But the GOP is at a disadvantage that is an outgrowth of its success in presidential politics. While the Democrats select new leaders from post–World War II generations, Republicans remain restrained by loyalty to an incumbent administration that is the last of its kind. The bright young minds and rising stars of the GOP find themselves struggling for freedom, not from Democrats, but from their own party. The contest has become one between two players, neither of whom can escape their past, but who must do so to achieve success.

For Republicans, to succeed requires a willingness to recognize that control of the presidency alone does not assure success. As the party has become more and more dependent on the presidency for financial and organizational muscle, it has become further and further removed from local-level political action. That distance threatens the ability of the GOP to fully understand generational dynamics of change. It must position itself to achieve not only executive but legislative success in the future and thus establish itself as the governing party at all levels of government.

Meeting the demographic challenge will demand political parties that have the capacity to abandon generational concerns and can move toward understanding opportunity not as defined by the political establishment, but as defined by the people who seek it. For Republicans, this means accepting the party proper as a dynamic, changing, and sometimes unstable institution. In doing this, the GOP would recreate itself in a form more closely related to the interest group coalition partners so important to future successes and better able to restore ideological power and credibility to its thesis of government.

PARTIES IN THE NEXT MILLENNIUM: A LOOK AHEAD

No doubt many great thinkers are thinking a lot of great thoughts about how to craft the successful party of the future. And, no doubt, a lot of data will be generated in an effort to predict what the electorate of post-2000 America will look like.

That's fine. But to understand what parties must do to succeed in the future, we must acknowledge that technology will drive party development. Voter groups must be viewed in the context of the social and technological world in which they will live. In a society as politically stable as ours, major shifts in partisanship or partisan control of government do not occur for reasons that are easily measured or discernable through traditional survey data.

Predicting what a successful party of the future will look like, how it will function, and what will be its basis depends upon an understanding of the progression of generations through their lives. How attitudes change as people age, and how the character of one generation affects that of another are the keys to understanding political evolution in America and, accordingly, to creating a model of political parties in the future.

The nature of the World War II generation now passing from American leadership has determined, in large part, many of the characteristics of those who follow. The so-called Baby Boomers are characterized by greater independence and a higher level of skepticism about government than the World War II generation. Baby Boomers have witnessed the failure of promises and confronted the complexity of managing the government their predecessors have created. And, as many corporate managers will attest to, it is easier to build an institution than to maintain it in the face of changing market conditions. Gaining the support of the Baby Boom generation will require communication on an entirely new level—one that moves away from geographically based mass organizing and toward socially based targeted communication using yet to be developed tools.

Those who follow the Baby Boom—the Baby Bust generation—aren't yet easily characterized. We can speculate that these individuals will retain the attributes of civic activism and pursuit of specific goals now emerging in American political society, but will also seek the opportunity to begin recreating government in a meaningful way. This will be true because their predecessors will have managed the failure of institutions built after World War II and will have left behind a cleaner slate than they were given. Through the lives of individuals from both of these generations, the desire to pursue specific policy goals and the culture of civic activism will become firmly rooted in American society. This in turn will make the study of interest groups critically important, and the move away from centralized political organization even more urgent than it is today.

We have devoted much time to the subject of interest groups, their power, their growth, their ability to withstand and survive instability, and their ability to focus on specific action. Groups are important because they have developed and evolved in the political marketplace of today, while the parties have essentially stood still. Many of the same attributes that enable success for interest groups will be necessary for parties to achieve real gains, real success into the next century.

For the Republican party, that means six main components must be developed, accepted, and put into place. They are: (1) the commitment by the party to be the main source of information to its members and identifiers; (2) the commitment to technology necessary to collect and deliver information; (3) the commitment to redemocratization of the party hierarchy and governing processes; (4) rededication of the party role as an advocate for its view of government; (5) the reestablishment of ideology and direction to the party platform; and (6) the redirection of party resources and attention to the state level.

PARTY AS SOURCE OF INFORMATION

In today's political world, information remains the province of news organizations. Whatever efforts are undertaken by the parties to communicate with identifiers and convey messages to the public, they are massively overshadowed by the news media and the information industry. Rapid advances in communications technology, including direct satellite broadcasting, the proliferation of television programming and on-line services, and the coming of addressable electronic advertising, will make possible the establishment of parties as providers of credible, unfiltered information to large sectors of the population. Success will depend in large part upon the ability of party organizations to seize this technology and eliminate their dependence upon the news media for publicity and communication. Absent the biased and cynical filter imposed by journalists, parties will finally be able to disseminate clear messages targeted to specific audiences for specific purposes.

COMMITMENT TO TECHNOLOGY

To fulfill the role of information provider, parties must make meaningful and long-term commitments to utilizing and developing communications technology to the fullest extent possible. This will include collecting information, editing, and distributing to identifiers and affiliates, and will also involve commitment by the party to make this resource available free of charge. Redirection of resources in this manner will force central party organizations to place greater emphasis on events outside of Washington, and will restore greater policy and ideological responsibility to the party itself.

REDEMOCRATIZATION OF PARTY HIERARCHY

As the national party commits itself to information and communication, it must transfer meaningful authority and power back to local leaders and away from Washington. In the case of the Republican party, this involves a fundamental change that will make the party less a captive of officeholders in general and the presidency in particular, and will build on the party as keeper and enforcer of the Republican ideology, or thesis of government. In the future, the party should not exist simply to serve elected officials and assist in campaigns as it does today, but rather should view itself as an active participant in government through its officeholders.

PARTY AS POLICY ADVOCATE

Restoration of the link between platform and public policy is essential if party identifiers and members are to be reenergized and persuaded to make commitments to partisan activity. This involves a near role reversal from the organizations of today. At present, the Republican National Committee acts not as a policy advocate/enforcer, but rather as the firewall between elected officials and the party platform. Delegates may write whatever platform they choose, but the party proper will play no role in enforcing that platform with elected officials.

Changing this relationship will have two important effects. First, it will make meaningful partisan growth possible again. And, second, by reestablishing a Republican thesis of government within policy circles, it will help to move away from the legislative gridlock that now characterizes the centrist Congress.

REESTABLISHMENT OF PARTISAN IDEOLOGY

To fulfill the role of advocate will require that the party abandon its current policy of ideological near-neutrality. Interest groups grow and flourish because they take stands and pursue objectives. The Republican

National Committee must once again become a national repository of political thought, rather than simply a center for tactical expertise as it has become.

REDIRECTION OF RESOURCES TO THE STATES

Finally, the Republican party must restore power and importance to state organizations. As discussed earlier, the argument can be made that the RNC has, in recent years, become a black hole for party resources, robbing states of needed revenues and offering little in return. To succeed into the next century, parties must offer the hope that political actions and affiliation by individuals can have some effect on policy. This can most easily be accomplished at the state and local level where government truly meets people.

To fulfill this need, Republicans will have to come to grips with the realization that they cannot expect to succeed and grow so long as Democrats retain pervasive control of government below the level of the presidency. To continue to expend huge percentages of party resources on control of the executive not only denies the existence of this problem, but offers no reason for activists to believe Republican policy objectives can be implemented.

CONCLUSION

What this listing describes is a party dedicated to communication and mobilization of people not along geographic lines, but rather within the context of social groupings and in the environment in which those people live, learn, and make decisions about their everyday lives. In short, to succeed in the future, the Republican party must restore meaning to its thesis of government, and use technology to make that thesis available to people and enforceable within party ranks.

Government, and a way of life, are what parties in America are about. Success in the future will require that parties reestablish the link between party and policy, and that policy once again becomes the focus of party organizations. Absent this, Americans have little to look forward to other than the continued collapse of policy to the center until another ideological president comes along.

AUTHOR INDEX

SUBJECT INDEX

Subject Index

emergence of pluralistic parties in Jacksonian era, 39–41
interest groups and partisanship, 35–38, 46–49
and organizational society, 41–46
Political Action Committees, 35, 48–49, 408
anti-party PACs, 420–421
and campaign finance, 62, 183, 190, 200, 207, 209, 218, 219–220, 256, 419, 420, 424, 477
and campaign finance reform, 520–528 *passim*, 531, 535, 536–538, 557
CIO's COPE, the first, 412, 419, 522
independent PACs, 422–423
leadership PACs, 477, 489n15
Political advertising, 205n15, 209
and campaign finance reform, 529–530, 531–532, 533–534
and congressional campaigns, 214–218
"genre" advertising, 188–189, 196
pre-testing, 196–197
Political appointments. *See* Patronage
Political culture, defined, 372
Political culture of Democratic and Republican parties
cohesion and commitment, 395–397
differences, 398–402
dissent and disloyalty, 391–395
organizational style, 383–391
party structure and flow of power, 373–381
world view, 381–383
"Political intelligence," 409
Political parties
accountability, 246, 267, 290, 296, 320
American and British systems compared, 131, 229n16, 289, 296–297, 298, 437
autonomy of congressional parties, 475–477
balance of power, 202–203
brokerage role, 228, 230n18, 424
coalitions, 131, 132–135, 143–148, 150n7
cohesion and commitment, 97, 395–397
competition, 44, 45, 47, 99–100
components, 233–235
constituency cross-pressuring, 84, 85, 86, 90, 94–96
cooperation and coordination, 238, 258–259
dealignment (*see also* Political realignment), 127–128, 149n2, 157, 232–233, 258, 259, 449
decline, 108–122, 124n17, 175, 203, 206–207, 306, 307, 310–311, 318–320, 323n8, 399, 408, 414, 437–449, 455

definition, 131, 150n7, 233
dissent and disloyalty, 391–395
elites, 345–349, 372–373, 395, 405n41, 493–512, 547, 550, 561–562, 569n39/40
and interest groups, 290–291, 407–426, 572, 573–574, 575
Johnson and the party system, 442–447
legitimacy, 320, 321, 378–381, 386
majority/minority parties, 253, 388, 402
nationalization, 398–399
Nixon and party system, 447–449
organizational style, 383–391
party-building, 188, 449–450, 455, 462n60
perceived differences, 109, 110, 113–118, 122, 123n9, 131–132, 407
political culture, 373–381, 398
pluralism, 39–41, 45–46
professionalization, 191, 198–200, 209, 213, 237–238, 399–400, 410, 414
purpose, 281–282
Reagan and party system, 449–453
realignment. *See* Political realignment
recruitment, 400–402
reforms. *See* Political reforms
resurgence, 198–203, 425–426
Roosevelt and party system, 437–442
social cleavage theory, 130–131, 148, 149n6
world view, 381–383
Political power flow and party structure, 373–381
Political realignment
of the coalitions, 130–131, 132–135, 149n6, 150n7
and dealignment, 127–128, 149n2, 157, 232–233, 259
and the Democratic control of Congress eroding, 555–559, 565
elections of 1896 and 1932, 86–102
and ideological polarization, 354, 364
literature, 149n1
and New Deal, 344–345
and partisan representation, 493–512
race and welfare issues, 140–141, 151n16
and Reagan, 335–339, 452, 461n58
and the South, 135–139, 143–148
"split-level" realignment, 300–301, 455, 556
"trickle-down" realignment, 557, 567n23
Political reforms, 9–10, 15, 18, 32, 42, 46, 47, 74, 291
in Congress, 108–109
and Democratic party, 12–13, 265–280, 378
in the nominating process, 292–296, 304–306, 414–418

598

AMERICAN POLITICAL PARTIES: A READER
Edited by Dana R. Gould, Hoffman Estates, Illinois
Production supervision by Kim Vander Steen, Palatine, Illinois
Cover design by Jeanne Calabrese, Berwyn, Illinois
Composition by Point West, Inc., Carol Stream, Illinois
Printed and bound by Braun-Brumfield, Inc., Ann Arbor, Michigan
Paper, Restorecote
The text is set in Palatino